Many-valued
Logic

Nicholas Rescher

RESEARCH PROFESSOR OF PHILOSOPHY
UNIVERSITY OF PITTSBURGH

Many-valued Logic

McGraw-Hill
Book Company

NEW YORK
ST. LOUIS
SAN FRANCISCO
LONDON
SYDNEY
TORONTO
MEXICO
PANAMA

Many-valued Logic

Copyright © 1969 by McGraw-Hill, Inc. All rights reserved.
Printed in the United States of America. No part of this
publication may be reproduced, stored in a retrieval system,
or transmitted, in any form or by any means, electronic,
mechanical, photocopying, recording, or otherwise, without
the prior written permission of the publisher.

Library of Congress Catalog Card Number 69-11708

51893

1 2 3 4 5 6 7 8 9 0   M A M M   7 6 5 4 3 2 1 0 6 9

950002

For Dorothy
spouse, helpmeet, and friend

*Cumque plurimas et maximas
commoditates amicitia contineat, tum illa
nimirium praestat omnibus, quod bonam
spem praelucet in posterum, nec
debilitari animos aut cadere patitur.*

Cicero, *De amicitia*, vii, 23

Preface

This is a basic textbook in many-valued logic, affording a general introduction to a wide cross-section of the principal problems and results of the
field. It may be used either (1) in an upperclass undergraduate logic course
in which at least part of the term is to be devoted to a more than superficial
examination of one important branch of nonclassical modern logic, or else (2)
in a graduate-level course devoted specifically to many-valued logic and
planned with the idea that, after covering the basic material of this book,
the class can profitably turn to the journal literature of the subject. (The
comprehensive Bibliography given in Chap. 4 is designed to facilitate this
last-named step.)

   At present there exists no well-rounded introduction to many-valued
logic that brings together at least a substantial part of the many contributions that have been made to this branch of logic since its inauguration as a
discipline less than half a century ago, surveying a wide variety of the numer-
ous systems that have been developed, relating them to one another,
examining their interpretations and applications, and the like. A coherent

exposition of the subject would seem to be very much needed: it has a great literature containing innumerable special results and affording interesting insights into points of detail, but this literature is disjointed and uncoordinated, and it certainly does not afford the beginning student an easy entry into the subject.

It might be asked: Why speak of many-valued *logic* at all, rather than many-valued *logics*, in view of the great proliferation of many-valued systems? The answer is that we do so just in order to distinguish between the comprehensive, variety-embracing subject matter (many-valued logic) on the one hand, and, on the other, the multitude of diverse systems (the many-valued logics) with which it deals. The case is analogous to that of the study of different geometric (or cryptographic) systems within the comprehensive discipline of geometry (or cryptography).

A book that seeks to deal with many-valued logic in general (and does not simply aim to present a certain group of technical results) is likely to emphasize either (1) the *metalogical* (primarily proof-theoretic and in any case the purely formal and near-algebraic) aspects of many-valued systems, or (2) the *semantical* considerations involved in the interpretation of such systems, or (3) the *applications* of many-valued logics in other branches of logical theory, in metamathematics, in physics, etc. While no well-rounded discussion can altogether neglect all three of these aspects, one or the other of them must set the dominant theme. This text exhibits the second, semantical direction of emphasis. Assuming that most students of many-valued logic will come to the subject with a background of preoccupation with philosophical issues, it was decided to adopt this as the most philosophically oriented perspective. This approach also provides the requisite background for the consideration (in Chap. 3) of the philosophically important issue of relativism in the fact of alternative systems of logic.

Although this is a textbook, it contains certain ideas and findings that represent the author's own contributions to the subject (some of which were aired in the journal literature on previous occasions). These points of originality include: (1) the concept of antidesignated truth-values and the distinction between nondesignation and antidesignation; (2) the conception of a quasi-truth-functional system of many-valued logic and the establishment of the metalogical characteristics of such systems; (3) the idea of a non-two-valued truth-value assignment operator and the concept of auto-descriptive systems; (4) the idea of the standard sequence of many-valued logic and some of its variants, and the exploration of their interrelationships; (5) the infinite-valued generalizations of the finite-valued systems of E. L. Post; (6) the alternative worlds approach and the Boolean systems interpretation of many-valued product logics; (7) the Post-style interpretation of systems of the sequence $S_n^{\mathfrak{D}}$; (8) the introduction of Mostowski-type quantifiers into many-valued logic; (9) the new departure in the examination of the status of the classical "laws of thought" in many-valued logic; (10) certain parts of the analysis of the consistency and relative completeness of many-valued logics; (11) the analysis of the key philosophical issue posed by the very existence of many-valued logics—the question of whether and to what extent the reality of such "alternative systems of logic" underwrites a warrant for relativism in logic. Going beyond such specific points of novelty, I would even hope that the organization and coordination of the otherwise scattered body of material dealt with here might itself count as a contribution to the subject.

In writing this book I have profited from helpful discussions with three of my University of Pittsburgh colleagues, Nuel D. Belnap, Jr., Joseph Camp, and especially Storrs McCall. I am also grateful to the members of a seminar on many-valued logic, held in the fall term of 1967, whose questions and discussions helped me in working out some of the material in Chap. 2. In gathering together the materials for the Bibliography I have been assisted by Anne Cross (Mrs. Michael) Pelon, Michael Pelon, Virginia Klenk, and Sandy Roper, whose assistance I acknowledge with sincere thanks. I am also very grateful to Miss Judy Bazy for her very patient and conscientious help in preparing this difficult manuscript and in helping to see it through press. Finally, I am indebted to Alasdair Urquhart for his able and substantial help in correcting the proofs.

NICHOLAS RESCHER

Contents

Chapter 1

A Historical Conspectus of Many-valued Logic

1 Prehistory

Throughout the orthodox mainstream of the development of logic in the West, the prevailing view was that every proposition is either true or else false—although which of these is the case may well neither be *necessary* as regards the matter itself nor *determinable* as regards our knowledge of it. This thesis, now commonly called the "Law of Bivalence", closely bound up with the historic "Law of the Excluded Middle", was, however, already questioned in antiquity. In Chap. 9 of his treatise *On Interpretation* (*De interpretatione*), Aristotle discussed the truth status of alternatives regarding "future-contingent" matters, whose occurrence—like that of the sea battle tomorrow—is not yet determinable by us, and may indeed actually be undetermined. His views on the matter are still disputed, but many commentators, both in antiquity and later, held him to maintain that propositions about future contingents, like that asserting the occurrence of the sea battle tomorrow, are neither actually true nor actually false, but potentially either, thus having—at least prior to the event—a third, indeterminate truth status. The acceptance of the principle of bivalence was, in antiquity, closely bound up with the doctrine of determinism. The Epicureans, who were indeterminists, rejected the Law of Bivalence; the Stoics (and above all Chrysippus), who were rigid determinists, insisted upon it.[1]

The very idea of truth-values other than the two orthodox truth-values of truth and falsity is obviously central to the conception of a "many-valued" logic. To obtain such a logic, we must contemplate the prospect of propositions that are neither definitely true nor definitely false, but have some other truth status such as *indeterminate* or *neuter*. Historically, the problem of future contingency provided a prime early impetus to the serious consideration of this prospect of propositions with such an unorthodox truth status.

In medieval times this problem of the truth status of future contingents was much discussed by logicians, both in the Islamic orbit and in Latin Europe.[2] One school of thought classed such propositions as indeterminate —i.e., neither true nor false—and correspondingly some historians have sought to find precursors of 3-valued logic in such thinkers as Duns Scotus and especially William of Ockham, who treat the *propositio neutra* as something quite distinct from the *propositio vera* and the *propositio falsa*.[3] This position asserting the truth indeterminacy of future contingents did not, however, appeal to the most prominent figures on the Islamic side (e.g., Alfarabi) or the Christian (e.g., Aquinas), because it involved theological difficulties—how can there be divine foreknowledge if future-contingent statements are neither true nor false? A particularly keen debate about these problems took place at the University of Louvain in the fifteenth century, with Peter de Rivo as the principal advocate of an "indeterminate" truth-value.[4] Difficulties about divine foreknowledge quite apart, it is difficult to justify granting to

[1]See N. Rescher, *Studies in the History of Arabic Logic* (Pittsburgh, 1963), pp. 43–44; and Łukasiewicz (1930) as tr. in S. McCall (ed.), *Polish Logic: 1920–1939* (Oxford, 1967), pp. 63–65. (Note that a name-date combination is used throughout to refer to the Bibliography given in Chap. 4.)

[2]Rescher, *op. cit.*, pp. 43–54. See also the historical references cited there, and on the medieval Latin debates see Philotheus Boehner's edition of William of Ockham's *Tractatus de Praedestinatione et de praescientia Dei* (St. Bonaventure, N.Y., 1945) as well as the references of note 4. Particularly important is the paper by K. Michalski, "Le problème de la volonté à Oxford et à Paris au XIVe siècle," *Studia philosophica*, vol. 2 (1937), pp. 233–365. Michalski adduces evidence that both William of Ockham and John Duns Scotus construed Aristotle's discussion in such a way as to require a third neutral truth-value apart from the classical ones of truth and falsity.

[3]See Michalski (1937) and Boehner (1945).

[4]See L. Baudry, *La querelle des futurs contingents* (*Louvain, 1465–1475*), *Textes inédits* (Paris, 1950). Cf. also Francisco Suarez' *Opusculum de scientia quam Deus habet in futuris contingentibus*, bk. II.

(1) "It will rain tomorrow" (asserted on April 12)

a truth status different from that of

(2) "It did rain yesterday" (asserted on April 14)

because both make (from temporally distinct perspectives) *precisely the same claim about the facts*, viz., rain on April 13. But be this as it may, the fact is that the idea of a third, indeterminate truth-value at issue in these historic discussions of future contingency provided the principal impetus and leading idea for Łukasiewicz' development of his 3-valued logic.[5]

The conception of propositional *modality* also provided an important source of inspiration for many-valued logic. Logicians since Aristotle have not been content to rest with the classification of the truth status of propositions into the simple dichotomy of *true* and *false*. Already in antiquity logicians devised a more refined modalized classification represented by the so-called *alethic* modalities:

> necessarily true
> contingently (i.e., actually but not necessarily) true
> contingently false
> necessarily false

Aristotle in fact devoted the bulk of his logical treatises to the systematization of the theory of such modal propositions. Alternatively, inspired by the development of probability theory in modern times, some logicians have considered the introduction of *probabilistic* modalities:

> certainly true
> probably true
> indifferent
> probably false
> certainly false

The idea of setting up a logic that reckons with such nondichotomous truth-values—and so opens up a realm of indeterminacy or contingency between actual truth and actual falsity—provided an important impetus for the development of many-valued logic.[6] (In the case of Peirce and Łukasiewicz the alethic modalities provided the motivating conception, whereas with MacColl the inspiration came from the probabilistic modalities.)

---

[5]For a fuller analysis of the principle of excluded middle in the context of many-valued logic see Sec. 23 of Chap. 2.
[6]On the lines of thought at issue here see Prior (1952) and (1955a).

2 Early History (1875–1916)

The founding fathers of many-valued logic were the Scotsman Hugh MacColl (1837–1909), the American Charles Sanders Peirce (1839–1914), and the Russian Nikolai A. Vasil'ev (1880–1940).

MacColl sketched a system of propositional logic in which propositions can take on several distinct "truth"-values, not only the traditional *true* and *false*, but also the modal values of *certainty* (necessity), *impossibility*, and *variability* (contingency).[1] He characterized his system as a "logic of three dimensions," in contrast with the symbolic systems of Schröder and Venn, which envisage only two dimensions (i.e., truth-values). A *certain* proposition is one which is always and necessarily true, an *impossible* proposition is always and necessarily false, and a *variable* proposition is sometimes true and sometimes false. As examples of bearers of these three truth-values, MacColl exhibited the three propositions: "$2 = 2$," "$3 = 2$," and "$x = 2$," or alternatively "$2 + 3 = 5$," "$2 + 3 \neq 5$," and "$2 + x = 5$," respectively. MacColl developed his system as an algebra of logic along the lines of previous systems, but based on three rather than two truth-values. He applied his logic of variable propositions especially to the calculus of probabilities, and he can be regarded as a precursor of those later logicians who sought to construe the nonclassical truth-values of many-valued logic along probabilistic lines.[2] MacColl's idea of proceeding along probabilistic lines is a particularly shrewd one because his truth-values, like probabilities, will not combine in a truth-functional way. If p is a variable proposition, then its conjunction with itself will be variable, and in this case variable-conjoined-with-variable will be variable. But if p is variable, then so is not-p, but in this case variable-conjoined-with-variable will be impossible rather than variable. (We shall later see that the system developed by Łukasiewicz some decades after MacColl's paper is deficient in just this respect.)

Peirce approached the ideas of many-valued logic from several points of departure. For one thing, he conceived of the idea of a neutral truth-value in the traditional context of Aristotle's problem of future contingency.[3] Moreover, in his (only posthumously published) essay entitled "Minute Logic" (dated 1902), Peirce envisaged a "trichotomic mathematics" which he interpreted as mathematics based on a 3-valued or "triadic" logic. Although Peirce is generally recognized as one of the inventors (along with

---

[1]See MacColl (1897) and also the discussion by Storrs McCall in the article on MacColl in *The Encyclopedia of Philosophy*, ed. by P. Edwards (New York, 1967), vol. 4, pp. 545–546.
[2]For a more detailed discussion of MacColl's ideas see also MacColl (1900–01).
[3]*Collected Papers of Charles Sanders Peirce*, ed. by C. Hartshorne and P. Weiss (6 vols., Cambridge, Mass., 1931–1935); see especially 4.12–20, and 4.257–265. But see also 3.366.

G. Frege) of the truth-table method for developing the classical, two-valued propositional calculus[4] his claims to be an originator of 3-valued logic have often been overlooked. There is now conclusive evidence that by early 1909 Peirce had—with considerable elaborateness—extended the truth-table method to 3-valued logic,[5] basing his three truth-values upon modal ideas that envisage a truth status intermediate between determinate truth and determinate falsity. Thus Peirce wrote to William James in 1909:

> I have long felt that it is a serious defect in existing logic that it takes no heed of the *limit* between two realms. I do not say that the Principle of Excluded Middle is downright *false;* but I *do* say that in every field of thought whatsoever there is an intermediate ground between *positive assertion* and *positive negation* which is just as Real as they. Mathematicians always recognize this, and seek for that limit as the presumable lair of powerful concepts; while metaphysicians and oldfashioned logicians,—the sheep & goat separators,— never recognize this. The recognition does not involve any denial of existing logic, but it involves a great addition to it.[6]

He considered a great many 3-valued connectives that were later to become well known in forms reinvented by others—Lukasiewicz' 3-valued negation, the cyclic 3-valued negation of E. L. Post, the T-function of Słupecki, the 3-valued conjunction and disjunction of Lukasiewicz, Bochvar's conjunction and disjunction (= Kleene's weak conjunction and disjunction), among others. Of course, Peirce did not work out these seminal ideas in any comprehensive way, nor did he publicize his discoveries. At least in part, the origin or at any rate the stimulus of Peirce's work in this area derives from his study of the published papers of MacColl, with whom he was also in touch through correspondence.[7] But Peirce expressed the view that a "trichotomic mathematics" cannot really be free from dichotomic (two-valued) ingredients, and was apparently not committed to the many-valued and/or modal approach to logic as deeply as MacColl.

In the period 1910–1914 Vasil'ev published several papers about what he called "imaginary non-Aristotelian logics."[8] In his paper of 1912, he

---

[4]See Alonzo Church, *Introduction to Mathematical Logic*, vol. I (Princeton, 1956), pp. 161–192.

[5]See Max Fisch and Atwell R. Turquette, "Peirce's Triadic Logic," *The Transactions of the Charles S. Peirce Society*, vol. 2 (1966), pp. 71–85. Our discussion is based upon this important account. See also A. R. Turqette, "Peirce's *Phi* and *Psi* Operators for Triadic Logic," *ibid.*, vol. 3 (1967), pp. 66–73.

[6]Quoted in Fisch and Turquette, *op. cit.*, p. 81.

[7]See Fisch and Turquette, *op. cit.*, pp. 82–84.

[8]See Vasil'ev (1910) and especially Vasil'ev (1912). Actually, (Aristotle himself is generally held to have assigned a third, neuter truth-value to future-contingent propositions. Consequently, logical systems with truth-values over and above *T* (true) and *F* (false) should not be characterized as "non-Aristotelian" but as "non-Chrysippean" after the Stoic logician Chrysippus, who explicitly insisted that all propositions are either true or else false.) (Cont'd on next page.)

described his work as an attempt to do for Aristotelian logic what an earlier professor at Kazan University, Nikolai Lobatchevski, had done for Euclidean geometry. Vasil'ev wanted to see what logical principles could be changed or eliminated from logic without its ceasing to be logic. On Vasil'ev's view, logic consists of (1) a fixed, unalterable body of metalogical principles, together with (2) a (potentially changeable) group of logical laws which have an *ontological* basis, being dependent upon the properties of known objects. Vasil'ev construed the Law of Contradiction in its Kantian form "No object can have a predicate which contradicts it," and construed the Law of Excluded Middle to say that "an object must either have a predicate or its negation." As such, he took both laws to pertain to the ontological sector of logic, rather than to what he called "metalogic," and so to be regarded as liable to change, pertaining to this actual world, not to every possible one. Correspondingly, he distinguished the Law of Contradiction from the Law of Non-Selfcontradiction, "One and the same judgment cannot be simultaneously true and false," which is an unalterable metalogical principle. Vasil'ev characterized a logic with an ontological basis different from that determined by our actual world as an "imaginary" logic, and sought to develop such a logic on a non-Aristotelian basis by dropping one or another of the aforementioned laws.

Thus Vasil'ev hypothesized a world where some objects have the predicate *A*, others its negation predicate *not-A*, and still others which simultaneously have both *A* and *not-A*. In the logic of this imaginary world the status of a proposition may be *affirmative* or *negative* or *indifferent* corresponding to the three "forms of judgment," viz. the *simple affirmation* "*S* is *P*" (or: *O* has *A*), the simple negation "*S* is *not-P*" (or: *O* has *not-A*), and the *combined affirmation and negation*, the indifferent judgment "*S* is both *P* and not-*P*" (or: *O* has both *A* and *not-A*). In such a world, unlike ours, the possession of *not-A* does not entail the absence of *A* (for then the Law of Selfcontradiction would be violated at the metalogical level). The logic of such a world is essentially three-valued, since a proposition ascribing a property to an object will correspond to one of three distinct states of affairs. Vasil'ev formulated a Law of Excluded Fourth which obtains in his three-state world as the Law of Excluded Third (*tertium non datur*) applies to ours in accordance with classical logic.

The most extensive discussion of the contribution of Vasil'ev is V. A. Smirnov's paper (in Russian) on "The Logical Views of N. A. Vasil'ev" in *Očérki po Istorii Logiki v Rossii* (Essays in the History of Logic in Russia) (Moscow, 1962), pp. 242–257. There is an extensive review of this paper by D. D. Comey in *The Journal of Symbolic Logic*, vol. 30 (1965), pp. 368–370, to which the present discussion is greatly indebted. See also George Kline, "N. A. Vasil'ev and the Development of Many-Valued Logics," in A. T. Tymieniecka (ed.), *Contributions to Logic and Methodology in Honor of J. M. Bocheński* (Amsterdam, 1965), pp. 315–326.

Vasil'ev even went on to generalize his three-state ontology to the case of n mutually exclusive and exhaustive states. In these systems neither the Law of Excluded Middle nor the Law of Contradiction will hold in their "ontological" form, although in the n-state system a "Law of Excluded $(n + 1)$st" will always be operative.

Although some of the governing motivations that led Vasil'ev to develop his "imaginary, non-Aristotelian" logics were identical with those guiding the development of many-valued logics, one cannot regard his systems as many-valued logics properly speaking. This is so because Vasil'ev himself never made the transition from his key idea of propositions about states of affairs corresponding to predications more complex than the classical on-off picture, to the concept that the truth status of a given proposition might be other than true or false, so that propositions can have truth-values other than the two classical ones.

Among the early steps toward many-valued logic we might also list the 1916 paper by another American, Edwin Guthrie. We quote a section of this paper:

> Not only can logic include more than the logic of Aristotle, as the modern logistic does, there might have been non-Aristotelian logics with principles different from the familiar laws of contradiction and excluded middle. What final authority would judge between the ultimate "correctness" of Aristotle's logic which offers two contradictories, obeying the laws: $x \cdot x' = 0$, $x + x' = 1$, $(x')' = x$, and a logic which would provide three contradictories, obeying the laws: $x \cdot x' \cdot x'' = 0$, $x + x' + x'' = 1$, $(x')' = x''$, $(x'')' = x$? It is true that we can only discuss other logics in terms of one logic, but this is no more a proof that they are therefore unreal than is the fact that an Englishman in discussing German must use English, a proof that English is the *a priori* condition of communication, valid for all times and all places.[9]

In this extract, Guthrie formulates in plain, straightforward fashion some of the main guiding ideas that stimulated the development of many-valued systems of logic. Regrettably he did not, however, elaborate his ideas so as to contribute to the further development of the subject.

3 The Pioneering Era (1920–1932)

The actual inauguration of many-valued logic must be dated from the pioneering papers of the Pole Jan Łukasiewicz and the American Emil L. Post, published in the early 1920s, in which the first developed systematiza-

[9]See Guthrie (1916), p. 336.

tions of many-valued logic are presented.[1] The systems at issue here and the motivating considerations of their development will be considered in detail in Chap. 2.

Łukasiewicz first publicized his 3-valued system of logic in a lecture before the Polish Philosophical Society in Lwów in 1920.[2] A report written by him (in Polish) giving the content of that lecture was published in the journal *Ruch Filozoficzy* later that year.[3] Łukasiewicz' paper of 1920 especially represents a thoroughgoing repudiation of two-valued logic and advocacy of a 3-valued system. The mainstream of the development of many-valued logic proceeded on the basis of elaborations of Łukasiewicz' ideas—especially in their formulation in his later papers in which the 3-valued logic was generalized to the many-valued, indeed even infinite-valued case.[4] Some of the relevant ideas were given wide circulation in the influential treatise on *Symbolic Logic* by Charles H. Langford and Clarence Irving Lewis published in 1932.[5] An important pioneering result was achieved by Mordchaj Wajsberg, who succeeded in 1931 in axiomatizing the 3-valued logic of Łukasiewicz[6] by the following elegant axiom set (together with the rules of *modus ponens* and substitution):

(1) $\alpha \to (\beta \to \alpha)$
(2) $(\alpha \to \beta) \to [(\beta \to \gamma) \to (\alpha \to \gamma)]$
(3) $(\neg\alpha \to \neg\beta) \to (\beta \to \alpha)$
(4) $[(\alpha \to \sim\alpha) \to \alpha] \to \alpha$

It must be noted that Łukasiewicz' thought about the nature of many-valued logic underwent a considerable change in the course of years. In his earlier papers, he held that only 3-valued and infinite-valued logic possessed philosophical interest and importance in application. Moreover,

---

[1]See Łukasiewicz (1920) and Post (1921). The former of these is translated in S. McCall (ed.), *Polish Logic: 1920-1939* (Oxford, 1967), pp. 16–18; and the latter is reprinted in J. van Heijenoort (ed.), *From Frege to Gödel: A Source Book in Mathematical Logic, 1879-1931* (Cambridge, Mass., 1967), pp. 265–283.

[2]However, Łukasiewicz had already published in 1910 his book on *The Principle of Non-Contradiction in Aristotle* [see Łukasiewicz (1910)] in which one principal motivating idea of the later development of his 3-valued logic—viz. the issue of future contingency—is already a major theme. For an account of the contributions of Łukasiewicz to symbolic logic, see Jordan (1945), Mostowski (1957), Scholz (1957), and Borkowski and Słupecki (1958).

[3]Vol. 5 (1920), p. 170.

[4]See especially Łukasiewicz (1930), tr. in S. McCall (ed.), *Polish Logic: 1920–1939* (Oxford, 1967), pp. 40–65. [Many writers have failed to appreciate that the contribution of Tarski to this paper was limited to one point of detail: the definition of the modal operator *M* by means of implication (*C*) and negation (*N*).] Łukasiewicz had already made the generalization to many-valued and infinite-valued systems by 1922. See Jordan (1945).

[5]See Lewis and Langford (1932), pp. 213–234.

[6]See Wajsberg (1931), tr. in S. McCall (ed.), *Polish Logic: 1920–1939* (Oxford, 1967), pp. 264–284.

he held that n-valued logics with finite $n > 3$ added no innovations of philosophical interest to 3-valued logic.[7] But late in life he changed his opinion and held a certain 4-valued logic to be the most important finitely many-valued logic.[8]

Post discovered his family of many-valued systems independently of the work of Łukasiewicz. His findings were presented in some six pages of his 1921 paper, and he never again returned to the subject in any publication. Whereas Łukasiewicz began with a 3-valued system that he afterwards generalized to n-values (and even to infinitely many values), Post presented his n-valued systems in full generality.[9] However, he did not contemplate the idea of infinite-valued systems, although his ideas for system construction can in fact be extended to the infinite-valued case (as will be shown in Chap. 2 below). Still, viewed as systems of many-valued *propositional* logic, Post's systems have a serious shortcoming. For Post's own semantical interpretation of his systems, the only one that has been devised to date, proceeds in terms of *sets* of propositions, and is not a propositional interpretation at all.

4 The Recent Period (1932–1965)

In the days since its inaugural, pioneering era—say the period 1920–1932—the theory and applications of many-valued logic have been developed along a great variety of lines. We shall now give a concise historical outline of some of the more important of these. Further details regarding many of these findings will be given in Chap. 2, and the reference data given in the classified register of the Bibliography should be consulted.

Various writers have recently carried further the study of the initial 3-valued logic of Łukasiewicz and his later many-valued generalizations of it. In this regard, apart from the continuing contributions of Łukasiewicz himself and the already mentioned results of Wajsberg, the work of other logicians of the Polish school—Alfred Tarski, Jerzy Słupecki, Bolesław Sobociński, and others—is especially important.[1] The joint work of James Barkley Rosser and Atwell R. Turquette is also important,[2] and recent

---

[7]See Łukasiewicz (1930), tr. in S. McCall (ed.), *Polish Logic: 1920–1939* (Oxford, 1967), pp. 40–65.
[8]See Łukasiewicz (1953b). Cf. pp. 97–98 below.
[9]Moreover, whereas the systems of Łukasiewicz allow for only one designated (truth-like) truth-value, Post introduced an arbitrary number of designated truth-values.
[1]For bibliographic data see the Author Listing of the Bibliography in Chap. 4.
[2]For the last see Rosser and Turquette (1952). The work on the Łukasiewiczian systems by logicians of the Polish school (Wajsberg, Słupecki, Sobociński, and others) is described in Sec. 5 of Jordan (1945), tr. in S. McCall (ed.), *Polish Logic: 1920–1939* (Oxford, 1967), pp. 389–395.

papers by Helena Rasiowa, Alan Rose, and Chen Chung Chang are particularly noteworthy in this connection.[3]

Many systems of propositional many-valued logic have been devised and studied apart from the original systems of Łukasiewicz. Along these lines we may cite especially contributions by Arend Heyting,[4] Kurt Gödel,[5] D. A. Bochvar,[6] and Stephen C. Kleene.[7] The papers by Bochvar and Kleene are of particular importance because they develop 3-valued systems of logic which, while fundamentally different from the system of Łukasiewicz, have significant applications in metamathematics (which will be discussed in Chap. 2). Two interesting procedures for creating new pluri-valued logics out of old ones—the methods of system *extension* and of forming the *product* of two systems—have been devised by Stanisław Jaśkowski.[8] The survey by Alonzo Church of unorthodox many-valued truth tables for classical propositional logic is of substantial interest.[9]

Certain special features of logical connectives serve to set many-valued systems of logic apart from their two-valued cousin. The need for special operators and connectives in many-valued logics, especially to assure truth-functional completeness, was recognized early in the development. Here the 1936 paper by J. Słupecki is a pioneering contribution.[10] Recent contributions to the study of special operators and connectives include papers by Norman M. Martin, A. Rose, Trevor Evans and Lane Hardy, and Eric Foxley.[11]

Negation must have special features in many-valued logic due to the absence of a *tertium non datur* principle. This establishes a certain generic kinship between many-valued logic and intuitionistic logic. The study of many-valued systems in the context of the intuitionistic propositional calculus (IPC) represents a fertile and important problem area. The pioneering spadework in this domain was done by the Dutch mathematician L. E. J. Brouwer,[12] but an important paper by the Russian mathematician A. N. Kolmogorov must also be cited.[13] Important contributions to the systema-

---

[3]See Rasiowa (1950), Rose (1950b), (1951f), and (1952b), and Chang (1959).
[4]See Heyting (1930).
[5]See Gödel (1932).
[6]See Bochvar (1939) and (1943).
[7]See Kleene (1938) and (1952).
[8]See the detailed discussion in Secs. 15 and 16 of Chap. 2 below.
[9]See Church (1953).
[10]See Słupecki (1936), tr. in S. McCall (ed.), *Polish Logic: 1920–1939* (Oxford, 1967), pp. 335–337.
[11]See N. M. Martin (1950), (1951), and (1952), Rose (1951a), (1953g), (1961a), and (1965), Evans and Hardy (1957), and Foxley (1962).
[12]See Brouwer (1925a) and (1925b). For a comprehensive listing of Brouwer's contributions see the bibliography in Heyting (1956).
[13]See Kolmogorov (1932).

tization of IPC were made by Arend Heyting,[14] who found a 3-valued logic that captures the calculus without being characteristic of it.[15] K. Gödel demonstrated that no finitely many-valued logic can be characteristic of IPC.[16] In the wake of Gödel's result, S. Jaśkowski was able to achieve the important result of constructing an infinite-valued logic that is characteristic of IPC.[17] An interesting further discussion is afforded in a more recent paper by Gene F. Rose.[18]

The construction of quantification theory for many-valued logic is a relatively late development. The adjustment of quantification theory to fit within the framework of many-valued logic was launched in 1939 in a pioneering paper by J. B. Rosser,[19] and the continuing collaborative work of Rosser and Turquette is of special importance in this connection.[20] A new point of departure was adopted in a 1964 paper by Nicholas Rescher.[21]

The axiomatization of systems of many-valued logic is a matter to which logicians have continued to give a good deal of attention. A detailed examination of the situation is made in the book by J. B. Rosser and A. R. Turquette.[22] Two 1961 papers by Andrzej Mostowski made a significant subsequent contribution.[23] In an important paper of 1955, Karl Schröter devised means for Gentzenizing systems of many-valued logic (i.e., axiomatizing them in a natural-deduction manner by using Gentzen's concept of sequents).[24] One recent significant result along axiomatic lines is the demonstration in 1958 by A. Rose and J. B. Rosser[25] of Łukasiewicz' conjecture that $Ł_{\aleph_0}$ (the denumerably many-valued system of Łukasiewicz) is axiomatized by the five axioms:

(1) to (3) as above
(4) $[(\alpha \to \beta) \to \beta] \to [(\beta \to \alpha) \to \alpha]$
(5) $[(\alpha \to \beta) \to (\beta \to \alpha)] \to (\beta \to \alpha)$

together with the rules of *modus ponens* and substitution.[26]

[14]See the discussion and references in Heyting (1956).
[15]See Heyting (1930), and cf. the discussion in Łukasiewicz (1938).
[16]See Gödel (1932).
[17]See Jaśkowski (1936).
[18]See Gene F. Rose (1953).
[19]See Rosser (1939).
[20]See Rosser and Turquette (1948), (1951), and (1952).
[21]See Rescher (1964).
[22]See Rosser and Turquette (1952).
[23]See Mostowski (1961a) and (1961b).
[24]See Schröter (1955) and G. Rousseau, "Sequents in Many-valued Logic: I," *Fundamenta Mathematica*, vol. 60 (1967), pp. 23–33. Considerable advances are made in this direction in Robert K. Meyer, Topics in Modal and Many-valued Logic (University of Pittsburgh doctoral dissertation, 1966), where unpublished contributions by Nuel D. Belnap, Jr., are also presented and developed.
[25]See Rose and Rosser (1958).
[26]That (4) is dispensable was proved independently in Meredith (1958) and in Chang 1958a.

The question of the semantic interpretation of many-valued logics—involving meaning specifications for truth-value assignments, and not simply viewing such assignments as themselves "semantical"—is a rather vexed one. Only relatively modest results have been achieved. Papers by A. N. Prior and by N. Rescher may be cited in this connection.[27]

No doubt the most important application of many-valued truth tables is their proof-theoretic application in propositional logic for demonstrating the nonderivability of theses and the independence of axioms. For a detailed exposition of this use, A. Church's *Introduction to Mathematical Logic* should be consulted.[28] Another interesting application of many-valued logics within the confines of logic itself is their use in the systematization of nonstandard systems of propositional logic. A joint paper by Alan Ross Anderson and Nuel D. Belnap, Jr., may be cited in this connection,[29] and also a paper by Storrs McCall.[30]

There have been various attempts to use many-valued logics for the study of modal logics, and to articulate ideas of modality by means of many-valuedness. For the earlier phases of such efforts a series of papers published by Robert Feys in 1937–38 should be consulted.[31] The work of K. Gödel is particularly important in this general context.[32] Following Gödel's approach, a 1940 paper by James Dugundji establishes that no finite characteristic matrix representation can be given for any of the Lewis systems S1 to S5.[33] As a consequence, an almost insuperable cleavage between the Lewis-style modal systems and finitely many-valued logic is made manifest.[34]

Systems of many-valued logic that are not actually truth-functional, but are based upon "truth functions" that are *many-valued* (and not single-valued in the orthodox way), have only recently begun to be studied. An early tentative effort in this direction was made by Zygmunt Zawirski in 1936.[35] The first systematic development of this approach was presented in a 1962 paper by N. Rescher.[36]

27See Prior (1955a) and Rescher (1965).
28See Church (1956).
29See Anderson and Belnap (1962).
30Storrs McCall, "Connexive Implication," *The Journal of Symbolic Logic*, vol. 31 (1966), pp. 415–433.
31See Feys (1937–38).
32See Gödel (1932).
33See Dugundji (1940).
34The gap can be bridged using infinite-valued truth tables (in a somewhat artificial way) by the method of Lindenbaum. (See p. 157 below.) Cf. also the more natural probabilistic (and hence non-truth-functional) approach developed for the interpretation of S5 in Rescher (1963).
35See Zawirski (1936a) and (1936b).
36See Rescher (1962).

The very earliest application of many-valued logics was to building up the logical groundwork of mathematical intuitionism. Such applications were envisaged as early as 1923 by L. E. J. Brouwer,[37] to whom the key insights in this area must be credited. Classic papers in this connection are due to John von Neumann and K. Gödel.[38] Important recent explorations of various aspects of the connection between many-valued logic and intuitionism have been made in papers by Takeo Sugihara, J. Łukasiewicz, A. Heyting, and Georg Kreisel.[39]

An important application of many-valued logic to an analysis of the foundational paradoxes in mathematics goes back to a 1939 paper by D. A. Bochvar,[40] who used the third, "indeterminate" truth-value of a 3-valued logic to mean *meaningless* or *undefined*, this truth-value being accorded to paradox-generating propositions.[41] Recently there have also been attempts to apply many-valued logic in the actual development of a paradox-free set theory. An early, rudimentary effort in this direction was made in a 1937 paper by Tameharu Shirai,[42] and a 1954 paper by Moh Shaw-kwei represents another pioneer effort in this direction.[43] Important advances have been made in recent papers by Thoralf Skolem and C. C. Chang.[44] Some logicians have also sought to apply many-valued logic to deal with the semantical paradoxes, especially the Liar paradox,[45] while others have argued that such paradoxes will recur within many-valued logic itself.[46]

The development of syllogistics in the context of many-valued logic has received very little attention. The earliest contribution here is a 1938 paper by Gregor C. Moisil,[47] who has been among the most active contributors to the field generally.

There has been much philosophical interest in many-valued logics. In the main, this has been motivated by preoccupation with the problem of future contingency and the idea of a *neutral* truth-value. Starting with J. Łukasiewicz[48] the idea of a neutral truth-value to reflect the special status of future-contingent propositions has been mooted. Especially the 3-valued

---

[37]See Brouwer (1925a) and (1925b).
[38]See von Neumann (1927) and Gödel (1932).
[39]See Sugihara (1951), Łukasiewicz (1952), Heyting (1956), and Kreisel (1962).
[40]See Bochvar (1939) and (1943).
[41]Compare also Moh Shaw-kwei (1954).
[42]See Shirai (1937). Cf. E. W. Beth, *The Foundations of Mathematics* (New York, 1966), p. 230.
[43]See Moh Shaw-kwei (1954).
[44]See Skolem (1957a) and Chang (1965), where further references are given. Skolem first presented his important work at the Fourth Austrian Mathematical Congress (Vienna, 1956).
[45]See Sec. 30 of Chap. 2 below.
[46]See especially Moh Shaw-kwei (1954).
[47]See Moisil (1938).
[48]See Łukasiewicz (1920).

system of Łukasiewicz has been studied from this standpoint by various writers.[49] In recent years, several papers by A. N. Prior have dealt with various facets of this approach.[50] Particular interest and importance attach to Prior's applications of infinite-series varieties of many-valued logic in the development of "tense logics," i.e., logical systems in which relations of propositions to the past, present, and future play a key role in determining their truth status.

Since the late 1920s a (highly sporadic) philosophical controversy has raged over the question of whether the several many-valued systems of logic represent logical theories alternative to the orthodox, two-valued logic. The earliest contributors to many-valued logic certainly looked on their efforts as providing such alternatives. For example, N. A. Vasil'ev called his system "imaginary" and characterized it as *non-Aristotelian*, drawing an explicit analogy with non-Euclidean geometries.[51] Some of the earlier discussions, apart from those on the (already-cited) papers by J. Łukasiewicz, are by C. I. Lewis and Paul Weiss.[52] In recent years, the Russian logician Aleksander Aleksandrovich Zinov'ev has been particularly active in discussions of this problem area.[53]

Various logicians have attempted to construct algebraic or topological models of many-valued logics. Attempts in the algebraic direction come as early as a 1929 paper by B. A. Bernstein.[54] One sort of topological model was presented by Carl G. Hempel in 1937.[55] The relationships between many-valued logics and lattices have been studied in a series of papers by A. Rose,[56] who has been among the most active contributors to the field generally, as has G. C. Moisil.[57]

From the standpoint of mathematical applications, special interest attaches to probabilistic approaches to many-valued logic which began to be explored around 1930 by the logicians of the Polish school. Z. Zawirski was one of the pioneers in this line of development.[58] Most of the Polish logicians, however, regarded the non-truth-functional character of probability assignments as a decisive obstacle against viewing a probabilistic system as a many-valued logic.[59] K. Ajdukiewicz, S. Mazurkiewicz, and A. Tarksi were of this mind[60]. Among the principal contributors to the

---

[49] A particularly important early development is that of Łukasiewicz (1930).
[50] See Prior (1953b) and (1957a).
[51] See Vasil'ev (1910) and cf. Kline (1965), p. 317.
[52] See Lewis (1932) and Weiss (1933).
[53] See especially Zinov'ev (1963).
[54] See Bernstein (1928).
[55] See Hempel (1937).
[56] See Rose (1950a), (1951d), (1951e), and (1958b).
[57] See Moisil (1939a), (1941b), (1945), and (1960a).
[58] See Zawirski (1934a), (1934b), (1935), (1936a), and (1936b).
[59] See Sec. 27 of Chap. 2 below.
[60] See Ajdukiewicz (1928), Mazurkiewicz (1932) and (1934), and Tarski (1935–36).

development of probabilistic logic were Hans Reichenbach and Rudolf Carnap.[61]

On the side of physical applications, a handful of writers have applied 3-valued logic in the context of indeterminacy situations of quantum mechanics. The ground was broken in a 1931 paper by Z. Zawirski,[62] but perhaps the most influential discussion is that of a paper published in 1936 by Garrett Birkhoff and J. von Neumann.[63] More recently, this line of approach has been pursued especially by H. Reichenbach[64] and Paulette Destouches-Février[65] and has been the arena for an ongoing discussion with many contributors.[66]

Great importance attaches to the use of many-valued logics for the formal analysis of electronic circuitry and in switching theory. Here the pioneering work is Claude E. Shannon's paper of 1938.[67] In later years, V. I. Shestakov[68] and G. C. Moisil[69] have been especially active in this area. (Shestakov's work is based on the 3-valued logic of Bochvar, while Moisil's is based on that of Łukasiewicz.) Among the most interesting ramifications of many-valued logics is their congeniality to computerized study, because of the considerable complexities of calculation that arise in working with many-valued systems. Various aspects of this phenomenon are illustrated in a spate of recent contributions to *The Journal of Computing Systems.*

In closing this brief historical survey, several points seem to be warranted. Many-valued logic is a very new subject whose original development in effect goes back only a single generation. Not only is it recent, but many-valued logic is also a very "unfinished" discipline at the present stage of its development. It is built up by a great mass of often rather isolated findings resulting from the work of a diverse group of contributors approaching the subject from many different directions. All this makes the task of integration (to which the present work is but a modest contribution) a particularly urgent one.[70]

It was virtually inevitable that many-valued logic would establish itself as an important branch of logic. This is clear from the range and

---

[61]See Reichenbach (1935), (1937), and (1949), and Carnap (1950).
[62]See Zawirski (1931).
[63]See Birkhoff and von Neumann (1936).
[64]See Reichenbach (1944), (1951), (1952–54), and (1954).
[65]See Destouches-Février (1951).
[66]See Margenau (1950), Putnam (1957), Törnebohm (1957), Feyerabend (1958), Kuznetzov (1959), and Turquette (1963a).
[67]See Shannon (1938). A part of Shannon's ideas regarding the analysis of electrical circuitry by means of Boolean algebra was developed independently in V. I. Shestakov's 1938 doctoral dissertation for the University of Moscow.
[68]See Shestakov (1946), (1953), and (1960b).
[69]See Moisil (1956a), (1956b), (1957a), and (1957b).
[70]The existing treatises in the field, apart from one very brief introduction—namely Robert Ackermann, *Many-Valued Logics* (London, 1967)—include only Turquette and Rosser (1952) and Zinov'ev (1963), both of which deal with a limited set of special topics.

variety of its applications and its connections with problems in other branches of inquiry. Moreover, many-valued logic is of particular interest from the philosophical point of view, because of its deep involvement with such philosophical issues as the question of future contingency, the problem of the logic of indeterminacy in quantum theory, and above all because the multiplicity of diverse systems of many-valued logic poses the question of "alternative logics" and the whole issue of relativism and conventionalism in logic.

The treatment of the historical aspect of many-valued logic in the present chapter has been deliberately compact. However, many further historical details going beyond these brief indications will be found in the discussion of specific systems in the text of Chap. 2.

Chapter 2

A Survey of Many-valued Logic

1 Symbolism, Notation, and Terminology

The object of this preliminary section is to describe some special items of symbolism, notation, and terminology that are to be used throughout the ensuing presentation. All these devices will be used repeatedly and should eventually become thoroughly familiar to the reader. It seems advisable to collect these descriptions together here, both by way of explanation and for handy reference.

A basic distinction is to be drawn between the classical *two-valued* logic and other systems that are *many-valued* in that they possess three or more truth-values. The term "pluri-valued" will be used generically to embrace both two-valued and many-valued systems. (Incidentally, we shall always write out "*two*-valued" but shall otherwise use: 3-valued, 4-valued, *n*-valued, etc.)

The letters of the following list:

$$p, q, r, \ldots$$

will be used as *metasystematic* variables for the well-formed formulas (wffs) of the particular system under discussion. For the propositional variables of the system itself we shall use lowercase Greek letters:

$\alpha, \beta, \gamma, \ldots$

This practice is the exact reverse of that which has become more usual in logic books. Since virtually our entire discussion is conducted on the metalinguistic level, this procedure has, however, been adopted here to give the text a more familiar-looking typographical appearance.

Systems of pluri-valued logic will always be denoted by capital letters in boldface; for example, the classical two-valued propositional calculus will be represented as $\mathbf{C_2}$.

We shall in general use the following symbolism for the propositional connectives of pluri-valued logics:

	Two-valued systems	Many-valued systems
Negation	$\sim$	$\neg$
Conjunction	$\&$	$\wedge$
Disjunction	$\vee$	$\vee$
Implication	$\supset$	$\rightarrow$, $\supset\!\!\!\!\cdot$
Equivalence	$\equiv$	$\leftrightarrow$, $\equiv$

Occasionally when several styles of many-valued connectives are being contrasted, further symbols may be introduced; for example, the group $\neg$, $\wedge$, $\vee$, $\Rightarrow$, and $\Leftrightarrow$; or again the group —, $\wedge$, $\vee$, $\leftrightarrow\!\!\!\!/$, and $\leftrightarrow$. With respect to the two double entries in the table given above it should be remarked that '$\rightarrow$' and '$\leftrightarrow$' will be used *in general*, with '$\supset\!\!\!\!\cdot$' and '$\equiv$' confined to the special case of the analogues for material implication:

$p \supset\!\!\!\!\cdot q$ FOR $\neg p \vee q$
$p \equiv q$ FOR $(p \supset\!\!\!\!\cdot q) \wedge (q \supset\!\!\!\!\cdot p)$

Definitional equivalences will be presented by using "FOR" in the just-indicated way.

Our attitude regarding the usual logicians' use of quotation marks is to adopt a practice that uses them in the most sparing possible way that is at all consonant with a recognition of the crucial distinction between meaning and use. Object-language symbols will be employed in the metalanguage in the usual autonymous way, and metalinguistic *formulas* will be given without any quotation marks. In general, quotes will be used only when talking about (1) *pieces of notation* (symbols, letters, etc.), (2) *intrasystematic formulas*, that is, formulas given within the language of the logical systems at issue, and (3) *verbal metalinguistic expressions*, viz. those that are not formulated wholly by symbolism, but involve English-language terms. We shall use only single and double quotes—single quotes around single letters and symbols, double quotes around more complex expressions.

The truth-value of a formula *p* will be represented by placing that formula within bars:

$/p/$

Identity and difference among truth-values will be indicated by the familiar symbolism, thus:

$$/p/ = /p \wedge p/$$
$$/p/ \neq /q/$$

Two abbreviations will be put to frequent use:

iff   FOR   *if and only if*
wff   FOR   *well-formed formula*

Apart from these special conventions, the standard symbolism of logic and of the elementary theory of sets will be used in the orthodox way with which the reader is expected to be familiar.

2 Two-valued Logic

Given a propositional logic of the familiar type, it is possible—once the rigorous *syntactical* (structure-oriented, grammatical) development of the system itself has been accomplished—to enter into the area of *semantical* (meaning-oriented) issues. The standard line of approach here is to consider the two truth-values *T* (for *truth*) and *F* (for *falsity*). Thereupon one introduces formal truth rules for the various propositional connectives, spelling out these rules by means of truth tables. Thus the truth rules for the usual connectives '$\sim$' (negation), '$\vee$' (disjunction), '&' (conjunction), '$\supset$' (material implication), and '$\equiv$' (material equivalence) are given by the following set of truth tables:

p	$\sim p$		q	$p \,\&\, q$		$p \vee q$		$p \supset q$		$p \equiv q$	
		p		T	F	T	F	T	F	T	F
T	F		T	T	F	T	T	T	F	T	F
F	T		F	F	F	T	F	T	T	F	T

The content—if not this particular form—of these truth tables will be entirely familiar to the reader.[1] In the second tabulation, the truth-value for p is given along the left-hand margin, and that for q along the top margin, so that the bottom right-hand entry of the &-table, for example—namely F—tells us that when p takes on the truth-value F (see its column entry), and q does likewise (see its row entry), then $p \& q$ will be false (i.e., takes on the truth-value F). Thus the truth table for conjunction contains the same four items of information often presented in the more familiar format:

p	q	$p \& q$
T	T	T
T	F	F
F	T	F
F	F	F

Given such a set of truth tables for certain connectives, we can think of the wffs involving these connectives in input-output terms. When certain truth-values are "fed into" a formula (wff), the formula guides us in using the truth tables to calculate an output truth-value. Thus consider the formula:

$$\alpha \supset (\beta \& [(\alpha \lor \beta) \supset (\gamma \equiv \alpha)])$$

When $/\alpha/ = T$, $/\beta/ = F$, and $/\gamma/ = T$, then this amounts to:

$$T \supset (F \& [(T \lor F) \supset (T \equiv T)])$$

Since the truth tables for $\lor$ and $\equiv$ inform us that $T \lor F = T$ and $T \equiv T = T$, this amounts to:

$$T \supset (F \& [(T) \supset (T)])$$

And since $T \supset T = T$, this amounts to:

$$T \supset (F \& [T])$$

---

[1] The truth tables are also often presented in an equivalent but variant numerical form, with 1 for T and 0 for F:

p	$\sim p$		q p	$p \& q$ 1 0	$p \lor q$ 1 0	$p \supset q$ 1 0	$p \equiv q$ 1 0
1	0		1	1 0	1 1	1 0	1 0
0	1		0	0 0	1 0	1 1	0 1

The construction of propositional logic by this method of truth tables had been originated by the American logician C. S. Peirce by around 1885.

But since $F \& T = F$, this amounts to:

$T \supset F$

which, by the truth table for $\supset$, amounts to F. This process illustrates how truth tables are used in the computation of the truth-values of complex formulas for specified assignments of truth-values to their constituent propositional variables. (The reader is assumed to be thoroughly familiar with the procedures involved here.)

It is possible to provide truth tables of this sort for all the propositional connectives that may be at issue, over and above the five indicated ones. All of these propositional connectives are—in view of their intended role and meaning—strictly *truth-functional*: they are such that, given the truth-values of the components, the truth-value of the resulting compound is always uniquely determined. For example, it is of the very essence of the meaning of '&' that a conjunction of the form $p \& q$ will be true just exactly when both components are true, and will always be false otherwise.

In the familiar case of the orthodox system of propositional logic we thus have to do with a two-valued—and strictly truth-functional—system of propositional logic. This system—which has been well known since the publication in 1910 by B. Russell and A. N. Whitehead of the first volume of their monumental *Principia Mathematica*—is the *classical* two-valued propositional calculus, which we shall designate as the system C_2. It represents the starting point for the development of many-valued systems of logic, and we shall assume that its principal features are familiar to the reader.

A (two-valued) tautology is a formula that always takes the truth-value T according to the indicated truth tables, regardless of what truth-values may be assigned to its component propositional variables. For example:

$\alpha \lor \sim\alpha$
$\sim(\alpha \& \sim\alpha)$
$\alpha \supset \alpha$

A particularly elegant axiomatization of C_2 is due to J. Łukasiewicz. It is based upon two rules of inference:

1. *Modus ponens*: If p and $p \supset q$ have been established as theorems, then q may be asserted as a theorem.
2. Substitution: Once p has been established as a theorem, one may assert as a theorem any other formula p' obtained from p by uniformly replacing all the occurrences in p of some propositional variable by any formula whatsoever.

Negation ($\sim$) and implication ($\supset$) are to be primitive, but the remaining propositional connectives can be introduced by the definitions:

$p \mathbin{\&} q$ FOR $\sim(p \supset \sim q)$
$p \vee q$ FOR $\sim p \supset q$
$p \equiv q$ FOR $(p \supset q) \mathbin{\&} (q \supset p)$

The axioms to be adopted are as follows:

(1) $(\sim\alpha \supset \alpha) \supset \alpha$
(2) $\alpha \supset (\sim\alpha \supset \beta)$
(3) $(\alpha \supset \beta) \supset [(\beta \supset \gamma) \supset (\alpha \supset \gamma)]$

From this basis, the entire system of classical propositional logic C_2 as systematized in *Principia Mathematica* can be developed axiomatically.

The objective of such an axiomatization of two-valued logic is to provide an economical list of theses from which all tautologies (but only the tautologies) can be derived as theorems by the rules of inference of the system (standardly the rules of substitution and *modus ponens*).[2] Such an axiom system, with respect to which every formula (wff) that is a theorem is also a two-valued tautology, and also conversely, so that every tautology is a theorem, is said to be *complete* for classical two-valued logic. (This mode of completeness involves ideas to which we shall return at considerable length below.)

It is important to stress that it is the semantical basis with its interpretation in terms of truth-values—and not the axiom system—that is the starting point for such an articulation of propositional logic. The truth tables provide a preexisting criterion of acceptability (viz. tautologousness) to which the axiom system must conform at the peril of inadequacy.

3 The 3-valued Logic of Łukasiewicz

A possible step beyond the simplest case of two-valued logic is the introduction of a third, "intermediate" or "neutral" or "indeterminate" truth-value *I*. This step was first taken by J. Łukasiewicz, who, in discussions beginning with a paper of 1920, pursued a line of thought that was motivated by ideas of *modality*, along the following lines:

> I can assume without contradiction that my presence in Warsaw at a certain moment of next year, e.g. at noon on 21 December, is at the present time determined neither positively nor negatively. Hence it is *possible*, but not *necessary*, that I shall be present in Warsaw at the given time. On this assumption the proposition "I shall be in Warsaw at noon on 21 December of next year," can at the present time be neither true nor false. For if it were

---

[2]This second rule is frequently also called the "rule of detachment."

true now, my future presence in Warsaw would have to be necessary, which is contradictory to the assumption. If it were false now, on the other hand, my future presence in Warsaw would have to be impossible, which is also contradictory to the assumption. Therefore the proposition considered is at the moment *neither true nor false* and must possess a third value, different from '0' or falsity and '1' or truth. This value we can designate by '$\frac{1}{2}$.' It represents "the possible," and joins "the true" and "the false" as a third value. The three-valued system of propositional logic owes its origin to this line of thought.[1]

Łukasiewicz thus implemented the idea—possessed of deep roots in the tradition of Aristotelian logic—that propositions regarding "future-contingent" matters have a truth status that does not correspond to either of the orthodox truth-values of truth and falsity.

In carrying out this idea, one must, of course, introduce corresponding ·complications into the truth rules for our propositional connectives. Łukasiewicz' solution to this problem consisted in effect in his putting forward the following truth tables:[2]

p	$\neg p$	q \ p	$p \wedge q$			$p \vee q$			$p \rightarrow q$			$p \leftrightarrow q$		
			T	I	F	T	I	F	T	I	F	T	I	F
T	F	T	T	I	F	T	T	T	T	I	F	T	I	F
I	I	I	I	I	F	T	I	I	T	T	I	I	T	I
F	T	F	F	F	F	T	I	F	T	T	T	F	I	T

Here again we have a strictly truth-functional system of propositional logic, but now one that is based upon three truth-values in place of the classical two. We shall designate this system, the 3-valued logic of Łukasiewicz, as $\mathbf{L_3}$. It is certainly the best-known of all pluri-valued systems alternative to the classical propositional calculus $\mathbf{C_2}$.

Actually, Łukasiewicz himself did not present his system in the all-at-once manner employed here. He used '¬' and '→' as primitives, subject to the given truth tables, and then defined the other connectives in terms of these as follows:

$p \vee q$ FOR $(p \rightarrow q) \rightarrow q$
$p \wedge q$ FOR $\neg(\neg p \vee \neg q)$
$p \leftrightarrow q$ FOR $(p \rightarrow q) \wedge (q \rightarrow p)$

[1]"Philosophische Bemerkungen zu mehrwertigen Systemen des Aussagenkalküls," *Comptes rendus des séances de la Société des sciences et des lettres de Varsovie*, Classe III, vol. xxiii (1930), pp. 51–77. An English translation of the paper is given in S. McCall (ed.), *Polish Logic 1920–1939* (Oxford, 1967), pp. 40–65 (see p. 53). In this paper Łukasiewicz discusses the prior history of his work with this system.
[2]We shall use T where Łukasiewicz used 1, and similarly shall replace his $\frac{1}{2}$ by I and his 0 by F.

These definitions lead from the truth tables for $\neg$ and $\rightarrow$ to those for the remaining connectives, as given above.

A system of many-valued logic is individuated by the formal structure among its connectives: the particular notational machinery deployed in its presentation is immaterial. Thus the following two sets of truth tables should also be viewed as merely alternative ways of presenting the system $Ł_3$:

p	$\neg p$		$p \wedge\!\!\wedge q$ 1 2 3	$p \vee\!\!\vee q$ 1 2 3	$p \Rightarrow q$ 1 2 3	$p \Leftrightarrow q$ 1 2 3
		$\begin{smallmatrix}q\\p\end{smallmatrix}$				
1	3	1	1 2 3	1 1 1	1 2 3	1 2 3
2	2	2	2 2 3	1 2 2	1 1 2	2 1 2
3	1	3	3 3 3	1 2 3	1 1 1	3 2 1

p	$-p$		$p \wedge q$ 1 ½ 0	$p \vee q$ 1 ½ 0	$p \leftrightarrow q$ 1 ½ 0	$p \leftrightarrow\!\!\leftrightarrow q$ 1 ½ 0
		$\begin{smallmatrix}q\\p\end{smallmatrix}$				
1	0	1	1 ½ 0	1 1 1	1 ½ 0	1 ½ 0
½	½	½	½ ½ 0	1 ½ ½	1 1 ½	½ 1 ½
0	1	0	0 0 0	1 ½ 0	1 1 1	0 ½ 1

The isomorphism (sameness of structure) between these truth tables and the initially given set assures that they all represent one and the same system of many-valued logic, despite whatever differences of symbolism may be involved.

The guiding principles of this system of 3-valued logic are readily explained:

(1) There are to be three truth-values, *T, I, F* (so ordered in terms of decreasing "truthfulness").

(2) The negation of a statement of given truth-values is its "opposite" in truthfulness.

(3) The truth-value of a conjunction is the falsest—and of a disjunction the truest—of the truth-values of its components.

(4) The truth-value of $p \rightarrow q$ is the same as that of $\neg p \vee q$, just as in classical propositional logic $p \supset q$ is equivalent with $\sim p \vee q$, *except* that the truth-value corresponding to $I \rightarrow I$ is set at *T* (to assure that "$\alpha \rightarrow \alpha$" will be tautologous by invariably assuming the truth-value *T*).

(5) The truth-value of $p \leftrightarrow q$ is to be the same as that of $(p \rightarrow q) \wedge (q \rightarrow p)$.

With a view to the future-contingency interpretation of the third truth-value *I*, Łukasiewicz introduced a modal operator of possibility and necessity (symbolically $\Diamond$ and $\Box$) into his 3-valued logic. These are to be subject to the truth table:

p	$\Diamond p$	$\Box p$
T	T	T
I	T	F
F	F	F

Thus, $\Diamond p$ is to be true if p is either true or indeterminate, but is false if p is definitely false. Alfred Tarski, then a pupil of Łukasiewicz', remarked that $\neg p \rightarrow p$ will—according to Łukasiewicz' 3-valued truth table—have exactly this same truth table and may thus be used as a definition of $\Diamond p$ within this framework.

In this connection it should be observed that Łukasiewicz' choice of '$\rightarrow$' as one of the primitives of his system was not an idle one. For his mode of implication '$\rightarrow$' could never be defined in terms of the truth tables for '$\neg$,' '$\wedge$,' and '$\vee$,' since each of these (and thus any combination thereof) yields an *I*-output for *I*-inputs, whereas $p \rightarrow p$ assumes the truth-value T when p takes on the truth-value *I*.

One of Łukasiewicz' principal motivations in the development of many-valued logic was the realization that a truth-functional treatment of the modalities was not possible in two-valued logic. The closest we can come to specifying modalities in C_2 along the indicated lines is

p	$\Diamond p$	$\Box p$
T	T	T
F	F	F

and then "$\alpha \equiv \Diamond \alpha$" and "$\Box \alpha \equiv \alpha$" and "$\Box \alpha \equiv \Diamond \alpha$" will all be logical truths (tautologies) so that modal distinctions collapse. In the 3-valued logic, however, we will have the desirable implications "$\alpha \rightarrow \Diamond \alpha$" and "$\Box \alpha \rightarrow \alpha$" and "$\Box \alpha \rightarrow \Diamond \alpha$," without being saddled with their undesirable converses, so that modal distinctions are preserved. Łukasiewicz attached great importance to this feature of his 3-valued logic.

It is an important facet of $Ł_3$ that the 3-valued truth table agrees with the usual two-valued ones when only T's and F's are involved, that is to say at the extreme or corner positions of the matrices for the individual connectives. This is rendered graphic if we mark out all entries in rows or columns headed by *I*:

			$p \wedge q$			$p \vee q$			$p \to q$			$p \leftrightarrow q$		
p	$\neg p$	$q\backslash p$	T	I	F	T	I	F	T	I	F	T	I	F
T	F	T	T	I	F	T	T	T	T	I	F	T	I	F
I	I	I	I	I	F	T	I	I	T	T	I	I	I	I
F	T	F	F	F	F	T	I	F	T	T	T	F	I	T

It follows from this that any 3-valued tautology—i.e., any formula (wff) that takes on the truth-value *T* regardless of the (3-valued) assignment to its variables of truth-values *T*, *I*, *F*—must also be a two-valued tautology (since it will then also take on *T* in the two-valued case, when only *T*'s and *F*'s are involved in an assignment—and thus *always* in the two-valued case by the agreement of the truth tables).

On the other hand, two-valued tautologies can take the truth-value *I* and thus fail to be tautologous in the 3-valued case—a "tautology" again being construed as a formula that uniformly takes on the truth-value *T* for all assignments of truth-values to the variables. Thus what is sometimes called the "Law of the Excluded Middle," namely the thesis "$\alpha \vee \neg \alpha$," fails to obtain as a tautology in $\mathbf{L}_3$, because this entire formula will take on the truth-value *I* when 'α' does so. Note that if Łukasiewicz had adopted a different disjunction relationship in place of his $\vee$, viz.

$$p \veebar q \quad \text{FOR} \quad \neg p \to q$$

whose truth table is

$q\backslash p$	$p \veebar q$		
	T	I	F
T	T	T	T
I	T	T	I
F	T	I	F

then the corresponding "Law of the Excluded Middle," viz. "$\alpha \veebar \neg \alpha$," would have been a tautology. (This law is thus not dependent upon two-valuedness; it may still obtain in the non-two-valued case.) Note, however, that the adoption of this revised mode of disjunction has certain undesirable side effects. For example, the 3-valued analogue of "$(\alpha \vee \alpha) \to \alpha$" is no longer a tautology if we change from $\vee$ to $\veebar$.

Some other examples of two-valued tautologies whose 3-valued analogues in $Ł_3$ fail to be tautologous are:

$$[(\alpha \to \beta) \to \alpha] \to \alpha$$
$$[\alpha \to (\alpha \to \beta)] \to (\alpha \to \beta)$$

However, the "paradoxes of material implication"

$$\alpha \to (\beta \to \alpha)$$
$$\sim\alpha \to (\alpha \to \beta)$$

will be $Ł_3$-tautologies. On the other hand, the "law of contradiction,"

$$\neg(\alpha \wedge \neg\alpha)$$

will fail to obtain: "$\alpha \wedge \neg\alpha$" takes the truth-value I when 'α' does so. In this regard, $Ł_3$ differs from the intuitionistic propositional logic of Brouwer and Heyting, for which the law of excluded middle also fails, but the law of contradiction does not.

If a formula (wff) never assumes F in $Ł_3$, then (since $Ł_3$ agrees with C_2 when only T's and F's are involved) it can never assume F in C_2 and is therefore a C_2-tautology. It might thus be surmised that if we redefine the conception of a "tautology," replacing the requirement that it "always takes on T" by requiring merely that it "always takes on either T or I," then the tautologies of this version of $Ł_3$ will be exactly those of C_2 itself. But this conjecture is erroneous, as shown by the example (due to A. R. Turquette) of the formula "$\neg(\alpha \to \neg\alpha) \vee \neg(\neg\alpha \to \alpha)$," whose two-valued counterpart is a C_2-tautology, but which assures F in $Ł_3$. when $/\alpha/ = I$.[3]

It is a noteworthy feature of $Ł_3$ that all its formulas that involve only '$\neg$,' '$\vee$,' and '$\wedge$' must take on the truth-value I when all of the propositional variables involved do so. This means that no such formulas—not even "$\alpha \wedge \neg\alpha$"—can be contradictions and uniformly take on the truth-value F for *all* assignments of truth-values to the variables. It is also curious that even a formula which, from the standpoint of interpretation, is as implausible as

$$(\alpha \wedge \neg\alpha) \leftrightarrow (\alpha \vee \neg\alpha)$$

can in appropriate circumstances take on T as its truth-value (viz. when $/\alpha/ = I$).

It is appropriate to make some further general observations about the fundamental motivation behind the idea of a third, indeterminate or

---

[3]This refutes the contention—encountered in various places in the literature—that no two-valued tautology can take on the truth-value F in $Ł_3$. This erroneous claim was made by A. N. Prior in the *Encyclopedia of Philosophy* ed. by P. Edwards (vol. 5, p. 3; New York, 1967) and echoed by the present writer in *Topics in Philosophical Logic* (Dordrecht, 1968), p. 66. I am grateful to Professor Prior for drawing the matter to my attention and notifying me of Turquette's finding as communicated in correspondence. For a further consideration of related issues see pp. 66–67 below.

"neuter," truth-value. Consider a highly inhomogeneous domain of objects (one that includes, say, sticks, stones, and numbers) and a corresponding range of descriptive or classificatory predicates of these objects (say "is granite," "is evergreen," "is a prime"). Now for an object *a* and a predicate *P*, three situations can be envisaged:

> (1) *Pa*, that is, *P* is *truly applicable* to *a*, in that (i) *P* can meaningfully be applied to *a* and (ii) the (meaningful) statement that results when *P* is applied to *a* is true.
> (2) $\overline{Pa}$, that is, *P* is *falsely applicable* to *a*, in that (i) just as before and (ii) the (meaningful) statement that results when *P* is applied to *a* is false.
> (3) Neither *Pa* nor $\overline{Pa}$, that is, *P* is *inapplicable* to *a*.

In a 3-valued logic these three cases are represented by classing *Pa* as true, false, and intermediate for these three cases. This leads to the following correspondences:

Situation	Truth status of *Pa*
1. *Pa*	*T*
2. $\overline{Pa}$	*F*
3. Neither *Pa* nor $\overline{Pa}$	*I*

Thus to say "*Pa* is not true" is to make the relatively weaker assertion that either Case 2 or Case 3 obtains, whereas to say "$\overline{Pa}$ is true" is to make the stronger, more specific assertion that Case 2 obtains. (These two modes of "negation" must then be carefully differentiated,[4] although in two-valued logic the distinctions at issue cannot even be drawn.)

These considerations indicate one general sort of purpose for which a 3-valued logic like that of Łukasiewicz will prove serviceable, viz. when situations like the above (and also Łukasiewicz' own problem case of future contingency) can be envisaged in which a proposition can only misleadingly or inappropriately be classed simply as true or as false, being such that its truth status is best indicated as being "indeterminate," "indefinite," "neuter," "undefined," or some such thing.

[4]They would correspond to the truth tables:

p	$N^w p$	$N^s p$
T	*F*	*F*
I	*T*	*F*
F	*T*	*T*

Note that the truth of $N^s p$ requires that of $N^w p$, but not conversely.

4 The 3-valued System of Bochvar

An important variant system of 3-valued logic was presented by the Russian logician D. A. Bochvar in a paper published in 1939.[1] Bochvar proposed to construe *I* as "undecidable" in a sense somewhat along the lines of "having *some* element of undecidability about it." On his construction, the Łukasiewiczian principle that the truth-value of a conjunction is the "falsest" of the truth-values of its components was abandoned, and the truth table for conjunction changed to:

	$p \wedge q$		
q	T	I	F
p			
T	T	I	F
I	I	I	I
F	F	I	F

That is to say, a Bochvarian conjunction agrees with the two-valued case when only *T*'s and *F*'s are involved, but will automatically take the truth-value *I* when either of its components takes this truth-value. (The fact that this happens when one of the components of the *conjunction* is false renders the semantics of the situation somewhat problematic.)

We are to think of *I* not so much as "intermediate" between truth and falsity but rather as *paradoxical* or even *meaningless*. We can think of such meaninglessness in terms of what is at issue in the classical semantical paradoxes—i.e., statements which, like "This sentence is false," one cannot viably class either as true or as false (if true it is false, if false, true). The effect of these motivating considerations is to make it plausible to take the view that the presence of an *I*-valued conjunct infects the entire conjunction with meaninglessness. The truth table is thus more suggestively presented as:

	$p \wedge q$		
q	T	F	I
p			
T	T	F	I
F	F	F	I
I	I	I	I

[1]See D. A. Bochvar, "Ob odnom tréhznačhom isčislénii i égo priménénii k analizu paradoksov kalssičéskogo rassirénnogo funkcional 'nogo isčislenija" (On a 3-valued logical calculus and its application to the analysis of contradictions), *Matématičeskij sbornik*, vol. 4 (1939), pp. 287–308. The paper is in Russian, but cf. the review by A. Church in *The Journal of Symbolic Logic*, vol. 4 (1939), pp. 98–99, and the correction, *ibid.*, vol. 5 (1940), p. 119. See also Bochvar's "K voprosu o neprotivorečivosti odnogo trexznačnogo isčislenija" (On the consistency of a three-valued calculus), *Matématičeskij sbornik*, vol. 54 (1943), pp. 353–369.

I now appears in a particularly strong role: its presence in a conjunction overpowers the whole and reduces it to *I* status.

Given the truth table for $\wedge$ as presented above, the other connectives in Bochvar's system are as follows:

(1) $\neg$ is defined as in the system of Łukasiewicz

(2) $\vee$ is defined by the definition:

$p \vee q$ FOR $\neg(\neg p \wedge \neg q)$

(3) $\rightarrow$ is defined by the definition:

$p \rightarrow q$ FOR $\neg(p \wedge \neg q)$

(4) $\leftrightarrow$ is defined by the definition:

$p \leftrightarrow q$ FOR $[(p \rightarrow q) \wedge (q \rightarrow p)]$

The truth tables for the whole group of connectives of Bochvar's system—let us call it B_3—will thus be as follows:

p	$\neg p$	q \ p	$p \wedge q$			$p \vee q$			$p \rightarrow q$			$p \leftrightarrow q$		
			T	I	F	T	I	F	T	I	F	T	I	F
T	F	T	T	I	F	T	I	T	T	I	F	T	I	F
I	I	I	I	I	I	I	I	I	I	I	I	I	I	I
F	T	F	F	I	F	T	I	F	T	I	T	F	I	T

In Bochvar's system, the usual concept of a *tautology* as a formula that is uniformly true, regardless of the truth-values assigned to its propositional variables, becomes inoperative. For once the truth-value *I* is an input into a formula, this formula is automatically I-assuming. The system B_3 is thus in need of further extensions if the usual concept of a tautology is to become applicable. (Or, alternatively, one could bring to bear the idea of a *quasi-tautology* as a formula that never assumes the truth-value *F*, regardless of the truth-values assigned to its propositional variables. Then one can show that the quasi-tautologies of Bochvar's B_3 are exactly the orthodox two-valued tautologies of C_2.)

In extending his system, Bochvar makes use of the idea of two distinct modes of *assertion:*

(1) The ordinary, straightforward, "internal" assertion of a formula *p* as simply *p*.

(2) The special mode of "external" assertion of a formula, represented by the special assertion operator *A*: *Ap*.

These two modes of assertion are characterized by the truth tables:

p	External assertion Ap	Internal assertion p
T	T	T
I	F	I
F	F	F

Subject to this conception, distinct "internal" and "external" versions can be defined for the various other connectives. Thus:

Connective	Internal form	External form[2]
Negation	$\neg p$	$\neg\!\!\neg p = \neg Ap$
Conjunction	$p \wedge q$	$p \,\barwedge\, q = Ap \wedge Aq$
Disjunction	$p \vee q$	$p \,\veebar\, q = Ap \vee Aq$
Implication	$p \rightarrow q$	$p \Rightarrow q = Ap \rightarrow Aq$
Equivalence	$p \leftrightarrow q$	$p \Leftrightarrow q = Ap \leftrightarrow Aq$

Thus when it comes to the "external" form of the connectives, we are throughout working simply with the two classical truth-values T and F, with respect to which even the internal 3-valued connectives agree entirely with the classical, two-valued case.[3] The truth tables for Bochvar's "external" connectives—whose interior will contain only T's and F's—will thus be as follows:

p	$\neg\!\!\neg p$	$\begin{array}{c} \\ q \\ p\diagdown \end{array}$	$p \barwedge q$ $T \ \ I \ \ F$	$p \veebar q$ $T \ \ I \ \ F$	$p \Rightarrow q$ $T \ \ I \ \ F$	$p \Leftrightarrow q$ $T \ \ I \ \ F$
T	F	T	$T \ \ F \ \ F$	$T \ \ T \ \ T$	$T \ \ F \ \ F$	$T \ \ F \ \ F$
I	F	I	$F \ \ F \ \ F$	$T \ \ F \ \ F$	$T \ \ T \ \ T$	$F \ \ T \ \ T$
F	T	F	$F \ \ F \ \ F$	$T \ \ F \ \ F$	$T \ \ T \ \ T$	$F \ \ T \ \ T$

We shall designate the system based on these connectives as $\mathbf{B}_3^{\mathrm{E}}$.

Thanks to their greater similarity to the familiar, two-valued case, the "external" connectives have certain obvious advantages *vis-à-vis* the "internal" ones as regards questions of interpretation. For example, consider "external" negation. The formula "$\alpha \barwedge \neg\!\!\neg\alpha$" will invariably come out

---

[2]Note that to obtain the "external" formula corresponding to an "internal" one, we simply put an 'A' before every occurrence of a propositional variable in the "internal" formula.

[3]The situation created by the introduction of "external" connectives would thus be exactly the same in any other system (e.g., that of Łukasiewicz) which agrees with the two-valued truth tables when only T's and F's are involved.

false, regardless of the value of 'α'; "$\alpha \lor \neg \alpha$" will invariably come out true; and one of the pair 'p' and "$\neg p$" will always take on the truth-value *false*. By contrast, it is an obvious disadvantage of Łukasiewicz' system that "$\alpha \land \neg \alpha$" does not inevitably come out false (specifically, it takes the truth-value I when 'α' does so).

It is easy to see that this Bochvarian system (as well as any other that resembles it in the relevant respects) will contain a fragment isomorphic with the classical, two-valued system $\mathbf{C_2}$: Let any classical tautology of $\mathbf{C_2}$ be rewritten with all the classical connectives replaced by their "external" counterparts in $\mathbf{B_3^E}$. Then the resulting formula must clearly be a tautology of $\mathbf{B_3^E}$ (since only T's and F's are involved, and the truth tables agree in the T-F case). Conversely, it is readily seen that every tautology of $\mathbf{B_3^E}$ will also be a tautology of $\mathbf{C_2}$, since the truth tables of $\mathbf{B_3^E}$ agree with those of $\mathbf{C_2}$ when only T's and F's are involved. It is thus an interesting feature of Bochvar's external system that it "includes" (in a certain sense) the whole of the classical, two-valued logic.

A very similar situation, however, obtains with regard to the original 3-valued system of Łukasiewicz. Consider a 3-valued logic with a mode of "weak assertion" W akin to Bochvar's external assertion A:

p	Wp
T	T
I	T
F	F

(Note that Wp would even be definable in $\mathbf{L_3}$ as: $\neg(p \land \neg p) \to p$.) Given some family of 3-valued connectives $\neg$, $\land$, $\lor$, $\to$, $\leftrightarrow$, we can introduce their "weak" counterparts $\neg$, $\barwedge$, $\veebar$, $\Rightarrow$, and $\Leftrightarrow$, exactly on analogy with Bochvar's approach:

Connective	Original form	Weak counterpart
Negation	$\neg p$	$\neg p = \neg Wp$
Conjunction	$p \land q$	$p \barwedge q = Wp \land Wq$
Disjunction	$p \lor q$	$p \veebar q = Wp \lor Wq$
Implication	$p \to q$	$p \Rightarrow q = Wp \to Wq$
Equivalence	$p \leftrightarrow q$	$p \Leftrightarrow q = Wp \leftrightarrow Wq$

Specifically for $\mathbf{L_3}$, the 3-valued system of Łukasiewicz one obtains the system $\mathbf{L_3^W}$:

p	$\neg p$	$\begin{smallmatrix}&q\\p&\end{smallmatrix}$	$p \wedge q$			$p \vee q$			$p \Rightarrow q$			$p \Leftrightarrow q$		
			T	I	F	T	I	F	T	I	F	T	I	F
T	F	T	T	T	F	T	T	T	T	T	F	T	T	F
I	F	I	T	T	F	T	T	T	T	T	F	T	T	F
F	T	F	F	F	F	T	T	F	T	T	T	F	F	T

When formulas (wffs) of C_2 are rewritten with *these* connectives, we have it that: a C_2-formula is a C_2-tautology iff its L_3^W-translation is an L_3^W-tautology. Thus L_3^W (and so also L_3, by whose means L_3^W has been set up) contains a *model* of the classical two-valued system C_2, i.e., has a subsector that is isomorphic with C_2[4].

Let us characterize a formula as *contradictory* within the 3-valued system if it never assumes the truth-value T for any assignment of the truth-values T, I, F to its propositional variables. With respect to tautologies and contradictions it should be noted that:

(1) "$\alpha \leftrightarrow \alpha$" is not a tautology in Bochvar's (internal) system (it takes the truth-value I when 'α' does so).

(2) "$\alpha \vee \neg\alpha$" is not a tautology of B_3 (for the same reason), although "$\alpha \vee \neg\alpha$" is.

(3) "$\alpha \wedge \neg\alpha$" is a contradiction of B_3—although its negation "$\neg(\alpha \wedge \neg\alpha)$" is not a tautology (while "$\neg(\alpha \wedge \neg\alpha)$" is).

Such features mark Bochvar's (internal) system as nonstandard in much the same way as is the case with Łukasiewicz' L_3.

In a 1954 paper,[5] the Chinese logician Moh Shaw-kwei suggested a Bochvarian interpretation for Łukasiewicz' 3-valued system L_3. He proposed that the intermediate truth-value I be construed as "paradoxical" and be assigned to propositions like "This statement is false" which will be false if classed as true and true if classed as false. This interpretation requires us to bear in mind a weaker mode of paradoxicality than Bochvar's all-contaminating *meaninglessness* since now $I \wedge F$ and $F \wedge I$ will both be F—and not I, as with Bochvar. Moreover, on Bochvar's interpretation it is clearly warranted to have $/p \wedge \neg p/ = I$ when $/p/ = I$, but on Moh Shaw-kwei's approach this step would be less plausible.

As will be seen later, B_3, the 3-valued (internal) system of Bochvar, is especially useful in dealing with semantical paradoxes and cognate situa-

---

[4]It should be noted in passing that L_3^W is in fact equivalent to C_2 in a very strong sense. For if we regard the I of L_3^W as an optical illusion for T, and set $I = T$ throughout the truth tables of L_3, this system will be at once reduced to C_2.

[5]See Moh Shaw-kwei, "Logical Paradoxes for Many-Valued Systems," *The Journal of Symbolic Logic*, vol. 19 (1954), pp. 37–40.

tions in which contradictions are encountered in formal systems (e.g., the paradoxes of set theory).

5 The 3-valued System of Kleene

Yet another way of setting up a system of 3-valued logic was introduced in 1938 by S. C. Kleene,[1] and we shall designate this system as the system K_3. In Kleene's system, a proposition is to bear the third truth-value I not for fact-related, ontological reasons but for knowledge-related, epistemological ones: it is not to be excluded that the proposition may *in fact* be true or false, but it is merely *unknown* or undeterminable[2] what its specific truth status may be.

Kleene introduced his 3-valued connectives by the truth tables:

p	$\neg p$		q	$p \wedge q$			$p \vee q$			$p \supset q$			$p \equiv q$		
		$p\backslash$		T	I	F	T	I	F	T	I	F	T	I	F
T	F		T	T	I	F	T	T	T	T	I	F	T	I	F
I	I		I	I	I	F	T	I	I	T	I	I	I	I	I
F	T		F	F	F	F	T	I	F	T	T	T	F	I	T

Here we have the standard Łukasiewiczian 3-valued truth tables for negation, conjunction, and disjunction. However, the principal novelty of Kleene's system *vis-à-vis* the system of Łukasiewicz relates to the concept of implication, for which the analogue of material implication is adopted: $p \supset q$ FOR $\neg p \vee q$. Consequently, it is not the case in Kleene's system that "$\alpha \supset \alpha$" is a tautology, since this formula takes the truth-value I when 'α' does so, nor (*a fortiori*) is "$\alpha \equiv \alpha$" tautologous.

Kleene motivated the construction of these truth tables in terms of a mathematical application. He has in mind the case of a mathematical predicate P (i.e., a propositional function) of a variable x ranging over a domain D where "$P(x)$" is defined for only a part of this domain. For example, we might have that

$$P(x) \quad \text{iff} \quad 1 \leq \frac{1}{x} \leq 2$$

[1]*Introduction to Metamathematics* (Amsterdam and Princeton, 1952), pp. 332–340. This system was originally presented by Kleene in an earlier paper, "On a Notation for Ordinal Numbers," *The Journal of Symbolic Logic*, vol. 3 (1938), pp. 150–155.
[2]Conceivably (in mathematical applications) "undeterminable" by certain specific methods, e.g., by an effective algorithm.

Here $P(x)$ will be:

(1) *true* when x lies within the range from $\frac{1}{2}$ to 1
(2) *undefined* (or undetermined) when $x = 0$
(3) *false* in all other cases (i.e., $[(x \neq 0) \,\&\, (x < \frac{1}{2})] \vee [1 < x]$)

Kleene presented his truth tables to formulate the rules of combination by logical connectives for such propositional functions. Thus he writes:

> From this standpoint, the meaning of $Q \vee R$ is brought out clearly by the statement in words: $Q \vee R$ is true, if Q is true (here nothing is said about R) or if R is true (similarly); false, if Q and R are both false; defined only in these cases (and hence undefined, otherwise).[3]

In addition to these truth tables for the propositional connectives that he designated as "strong," Kleene also introduced a family of "weak" connectives, characterized by the feature that the truth table of such a connective automatically shows the "output" truth-value I when any one of the "input" truth-values is I. (The system based on these weak connectives will thus turn out to be the same as Bochvar's $\mathbf{B_3}$.) By this rule, the "weak" versions of negations and equivalence will be identical with the "strong" ones, but new versions will be obtained for other connectives. The resulting system is as follows:

p	$\neg p$	q	$p \wedge\!\!\!\wedge q$			$p \vee\!\!\!\vee q$			$p \Rightarrow q$			$p \Leftrightarrow q$		
		p	T	I	F	T	I	F	T	I	F	T	I	F
T	F	T	T	I	F	T	I	T	T	I	F	T	I	F
I	I	I	I	I	I	I	I	I	I	I	I	I	I	I
F	T	F	F	I	F	T	I	F	T	I	T	F	I	T

Kleene motivated these truth tables in terms of arithmetical propositional functions (as before) with respect to which the key issue is that of recursiveness, i.e., of being able to decide the truth status of the statement by means of an effective calculating procedure. We can think here of a mechanism that is simply *incapable of processing indeterminate* (I-*assuming*) *statements*, so that it gives us output value I whenever it receives an input value of I, even if it does so in a context like I-*and*-F or I-*or*-T. Here I plays the role of a factor of all-corrupting meaninglessness, exactly as in the system $\mathbf{B_3}$ of Bochvar. Indeed, Kleene's "weak" connectives are identical

---

[3]*Introduction to Metamathematics*, p. 336. Some interesting philosophical applications of a system that is a minor variant of $\mathbf{K_3}$ are discussed in Lennart Åqvist, "Reflections on the Logic of Nonsense," *Theoria*, vol. 28 (1962), pp. 138–157.

with Bochvar's "internal" ones: this kinship is not surprising, since the motivating considerations of the two approaches are quite similar.

6 Many-valued Generalizations of the 3-valued Logic of Łukasiewicz

In several papers published in the early 1930s Łukasiewicz generalized his 3-valued logic to the case of still more truth-values, indeed to infinite-valued systems. Let these truth-values be represented by real numbers from the interval 0 to 1 (with 0 playing the role of *false* and 1 as *true*). Łukasiewicz' 3-valued system can be developed from the three truth-values $0, \frac{1}{2}, 1$ using the truth tables based on the arithmetical rules:

$$/\neg p/ \; = 1 - /p/$$
$$/p \vee q/ = \max [/p/,/q/]$$
$$/p \wedge q/ = \min [/p/,/q/]$$
$$/p \to q/ = \left\{ \begin{array}{l} 1 \\ 1 - /p/ + /q/ \end{array} \right\} \text{ according as } /p/ \text{ is } \left\{ \begin{array}{l} \leq /q/^1 \\ > /q/ \end{array} \right.$$
$$/p \leftrightarrow q/ = /(p \to q) \wedge (q \to p)/ = 1 - |/p/ - /q/|^2$$

Actually, Łukasiewicz' own approach was (as we have seen) to take negation ($\neg$) and implication ($\to$) as primitives, subject to the just-indicated principles for constructing their truth tables, and then to define disjunction ($\vee$) and conjunction ($\wedge$) in terms of them as follows:

$$p \vee q \quad \text{FOR} \quad (p \to q) \to q$$
$$p \wedge q \quad \text{FOR} \quad \neg(\neg p \vee \neg q).$$

Such a numerical development of many-valued logic is readily generalized. Let us now divide the interval from 0 to 1 by inserting evenly spaced division points, for a total of n points ($n \geq 2$):

n	Division points (=truth-values)	
2	1/1, 0/1	(1,0)
3	2/2, 1/2, 0/2	$(1,\frac{1}{2},0)$
4	3/3, 2/3, 1/3, 0/3	$(1,\frac{2}{3},\frac{1}{3},0)$
.		
.		
.		
n	$1 = \dfrac{n-1}{n-1}, \dfrac{n-2}{n-1}, \cdots, 2/n-1, 1/n-1, 0/n-1 = 0$	

Given the propositional connectives based on the arithmetical rules listed in the first paragraph, and taking the members *of this series* as truth-values,

----

[1]An equivalent alternative formulation is $/p \to q/ = \min \{1, 1 - /p/ + /q/\}$.
[2]The vertical slashes here represent the *absolute value* of the difference.

we obtain the series $\mathbf{L}_n$ of Łukasiewiczian many-valued logics. It is readily seen that:

(1) $\mathbf{L}_2$ is identical with $\mathbf{C}_2$ if we identify 1 with T and 0 with F.

(2) $\mathbf{L}_3$ is identical with the 3-valued system of Łukasiewicz, if we identify 1 with T, $\frac{1}{2}$ with I, and 0 with F.

It is therefore clear that the systems of the series will be many-valued generalizations both of the classical two-valued system $\mathbf{C}_2$ and of the Łukasiewiczian 3-valued system $\mathbf{L}_3$.

Moreover, one can envisage the further possibility of obtaining two infinite-valued systems, as follows:

(1) For the system $\mathbf{L}_{\aleph_0}$ we take 0 and 1 together with all the *rational* numbers (i.e., all fractions n/m) between 0 and 1 as truth-values.

(2) For the system $\mathbf{L}_{\aleph_1}$ we take all the real numbers from the interval 0 to 1 as truth-values.

The first of these systems has a set of truth-values that is of denumerably infinite cardinality, having the cardinality of the set of integers (i.e., is of cardinality $\aleph_0$). The set of truth-values of the second system is not denumerably infinite, but has the cardinality of the continuum (i.e., is of cardinality $\aleph_1$). These systems are (as we shall see below) essentially equivalent.[3]

Let a formula be characterized as a *tautology* if it uniformly takes on truth-value 1 for all assignments of truth-values to its variables. It is not hard to establish the fact that:

Every tautology of (any one of the) $\mathbf{L}_n$ is a tautology of the classical, two-valued propositional calculus $\mathbf{C}_2$.

This is so because the truth tables for every $\mathbf{L}_n$ will *agree* with the two-valued ones when only 0 and 1 (i.e., F and T) are involved, so that a wff that always yields 1 as output for inputs from the larger group of values will always do so when the only inputs are 0s and 1s.

On the other hand, there will in general be tautologies of $\mathbf{C}_2$ that are not tautologies of $\mathbf{L}_n$ (with $n > 2$). Thus let us consider $\mathbf{L}_4$:

p	$\neg p$	$\diagdown^q_p$	$p \vee q$				$p \wedge q$				$p \rightarrow q$				$p \leftrightarrow q$			
			1	$\frac{2}{3}$	$\frac{1}{3}$	0	1	$\frac{2}{3}$	$\frac{1}{3}$	0	1	$\frac{2}{3}$	$\frac{1}{3}$	0	1	$\frac{2}{3}$	$\frac{1}{3}$	0
1	0	1	1	1	1	1	1	$\frac{2}{3}$	$\frac{1}{3}$	0	1	$\frac{2}{3}$	$\frac{1}{3}$	0	1	$\frac{2}{3}$	$\frac{1}{3}$	0
$\frac{2}{3}$	$\frac{1}{3}$	$\frac{2}{3}$	1	$\frac{2}{3}$	$\frac{2}{3}$	$\frac{2}{3}$	$\frac{2}{3}$	$\frac{2}{3}$	$\frac{1}{3}$	0	1	1	$\frac{2}{3}$	$\frac{1}{3}$	$\frac{2}{3}$	1	$\frac{2}{3}$	$\frac{1}{3}$
$\frac{1}{3}$	$\frac{2}{3}$	$\frac{1}{3}$	1	$\frac{2}{3}$	$\frac{1}{3}$	$\frac{1}{3}$	$\frac{1}{3}$	$\frac{1}{3}$	$\frac{1}{3}$	0	1	1	1	$\frac{2}{3}$	$\frac{1}{3}$	$\frac{2}{3}$	1	$\frac{2}{3}$
0	1	0	1	$\frac{2}{3}$	$\frac{1}{3}$	0	0	0	0	0	1	1	1	1	0	$\frac{1}{3}$	$\frac{2}{3}$	1

[3]Whenever a given procedure for system construction yields two essentially equivalent infinite systems $\mathbf{X}_{\aleph_0}$ and $\mathbf{X}_{\aleph_1}$, we shall treat these as variants of one common system, to be designated $\mathbf{X}_\aleph$. (From this standpoint, it is notationally convenient to assume the "continuum hypothesis" that $\aleph_1$ is the cardinality of the real number continuum.)

Note now that the two-valued tautology "$\alpha \vee \neg\alpha$" will not be a tautology of $\mathbf{L}_4$, for when $/\alpha/ = \frac{1}{3}$, then:

$$/\alpha \vee \neg\alpha/ = \tfrac{1}{3} \vee \neg\tfrac{1}{3} = \tfrac{1}{3} \vee \tfrac{2}{3} = \tfrac{2}{3} \neq 1$$

This finding reflects a general situation: When $m < n$, there will inevitably be tautologies in $\mathbf{L}_n$ that are not tautologies of $\mathbf{L}_m$. (This loss-of-tautologies-with-an-increase-in-truth-values principle follows from a consideration of the Dugundji sequence of formulas Δi discussed in Sec. 25 below.) The critical relationship among the Łukasiewicz systems is represented by the following thesis:

> The tautologies (i.e., uniformly T-assuming wffs) of $\mathbf{L}_n$ will be included among those of $\mathbf{L}_m$ iff $m - 1$ is a divisor of $n - 1$ (i.e., iff there is a positive integer k such that $k(m - 1) = n - 1$).[4]

Let $T(\mathbf{X})$ represent the set of all tautologies of the system $\mathbf{X}$. Then as a result of this relationship we obtain for every prime number k the containment series:

$$T(\mathbf{L}_{\aleph}) \subset T(\mathbf{L}_{n(k+1)}) \subset \cdots \subset T(\mathbf{L}_{2(k+1)}) \subset T(\mathbf{L}_{1(k+1)}) \subset T(\mathbf{L}_2) = \mathbf{C}_2$$

On the other hand, when $i - 1$ and $j - 1$ are such that one is not a divisor of the other, then the systems $\mathbf{L}_i$ and $\mathbf{L}_j$ are distinct in their tautologies, i.e., each has tautologies that are not tautologies of the other. Since—as we have already seen—there are tautologies in $\mathbf{L}_{\aleph}$ (e.g., "$\alpha \rightarrow \alpha$"), we know also that there are tautologies common to all the systems $\mathbf{L}_n$. The sequence of Łukasiewicz systems $\mathbf{L}_n$ thus affords an infinite variety of tautology-distinct systems (all of which, however, contain the tautologies of $\mathbf{L}_{\aleph}$ and are contained in those of $\mathbf{L}_2 = \mathbf{C}_2$).

To return to the infinite systems, it is readily shown that the difference between $\mathbf{L}_{\aleph_0}$ and $\mathbf{L}_{\aleph_1}$ is not a logically crucial one because both systems have exactly the same stock of tautologies.[5] This is established by the following reasoning. Since the truth rules of the two systems are exactly the same, the fact that the truth-values of $\mathbf{L}_{\aleph_0}$ form a subset of those of $\mathbf{L}_{\aleph_1}$ suffices to show that every $\mathbf{L}_{\aleph_1}$-tautology must be an $\mathbf{L}_{\aleph_0}$-tautology. The converse can also be shown. Łukasiewicz had conjectured and Wajsberg subsequently shown that the set of tautologies of $\mathbf{L}_{\aleph_0}$ can be axiomatized (by the rules of substitution and *modus ponens*) with the axioms:

---

[4]We shall not here present the (somewhat complex) demonstration of this fact, but refer the reader to R. Ackermann, *Introduction to Many-Valued Logics* (London, 1967), pp. 60–63.

[5]That is, the difference between these systems is not "logically crucial" for *propositional* logic. In quantificational logic critical differences do come to the fore. For discussions of this matter in the literature, see division I5 of the Topically Classified Register given in Chap. 4.

(1) $\alpha \rightarrow (\beta \rightarrow \alpha)$
(2) $(\alpha \rightarrow \beta) \rightarrow [(\beta \rightarrow \gamma) \rightarrow (\alpha \rightarrow \gamma)]$
(3) $(\neg\alpha \rightarrow \neg\beta) \rightarrow (\beta \rightarrow \alpha)$
(4) $[(\alpha \rightarrow \beta) \rightarrow \beta] \rightarrow [(\beta \rightarrow \alpha) \rightarrow \alpha]$
(5) $[(\alpha \rightarrow \beta) \rightarrow (\beta \rightarrow \alpha)] \rightarrow (\beta \rightarrow \alpha)$

All of these can be shown (by procedures to which we shall shortly return) also to be $\mathbf{L}_{\aleph_1}$-tautologies, and thus all of their consequences (by *modus ponens* and substitution) must also be $\mathbf{L}_{\aleph_1}$-tautologies, since these rules will preserve tautologousness. This, then, establishes the claimed identity of the tautology groups of the two systems. We may thus treat $\mathbf{L}_{\aleph_0}$ and $\mathbf{L}_{\aleph_1}$ as variants of one common infinite-valued Łukasiewiczian system $\mathbf{L}_{\aleph}$.

We have claimed that axioms (1) to (4) can be shown to be $\mathbf{L}_{\aleph_1}$-tautologies. We shall substantiate this claim only in part, by showing in detail how the $\mathbf{L}_{\aleph_1}$-tautologousness of (1) can be established. Analogous procedures can be applied to the other axioms.

Abstractly speaking, three possibilities are conceivable for $p \rightarrow (q \rightarrow p)$:

Case (1): $/p/ \le /q \rightarrow p/$
Case (2): $/p/ > /q \rightarrow p/$
Case (2a): $/q/ \le /p/$
Case (2b): $/q/ > /p/$

Now Case (2a) cannot arise, because when it does, $/q \rightarrow p/ = 1$, and then we cannot have $/p/ > /q \rightarrow p/$. Nor can Case (2b) arise. For then:

$$/q \rightarrow p/ = 1/ - /q + /p/$$

But since $/p/ > /q \rightarrow p/$, then:

$$/p/ > 1 - /q/ + /p/$$

Hence, we have:

$$1 - /q/ \ / < 0$$

But then:

$$/q/ > 1$$

and the last of these is impossible, so that this case cannot result. Thus Case (1) is the only possibility. But in this case

$$/q \rightarrow (p \rightarrow q)/ = 1$$

and so the tautologousness of "$\alpha \rightarrow (\beta \rightarrow \alpha)$" is established.

It should be stressed, moreover, that other, radically different systems of infinitely many-valued logics are possible which can also qualify as generalizations of the basic 3-valued logic of Łukasiewicz, $\mathbf{L}_3$. For example, let the value of a proposition be any real number from the interval from -1 to $+1$ (construing -1 as *false*, $+1$ as *true*, and 0 as *neutral*):

$$-1 \le /p/ \le +1$$

Let us introduce truth tables for the propositional connectives by the rules:

$$/\neg p/ = -/p/$$
$$/p \wedge q/ = \min [/p/,/q/]$$

The truth tables for other propositional connectives can then be construed on this basis, if these connectives are introduced by definition in terms of the primitives '$\neg$' and '$\wedge$':

$$p \vee q \quad \text{FOR} \quad \neg(\neg p \wedge \neg q)$$
$$p \supset q \quad \text{FOR} \quad \neg p \vee q$$

We would consequently have it that:

$$/p \vee q/ = \max [/p/,/q/]$$
$$/p \supset q/ = \max [-/p/,/q/]$$

It deserves remark that we can introduce into the systems of this discussion a new style of implication $\rightarrow$ (distinct from $\supset$) by the rule:

$$/p \rightarrow q/ \text{ is } \begin{Bmatrix} 1 \\ 0 \\ -1 \end{Bmatrix} \text{ according as } /p/ - /q/ \text{ is } \begin{cases} \le 0 \\ > 0 \text{ but } \le 1 \\ > 1 \end{cases}$$

Thus while our propositional logic may be infinite-valued, a $\rightarrow$ implication must always be true, false, or neutral.

The system obtained in this way will be characterized as $\mathbf{U}_{\aleph}$. This system also has finite counterparts: let the truth-values be the totality of integers between (and including) $-\dfrac{n-1}{2}$ and $+\dfrac{n-1}{2}$. Note that this totality will always be odd-numbered, but that even-valued systems can always be obtained by dropping 0 as a truth-value. Then the preceding truth rules will generate a family of finitely valued systems $\mathbf{U}_n$.

Let us for the moment limit our horizon to the special case of three values $+1$, 0, -1. We now obtain, in virtue of the rules laid down for the mode of many-valued logics at issue, the following truth tables for $\mathbf{U}_3$:

p	$\neg p$	q over p	$p \wedge q$			$p \vee q$			$p \supset q$			$p \rightarrow q$		
			1	0	-1	1	0	-1	1	0	-1	1	0	-1
1	-1	1	1	0	-1	1	1	1	1	0	-1	1	0	-1
0	0	0	0	0	-1	1	0	0	1	0	0	1	1	0
-1	1	-1	-1	-1	-1	1	0	-1	1	1	1	1	1	1

Provided, then, that we adopt → (and not ⊃) as our basic mode of implication, we see that the family of systems U_n just described represents yet another, distinctly different way of generalizing Ł₃.

In the specific case of U_5 we shall obtain:

p	$\neg p$	q over p\	$p \wedge q$ 1	½	0	-½	-1	$p \vee q$ 1	½	0	-½	-1	$p \to q$ 1	½	0	-½	-1
1	-1	1	1	½	0	-½	-1	1	1	1	1	1	1	0	0	-1	-1
½	-½	½	½	½	0	-½	-1	1	½	½	½	½	1	1	0	0	-1
0	0	0	0	0	0	-½	-1	1	½	0	0	0	1	1	1	0	0
-½	½	-½	-½	-½	-½	-½	-1	1	½	0	-½	-½	1	1	1	1	0
-1	1	-1	-1	-1	-1	-1	-1	1	½	0	-½	-1	1	1	1	1	1

In view of the similarity in their mode of construction, the close resemblance of this system to Ł₅ is not surprising.

As this example illustrates, a great many varieties of many-valued—and indeed also infinite-valued—generalizations of the initial 3-valued logic of Łukasiewicz can be constructed. We could introduce into this family of systems the idea that a formula is "acceptable" if it must *invariably* assume nonnegative truth-values, i.e., does so uniformly for any and every assignment of truth-values to its constituent propositional variables. Note that:

1. If p and $p \to q$ are both acceptable (in this sense), then q must be acceptable so that the rule of *modus ponens* obtains with respect to acceptable propositions. (It is obvious that if a wff is acceptable, any of its substitution instances must also be, so that the rule of inference by substitution from acceptable propositions will then obtain.)

2. It can be shown that the following formulas are all acceptable in all of the systems U_n (even in $U_{\aleph}$):

$$\alpha \to \alpha$$
$$(\alpha \wedge \beta) \to \alpha$$
$$\alpha \to (\neg \alpha \to \beta)$$

The following sample calculation establishes the acceptability of "$\alpha \to (\neg \alpha \to \beta)$":

$$
\begin{aligned}
/\alpha \to (\neg\alpha \to \beta)/ &= \max\,[-/\alpha/,/\neg\alpha \to \beta/] \\
&= \max\,[-/\alpha/, \max\,[/\alpha/,/\beta/]] \\
&= \max\,[-/\alpha/,/\alpha/,/\beta/] \\
&= \max\,[-/\alpha/,/\alpha/, \text{(other entries)}] \geq 0
\end{aligned}
$$

It deserves remark that one can introduce into infinite-valued logics operators fundamentally different from, but interestingly analogous to, two-valued ones. Thus let us add to the machinery of $\mathbf{L_\aleph}$ the averaging operator $\sqcap$ defined so that the truth-values of the resulting composite is *the average* truth-value of the constituent components:

$$/p \sqcap q/ = \tfrac{1}{2}(/p/ + /q/)$$

It is clear that $\sqcap$ is fundamentally different from any classical connective since its truth table will not yield a 0-or-1 output for 0-and-1 inputs.[6] Indeed, $\sqcap$ has no counterpart in any finitely many-valued system, since $v \sqcap v'$ will fail to be defined in any such system when v and v' are adjacent truth-values. Note that if 1 alone is designated, we shall have the following as tautologies of $\mathbf{L_\aleph}$:[7]

$$(\alpha \wedge \beta) \rightarrow (\alpha \sqcap \beta)$$
$$(\alpha \sqcap \beta) \rightarrow (\alpha \vee \beta)$$
$$(\alpha \sqcap \beta) \leftrightarrow (\beta \sqcap \alpha)$$
$$(\alpha \sqcap \alpha) \leftrightarrow \alpha$$

These tautologies tend to suggest that $\sqcap$ is a somehow strengthened mode of disjunction or a somehow weakened mode of conjunction. But observe we shall not have a principle of association for $\sqcap$ in $\mathbf{L_\aleph}$, since

$$[\alpha \sqcap (\beta \sqcap \gamma)] \leftrightarrow [(\alpha \sqcap \beta) \sqcap \gamma]$$

is not a tautology.[8] On the other hand, if all the truth-values $\geq \tfrac{1}{2}$ are treated as designated (i.e., classed as truth-like), then this thesis will also be a tautology. Let a, b, c be $/\alpha/$, $/\beta/$, and $/\gamma/$, respectively. Then the absolute value of the difference between the truth-values of the two sides of the equivalence will be:

$$d = |\tfrac{1}{2}[a + \tfrac{1}{2}(b + c)] - \tfrac{1}{2}[\tfrac{1}{2}(a + b) + c]|$$
$$= |\tfrac{1}{2}a + \tfrac{1}{4}b + \tfrac{1}{4}c - \tfrac{1}{4}a - \tfrac{1}{4}b - \tfrac{1}{2}c|$$
$$= |\tfrac{1}{4}a - \tfrac{1}{4}c| = \tfrac{1}{4}|a - c| \leq \tfrac{1}{2}$$

Therefore the equivalence will always assume a truth-value $\geq \tfrac{1}{2}$, and so will be tautologous. In fact if all truth-values $\geq \tfrac{1}{2}$ are designated, then $\sqcap$ will, in effect, approximate both to $\wedge$ and to $\vee$ (which—as we have seen above—will in this case behave very much like their two-valued counterparts), since

$$(\alpha \sqcap \beta) \leftrightarrow (\alpha \vee \beta)$$
$$(\alpha \sqcap \beta) \leftrightarrow (\alpha \wedge \beta)$$

[6]This also establishes the fact that $\sqcap$ cannot be defined in terms of the primitive connectives of $\mathbf{L_\aleph}$.
[7]And indeed of any of the infinite-valued systems such that $/p \rightarrow q/$ is designated (i.e., truth-like) whenever $/p/ \leq /q/$ and $/p \leftrightarrow q/$ is designated whenever $/p/ = /q/$.
[8]Note moreover, that if the truth rule for negation is the usual $/\neg p/ = 1 - /p/$, then $\sqcap$ will be self-dual in that:

$$/p \sqcap q/ = /\neg(\neg p \sqcap \neg q)/$$

will become tautologous. For the absolute value of the difference between the two sides of the first equivalence will be:

$$d = |\tfrac{1}{2}(a + b) - \max [a,b]| = \tfrac{1}{2}|a + b - 2 \max [a,b]|$$
$$= \tfrac{1}{2} \times \text{(a quantity } \leq 1) \leq \tfrac{1}{2}$$

Therefore the equivalence will always assume a truth-value $\geq \tfrac{1}{2}$, and so will be tautologous. An analogous demonstration can be given for the second equivalence also. Moreover, the approximation of $\sqcap$ to disjunction in this case is further shown by the (readily verified) tautologousness of:

$$\alpha \rightarrow (\alpha \sqcap \beta)$$
$$\alpha \sqcap \neg\alpha$$

It should be noted that the question of the *consistency* within the set of tautologous (i.e., uniformly *T*- or 1-assuming) propositions of the logical systems that are constructed in this way is not very interesting because it is too readily settled in the affirmative. The very manner of construction of the system provides an arithmetical model that guarantees that its set of accepted propositions will be consistent, since if p uniformly takes on the value 1, then $\neg p$ cannot possibly do so. (The topic of consistency will be explored in greater detail in Sec. 23.)

7 Some Infinite-valued Logics That Are Not Generalizations of Ł₃

The infinite-valued systems dealt with in the preceding sections were all generalizations of the 3-valued system of Łukasiewicz. But other (infinite) families of many-valued systems are, of course, possible; systems constructed on principles that will not yield $Ł_3$ in the 3-valued case.

Thus consider the following family of systems, which we shall designate as B_n, since they are based upon the guiding intuition of the 3-valued system of Bochvar and yield his system B_3 when $n = 3$. The range of values is to consist (as with $Ł_n$) of the evenly spaced division points between 0 and 1[1] (or, for $B_\aleph$, of all of the numbers from this interval), with 1 playing the role of *T* (true) and 0 that of *F* (false). The truth rules are as follows:

$$/\neg p/ = 1 - /p/$$

$$/p \wedge q/ = \begin{cases} /p/ \times /q/ & \text{if both } /p/ \text{ and } /q/ \text{ belong to the set } \{0,1\} \\ Z(n) \text{ otherwise [\textsc{note}: } Z(n) = \tfrac{1}{2} \text{ or } \dfrac{n-2}{2(n-1)} \text{ according as } n \text{ is odd or} \\ \quad \text{even. For } B_\aleph, Z(\aleph) \text{ is to be taken as simply } \tfrac{1}{2}]. \end{cases}$$

[1] That is, the values $\dfrac{k-1}{n-1}$ with $k = 1, 2, \ldots, n$.

$$/p \vee q/ = \begin{cases} \min \left[1, /p/ + /q/\right] & \text{if both } /p/ \text{ and } /q/ \text{ belong to } \{0,1\} \\ Z(n) & \text{otherwise} \end{cases}$$

$$/p \rightarrow q/ = \begin{cases} \min \left[1, 1 - /p/ + /q/\right] & \text{if both } /p/ \text{ and } /q/ \text{ belong to } \{0,1\} \\ Z(n) & \text{otherwise} \end{cases}$$

$$/p \leftrightarrow q/ = \begin{cases} 1 - /p/ - /q/ + 2[/p/ \times /q/] & \text{if both } /p/ \text{ and } /q/ \text{ belong to } \{0,1\} \\ (Z\{n\}) & \text{otherwise} \end{cases}$$

Note that a proposition whose main connective *binary* can only assume the three truth-values 0, $\frac{1}{2}$ $\left(\text{or } \dfrac{n-2}{2(n-1)}\right)$, and 1, even when the system itself is infinite-valued.

A perhaps more interesting—but in any case less cumbersome—example of a many-valued logic that is not a generalization of $\mathbf{L}_3$ results when, with the same truth-values as above, we take the truth rules:

$$/{\neg}p/ = 1 - /p/$$
$$/p \wedge q/ = \min \left[/p/, /q/\right]$$
$$/p \vee q/ = \max \left[/p/, /q/\right]$$
$$/p \supset q/ = /{\neg}p \vee q/$$
$$/p \equiv q/ = /(p \supset q) \wedge (q \supset p)/$$

These rules lead to the family of systems $\mathbf{S}_n^{\supset}$ whose characteristics will be examined in considerable detail in the next section. In the 3-valued case, the system $\mathbf{S}_3^{\supset}$—based on the truth-values $0, \frac{1}{2}, 1$—will be as follows:

p	$\neg p$	$\begin{array}{c}\\ \diagdown{}^{q}_{p}\end{array}$	$p \wedge q$ $1 \quad \frac{1}{2} \quad 0$	$p \vee q$ $1 \quad \frac{1}{2} \quad 0$	$p \supset q$ $1 \quad \frac{1}{2} \quad 0$	$p \equiv q$ $1 \quad \frac{1}{2} \quad 0$
1	0	1	$1 \quad \frac{1}{2} \quad 0$	$1 \quad 1 \quad 1$	$1 \quad \frac{1}{2} \quad 0$	$1 \quad \frac{1}{2} \quad 0$
$\frac{1}{2}$	$\frac{1}{2}$	$\frac{1}{2}$	$\frac{1}{2} \quad \frac{1}{2} \quad 0$	$1 \quad \frac{1}{2} \quad \frac{1}{2}$	$1 \quad \frac{1}{2} \quad \frac{1}{2}$	$\frac{1}{2} \quad \frac{1}{2} \quad \frac{1}{2}$
0	1	0	$0 \quad 0 \quad 0$	$1 \quad \frac{1}{2} \quad 0$	$1 \quad 1 \quad 1$	$0 \quad \frac{1}{2} \quad 1$

This is Kleene's system $\mathbf{K}_3$, so that the system $\mathbf{S}_n^{\supset}$ will not be many-valued generalizations of the 3-valued system of Łukasiewicz.

Yet another family of many-valued systems, to be designated $\mathbf{G}_n$, are due to Kurt Gödel.[2] They result when, under the same circumstances as before, we adopt the truth rules:

$$/{\neg}p/ = \begin{Bmatrix} 1 \\ 0 \end{Bmatrix} \text{ according as } \begin{cases} /p/ = 0 \\ /p/ \neq 0 \end{cases}$$

$$/p \wedge q/ = \min \left[/p/, /q/\right]$$
$$/p \vee q/ = \max \left[/p/, /q/\right]$$

$$/p \rightarrow q/ = \begin{Bmatrix} 1 \\ /q/ \end{Bmatrix} \text{ according as } \begin{cases} /p/ \leq /q/ \\ /p/ > /q/ \end{cases}$$

$$/p \leftrightarrow q/ = /(p \rightarrow q) \wedge (q \rightarrow p)/ = \begin{Bmatrix} 1 \\ \min \left[/p/, /q/\right] \end{Bmatrix} \text{ according as } \begin{cases} /p/ = /q/ \\ /p/ \neq /q/ \end{cases}$$

[2]See Alonzo Church, *Introduction to Mathematical Logic* (Princeton, 1956), p. 145 (exercise 26.10).

In the 3-valued case, these truth rules will lead to the following 3-valued system G_3, originally devised by A. Heyting:

p	$\neg p$	$\begin{smallmatrix}&q\\p&\end{smallmatrix}$	$p \wedge q$			$p \vee q$			$p \rightarrow q$			$p \leftrightarrow q$		
			1	$\frac{1}{2}$	0	1	$\frac{1}{2}$	0	1	$\frac{1}{2}$	0	1	$\frac{1}{2}$	0
1	0	1	1	$\frac{1}{2}$	0	1	1	1	1	$\frac{1}{2}$	0	1	$\frac{1}{2}$	0
$\frac{1}{2}$	0	$\frac{1}{2}$	$\frac{1}{2}$	$\frac{1}{2}$	0	1	$\frac{1}{2}$	$\frac{1}{2}$	1	1	0	$\frac{1}{2}$	1	0
0	1	0	0	0	0	1	$\frac{1}{2}$	0	1	1	1	0	0	1

This system G_3 is of particular interest from a logical point of view because all of the theorems of the intuitionistic propositional calculus (**IPC**)[3] are G_3-tautologies (i.e., are uniformly 1-assuming wffs), whereas such definitive nontheses of **IPC** as

$$\alpha \vee \neg\alpha$$
$$\neg\neg\alpha \rightarrow \alpha$$
$$(\neg\alpha \rightarrow \neg\beta) \rightarrow (\beta \rightarrow \alpha)$$

will not be G_3-tautologies.[4] On the other hand, certain G_3-tautologies are unfortunately not theorems of **IPC**—for example, "$(\alpha \rightarrow \beta) \vee (\beta \rightarrow \alpha)$" and "$(\neg\neg\alpha \rightarrow \alpha) \rightarrow (\alpha \vee \neg\alpha)$."[5]

An infinite-valued system $G_\aleph$ can also be obtained by letting the truth-values be the real or the rational numbers from 0 to 1 (inclusive), and keeping exactly the same truth rules as for the finite-valued G_n. This system is also such that all $G_\aleph$-tautologies are again **IPC**-theorems. This family of many-valued systems thus affords useful instruments for the study of one important branch of nonclassical propositional logic.[6]

[3] See A. Heyting, *Intuitionism* (Amsterdam, 1956). An elegant variant axiomatization of **IPC** is given in J. Łukasiewicz, "On the Intuitionist Theory of Deduction," *Indagationes Mathematicae*, vol. 14 (1952), pp. 202–212. Incidentally, the converse of the just-stated claim, viz. that all G_3-tautologies are **IPC**-theorems does not obtain, so that the many-valued system G_3 will not be characteristic of **IPC**. (For the ideas at issue here, see Sec. 24 below.)
[4] Note that if a "tautology" is construed to be a uniformly 1-or-$\frac{1}{2}$-assuming formula, then all classical tautologies will be tautologies of G_3 *in this sense*. For if $\frac{1}{2}$ is treated as an optical illusion for 1 throughout the truth tables of G_3, then these truth tables in fact collapse into those of C_2. (This fact, as we shall see, serves to assure that all the C_2-tautologies will be G_3-tautologies—in the new sense.)
[5] On the relationship between G_3 and **IPC** see also Zawirski (1946), Kleene (1952), and Kotarbiński (1957).
[6] The exact relationship of G_i-systems to **IPC** is as follows: K. Gödel has shown that no finitely many-valued system can be such that its tautologies correspond exactly to the **IPC**-theorems. However, it has been shown by M. A. E. Dummett that the axiom system obtained from **IPC** by adding the axiom "$(\alpha \rightarrow \beta) \vee (\beta \rightarrow \alpha)$" is such that its theorems are exactly the $G_\aleph$-tautologies. And Łukasiewicz (*loc. cit.*) has stated that if "$(\neg\alpha \rightarrow \beta) \rightarrow [([\beta \rightarrow \alpha] \rightarrow \beta) \rightarrow \beta]$" is added to **IPC** as a new axiom, then the theorems of this system are exactly the G_3-tautologies. Moreover, S. Jaśkowski has produced an infinite-valued system (distinct from $G_\aleph$) whose tautologies correspond exactly to the **IPC**-theorems. (Fuller details regarding the publications at issue in regard to these contributions can be found in the Bibliography.)

8 The "Standard Sequence" S_n of Many-valued Systems and Its Variants

Consider the following set of rules for generating systems of many-valued logic:

1. The system has n truth-values ($n \geq 2$) which comprise, in addition to the orthodox values T and F, the "intermediate" truth-values $I_1, I_2, \ldots, I_{n-2}$. All n of these truth-values may be arranged in an "order of truth," or rather in order of increasing "falsity," as follows:

   $$T, I_1, I_2, \ldots, I_{n-2}, F$$

2. The truth table for negation ($\neg$) has the "mirror-image" feature, that is, negation is such as to take a given truth-value into its opposite in the order of truth:

p	$\neg p$
T	F
I_1	I_{n-2}
I_2	I_{n-3}
.	
.	
.	
I_{n-3}	I_2
I_{n-2}	I_1
F	T

3. The truth table for conjunction ($\wedge$) is such that the truth-value of a conjunct is the falsest of the truth-values of its members.
4. The truth table for disjunction ($\vee$) is such that the truth-value of a disjunct is the truest of the truth-values of its members.
5. The truth table for implication ($\rightarrow$) is such that an implication is true (T) whenever the antecedent is no less true (i.e., as true or truer) than the consequent and false (F) otherwise.
6. The truth table for equivalence is to be derived from that for implication by the rule:

   $$/p \leftrightarrow q/ = /(p \rightarrow q) \wedge (q \rightarrow p)/$$

The systems of the standard sequence we shall symbolize as S_n, with n to indicate the number of truth-values involved.[1] It is obvious that

---

[1] We shall abbreviatively characterize a "system of the standard sequence" as a "standard system."

$S_2 = C_2$, so that the standard systems are yet another mode of generalization of the orthodox two-valued logic. Moreover, S_3 and S_4 will be as follows:

p	$\neg p$	$q\backslash p$	$p \wedge q$ T	I	F	$p \vee q$ T	I	F	$p \to q$ T	I	F	$p \leftrightarrow q$ T	I	F
T	F	T	T	I	F	T	T	T	T	F	F	T	F	F
I	I	I	I	I	F	T	I	I	T	T	F	F	T	F
F	T	F	F	F	F	T	I	F	T	T	T	F	F	T

p	$\neg p$	$q\backslash p$	$p \wedge q$ T	I_1	I_2	F	$p \vee q$ T	I_1	I_2	F	$p \to q$ T	I_1	I_2	F	$p \leftrightarrow q$ T	I_1	I_2	F
T	F	T	T	I_1	I_2	F	T	T	T	T	T	F	F	F	T	F	F	F
I_1	I_2	I_1	I_1	I_1	I_2	F	T	I_1	I_1	I_1	T	T	F	F	F	T	F	F
I_2	I_1	I_2	I_2	I_2	I_2	F	T	I_1	I_2	I_2	T	T	T	F	F	F	T	F
F	T	F	F	F	F	F	T	I_1	I_2	F	T	T	T	T	F	F	F	T

Note that the truth tables for S_3 differ from those for all the 3-valued systems ($Ł_3, B_3, K_3$) we have considered. However, the connectives $\neg$, $\wedge$, and $\vee$ of the standard systems S_n are in general identical with those of the Łukasiewicz systems $Ł_n$, so that the only points of difference arise in regard to implication (thus also affecting equivalence, etc.).

We can also introduce the idea of an infinite-valued standard system $S_\aleph$ with numbers drawn from the interval from 0 to 1 as truth-values (with 0 corresponding to falsity and 1 to truth), and the following truth rules for negation, disjunction, and conjunction:

$$/\neg p/ = 1 - /p/$$
$$/p \wedge q/ = \min [/p/,/q/]$$
$$/p \vee q/ = \max [/p/,/q/]$$

As regards implication, we have the truth rule:

$$/p \to q/ = \begin{Bmatrix} 1\ (T) \\ 0\ (F) \end{Bmatrix} \text{ according as } \begin{cases} /p/ \leq /q/ \\ /p/ > /q/ \end{cases}$$

Equivalence can be obtained from $\to$ and $\wedge$ in the usual way: $(/p \leftrightarrow q/ = /(p \to q) \wedge (q \to p)/$.

The system $S_{[\aleph]}$—obtained from $S_\aleph$ by deleting $\frac{1}{2}$ from its range of truth-values—is a significant variant. Every $S_\aleph$-tautology must obviously also be a tautology of $S_{[\aleph]}$, but there will be various tautologies of $S_{[\aleph]}$ that are not $S_\aleph$-tautologies. An example is:

$$\neg(\alpha \leftrightarrow \neg\alpha)$$

If $\frac{1}{2}$ is not within the range of values, then always $/p/ \neq /\neg p/$, and thus always either $/p \to \neg p/$ or $/\neg p \to p/$ will be 0 (i.e., *F*).

These standard systems have certain significant relationships to C_2 (the classical two-valued logic) and to one another that must be considered.

First of all, it is clear that if we disregard all the "intermediate" truth-values, that is, consider only those truth-table entries which derive from *T*'s and *F*'s alone, then the truth tables for any standard system will agree with those for the classical two-valued system C_2. From this, it at once follows that every tautology (that is, formula which uniformly takes on the truth-value *T* for *every* assignment of truth-values to the propositional variables involved) of any such system S_n will also be a tautology of C_2. Thus all the standard systems will be subsystems of C_2, in the sense that any S_n-tautology will be a C_2-tautology.

By analogous reasoning it can be seen that all the odd-valued standard systems (i.e., those having an odd number of truth-values) are such that the tautologies of any odd-valued system will include those of the next-largest odd-valued one. For example, notice that with respect to S_3 and S_5 the truth table for every connective (e.g., conjunction) of the smaller system is contained bodily within that of the larger system:

And this situation is a general one. It is readily verified that when, in the $(k + 1)$st odd-valued standard system, we systematically suppress the second and the next-to-last rows and columns of the truth tables, then the truth tables for the kth odd-valued standard system will result. And exactly the same relationship holds within the sequence of even-valued systems. Moreover, every odd-valued standard system bodily contains the next-smaller even-valued one. This is readily seen by suppressing throughout the truth tables of the larger system the rows and columns for the "central" truth-value, i.e., that truth-value v for which:

$$v = \neg v$$

Now we shall see (in Sec. 11) that whenever one many-valued system can be reduced to another by such suppressions, then the tautologies (i.e., uniformly *T*-assuming wffs) of the larger system are also tautologies of the smaller system. In virtue of this, the relationships established in the preceding paragraph suffice to establish the key relationship among the standard systems embodied in the facts that (letting $T(\mathbf{X})$ represent the set of tautologies of the system $\mathbf{X}$):

1. Whenever n is odd, then for *any $m < n$*:

$$T(\mathbf{S_\aleph}) \subset T(\mathbf{S}_n) \subset T(\mathbf{S}_m) \subset T(\mathbf{S}_3) \subset T(\mathbf{C}_2)$$

2. Whenever n is even, then for *any even $m < n$*:

$$T(\mathbf{S_\aleph}) \subset T(\mathbf{S}_{[\aleph]}) \subset T(\mathbf{S}_n) \subset T(\mathbf{S}_m) \subset T(\mathbf{S}_2) = T(\mathbf{C}_2)$$

However, when n is even, then $\mathbf{S}_n$ will include a tautology that is not a tautology of any odd-valued standard system with fewer than n truth-values. This is shown by considering

$$\neg[(\alpha \rightarrow \neg\alpha) \wedge (\neg\alpha \rightarrow \alpha)] = \neg(\alpha \leftrightarrow \neg\alpha)$$

which is tautologous in every even-valued $\mathbf{S}_n$, but not in $\mathbf{S}_3$ (and therefore not in any odd-valued standard system).

We have observed that it is a feature of the odd-valued standard systems that they include a truth-value v for which $v = \neg v$. Note that $\mathbf{S_\aleph}$ counts with the odd-valued systems in this regard, since $\frac{1}{2}$ will play the role of such a truth-value v. On the other hand, $\mathbf{S}_{[\aleph]}$ counts with the even-valued systems.

The relationship between $\mathbf{L}_3$ and $\mathbf{S}_3$ is not a simple one, despite the superficial similarity between these systems. For "$\alpha \rightarrow (\beta \rightarrow \alpha)$," which is a tautology of $\mathbf{L}_3$, is not a tautology of $\mathbf{S}_3$. And "$[(\alpha \rightarrow \beta) \rightarrow (\gamma \rightarrow \delta)] \vee [\neg(\alpha \rightarrow \beta) \rightarrow (\gamma \rightarrow \delta)]$," which is a tautology of $\mathbf{S}_3$, is not a tautology of $\mathbf{L}_3$. Thus neither system is included within the other. In consequence, because of the tautology-containment relationships obtaining *within* the $\mathbf{L}_n$ series and the $\mathbf{S}_n$ series, such a discrepancy between the corresponding members of this series will obtain throughout.

We shall now consider a variant of the standard systems. This is the series having the same truth tables for negation ($\neg$), conjunction ($\wedge$), and disjunction ($\vee$), but with the variant (although by now familiar) mode of implication

$$p \supset q \quad \text{FOR} \quad \neg p \vee q$$

and the corresponding mode of equivalence:

$$p \equiv q \quad \text{FOR} \quad (p \supset q) \wedge (q \supset p)$$

These stipulations lead to a sequence of variant-standard systems that we shall call $\mathbf{S}_n^\supset$. Clearly we shall have it that $\mathbf{S}_2^\supset = \mathbf{C}_2$, so that the variant-standard systems again represent a mode of generalization of orthodox two-valued logic. Moreover, $\mathbf{S}_3^\supset$ and $\mathbf{S}_4^\supset$ will be as follows:

p	$\neg p$	$\diagdown q$ $p\diagdown$	$p \wedge q$			$p \vee q$			$p \supset q$			$p \equiv q$		
			T	I	F	T	I	F	T	I	F	T	I	F
T	F	T	T	I	F	T	T	T	T	I	F	T	I	F
I	I	I	I	I	F	T	I	I	T	I	I	I	I	I
F	T	F	F	F	F	T	I	F	T	T	T	F	I	T

p	$\neg p$	$\diagdown q$ $p\diagdown$	$p \wedge q$				$p \vee q$				$p \supset q$				$p \equiv q$			
			T	I_1	I_2	F	T	I_1	I_2	F	T	I_1	I_2	F	T	I_1	I_2	F
T	F	T	T	I_1	I_2	F	T	T	T	T	T	I_1	I_2	F	T	I_1	I_2	F
I_1	I_2	I_1	I_1	I_1	I_2	F	T	I_1	I_1	I_1	T	I_1	I_2	I_2	I_1	I_1	I_2	I_2
I_2	I_1	I_2	I_2	I_2	I_2	F	T	I_1	I_2	I_2	T	I_1	I_1	I_1	I_2	I_2	I_1	I_1
F	T	F	F	F	F	F	T	I_1	I_2	F	T	T	T	T	F	I_2	I_1	T

Thus $\mathbf{S}_3^{\supset} = \mathbf{K}_3$, so that these variants of the standard systems can also be regarded as many-valued generalizations of the 3-valued system of Kleene.[2] Moreover, it is readily shown that $\mathbf{S}_n^{\supset} = \mathbf{U}_n$ (cf. p. 40), provided that $\supset$ is taken as the implication relationship for $\mathbf{U}_n$.

The systems of the series $\mathbf{S}_n^{\supset}$ are related by some significant interconnections. When n is odd, then the suppression in all truth tables for $\mathbf{S}_n^{\supset}$ of all of the rows and columns that are headed by that truth-value v such that $\neg v = v$ will reduce $\mathbf{S}_n^{\supset}$ to $\mathbf{S}_{n-1}^{\supset}$. On the other hand, when n is even, then the suppression in all of the truth tables of $\mathbf{S}_n^{\supset}$ of the rows and columns headed by the second and the next-to-last truth-values of the sequence $T, I_1, I_2, \ldots, I_{n-2}, F$ will reduce $\mathbf{S}_n^{\supset}$ to $\mathbf{S}_{n-2}^{\supset}$. As a result of this (as will be seen below), we shall have it that

$$T(\mathbf{S}_n^{\supset}) \subset T(\mathbf{S}_m^{\supset}) \quad \text{for any } m < n$$

when tautologousness is determined in $\mathbf{S}_n^{\supset}$ and $\mathbf{S}_m^{\supset}$ in a uniform way.

Up to this point of the present section we have understood a "tautology" to be a formula (wff) that uniformly takes on the truth-value T (truth) for all assignments of values to its variables. This conception of the matter has serious limitations. It is easily shown that the systems $\mathbf{S}_n^{\supset}$ will have *no tautologies whatsoever* in this sense of the term. For all of the connectives of $\mathbf{S}_n^{\supset}$ are such that when nonclassical truth-values (i.e., those distinct from T and F) are inputs, nonclassical truth-values result as outputs. Since all the basic connectives are of this sort, all of the wffs generated from

---

[2]The first systematic study of the systems of this variant-standard sequence was made in Z. P. Dienes, "On an Implication Function in Many-Valued Systems of Logic," *The Journal of Symbolic Logic*, vol. 14 (1949), pp. 95–97. See also the review of this paper by A. Church and N. Rescher, *ibid.*, vol. 15 (1950), pp. 69–70.

them will also be so. Hence there can be no wff that takes on T uniformly for all assignments of truth-values to its component propositional variables. Let us thus consider now a new, modified definition of tautologousness:

> A wff will be regarded as a tautology if it never assumes the truth-value F (falsity) for any assignment of values to its variables.

It is now possible to show that all two-valued tautologies will be many-valued tautologies (in *this* sense) in all of the systems $S_n^{\supset}$. (The converse, viz. that the many-valued tautologies will also be two-valued ones, is again obvious by the agreement of the many-valued truth tables with the two-valued ones in the T-F case.) The proof is as follows:

We shall show that if a wff can ever take on F for some truth-value assignment to its variables in the many-valued case, then it can also do so in the two-valued case, so that if it is not a many-valued tautology, then it cannot be a two-valued one. From the design of the truth tables for $S_n^{\supset}$ it is readily seen that the connectives $\neg$, $\vee$, $\supset$, and $\equiv$ are all such that they can only yield the truth-value F with classical T-F inputs (and then they reflect the two-valued output). Moreover, the truth table for $\wedge$ is such that $/p \wedge q/$ can only yield F as output when either $/p/ = F$ or $/q/ = F$, so that in this case too an F output would be reflected in the two-valued case. Thus any formula built up with the whole list of connectives can only yield F in the many-valued case under circumstances when it does so in the two-valued case.

We have thus shown that subject to a suitable redefinition of "tautology"[3] all of the systems of the standard sequences $S_n^{\supset}$—specifically including $S_{\aleph}^{\supset}$—will have exactly the same stock of tautologies as the classical two-valued system C_2.

Yet another interesting variant of the standard systems is obtained by letting $\neg$, $\wedge$, and $\vee$ be defined as above, but taking implication to be characterized by the truth rule:

$$/p \to q/ = \begin{Bmatrix} T \\ /q/ \end{Bmatrix} \text{ according as } \begin{cases} /p/ \leq /q/ \\ /p/ > /q/ \end{cases}$$

Equivalence may then be defined as usual

$$p \leftrightarrow q \quad \text{FOR} \quad (p \to q) \wedge (q \to p)$$

with the result that

$$/p \leftrightarrow q/ = \begin{Bmatrix} T \\ \min\,[/p/,/q/] \end{Bmatrix} \text{ according as } \begin{cases} /p/ = /q/ \\ /p/ \neq /q/ \end{cases}$$

[3]That is to say, in the vocabulary to be introduced in Sec. 10 below, if sufficiently many truth-values are "designated."

This gives rise to the sequence of systems S_n^*, which obviously also has infinite-valued members $S_{\aleph_0}^*$ and $S_{\aleph_1}^*$, obtained in the usual way, by taking as truth-values all the real numbers from the interval from 0 to 1 (inclusive). The systems S_3^* and S_4^* will be as follows:

p	$\neg p$	$q \backslash p$	$p \wedge q$			$p \vee q$			$p \to q$			$p \leftrightarrow q$		
			T	I	F	T	I	F	T	I	F	T	I	F
T	F	T	T	I	F	T	T	T	T	I	F	T	I	F
I	I	I	I	I	F	T	I	I	T	T	F	I	T	F
F	T	F	F	F	F	T	I	F	T	T	T	F	F	T

p	$\neg p$	$q \backslash p$	$p \wedge q$				$p \vee q$				$p \to q$				$p \leftrightarrow q$			
			T	I_1	I_2	F	T	I_1	I_2	F	T	I_1	I_2	F	T	I_1	I_2	F
T	F	T	T	I_1	I_2	F	T	T	T	T	T	I_1	I_2	F	T	I_1	I_2	F
I_1	I_2	I_1	I_1	I_1	I_2	F	T	I_1	I_1	I_1	T	T	I_2	F	I_1	T	I_2	F
I_2	I_1	I_2	I_2	I_2	I_2	F	T	I_1	I_2	I_2	T	T	T	F	I_2	I_2	T	F
F	T	F	F	F	F	F	T	I_1	I_2	F	T	T	T	T	F	F	F	T

The suppression relationship that takes these truth tables of this sequence into those of smaller-valued systems will be exactly the same as with $S_n^{\supset}$. As a result, we shall have:

$$T(S_n^*) \subset T(S_m^*) \qquad \text{for any } m < n^4$$

9 The Many-valued Systems of Post

All of the finite systems of many-valued logic with which we have dealt to this point have a mode of negation that has the *mirror-image* feature: the second column of the negation truth table is the reverse of the first column. It is of interest also to consider systems that do not fall into this pattern. In a paper of 1921, Emil L. Post presented a system of finitely many-valued propositional logic based on the m different truth-values for which, for the sake of simplicity, we shall use the first m positive integers $1, 2, 3, \ldots, m$ (rather than adopting Post's own practice of using subscripted t's),[1] with 1 playing the role of *true* and m that of *false*. Following in the steps of Russell and Whitehead's *Principia Mathematica*, where

[4] And this result will obtain regardless of the designations used to define tautologousness in S_n^*, provided there is uniformity with S_m^*. For the concepts at issue here see Sec. 13 below.
[1] See E. L. Post, "Introduction to a General Theory of Elementary Propositions," *American Journal of Mathematics*, vol. 43 (1921), pp. 163–185. Cf. W. and M. Kneale, *The Development of Logic* (Oxford, 1962), pp. 568–569.

negation ($\sim$) and disjunction ($\lor$) are taken as primitives, Post introduced m-valued variants of these connectives $\overset{m}{\neg}$ and $\overset{m}{\lor}$. Negation is governed by the truth table:

p	$\overset{m}{\neg}p$
1	2
2	3
3	4
.	.
.	.
.	.
$m-2$	$m-1$
$m-1$	m
m	1

Thus negation becomes, in effect, an operation which makes a *cyclic shift* in the truth-values and so departs radically from the mode of negation of the standard systems. Disjunction is governed by a truth table based on the principle (familiar from the $\mathbf{L}_n$ and $\mathbf{S}_n$ sequences) that the truth-value of a disjunct is simply the "truest"—i.e., smallest—of the truth-values of its constituents (in Post's formulation the one higher in its subscripted index), so that $/p \overset{m}{\lor} q/ = \min\,[/p/,/q/]$. The remaining propositional connectives can then be introduced in terms of these in the usual way, as follows:

$$p \overset{m}{\land} q \quad \text{FOR} \quad \overset{m}{\neg}(\overset{m}{\neg}p \overset{m}{\lor} \overset{m}{\neg}q)$$
$$p \overset{m}{\supset} q \quad \text{FOR} \quad \overset{m}{\neg}p \overset{m}{\lor} q$$
$$p \overset{m}{\equiv} q \quad \text{FOR} \quad (p \overset{m}{\supset} q) \overset{m}{\land} (q \overset{m}{\supset} p)$$

Thus we obtain the Postian family of many-valued systems $\mathbf{P}_m$. Actually, Post contemplated a two-parameter family of systems $\mathbf{P}_m^\mu$, obtained by treating as truth-like (that is, as "designated") the first μ of the m truth-values of $\mathbf{P}_m$.

Specifically, $\mathbf{P}_3$ will be as follows. (We shall henceforth suppress the m-indicator for the connectives.)

p	$\neg p$	$q \backslash p$	$p \land q$ 1	2	3	$p \lor q$ 1	2	3	$p \supset q$ 1	2	3	$p \equiv q$ 1	2	3
1	2	1	3	3	2	1	1	1	1	2	2	3	3	3
2	3	2	3	1	2	1	2	2	1	2	3	3	1	2
3	1	3	2	2	2	1	2	3	1	1	1	3	2	3

It is clear that while "$\alpha \lor \neg\alpha$" is not a tautology (i.e., uniformly 1-assuming wff) of $\mathbf{P}_3$, "$\alpha \lor \neg\alpha \lor \neg\neg\alpha$" will be.

Even though this was not done by Post himself, it is possible to set up an infinite-valued Post-style system $\mathbf{P}_{\aleph_0}$ as follows. Truth-values are to be the numbers 1 (true) and 0 (false) and all fractions of the form $(\frac{1}{2})^k$ with integral exponents k:

$$1, \tfrac{1}{2}, \tfrac{1}{4}, \tfrac{1}{8}, \ldots, (\tfrac{1}{2})^k, \ldots, 0$$

The truth rules for the various connectives go as follows:

$$/\neg p/ \ = \ \begin{cases} 1 \\ \tfrac{1}{2} \times /p/ \end{cases} \text{ according as } /p/ \begin{cases} = 0 \\ \neq 0 \end{cases}$$

$/p \vee q/ = \max [/p/, /q/]^2$

$/p \wedge q/ = /\neg(\neg p \vee \neg q)/$

$/p \supset q/ = /\neg p \vee q/$

$/p \equiv q/ = /(p \supset q) \wedge (q \supset p)/$

These same truth rules also yield Post-style systems with a non-denumerable set of truth-values, $\mathbf{P}_{\aleph_1}$, if we simply let the truth-values be all of the real numbers from the interval from 0 to 1 (inclusive).

An interesting feature of $\mathbf{P}_{\aleph_0}$ is that *there are no tautologies* (uniformly 1-assuming wffs). For no formula (wff) of the form $\neg p$ can yield a 0-or-1 output unless there is a 0-or-1 input (in fact, a 0 input), nor can a formula of the form $p \vee q$ yield a 0-or-1 output unless there is a 0-or-1 input. It is thus easy to show (by mathematical induction on the number of primitive connectives [$\neg$ or $\vee$] occurring in a formula) that no formula can be tautologous in $\mathbf{P}_{\aleph_0}$.[3] On the other hand, it is easy to see that every finite-valued system $\mathbf{P}_n$ will have tautologies—and indeed tautologies in the sequence of "Laws of the Excluded nth":

$\alpha \vee \neg\alpha$

$\alpha \vee \neg\alpha \vee \neg\neg\alpha$

$\alpha \vee \neg\alpha \vee \neg\neg\alpha \vee \neg\neg\neg\alpha$

etc.

So far, the exposition of the system has proceeded as an exercise in purely abstract manipulation that does little to provide a basis for construing the values at issue to be *truth*-values. And the finding of such a construction is not a trivial matter. For there is no way of identifying truth-values $i = T$ and $j = F$ within the finite Postian systems $\mathbf{P}_m$ (with $2 < m < \aleph_0$) so that the truth tables for the propositional connectives become *normal* in the sense of agreeing with the usual two-valued connectives when only T's and F's are involved. (This is clear from the cyclic character of the truth table for negation.) All the same, Post did manage to

---

[2]In this truth-value series the earlier (truer) member is the maximum, rather than the minimum as in the series 1,2,3,...,n.

[3]And *a fortiori* not in $\mathbf{P}_{\aleph_1}$.

present a semantical interpretation for his nonstandard m-valued logic. Post's interpretation goes essentially as follows:

1. Let the "propositions" at issue (represented by *capital* letters) be $(m - 1)$-tuples of ordinary, two-valued propositions (represented by small letters), subject, however, to the convention that the *true propositions are listed before the false.*

2. Let P assume the truth-value i when exactly $i - 1$ elements of P are false (i.e., when $m - i$ are true).

3. Let $\overset{m}{\neg} P$ be formed by replacing the first false element of P by its denial—but if there is no false element, then all are to be denied. (The negation at issue here is $\sim$, the usual, classical propositional negation.)

4. When $P = (p_1, p_2, \ldots, p_{m-1})$ and $Q = (q_1, q_2, \ldots, q_{m-1})$, then

$$P \overset{m}{\vee} Q = (p_1 \vee q_1, p_2 \vee q_2, \ldots, p_{m-1} \vee q_{m-1})$$

(The disjunction on the right-hand side of this last equation is the usual, classical propositional disjunction.)

On the basis of this interpretation of the connectives, satisfaction of the truth tables of Post's m-valued propositional logic is guaranteed. The interpretation of the logic in terms of $(m - 1)$-tuples of propositions thus provides a means for constructing Post's m-valued system out of the orthodox, two-valued system. Note, however, that this is not a *propositional* interpretation, but one that proceeds in terms of *sets* of propositions. Here greater flexibility is available, but this fact should not block our vision of the nonstandard nature of the interpretation. We now have to do, in effect, not with a many-valued *propositional* logic, but with a many-valued logic of (duly ordered) *sets of propositions;* and with propositional operators that represent "negation" and "disjunction" (etc.) in only a strained or extended sense of those terms.

10 Some Structural Features of Many-valued Logics

It is helpful for present purposes to consider some important abstract, structural features that characterize many (though not necessarily all) of the most familiar systems of many-valued logic.

(1) The truth table for a propositional connective that is the many-valued analogue of one of the two-valued connectives will be said to be *normal* if (1) it includes at least one true-analogous or "designated" truth-value T (which may, however, be represented

56   Many-valued Logic

by 0 or 1 or *n* or in some other way) and at least one false-analogous or "antidesignated" truth-value *F* (also perhaps represented differently) and (2) it *agrees entirely with the standard two-valued one for the connective* C_2 *when only the two truth-values T and F are involved.*

A many-valued logic may be said to be *normal* (as a whole) if the truth tables for all of its basic connectives are normal (throughout with respect to one and the same pair of truth-values *T, F*).[1]

With the exception of the Postian systems, all of the systems of many-valued logic we have considered thus far are normal in this sense.

The key feature of all of the normal systems of many-valued logic is inherent in the following principle:

Every uniformly *T*-assuming tautology in any normal system (i.e., every wff that invariably takes on the truth-value *T* for all possible assignments of truth-values to its constituent propositional variables) will be a tautology of the two-valued system C_2.

The demonstration of this important fact is very simple: If the wff uniformly takes on *T* whenever its variables assume values from the list $T, I_1, I_2, \ldots, I_n, F$, then this wff will also take on *T* whenever its variables take values from the abbreviated list *T, F*—and so the wff must also be a two-valued tautology. The set of tautologies of any normal system is thus a subset of the set of the standard, two-valued tautologies. In this (tautology-containment) sense all of the standard systems of many-valued logic are included within the classical, two-valued system C_2 as so-called "fragments" thereof. But, of course, perfectly self-consistent and serviceable systems of many-valued logic can (as we shall see below) fail to be normal and may then encompass as tautologous formulas wffs that are not two-valued tautologies.

If many-valued connectives are normal and agree with their two-valued counterparts when only *T*'s and *F*'s are involved, then the many-valued tautologies (and contradictions) must also be—as we have seen—two-valued tautologies (and contradictions). But the converse is not the case: two-valued tautologies and contradictions need not correspond to those involving their normal many-valued counterparts. Thus consider the 3-valued connective † and its two-valued relative ‡:

---

[1]This idea of normality differs from what Jan Łukasiewicz in his 1941 paper calls "normal" —viz. the feature that *modus ponens* obtains for the system so characterized, in that its truth table for → is such that whenever *p* and *p* → *q* both take on designated truth-values, then *q* will also do so. See p. 70.

p	$\ddagger\alpha$	p	$\dagger\alpha$
T	F	T	F
F	F	I	T
		F	F

While "$\ddagger\alpha$" is a contradiction, "$\dagger\alpha$" is not; and while $\sim$"$\ddagger\alpha$" is a tautology, $\neg\dagger\alpha$ is not. Incidentally, this connective is of special interest because it may be used to formulate in the standard systems of 3-valued logic the analogue of the two-valued "Law of Excluded Middle" (or "Principle of Excluded Third"), viz.: "$\alpha \lor \sim\alpha$." For in such 3-valued systems we do not have "$\alpha \lor \neg\alpha$" as a tautology, but we do have: "$\alpha \lor \neg\alpha \lor \dagger\alpha$." This thesis is frequently referred to as the "principle of excluded fourth" for 3-valued logic. (Analogous principles—of "excluded fifth," "excluded sixth," and so on—can also be devised for higher-valued systems.)

> (2) We shall characterize the many-valued truth table of a connective as *uniform* if, whenever the T- and F-headed positions in a given row (or column) both agree in having the same entry, then the entire row (column) uniformly shows this agreeing truth-value. In a uniform truth table, agreement in the T-F case turns out to be decisive throughout. The uniformity of a truth table in this sense may be looked on as a "forcing principle" to the effect that when the two extreme entries of a row (column) agree in the T and F cases, this forces agreement throughout this row (column). That is, if it makes no difference in the outcome truth-value whether the input truth-value is T or F, then it will simply not matter at all what the input truth-value is.
>
> A many-valued logic may be called *uniform* (as a whole) if the truth tables for all of its basic connectives are so.

K_3 the (strong) 3-valued logic of Kleene and all of the standard systems of many-valued logic based on $\supset$ and $\equiv$ are uniform in this sense, but the 3-valued system B_3 of Bochvar is not (see the truth table for $\rightarrow$), nor is that of Łukasiewicz, as is shown by his truth table for $\leftrightarrow$ (but note that the truth table for $\rightarrow$ is uniform):

$p \backslash^q$	$p \rightarrow q$			$p \leftrightarrow q$		
	T	I	F	T	I	F
T	T	I	F	T	I	F
I	T	T	I	I	T	I
F	T	T	T	F	I	T

This consideration brings out a significant fact, viz. that nonuniform connectives can be introduced definitionally in terms of uniform ones. For Łukasiewicz' truth tables for implication ($\rightarrow$) and conjunction ($\wedge$) are both uniform, but his equivalence ($\leftrightarrow$) which is defined as

$$p \leftrightarrow q \quad \text{FOR} \quad (p \rightarrow q) \wedge (q \rightarrow p)$$

is (as we have just seen) not uniform.

   (3) The truth table for a many-valued connective is *regular in the sense of Kleene* (K-regular) if it never contains T (or F) as an entry in a row (or column) for one of the "intermediate" values different from T and F unless this entry T (or F) occurs uniformly throughout its entire column (or row, respectively). In other words, in a K-regular truth table a classical, definite truth-value (T or F) will occur in a position governed by an intermediate truth-value only if this definiteness is required by the forcing principle of uniformity (i.e., by agreement of the extreme T and F positions).
   A many-valued system will be said to be *K-regular* (as a whole) if the truth tables for all of its basic connectives are so.

The truth tables for Kleene's (strong) system $\mathbf{K}_3$ of 3-valued logic and those for the system $\mathbf{B}_3$ of Bochvar have this property, as do the truth tables for $\wedge$ and $\vee$ in all the standard systems of many-valued logic. But the truth tables for $\rightarrow$ and $\leftrightarrow$ in the 3-valued logic of Łukasiewicz violate it:

$_p\backslash^q$	$p \rightarrow q$			$p \leftrightarrow q$		
	T	I	F	T	I	F
T	T	I	F	T	I	F
I	T	T	I	I	T	I
F	T	T	T	F	I	T

Note that these tables would become K-regular by changing the central T to I, a change resulting in Kleene's system $\mathbf{K}_3$.

   Kleene rightly observes that his (strong) system is uniquely determined as the 3-valued system that combines three features:

   1. It is *normal* in being an extension of two-valued logic, and so agreeing with it when only T's and F's are involved.
   2. It is *K-regular*.
   3. It is *the strongest such system*, in the sense that its truth tables have the classical truth-value T or F whenever this is possible for a 3-valued system that is both normal and K-regular.

We shall verify this fact only with respect to the truth table for disjunction. We begin with a truth table of the following form, the corner entries being determined by the assumption of normality:

$p \backslash q$	T	I	F
		$p \vee q$	
T	T	(1)	T
I	(2)	(3)	(4)
F	T	(5)	F

Entry (1) will be T, since it should be T or F (the truth table being the strongest), but it cannot be F (by K-regularity). And exactly the same reasoning applies to entry (2). This brings us to the truth table:

$p \backslash q$	T	I	F
		$p \vee q$	
T	T	T	T
I	T	(3)	(4)
F	T	(5)	F

Now entry (4) cannot be T or F (by K-regularity), and hence is I. And exactly the same reasoning applies to entry (5). And finally, entry (3) cannot now be T or F (by K-regularity). Thus all three remaining entries must be I, and the expected truth table for $\vee$ is therefore uniquely determined.

In this connection, however, it is also interesting to observe that Kleene's (strong) system is also uniquely characterized among 3-valued systems as *the weakest uniform normal system:* weakest in the sense of introducing a nonclassical truth-value (viz. I) whenever possible. This finding actually characterizes the intended applications of this system better than the preceding one does: Whenever the nonclassical indeterminate I enters the scene, the connective yields I as an output value—unless this output truth-value is otherwise fixed by agreement of the T and F inputs for this case (which would show that the input truth-values are, in a sense, immaterial, so that it does not affect matters even if they are "intermediate" [undecided, unknown, indeterminate, or whatever]).

To make the next point, two further structural features of a wide variety of many-valued systems must first be delineated:

(4) The truth table for a propositional connective in a system of many-valued logic is *strongly uniform* (S-uniform) if it is such

that whenever *the same* truth-value occurs at *any* two positions in a certain row (or column)—not necessarily at just the extremes—then all of the intermediate positions of this row (or column) are filled by the same entry.

(5) Let a many-valued logic be based on a truth-value series $T, I_1, I_2,$ ..., I_n, F. Then the truth table for a connective will be said to be *continuous* if every row (or column) that begins with T and ends with F (or the reverse) has the intervening positions filled with *all the intermediate truth-values in proper order*.

The 3-valued systems we have considered (Łukasiewicz, Bochvar, Kleene) are strongly uniform (trivially so, since they are both uniform and 3-valued), and so also are all the standard systems. Moreover, all these 3-valued systems are continuous and all the standard systems also.

It is a fact of considerable interest that:

The many-valued systems of the sequence S_n or $Ł_n$ are uniquely determined—apart from their specific mode of implication—as *the normal, S-uniform, and continuous systems whose truth tables for $\land$ and $\lor$ have "the diagonal property,"* viz. that whenever two identical truth-values occur as inputs, then this same value will also be the output truth-value.

This feature of the systems S_n and $Ł_n$ is obvious with regard to their truth table for negation. For the truth table for $\neg$ will here take the form:

p	$\neg p$
T	F
I_1	?
.	.
.	.
.	.
I_n	?
F	T

The T-F entries are fixed as indicated by the requirement of normality, and then the intervening entries are all determined (in the proper way) by the requirement of continuity.

To illustrate the process of verification in the case of the binary connectives, we shall carry through the argument for $\land$ in S_4. We begin with:

$_p\backslash^q$	T	I_1	I_2	F
T	T	(1)	(2)	F
I_1	(3)			(5)
I_2	(4)			(6)
F	F	(7)	(8)	F

with column header $p \land q$

The four corner positions are fixed as indicated by the requirement of normality. By S-uniformity, $(5) = (6) = F$ and $(7) = (8) = F$. By continuity $(1) = I_1$ and $(2) = I_2$; and also $(3) = I_1$ and $(4) = I_2$. This brings us to:

$\overset{q}{\underset{p}{\diagdown}}$	$p \wedge q$			
	T	I_1	I_2	F
T	T	I_1	I_2	F
I_1	I_1	(a)	(b)	F
I_2	I_2	(c)	(d)	F
F	F	F	F	F

By the diagonal property (a) $= I_1$ and (d) $= I_2$. But then by S-uniformity, (b) $= I_2$ (since it is caught between two I_2's in its column), and similarly (c) $= I_2$ (since it is caught between two I_2's in its row). This completes the requisite derivation that uniquely determines this truth table. This line of argument is readily generalized to all the other relevant cases.

Yet other significant features of certain many-valued truth tables are as follows:

(6) The truth table for a propositional connective is *decisive* if only T's and F's ever occur as output truth-values, so that a *classically definite* truth-value (i.e., T or F) will result in every case.

Bochvar's external system $\mathbf{B}_3^{\mathrm{E}}$ is decisive in the specified sense, each of its truth tables having the feature of decisiveness. (It seems scarcely worth mentioning that $\mathbf{C}_2$ is decisive.) The implication and equivalence relationships of all the standard systems $\mathbf{S}_n$ are decisive (but not their modes of negation, disjunction, and conjunction).

Two further structural features of many-valued truth tables are of interest:

(7) The truth table for a propositional connective is *categorical* if there is a classical (T or F) output whenever there is a classical input.

(8) The truth table for a propositional connective is *anticategorical* if there is a nonclassical (indeterminate, non-T/F) output whenever there is a nonclassical input.

Clearly, decisiveness will entail categoricity, so that our various examples of categorical connectives will illustrate this feature also. Moreover, the connectives of Bochvar's system $\mathbf{B}_3$ are all anticategorical.

It is worth noting that decisiveness, categoricity, and anticategoricity all have the feature of *definitional transmission:* given connectives with one of these properties as primitives, those other connectives definable by means of them will also all have this property. It follows, e.g., that only decisive connectives can be defined within $\mathbf{B}_3^*$, and that only anticategorical connectives can be defined within $\mathbf{B}_3$. Indeed, the three conditions of 3-valuedness, normality (i.e., agreement with the two-valued case when only T's or F's are involved), and anticategoricity suffice to determine uniquely the system $\mathbf{B}_3$ of Bochvar.

It is interesting to note that the truth table for a many-valued binary connective $\varnothing$ will be both decisive and K-regular only if it contains only F's or only T's as its interior entries. For consider such a truth table:

q $\backslash$ p	T	I_1	I_2	...	I_n	F
T						
I_1	v					
I_2						
.						
.						
.						
I_n						
F						

(with heading $p \varnothing q$)

By decisiveness v must be T or F. Suppose it is T. Then K-regularity has it that T must occur uniformly throughout the entire second column and the entire second row. And then T must occur homogeneously throughout the entire truth table. (And an analogous argument holds if v had been F.)

11 Truth-functional Completeness in Many-valued Logic

The number of distinct, strictly truth-functional propositional connectives that can be defined within a many-valued logic is vastly greater than that of two-valued logic. For in n-valued logic any given place in the truth table can be occupied by n—and not just two—truth-values. Since the truth table for a k-place connective has room for

$$n \times n \times \cdots \times n \, (k \text{ times}) = n^k$$

entries, for each of which there will be any one of n possibilities, we will have

$$n \times n \times \cdots \times n \, (n^k \text{ times}) = n^{n^k}$$

possible k-place truth tables in an n-valued logic. This, of course, is a number that grows astronomically with an increase in n:[1]

---

[1] I take these calculations from J. Łukasiewicz, "Die Logik und das Grundlagenproblem," *Les Entretiens de Zürich sur les fondements et la méthode des sciences mathématiques*, 6–9 décembre 1938, ed. by F. Gonseth (Zürich, 1941).

No. of truth-values	No. of 1-place connectives	No. of 2-place connectives
2	4	16
3	27	19,683
4	256	4,294,967,269

It is clear that the number of possible connectives in a many-valued logic—and thus the number of distinct modes of logical interrelation that can be described therein—will vastly exceed that of two-valued logic.

A system of truth-functional logic is characterized as being "truth-functionally complete" if the truth tables for its basic connectives are such that *every possible truth-value function* can be defined in terms of these basic connectives. This mode of completeness is thus a matter of being able to generate all possible truth tables for all possible connectives by means of combining the members of a starter set of truth tables for a given group of connectives. Such completeness is readily established for the standard two-valued system (based on the connectives $\sim$, &, $\vee$, $\supset$, $\equiv$) by extending the reasoning of the following example:

p	q	r	$\Phi(p,q,r)$
T	*T*	*T*	$\sqrt{}$
T	*T*	*F*	$\sqrt{}$
T	*F*	*T*	x
T	*F*	*F*	x
F	*T*	*T*	x
F	*T*	*F*	$\sqrt{}$
F	*F*	*T*	$\sqrt{}$
F	*F*	*F*	x

Suppose we wish to define a truth function Φ for the three variables p, q, r, which is to be true at exactly those places marked $\sqrt{}$ (and false elsewhere, i.e., at those marked x). All we need to do is to form the disjunction of the conjunctive compounds corresponding to the rows marked with a $\sqrt{}$. This, in the present case, leads to:

$$\Phi(p, q, r) = (p \& q \& r) \vee (p \& q \& \sim r) \vee (\sim p \& q \& \sim r) \vee (\sim p \& \sim q \& r)$$

By a process of exactly this sort, any arbitrary truth function of propositional variables can be represented in terms of the truth tables for the three basic connectives $\sim$, &, and $\vee$.

But this situation is radically altered in a many-valued system of logic. For example, in all of the "normal" systems of many-valued logic (and thus with virtually all of the systems we have been considering) the truth tables for the connectives will *agree with the classical two-valued truth tables when only the two classical truth-values T and F are involved.* Consequently, it will obviously be impossible to define by means of them a truth function such as the following (drawing our example from the 3-valued case)

p	Tp
T	I
I	I
F	I

i.e., a one-place truth function which *uniformly* takes on the truth-value I (i.e., assumes this value for *all* possible inputs). The impossibility of introducing this connective—the "T-function" first introduced by the Polish logician Jerzy Słupecki in 1936—establishes the *truth-functional* incompleteness of these systems of many-valued logic.[2] Such systems are properly characterized as "incomplete" because they do not afford the means for introducing certain specifiable truth functions.

If one adds to the connectives of $Ł_3$, 3-valued logic of Łukasiewicz, the operator Tp—defined as above—then the resulting system will be that based on the truth tables:

p	$\neg p$	Tp	$\begin{smallmatrix}&q\\p&\end{smallmatrix}$	$p \wedge q$ T I F	$p \vee q$ T I F	$p \rightarrow q$ T I F	$p \leftrightarrow q$ T I F
T	F	I	T	T I F	T T T	T I F	T I F
I	I	I	I	I I F	T I I	T T I	I T I
F	T	I	F	F F F	T I F	T T T	F I T

Let us designate this system as $Ł_3^S$, that is, as the Słupecki variant of $Ł_3$. It was shown by Słupecki that this T-supplemented 3-valued system is truth-functionally complete.[3] The truth-functional completeness of different groups of connectives in 3-valued logic has also been explored. For example, the following group can also be shown to be complete:

[2]Jerzy Słupecki, "Der volle dreiwertige Aussagenkalkül," *Comptes rendus des séances de la Société des sciences et des lettres de Varsovie*, Classe III, vol. xxix (1936), pp. 9–11. Tr. as "The Full Three-Valued Propositional Calculus" in S. McCall (ed.), *Polish Logic: 1920–1939* (Oxford, 1967), pp. 335–337. Słupecki used T for *tertium* to suggest the key role here of the third (intermediate) truth-value.
[3]This will not hold true if one considers either Kleene's system K_3 or Bochvar's system B_3 in place of $Ł_3$ as the basic system to which T is added. For in both cases there will be no way of combining the connectives of the augmented system to obtain a formula that yields a classical truth-value (T or F) as output when the input truth-values are all uniformly I.

				$p \wedge q$			$p \vee q$		
p	$\neg p$	$\dashv p$	$\diagdown \overset{q}{\underset{p}{}}$	1	2	3	1	2	3
1	3	2	1	1	2	3	1	1	1
2	2	3	2	2	2	3	1	2	2
3	1	1	3	3	3	3	1	2	3

Here the connectives $\neg$, $\vee$, and $\wedge$ have the standard features of 3-valued negation, disjunction, and conjunction, while $\dashv$ is Post's cyclical "negation."

The issue of functional completeness for n-valued propositional logic has also been explored extensively. Basing an n-valued system upon the natural numbers $1, 2, \ldots, n$, as truth values, the following set is known to be complete:

$\circledcirc$: where $/\circledcirc(p)/ = i$ for $1 \leq i \leq n$, uniformly regardless of the value of $/p/$

$\boxed{i}$: where $/\boxed{i}(p)/ = \begin{Bmatrix} 1 \\ n \end{Bmatrix}$ according as $\begin{cases} /p/ = i \\ /p/ \neq i \end{cases}$ with $1 \leq i \leq n$

$[\![m]\!]$: where $/p[\![m]\!]q/ = \min \{/p/,/q/\}$

$[\![M]\!]$: where $/p[\![M]\!]q/ = \max \{/p/,/q/\}$

(Here the connectives where i figures as a parameter are in fact families of n connectives.) More economically, the following pair of connectives will also be truth-functionally complete:

$[\![M]\!]$: as above

$\overset{n}{\dashv}$: where $/\overset{n}{\dashv}p/ = /p/ + 1 \pmod{n+1}$[4]

Since $[\![M]\!]$ has the essential maximizing feature of Postian disjunction, it follows that all of the systems in Post's sequence $\mathbf{P}_n$ are truth-functionally complete. In fact, D. Webb has shown that all possible truth-functional connectives for an n-valued logic can be defined using one single binary connective:[5]

$[\![W]\!]$: where $/p[\![W]\!]q/ = [\max \{/p/,/q/\} + 1] \pmod{n+1}$

The truth-functional completeness of a set of many-valued connectives is an interesting feature from the purely formal, algebraic point of view. From other points of consideration, this feature may in some ways be desirable, but it is certainly not essential. Indeed one must be prepared to

---

[4]Exactly as with the negation operator in Post's system $\mathbf{P}_n$, with integers now used as truth-values. (Here "mod" represents the mathematical modulus notation, with which the reader is assumed to be familiar.)

[5]See D. L. Webb, "Generation of Any n-Valued Logic by One Binary Operation," *Proceedings of the National Academy of Sciences*, vol. 21 (1935), pp. 252–254. M. Wajsberg had made this finding in the 1920s. See Wajsberg (1937) as translated in McCall, *Polish Logic* (*op. cit.*), pp. 317–318.

abandon it as a desideratum if one wants to deal with infinite-valued logics. For it is obvious that no finite set of connectives can be truth-functionally complete for any infinite-valued logic.

We shall not pursue this theme of truth-functional completeness for connectives in many-valued logic any further here. A substantial literature has grown up around this topic, and readers who wish to pursue the matter will find guidance in the Bibliography. The considerations primarily involved in the issue of truth-functional completeness are algebraic and syntactical: they are rather remote from the semantical and meaning-related side of logic with which we are primarily concerned here.

12 Tautologousness and Designated Truth-values

The concept of a *tautology* familiar from the two-valued case is as follows: a tautology is a formula that *uniformly takes on the truth-value T for any and every assignment of truth-values to its propositional variables.* This concept is readily generalized to apply to many-valued systems of logic. Given a many-valued system of anything like the normal variety, we can classify certain of its truth-values as *designated*—i.e., as representing "truth-like" truth-values. A formula will then be a *tautology* of the many-valued logic in question—subject to the specified designations of truth-values— if it uniformly takes on a designated truth-value for any and every assignment of truth-values to its propositional variables. We shall speak of a formula as *satisfying* a set of many-valued truth tables (with specified designations) when it is a tautology with respect to them.

The case of Łukasiewicz' 3-valued logic is instructive. Consider again the truth table for $Ł_3$:

p	$\neg p$	$q \backslash p$	$p \wedge q$			$p \vee q$			$p \rightarrow q$			$p \leftrightarrow q$		
			T	I	F	T	I	F	T	I	F	T	I	F
T	F	T	T	I	F	T	T	T	T	I	F	T	I	F
I	I	I	I	I	F	T	I	I	T	T	I	I	T	I
F	T	F	F	F	F	T	I	F	T	T	T	F	I	T

If we designate T alone, we obtain the usual tautologies of $Ł_3$, including, say, "$\alpha \rightarrow \alpha$" but not "$\alpha \vee \neg\alpha$" or "$\neg(\alpha \wedge \neg\alpha)$." But if we designate both T and I, then *many of the classical tautologies (i.e., tautologies of C_2) that fail to hold in L_3 will satisfy the revised 3-valued system* (subject to the usual correspondence between the propositional connectives). Some examples of this are: "$\alpha \vee \neg \alpha$" and "$\neg(\alpha \wedge \neg \alpha)$." However, as we have already seen on page 27, not all of the C_2-tautologies will now obtain in the revised system: specifically the classical tautology "$\neg(\alpha \rightarrow \neg \alpha) \vee \neg(\neg \alpha \rightarrow \alpha)$" will continue to fail in the three-valued case. Thus the revised system is a many-valued logic somehow intermediate between $Ł_3$ and C_2.[1] As this example shows, it makes a great difference for determining the accepted theses (i.e., tautologies) of a many-valued system which truth-values are selected for "designation."

The concept of contradictoriness can also be extended to many-valued logics. In the two-valued case, a formula is, of course, a contradiction if it uniformly takes on the truth-value F for any and every assignment of truth-values to its propositional variables. Now in a many-valued system of anything like the normal variety, we can classify certain of its truth-values as *antidesignated*—i.e., as representing "false-like" truth-values. A formula will then be a *contradiction* of the many-valued logic in question —subject to the specified antidesignations of truth-values—if it takes on an antidesignated truth-value for any and every assignment of truth-values to its propositional variables.

The reasons for introducing *antidesignated* truth-values, and not simply getting by with nondesignated ones, are readily illustrated. Consider K_3. If we designate T alone, there will be no tautologies (since every formula takes I when all its variables do). To obtain tautologies, we must designate both T and I (and then the usual tautologies of C_2 result). Now if a contradiction is a formula that "uniformly assumes *nondesignated* truth-values" —i.e., that uniformly takes on F—then there will be no contradictions (again, since every formula takes I when all its variables do). We must therefore characterize contradictions in terms of something other than the nondesignated truth-values, and the machinery of antidesignated truth-values is intended to provide this needed resource.

The choice of designated and antidesignated truth-values is not to be looked upon as an arbitrary matter. We would obviously want the tautologies (and contradictions) determined by means of the designation specifications to bear *some* relation to the familiar situation in the classical, two-valued case. For example, we would not want it to happen that there is some truth-value v which is both designated and antidesignated when it is also the case that there is some formula which uniformly assumes this truth-value, for then this formula would be both a tautology and a contradiction.

---

[1] The axiomatization of this 3-valued system is an open question.

The situation with respect to $\mathbf{L}_3$ is again instructive. If we antidesignate F alone, there will be various contradictions, including "$\neg(\alpha \to \alpha)$" and "$\neg[\beta \to (\alpha \to \alpha)]$" and "$\neg[\neg(\alpha \to \alpha) \to \beta]$." (Note, however, that there can then be no contradiction involving only $\neg$, $\wedge$, and $\vee$, since the truth tables at issue are such that any formula involving only these connectives will uniformly yield I as output truth-value when *all* the input truth-values are I. Thus specifically "$\alpha \wedge \neg\alpha$" and "$\neg(\alpha \vee \neg\alpha)$" will not be contradictions.) On the other hand, if we antidesignate both F and I, then all of the classical contradictions (i.e., all contradictions of $\mathbf{C}_2$) will become contradictions of $\mathbf{L}_3$. (This is established by considerations that parallel the preceding argument that if both T and I are designated in $\mathbf{L}_3$, then all the classical tautologies will result.)

The preceding remark sets the stage for an important point, viz. that in the consideration of some systems of many-valued logic there may be good reason for *letting one and the same truth-value be both designated and antidesignated.* The principle of the classical two-valued case that all (and only) nondesignated truth-values are automatically to be treated as antidesignated does not apply in the many-valued situation, where the set of antidesignated truth-values may set up as being *either smaller or larger* than the set of nondesignated ones.

The classical negation principle that *the negation of a tautology is a contradiction, and vice versa*, must be reexamined in the light of these considerations. For this principle will hold, in general, only if a rather special condition is satisfied:

> That the truth table for negation has the orthodox reflection feature of taking all designated truth-values into antidesignated ones, and vice versa.

Once this special condition is satisfied, the operativeness of the classical principle of the negation correspondence between contradictions and tautologies will be restored in the context of many-valued logic.

Some points of notation must be introduced. In setting up the truth tables for pluri-valued connectives, we shall frequently mark a truth-value with a plus or minus, $+v$ and $-v$ being used to indicate that the truth-value at issue is designated or antidesignated, respectively. The set of all designated values of the system $\mathbf{X}$ will be represented as $D^+(\mathbf{X})$ and the set of all its antidesignated values as $D^-(\mathbf{X})$. The set of all tautologies of $\mathbf{X}$ is indicated as

$$T(\mathbf{X})$$

and the set of all of its contradictions as

$$C(\mathbf{X})$$

Thus to indicate that p is or is not an **X**-tautology, we shall write $p \in T(\mathbf{X})$ or $p \notin T(\mathbf{X})$, respectively, and to indicate that q is or is not an **X**-contradiction, we shall write $q \in C(\mathbf{X})$ or $q \notin C(\mathbf{X})$, respectively.

Putting this notation to work, we may observe that we have already shown with regard to $\mathbf{L}_3$, the 3-valued system of Łukasiewicz, that if we adopt the designations

$$+T$$
$$\pm I$$
$$-F$$

then both:

$$T(\mathbf{L}_3) = T(\mathbf{C}_2)$$
$$C(\mathbf{L}_3) = C(\mathbf{C}_2)$$

To go beyond this established finding, let us reexamine $\mathbf{B}_3$, the 3-valued logic of Bochvar, with respect to the same group of designations:

p	$\neg p$	$\begin{smallmatrix}q\\p\end{smallmatrix}$	$p \wedge q$ $T\ \ I\ \ F$	$p \vee q$ $T\ \ I\ \ F$	$p \rightarrow q$ $T\ \ I\ \ F$	$p \leftrightarrow q$ $T\ \ I\ \ F$
$+T$	F	$+T$	$T\ \ I\ \ F$	$T\ \ I\ \ T$	$T\ \ I\ \ F$	$T\ \ I\ \ F$
$-I$	I	$-I$	$I\ \ I\ \ I$	$I\ \ I\ \ I$	$I\ \ I\ \ I$	$I\ \ I\ \ I$
$\pm F$	T	$\pm F$	$F\ \ I\ \ F$	$T\ \ I\ \ F$	$T\ \ I\ \ T$	$F\ \ I\ \ T$

These connectives are such that:

1. Any formula (wff) will take the $\mathbf{C}_2$-dictated truth-value when only T's and F's are involved.
2. Any formula (wff) will automatically take on the truth-value I whenever I enters upon the scene as an input.

It is clear therefore that two-valued tautologies, and only these, can be tautologies of $\mathbf{B}_3$ subject to the specified designations. Similarly, the two-valued contradictions, and only these, can be contradictions of $\mathbf{B}_3$. Thus we shall also have:

$$T(\mathbf{B}_3) = T(\mathbf{C}_2)$$
$$C(\mathbf{B}_3) = C(\mathbf{C}_2)$$

Despite the very substantial differences among the three pluri-valued systems $\mathbf{C}_2$, $\mathbf{L}_3$, and $\mathbf{B}_3$, they will all yield exactly the same tautologies and exactly the same contradictions (subject to the designations $+T$, $\pm I$, and $-F$ for the two 3-valued systems).[2]

[2]This finding can also be extended to $\mathbf{K}_3$, the 3-valued system of Kleene.

In this context it should, however, be observed that a normal 3-valued logic whose "intermediate" truth-value is designated need not yield all the tautologies of C_2, but may yield only a fragment. Thus consider the system:[3]

p	$\neg p$	q\p	$p \wedge q$			$p \vee q$			$p \supset q$			$p \equiv q$		
			T	I	F	T	I	F	T	I	F	T	I	F
$+T$	F	$+T$	T	T	F	T	T	T	T	F	F	T	F	F
$+I$	I	$+I$	T	I	F	T	I	F	T	I	F	F	I	F
$-F$	T	$-F$	F	F	F	T	F	F	T	T	T	F	F	T

That the two-valued tautology "$\alpha \supset (\beta \supset \alpha)$" is not a tautology of this system is apparent when $/\alpha/ = I$ and $/\beta/ = T$.[4]

It is necessary to distinguish between two ways in which a *modus ponens* principle can be operative in a system of many-valued logic, viz.

(i) Whenever $/p/$ and $/p \rightarrow q/$ are both designated truth-values, then $/q/$ must also be a designated value.

(ii) Whenever p and $p \rightarrow q$ are both tautologies, then q must also be a tautology.

It can be seen that (i) entails (ii), but the reverse is not the case. Thus consider the truth table for K_3 with both T and I designated:

p\q	$p \supset q$		
	T	I	F
$+T$	T	I	F
$+I$	T	I	I
F	T	T	T

A *modus ponens* principle in form (ii) holds; for assume that p and $p \rightarrow q$ are both tautologies, but that q is not. Now this can only be when for some assignment of values to the variables in p and q it results that $/p/ = I$ and $/p \rightarrow q/ = I$, and $/q/ = F$. But then under the modified assignment obtained by replacing each I in the initial one by T, we shall have it that: $/q/ = F$, and either $/p/ = F$ or $/p \rightarrow q/ = F$, contrary to assumption. Thus (ii) must obtain. But (i) obviously fails because $I \rightarrow F = I$, and F is not designated.

[3]This 3-valued system is due to B. Sobociński and has been axiomatized by him. See his paper "Axiomatization of a Partial System of Three-Valued Calculus of Propositions," *The Journal of Computing Systems*, vol. 1 (1952), pp. 23–55.
[4]Indeed Sobociński has shown (*op. cit.*) that no formula in which some variable occurs only once can be a tautology of this 3-valued system.

Whenever we speak of *modus ponens* as a "rule of inference" in the context of many-valued logic, it is the weaker condition (ii) that is at issue. For this suffices to guarantee the essential feature of any *rule of inference* that it be tautologousness-preserving: applied to tautologies as premisses it must yield a tautologous conclusion. Note that two comparably different versions will also pertain to the other rules of inference, viz. either the (stronger) formulation of invariably leading from designated premisses to designated conclusions, or else the weaker formulation of leading from invariably-designated (tautologous) premisses to invariably-designated (tautologous) conclusions.

13 Containment Relationships between Many-valued Logics

One many-valued system can be said to be "contained" in another in several distinct senses, three of which are especially important for our purposes. (We suppose that the systems at issue are based upon notationally the same propositional connectives, so that the formulas involved are the same throughout.)

(I) The system **Y** may "contain" the system **X** in the sense that every tautology of **X** (according to its truth tables and their designated values) is a tautology of **Y** (under the same conditions). We shall then say that **X** *T-contains* **Y**—i.e., contains **Y** in respect of *tautologies*. In this sense, for example, all of the normal systems are contained in **C₂**.

(II) The system **X** may "contain" the system **Y** in the sense that (1) all the truth-values of **Y** are also truth-values of **X** and (2) if throughout the truth tables for **X** one suppresses (i.e., erases) all of those rows and columns headed by those truth-values of **X** that are additional to those of **Y**, then what remains will simply be the truth tables of **Y**. We shall then say that **X** *S-contains* **Y**—i.e., contains **Y** subject to certain *suppressions*. For example, consider the following 4-valued logic.

p	$\neg p$	q \ p	$p \wedge q$ T	I	I*	F	$p \vee q$ T	I	I*	F	$p \supset q$ T	I	I*	F	$p \equiv q$ T	I	I*	F
$+T$	F	$+T$	T	I	I*	F	T	T	T	T	T	I	I*	F	T	I	I*	F
I	I	I	I	I	I*	F	T	I	I	I	T	I	I*	I	I	I	I	I
$I*$	I	$I*$	I*	I*	I*	F	T	I	I*	I*	T	I	I	I	I*	I	I	I
F	T	F	F	F	F	F	T	I	I*	F	T	T	T	T	F	I	I	T

As the boxings show, if we suppress the rows and columns correspondingly to I^*, the residual system will be Kleene's system K_3, which is thus S-contained in the initial 4-valued system.

(III) The system X also "contains" the system Y if we obtain Y from X by identifying each of the truth-values of X with one of the truth-values of Y, possibly collapsing several X-truth-values in the process. We shall then say that X *I-contains* Y—i.e., contains Y subject to the compression effected bycer taini *dentifications*.[1]

Thus consider the system $S_4^{\supset}$ of the variant-standard sequence:

p	$\neg p$	$\begin{smallmatrix}&q\\p&\end{smallmatrix}$	$p \wedge q$ T I I^* F	$p \vee q$ T I I^* F	$p \supset q$ T I I^* F	$p \equiv q$ T I I^* F
$+T$	F	$+T$	T I I^* F	T T T T	T I I^* F	T I I^* F
I	I^*	I	I I I^* F	T I I I	T I I^* I^*	I I I I^*
I^*	I	I^*	I^* I^* I^* F	T I I^* I^*	T I I I	I^* I I I
$-F$	T	$-F$	F F F F	T I I^* F	T T T T	F I^* I T

Notice that if we establish the following compression of the truth-values of the 4-valued tables T,I,I^*,F into the truth-values of a 3-valued logic

T goes into T $\quad$ I^* goes into I
I goes into I $\quad$ F goes into F

that is to say if we simply identify $I = I^*$, then these truth tables become:

p	$\neg p$	$\begin{smallmatrix}&q\\p&\end{smallmatrix}$	$p \wedge q$ T I F	$p \vee q$ T I F	$p \supset q$ T I F	$p \equiv q$ T I F
$+T$	F	$+T$	T I F	T T T	T I F	T I F
I	I	I	I I F	T I I	T I I	I I I
$-F$	T	$-F$	F F F	T I F	T T T	F I T

That is, subject to the indicated identifications, we compress $S_4^{\supset}$ into the 3-valued system $S_3^{\supset} = K_3$, so that $S_4^{\supset}$ is seen to I-contain this system.

It should be observed in general that no many-valued system which—like all of the 3-valued logics we have considered—contains a self-negating truth-value v for which

$\neg v = v$

---

[1] To put the matter in algebraic language: X S-contains Y iff Y is a subalgebra of X, and X *I*-contains Y iff Y is a homomorphic image of X. Universal algebra apparently affords no counterpart to T-containment.

can possibly I-contain the classical two-valued system C_2, since v cannot then be identified either with T or with F.

It should be noted that:

(1) S-containment implies (reverse) T-containment, but not conversely.
(2) I-containment does not in general imply (reverse) T-containment (though it will do so in special circumstances) nor, conversely, does T-containment imply I-containment.
(3) S-containment does not imply I-containment, nor, conversely, does I-containment imply S-containment.

That S-containment yields (reverse) T-containment is obvious: if for some truth tables a formula takes a designated truth-value always and in general, then it must continue to do so within the postsuppression truth tables. That (reverse) T-containment does not entail S-containment can be seen from the fact that smaller many-valued logics can be T-contained in larger ones.

That T-containment does not imply (reverse) I-containment can be seen by the fact that $Ł_3$ is T-contained in C_2, but C_2 is not I-contained in $Ł_3$. That I-containment does not imply (reverse) T-containment can be seen by the example of:

p	$\neg p$			$p \wedge q$			$p \vee q$		
		q	1	2	3	1	2	3	
		p							
+1	3	+1	1	2	3	1	1	1
+2	3	+2	2	2	3	1	2	2
3	1	3	3	3	3	1	2	3

The compression

1 goes into F
2 goes into F
3 goes into T

will yield the two-valued system

p	$\neg p$			$p \wedge q$		$p \vee q$	
		q	T	F	T	F	
		p					
T	F	T	T	T	F	F
F	T	F	T	F	F	T

But "$\alpha \wedge \neg \alpha$" is a tautology of the two-valued system, though not of the 3-valued one. And "$\neg(\alpha \wedge \neg \alpha)$" is a tautology of the 3-valued system, though not of the two-valued one. Thus neither system can T-contain the other.

However, in the special case that the I-containment-generating compression is such that undesignated values never go into designated values, it can be shown that I-containment implies (reverse) T-containment. The argument goes as follows. Assume **X** I-contains **Y**. Suppose now that some formula that is a **Y**-tautology were not an **X**-tautology. Then there would be a truth-value assignment in **X** for which this formula would take on an **X**-undesignated value. But now consider this assignment in **X** and let each of its value specifications be subjected to the indicated identifications to yield an assignment in **Y**. Then the **Y**-value of the formula must also take on an undesignated value (because undesignated values are never to be mapped into designated ones by identifications). But then this formula will not be a **Y**-tautology, contrary to assumption. Thus we may define a *natural* compression as one which—unlike the "unnatural" one specified in the last paragraph—will have the features that it:

1. Always takes designated values into designated ones.
2. Never takes undesignated values into designated ones.
3. Always takes antidesignated values into antidesignated ones.
4. Never takes not antidesignated values into antidesignated ones.

With all such natural compressions, the tautologies and contradictions of the precompressed system must always be included among those of the compressed one. Thus, for example, since—as we saw above—$S_4^{\mathfrak{D}}$(with the designations $+T, I_1, I_2, -F$) can be shown by means of a normal compression to I-contain Kleene's system K_3 (with the designations $+T, I, -F$), we know that all $S_4^{\mathfrak{D}}$-tautologies are K_3-tautologies.

That S-containment does not imply I-containment can be seen from the fact that $Ł_3$ S-contains C_2, but does not I-contain it. That I-containment does not imply S-containment can be seen from the fact that $S_4^{\mathfrak{D}}$ I-contains K_3 (as above), but that it is readily seen—from the inspection of its truth tables—that $S_4^{\mathfrak{D}}$ does not S-contain K_3.

It is sometimes said that any viable system of many-valued logic must be a subsystem (fragment) of the classical two-valued system C_2, being T-contained in it. Now it is unquestionably true that most of the systems of many-valued logic considered to date do have this property. But this is by no means inevitable. Consider, for example, the 3-valued system:

p	$\neg p$		$p \vee q$			$p \to q$		
		$_p\backslash^q$	T	I	F	T	I	F
$+T$	F	$+T$	T	T	T	T	I	I
I	I	I	T	T	T	T	T	T
$-F$	T	$-F$	T	T	F	T	T	T

This system is orthodox in many respects and, in particular, has the following features:

(1) The truth tables for $\neg$ and $\vee$ are normal (in that they agree with the usual two-valued ones when only T's and F's are involved).
(2) The implication-relationship
    (a) is reflexive (i.e., $p \rightarrow p$ is always designated)
    (b) is transitive (i.e., if $p \rightarrow q$ and $q \rightarrow r$ are both designated, then $p \rightarrow r$ is designated)
    (c) is nonsymmetric (i.e., $q \rightarrow p$ can fail to be designated when $p \rightarrow q$ is designated)
    (d) is such that *modus ponens* holds (i.e., when $p \rightarrow q$ and p are both designated, so is p)

Moreover, the resulting system is nontrivial: many formulas will fail to be tautologous, e.g., "$\alpha \rightarrow \neg\alpha$." However, it is easy to see that the system has tautologies that are not two-valued tautologies. An example is:

$$(\alpha \rightarrow \beta) \vee (\alpha \rightarrow \gamma)$$

For we note by the truth tables that $/p \rightarrow q/ = (T\text{-or-}I)$ and that $(T\text{-or-}I) \vee (T\text{-or-}I) = T$. But it is easy to check that "$(\alpha \supset \beta) \vee (\alpha \supset \gamma)$" is not a two-valued tautology. This example shows that there can be viable systems of many-valued logic whose tautologies include some formulas that are not two-valued tautologies. Consequently, it cannot be maintained in general that many-valued systems of logic must be subsystems of C_2.

We must not close the present section without at least mentioning yet another sense in which one system of many-valued logic can be "contained" in another—viz. when all of the connectives of the one can be defined in terms of those of the other. When this occurs, the truth functions of the one system will be said to be D-contained (*definitionally* contained) in those of the other. For example, the connectives of K_3, the 3-valued system of Kleene, can be defined by means of those of L_3, the 3-valued system of Łukasiewicz. Let, $\neg$, $\wedge$, $\vee$, $\rightarrow$, and $\leftrightarrow$ be negation, conjunction, disjunction, implication, and equivalence (respectively) in L_3, and let $\rightrightarrows$, $\bigwedge$, $\bigvee$, $\Rightarrow$, and $\Leftrightarrow$ be the corresponding connectives of K_3. Then we can effect the following definitions:

$$\rightrightarrows p \quad \text{FOR} \quad \neg p$$
$$p \bigwedge q \quad \text{FOR} \quad p \wedge q$$
$$p \bigvee q \quad \text{FOR} \quad p \vee q$$
$$p \Rightarrow q \quad \text{FOR} \quad \neg p \vee q$$
$$p \Leftrightarrow q \quad \text{FOR} \quad (\neg p \vee q) \wedge (\neg q \vee p)$$

On the other hand, K_3 does not include L_3 in this sense. We cannot possibly define all connectives of L_3 (specifically $\rightarrow$ implication by means of those of

$\mathbf{K}_3$. This is so because each of the connectives of $\mathbf{K}_3$ will always yield the truth-value I as output when only I's occur as inputs, and this feature will continue operative no matter how these connectives may be combined to provide a complex definition.

This sense of system "containment" (applicable only to systems of the same degree of many-valuedness) relates to purely formal, algebraic features of the truth tables at issue, rather than to more closely meaning-related considerations. Thus we shall not pursue this matter any further here.

14 The Parametric-operator Development of Pluri-valued Logics

We shall explore a new procedure for the development of systems of many-valued logic. The basis of this approach is the concept of a parametric one-place propositional operator $\mathbf{V}v$, where v is a truth-value (an integer or else a more traditional-looking truth-value like T or F or I, etc.). The guiding idea is that "$\mathbf{V}vp$" is to be read and understood as "the truth-value of p is v" or "v is the truth-value of p." $\mathbf{V}v$ is thus a one-parameter propositional truth-value assignment operator, with "$\mathbf{V}vp$" playing the role of a proposition about the truth-value status of a proposition.

For the present it shall be supposed that the truth-values at issue are the integers $1, 2, \ldots, n$ and that these values constitute the range of the parameter v. We suppose that 1 is the truth-value T (truth) and that n is the truth-value F (falsity). For the sake of simplicity we shall in general restrict ourselves to the 3-valued case ($n = 3$), but our remarks can readily be extended to the general case.

A proposition of the form "$\mathbf{V}vp$" is—so we shall for the time being postulate—capable of assuming only the classical truth-values T and F. We shall thus for the present lay down the principles:

  (i) If $\mathbf{V}vp = u$, then u will have to be 1 or n.
  (ii) $/\mathbf{V}vp/ = 1$ iff $v = /p/$

In the 3-valued case, we have it under this assumption that the truth table for $\mathbf{V}vp$ is as follows:

$_v\backslash^p$	$\mathbf{V}vp$		
	1	2	3
+1	1	3	3
2	3	1	3
−3	3	3	1

Note that $/\mathbf{V}vp/$ will:

(1) always be either 1 or 3
(2) always be 1 when $/p/ = v$
(3) always be 3 when $/p/ \neq v$

Thus the truth table for $\mathbf{V}vp$ is decisive—since only T's and F's (i.e., 1s and 3s) occur as entries within its defining matrix—and so the truth-value assignment operator is classically two-valued.

Our first principal observation is that the truth tables upon which an n-valued logic is based can always be presented as statements combining expressions of the form $\mathbf{V}vp$ with the classical two-valued connectives. Thus, consider the usual truth table for 3-valued negation:

p	$\neg p$
$+1$	3
2	2
-3	1

The content of this table is exhaustively presented by the three equivalences:

$\mathbf{V}3 \neg p$ iff $\mathbf{V}1p$
$\mathbf{V}2 \neg p$ iff $\mathbf{V}2p$
$\mathbf{V}1 \neg p$ iff $\mathbf{V}3p$

Note that on the right-hand side of these equivalences the many-valued connectives have been eliminated.

Again, the 3-valued truth table for disjunction is:

$\diagdown \ q$ $p \diagdown$	$p \vee q$ 1	2	3
$+1$	1	1	1
2	1	2	2
-3	1	2	3

The content of this table is exhaustively presented by the three equivalences:

$\mathbf{V}1(p \vee q)$ iff $\mathbf{V}1p \mathbf{V} \mathbf{V}1q$
$\mathbf{V}2(p \vee q)$ iff $[\mathbf{V}2p \,\&\, {\sim}\mathbf{V}1q] \mathbf{V} [\mathbf{V}2q \,\&\, {\sim}\mathbf{V}1p]$
$\mathbf{V}3(p \vee q)$ iff $\mathbf{V}3p \,\&\, \mathbf{V}3q$

Here again, no many-valued connectives occur on the right-hand side of these equivalences. (We continue with our established procedure of taking $\sim, \&, \mathbf{V}, \supset, \equiv$ for the classical, two-valued propositional connectives, and $\neg, \wedge, \vee, \rightarrow, \leftrightarrow$ as their many-valued counterparts.)

As these examples show, a many-valued truth table for a propositional connective can be developed within the two-valued logic by introducing the truth-value assignment operator $\mathbf{V}vp$ subject to suitable axiomatic stipulations. For example, we would want to postulate in general the condition of single-valuedness:

$(\mathbf{V}vp\ \&\ \mathbf{V}up) \supset v = u$

And in a specifically 3-valued logic (based on 1, 2, 3) we would want to postulate:

$\mathbf{V}1p\ \vee\ \mathbf{V}2p\ \vee\ \mathbf{V}3p$

Note that the preceding specifications for $\neg$ and $\vee$ are consonant with this postulation, in that

$\mathbf{V}1(\neg p)\ \vee\ \mathbf{V}2(\neg p)\ \vee\ \mathbf{V}3(\neg p)$
$\mathbf{V}1(p\ \vee\ q)\ \vee\ \mathbf{V}2(p\ \vee\ q)\ \vee\ \mathbf{V}3(p\ \vee\ q)$

are assured as tautologies given the Law of Excluded Fourth: $\mathbf{V}1p\ \vee\ \mathbf{V}2p\ \vee\ \mathbf{V}3p$.

We shall need to refer to the truth table for 3-valued Łukasiewiczian implication:

$\stackrel{\textstyle q}{p}$	$p \rightarrow q$ 1	2	3
$+1$	1	2	3
2	1	1	2
-3	1	1	1

This can be represented as:

$\mathbf{V}1(p \rightarrow q)$ iff $\mathbf{V}3p \vee \mathbf{V}1q \vee (\mathbf{V}2p\ \&\ \mathbf{V}2q)$
$\mathbf{V}2(p \rightarrow q)$ iff $(\mathbf{V}1p\ \&\ \mathbf{V}2q) \vee (\mathbf{V}2p\ \&\ \mathbf{V}3q)$
$\mathbf{V}3(p \rightarrow q)$ iff $\mathbf{V}1p\ \&\ \mathbf{V}3q$

All the tautologies according to the many-valued truth tables will now become theorems of two-valued logic. To verify, for example, that "$\alpha \rightarrow \alpha$" is a 3-valued tautology, we must establish that the two-valued counterpart of "$\mathbf{V}1(\alpha \rightarrow \alpha)$" is a (two-valued) tautology, which is evident from the specified equivalences. For $\mathbf{V}1(p \rightarrow p)$ now amounts to

$(\mathbf{V}3p \vee \mathbf{V}1p \vee [\mathbf{V}2p\ \&\ \mathbf{V}2p]) = (\mathbf{V}1p \vee \mathbf{V}2p \vee \mathbf{V}3p)$

which we have postulated for the $\mathbf{V}$-operator (and whose tautologousness follows from the (two-valued) truth table for $\mathbf{V}vp$). Moreover, $\mathbf{V}2(p \rightarrow p)$ and $\mathbf{V}3(p \rightarrow p)$ can never be true. For, by the given equivalences, the first becomes

$(\mathbf{V}1p\ \&\ \mathbf{V}2p) \vee (\mathbf{V}2p\ \&\ \mathbf{V}3p)$

and the second

$V1p \& V3p$

The necessary falsity of these two statements is obvious from the postulated single-valuedness of the V-operator, according to which we cannot have it that $Vvp \& Vup$ is true when $v \neq u$.

This example illustrates a general fact: The status of many-valued theses as tautologous, contradictory, or contingent can always be verified by tautology calculation on the Vvp's in the two-valued case. Thus, finitely many-valued truth tables can be represented within two-valued logic, using the machinery of the numerical assignment operation Vv and representing the truth tables as intrasystematic equivalences. Indeed, any system of (finitely) many-valued logic whatsoever can be constructed along such lines within the classical two-valued system C_2.[1] This fact was first observed by the Russian logician V. I. Shestakov.[2]

With the explicit introduction of quantifiers, standardly metatheoretic principles for a many-valued logic become expressible in the two-valued system based on the parametric operation Vv. Thus consider the following renditions of meta-theses:

(1) The truth table for $\vee$ exhibits diagonal homogeneity:

$$(\forall v)(\forall p)(\forall q)[(Vvp \& Vvq) \supset Vv(p \vee q)]$$

(2) The truth table for $\vee$ exhibits diagonal symmetry:

$$(\forall p)(\forall q)(\forall w)(Vw[p \vee q] \equiv Vw[q \vee p])$$

(3) The system at issue is n-valued:

$$(\forall p)[V1p \vee \ldots \vee Vnp]$$

(4) The system at issue is strictly truth-functional:

$$(\forall v)(\forall u)(\forall p)[(Vvp \& Vup) \supset v = u]$$

(5) The system is such that each truth-value is identically assumed by some formula:

$$(\forall v)(\exists p)(\forall q)[Vvq \equiv (q \equiv p)]$$

These examples illustrate how various meta-theses about a many-valued propositional logic can be cast intrasystematically by means of quantifiers and our parametrized V-operator.

---

[1] This, however, does not earn any sort of absolute preeminence for C_2, since the reverse is also true—viz. that C_2 can be constructed within various systems of many-valued logic. (See, for example, p. 33.)

[2] For a presentation of Shestakov's finding see A. A. Zinov'ev, *Philosophical Problems of Many-Valued Logic* (Dordrecht, 1963), pp. 38–39.

It deserves remark that one can lay down certain theses for a para-metric propositional operator that would entirely *preclude* its interpretation as a value-assignment functor of a many-valued logic. Consider for example:

$$(\forall v)[\mathbf{V}v(p \,\&\, q) \equiv (\mathbf{V}vp \,\&\, \mathbf{V}vq)]$$

For suppose that **V** represented a truth-value assignment (say in the 3-valued case). If the truth-value of p is 1 and that of q is 2, what truth-value can now possibly be accorded to $p \,\&\, q$? Clearly the thesis at issue precludes *every such assignment whatsoever!*

In the light of the $\mathbf{V}vp$-operator let us consider the Tarski criterion of truth:

(T) $\mathbf{V}1p \leftrightarrow p$

This has two parts:

(T1) $\mathbf{V}1p \to p$
(T2) $p \to \mathbf{V}1p$

(T1) is readily verified to be tautologous for our 3-valued $\mathbf{V}vp$ operator:

$\mathbf{V}11 \to 1 = 1 \to 1 = 1$
$\mathbf{V}12 \to 2 = 3 \to 2 = 1$
$\mathbf{V}13 \to 3 = 3 \to 3 = 1$

But (T2), interestingly enough, is not tautologous (if 2 is not designated):

$1 \to \mathbf{V}11 = 1 \to 1 = 1$
$2 \to \mathbf{V}12 = 2 \to 3 = 2$
$3 \to \mathbf{V}13 = 3 \to 3 = 1$

The Tarski criterion of truth in the specific form (T) cannot, therefore, be postulated for many-valued logics in general.

In the cases we have considered, we have it that, although p is 3-valued (i.e., can take on the truth-values T,I,F), $\mathbf{V}vp$ is two-valued—that is, only T's and F's occur *within* the table:

$_p\diagdown_v$	T	$\mathbf{V}vp$ I	F
$+T$	T	F	F
I	F	T	F
$-F$	F	F	T

This two-valuedness of $\mathbf{V}vp$ is, in effect, the basis for our embedding the many-valued logic at issue within a two-valued framework. It is clear that this stratagem would not have worked if the truth table for $\mathbf{V}vp$ had not been decisive and had itself been 3-valued; if, for example, it had been like the truth table for Łukasiewiczian equivalence:

$\overset{p}{v}\diagdown$	$\mathbf{V}vp$		
	T	I	F
$+T$	T	I	F
I	I	T	I
$-F$	F	I	T

From this point of view, there is always a certain fuzzy penumbra surrounding the allocation of truth-values. This observation embodies an important lesson. If one is seriously convinced of the irreducible need for a many-valued logic, then it would seem that one must opt for a value-assignment functor $\mathbf{V}vp$ whose application is itself not a true-false, on-off matter, but is subject to the semantic shadings of multiple truth-values. Indeed there is no reason why the truth-value assignment operator for an infinite-valued system could not be infinite-valued, for example: Thus let the truth-values at issue range from 0 to 1 (with 1 designated). We could then specify:

$$/\mathbf{V}vp/ = 1 - |v - /p/|$$

Here $\mathbf{V}v$ is now a *parametrized* propositional operator generating propositions whose truth-value is subject to the indicated truth rule. The only requirement we would want to impose upon this operator in general is:

$$/\mathbf{V}vp/ \in D^+ \quad \text{iff} \quad v = /p/$$

It is interesting to observe that if the just-mentioned 3-valued truth table is adopted for $\mathbf{V}vp$, then the validity of the Tarski criterion of truth

(T) $\quad \mathbf{V}1p \leftrightarrow p$

is preserved (i.e., this formula is now tautologous with respect to the 3-valued equivalence of $\mathbf{L}_3$ and $\mathbf{S}_3$). Moreover, in some many-valued logics conditions even stronger than the Tarski criterion can be established. Thus consider the 4-valued logic based on:

$\overset{p}{v}\diagdown$	$\mathbf{V}vp$			
	1	2	3	4
$+1$	1	2	3	4
$+2$	2	1	3	4
3	3	3	1	3
-4	4	4	3	1

$\overset{q}{p}\diagdown$	$p \leftrightarrow q$			
	1	2	3	4
$+1$	1	2	4	4
$+2$	2	1	3	4
3	4	3	1	3
-4	4	4	3	1

Note that here we have not only the Tarski condition that (T) is tautologous, but that so is the following stronger condition that whenever v is designated, then

(T′) $p \leftrightarrow \mathbf{V}vp$

is tautologous. Moreover, since $\leftrightarrow$ is here transitive for designated values (i.e., if $p \leftrightarrow q$ and $q \leftrightarrow r$ take designated values, so must $p \leftrightarrow r$), it follows that the equivalence

$\mathbf{V}vp \leftrightarrow \mathbf{V}up$

will represent a tautology whenever v and u are designated values.

Some structural features of the aforementioned genuinely 3-valued defining matrix of $\mathbf{V}vp$ should be noted:

(1) Values other than those corresponding to the classical ones (viz. T and F) are not ruled out as possible values of $\mathbf{V}vp$.

(2) If $/\mathbf{V}vp/ = T$, then $/p/ = v$ (so that if we know either $/p/$ or v, the other is fixed).

(3) If $/\mathbf{V}vp/ = F$, then one of v and $/p/$ must be T and the other F.

(4) If $/\mathbf{V}vp/ = I$, then one of v and $/p/$ must be I and the other T or F.

(5) The truth-value assigned to $\mathbf{V}vp$ by an iterative use of the V-operator must reflect the relationship between $/p/$ and v. Specifically, it cannot happen that:

  (a) $/\mathbf{V}T\mathbf{V}vp/ = T$ and $/p/ \neq v$
  (b) $/\mathbf{V}F\mathbf{V}vp/ = T$ and $/p/ = v$
  (c) $/\mathbf{V}I\mathbf{V}vp/ = T$ and both $/p/ \neq I$ and $v \neq I$

The question of whether a many-valued logic can be used as the metalogical basis for articulating a system that is itself a many-valued system of logic—or whether, on the other hand, all of the many-valued systems must themselves be developed from the two-valued point of view—must be considered in detail. For if many-valued systems inevitably presuppose a two-valued metalogic, then two-valued logic would enjoy a conceptual priority and fundamentality of a most significant kind.

Various writers have claimed that this question can be resolved in favor of two-valued logic. For example, in his recent book on many-valued logic the Russian logician A. A. Zinov'ev has stated that: "All known constructions [of many-valued logics] ... start from the presupposition of the two-valuedness of the propositions [that assign truth-values]."[3] This may be so, but the question remains open whether it describes a

[3]*Ibid.*, p. 83.

contingent and not a necessary circumstance, Zinov'ev's own assertion to the contrary notwithstanding.[4] Moreover, Zinov'ev flatly maintains that:

> The metalanguage of the language of three-valued logic belongs to two-valued logic; i.e., propositions of the type "*p* has the truth value *i*" are two-valued. (p. 33)

This contention, of course, goes counter to the motivating spirit of many-valued logic, and would, if true, seriously impair the claims of such logics to a status coequal with classical, two-valued logic. Thus, it remains to be considered whether many-valued logics can be built up in a coherent way if one begins from such a many-valued point of departure. Until this has been settled, the prospect remains that two-valued logic is somehow fundamental to the construction of all systems of pluri-valued logic in general. We shall here contend, and indeed demonstrate, that many-valued systems can themselves provide the metalogics needed for the development of many-valued systems of logic.

Quite in general, a many-valued system is presented by matrices of the form (for an arbitrary binary connective represented by $\varnothing$):

$$
\begin{array}{c|ccc}
 & & p \varnothing q & \\
\diagdown q & \cdots & v_j & \cdots \\
p \diagdown & & & \\
\hline
\vdots & & & \\
v_i & & \langle v_i \varnothing v_j \rangle = v_k & \\
\vdots & & &
\end{array}
$$

An entry within such a matrix is intended to present a fact of the following kind:

$$\text{If } /p/ = v_i \text{ and } /q/ = v_j, \text{ then } /p \varnothing q/ = \langle v_i \varnothing v_j \rangle = v_k$$

For it to be possible to represent theses of this sort within a many-valued system—i.e., by using the machinery of the system as the language of discourse—this system will have to afford us counterparts of three meta-systematic or presystematic logical concepts:

> if . . . , then —
> both . . . and —
> the truth-value *v* represents the truth status of the proposition —

[4]*Ibid.*, p. 84.

Once the system affords this machinery, we can use it to make the appropriate descriptive statements about itself—provided the system is suitably "well behaved."

In tracing out what is involved here, we shall assume (as we may do without any loss of generality) that the truth-values are positive integers $1, 2, \ldots, n$. Consider now an entry in an n-valued truth table for a two-place connective $\varnothing$.

$$
\begin{array}{c|c}
\diagdown\,^{q}\!\!\!\! & p \varnothing q \\
_{p}\diagdown & j \\
\hline
i & \langle i \varnothing j \rangle
\end{array}
\qquad \text{where } i \text{ and } j \text{ and } \langle i \varnothing j \rangle \text{ are all elements of } 1, 2, \ldots, n
$$

Such an entry says: "If the truth-value of p is i and that of q is j, then that of $p \varnothing q$ is to be $\langle i \varnothing j \rangle$." We can translate this quoted statement into the vocabulary of the many-valued system itself whenever this system affords us three pieces of machinery: (i) an implication connective $\rightarrow$ for "if-then" (which is assumed to have the *modus ponens* feature that if p and $p \rightarrow q$ take designated truth-values, then so does q); (ii) a conjunction connective $\wedge$ for "both-and" (which is assumed to have the feature that if p and q both take designated truth-values, then $p \wedge q$ does so); and (iii) a truth-value assignment operator $\mathbf{V}ip$ for "the truth-value of p is i" (which is assumed to have the feature that $\mathbf{V}ip$ takes a designated truth-value iff i is the truth-value of p). The above-quoted statement can then be rendered *intrasystematically* as:

(1) $(\mathbf{V}ip \wedge \mathbf{V}jq) \rightarrow \mathbf{V}\langle i \varnothing j \rangle(p \varnothing q)$

(The translation of the truth table for a one-place connective is to be handled analogously.)

A many-valued system that affords this machinery will be termed *autodescriptive* with respect to its truth-value assignment operator $\mathbf{V}ip$ if *the translation into the system of the information enshrined in each and every one of its truth-table entries in the manner of proposition (1) will be a tautology of the system.* The essential feature of such a system will be that it can be described by means of its own machinery, and this description constitutes a group of logical truths. The condition at issue is, of course, an extremely powerful and restrictive one, since in an n-valued system—when $i, j, /p/$, and $/q/$ can each take any of n values—$n \times n \times n \times n = n^4$ cases must work out properly for (1) to be tautologous.

Given the above-listed conditions upon the propositional connectives and the truth-value assignment operator $\mathbf{V}ip$, it follows that:

(a) $\mathbf{V}ip \wedge \mathbf{V}jq \wedge \mathbf{V}k(p \oslash q)$ can never assume a designated value when $k \neq \langle i \oslash j \rangle$.

(b) $\mathbf{V}ip \wedge \mathbf{V}j\mathbf{V}ip$ can never assume a designated truth-value when j is undesignated.

(c) Whenever 1 is the only designated truth-value, then both $p \rightarrow \mathbf{V}1p$ and $\mathbf{V}1p \rightarrow p$ are tautologies, and so $p \leftrightarrow \mathbf{V}ip$ is also.

The truth-value assignment operator of an n-valued system will be said to be *diversified* if statements of the form $\mathbf{V}ip$ can assume *all* of the truth-values (not just the two corresponding to *truth* and *falsity*). The defining matrix for a diversified truth-value assignment operator has the crucial and interesting feature that it contains entries other than 1 (true) and n (false), so that the truth-value assigning statements of the form "the truth-value of p is i" are not viewed as inherently two-valued (in a way alien to the spirit of many-valued logic).

The 3-valued system $\mathbf{L}_3$ of Łukasiewicz is an example of a system that is autodescriptive in this sense with respect to the now-to-be-specified diversified truth-value assignment operator:

$\substack{p \\ i}$	$\mathbf{V}ip$			$\substack{q \\ p}$	$\neg p$	$p \wedge q$			$p \rightarrow q$		
	1	2	3			1	2	3	1	2	3
+1	1	2	3	+1	3	1	2	3	1	2	3
2	2	1	2	2	2	2	2	3	1	1	2
−3	3	2	1	−3	1	3	3	3	1	1	1

Quite in general, whenever the matrix for $\mathbf{V}ip$ has the features that (1) $/\mathbf{V}ip/$ is designated if and only if $i = /p/$, (2) implication has the *modus ponens* feature, and (3) conjunction has the feature that if $p \wedge q$ assumes a designated value, then both p and q must do so, then—when these three conditions are met—it is not difficult to show that the system must be autodescriptive. For then (a) above could fail to assume a designated truth-value only when its antecedent is designated and its consequent undesignated. But the former can now happen only when both $\mathbf{V}ip$ and $\mathbf{V}jq$ take designated values, i.e., iff both $i = /p/$ and $j = /q/$. But in this case $\mathbf{V}\langle i \oslash j \rangle(p \oslash q)$ has the form $\mathbf{V}vr$ where $v = /r/$, so that this complex must assume a designated value, not an undesignated one. (Thus—as a consequence of this result—the aforementioned diversified truth-value assignment operator $\mathbf{V}ip$ will also underwrite the autodescriptivity of Kleene's $\mathbf{K}_3$.)

On the basis of these considerations it is easy to see that infinite-valued systems can also be autodescriptive. Indeed, it is readily verified that subject to the truth-value assignment operator

$$/\mathbf{V}vp/ \;=\; 1 - |v - /p/|$$

the following infinite-valued systems (with truth-values from the range 0 to 1, inclusive—and *with 1 as the only designated truth-value*) will all be autodescriptive: $\mathbf{L_{\aleph}, G_{\aleph}, S_{\aleph}, S_{\aleph}^{\supset}, S_{\aleph}^{*}}$.

Autodescriptivity in the face of a diversified truth-value assignment operator is by no means a routine feature of many-valued systems, for it will certainly be absent in many cases. The 3-valued system $\mathbf{B_3}$ of Bochvar, for example, is not autodescriptive for the 3-valued truth-value assignment operator:

v \ p	**V**vp		
	T	*I*	*F*
+*T*	*T*	*I*	*F*
I	*I*	*T*	*I*
F	*F*	*I*	*T*

For we have it that

$$[(\mathbf{V}IT \wedge \mathbf{V}IF) \to \mathbf{V}\langle I \wedge I\rangle(T \wedge F)] = I \to \mathbf{V}IF = I \to I = I$$

and so autodescriptivity must fail, though it does not do so for the classical truth-value assignment operator:

v \ p	**V**vp		
	T	*I*	*F*
+*T*	*T*	*F*	*F*
I	*F*	*T*	*F*
F	*F*	*F*	*T*

The key feature of an autodescriptive logic is that it can be regarded as providing the presystematic or metasystematic groundwork needed for its own development. In the case of an autodescriptive system of many-valued logic with a diversified truth-value assignment operator, one can take the view that the system can be presented by means of a many-valued metalanguage and does not require the usual two-valued one. The existence of such many-valued systems which could themselves serve as their own metalanguage refutes the position of various writers who view two-valued logic as fundamental *vis-à-vis* many-valued logic on the grounds that many-valued systems must invariably be developed by means of two-valued logical machinery used at the metalinguistic level.[5]

Autodescriptivity—at least with a classically two-valued truth-value assignment operator—is an essential aspect of adequacy in many-valued systems of logic. For if a formal system is to qualify as an adequate system of logic it must at the very least provide a logical apparatus that suffices at the metalinguistic level for the description of this system itself. In this perspective an adequate system of pluri-valued logic must be capable of providing its own metalanguage.[6]

It might seem at first thought that use of a 3-valued truth-value assignment operator would immediately enable us to avert the semantical paradoxes of self-reference along such lines as the following. Consider the proposition that generates the so-called Liar paradox:

(1) This proposition—viz. the proposition (1)—is false.

Here we have that

$(1) = VF(1)$

and therefore

$/(1)/ = /VF(1)/$

If the truth-value assignment operator is the two-valued

$\underset{v}{\overset{p}{\diagdown}}$	Vvp	
	T	F
$+T$	T	F
$-F$	F	T

then we of course have the paradoxical results that:

If $/VF(1)/ = T$, then both $/(1)/ = T$ and $/(1)/ = F$
If $/VF(1)/ = F$, then both $/(1)/ = F$ and $/(1)/ = T$

But if the truth-value assignment operator is the 3-valued

p \\ v	$\mathbf{V}vp$		
	T	I	F
$+T$	T	I	F
I	I	T	I
$-F$	F	I	T

then we can obtain the perfectly consistent result:

$$/\mathbf{V}F(1)/ = /(1)/ = I$$

This eliminates the paradox generated by (1).

But the matter is not all that easy. For consider now the analogous proposition:

(2) This proposition—viz. the proposition (2)—is indeterminate.

Thus

$$(2) = \mathbf{V}I(2)$$

But note that:

If $/\mathbf{V}I(2)/ = T$, then both $/(2)/ = T$ and $/(2)/ = I$
If $/\mathbf{V}I(2)/ = I$, then $/(2)/ = I$ and either $/(2)/ = T$ or $/(2)/ = F$
That $/\mathbf{V}I(2)/ = F$ is impossible, since in no case can $\mathbf{V}Ip$ take the truth-value F.

It thus becomes plain that, unfortunately, revised versions of the Liar paradox will arise also with certain many-valued truth-value assignment operators.[7]

The obstacles involved do not, however, seem to be insuperable. Let our 3-valued truth-value assignment operator be changed to:

[7]Exactly parallel considerations vitiate a recent proposal to eliminate the Liar paradox by a device equivalent to adopting the truth-value assignment operator:

p \\ v	$\mathbf{V}vp$		
	T	I	F
$+T$	T	F	F
I	I	T	I
$-F$	F	F	T

(See M. J. O'Carroll, "A Three-Valued Non-Levelled Logic Consistent for All Self-Reference," *Logique et Analyse*, vol. 10 (1967), pp. 173–178.) For while this resolves the problem raised by (1) = $\mathbf{V}F(1)$, the situation with regard to (2) = $\mathbf{V}I(2)$ is here exactly as with the preceding case.

$$
\begin{array}{c|ccc}
 & \multicolumn{3}{c}{\mathbf{V}vp} \\
{}_{p}\diagdown{}^{v} & T & I & F \\
\hline
+T & T & I & F \\
I & I & T & F \\
-F & F & I & T \\
\end{array}
$$

Now the three self-referential statements

(1) $= \mathbf{V}F(1)$
(2) $= \mathbf{V}I(2)$
(3) $= \mathbf{V}T(3)$

will not be paradoxical, but will simply take on the truth-values I, F, and T, respectively. But difficulty is still upon us, now in the form of complex statements about truth-values. For consider:

(4) This proposition—viz. the proposition (4)—is either indifferent or false.

We now have:

(4) $= [\mathbf{V}I(4) \lor \mathbf{V}F(4)]$

But then:

If $/(4)/ = T$, then $/(4)/ = I \lor F$
If $/(4)/ = I$, then $/(4)/ = T \lor F = T$
If $/(4)/ = F$, then $/(4)/ = F \lor T = T$

To make this viable, we would be forced to the unpalatable expedient of having the truth table for $\lor$ be such that $T = I \lor F$.

Elimination of the paradoxes of self-reference by means of a many-valued truth-value assignment operator—if indeed possible at all—will require sophisticated procedures and is probably most efficiently accomplished in an infinite-valued logic. For in such a logic, with numerical truth-values ranging from 0 to 1, inclusive, let:

$\mathbf{V}vp = 1 - |v - /p/|$

Then the Liar paradox condition

$(n) = \mathbf{V}v(n)$

will *always* be solvable, since for every value of v there will always be a value u such that: $u = 1 - |v - u|$ or equivalently $|v - u| = 1 - u$. (The function $u = \frac{1}{2}(1 + v)$ establishes the requisite relationship.)

Moreover, the negative Liar paradox condition

$(m) = \neg \mathbf{V}v(m)$

now requires that for every value v there is some value u such that:

$$u = /\neg V v u / = 1 - (1 - |v - u|)$$
$$u = |v - u|$$

But this can similarly be shown by noting that the function $u = \frac{1}{2}v$ establishes the requisite relationship. Again, a statement of the form

$$(m) = [Vv(m) \lor Vv'(m)]$$

requires that for every v,v' there is a u such that:

$$u = /(1 - |v - u|) \lor (1 - |v' - u|)/$$

That this condition can always be satisfied (when, as usual, $/p \lor q/ = \max [/p/,/q/]$) can also be shown. Thus the various analogue versions of the Liar paradox all turn out to be nonparadoxical in the infinite-valued case.

Appendix

J. B. Rosser and A. R. Turquette have made a special study of a special operator J defined for the Łukasiewicz systems L_n (and for suitably cognate systems).[8] This operator is governed by the truth rule that for the system L_n:

$$J[i,n](p) = \begin{cases} 1 \text{ (true)} \\ 0 \text{ (false)} \end{cases} \text{ according as } /p/ \begin{cases} = \dfrac{i}{n-1} \\ \neq \dfrac{i}{n-1} \end{cases}$$

Here $0 \le i \le n - 1$, so that an n-valued system L_n will have exactly n such J-operators. Rosser and Turquette have shown how in every L_n these J-operators can be defined in terms of '$\rightarrow$' and '$\neg$.' We shall not here enter into the details of this defining procedure. Suffice it here to note that for L_3, it results in the following three J-operators:

$$J[2,3](p) = \neg(p \rightarrow \neg p)$$
$$J[1,3](p) = [(\neg[p \rightarrow \neg p] \rightarrow \neg[\neg p \rightarrow p]) \rightarrow \neg(\neg p \rightarrow p)]$$
$$J[0,3](p) = \neg[\neg p \rightarrow p]$$

It is readily shown (by calculation with the truth tables of L_3) that these formulas will yield the following truth tables:

p	$J[2,3](p)$	$J[1,3](p)$	$J[0,3](p)$
$+1$	1	0	0
$\frac{1}{2}$	0	1	0
-0	0	0	1

It is thus clear that these J-operators for L_3 have the requisite characteristics.

[8]See Rosser and Turquette, *Many-Valued Logics* (Amsterdam, 1952), pp. 16–23.

The construction of these *J*-operators for the $\mathbf{L}_n$ systems is of special interest because they can be regarded as representing a parametric truth-value assignment operator $\mathbf{V}vp$. For any $\mathbf{L}_n$, the truth table for $J[i,n](p)$ will be identical to that for the classically *T-F*-valued—i.e., two-valued—V-operator $\mathbf{V}\left(\dfrac{i}{n-1}\right)p$. This operator has the feature that (quite in general):

$$\mathbf{V}vp = \begin{Bmatrix} 1 \text{ (true)} \\ 0 \text{ (false)} \end{Bmatrix} \text{ according as } /p/ \begin{cases} = v \\ \neq v \end{cases}$$

And this stipulation agrees entirely with the *J*-operator for the system $\mathbf{L}_n$. Being formulas internal to the system at issue, the *J*-operators therefore enable us to reflect within that system itself the structure of its own truth-value assignments. (This fact can also be exploited in axiomatizing systems $\mathbf{L}_n$ by a procedure, due to J. B. Rosser and A. R. Turquette, to which we shall return in Sec. 22.[9])

When this sort of internal V-operator representation—afforded in the case of the $\mathbf{L}_n$ systems by the Rosser-Turquette *J*-operators—can obtain in the case of an autodescriptive system, the result is of particular interest because then the entire truth-functional structure of the system can be represented within itself in a rather illuminating way.

15 The Extension of n to (n + 1)-valued Logic

We shall now consider a technique for "extending" any given *n*-valued logic into an $(n + 1)$-valued logic. This extension procedure is, in its essentials, due to Stanisław Jaśkowski.[1]

Let $\neg$, $\wedge$, $\vee$, $\rightarrow$, and $\leftrightarrow$ be the connectives of the given *n*-valued logic (whose truth-values we shall assume to be $1, 2, \ldots, n$). Correspondingly, $\rightharpoondown$, $\bigwedge$, $\bigvee$, $\Rightarrow$, and $\Leftrightarrow$ are to be the connectives of the $(n + 1)$-valued system being constructed. Moreover, if i and j are two *n*-valued truth-values, then:

(1) $\langle \neg i \rangle$ is to be the truth-value assigned by the initial *n*-valued truth table for negation ($\neg$) to the negation of the truth-value i.

(2) $\langle i \oslash j \rangle$ is to be the truth-value assigned by the initial *n*-valued truth table for the binary connective $\oslash$ (any arbitrary binary connective) to the truth-value combination i,j.

One can now construct a family of $(n + 1)$-valued truth tables in accordance with the following principles. Negation is to be extended according to the rule:

[9]For full details, see Rosser and Turquette, *op. cit.*
[1]See Jaśkowski, "Recherches sur le système de la logique intuitioniste," *Actes du Congrès International de Philosophie Scientifique*, vol. VI (Paris, 1936), pp. 58–61; tr. in S. McCall (ed.), *Polish Logic: 1920–1939* (Oxford, 1967). Cf. Zinov'ev, *Philosophical Problems of Many-Valued Logic* tr. by G. Küng and D. D. Comey (Dordrecht, 1963), pp. 23–25.

p	$\neg p$
1	$n+1$
$i(\neq 1)$	$\langle \neg (i-1) \rangle$

The binary connectives are to be extended as follows:

	$p \barwedge q$		$p \veebar q$		$p \Rightarrow q$	
$\overset{\textstyle q}{\diagdown}$ p	$j(\neq n+1)$	$n+1$	$j(\neq n+1)$	$n+1$	$j(\neq n+1)$	$n+1$
$i(\neq n+1)$	$\langle i \wedge j \rangle$	$n+1$	$\langle i \vee j \rangle$	i	$\langle i \to j \rangle$	$\langle i \to n \rangle + 1$
$n+1$	$n+1$	$n+1$	j	$n+1$	1	1

This construction procedure provides an automatic means for expanding an *n*-valued logic to an $(n+1)$-valued system.

By way of illustration, when we start with the usual two-valued conjunction (now with $1 = T$ and $2 = F$)

	$p \,\&\, q$	
$\overset{\textstyle q}{\diagdown}$ p	1	2
1	1	2
2	2	2

then this extension procedure will yield the following sequence:

	$p \barwedge q$		
$\overset{\textstyle q}{\diagdown}$ p	1	2	3
1	1	2	3
2	2	2	3
3	3	3	3

	$p \barwedge q$			
$\overset{\textstyle q}{\diagdown}$ p	1	2	3	4
1	1	2	3	4
2	2	2	3	4
3	3	3	3	4
4	4	4	4	4

	$p \barwedge q$				
$\overset{\textstyle q}{\diagdown}$ p	1	2	3	4	5
1	1	2	3	4	5
2	2	2	3	4	5
3	3	3	3	4	5
4	4	4	4	4	5
5	5	5	5	5	5

Note that, as the extension procedure specifies, we always simply copy the old truth table in the upper left-hand corner of the new one and fill in all the remaining places with the "new" truth-value.

Moreover, the two-valued negation

p	$\sim p$
1	2
2	1

gives rise to the following sequence:

p	$\neg p$	p	$\neg p$	p	$\neg p$
1	3	1	4	1	5
2	2	2	3	2	4
3	1	3	2	3	3
		4	1	4	2
				5	1

Note that the new negation column always begins with the "new" truth-value, and that the old negation column is then just copied in underneath.

Given a many-valued system **X**, we shall designate its expanded counterpart according to this specific procedure by $E(\mathbf{X})$. It ought to go without saying that different extension procedures that depart from the specified features of E can of course be envisaged.

The key feature of E is that if we start with a system **X** that is in the Łukasiewicz sequence $\mathbf{Ł}_n$, then $E(\mathbf{X})$ will also always be a Łukasiewiczian system, so that $E(\mathbf{Ł}_n) = \mathbf{Ł}_{n+1}$. Let us begin with the classical two-valued calculus $\mathbf{C}_2$. Then $E(\mathbf{C}_2)$ will be as follows:

p	$\neg p$		q	$p \wedge q$ 1 2 3	$p \vee q$ 1 2 3	$p \Rightarrow q$ 1 2 3
1	3		1	1 2 3	1 1 1	1 2 3
2	2		2	2 2 3	1 2 2	1 1 2
3	1		3	3 3 3	1 2 3	1 1 1

But this is exactly the 3-valued logic of Łukasiewicz, so that we have established that:

$$E(\mathbf{C}_2) = \mathbf{Ł}_3$$

Continuing the process one iteration further, we have it that $E(\mathbf{Ł}_3)$ is as follows:

p	$\neg p$		q	$p \wedge q$ 1 2 3 4	$p \vee q$ 1 2 3 4	$p \Rightarrow q$ 1 2 3 4
1	4		1	1 2 3 4	1 1 1 1	1 2 3 4
2	3		2	2 2 3 4	1 2 2 2	1 1 2 3
3	2		3	3 3 3 4	1 2 3 3	1 1 1 2
4	1		4	4 4 4 4	1 2 3 4	1 1 1 1

This is the system $Ł_4$. And in general, if one introduces the abbreviation

$$E^n(X) = \underbrace{E[E[E[\ldots[E(X)]\ldots]}_{n \text{ times}}$$

then it is not difficult to show (by mathematical induction) that:

$$E^n(C_2) = Ł_{n+2}$$

By way of contrast with this sequence of extended systems starting from C_2, let us begin with an initial 3-valued system that is based on the following truth table for implication:

	$p \to q$		
$\diagdown q$ p	1	2	3
1	1	2	3
2	1	2	2
3	1	1	1

In this event the E-extended 4-valued truth table for implication would be:

	$p \Rightarrow q$			
$\diagdown q$ p	1	2	3	4
1	1	2	3	4
2	1	2	2	3
3	1	1	1	2
4	1	1	1	1

It should be noted that this construction procedure for the extension E is such that if all the truth-values are designated in $E(X)$ that were designated in X, then every tautology of $E(X)$ will also be a tautology of X. Thus the E-extended version of a many-valued logic will always be T-contained in the original system (subject to the indicated supposition about designation).

For the sake of comparison let us now consider another extension method F, which differs from E only as regards implication, replacing the procedure of E by:

	$p \Rightarrow q$	
$\diagdown q$ p	1	$j \neq 1$
$i (\neq n + 1)$	1	$\langle i \to (j - i) \rangle$ $+1$
$n + 1$	1	1

Note that C_2, $F(C_2)$, and $F^2(C_2)$ has the implication truth tables:

$p \supset q$				$p \Rightarrow q$					$p \Rightarrow q$				
$\stackrel{q}{{}_p\backslash}$	1	2		$\stackrel{q}{{}_p\backslash}$	1	2	3		$\stackrel{q}{{}_p\backslash}$	1	2	3	4
1	1	2		1	1	2	3		1	1	2	3	4
2	1	1		2	1	2	2		2	1	2	3	3
				3	1	1	1		3	1	2	2	2
									4	1	1	1	1

Thus F yields Kleene's 3-valued logic $\mathbf{K_3} = \mathbf{S}_3^{\supset}$ (rather than $\mathbf{L_3}$ as with E) as the extension of C_2. Moreover, we can see in general that F is such that:

$$F^n(C_2) = \mathbf{S}_{n+2}^{\supset}$$

The following fact deserves to be noted in the context of the extension of many-valued systems:

> Given truth tables for any set of connectives within an n-valued logic, one can always specify counterpart connectives in an extended $(n + 1)$-valued logic that will yield *exactly the same* set of tautologies.

In showing this we shall again make use of another extension procedure G that also differs from E. Let the original n-valued truth tables be of the type

p	$\perp p$		$\stackrel{q}{{}_p\backslash}$	$p \varnothing q$
				j
i	z_i		i	$x_{i,j}$

where $1 \leq i \leq n$, $1 \leq j \leq n$, with $\perp$ an arbitrary one-place connective and $\varnothing$ an arbitrary binary connective. We shall now specify the extended, $(n + 1)$-valued truth tables to be

p	Ψp		$\stackrel{q}{{}_p\backslash}$	$j \leq n$	$p \Phi q$ $n+1$
$i \leq n$	$z_i = \langle \perp i \rangle$		$i \leq n$	$x_{i,j} = \langle i \varnothing j \rangle$	$x_{i,n}$
$n+1$	z_n		$n+1$	$x_{n,j}$	$x_{n,n}$

where again $1 \leq i \leq n$, $1 \leq j \leq n$.

Thus if we begin with $\mathbf{K_3} = \mathbf{S}_3^{\supset}$

p	¬p	q\p	$p \wedge q$ 1 2 3	$p \vee q$ 1 2 3	$p \supset q$ 1 2 3	$p \equiv q$ 1 2 3
1	3	1	1 2 3	1 1 1	1 2 3	1 2 3
2	2	2	2 2 3	1 2 2	1 2 2	2 1 2
3	1	3	3 3 3	1 2 3	1 1 1	3 2 1

then we shall obtain $G(\mathbf{K}_3)$ as follows:

p	=p	q\p	$p \hat{\wedge} q$ 1 2 3 4	$p \vee\!\!\!\vee q$ 1 2 3 4	$p \Rightarrow q$ 1 2 3 4	$p \Leftrightarrow q$ 1 2 3 4
1	3	1	1 2 3 3	1 1 1 1	1 2 3 3	1 2 3 3
2	2	2	2 2 3 3	1 2 2 2	1 2 2 2	2 1 2 2
3	1	3	3 3 3 3	1 2 3 3	1 1 1 1	3 2 1 1
4	1	4	3 3 3 3	1 2 3 3	1 1 1 1	3 2 1 1

This example illustrates that the *G*-extended system is such that when we identify the new $(n + 1)$st truth-value with the old *n*th one—that is, identify 3 and 4—we simply obtain back the initial, *n*-valued truth tables. In general, these $(n + 1)$-valued truth tables thus have the feature that (1) they wholly agree with the *n*-valued truth tables when only values of the *n*-valued systems are at issue (so that we would simply get the old truth tables back if we suppressed the rows and columns corresponding to the new truth-values) and (2) they treat the truth-value $n + 1$ exactly like the truth-value *n*. From (1) it is clear that any $(n + 1)$-valued tautology must be an *n*-valued tautology, and from (2) we obtain the converse that every *n*-valued tautology must be an $(n + 1)$-valued tautology. The two systems will thus yield exactly the same set of tautologies. It follows that for any finitely many-valued system one can always find another system of many-valued logic of arbitrarily greater size that will have exactly the same set of tautologies.

Is the reverse of this the case: can one always find *n*-valued counterparts to the truth tables for $(n + 1)$-valued connectives in such a way that the set of *n*-valued tautologies will be the same as that of the $(n + 1)$-valued ones? The negative answer that must be given to this question inheres in the fact that a truth-functionally complete set of connectives in $(n + 1)$-valued logic always yields a vastly greater number of distinct, nonredundant connectives (and thus of nonequivalent propositions of a given length) than is available with the more modest resources of an *n*-valued logic.

16 Products of Pluri-valued Logics

Suppose two systems of pluri-valued logic, $\mathbf{X}_1$ and $\mathbf{X}_2$, to be given. We can then form a new, many-valued system—to be designated $\mathbf{X}_1 \times \mathbf{X}_2$—as the product (the "Cartesian" product) of these two systems. This is to be done in accordance with the following three rules:

(1) The truth-values of the system $X_1 \times X_2$ are to be *ordered pairs* $\langle v_1, v_2 \rangle$ of truth-values, the first of which, v_1, is a truth-value of X_1 and the second of which, v_2, is one of X_2.

(2) The truth-value of a proposition is to be $\langle v_1, v_2 \rangle$ in $X_1 \times X_2$ if and only if its truth-value is v_1 in X_1 and is v_2 in X_2.

(3) Correspondingly, negation ($\neg$) and the primitive binary logical connectives ($\varnothing$ an arbitrary such connective) are to be so specified for $X_1 \times X_2$ that their truth tables are governed by the rules:

$$\neg \langle v_1, v_2 \rangle = \langle \neg v_1, \neg v_2 \rangle$$
$$\langle v_1, v_2 \rangle \, \varnothing \, \langle v_1', v_2' \rangle = \langle v_1 \, \varnothing \, v_1', v_2 \, \varnothing \, v_2' \rangle$$

Subject to these principles, the product of two pluri-valued logics is always a well-defined system of many-valued logic; and specifically, the product of an n-valued system with an m-valued system is an ($n \times m$)-valued system.

This method of forming the product of two pluri-valued systems was devised in the late 1930s by the Polish logician Stanisław Jaśkowski.[1] In a late paper, J. Łukasiewicz displayed great partiality for product systems— or at any rate for the particular system $C_2 \times C_2$, to which we now turn.

Let us consider some cases of the working of these ideas. The product of the classical two-valued propositional calculus C_2 with itself—that is, $C_2 \times C_2$—will be as follows. We shall again write 1 for T and 0 for F. (Note: When only a small number of truth-values are involved, we may omit writing the brackets of $\langle v_1, v_2 \rangle$.)

p	$\neg p$	$\begin{matrix} & \backslash q \\ p & \end{matrix}$	$p \wedge q$ 11 10 01 00	$p \vee q$ 11 10 01 00	$p \supset q$ 11 10 01 00	$p \equiv q$ 11 10 01 00
11	00	11	11 10 01 00	11 11 11 11	11 10 01 00	11 10 01 00
10	01	10	10 10 00 00	11 10 11 10	11 11 01 01	10 11 00 01
01	10	01	01 00 01 00	11 11 01 01	11 10 11 10	01 00 11 10
00	11	00	00 00 00 00	11 10 01 00	11 11 11 11	00 01 10 11

[1]See his "Recherches sur le système de la logique intuitioniste," *Actes du Congrès International de Philosophie Scientifique*, vol. VI (Paris, 1936), pp. 58–61; tr. in S. McCall (ed.), *Polish Logic: 1920–1939* (Oxford, 1967). Jaśkowski's method is described in detail in Z. Zawirski, "Geneza i rozwoj logiki intuicjonistycznej," *Kwartalnik filozoficzny*, vol. 16 (1946), pp. 165–222. A convenient entrée into these ideas is A. A. Zinov'ev's *Philosophical Problems of Many-Valued Logic*, tr. by G. Küng and D. D. Comey (Dordrecht, 1963), pp. 23–27. A device fundamentally akin to the formation of product systems was employed in a 1938 paper by the Czech O. V. Zich, known to me only through the review by K. Reach in *The Journal of Symbolic Logic*, vol. 4 (1939), pp. 165–166.

Since we may simply rewrite the truth-values as $11 = 1$, $10 = 2$, $01 = 3$, $00 = 4$, we note that these truth tables are identical with the system:

p	p	${}^q\!\diagdown_p$	$p \wedge q$				$p \vee q$				$p \supset q$				$p \equiv q$			
			1	2	3	4	1	2	3	4	1	2	3	4	1	2	3	4
1	4	1	1	2	3	4	1	1	1	1	1	2	3	4	1	2	3	4
2	3	2	2	2	4	4	1	2	1	2	1	1	2	3	2	1	4	3
3	2	3	3	4	3	4	1	1	3	3	1	2	1	2	3	4	1	2
4	1	4	4	4	4	4	1	2	3	4	1	1	1	1	4	3	2	1

This system has a special historical significance. Late in life, J. Łukasiewicz came to regard this 4-valued product system $C_2 \times C_2$ as the many-valued system of principal importance from the philosophical point of view. In his 1953 paper,[2] he published the following astonishing retraction:

> When I had discovered in 1920 a 3-valued system of logic, I called the third value, which I denoted by $\frac{1}{2}$, "possibility." Later on, after having found my n-valued modal systems, I thought that only two of them may be of philosophical importance, viz., the 3-valued and the $\aleph_0$-valued system. For we can assume, I argued, that either possibility has no degrees at all getting thus the 3-valued system, or that it has infinitely many degrees, as in the theory of probabilities, and then we have the $\aleph_0$-valued system. This opinion, as I see it today, was wrong. The L-modal logic is a 4-valued system with two values . . . denoting possibility . . .

For a second example of a product system, consider the product of the classical two-valued system C_2 (now with 1,2 for T,F) with Łukasiewicz' L_3 (with 1,2,3 for T,I,F), leading to the system $C_2 \times L_3$:

p	$\neg p$	${}^q\!\diagdown_p$	$p \wedge q$						$p \vee q$						$p \supset q$					
			11	12	13	21	22	23	11	12	13	21	22	23	11	12	13	21	22	23
11	23	11	11	12	13	21	22	23	11	11	11	11	11	11	11	12	13	21	22	23
12	22	12	12	12	13	22	22	23	11	12	12	11	12	12	11	11	12	21	21	22
13	21	13	13	13	13	23	23	23	11	12	13	11	12	13	11	11	11	21	21	21
21	13	21	21	22	23	21	22	23	11	11	11	21	21	21	11	12	13	11	12	13
22	12	22	22	22	23	22	22	23	11	12	12	21	22	22	11	11	12	11	11	12
23	11	23	23	23	23	23	23	23	11	12	13	21	22	23	11	11	11	11	11	11

In general, it is clear that the product of the n-valued system X_1 with an m-valued system X_2 will be a system $X = X_1 \times X_2$ which is $(n \times m)$-valued, and which will be closely related to the initial systems (in ways yet to be explored).

[2] "A System of Modal Logic," *The Journal of Computing Systems*, vol. 1 (1952), pp. 111–189 (see p. 129).

We shall introduce the notation $\Pi_k(X)$ for the k-fold product of the pluri-valued system X with itself. Thus:

$$\Pi_k(X) = X \times X \times \cdots \times X \;(k \text{ repetitions})$$

Note that if X is an n-valued system, then $\Pi_k(X)$ is n^k-valued. We adopt also the convention that $\Pi_{\aleph_0}(X)$ is the infinite product of X with itself:

$$\Pi_{\aleph_0}(X) = X \times X \times X \times \cdots(ad\ infinitum)$$

Given any pluri-valued system as a starting point, an infinite variety of distinct product systems can be generated from it. The logical relationships among these systems must be considered.

In general, the tautologies of a product system will bear interesting relations to those of the component systems. To exhibit this, we shall again make use of two abbreviations introduced above. If X is a many-valued system, then let:

$D^+(X)$ = the set of the designated truth-values of X
$T(X)$ = the set of tautologous formulas (wffs) of X

One basic question to be resolved before a cogent consideration of the tautologies of a product system becomes possible is: What are to be the designated truth-values of $X_1 \times X_2$? Here two major alternatives lie open:

Policy 1
$\langle v,u \rangle \in D^+(X_1 \times X_2)$ iff both $[v \in D^+(X_1)]$ and $[u \in D^+(X_2)]$
Policy 2
$\langle v,u \rangle \in D^+(X_1 \times X_2)$ iff either $[v \in D^+(X_1)]$ or $[u \in D^+(X_2)]$

For the sake of notational convenience we shall say that these two policies result in the systems $X_1 \;\boxed{x}\; X_2$ and $X_1 \;\circledast\; X_2$, respectively. A substantial difference between these two systems is readily established, although it is obvious that we shall in general have:

$$T(X_1 \;\boxed{x}\; X_2) \subseteq T(X_1 \;\circledast\; X_2)$$

First, we shall prove the theorem:

$$T(X_1 \;\boxed{x}\; X_2) = T(X_1) \cap T(X_2)$$

The demonstration of this result may be divided into two parts as follows:

(i) To begin with, let us assume that $p_1 \in T(X_1 \;\boxed{x}\; X_2)$. It will then be the case that p_1 will take on a designated two-place truth-value in $X_1 \;\boxed{x}\; X_2$ for *every* assignment of two-place truth-values to its variables, and must therefore take on an X_1-designated value for any assignment in X_1 and also an X_2-designated value for any assignment in X_2. This establishes half of our theorem, viz. $T(X_1 \;\boxed{x}\; X_2) \subseteq T(X_1) \cap T(X_2)$.

(ii) Secondly, and conversely, assume that both $p_1 \in T(X_1)$ and $p_1 \in T(X_2)$. Then p_1 will always take on a designated value in X_1 and will always take on a designated value in X_2. But in this circumstance, it must also always take on a designated two-place value in $X_1 \boxed{x} X_2$. This establishes the remaining half of the theorem.

Note, moreover, that the theorem has the immediate consequence that:

$$T(X \boxed{x} X) = T(X)$$

It is of interest to observe that $X_1 \boxed{x} X_2$ will S-contain both X_1 and X_2. This can be seen by suppressing all rows (columns) of the $X_1 \boxed{x} X_2$ truth tables whose second (respectively first) place entry (as a two-place truth-value differs) from any one certain value (say T). Moreover, $X_1 \boxed{x} X_2$ will also I-contain both X_1 and X_2. This can be seen by identifying all truth-values of $X_1 \boxed{x} X_2$ that have the same first (or respectively second) place entry in the two-place truth-value.

We turn now to the consequences of adopting Policy 2. Here we can prove the theorem:

$$T(X_1 \circledcirc X_2) = T(X_1) \cup T(X_2)$$

We shall again present the proof in two parts: (i) First suppose that:

$$p_1 \in T(X_1) \cup T(X_2)$$

Then either $p_1 \in T(X_1)$ or $p_1 \in T(X_2)$—or both. But if $p_1 \in T(X_1)$, then p_1 will, for all assignments of X_1 truth-values to its variables, uniformly take on a designated value in X_1. But then, by Policy 2, p_1 will uniformly take on a designated value in $X_1 \circledcirc X_2$. Exactly parallel reasoning applies when we assume $p_1 \in T(X_2)$. Consequently $p_1 \in T(X_1 \circledcirc X_2)$ in either case, and this fact establishes that:

$$T(X_1) \cup T(X_2) \subseteq T(X_1 \circledcirc X_2)$$

(ii) It remains to prove the converse of this finding, viz.:

$$T(X_1 \circledcirc X_2) \subseteq T(X_1) \cup T(X_2)$$

We shall proceed by *reductio ad absurdum*. Suppose that the indicated relationship fails, so that there is some formula p_1 such that:

(1) $p_1 \in T(X_1 \circledcirc X_2)$
(2) $p_1 \notin T(X_1)$
(3) $p_1 \notin T(X_2)$

By (2) we have it that in X_1 there is some assignment of truth-values to the variables of p_1 for which p_1 fails to take on an X_1-designated value. Let this assignment be:

$$v_1, v_2, \ldots, v_n$$

By (3) we have a similar assignment in X_2 for which p_1 fails to take on an X_2-designated value, say:

$$v_1', v_2', \ldots, v_n'$$

But now consider the $X_1 \circledast X_2$ assignment:

$$\langle v_1, v_1' \rangle, \langle v_2, v_2' \rangle, \ldots, \langle v_n, v_n' \rangle$$

With this assignment p_1 will now take on a two-place truth-value undesignated in $X_1 \circledast X_2$. Thus $p_1 \not\subseteq T(X_1 \circledast X_2)$. But this contradicts (1), as we planned to show.

It is also an immediate consequence of the theorem that:

$$T(X \circledast X) = T(X) = T(X \boxed{x} X)$$

In a *self-product* system, it does not matter for tautologousness which of our two designation policies is adopted. The added designations of Policy 2 cannot add to the stock of tautologies. The reasons for this lie in the fact that under one policy tautologousness in the product system requires tautologousness in both member systems and under the other it requires tautologousness in one of the systems: since the systems are the same, these two requirements will automatically coincide. Regardless of the value of n, all the infinite variety of product systems $\Pi_n(X)$ will have exactly the same tautologies as the initial system X itself. This finding can also be extended to the infinite product system so that:

$$T(\Pi_{\aleph_0}(X)) = T(X)$$

Appendix

It is also possible to form the product of two *different* connectives so as to develop new connectives in higher-valued systems. Thus consider the binary (let us assume) connective $\varnothing$ of the many-valued system X_1 and the binary connective $\mathscr{S}$ of the system X_2. We can then form the product of these two connectives in the product system $X_1 \times X_2$ by multiplying them as follows

$$/p[\varnothing \times \mathscr{S}]q/ = \langle /p \varnothing q/_1, /p \mathscr{S} q/_2 \rangle$$

where $/p/_i$ is the truth-value of p in the system X_i (with $i = 1$ or $i = 2$). Thus if $\varnothing$ is the classical two-valued equivalence ($\equiv$) of C_2 and $\mathscr{S}$ is the implication ($\rightarrow$) of Łukasiewicz' 3-valued system L_3

$p \equiv q$				$p \rightarrow q$		
$\diagdown q$ $\llap{$p$}$	T	F		$\diagdown q$ $\llap{$p$}$	T	I	F
T	T	F		T	T	I	F
F	F	T		I	T	T	I
				F	T	T	T

then we have that [≡ × →] corresponds to the 6-valued truth table:

$\begin{matrix}\backslash q\\p\backslash\end{matrix}$	$p[\equiv \times \to]q$ TT	TI	TF	FT	FI	FF
TT	TT	TI	TF	FT	FI	FF
TI	TT	TT	TI	FT	FT	FI
TF	TT	TT	TT	FT	FT	FT
FT	FT	FI	FF	TT	TI	TF
FI	FT	FT	FI	TT	TT	TI
FF	FT	FT	FT	TT	TT	TT

One interesting finding regarding this way of multiplying connectives is due to Helena Rasiowa, who has studied the product of the implication ($\supset$) and equivalence ($\equiv$) of classical two-valued logic, [$\supset \times \equiv$], or $\Rightarrow$ for short:

$\begin{matrix}\backslash q\\p\backslash\end{matrix}$	$p \supset q$ T	F
+T	T	F
−F	T	T

by

$\begin{matrix}\backslash q\\p\backslash\end{matrix}$	$p \equiv q$ T	F
+T	T	F
−F	F	T

yields

$\begin{matrix}\backslash q\\p\backslash\end{matrix}$	$p \Rightarrow q$ TT	TF	FT	FF
+TT	TT	TF	FT	FF
TF	TF	TT	FF	FT
FT	TT	TF	TT	TF
−FF	TF	TT	TF	TT

Rasiowa has demonstrated that the tautologies involving $\Rightarrow$ alone (with only *TT* designated) are axiomatized by the three formulas (with *modus ponens* and substitution as rules of inference):[3]

$$(\alpha \Rightarrow \beta) \Rightarrow [(\beta \Rightarrow \gamma) \Rightarrow (\alpha \Rightarrow \gamma)]$$
$$\alpha \Rightarrow [\beta \Rightarrow (\beta \Rightarrow \alpha)]$$
$$[(\alpha \Rightarrow \beta) \Rightarrow (\alpha \Rightarrow \beta) \Rightarrow \alpha] \Rightarrow \alpha$$

The tautologies of this system will consist of all those tautologies of C_2 which (1) involve only the implication connective ($\supset$) and (2) remain tautologous when '$\supset$' is replaced by '$\equiv$.'

17 The Purely Abstract Approach to Many-valued Logic

We characterize as "abstract" that approach to many-valued logic which proceeds on the basis that we are dealing with assignments of values of some *unspecified* kind, that are not necessarily *truth*-values at all. On such an approach, we overlook wholly the relevance of the "values" at issue to

[3]See Rasiowa, "O pewnym fragmencie implikacyjnego rachunku zdan," (On a fragment of the implicative propositional calculus), *Studia Logica*, vol. 3 (1955), pp. 208–226. Cf. the discussion of Zinov'ev, *op. cit.*, p. 27.

semantical considerations regarding truth and falsity: The assignment of values to propositions is simply viewed as a formal exercise, a (possibly very useful) abstract sort of symbolic game. (Following custom, we shall, however, continue to speak of "truth tables" and "truth-values" in this context also.) This (perhaps seemingly unfruitful) procedure is of the greatest usefulness in the study of proof-theoretic issues regarding systems of propositional logic.

Its main application is in the presentation of *demonstrations of non-derivability* in propositional logic. To show that some formula (wff), say p_1, is not provable from certain axioms $A_1, A_2, \ldots, A_n$, we may present a set of many-valued truth tables such that:

(1) Each of the axioms has some feature θ that can be articulated by means of these truth tables. (This feature θ may, for example, be "uniformly taking the truth-value v for all assignments of truth-values to the propositional variables involved," or "never taking the truth-value v for any assignment of truth-values to the propositional variables involved," or "always taking one of the truth-values $v_1, v_2, \ldots, v_n$ for any assignment of truth-values to the propositional variables involved.")

(2) The rules of inference are feature-preserving (i.e., θ-preserving) in the sense that when applied to formulas that are feature-possessing, they must lead to a result formula that is feature-possessing.

(3) The formula p_1 lacks the feature θ.

In such circumstances it is clear that p_1 cannot be derived from the axioms. For a proof of p_1 would be a list of formulas:

F_1
F_2
.
.
.
$F_n = p_1$

All of these formulas up to some F_j are axioms, and all formulas after F_j are obtained from preceding formulas by the rules of inference. But if the axioms are feature-possessing, and the rules of inference feature-preserving, then *every* formula in the list for a valid proof must be feature-possessing. Then we could never arrive at the feature-lacking formula p_1, thus demonstrating its unprovability from the axioms and its nontheorematic status in the axiom system at issue.

This method of establishing nonprovability is especially useful in the study of axiomatized systems of propositional logic (and to a certain extent quantificational logic also) for purposes of showing the *independence* of the axioms—one axiom being "independent" of the rest when it is not derivable from them. The origination of this abstract application of many-valued logic is to be credited to Paul Bernays.[1]

As an example of this technique, consider the following standard set of axioms for the classical propositional calculus[2] (based on the rules of substitution and *modus ponens* as rules of inference). For the axiomatization '$\lor$' and '$\sim$' are taken as primitive, adopting the definitions:

$p \supset q$ FOR $\sim p \lor q$
$p \,\&\, q$ FOR $\sim(\sim p \lor \sim q)$

The axioms are as follows:

(A1) $(\alpha \lor \alpha) \supset \alpha$
(A2) $\alpha \supset (\beta \lor \alpha)$
(A3) $(\alpha \lor \beta) \supset (\beta \lor \alpha)$
(A4) $[\alpha \lor (\beta \lor \gamma)] \supset [\beta \lor (\alpha \lor \gamma)]$
(A5) $(\beta \supset \gamma) \supset [(\alpha \lor \beta) \supset (\alpha \lor \gamma)]$

Consider now the following set of 3-valued truth tables (with $\neg$, $\land$, $\lor$, $\eqsupset$, and $\equiv$ as the many-valued counterparts of the classical $\sim$, $\&$, $\lor$, $\supset$, and $\equiv$, respectively):

p	$\neg p$	$\diagdown q$ $p \diagup$	$p \land q$ 1 2 3	$p \lor q$ 1 2 3	$p \eqsupset q$ 1 2 3	$p \equiv q$ 1 2 3
+1	3	+1	1 2 3	1 1 1	1 2 3	1 2 3
2	2	2	2 1 3	1 1 2	1 1 2	2 1 2
−3	1	−3	3 3 3	1 2 3	1 1 1	3 2 1

With regard to these connectives, we observe that their defining truth tables are such that: (1) they are in accord with the usual definitions of '$\land$,' '$\eqsupset$,' and '$\equiv$' in terms of the primitives '$\lor$' and '$\neg$,' with 1 construed as truth and 3 as falsity; (2) the rule of substitution obtains, since a substituted formula must take on a subset of the truth-values initially assumed by the

[1]See Jan Łukasiewicz, "Die Logik und das Grundlagenproblem" in F. Gonseth (ed.), *Les Entretiens de Zürich sur les fondements et la méthode des sciences mathématiques 6–9 décembre 1938* (Zürich, 1941), pp. 82–100 (see p. 89).
[2]These are, essentially, the axioms for propositional logic given in B. Russell and A. N. Whitehead, *Principia Mathematica*, vol. 1 (Cambridge, 1910). This axiom set can be simplified by deleting (A4). See Paul Bernays, "Axiomatische Untersuchung des Aussagen-Kalküls der *Principia Mathematica*," *Mathematische Zeitschrift*, vol. 25 (1926), pp. 305–320.

variable substituted for; (3) the rule of *modus ponens* obtains since if an implication and its antecedent both have the truth-value 1, the consequent must also have the truth-value 1; and (4) the rule of replacement of equivalents holds, since an equivalence obtains the truth-value 1 only when both its members bear exactly the same truth-value.

Returning to the specified axioms, it is easily verified that all of these axioms except for axiom (A1) will assume the truth-value 1 *identically* (for all assignments of truth-value to its propositional components). However, axiom (A1) does not have this 1-assuming feature, for when 'α' takes on 2, then "$\alpha \lor \alpha$" takes on 1, and so "$(\alpha \lor \alpha) \supset \alpha$" assumes the value 2, and not 1. However, since all the other axioms are uniformly 1-assuming, and since the rules of inference will preserve this feature, this proves that *axiom (A1) cannot possibly be derived from the rest and so is independent of them.* This significant metasystematic fact is readily brought out by means of our "truth-table" considerations.

The important thing to notice about these tables is that we cannot really make semantical sense of the "*truth*"-values at issue. We cannot construe 2 as an analogue to *truth* or to *falsity* (for then $\neg p$ could not take on 2 when p takes on 2). Moreover, according to the truth table for '$\equiv$,' we have it that both $(2 \equiv 1) = 2$ and $(2 \equiv 3) = 2$, which suggests that 2 can be neither true-like nor false-like. In sum, the values of the "truth tables" at issue do not admit a semantical interpretation as representing "*truth*"-values.

A second, somewhat more elegant example of this abstract use of many-valued logics to demonstrate the independence of axioms is as follows. It has been shown (by Łukasiewicz) that the classical propositional calculus can also be based upon the following three axioms, with '$\sim$' and '$\supset$' taken as primitives, and the rules of inference again being substitution and *modus ponens:*

[A1] $(\sim\alpha \supset \alpha) \supset \alpha$
[A2] $\alpha \supset (\sim\alpha \supset \beta)$
[A3] $(\alpha \supset \beta) \supset [(\beta \supset \gamma) \supset (\alpha \supset \gamma)]$

The independence of these axioms can be seen by means of the following three sets of truth tables:

Set 1						Set 2						Set 3					
p	$\sim p$		$\begin{array}{c}\\ {}_{p}\diagdown^{q}\end{array}$	$p \supset q$		p	$\sim p$		$\begin{array}{c}\\ {}_{p}\diagdown^{q}\end{array}$	$p \supset q$		p	$\sim p$		$\begin{array}{c}\\ {}_{p}\diagdown^{q}\end{array}$	$p \supset q$	
				0	1					0	1					1 2 3	
+0	1		+0	0	1	+0	0		+0	0	1	+1	3		+1	1 3 3	
1	1		1	0	0	1	0		1	0	0	2	2		2	1 3 1	
												3	1		2	1 1 1	

Each of these sets of truth tables accommodates both rules of inference, but they are so designed that:

> With respect to Set i, all the axioms except [Ai] are
> tautologies, but [Ai] is nontautologous (with $i = 1, 2, 3$).

These three sets of "truth tables" therefore exhibit the independence of each of the axioms from the other two. However, the claims of the values at issue to represent *truth*-values are problematic, to say the least. (This is rendered obvious in the case of Sets 1 and 2 by inspecting the table for negation.)

Another abstract employment of many-valued logics in the study of axiomatic systems, closely related to the case of demonstrations of non-derivability, is their use in demonstrating the consistency of an axiom system. An axiom system is *consistent* if not every formula is a theorem, i.e., when there is some nonderivable thesis. The preceding device for demonstrating nonderivability can thus be employed also for establishing consistency. (We shall resume this topic of consistency at greater length in Sec. 25.) In effect, this use of pluri-valued systems for providing demonstrations of consistency derives from E. L. Post's classic paper of 1921.[3]

This "abstract" use of many-valued truth tables in the construction of metasystematic independence proofs and consistency proofs is one of their main uses in symbolic logic. It is, however, a very specialized use of such systems, and in general the systems involved qualify as many-valued *logics* only by courtesy. Their "truth-values" have in fact cut loose from the moorings of a semantical construction in *truth*-relevant terms, and correspondingly the assignment of such values to propositions has little bearing (indeed no direct bearing) on the characterization of inferences and processes of reasoning. Consequently such technical constructs can be characterized as "systems of logic" only by metonymy. To say this is not to impugn the possible interest of such systems from a certain point of view. The algebraic analysis of formal properties of multivalent propositional systems may well be of considerable value in its own right. But one should note that it would be misleading to characterize such an abstract mechanism as presenting a "logic." It is not even quite enough, it would seem, that the many-valued system should (with appropriate value designations) single out as tautologies the asserted theses of some viable system of propositional logic. For although this does go *some* way toward giving the many-valued system the aspect of a logic, it does not go far enough. We would now merely have a purely algebraic or combinational device that serves as a "correct formula selector." Without an adequate semantical underpinning such a combina-

[3]"Introduction to a General Theory of Elementary Propositions," *American Journal of Mathematics*, vol. 43 (1921), pp. 163–185, reprinted in J. van Heijsuoort, *From Frege to Gödel* (Cambridge, Mass., 1967).

tional instrumentality may well be a logically useful mechanism, but does not—it is clear—really qualify as itself constituting a logic.

To have what deserves to be called "many-valued *logic*," some appropriate semantical link of the "truth"-values at issue to the standard conception of truth-falsity must be present. This link need not necessarily be a direct one. For example, it need not lead to the categorical true-false distinction, but to truth and falsity *relative to assumptions*, thus invoking the concept of inferential validity. But *some* involvement with truth—be it categorical or hypothetical—is essential to make the "truth"-values of a many-valued system into *truth*-values, thus establishing the semantical link which alone can make the many-valued system into a *logic*.

The semantical interpretation of infinite-valued logic is thus on the one hand a matter of substantial importance and on the other a matter of substantial difficulty. There is no known general solution to this interpretation problem. In fact there is no known satisfactory interpretation for some of the best-known systems of many-valued logic, specifically including the historic and influential family $\mathbf{L}_n$ of Łukasiewicz. However, a satisfactory semantics can be provided for (1) the product logics of systems that themselves have a satisfactory semantics—and so specifically for the entire sequence of systems $\Pi_n(\mathbf{C}_2)$—and (2) for systems of the sequence $\mathbf{S}_n^2$. The presentation of the semantical interpretations at issue here will be the task of the following two sections.

18 Difficulties in the Semantical Interpretation of Many-valued Logics and a Mode of Resolution for Product Logics and for Boolean Logics

The question of the semantical interpretation of many-valued logics is a pivotal issue. For, as we have just argued, without an interpretation that gives some semantical rationale for its truth-values—somehow connecting them with the conception of the *truth status* of propositions—a many-valued system may be an interesting abstract mechanism, but is deficient in its claim to the rubric of a "logic." On our view the problem of semantical interpretation is absolutely fundamental in the study of many-valued logics. One very able logician has written:

> The problem of finding an interpretation for the truth-values is still far from a satisfactory solution, at least in the general *n*-valued case. This need not deter us. The abstract nature of truth-values has been indicated already by Peirce. And in the formal development of many-valued logic the semantical meaning of truth-values is quite unessential.[1]

[1] Arto Salomaa, "On Many-Valued Systems of Logic," *Ajatus*, vol. 22 (1959), pp. 115–159 (see p. 121).

To be sure, if one is interested simply in the formal development of an abstract corpus of symbolic apparatus, the matter of the interpretation of the values involved is quite irrelevant. But if one is to consider such systems as systems *of logic*—and not as abstract games—then the issue of interpretation becomes absolutely crucial. Otherwise one is forced to take the position of the eminent German logician Heinrich Scholz,[2] who insisted that one should speak of *n*-valued *calculi* rather than of *n*-valued *logics* (or *logical* calculi), or, similarly, to agree with Paul F. Linke,[3] who holds that we have to do here not with logic, but with logic-like formalisms (*"logoide Formalismen"*). The critical considerations have been formulated with clarity and force by Z. Jordan:

> The difficulty with the *n*-valued systems does not consist so much in technical problems, considerable as these are, as in finding an interpretation of the *n* "truth-values" involved in the system. Without an interpretation assigning a definite logical meaning to the *n* "truth-values" any given *n*-valued calculus remains an abstract structure. The importance of studying such structures cannot be denied. But according to the accepted opinion, coming ultimately from Wittgenstein, the value of a logical system consists in providing a set of rules (possessing definite properties) for transforming expressions of a given meaning into other expressions, and thus in revealing their hidden properties and relations. This requirement is not satisfied by an abstract *n*-valued calculus.[4]

It is necessary to consider the principal alternatives that have been proposed for the semantical *interpretation* of the (nonstandard) truth-values of many-valued logic. An examination of the literature of the subject shows that the various principal possibilities here are as follows. (They have generally been articulated for the 3-valued case. The semantics of the richer systems of many-valued logic is—as apart from Cases (I) and (III) below—a relatively unexplored domain.)

> (I) One major alternative is to let the truth-values be assigned not to individual propositions but to ordered *sets* of propositions, and then to reinterpret such assignments in terms of allotment of the classical truth-values *T, F* to the propositions comprised in these sets. (E. L. Post) (This prospect will be explored more extensively in Sec. 20.)

[2]Heinrich Scholz, "In Memoriam Jan Łukasiewicz," *Archiv für mathematische Logik und Grundlagenforschung*, vol. 3 (1957), pp. 3–18.
[3]"Die mehrwertigen Logiken und das Wahrheitsproblem," *Zeitschrift für philosophische Forschung*, vol. 3 (1948), pp. 378–398, 530–536. Also cf. his "Eigentliche und uneigentliche Logik," *Methodos*, vol. 4 (1952), pp. 165–168.
[4]Z. Jordan, "The Development of Mathematical Logic in Poland between the Two Wars" in S. McCall (ed.), *Polish Logic: 1920–1939* (Oxford, 1967), pp. 346–397 (see pp. 393–394).

(II) Another approach is to consider the assignment of truth-values not to definite but to *variable propositions*—i.e., propositional functions of a parameter. Then a 3-valued logic emerges in a natural way, with T representing "unqualifiedly (i.e., uniformly) true," i.e., true for all values of the parameter, F representing "unqualifiedly (i.e., uniformly) false," and I representing "sometimes true and sometimes false." The main possibility that has been explored in this direction is that of a *temporal* parameter, an approach which can give rise to an n-valued logic with arbitrarily large n, and even to an infinite-valued logic. (A. N. Prior)

(III) Again, in a related way the propositions at issue can be taken to be specific substitution instances of mathematical functions that may be undefined for some values of the dependent (numerical) variable (as $1/x$ is undefined for $x = 0$). Then the "intermediate" truth-value I comes to represent not variability (as before) but literal meaninglessness in the sense of lack of definition or determination. (S. C. Kleene's strong system)

(IV) A related approach is to let the truth-values reflect the semantical status of propositions within the schematism: true, meaningless, false. The idea is to take account of the prospect of paradoxical statements—e.g., those involved in the semantical paradoxes—that cannot viably be classed either as true or as false. (D. A. Bochvar, S. C. Kleene's weak system)

(V) Another approach is to let the truth-values reflect the *modal* (or the ontological) status of propositions within some such schematism as:

> necessarily false, actually false, indeterminate, actually true, necessarily true

By aggregation to three cases one arrives at the traditional 3-valued case: true, indeterminate, false.[5] (J. Łukasiewicz)

(VI) A kindred approach—and one that exhibits the same strengths and weaknesses as the preceding—is to have the truth-values represent the *probabilistic* status of propositions. Here one obtains such categorizations as:

> certainly true, probably true, as likely as not, probably false, certainly false

---

[5]The major shortcoming of an approach along these lines is that all attempts to implement it in a natural way must result in a failure of truth functionality.

This probabilistic line of approach dates back to MacColl and has in recent years been followed by many writers. (Z. Zawirski, H. Reichenbach, etc.)

(VII) A further possibility is to let the truth-values reflect the *epistemic* status of propositions, within some such schematism as:

> known to be or demonstrably (provably) false
> neither known to be (provable as) true nor known to be (provable as) false
> known to be or demonstrably (provably) true

In this way one can, for example, attempt a many-valued treatment of intuitionistic logic. (J. B. Rosser)

(VIII) A close analogue of the preceding case arises when the discussion is built upon a basic *set of axioms*, and one takes a proposition p to assume one of the three truth-values T,F,I, according as:

1. p is derivable from the axioms
2. not-p is derivable from the axioms
3. neither p nor not-p is derivable from the axioms

On this approach, it is not absolute truth or falsity that is at issue in the allocation of truth-values, but truth or falsity *relative to assumptions*.

We must examine the possibilities along these lines in somewhat greater detail. Let us begin with 3-valued logic. The task of providing a plausible semantical interpretation for 3-valued logic is—to put it mildly— a most difficult one. For consider the set of (incomplete) truth tables:

p	$\neg p$		$p \wedge q$			$p \vee q$		
		q / p	T	I	F	T	I	F
T	F	T	T		F	T		T
I	I	I		X				
F	T	F	F		F	T		F

These truth tables agree (as is customary) with the usual, two-valued truth tables whenever only T's and F's alone are involved. But how is the rest of the tables to be filled in? Let us concentrate for the moment on the entry x. What is its value to be: T, I, or F? Here the following two lines of thought can be brought to bear:

1. Obviously we must have it that $/p \wedge p/ = /p/$. Thus when $/p/ = I$, then also $/p \wedge p/ = I$. Thus we must have it—by this

line of thought—that x, the truth-value corresponding to the case $I \wedge I$ must be I.

2. Obviously $/p \wedge \neg p/$ must be F, regardless of what $/p/$ may be. But when $/p/ = I$, we also have it that $/\neg p/ = I$. Now since $/p \wedge \neg p/ = F$, by our initial principle we must have it—on this line of thought—that x, the truth-value corresponding to the case $I \wedge I$, must be F.

This pair of findings poses a dilemma for the issue of semantical interpretation: there *just is no way* at all of arriving at an unproblematically satisfactory specification of the value x.

This shortcoming of 3-valued logic—on any halfway plausible semantical basis—inheres in the fact that there will here be a self-negating truth-value, that is, a truth-value v such that $\neg v = v$. The natural step to overcome this obstacle is to proceed to a 4-valued system. Let us see what can be done along these lines.

It would appear on first thought that the most plausible and tempting possibility of interpreting the truth-values of a 4-valued system of propositional logic would be along some such lines as the following:

Truth-value	Interpretation (A)	Interpretation (B)
+1	necessarily true	true
+2	contingently true	probably true
3	contingently false	probably false
4	necessarily false	false

It is plain that both 1 and 2 must be taken as *designated* truth-values in this scheme—i.e., "truth-like" truth-values which a formula must always take on if it is to avoid losing the status of a tautology, since we wish to keep to the customary meaning of a "tautology" as a propositional schema that is "uniformly *true* for every truth-value assignment to its constituents."

In both instances, negation would be characterized by the familiar truth table:

p	$\neg p$
+1	4
+2	3
3	2
4	1

Along these lines we might think to obtain a 4-valued system discussed by A. N. Prior.[6] For let the four truth-values 1 to 4 be so construed that their assignment to a proposition has the following significance:

1 true and purely formal
2 true but involving reference to facts
3 false but involving reference to facts
4 false and purely formal

The propositions at issue are thus classified according to whether they are "pure," i.e., strictly formal (abstract or mathematical in subject matter), or "impure" in involving a reference to facts about natural objects. Such "impurity" infects any proposition into which it enters conjunctively: "The cat is on the mat and $2 + 2 = 5$" thus automatically takes the truth-value 3 (despite the logical falsity of its second conjunct). Then we might think to have the following truth table for conjunction in this case:

$$
\begin{array}{c|cccc}
 & \multicolumn{4}{c}{p \wedge q} \\
{}^{q}_{p} & 1 & 2 & 3 & 4 \\
\hline
1 & 1 & 2 & 3 & 4 \\
2 & 2 & 2 & 3 & 3 \\
3 & 3 & 3 & 3 & 3 \\
4 & 4 & 3 & 3 & 4 \\
\end{array}
$$

Unfortunately, however, the same vitiating difficulty arises alike with all these cases with regard to the matrix for conjunction. Consider what entry is to correspond to $2 \wedge 3$. In Interpretation (B), it is obvious that this cannot be specified as simply 3, since, in the instance of $p \wedge \neg p$ with $/p/ = 2$ the obviously appropriate entry would be 4. Again, in Interpretation (A), the entry corresponding to $2 \wedge 3$ will in general be 3, but will have to be 4 if—again as in the case of $p \wedge \neg p$ with $/p/ = 2$—the conjuncts are mutually exclusive. The result is a breakdown of truth functionality along the lines of this interpretation. The root difficulty is that in the case of either interpretation it is impossible to carry through a semantically adequate truth-functional specification of a matrix for conjunction.

The approach now to be presented is related to the above, but different from it at a crucial point. It is based on a modification of Interpretation (A) which—by an appropriate but minor change in the intended meaning of the truth-values—*removes* the possibility that conjunctions corresponding

[6]See his article, "Logic, Many-Valued" in *The Encyclopedia of Philosophy*, ed. by P. Edwards (New York, 1967), vol. 5, pp. 1–5 (see p. 4).

to the truth-value compounds 2 $\wedge$ 3 or 3 $\wedge$ 2 can possibly be self-consistent, i.e., can yield a value of 3 as well as 4.

Let it be supposed that there are just two possible alternatives (i.e., incompatible states of affairs), the *actual* world (or state) X and the *possible alternative* world (or state) Y. To any proposition whatever, we will assign the truth-value 1, 2, 3, or 4 according as it is:

(1) true in X and in Y (i.e., is necessarily true)
(2) true in X but not in Y (i.e., is actually but not necessarily true)[7]
(3) false in X but true in Y (i.e., is actually but not necessarily false)
(4) false in both X and in Y (i.e., is necessarily false)

This interpretation of the truth-values[8] clearly gives rise to the following truth tables for negation and conjunction:

p	$\neg p$
+1	4
+2	3
3	2
4	1

$p \wedge q$ q / p	1	2	3	4
+1	1	2	3	4
+2	2	2	4	4
3	3	4	3	4
4	4	4	4	4

The system here at issue is clearly the product logic $C_2 \times C_2$. The line of interpretation afforded by (1) to (4) above provides a perfectly viable semantical interpretation for this system of 4-valued logic. *Thus at least some many-valued logics can be fitted out with a meaningful semantics.* (We may note, incidentally, that this characterization of negation and conjunction in fact coincides with one of the 4-valued truth tables ["matrices"] originally proposed by W. T. Parry.[9])

A very similar interpretation for this same system is provided by examining propositions which can be true (or false) in two different systematic settings S_1 and S_2—say in two systems of logic or in two different systems of geometry. Then the four truth-values could be interpreted as:

[7]Both (1) and (2) will now of course be *designated* truth-values.
[8]This approach has been evolved, albeit with crucial modifications, from a proposal put forward by A. N. Prior in a paper on "Many-Valued and Modal Systems: An Intuitive Approach," *The Philosophical Review*, vol. 64 (1955), pp. 626–630.
[9]C. I. Lewis and C. H. Langford, *Symbolic Logic* (New York, 1932; reprinted 1959). See Appendix II. All references here to "Lewis and Langford" are to this appendix which was, however, written by Lewis. Actually, the method of interpretation that is here at issue is due in its essentials to O. V. Zich. See the review of his 1938 paper by K. Reach in *The Journal of Symbolic Logic*, vol. 9 (1939), pp. 165–166.

$1 = $ true in S_1 and S_2
$2 = $ true in S_1 but not in S_2
$3 = $ false in S_1 but not in S_2
$4 = $ false in both S_1 and S_2

Along just these same lines, Alan Rose constructed an 8-valued ($8 = 2^3$) system with geometric propositions—the values indicating their truth status in the three systems of Euclidean, Riemannian, and Lobatchevskian geometry.[10]

In general, other systems will arise along these lines when more than the two alternative worlds X, Y are involved. When there are k such worlds $X_1, X_2, \ldots, X_k$, then the corresponding logic will be the product system $\Pi_k(\mathbf{C}_2)$, with $m = 2^k$ truth-values. The situation would be analogous but more complicated yet if the basic logic were not two-valued, but 3-valued, adding an "indeterminate" (undefined, neutral) truth status to the usual *true* and *false*. With k basic cases we would then get a system $\Pi_k(\mathbf{Ł}_3)$ or $\Pi_k(\mathbf{B}_3)$ or $\Pi_k(\mathbf{K}_3)$—with $m = 3^k$ truth-values—depending upon which 3-valued logic is used as the basis.[11]

What we have thus accomplished amounts, in effect, to providing a semantical interpretation for one important family of many-valued systems —viz. those that can be represented as products of lesser-valued systems for which a semantical interpretation is already in hand. This line of approach may be characterized as *the alternative worlds interpretation* of product logics.

This way of interpreting product logics is so important that a detailed study deserves to be made of its systematization.

Let us consider a way of building up many-valued systems using a "truth-set" interpretation of the truth-values as our starting point. Let there be a given set of "possible worlds":

$$W = \{w_1, w_2, \ldots\}$$

As the truth-value of a proposition we shall take a certain *semantically determined set*, namely that subset of W comprising all those possible

---

[10]See his "Eight-Valued Geometry," *Proceedings of the London Mathematical Society*, series 3, vol. 2 (1952), pp. 30–44. For an earlier suggestion that goes in the same direction see O. V. Zich's Russian paper of 1938 on the sentential calculus with complex values, reviewed by K. Reach in *The Journal of Symbolic Logic*, vol. 4 (1939), pp. 165–166.
[11]Some of the material presented in this section has been drawn from the writer's paper "An Intuitive Interpretation of Systems of Four-Valued Logic," *Notre Dame Journal of Formal Logic*, vol. 6 (1965), pp. 154–156.

worlds in which p is true:

$$/p/ = \{w \mid w \in W \ \& \ p \text{ is true in } w\}^{12}$$

Thus the basis of the very construction of these systems is a semantical guiding principle. This leads immediately to the many-valued system based on the truth-values:

$$/\neg p/ \ \ = /p/' \quad \text{(NOTE: The prime here represents set complementation in } W\text{)}$$
$$/p \wedge q/ = /p/ \cap /q/$$
$$/p \vee q/ = /p/ \cup /q/$$
$$/p \supset q/ = /\neg p \vee q/$$
$$/p \equiv q/ = /(p \supset q) \wedge (q \supset p)/$$

The system is, in effect, a Boolean algebra of truth-values, or rather, the truth-value structure is a Boolean algebra of sets. When there are m elements in the set W, then we obtain the many-valued system Σ_n, where $n = 2^m$, which we may characterize as the Boolean sequence of systems.[13]

Suppose there is just one possible world:

$$W = \{w\}$$

Then there will be just two truth-values, $0 = \Lambda$ and $1 = \{w\} = W = V$. The truth tables of this system Σ_2 will be:

p	$\neg p$		q	$p \wedge q$		$p \vee q$		$p \supset q$		$p \equiv q$	
			p	0	1	0	1	0	1	0	1
0	1		0	0	0	0	1	1	0	1	0
1	0		1	0	1	1	1	1	1	0	1

This is exactly the classical two-valued system C_2, so that $\Sigma_2 = C_2$, and the Σ_i are thus many-valued generalizations of classical propositional logic.

Suppose there are just two possible worlds:

$$W = \{w_1, w_2\}$$

---

[12]Actually, the elements of W need not be alternative possible worlds, but could be temporal periods in the history of this actual world, provided the propositions are temporally indefinite, i.e., are of the type "It rains today" or "It rained a week ago," so that they can be true for one time period and false for another. We shall explore this line of approach below in further detail.

[13]Note that the propositional modalities are readily accommodated to this approach by the truth rules:

$$/\Box p/ = \begin{Bmatrix} V = W \\ \Lambda \end{Bmatrix} \text{ according as } /p/ \begin{cases} = V \\ \neq \Lambda \end{cases}$$

$$/\Diamond p/ = \begin{Bmatrix} V = W \\ \Lambda \end{Bmatrix} \text{ according as } /p/ \begin{cases} \neq \Lambda \\ = \Lambda \end{cases}$$

Then there will be four truth-values, as follows:

$$1 = \{w_1, w_2\} = W = V$$
$$2 = \{w_1\}$$
$$3 = \{w_2\}$$
$$4 = \Lambda$$

The corresponding 4-valued systems Σ_4 is:

p	$\neg p$	$\begin{smallmatrix}q\\p\end{smallmatrix}$	$p \wedge q$ 1 2 3 4	$p \vee q$ 1 2 3 4	$p \supset q$ 1 2 3 4	$p \equiv q$ 1 2 3 4
1	4	1	1 2 3 4	1 1 1 1	1 2 3 4	1 2 3 4
2	3	2	2 2 4 4	1 2 1 2	1 1 3 3	2 1 4 3
3	2	3	3 4 3 4	1 1 3 3	1 2 1 2	3 4 1 2
4	1	4	4 4 4 4	1 2 3 4	1 1 1 1	4 3 2 1

But this system is identical with $C_2 \times C_2$. In the three-world case $W = \{w_1, w_2, w_3\}$ we would obtain an 8-valued logic identical with $C_2 \times C_2 \times C_2$, based on the truth-values

$$1 = \{w_1, w_2, w_3\} = V \qquad 5 = \{w_1\}$$
$$2 = \{w_1, w_2\} \qquad\qquad 6 = \{w_2\}$$
$$3 = \{w_1, w_3\} \qquad\qquad 7 = \{w_3\}$$
$$4 = \{w_2, w_3\} \qquad\qquad 8 = \Lambda$$

And this finding is readily generalized (by mathematical induction) to show that $\Sigma_{2^m} = \Pi_m(C_2)$. The key fact regarding the Boolean systems is that they are exactly the C_2 self-product logics. (Thus all these systems will have the same tautologies as C_2.[14])

Many-valued systems having this property—that of I-containing C_2 in this way—are called "normal in the sense of Carnap" (C-normal) by Alonzo Church, who has made an extensive study of the relevant issues.[15] An interesting example of a system which has the same tautologies as C_2 but is not C-normal is the following system, viz. $S_3^{\supset}$ with 1 and 2 both designated:[16]

---

[14]Actually, whenever the truth-values of a pluri-valued system form a Boolean algebra in which V, the unit of the algebra, is designated, then the tautologies of this system will be the same as those of C_2.

[15]See A. Church, "Non-Normal Truth-Tables for the Propositional Calculus," *Boletin de la Sociedad Matematica Mexicana*, vol. 10 (1953), pp. 41–52. See also Church's *Introduction to Mathematical Logic* (Princeton, 1956), p. 117 (sec. 19.10).

[16]For a discussion of the relevant features of this system see Church, "Non-Normal Truth-Tables for the Propositional Calculus," *op. cit.* That these truth tables define the same tautologies as C_2, but that nevertheless no Boolean algebra is homomorphic to them, was remarked by A. Church and N. Rescher in a review in *The Journal of Symbolic Logic*, vol. 15 (1950), pp. 69–70.

p	$\neg p$	$\substack{q \\ p}$	$p \wedge q$ 1 2 3			$p \vee q$ 1 2 3			$p \supset q$ 1 2 3			$p \equiv q$ 1 2 3		
+1	3	+1	1	2	3	1	1	1	1	2	3	1	2	3
+2	2	+2	2	2	3	1	2	2	1	2	2	2	2	2
3	1	3	3	3	3	1	2	3	1	1	1	3	2	1

In the family of systems Σ_n, based on a plurality of possible worlds, we further have a natural construction for the concept of a "designated" truth-value. For let some possible world $w^* \in W$ be supposed to be the actual world. Then one can take all truth-values (i.e., subsets of W) that include w^* to be designated. Thus, if in the preceding example w_1 is assumed to be the actual world, so that $w^* = w_1$, then 1 and 2 will be the designated truth-values. (It is not hard to see that any Boolean system Σ_n will collapse into $\Sigma_2 = C_2$ if all of its so-designated truth-values are identified with one another and all of its nondesignated truth-values are identified.)

A variant of the preceding approach is of interest. Suppose the "propositions" at issue ($p, q, \dots$) are propositional functions of a numerical parameter ranging over a specified domain $\mathfrak{D}$, say $\mathfrak{D}$ is the set of all nonnegative integers $\{0, 1, 2, \dots\}$. Thus p—or better $p(x)$—might be, say, $x + 2 = 13$ or $x - 3 < 5$. Now let the truth-values of $p(x)$ be the set of all values of x for which $p(x)$ is true:

$$/p/ = /p(x)/ = \{x \mid x \in \mathfrak{D} \ \& \ p(x) \text{ is true}\}$$

Then the same truth rules as before are again operative and a system of many-valued logic can be built up exactly as before, and the resultant n-valued system will be isomorphic with Σ_n. (As we shall shortly see, exactly the same situation will also obtain if $p = p(t)$ is a propositional function of a temporal parameter.)

To show that a product logic can be given yet another sort of semantical interpretation, we shall consider an application to chronological logic.[17] Let time be divided into n intervals, beginning with "the present" interval I_1:

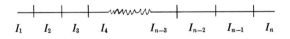

$$I_1 \quad I_2 \quad I_3 \quad I_4 \qquad I_{n-3} \quad I_{n-2} \quad I_{n-1} \quad I_n$$

Let the propositions p, q, etc., that are at issue be temporally indefinite,

[17]This particular application is due in its essentials to A. N. Prior. See his *Time and Modality* (Oxford, 1957; 2d ed., 1962). The fundamental idea at issue was first developed in O. V. Zich's 1939 paper cited in note 18 below.

so that they can—like "It is raining today"—be false at one time yet true at another. Then a proposition will take on an n-place truth-value,

$$\langle v_1, v_2, \ldots, v_n \rangle$$

where v_i is T or F according as p is true or false in the ith interval I_i. This temporal construction of many-valued logic represents a perfectly plausible interpretation for the product logic:

$$\mathbf{C}_2 \times \mathbf{C}_2 \times \cdots \times \mathbf{C}_2 \text{ (n repetitions)}$$

We thus have an illustration of a semantical interpretation of a tense-logical variety for a product logic. Infinite-product systems can also be given a temporal interpretation along the already-indicated lines, time being divided into denumerably many intervals. In just this way A. N. Prior provides the means for interpreting the infinite self-product of a 3-valued logic by letting time start with "the present" and construing the three truth-values as follows:

1 = determinately true (i.e., always true)
3 = determinately false (i.e., always false)
2 = future contingent (i.e., neither determinately true nor determinately false)

Such a temporal construction can provide an interpretation for an infinite-valued system of propositional logic.[18] This line of approach may be called *the time-series interpretation* of product logics.

Cognate interpretations can be provided along essentially the same lines for many-valued product systems. Thus let the systems $\mathbf{Z}_i$ be n different axiom systems for propositions expressed in one common language—e.g., different systems of Euclidean and non-Euclidean geometry.[19] Then let the truth-value of p be

$$\langle v_1, v_2, \ldots, v_i, \ldots, v_n \rangle$$

where v_i is T (or F, or I) according as p is provable (or $\neg p$ is provable, or neither) in the system $\mathbf{Z}_i$. Or, to take a somewhat more general stance, the $\mathbf{Z}_i$ need not be axiom systems specifically, but merely *assertors* of some kind, and then $/p/$ will have T, F, or I in the ith place according as the ith assertor asserts p, asserts $\neg p$, or neither.[20] Both these approaches yield a

---

[18]Prior does not notice, however, that this 3-valued logic cannot be strictly truth-functional (in the sense to be specified in Sec. 26 below). For 2 conjoined with 2 may result either in 2 or in 3, and 2 disjoined with 2 may result either in 2 or in 1.

[19]This interpretation is in its essentials due to Alan Rose. See his paper "Eight-Valued Geometry," *op. cit.*

[20]The way in which many-valued logics arise in the logic of assertion is considered in detail in Chap. XIV, "Assertion Logic" in N. Rescher, *Topics in Philosophical Logic* (Dordrecht, 1968).

readily intelligible and workable semantical interpretation for a 3-valued product logic, which we may designate as *the alternative-systems interpretation* of such product logics.

Appendix

The procedures presented for the construction of the (Boolean) product systems $\Sigma_{2m} = \Pi_m(C_2)$ can be generalized in an interesting way. This construction went as follows. We began with a set

$$W = \{w_1, w_2, \ldots\}$$

of possible worlds. With respect to the members of this set, a basic truth-value assignment that is essentially two-valued was postulated above, so that $/p/_w$—i.e., the truth-value of the proposition p is the possible world $w \in W$—must always be either T or F. We then let the derivative truth-value of p be the set of all w within W for which $/p/_w$ is true:

$$/p/ = \{w \mid w \in W \ \& \ /p/_w = T\}$$

The truth rules for $/p/$ were, as we saw, simply the Boolean operators.

But suppose that the logic for the initial truth-value assignment $/p/_w$ were not two-valued but finitely many-valued, based (say) on the truth-values $1, 2, \ldots, n$. Then we can introduce the complex, n-place truth-value

$$/p/ = \langle 1(p), 2(p), \ldots, n(p) \rangle$$

where $i(p)$ is the set of all those possible worlds in which p takes the truth-value i:

$$i(p) = \{w \mid w \in W \ \& \ /p/_w = i\}$$

(We may assume that the sets $i(p)$ are mutually exclusive and exhaustive.[21]) If W contains a designated element w^*, then we may class the truth-value

$$/p/ = \langle 1(p), 2(p), \ldots, n(p) \rangle$$

as designated whenever $w^* \in 1(p)$ (or, alternatively, whenever $w^* \in 1(p) \cup 2(p) \cup \ldots \cup k(p)$, for some $k < n$, the designated values of the initial system being $1, 2, \ldots, k$).

The truth rules will obviously now have to depend upon those of the underlying logic. Thus suppose the latter to be:

p	$\neg p$		q	$p \wedge q$			$p \vee q$		
		p		1	2	3	1	2	3
+1	3		+1	1	2	3	1	1	1
2	2		2	2	2	3	1	2	2
3	1		3	3	3	3	1	2	3

[21]See pp. 180–182 below for the consequences of dropping this assumption.

If $/p/ = \langle P_1, P_2, P_3 \rangle$ and $/q/ = \langle Q_1, Q_2, Q_3 \rangle$, then:

$$/\lnot p/ = \langle P_3, P_2, P_1 \rangle$$
$$/p \mathbin{\hat{\wedge}} q/ = \langle P_1 \cap Q_1, (P_1 \cap Q_1) \cup (P_2 \cap Q_1) \cup (P_2 \cap Q_2), P_3 \cup Q_3 \rangle$$
$$/p \mathbin{\hat{\vee}} q/ = \langle P_1 \cup Q_1, (P_2 \cap Q_2) \cup (P_2 \cap Q_3) \cup (P_3 \cap Q_2), P_3 \cap Q_3 \rangle$$

Thus consider again a family of possible worlds $W = \{w_1\}$ with one single element. There will now be three three-place truth-values (whose entries are the only two available sets $W = \{w_1\} = V$ and Λ):

$$\text{I} = \langle V, \Lambda, \Lambda \rangle$$
$$\text{II} = \langle \Lambda, V, \Lambda \rangle$$
$$\text{III} = \langle \Lambda, \Lambda, V \rangle$$

The resulting 3-valued logic, as derived from the specified truth rules, will be:

p	$\lnot p$	$q \atop p \diagdown$	$p \mathbin{\hat{\wedge}} q$ I	II	III	$p \mathbin{\hat{\vee}} q$ I	II	III
+I	III	+I	I	II	III	I	I	I
II	II	II	II	II	III	I	II	II
III	I	III	III	III	III	I	II	III

Thus in this special case of a single-element family of possible worlds, the derived many-valued logic will be identical with the initial 3-valued system.

If the initial family of possible worlds is the two-element set $W = \{w_1, w_2\}$, then there will be nine truth-values:

$$\text{I} = \langle \{w_1, w_2\}, \Lambda, \Lambda \rangle$$
$$\text{II} = \langle \{w_1\}, \{w_2\}, \Lambda \rangle$$
$$\text{III} = \langle \{w_1\}, \Lambda, \{w_2\} \rangle$$
$$\text{IV} = \langle \{w_2\}, \{w_1\}, \Lambda \rangle$$
$$\text{V} = \langle \{w_2\}, \Lambda, \{w_1\} \rangle$$
$$\text{VI} = \langle \Lambda, \{w_1, w_2\}, \Lambda \rangle$$
$$\text{VII} = \langle \Lambda, \{w_1\}, \{w_2\} \rangle$$
$$\text{VIII} = \langle \Lambda, \{w_2\}, \{w_1\} \rangle$$
$$\text{IX} = \langle \Lambda, \Lambda, \{w_1, w_2\} \rangle$$

The resulting 9-valued logic can be shown to be the product of the initial 3-valued logic with itself. (If w_1 is the designated world, then I, II, III will be designated truth-values.)

In general, if the initial system is X, then the indicated type of construction procedure will generate as the derived system the product logic $\Pi_n(X)$ for an n-element family W of possible worlds.

19 A Variant Semantical Approach to Many-valued Logics of the Sequence $\mathbf{S}_n^{\supset}$

A semantic interpretation can be provided for one important family of systems of many-valued logic—viz. the systems of the variant-standard sequence $S_n^{\supset}$—by a variation upon Post's approach described in Sec. 9 above. These systems at issue are based on a family of truth-values

$$T, I_1, I_2, \ldots, I_{n-2}, F$$

construed as arranged in a decreasing "order of truth." The truth table for negation is assumed to obey the mirror-image rule (the truth-table column being written in the reverse order), and so is such as to take a truth-value into its "opposite in truth." The truth tables for conjunction ($\wedge$) and disjunction ($\vee$) are given in accordance with the rules that the truth-value of a conjunct is the falsest of the truth-values of its members, and the truth-value of a disjunct is the truest of the truth-values of its members. The truth rules for implication ($\supset$) and equivalence $(\equiv)$ are then assumed to be given in terms of those for the preceding connectives via the usual definitions:

$p \supset q$ FOR $\neg p \vee q$
$p \equiv q$ FOR $(p \supset q) \wedge (q \supset p)$

To provide a semantical interpretation for the systems of this standard sequence $S_n^{\supset}$, let us return to the basic idea of Post's system:

(1) Again, let the "propositions" at issue (represented once more by capital letters) be n-tuples of ordinary, two-valued propositions (represented by small letters) subject to the convention that *all the true propositions are listed before the false:*

$$P = \underbrace{(p_1, p_2, \ldots, p_n)}_{\text{All true} \quad \text{All false}}$$

(2) Let P assume the truth-value I_i if exactly $i - 1$ elements of P are false; adopting the convention that $I_0 = T$ and $I_{n-1} = F$.

(3) When $P = (p_1, p_2, \ldots, p_n)$, then:

$$\neg P = (\sim p_n, \ldots, \sim p_2, \sim p_1)$$

(4) When $P = (p_1, p_2, \ldots, p_n)$ and $Q = (q_1, q_2, \ldots, q_n)$, then:

$$P \wedge Q = (p_1 \& q_1, p_2 \& q_2, \ldots, p_n \& q_n)$$

(5) When P and Q are as in (4) above, then:

$$P \vee Q = (p_1 \vee q_1, p_2 \vee q_2, \ldots, p_n \vee q_n)$$

It being assumed that the connectives $\supset$ and $\equiv$ are defined in terms of $\neg$, $\wedge$, and $\vee$ in the familiar way, their interpretation can be derived from the preceding stipulations. Thus, subject to this interpretation of the connectives, satisfaction of all the rules for the family $S_n^{\supset}$ of many-valued systems is guaranteed.

This approach to truth-value assignments in terms of n-tuples of propositions thus provides a means for constructing an interpretation for the standard systems of many-valued logic out of the semantics of the classical two-valued logic based on the orthodox connectives ($\sim$, &, $\lor$). A qualification that was already made in the discussion of Post's interpretation of his many-valued systems $\mathbf{P}_n$ (in Sec. 9 above) must be repeated here. This interpretation is not an interpretation of the systems as *propositional* logics at all, but one that proceeds in terms of *sets* of propositions. Here greater flexibility is available, but this fact should not block our vision of the nonstandard nature of the interpretation. We now have to do, in effect, not with a many-valued *propositional* logic, but with a many-valued logic of (duly ordered) *sets of propositions,* and with propositional operators that represent "negation" and disjunction" (etc.) in only a strained or extended sense of those terms.

Moreover, the existence of such a two-valued interpretation for the systems $\mathbf{S}_n^{\supseteq}$ does not show anything as to the relative conceptual *fundamentality* of the pluri-valued logics involved. To be sure, we can devise such a two-valued interpretation for various systems of many-valued logic. But the converse is just as true: given virtually any reasonably well-behaved system of many-valued logic, one can generally use it as a basis for devising a many-valued interpretation of the orthodox two-valued system. The fact that one system can be interpreted within the other does not cut any ice with respect to the interesting (if somewhat vague) issue of which of the systems is the more "fundamental."[1]

20 Varieties of Negation in Many-valued Logic

In a many-valued logic, various types of "negation" are always possible. We may say that a propositional operator (one-place connective) $\mathbf{N}$ represents a mode of negation if it can never, under any circumstances, happen that the members of the pair $p, \mathbf{N}p$ are both true or are both false (i.e., both never take T and both never take F, or whatever other truth-values represent truth and falsity). When T and F—or their surrogates—are not included among the truth-values of the many-valued system, then one can apply the preceding formula only by substituting *designated* for "true" and *antidesignated* for "false." In this form, however, the condition is too strong to be imposed as a plausible general requirement for negation, as we shall show

---

[1]This point was already observed by E. L. Post, who suggested, at the end of his classic article of 1921, that his analysis might be recast with the language of a many-valued system taken as basic, so that then the two-valued system would—by reversing the steps of the construction—be constructed out of the many-valued system: the latter would then appear as fundamental, the former as a constructed artifact. The entire issue of the relative conceptual priority of two-valued as contrasted with many-valued logic will be resumed in the next chapter.

below. We shall in this case have to add an exception clause, as follows: **N** is a mode of negation if p and **N**p are never both designated or both antidesignated unless it should happen that $/p/ = /$**N**$p/$. Thus considering the following possibilities for a negative operator one notes that the first

p	N_1p		p	N_2p		p	N_4p		p	N_3p		p	N_5p		p	N_6p
$+T$	F		$+T$	F		$+T$	F		$+T$	F		$+T$	F		$+T$	F
I	I		$+I$	I		$+I$	F		$-I$	T		$+I$	T		$-I$	F
$-F$	T		$-F$	T		$-F$	T		$-F$	T		$-F$	T		$-F$	T

four N_i will all qualify as modes of negation according to the present criterion, whereas the last two will not.

We regard this requirement as representing the minimal requisite (necessary condition) in qualifying a one-place propositional connective as a negation operator. It should be noted that even the rather far-fetched mode of "negation" at issue in the Postian systems (see Sec. 7) satisfies this necessary condition.

This requirement not only preserves an evident point of kinship with the ordinary (two-valued) situation, but assures other points of orthodoxy as well, for example:

If a conjunction ($\wedge$) takes the "falsest" and a disjunction ($\vee$) the "truest" truth-value, then:

$p \wedge$ **N**p can never be T
$p \vee$ **N**p can never be F

Note that it would surely not be plausible to subject negation to the requisite that either:

1. At least one member of the pair p,**N**p must always be true (or *must always be designated*)
2. At least one member of the pair p,**N**p must always be false (or *must always be antidesignated*)

For these conditions would exile from among the modes of negation all the traditional 3-valued logics which (like those of Łukasiewicz, Bochvar, and Kleene) are based on the truth table:

p	$\neg p$
$+T$	F
I	I
$-F$	T

A characterization of the concept that disqualified the mode of negation operative in such typical and historically significant systems would not be acceptable.

We may now introduce several styles of "negation" (in the specified sense) over and above that of Łukasiewicz ($\neg$):

p	$\daleth p$	$\neg p$
$+T$	F	F
I	F	T
$-F$	T	T

Apart from $\neg$, these modes of negation, the "intuitionist" negation $\daleth$[1] and its variant —, are the only possible 3-valued negations that are "normal" in the sense of conforming to the truth table for negation in the two-valued case (when only T's and F's are involved). If we drop this requirement of normality, still other modes of 3-valued negation become possible, such as:

p	$\overset{\frown}{\neg} p$	$\approx p$	$\simeq p$	$\widetilde{\approx} p$	$\overset{\circ}{\approx} p$	$\simeq$
$+T$	I	I	F	I	I	I
I	T	I	T	I	F	F
$-F$	I	T	I	I	I	T

Given any arbitrary mode of conjunction ($\wedge$), we can measure the *strength* of a specified mode of negation—with respect to this mode of conjunction— by the proportion of cases in which "$\alpha \wedge \mathbf{N}\alpha$" takes the truth-value F (or takes an antidesignated truth-value). Thus let the 3-valued conjunction be the familiar:

$\overset{q}{\underset{p}{\diagdown}}$	$p \wedge q$		
	T	I	F
$+T$	T	I	F
I	I	I	F
$-F$	F	F	F

Then notice that the strength of a mode of negation cannot in this case be less than $\frac{1}{3}$, since the conjunction takes the truth-value F when $/\alpha/ = F$, regardless of the truth-value of $\mathbf{N}p$. Thus we have:

[1]See Jan Łukasiewicz, "Die Logik und das Grundlagenproblem," *Les Entretiens de Zürich sur les fondements et la méthode des sciences mathématiques*, 6–9 décembre 1938, ed. by F. Gonseth (Zürich, 1941), pp. 82–100.

N	Strength
¬	$\frac{2}{3}$
⌐	$\frac{3}{3}$
—	$\frac{2}{3}$
⇁	$\frac{1}{3}$
≈	$\frac{1}{3}$
∼	$\frac{2}{3}$
≋	$\frac{1}{3}$
⇔	$\frac{2}{3}$
⇌	$\frac{2}{3}$

Of course, some of the weaker modes of negation will appear in a very strange light when one contrasts the principles (acceptable theses) that govern them with those obtaining for orthodox negation. Consider, for example, the thesis

$$(\alpha \leftrightarrow N\alpha) \leftrightarrow N(\alpha \leftrightarrow N\alpha)$$

(being of the form $p \leftrightarrow Np$) where $\leftrightarrow$ is Łukasiewiczian equivalence:

p＼^{q}	T	I	F
+T	T	I	F
I	I	T	I
−F	F	I	T

This thesis is clearly a distinctly odd one. Yet it is a logical truth (i.e., is tautologous or uniformly true) if either ⇁ or ≈ is taken to be the mode of negation (N) in question. However, this sort of anomaly cannot arise when all of the propositional connectives are normal and so conform to the two-valued case whenever only T's and F's are involved. This is so because the many-valued tautologies must then form a subset of the two-valued ones, so that the many-valued system is a fragment of the classical two-valued propositional calculus.

Let us call a many-valued mode of negation *natural* if there is no self-negating truth-value, i.e., no truth-value v such that:

$$\neg v = v$$

As discussed in Sec. 10, a mode of negation will be K-regular if only the classical, definite truth-values (T and F) yield a definite truth-value for their negation. It is then clear that:

(1) No 3-valued negation can be both natural and K-regular.

(2) The only 4-valued negation that is natural, normal, and K-regular is:

p	$\neg p$
T	F
I_1	I_2
I_2	I_1
F	T

That is, the conditions of normality, naturalness, and K-regularity uniquely determine this mode of negation in the 4-valued case.

(3) Whenever more than four truth-values are involved, then obviously various different modes of negation that are normal, natural, and K-regular can be devised.

Finally, let us characterize a mode of negation as having the *inversion* or *mirror-image* property if the truth-values at issue can be arranged in an "order of truth" and the truth table for negation simply assigns the opposite truth-value (as is the case with most of the system families we have encountered):

p	$\neg p$
T	F
I_1	I_n
I_2	I_{n-1}
.	.
.	.
.	.
I_{n-1}	I_2
I_n	I_1
F	T

A negation operator that has this mirror-image property will automatically be normal (i.e., in agreement with the two-valued case) and K-regular. It will, moreover, also have to be natural whenever an even number of truth-values are involved (though never otherwise).

The *general* situation regarding negation in many-valued logic is best approached with a view to the distinction between designated and anti-designated truth-values as introduced above. We may then contemplate the following conditions upon what is to be recognized as a many-valued variety of "negation":

(N1a) If $/p/ \in D^+(X)$, then $/\neg p/ \not\in D^+(X)$
(N1b) If $/p/ \in D^+(X)$, then $/\neg p/ \in D^-(X)$
(N2a) If $/p/ \not\in D^+(X)$, then $/\neg p/ \in D^+(X)$
(N2b) If $/p/ \in D^-(X)$, then $/\neg p/ \in D^+(X)$
(N1b′) If $/\neg p/ \in D^+(X)$, then $/p/ \in D^-(X)$
(N2b′) If $/\neg p/ \in D^-(X)$, then $/p/ \in D^+(X)$
(N3a) If $/\neg p/ \in D^-(X)$, then $/p/ \not\in D^-(X)$

Here only the pair of nonmixed conditions (N1a), and (N3a) were included among the requirements stipulated for negation in the first paragraph of this section, and even these conditions are too strong in the aggregate (since they preclude designating the I of $\mathbf{L}_3$ and $\mathbf{K}_3$, a step we noted as possibly desirable). (If *all* the rest are added, we are forced to identify the antidesignated truth-values with the nondesignated ones!) We may note that the standard 3-valued negation

p	$\neg p$
$+T$	F
I	I
$-F$	T

will satisfy *all* of these conditions if T is alone designated and F alone antidesignated. Moreover, the familiar 4-valued negation

p	$\neg p$
T	F
I_1	I_2
I_2	I_1
F	T

will satisfy all these conditions if $D^+(X) = \{T\}$ and $D^-(X) = \{F\}$, and will also do so if $D^+(X) = \{T, I_1,\}$ and $D^-(X) = \{F, I_2\}$. However, the reader can verify that even (N1a) and (N2a) are unworkable in an odd-valued Postian system $\mathbf{P}_n$, and that these two conditions would lead to designating *alternate* truth-values in an even-valued Postian system, which—given that the truth tables for conjunction and disjunction there treat the truth-values as put into an "order of truth"—would make this propositional operator unintelligible as a mode of "negation."

The listed conditions in effect come down to a series of restrictive instructions regarding designation:

(N1a) Never designate the negation of a designated value.

(N1b) Always antidesignate the negation of a designated value.

(N2a) Always designate the negation of a nondesignated value.

(N2b) Always designate the negation of an antidesignated value, etc.

These conditions will certainly be violated in some plausible cases. For example, both the 3- and the 4-valued negations just considered will violate condition (N1a) if the intermediate truth-values involved are also designated.

In the aggregate, moreover, the conditions are quite restrictive. They come down to the stipulation that the following three states of affairs are to be equivalent:

$$/p/ \not\in D^+(\mathbf{X}) \qquad /\neg p/ \in D^+(\mathbf{X}) \qquad /p/ \in D^-(\mathbf{X})$$

That is, the negation of a designated value must be nondesignated, and all nondesignated values must be antidesignated. This requires a partition of the truth-values into the two (exclusive and exhaustive) sets $D^+(\mathbf{X})$ and its complement $[D^+(\mathbf{X})]' = D^-(\mathbf{X})$ and stipulates that negation effects a "reflection" of the one set into the other. So strong a condition will certainly not be satisfied by the otherwise plausible negation operators of many-valued logics in general.

On the other hand, conditions (N1b) and (N2b)—and their primed counterparts—represent relatively plausible and pretty generally acceptable requirements (though not, as we have seen, universally applicable ones). A mode of negation may be characterized as having *the reflection property* (with respect to a fixed group of designation specifications) if the negation of a designated truth-value is always antidesignated, and conversely; i.e., if conditions (N1b) and its converse (N2b) are met. This feature at least assures that the negation of a tautology will be a contradiction and conversely.

Some further plausible conditions upon a many-valued mode of negation are as follows:

(N4) In a many-valued system involving the classical truth-values T and F (or their counterparts), negation must be *normal* in agreeing with the two-valued case when these truth-values alone are involved, so that $\neg T = F$ and $\neg F = T$.

(N5) In a many-valued system whose truth-values are arranged in an "order of truth" (such as $T, I_1, I_2, \ldots, I_n, F$), negation must have the *contraposition* property:

If $/p/ \leq /q/$, then $/\neg q/ \leq /\neg p/$ (where $\leq$ represents precedence in the ordering.

Yet another viable—but in the light of intuitionist criticisms again not necessarily plausible—restriction on many-valued negation is represented by the principle:

(N6) $/\neg\ \neg p/ = /p/$

The addition of this principle would render (N2a) and (N2b) the converses of (N1a) and (N1b), respectively, and would, moreover, render all of the primed principles derivable from their unprimed counterparts.

The Russian logician A. A. Zinov'ev has made the following claim:

> In two-valued logic the negation of truth is falsity, and the negation of falsity, truth. In many-valued logic this should be preserved in some form: if i is the truth value corresponding to truth, and k the one corresponding to falsity, then $Ni = k$ and $Nk = i$ should be the case. Without this condition every comparison becomes meaningless.[2]

On this contention the systems with a nonnormal mode of negation would be ruled out altogether. But this is doubtless too drastic a step. The workings of systems with nonnormal modes of "negation"—such as that of Postian systems—can be perfectly coherent and intelligible. Viable semantic interpretations can be provided for them (as we have seen for Post's systems and—in a different way—shall see below in the consideration of non-truth-functional systems of many-valued logic). The most that can be said is that such a system represents yet another degree of anomaly from the two-valued standpoint, so that its claims to be a system of "logic" become the more tenuous.[3] For not only are there orthodox theses of logic (viz. two-valued tautologies) which these systems do not accept—a circumstance common-place among the many-valued systems in general—but they will render accepted (tautologous) certain theses that are anomalous in that they neither are nor are analogous to two-valued tautologies.

21 Many-valued Generalizations of the Standard Two-place Connectives

One might reasonably expect a many-valued analogue of conjunction to have the following features:

---

[2]*Philosophical Problems of Many-Valued Logic* (Dordrecht, 1963), p. 91.
[3]Inherent in this way of viewing the matter is the idea that the further a system departs from orthodox logic—e.g., by including among its tautologies the outright contradictions of various customary principles such as "$\alpha \wedge \neg\alpha$" or "$\neg(\alpha \vee \neg\alpha)$" or "$\neg(\alpha \to \alpha)$"—the more tenuous its claims to constitute a "logic" will become.

(C1) When the many-valued system includes the classical truth-values T and F, then:

$$\text{If } /p/ = F, \text{ then } /p \wedge q/ = /q \wedge p/ = F$$
$$\text{If } /p/ = T, \text{ then } /p \wedge q/ = /q \wedge p/ = /q/$$
$$\text{If } /p \wedge q/ = T, \text{ then both } /p/ = T \text{ and } /q/ = T$$
$$\text{If } /p \wedge q/ = F, \text{ then either } /p/ = F \text{ or } /q/ = F$$

These conditions assure normality for this connective, i.e., agreement with two-valued conjunction when only T's and F's are involved.

(C2) When the many-valued system envisages certain truth-values as designated and some as antidesignated, we have it that:

(a) If $/p \wedge q/ \in D^+(\mathbf{X})$, then both $/p/ \in D^+(\mathbf{X})$ and $/q/ \in D^+(\mathbf{X})$
(b) If $/p \wedge q/ \notin D^+(\mathbf{X})$, then either $/p/ \notin D^+(\mathbf{X})$ or $/q/ \notin D^+(\mathbf{X})$
(c) If $/p \wedge q/ \in D^-(\mathbf{X})$, then either $/p/ \in D^-(\mathbf{X})$ or $/p/ \in D^-(\mathbf{X})$
(a') the converse of (a)
(b') the converse of (b)
(c') the converse of (c)

(C3) That the following three identity relationships hold in general:
(a) Redundancy

$$/p \wedge p/ = /p/$$

(b) Symmetry

$$/p \wedge q/ = /q \wedge p/$$

(c) Associativity

$$/(p \wedge q) \wedge r/ = /p \wedge (q \wedge r)/$$

These conditions are quite restrictive in the aggregate. Thus consider the five truth-values:

$$+T, +I_1, I_2, -I_3, -F$$

Condition (C1) above leads us to

$_p\diagdown^q$	T	I_1	I_2	I_3	F
$+T$	T	I_1	I_2	I_3	F
$+I_1$	I_1				F
I_2	I_2				F
$-I_3$	I_3				F
$-F$	F	F	F	F	F

$p \wedge q$

where no T's or F's can occur at the unmarked positions. If we also impose condition (C3), we obtain

$\backslash q$ $p\backslash$	T	I_1	I_2	I_3	F
			$p \wedge q$		
$+T$	T	I_1	I_2	I_3	F
$+I_1$	I_1	I_1	x	y	F
I_2	I_2	x	I_2	z	F
$-I_3$	I_3	y	z	I_3	F
$-F$	F	F	F	F	F

with x, y, and z all $\neq T$ and all $\neq F$. By (C2a) and (C2b) we have $x = I_2$. By (C2c) y must be I_3, and z must be I_3. Thus with the indicated designations (C1) to (C3) will uniquely determine the truth table:

$\backslash q$ $p\backslash$	T	I_1	I_2	I_3	F
			$p \wedge q$		
$+T$	T	I_1	I_2	I_3	F
$+I_1$	I_1	I_1	I_2	I_3	F
I_2	I_2	I_2	I_2	I_3	F
$-I_3$	I_3	I_3	I_3	I_3	F
$-F$	F	F	F	F	F

We now resume the listing of plausible conditions for many-valued modes of conjunction.

(C4) When the truth-values can be arranged in an "order of truth" (say $T, I_1, I_2, \ldots, I_n, F$ or some numerical analogue), then $/p \wedge q/$ must be the "falsest" of $/p/$ and $/q/$. When operative, this requirement encompasses (C1) and (C2) above. Moreover, when designation applies to only an initial part of the list and antidesignation to only a terminal part, then this requirement also encompasses (C2) above.

(C5) When the truth-values can be arranged in an "order of truth," then:

1. If $/p/ \le /q/$, then $/p \wedge r/ \le /q \wedge r/$, for any r
2. If $/p/ \le /q/ \le /r/$, then $/p \wedge q/ \le /p \wedge r/$

The situation is analogous with regard to a many-valued analogue of disjunction. One might reasonably expect a many-valued analogue of disjunction to have the following features:

(D1) When the many-valued system includes the classical truth-values T and F, then:

> If $/p/ = T$, then $/p \lor q/ = /q \lor p/ = T$
> If $/p/ = F$, then $/p \lor q/ = /q \lor p/ = /q/$
> If $/p \lor q/ = T$, then either $/p/ = T$ or $/q/ = T$
> If $/p \lor q/ = F$, then both $/p/ = F$ and $/q/ = F$

These conditions assure normality for this connective, i.e., agreement with two-valued disjunction when only T's and F's are involved.

(D2) When the many-valued system envisages certain truth-values as designated and others as antidesignated, we have it that:

    (a) If $/p \lor q/ \in D^+(\mathbf{X})$, then either $/p/ \in D^+(\mathbf{X})$ or $/q/ \in D^+(\mathbf{X})$, or both

    (b) If $/p \lor q/ \notin D^+(\mathbf{X})$, then both $/p/ \notin D^+(\mathbf{X})$ and $/q/ \notin D^+(\mathbf{X})$

    (c) If $/p \lor q/ \in D^-(\mathbf{X})$, then both $/p/ \in D^-(\mathbf{X})$ and $/q/ \in D^-(\mathbf{X})$

    (a') the converse of (a)

    (b') the converse of (b)

    (c') the converse of (c)

(D3) That the following two identity relationships hold in general:

    (a) Redundancy

$$/p \lor p/ = /p/$$

    (b) Symmetry

$$/p \lor q/ = /q \lor p/$$

    (c) Associativity

$$/(p \lor q) \lor r/ = /p \lor (q \lor r)/$$

In the aggregate these conditions are quite restrictive. Let us again consider the five truth-values:

$$+T, +I_1, I_2, -I_3, -F$$

There it is readily verified that conditions (C1) to (C3) will uniquely determine the truth table:

$p \backslash q$	T	I_1	I_2	I_3	F
T	T	T	T	T	T
I_1	T	I_1	I_1	I_1	I_1
I_2	T	I_1	I_2	I_2	I_2
I_3	T	I_1	I_2	I_3	I_3
F	T	I_1	I_2	I_3	F

$p \lor q$

We thus see that the preceding conditions for "well-behaved" modes of conjunction and disjunction narrow the field quite drastically. Specifically in the 5-valued example considered they restrict our horizon to the two most familiar cases.

We now continue with the listing of plausible conditions for many-valued modes of disjunction.

(D4) When the truth-values can be arranged in "order of truth"

$$T, I_1, I_2, \ldots, I_n, F$$

then $/p \vee q/$ must be the "truest" of $/p/$ and $/q/$. When operative, this requirement encompasses (D1) and (D2) above. Moreover, when designation applies to only an initial part of the list and antidesignated to only a terminal part, then this requirement also encompasses (D2) above.

(D5) When the truth-values can be arranged in an "order of truth," then:

1. If $/p/ \leq /q/$, then $/p \vee r/ \leq /q \vee r/$, for any r
2. If $/p/ \leq /q/ \leq /r/$, then $/p \vee q/ \leq /q \vee r/$

These final two requirements represent powerfully restrictive conditions. They automatically restrict us—as (C4) and (C5) above do also—to the connectives at issue in the $\mathbf{L}_n$ or $\mathbf{S}_n$ sequence.

Many of the systems of many-valued logic we have encountered (e.g., the sequences $\mathbf{L}_n$ and $\mathbf{S}_n$) meet all of these conditions (when they are applicable). An interesting exception, however, is formed by the product logics. Consider again the many-valued system $\mathbf{C}_2 \times \mathbf{C}_2$:

p	$\neg p$	$\begin{matrix}\diagdown q\\p\diagdown\end{matrix}$	$p \wedge q$ TT	TF	FT	FF	$p \vee q$ TT	TF	FT	FF
TT	FF	TT	TT	TF	FT	FF	TT	TT	TT	TT
TF	FT	TF	TF	TF	FF	FF	TT	TF	TT	TF
FT	TF	FT	FT	FF	FT	FF	TT	TT	FT	FT
FF	TT	FF	FF	FF	FF	FF	TT	TF	FT	FF

Suppose that *TT* alone is designated and *FF* alone antidesignated. Then since

$$TF \vee FT = TT$$

we have it that $/p \vee q/ \in D^+$ can happen when neither $/p/ \in D^+$ nor $/q/ \in D^+$. (When the context permits, we may—as here—suppress explicit reference to a system after D^+ or D^-.) And since

$$TF \wedge FT = FF$$

we have it that $/p \wedge q/ \in D^-$ can happen when neither $/p/ \in D^-$ nor $/q/ \in D^-$. Thus both principles (C2b) and (D2a) are violated by this perfectly viable system of many-valued logic, which can also be seen to violate conditions (C4), (C5), (D4), and (D5).

The situation regarding the implication relationships of many-valued logic is extremely complex. One might reasonably expect a many-valued mode of implication to have the following features:

(I1) When the many-valued system includes the classical truth-values T and F, then for any and every truth-value v:

$$T \rightarrow v = v \text{ (i.e., if } /p/ = T, \text{ then } /p \rightarrow q/ = /q/)$$
$$v \rightarrow F = \neg v \text{ (i.e., if } /q/ = F, \text{ then } /p \rightarrow q/ = /\neg p/)$$

This suffices to assure normality for implication (i.e., agreement with the two-valued case).

(I2) When the many-valued system envisages certain truth-values as designated and others as antidesignated, we have the following conditions:

(a) Reflexivity

Always: $/p \rightarrow p/ \in D^+(\mathbf{X})$

(b) Transitivity

Whenever both $/p \rightarrow q/ \in D^+(\mathbf{X})$ and $/q \rightarrow r/ \in D^+(\mathbf{X})$, then $/p \rightarrow r/ \in D^+(\mathbf{X})$

(c) Nonsymmetry

For some p,q: $/p \rightarrow q/ \in D^+(\mathbf{X})$ but $/q \rightarrow p/ \notin D^+(\mathbf{X})$

(d) *Modus ponens* condition

Whenever both $/p/ \in D^+(\mathbf{X})$ and $/p \rightarrow q/ \in D^+(\mathbf{X})$, then $/q/ \in D^+(\mathbf{X})$

(e) *Modus tollens* condition

1. Whenever $/p \rightarrow q/ \in D^+(\mathbf{X})$ and $/q/ \notin D^+(\mathbf{X})$, then $/p/ \notin D^+(\mathbf{X})$
2. Whenever $/p \rightarrow q/ \in D^+(\mathbf{X})$ and $/q/ \in D^-(\mathbf{X})$, then $/p/ \in D^-(\mathbf{X})$

(f) *Modus ponens* applicability

For some p,q: $/p \rightarrow q/ \in D^+(\mathbf{X})$ and $/p/ \in D^+(\mathbf{X})$

(g) *Modus tollens* applicability

1. For some p,q: $/p \rightarrow q/ \in D^+(\mathbf{X})$ and $/q/ \notin D^+(\mathbf{X})$
2. For some p,q: $/p \rightarrow q/ \in D^+(\mathbf{X})$ and $/q/ \in D^-(\mathbf{X})$

(h) Designation enhancement

1. If $/p/ \notin D^+(\mathbf{X})$ and $/q/ \in D^+(\mathbf{X})$, then $/p \rightarrow q/ \in D^+(\mathbf{X})$
2. If $/p/ \in D^-(\mathbf{X})$ and $/q/ \in D^+(\mathbf{X})$, then $/p \rightarrow q/ \in D^+(\mathbf{X})$

(i) Designation degradation

1. If $/p/ \in D^+(\mathbf{X})$ and $/q/ \notin D^+(\mathbf{X})$, then $/p \rightarrow q/ \notin D^+(\mathbf{X})$
2. If $/p/ \in D^+(\mathbf{X})$ and $/q/ \in D^-(\mathbf{X})$, then $/p \rightarrow q/ \in D^-(\mathbf{X})$

It must be stressed that, in the light of such requirements, the capacity of a many-valued connective to serve as a mode of implication (or whatever) will not depend solely upon its defining truth table, but will also hinge essentially on the designation choices that are made. Consider, for example, the 3-valued implication of Łukasiewicz:

$q \backslash p$ $p \to q$	T	I	F
T	T	I	F
I	T	T	I
F	T	T	T

If *T* alone is designated, then this implication will satisfy the *modus ponens* condition, but if *I* is also designated, then this condition will fail. For then *I* is designated, and $I \to F$ is designated, but *F* is not designated.

It deserves note that the totality of these conditions is not strong enough to determine uniquely even a 3-valued implication. Thus, consider the 3-valued implication:

$p \to q$	T	I	F
+T	T		
I		T	
−F			T

We suppose that *T* alone is designated and *F* alone antidesignated. Then the *T*'s in the diagonal are determined by condition (a). Condition (h) guarantees that all other entries of the first column will be *T*. Condition (i) guarantees that all other entries of the first row will be *F*. This produces:

$p \to q$	T	I	F
+T	T	F	F
I	T	T	x
−F	T	y	T

Condition (e) requires that $x \neq T$. Conditions (b), (c), (d), and (f) are now assured. There will thus be *six* 3-valued implication matrices (two chosen for *x* *times* three choices for *y*) that will satisfy all of the conditions (a) to (i). The failure of these conditions to be more narrowly determinative in even this 3-valued case can be taken as an indication of the relative weakness of these conditions. On the other hand, it is certainly the case that not every plausible many-valued implication will satisfy all of these conditions. For example, the 3-valued implication of Łukasiewicz (given above) will not satisfy condition (*I*2d) if T and I alone are designated and F alone anti-designated.

We continue now to list some further features that one might reasonably expect of a many-valued mode of implication:

(I3) That the following identity relationship holds in general:

If $/p \to q/ = /q \to p/$, then $/p/ = /q/$ (or equivalently: Whenever $/p/ \neq /q/$, then $/p \to q/ \neq /q \to p/$)

(I4) When the truth-values can be arranged in "order of truth"

$$T, I_1, I_2, \ldots, I_n, F$$

then (using the mathematical $\geq$, to indicate the order relationship of this sequence), we will have:

(a) Always $/p \to q/ \geq /q/$
(b) Always $/p \to q/ \geq \exists/p/$ (where $\exists v$ is *the opposite* of the truth-values of v in the "order of truth," its counterpart in the *reversed* order)
(c) Whenever $/p/ \geq /q/$, then $/r \to p/ \geq /r \to q/$
(d) Whenever $/q/ \geq /p/$, then $/p \to r/ \geq /q \to r/$
(e) Whenever $/p \to q/ = T$, then $/q/ \geq /p/$
(f) Whenever $/q/ \geq /p/$, then $/p \to q/ = T$
(g) Whenever $/p \to q/ \in D^+$, then $/q/ \geq /p/$
(h) Whenever $/q/ \geq /p/$, then $/p \to q/ \in D^+$

This last group of principles, (I4), requires some discussion. Consider the implication matrix:

$\searrow^q$ $p\searrow$	T	I_1	I_2	$\cdots$	I_n	F
T	T					
I_1	T					
I_2	T					
.	.					
.	.					
.	.					
I_n	T					
F	T	T	T	$\cdots$	T	T

Principle (a) asserts that no entry in the matrix can be "falser" than its column heading. Principle (b) asserts that no entry can be "falser" than the *opposite* of its row heading. These two principles assure the T entries that are given in the matrix. Principle (c) asserts that every column must "dominate" its succeeding column in truth. Principle (d) states that every row is dominated by its succeeding row in truth. Principles (e) and (f) are very strong conditions that can certainly not be expected to hold in general. Specifically principle (e) asserts that only T's will occur at and below the main diagonal, and principle (f) asserts that no T's will be found above the main diagonal.[1] (The implication matrix of the standard systems S_n represents the most emphatic way of satisfying this requirement.[2])

If implication observes the (somewhat implausible) principle

(1) $/p \rightarrow q/ \in D^+(X)$ iff $/p/ \notin D^+(X)$ or $/q/ \in D^+(X)$

then $\rightarrow$ will satisfy all the axioms of the system $\mathbf{C}_2^{\supset}$, the purely implicational fragment of $\mathbf{C}_2$. The axioms of $\mathbf{C}_2^{\supset}$ are:

($\supset$1) $\alpha \supset (\beta \supset \alpha)$
($\supset$2) $[(\alpha \supset \beta) \supset \alpha] \supset \alpha$
($\supset$3) $(\alpha \supset \beta) \supset [(\beta \supset \gamma) \supset (\alpha \supset \gamma)]$

That an implication obeying (1) will satisfy these axioms can be seen by letting '$\in$' represent "$\in D^+$" and '$\notin$' represent "$\notin D^+$" and then tabulating the resultant relationships in a truth-table fashion. Thus consider the following implication of ($\supset$1):

p	q	$q \supset p$	$p \supset (q \supset p)$
$\in$	$\in$	$\in$	$\in$
$\in$	$\notin$	$\in$	$\in$
$\notin$	$\in$	$\notin$	$\in$
$\notin$	$\notin$	$\in$	$\in$

Similar reasonings can be carried through for ($\supset$2) and ($\supset$3). Since (1) also guarantees *modus ponens*, it follows that any many-valued logic whose truth table for implication obeys (1) will include the entire pure implicational fragment of $\mathbf{C}_2$. Thus, both of the following 3-valued implications will yield this fragment:

$\begin{array}{c}\\[-0.5em]{}^q\diagdown\\[-0.5em]{}^p\end{array}$	$p \rightarrow q$		
	T	I	F
$+T$	T	I	F
$+I$	T	T	F
F	T	T	T

$\begin{array}{c}\\[-0.5em]{}^q\diagdown\\[-0.5em]{}^p\end{array}$	$p \rightarrow q$		
	T	I	F
$+T$	T	I	F
$+I$	T	I	F
F	T	T	T

---

[1] For a quite extensive discussion of many-valued connectives that considers many of the conditions discussed in this section, see Arto Salomaa, "On Many-Valued Systems of Logic," *Ajatus*, vol. 22 (1959), pp. 115–159.

[2] The consequences of adopting various combinations of the implication conditions set forth here are discussed in Arto Salomaa, *op. cit.* (see pp. 128–135).

Along strictly similar lines it is possible to show that if we supplement (1) with

(2) $/\neg p/ \in D^+(\mathbf{X})$ iff $/p/ \notin D^+(\mathbf{X})$

then the resulting system must yield the entire negation-implication fragment of the classical propositional calculus, and must thus contain a model of this entire system itself. An example of a many-valued system satisfying these conditions is:

p	$\neg p$		q	$p \to q$			
		p		T	I_1	I_2	F
$+T$	F	$+T$		T	I_1	F	F
$+I_1$	I_2	$+I_1$		T	I_1	I_2	F
I_2	I_1	I_2		T	I_1	I_1	I_1
F	T	F		T	T	T	T

We shall deal wtih the conditions upon equivalence in many-valued logic somewhat more briefly. The principal conditions are:

(E1) Equivalence must be reflexive, symmetric, and transitive (i.e., it must be an "equivalence relation"). In general, then

(a) $/p \leftrightarrow p/ \in D^+(\mathbf{X})$, for all p
(b) $/p \leftrightarrow q/ \in D^+(\mathbf{X})$ iff $/q \leftrightarrow p/ \in D^+(\mathbf{X})$
(c) If $/p \leftrightarrow q/ \in D^+(\mathbf{X})$ and $/q \leftrightarrow r/ \in D^+(\mathbf{X})$, then $/p \leftrightarrow r/ \in D^+(\mathbf{X})$

When the specified truth-value T (truth) or a counterpart is among the truth-values at issue, then:

(a') $/p \leftrightarrow p/ = T$
(b') $/p \leftrightarrow q/ = T$ iff $/q \leftrightarrow p/ = T$
(c') If $/p \leftrightarrow q/ = T$ and $/q \leftrightarrow r/ = T$, then $/p \leftrightarrow r/ = T$

Moreover, the symmetry condition might be strengthened to:

(b'') $/p \leftrightarrow q/ = /q \leftrightarrow p/$

(E2) The truth status of $p \leftrightarrow q$ must hinge upon a close kinship between the truth-values of p and q:

(a) $/p \leftrightarrow q/ \in D^+(\mathbf{X})$ iff $/p/ = /q/$
(b) $/p \leftrightarrow q/ = T$ iff $/p/ = /q/$
(c) $/p \leftrightarrow q/ \in D^-(\mathbf{X})$ iff $/p/ \neq /q/$
(d) $/p \leftrightarrow q/ = F$ iff $/p/ \neq /q/$
(e) If $/p/ \in D^+(\mathbf{X})$ and $/q/ \notin D^+(\mathbf{X})$, then $/p \leftrightarrow q/ \notin D^+(\mathbf{X})$
(f) If $/p/ \in D^+(\mathbf{X})$ and $/q/ \in D^-(\mathbf{X})$, then $/p \leftrightarrow q/ \in D^-(\mathbf{X})$
(g) If $/p/ \in D^+(\mathbf{X})$ and $/q/ \notin D^+(\mathbf{X})$, then $/p \leftrightarrow q/ \in D^-(\mathbf{X})$

(E3) The truth status of an equivalence is closely bound up with certain other connectives:

(a) $/p \leftrightarrow q/ \in D^+(X)$ iff both $/p \rightarrow q/ \in D^+(X)$ and $/q \rightarrow p/ \in D^+(X)$
(b) $/p \leftrightarrow q/ = T$ iff both $/p \rightarrow q/ = T$ and $/q \rightarrow p/ = T$
(c) $/p \leftrightarrow q/ = /(p \rightarrow q) \wedge (q \rightarrow p)/$

It deserves note that conditions (E2b) and (E3a) are independent in that neither of these conditions entails the other. That (E2b) need not be satisfied when (E3a) is, is obvious. That (E3a) need not be satisfied when (E2b) is, is shown by the system $\mathbf{K_3}$:

p	$\neg p$	$\begin{smallmatrix}q\\p\end{smallmatrix}$	$p \wedge q$			$p \vee q$			$p \rightarrow q$			$p \leftrightarrow q$		
			T	I	F	T	I	F	T	I	F	T	I	F
$+T$	F	$+T$	T	I	F	T	T	T	T	I	F	T	I	F
I	I	I	I	I	F	T	I	I	T	I	I	I	I	I
F	T	F	F	F	F	T	I	F	T	T	T	F	I	T

(E4) If the truth-values can be arranged in an "order of truth" (as with $T, I_1, I_2, \ldots, I_n, F$), then

(a) $/p \rightarrow q/ \geq /p \leftrightarrow q/$
(b) If $/p/ \geq /q/ \geq /r/$, then $/p \leftrightarrow q/ \geq /p \leftrightarrow r/$

(E5) When only the specific truth-values T and F (or their analogues) are involved, we have agreement with the two-valued case:

$$T \leftrightarrow T = F \leftrightarrow F = T$$
$$T \leftrightarrow F = F \leftrightarrow T = F$$

To this point we have discussed the more or less plausible conditions upon the different many-valued connectives pretty much in isolation. It is, however, of substantial interest to investigate the properties of systems that conform to various constellations of these principles.

Consider any many-valued system that is built up on the following set of principles:[3]

(1) $/\neg p/ \in D^+(X)$ iff $/p/ \notin D^+(X)$
(2) $/p \wedge q/ \in D^+(X)$ iff both $/p/ \in D^+(X)$ and $/q/ \in D^+(X)$
(3) $/p \vee q/ \in D^+(X)$ iff either $/p/ \in D^+(X)$ or $/q/ \in D^+(X)$
(4) $/p \rightarrow q/ \in D^+(X)$ iff either $/p/ \notin D^+(X)$ or $/q/ \in D^+(X)$
(5) $/p \leftrightarrow q/ \in D^+(X)$ iff both $/p \rightarrow q/ \in D^+(X)$ and $/q \rightarrow p/ \in D^+(X)$

The truth tables of any such system will obviously be reduced to those of $\mathbf{C_2}$ if all of the designated truth-values are identified with one another and

---

[3]These conditions are called the "standard conditions" for the several connectives by J. B. Rosser and A. R. Turquette. See their *Many-Valued Logic* (Amsterdam, 1952), p. 26.

all of the undesignated truth-values are also identified with one another.[4] It thus follows that the stock of tautologies of such a system will be exactly the same as the tautologies of C_2. In a significant sense, then, an insistence upon the whole group of principles (1) to (5) amounts to a choice of classical two-valued logic.

It is of interest to examine in the light of the preceding paragraph the infinite-valued system whose truth-values are taken from the interval 0 to 1 (inclusive) with 1 alone designated, and which is subject to the truth rules:

$$
\begin{aligned}
/{\neg}p/ &= 1 - /p/ \\
/p \wedge q/ &= \min \left[/p/,/q/\right] \\
/p \vee q/ &= \max \left[/p/,/q/\right] \\
/p \to q/ &= \left\{ \begin{matrix} 1 \\ 0 \end{matrix} \right\} \text{ according as } \left\{ \begin{matrix} \text{either } /p/ \neq 1 \text{ or } /q/ = 1 \\ \text{otherwise} \end{matrix} \right. \\
/p \leftrightarrow q/ &= /(p \to q) \wedge (q \to p)/
\end{aligned}
$$

Since this system—let us call it $S_\aleph^*$—is so designed as to satisfy all of the principles (1) to (5), it follows immediately that it will have exactly the same tautologies as C_2.

It is of incidental interest that any even-valued system $S_{2k}^{\mathfrak{D}}$ with exactly the first half of its truth-values designated[5] will obey all of the principles (1) to (5). Therefore every even-valued $S_n^{\mathfrak{D}}$ (with the indicated designations) will—as we have already seen for another point of view—have to be such that:

$$T(S_n^{\mathfrak{D}}) = T(C_2)$$

And exactly the same will be true of the system $S_{[\aleph]}^{\mathfrak{D}}$, the system whose truth-values are all the real numbers from 0 to 1 inclusive *except for* $\frac{1}{2}$, with all of the values v such that $\frac{1}{2} < v \leq 1$ as designated values, and with exactly the same truth rules as those for $S_\aleph^{\mathfrak{D}}$. Thus we have

$$T(S_{[\aleph]}^{\mathfrak{D}}) = T(C_2)$$

so that we have here an example of infinite-valued systems whose stock of tautologies is exactly the same as that of classical two-valued logic.

In view of the restrictiveness of the foregoing set of conditions (1) to (5), it is of interest to consider the somewhat weakened set:

---

[4]This is the defining feature of the many-valued systems Alonzo Church characterizes as "normal" in the sense of R. Carnap (C-normal) and regarding whose abstract features he offers some interesting observations in his *Introduction to Mathematical Logic*, vol. I (Princeton, 1956), p. 117 (sec. 19.10).

[5]That is, with the designations $+T, +I_1, +I_2, \ldots, +I_{k-1}, I_k, \ldots, I_{k-2}, F$.

(1') $/p/ \notin D^+(\mathbf{X})$ if $/\neg p/ \in D^+(\mathbf{X})$
(2) $/p \wedge q/ \in D^+(\mathbf{X})$ iff both $/p/ \in D^+(\mathbf{X})$ and $/q/ \in D^+(\mathbf{X})$
(3) $/p \vee q/ \in D^+(\mathbf{X})$ iff either $/p/ \in D^+(\mathbf{X})$ or $/q/ \in D^+(\mathbf{X})$
(4') $/p \rightarrow q/ \notin D^+(\mathbf{X})$ if $/p/ \in D^+(\mathbf{X})$ and $/q/ \notin D^+(\mathbf{X})$[6]
(5) $/p \leftrightarrow q/ \in D^+(\mathbf{X})$ iff both $/p \rightarrow q/ \in D^+(\mathbf{X})$ and $/q \rightarrow p/ \in D^+(\mathbf{X})$

All conditions will be satisfied by the even-valued standard systems (and variants) and for the odd-valued ones if only truth-values before the self-negating one (in the "order of truth") are designated.[7] That this modified set of conditions is in fact enormously weaker than the initial set is shown by the system $\mathbf{K}_3$ which, while satisfying all the conditions, yields no tautologies whatsoever (since any formula must take on the truth-value 2 when all its constituent propositional variables do so):

p	$\neg p$		$p \wedge q$ 1 2 3	$p \vee q$ 1 2 3	$p \rightarrow q$ 1 2 3	$p \leftrightarrow q$ 1 2 3
+1	3	+1	1 2 3	1 1 1	1 2 3	1 2 3
2	2	2	2 2 3	1 2 2	1 2 2	2 2 2
3	1	3	3 3 3	1 2 3	1 1 1	3 2 1

A delicate situation arises with regard to such lists of "requirements" for many-valued connectives. As indicated in the earlier discussion, one would certainly not want to stipulate that a many-valued connective satisfies *all* of the relevant requirements, and so be driven back again to the system $\mathbf{C}_2$ (by contemplation of which they were originally arrived at). On the other hand, if the connectives of a system did not satisfy *many or most* of the pertinent requirements, we would hardly be tempted to speak of these connectives as many-valued versions of "conjunction" or "disjunction" or "implication," etc. But we must recognize that the question of the capacity of many-valued connectives to serve in such a role is invariably a matter of degree, of more or less, which cannot be settled in a hard-and-fast yes-or-no manner.

These conditions point toward the difficult and complex question:

> By what criteria can one go about deciding whether an arbitrary, abstractly given set of truth tables for otherwise nondescript wff-generating operators represents a "logic"?

It would seem that at least conditions of the following general type would figure among the operative criteria:

---

[6]Note that (4') is equivalent with the *modus ponens* condition:

    If $/p/ \in D^+(\mathbf{X})$ and $/p \rightarrow q/ \in D^+(\mathbf{X})$, then $/q/ \in D^+(\mathbf{X})$

[7]If the self-negating truth-value is designated, condition (1') will be violated.

(1) There must be a subset of the truth-values such that if all these are designated, then some formulas (wffs) will be tautologous (i.e., uniformly take on truth-values from this subset). And presumably one would want to add another analogous requirement for antidesignated truth-values to generate contradictions.

(2) There must be some way of interpreting the operators in terms of the orthodox logical conceptions of negation, disjunction, conjunction, etc. Ideally, there should be outright negation analogues, disjunction analogues, etc., conforming in significant measure to the principles of orthodoxy specified in the present section. (Note that the determinations about this have to be made in an interlocked way and that the issue is one of a matter of degree.)

(3) Once certain operators have been identified as analogues of the orthodox ones according to condition (2), then these operators will have to conform to condition (1) in that the tautologous formulas in which they alone figure must bear an appropriately close relationship to the two-valued situation, and ideally—but not, as we have seen, inevitably—will be a subset of their counterpart tautologies in the classical, two-valued logic.

(4) It would appear, moreover, that if the formalism is to be adequate as a logic it must have the key feature of autodescriptivity with respect to a classically two-valued truth-value assignment operator (in the manner examined in some detail in Sec. 14). It must be capable of furnishing at least the logical machinery needed at the metalinguistic level for its own formal development.

It seems anomalous that one cannot deal with the question of what constitutes a many-valued "logic" in a sharper, less indecisive way. But the complexities of the issue preclude a simpler solution. (We shall resume the topic at greater length in Chap. 3.)

Appendix

It is useful to consider a concrete example of a many-valued system which, while not entirely implausible in its conception, has rather wild and unacceptable consequences. The system to be adduced will satisfy conditions (1) and (2) set forth at the close of the preceding discussion, but will violate condition (3).

Consider an infinite-valued logic whose truth-values are the real numbers from 0 to 1 (inclusive), with all values $\geq \frac{1}{2}$ as designated. Let the truth rule for negation be as usual, and let conjunction be represented by the averaging operator

Δ discussed in Sec. 6 above. Disjunction, implication, and equivalence can be defined as usual:

$$p \lor q \quad \text{FOR} \quad \neg(\neg p \land \neg q)$$
$$p \supset q \quad \text{FOR} \quad \neg p \lor q$$
$$p \equiv q \quad \text{FOR} \quad (p \supset q) \land (q \supset p)$$

This leads to the group of truth rules:

$$/\neg p/ \ = 1 - /p/$$
$$/p \land q/ = \tfrac{1}{2}(/p/ + /q/)$$
$$/p \lor q/ = /\neg(\neg p \land \neg q)/ = \tfrac{1}{2}(/p/ + /q/) = /p \land q/$$
$$/p \supset q/ = /\neg p \lor q/ = \tfrac{1}{2}(1 - /p/ + /q/) = /\neg(p \land \neg q)/$$
$$/p \equiv q/ = /(p \supset q) \land (q \supset p)/ \ (\text{NOTE: This will invariably be} = \tfrac{1}{2}!)$$

This system has various plausible characteristics such as the tautologousness of the following:

$$\alpha \lor \neg\alpha$$
$$\alpha \supset \alpha$$
$$(\alpha \land \beta) \supset \alpha$$

Moreover, the implication relationship of the system is well behaved in that it has the *modus ponens* feature: If $/p/$ and $/p \supset q/$ are designated, then $/q/$ must also be designated. But the system has certain wildly peculiar features, of which perhaps the strangest is that *any proposition will be tautologously equivalent to any other proposition*. Thus despite its large degree of similarity to viable systems of many-valued logic, a system such as this cannot lay claim to representing a "system of *logic*."

22 The Law of Contradiction in Many-valued Logic

The motivation afforded by the idea of overcoming the classical "Law of Contradiction"—sometimes also referred to as the "Law of Noncontradiction"—was one major impetus in the development of many-valued logics. There has, however, been considerable disagreement as to the exact content of this law, and it can certainly be construed along various divergent lines.

Traditional logicians generally construed the Law of Contradiction to say that *nothing can be both A and not-A*, or, in a somewhat different formulation, that "*B is A*" and "*B is not-A*" cannot both be true together— at least one member of the pair must be false. Though this traditional formulation casts it within the language of predication, the principle is often identified with a theorem of orthodox propositional logic: $\sim(\alpha \ \& \sim\alpha)$. Actually, a counterpart of this in predicate logic, namely "$\sim(\exists x)(Px \ \& \sim Px)$," might seem a more appropriate formulation.

At any rate, in the context of many-valued logic, this "law" can take on a variety of forms. In a canvass of the primary possibilities, it will emerge that the Law of Contradiction can be construed as:

(i) The principle that the thesis

$$\alpha \wedge \neg\alpha$$

is to be rejected as a logically false (self-contradictory) proposition.[1]

(ii) The principle that the thesis

$$\neg(\alpha \wedge \neg\alpha)$$

is to be accepted as an asserted (logically true or tautologous) proposition.[2]

(iii) The principle that at least one member of the pair $p, \neg p$ must inevitably be false:

Not both $/p/ \neq F$ and $/\neg p/ \neq F$

that is:

$(/p/ = F)$-or-$(/\neg p/ = F)$

(iv) The "exclusion principle" that p and $\neg p$ cannot both be true together, i.e., at most one can be true. We cannot have both $/p/ = T$ and $/\neg p/ = T$, that is

$(/p/ \neq T)$-or-$(/\neg p/ \neq T)$

(v) A proposition cannot be both true and false. At least one member of the pair

$$/p/ = T \qquad /p/ = F$$

must be false, that is:

$(/p/ \neq T)$-or-$(/p/ \neq F)$

(vi) A proposition can assume only a single truth-value: it is always false to say that a certain proposition both takes a certain truth-value and yet takes another different one. Whenever $v \neq v'$, then at least one member of the pair

$$/p/ = v \qquad /p/ = v'$$

must be false.

---

[1] More fully, the rejected thesis at issue could be formulated as: $(\exists\alpha)(\alpha \wedge \neg\alpha)$.
[2] More fully, the accepted thesis at issue could be formulated as: $(\forall\alpha)\neg(\alpha \wedge \neg\alpha)$.

The question of whether the Law of Contradiction obtains in many-valued logic is thus a *complex* question that is subject to a variety of distinctly divergent interpretations. The following observations are in order:

(1) With respect to construction (i), there is no reason why this version of the principle should not obtain in a system of many-valued logic, and in fact "$\alpha \land \neg\alpha$" is a contradiction in many of the systems we have considered. It is not, however, a contradiction in all of them. In particular (and this is of considerable historical importance) it fails for the system $Ł_3$ of Łukasiewicz (with F alone antidesignated), as well as for the 3-valued systems P_3, B_3, and K_3 of Post, Bochvar, and Kleene.

(2) In construction (ii), the principle holds in many systems of many-valued logic. Again, it fails for $Ł_3$ (with T alone designated), as well as the 3-valued systems P_3, B_3, and K_3. It should be noted, moreover, that whenever the negation operator $\neg$ has the reflection property (the reversal feature of taking antidesignated values into designated ones, and conversely), then this second version of the principle is equivalent with the first.

(3) In construction (iii), the principle comes down to a highly restrictive condition on the truth table for negation:

p	$\neg p$
T	F
I_1	(1)
I_2	(2)
.	
.	
.	
I_n	(n)
F	?

Construction (iii) asserts in effect that all the positions (1) to (n) must be filled with F's (though we are left free to fill in the ?-position as we please).

(4) Construction (iv) represents a very weak (and highly plausible) construction of the principle. All of the many-valued systems we have considered obey this version of the principle, and for a very good reason. In this version the principle would be violated only if it happened that the truth tables for $\neg$ had the feature that:

$$\neg T = T$$

But in this case ¬ could hardly be conceived of as representing a mode of "negation."

(5) It should be noted that construction (iii) yields (iv) (since $\neg T = F$ and $\neg F = T$).

(6) Construction (v) in effect claims that the truth status of a proposition can never be so irregular that the proposition would take both T and F as its truth-value. Though this principle is very plausible, we shall see in Sec. 26 that it is not an inevitable principle of many-valued logic.

(7) In construction (vi), the principle comes down to legislating the two-valued point of view with respect to one special category of proposition, viz. truth-value assignment statements themselves. Given this construction of the principle, if a statement of the form

$$/p/ = v$$

is ever *true* (and if not, we cannot say that a family of many-valued truth-values is at issue), then all statements of the form

$$/p/ = v'$$

will be *false* whenever $v' \neq v$. In short, only the classical truth-values T and F come into view when the question is one of the truth-value status of the truth-value assignment propositions themselves. That this version of the principle does not represent a necessary feature of many-valued logics should be apparent from Sec. 14. As we have seen on page 85, this plausible feature which holds for virtually all systems of many-valued logic considered to date is not to be regarded as a necessary characteristic of many-valued logics in general.

(8) It should be noted that construction (vi) yields (v) (since $T \neq F$).

(9) Constructions (i) and (ii) differ from the rest in that both negation and conjunction are involved. Constructions (iii) and (iv) involve only negation, while (v) and (vi) involve no connectives at all.

We may thus see that there are several distinct versions of the Law of Contradiction for many-valued logic, and that only one version of the principle—viz. construction (iv)—can plausibly be held to represent a strictly necessary feature of many-valued logics in general.

It remains to reconsider the topic from a variant perspective. Let us assume the many-valued point of view with the classical *truth* and *falsity* generalized to a multiplicity of *designated* (truth-like) and *anti-designated* (false-like) truth-values. Some of the aforementioned versions of the Law of Contradiction can then be reshaped accordingly.

Let us again adopt two items of notation, namely let:

$D^+ = D^+(X) =$ the (set of) designated truth-values of the system **X**
$D^- = D^-(X) =$ the (set of) antidesignated truth-values of the system **X**

We can now effect a reformulation of two of the previously considered versions of the Law of Contradiction. Items (iii) to (v) will have the following counterparts:

(iii′) The principle that at least one member of the pair p, $\neg p$ must inevitably take on an antidesignated truth-value:

$$[/p/ \in D^-(X)]\text{-or-}[/\neg p/ \in D^-(X)]$$

(iv′) The "exclusion principle" that p and $\neg p$ cannot both take on designated truth-values:

$$[/p/ \not\subseteq D^+(X)]\text{-or-}[/\neg p/ \not\subseteq D^+(X)]$$

(v′) The principle that a proposition cannot take both a designated and an antidesignated truth-value:

$$(/p/ \not\subseteq D^+(X))\text{-or-}(/p/ \not\subseteq D^-(X))$$

Several observations are in order with respect to these reformulations:

(1) Principle (iii′) can be looked on as a procedural rule governing the designation status of truth-values: *Be sure to antidesignate the truth-values so that either v or $\neg v$ is antidesignated in every case.* We are enjoined to make sure—subject to the guidance of the truth table for negation—that sufficiently many truth-values have been antidesignated.

(2) By contrast, principle (iv′) has the character of an economy principle. This too can be looked on as a procedural rule governing the designation status of truth-values: *Be sure to designate truth-values sufficiently sparingly so that it never happens that v and $\neg v$ are both designated.* We are enjoined to make sure—subject to the guidance of the truth table for negation—that sufficiently few truth-values have been designated.[3]

(3) In this version the principle amounts to:

$D^- \subseteq D'$, where D' is the set complement of D^+

That is, it claims that every antidesignated truth-value must be nondesignated, or, equivalently, that there is no truth-value that is both designated and antidesignated. This also can be

---

[3]And also, incidentally, to see to it that no self-negating truth-value (for which $v = \neg v$) is designated.

looked upon as a procedural rule governing the designation of truth-values: *Never designate a truth-value that is also anti-designated.*

(4) Although (iii) yields (iv), it is definitely not the case that (iii′) yields (iv′). On the other hand, (iii′) and (iv′) will be equivalent in the special (reflection property) case when D^- is taken to be the set complement of D^+, and in this case (v′) will automatically be satisfied.

In concluding this section, it is appropriate to remark that in many-valued logic the Law of Contradiction is best looked upon as a restrictive principle governing the mode of negation at issue. It seeks to assure that the truth table for negation is relatively well behaved (in one of several ways) with respect to the distribution of T's and F's—or of designated and antidesignated truth-values. By and large when the principle fails, one can plausibly take the view that—assuming a reasonable mode of conjunction ($\wedge$) for versions (i) and (ii)—the mode of negation ($\neg$) at issue is of an aberrant variety.

23 The Law of the Excluded Middle in Many-valued Logic

The "Law of the Excluded Middle" is generally given by traditional logicians as the principle that *everything is either A or not-A*, or, in a somewhat different formulation, that one member of the pair "*B is A*" and "*B is not-A*" must be true, so that both cannot be false. Though its traditional formulation casts it within the language of predication, the principle is often identified with a thesis of orthodox propositional logic: "$\alpha \vee \sim\alpha$." Actually, a counterpart of this assertion in predicate logic, namely the thesis "$(\forall x)(Px \vee \sim Px)$," might seem a formulation more appropriate to the historical version.

The Law of the Excluded Middle has an interesting history into the details of which we cannot enter here. Aristotle was certainly familiar with the principle at issue and accepted it as holding by and large, although (according to many interpreters) he rejected it with respect to the so-called *future-contingent propositions* which involve the outcome of free human choices.[1] The law was clearly insisted upon in a thoroughly unqualified way

---

[1]For many historical details—and references to the ramified literature of the topic—see N. Rescher, "An Interpretation of Aristotle's Doctrine of Future Contingency and Excluded Middle" in *Studies in the History of Arabic Logic* (Pittsburgh, 1963). The pioneering study is that of J. Łukasiewicz. See Łukasiewicz' paper of 1930, tr. as "Philosophical Remarks on Many-Valued Systems of Propositional Logic" in S. McCall (ed.), *Polish Logic: 1920–1939* (Oxford, 1967), pp. 40–65 (see especially the Appendix "On the History of the Law of Bivalence," pp. 63–65).

by Chrysippus, one of the founders of the Stoic school. Accordingly, many recent writers follow J. Łukasiewicz in referring to logical systems that abandon the Law of Excluded Middle as *non-Chrysippean* systems—rather than as "non-Aristotelian" systems, as earlier writers on the subject tended to do. K. Michalski has made an extensive study of the history of the Law of the Excluded Middle in medieval times.[2] It can be shown that in the Middle Ages various logicians—preeminently Duns Scotus and William of Ockham—construed Aristotle's discussion in chap. 9 of *De interpretatione* in the manner referred to above and argued the need for a third, neutral truth-value to accommodate propositions referring to future-contingent events. Thus Michalski writes:

> . . . in the reasoning of Ockham, the idea of a third truth-value in logic is not the result of a theological discussion, but is a logical tool taken from Aristotle's treatise *De interpretatione*. John Duns Scotus unquestionably relied upon this same treatise when he explicated the essence of propositions that are neither true nor false as *complexa neutra*.[3]

More than any other orthodox principle of traditional logic, the Law of Excluded Middle has been the subject of doubt and denial throughout the course of logical history.

In any case, in the context of many-valued logic, the rubric "Law of the Excluded Middle" actually applies to a variety of distinct though related principles. It can, *inter alia*, be construed as:

(i) The principle that the thesis

$$\alpha \lor \neg\alpha[4]$$

is to be included among the assertions (i.e., tautologies) of a logical system.

(ii) The "Principle of Bivalence" or the "*Tertium non datur* Principle" to the effect that a proposition must be either true or else false:

$$(/p/ = T)\text{-or-}(/p/ = F)$$

This "Law of an Excluded Third" in effect rules out any other truth-values than T and F.[5]

(iii) Of a proposition and its contradictory *at least one* must be true:

$$(/p/ = T)\text{-or-}(/\neg p/ = T)$$

---

[2]K. Michalski, "Le problème de la volonté à Oxford et à Paris au XIVe siècle," *Studia philosophica*, vol. 2 (1937), pp. 233–365 (see especially pp. 285–331).
[3]*Op. cit.*, p. 301.
[4]That is, $(\forall\alpha)(\alpha \lor \neg\alpha)$.
[5]The Principle of Bivalence in this form is obviously the key roadblock to the development of many-valued systems of logic. The history of the principle was first surveyed in Łukasiewicz' paper cited in note 1 above.

or equivalently

If $/p/ \neq T$, then $/\neg p/ = T$

When this is supplemented by a version of the Law of Contradiction to the effect that a proposition and its negation cannot both be true, it then follows that the italicized "*at least one*" of the formula can be strengthened to "*exactly one*."[6]

(iv) A proposition cannot be true and its denial fail to be false, or its denial be false and it fail to be true. A proposition is true if and only if its negation (contradictory or denial) is false, and conversely:

$$/p/ = T \text{ iff } /\neg p/ = F$$
$$/\neg p/ = T \text{ iff } /p/ = F$$

This principle is perhaps less a version of the Law of Excluded Middle than a (rather restrictive) formulation of the truth conditions for the denial (negation) of propositions. We include the principle here because its main consequence is

If $/p/ \neq T$, then $/\neg p/ \neq F$

which obviously is closely related to (iii) above. [Moreover, (iv) establishes immediately the equivalence of (ii) and (iii).]

(v) Every proposition either takes a given truth-value or else does not. Even if ground-floor statements like p or q are not necessarily bivalent, at any rate truth-value assigning statements of the type

$$/p/ = v$$

are invariably either true or false.

The question of whether the Law of the Excluded Middle can be maintained in many-valued logic is thus a *complex* question that is also subject to a variety of distinctly divergent constructions. The following observations are in order regarding these different interpretations of the principle:

(1) With respect to construction (i), there is no reason of principle why this version of the principle could not be maintained in certain systems of many-valued logic: in fact, "$\alpha \lor \neg\alpha$" is an asserted thesis (tautology) in various such systems. On the other hand, it must also be recognized that this formula may very well fail to secure the status of an asserted thesis (tautology) in other, perfectly viable systems of many-valued logic (e.g., $Ł_3$).

---

[6]For a historical discussion of (ii) and (iii) in the light of their relationship to the issue of future contingency, see Rescher, *op. cit.*, in note 1 above.

(2) In construction (ii), the principle cannot be maintained in any system of many-valued logic whatsoever. Indeed, the deliberate violation of this principle is the very basis of and reason for the construction of systems of *many*-valued logic.

(3) With respect to construction (iii), there is again no reason why a system of many-valued logic could not incorporate this version of the principle, though, of course, not all will do so, as we have seen. Consider the truth table for any normal mode of many-valued negation:

p	$\neg p$
T	F
I_1	(1)
I_2	(2)
.	.
.	.
.	.
I_n	(n)
F	T

The applicability of the principle at the extreme positions being assured by normality, it remains to consider positions (1) to (n). All these positions must, according to the principle, be filled by the entry T.

(4) Version (iv) of the principle can readily be maintained in systems of many-valued logic. Consider the truth table for the negation operator:

p	$\neg p$
T	(1)
I_1	?
I_2	?
.	.
.	.
.	.
I_n	?
F	(2)

By the first half of the principle, F must occur at position (1) and *can occur at this position only*. By the second half, T must appear at position (2) and *can occur at this position only*. Hence all the positions marked ? will have to be occupied by "intermediate" truth-values distinct from the classical T and F. It follows that version (iv) of the principle will obtain in any and every system of many-valued logic whose truth table for negation is both normal and K-regular (and so always gives an intermediate, nonclassical output when there is an intermediate input).

(5) Version (v) of the principle obtains with respect to virtually all of the systems of many-valued logic that have been studied to date. But it is not an essential principle which must in the nature of things apply in all cases, as is shown by our discussion on pages 80–87.

(6) Version (i) is an object-language formulation of the principle, versions (ii) to (iv) are metalanguage formulations, and version (v) is a meta-metalanguage formulation.

(7) Version (i) involves both negation and disjunction (at the object-language level), and versions (iii) and (iv) involve only negation. Only versions (ii) and (v) involve no special reference to any connectives of the system.

(8) These versions of the principle are all independent except for the following significant interrelationships (and their consequences):

$$\left.\begin{array}{l}\text{(ii) and (iv) yield (iii)}\\ \text{(iii) and (iv) yield (ii)}\end{array}\right\} \text{ thus (ii) and (iii) are equivalent given (iv)}$$

(ii) yields (v)

We thus see that of the many possible alternative versions of the Law of the Excluded Middle the only one that *must* inevitably be yielded up in the context of a many-valued logic is the Principle of Bivalence (or *tertium non datur* principle), although the others *may* be given up in certain cases. Abandonment of the Law of the Excluded Middle is therefore far from being an automatic result when we take the step from two-valued to many-valued logic.

Once a thoroughly many-valued point of view has been assumed, and the ideas of definite *truth* and *falsity* generalized to those of *designated* (truth-like) and *antidesignated* (false-like) truth-values, then some of the foregoing versions of the Law of Excluded Middle can be reshaped accordingly. As before, let:

$D^+ = D^+(\mathbf{X})$ = the designated truth-values of the system $\mathbf{X}$
$D^- = D^-(\mathbf{X})$ = the antidesignated truth-values of the system $\mathbf{X}$

We can now reformulate three of the above versions of the Law of the Excluded Middle into the counterparts:

(ii′) $[/p/ \in D^+(\mathbf{X})]\text{-or-}[/p/ \in D^-(\mathbf{X})]$
(iii′) $[/p/ \in D^+(\mathbf{X})]\text{-or-}[/\neg p/ \in D^+(\mathbf{X})]$
(iv′) $\begin{cases} /p/ \in D^+(\mathbf{X}) \text{ iff } /\neg p/ \in D^-(\mathbf{X}) \\ /\neg p/ \in D^+(\mathbf{X}) \text{ iff } /p/ \in D^-(\mathbf{X}) \end{cases}$

The following comments are in order with respect to these reformulations:

(1) Principle (ii′) can be looked on as a procedural rule governing the designation of truth-values: *Be sure to antidesignate all nondesignated truth-values* (or, viewing the matter in reverse, be sure to designate all those truth-values that are not antidesignated). As we have seen, many-valued logics in some cases do obey this rule, but need not invariably do so. (Note that whenever D^- is taken simply as D', the set *complement* of D^+, then conformity to this rule is assured.)

(2) Principle (iii′) can also be taken as a procedural rule governing the designation of truth-values: *Be sure to designate the truth-values so that either v or ¬v is designated in any given case.* Again, many-valued systems of logic in some cases do obey this rule of liberality in designation, but need not invariably do so. For example, $Ł_3$ does not do so on Łukasiewicz' own approach. Since *I* is not designated, neither *I* nor $¬I(=I)$ is designated. (Of course, if one should choose also to designate *I*, then $Ł_3$ will conform to the rule.)

(3) Choices about designation and antidesignation alone can thus assure principles (ii′) and (iii′). This is also true with regard to (iv′), but in a much more restrictive way. Consider, for example, Post's cyclical negation in a 3-valued case:

p	$¬p$
1	2
2	3
3	1

Suppose $1 \in D^+$. Then $2 \in D^-$, since $¬1 = 2$. Then $3 \in D^+$, since $¬2 = 3$. But then $1 \in D^-$, since $¬3 = 1$. But then $2 \in D^+$, since $¬1 = 2$. But then $3 \in D^-$, since $¬2 = 3$. Thus *all* the truth-values will belong to D^+, and all the truth-values will also belong to D^-. But this result is patently unacceptable, since it defeats the whole idea of designation. The lesson is clear. We can *always* assure (iv′) by an appropriate designation policy, viz. to designate and antidesignate each and every truth-value. But a reasonable working out of (iv′)—in those plausible cases in which at least some truth-values are not designated and at least some are not antidesignated—will require a suitably well-behaved mode of negation.

(4) The following minor variant of (iv′) is possible:

(iv″) $/p/ \in D^+(\mathbf{X})$ iff $/¬p/ \notin D^+(\mathbf{X})$

This amounts to the conjunction of two theses:

(a) [/p/ $\in$ D^+(**X**)]-or-/$\neg p$/ $\in$ D^+(**X**)]
(b) [/p/ $\notin$ D^+(**X**)]-or-[/$\neg p$/ $\notin$ D^+(**X**)]

The former of these is identical with (iii'), so (b) alone introduces a new precept: *Be sure to designate the truth-values so that either v or ¬v is nondesignated in any given case.*

By and large, the Law of Excluded Middle should also be looked upon as a means for assuring that the truth table for negation is relatively well behaved (in one of several ways) with regard to the distribution of *T*'s and *F*'s—or of designated and antidesignated truth-values. When the principle fails, this failure can again by and large be blamed upon aberrations in the mode of negation at issue.

24 *Axiomatizability, Relative Completeness, and Characteristic Sets of Truth Tables*

Many-valued systems of logic are conceived along fundamentally semantical lines: it is a secondary and, as it were, extra step to accord them an axiomatic treatment. Nevertheless, the problems involved in questions of axiomatization are among the most important and interesting logical issues in this area and serve to shed much light upon the logical characteristics and interrelationships of the systems at issue.

Consider on the one hand (1) a set of truth tables and truth-value designations determining a conception of tautologousness within some family of formulas (wffs) of a propositional logic, and on the other hand (2) an ensemble of axioms and rules of inference for a system of propositional logic determining the set of its theorems. The first of these defines a system of many-valued logic **X**, the second defines an axiom system **A**. (We may, as usual, write $p \in T(\mathbf{X})$ when p is an **X**-tautology and $\vdash p$ when p is an **A**-theorem.) Then we may define:

(1) The many-valued system **X** is *adequate* for the axiom system **A** if the theorems of **A** satisfy the truth tables of **X**—or, to put it inversely, if the truth tables "verify" all the axioms—that is, if every **A**-theorem is an **X**-tautology, and so if:

Whenever $\vdash p$, then $p \in T(\mathbf{X})$

(2) The axiom system **A** *captures* the many-valued system **X** if every **X**-tautology is an **A**-theorem, and so if:

Whenever $p \in T(\mathbf{X})$, then $\vdash p$

(3) The many-valued system $\mathbf{X}$ is *characteristic* for the axiom system of **A**—or equivalently but inversely, the axiom system **A** *axiomatizes* the many-valued system $\mathbf{X}$ ("gives an axiomatization *that is* complete relative to the many-valued system $\mathbf{X}$")—if both (1) and (2), and so if:

$p \in T(\mathbf{X})$ iff $\vdash p$

The completeness at issue here warrants comment. It is not of any absolute sort, but a *relative* one that obtains with respect to a certain prior specification of tautologousness. The idea of "relative completeness" is deployed as follows: that when **A** axiomatizes $\mathbf{X}$, then **A** provides an axiomatic development of the set of acceptable formulas (tautologies) of $\mathbf{X}$, and so **A** is "complete" *relative to* the system $\mathbf{X}$ with its given mode of tautologousness. This issue of axiomatization is an important one, for systems can often be most effectively compared and contrasted in their axiomatic form.

Two general types of problems can thus be posed in connection with the topic of relative completeness. We may begin with a set of truth tables and be asked to *axiomatize* (i.e., find a relatively complete axiomatization for) the corresponding set of tautologies. Conversely, we may begin with a set of axioms and be asked to devise a *characteristic set of many-valued truth tables* for them. Both of these approaches must be considered.

The classic result in the area of axiomatization of preexisting many-valued logic is M. Wajsberg's axiomatization in 1931 of the 3-valued logic of Łukasiewicz.[1] Wajsberg showed that, given *modus ponens* and substitution as rules of inference, the following postulates will provide a (very elegant) axiomatization of $\mathbf{L}_3$.

(W1) $\alpha \to (\beta \to \alpha)$
(W2) $(\alpha \to \beta) \to [(\beta \to \gamma) \to (\alpha \to \gamma)]$
(W3) $(\neg\beta \to \neg\alpha) \to (\alpha \to \beta)$
(W4) $[(\alpha \to \neg\alpha) \to \alpha] \to \alpha$

Moreover, it was shown by Słupecki that $\mathbf{L}_3^S$, the T-supplemented version of $\mathbf{L}_3$, is axiomatized by adding to (W1)–(W4) the further axioms:

(S1) $\mathsf{T}\alpha \to \neg\mathsf{T}\alpha$
(S2) $\neg\mathsf{T}\alpha \to \mathsf{T}\alpha$

[1] For the full reference to Wajsberg's original paper see the Bibliography. An English translation of the paper is given under the title "Axiomatization of the Three-Valued Propositional Calculus" in S. McCall (ed.), *Polish Logic: 1920–1939* (Oxford, 1967), pp. 264–284.

At the other end of the L_n spectrum, it has been shown that $L_{\aleph_1}$ is axiomatized (with respect to the same rules of inference) by the axioms:[2]

(L1) $\beta \to (\alpha \to \beta)$ [= (W1)]
(L2) $(\alpha \to \beta) \to [(\beta \to \gamma) \to (\alpha \to \gamma)]$ [= (W2)]
(L3) $(\neg \beta \to \neg \alpha) \to (\alpha \to \beta)$ [= (W3)]
(L4) $[(\alpha \to \beta) \to \beta] \to [(\beta \to \alpha) \to \alpha]$

As regards the intermediate L_n, the situation is as follows. Wajsberg has shown that every propositional logic based on $\to$ and $\neg$ that contains the following axioms will be finitely axiomatizable.[3] (An axiom system is said to be finite when it is based upon a finite list of axioms and has *modus ponens* and substitution as its only rules of inference.)

(A) $(\alpha \to \beta) \to [(\beta \to \gamma) \to (\alpha \to \gamma)]$
(B) $(\alpha \to \beta) \to [(\gamma \to \alpha) \to (\gamma \to \beta)]$
(C) $(\beta \to \gamma) \to (\alpha \to \alpha)$
(D) $(\alpha \to \beta) \to (\neg \beta \to \neg \alpha)$
(E) $\neg \beta \to [(\alpha \to \beta) \to \neg \alpha]$

Now all of these can be shown to be theorems of $L_\aleph$ and are therefore theorems of every L_m.[4] It follows at once that every L_m is finitely axiomatizable. Indeed a procedure for constructing axiomatizations for all the L_m has been devised by J. B. Rosser and A. R. Turquette.[5] Due to its high degree of generality, their procedure results in highly uneconomical and inelegant axiomatizations.[6] In any event, the considerations involved in the axiomatization of particular systems are highly technical and complex. We shall not pursue the matter here, apart from setting forth below the broad outlines of the general strategy used in establishing the axiomatic completeness of a postulate system for a given many-valued logic.

The reverse procedure arises when a certain set of axioms is given and the problem is to discover a characteristic set of many-valued truth tables for them. If one restricts the range of consideration to finitely many-valued

[2]See A. Rose and J. B. Rosser, "Fragments of Many-Valued Statement Calculi," *Transactions of the American Mathematical Society*, vol. 87 (1958), pp. 1–53. See also C. A. Meredith, "Dependence of an Axiom of Łukasiewicz," *ibid.*, p. 54, as well as C. C. Chang, "Proof of an Axiom of Łukasiewicz," *ibid.*, pp. 55–56. An excellent presentation of the whole range of considerations at issue here is J. B. Rosser, "Axiomatization of Infinite-Valued Logics," *Logique et Analyse*, vol. 3 (1960), pp. 137–153.
[3]"Beiträge zum Metaaussagenkalkül, I," *Monatshefte für Mathematik und Physik*, vol. 42 (1935), pp. 221–242.
[4]The details are presented in Rose and Rosser, *op. cit.*
[5]See Rosser and Turquette, *op. cit.*
[6]They proceed essentially by a piecemeal representation by means of the *J*-operators (see the Appendix of Sec. 12) of the appropriate truth-table characterization of the basic connectives $\neg$ and $\to$.

logics, then it may very well happen that no characteristic set of truth tables can be found for the initially given axiom system. For example, we shall see below (in Sec. 25) that the axiom sets for C. I. Lewis's various systems of "strict implication" cannot be provided with any finitely many-valued sets of truth tables that are characteristic of the system.

Quite in general, it is, however, readily shown—by an ingenious argument due to A. Lindenbaum[7]—that the set of theorems of any and every axiom system of logic subject to a rule of inference by substitution will have a correspondingly characteristic many-valued logic if one is willing to go to infinite-valued logics. For let the "truth-values" of the many-valued logic be the system's formulas themselves, the "designated" truth-values being its theorems. Let an "assignment of truth-values to a formula of the system" consist in the substitution of these truth-values (i.e., formulas) for the variables of this formula. This setup must yield a characteristic set of truth tables for the axiom system. For every theorem must uniformly take on a designated truth-value (since all its substitution instances will be theorems). Conversely, every nontheorem will take on a nondesignated truth-value for some assignment of truth-values (for let every variable simply be put for itself). This construction of the matter trivializes the affirmative reply to the question: *Can every axiomatic system of logic be represented as a many-valued logic?*[8] (To be sure, it does so in a somewhat unnatural and contorted manner.)

Thus every axiom system can be represented as a many-valued logic. It is of interest to raise the converse question: Can every many-valued logic that comprises a reasonable mode of implication be developed axiomatically using only *modus ponens* and substitution as the rules of inference? That this question must be answered in the negative can be seen from the following demonstration that *not every (finite) many-valued logic is finitely axiomatizable with substitution and modus ponens.*

Consider a 3-valued logic based on the truth-values T,I,F. Let T and I be the designated truth-values.

Let the matrix for implication ($\rightarrow$) be such that: (1) T is the only designated truth-value it ever yields as output and (2) it will only yield T with a designated antecedent when the consequent is T. The following truth table meets these conditions:

[7]See J. Łukasiewicz and A. Tarski, "Untersuchungen über den Aussagenkalkül," *Comptes rendus des séances de la Société des Sciences et des Lettres de Varsovie*, Classe III, vol. 23 (1930), pp. 1–21.
[8]On the result of this paragraph, due to Lindenbaum, see also the discussion in J. C. C. McKinsey and A. Tarski, "Some Theorems About the Sentential Calculi of Lewis and Heyting," *The Journal of Symbolic Logic*, vol. 13 (1948), pp. 1–13.

| $p \to q$ | | |
$\begin{smallmatrix}&q\\p&\end{smallmatrix}$	T	I	F
+T	T	F	F
+I	T	F	F
F	T	T	T

It is to be stressed that this implication relationship meets many of the usual requirements for a mode of implication.[9] Specifically:

1. It is *normal* in that it agrees with two-valued (material) implication when only *T*'s and *F*'s are involved.
2. It satisfies the "*modus ponens* condition" in assuring that when *p* and $p \to q$ take designated values, then so does *q*.
3. It satisfies the "transitivity condition" in assuring that when $p \to q$ and $q \to r$ take designated values, then so does $p \to r$.

Given this truth table for →, it is clear that the only formulas that can ever be established by *modus ponens* are ones that identically take on the truth-value *T*. Consequently, no formula that identically assumes the (designated) truth-value *I* can ever be obtained by *modus ponens*.

We now introduce one further binary connective into our many-valued logic, namely the connective ☆. This is to be introduced in such a way that all the formulas of the following series are tautologies that uniformly take on the truth-value *I*:

$\alpha \bigstar \alpha$
$\alpha \bigstar (\alpha \bigstar \alpha)$
$\alpha \bigstar (\alpha \bigstar (\alpha \bigstar \alpha))$
etc.

The relevant feature of this sequence is that no formula in it can be obtained from any shorter formula by uniform substitution. Given the irrelevance of *modus ponens*, there will thus be no way of deriving the members of this series of tautologies from any finite list of axioms.

A truth table which yields the appropriate properties for this connective is:

| $p \bigstar q$ | | |
$\begin{smallmatrix}&q\\p&\end{smallmatrix}$	T	I	F
+T	I	I	F
+I	F	I	F
F	F	I	I

[9]But obviously not all of them. For example "$\alpha \to \alpha$" is not a tautology.

We have thus demonstrated that the 3-valued logic based on these truth-values is not axiomatizable with respect to inference procedures provided by the rules of substitution and *modus ponens* for →.

It is not difficult to see that nothing fundamental would be altered in the preceding discussion by augmenting our 3-valued logic by introducing the (usual) truth tables for such further connectives as negation ($\neg$), conjunction ($\wedge$), and disjunction ($\vee$). Formulas involving only → and ☆ that are not otherwise derivable from axioms involving these connectives alone would not become derivable by the addition of further axioms involving also $\neg$, $\wedge$, and $\vee$. Thus many-valued logics with a plausible mode of implication need not invariably be finitely axiomatizable (subject to substitution and *modus ponens* as rules of inference). But such systems must invariably be subject to infinite axiomatizations—trivially so, since we can sift through the wffs in order of length, adding each new tautology as an axiom.

The upshot of this discussion of axiomatizability and truth-table representation can thus be summarized as follows:

Given	One can
(1) An (arbitrary) axiom system for connectives of propositional logic (with *modus ponens* and substitution as rules of inference)	(1a) Always find a denumerably infinite-valued set of characteristic truth tables (athough it may not be possible to do this in an "effective" way)
	(1b) Sometimes *but not always* find a finite set of characteristic truth tables
(2) An (arbitrary) group of finite-valued truth tables for connectives of propositional logic (with a "well-behaved" mode of implication)	(2a) Always find a denumerably infinite axiomatization
	(2b) Sometimes *but not always* find a finite axiomatization (with *modus ponens* and substitution as rules of inference)

The process of establishing in detail that a certain axiomatization (e.g., that of Wajsberg) is provability-complete for a particular many-valued logic (that of Łukasiewicz) is of an order of complication beyond the scope of this book. We shall limit ourselves to setting forth the general *strategy* of such a proof, but omit details.

The leading idea is to identify truth-values with *formulas* (wffs) such that what the truth tables say is provable within the system itself. Confining ourselves (for the sake of simplicity) to 3-valued logic, we may represent the correspondence abstractly:

$$T \simeq T(p)$$
$$I \simeq I(p)$$
$$F \simeq F(p)$$

where $T(p)$, $I(p)$, and $F(p)$ are *formulas* of an appropriate kind, involving p. For example, we might have:

$$T \simeq p \to p$$
$$F \simeq \neg(p \to p)$$

The truth table for negation is then transformed as follows:

p	$\neg p$		p	$\neg p$
T	F		$T(p)$	$F(p) \leftrightarrow \neg T(p)$
I	I	leads to	$I(p)$	$I(p) \leftrightarrow \neg I(p)$
F	T		$F(p)$	$T(p) \leftrightarrow \neg F(p)$

To capture this truth table in theorematic form, we must thus prove (or postulate) certain equivalences among formulas, to wit:

$$F(\alpha) \leftrightarrow \neg T(\alpha)$$
$$I(\alpha) \leftrightarrow \neg I(\alpha)$$
$$T(\alpha) \leftrightarrow \neg F(\alpha)$$

Exactly the same considerations hold for binary connectives. Thus consider Łukasiewiczian implication, for example:

$p \backslash^q$	$p \to q$ T	I	F		$p \backslash^q$	$T(p)$	$p \to q$ $I(p)$	$F(p)$
T	T	I	F		$T(p)$	$T(p) \leftrightarrow T(p) \to T(p)$	$I(p) \leftrightarrow T(p) \to I(p)$	$F(p) \leftrightarrow T(p) \to F(p)$
I	T	T	I		$I(p)$	$T(p) \leftrightarrow I(p) \to T(p)$	$T(p) \leftrightarrow I(p) \to I(p)$	$I(p) \leftrightarrow I(p) \to F(p)$
F	T	T	T		$F(p)$	$T(p) \leftrightarrow F(p) \to T(p)$	$T(p) \leftrightarrow F(p) \to I(p)$	$T(p) \leftrightarrow F(p) \to F(p)$

Thus the nine equivalences internal to the right-hand matrix would have to be proved (or postulated). And the same process has to be carried out for the truth tables of the other connectives.

Several further demands must then be made on the axiomatization. We must establish on the metatheoretic level that:

> If a formula involving p is provably equivalent to $T(p)$ in all three *special* cases that p is $T(p)$, $I(p)$, and $F(p)$, then this formula is provably equivalent to $T(p)$ in general.

Moreover, we shall need to establish (1) that $T(p)$ is provable and (2) the substitutivity of provable equivalents. For then it follows that a formula involving p will be provable in general if it is provably equivalent to $T(p)$ in the three special cases envisaged above (p as $T(p)$, $I(p)$, and $F(p)$, respectively).

Now once all this is done, it is easy to see that *the process of checking tautologousness can be transformed into a proof procedure* (so that *every* tautology is provable). For example, consider:

$$\alpha \to \alpha$$

The tautologousness of this formula is established by showing that

$$T \rightarrow T = T$$
$$I \rightarrow I = T$$
$$F \rightarrow F = T$$

But from the design of the truth tables, these relationships will hold iff

$$[T(\alpha) \rightarrow T(\alpha)] \leftrightarrow T(\alpha)$$
$$[I(\alpha) \rightarrow I(\alpha)] \leftrightarrow T(\alpha)$$
$$[F(\alpha) \rightarrow F(\alpha)] \leftrightarrow T(\alpha)$$

are all provable, and this is indeed so as we supposed above. Thus the question of tautologousness of the formula "$\alpha \rightarrow \alpha$" amounts to the demonstrable equivalence to $T(p)$ of the three substitution instances of this formula with α as $T(\alpha)$, $I(\alpha)$, and $F(\alpha)$, respectively. Since "$\alpha \rightarrow \alpha$" is a tautology, all three of these must—from the design of the truth table—be provably equivalent to $T(\alpha)$. And therefore, this formula will be provable on the basis of the metatheorem stated above.[10]

This shows that if we have introduced on the axiomatic side enough machinery to establish the theorems and metatheorems mentioned above as being needed, then we can show that every tautology is provable as a theorem, i.e., that the axiom system captures the many-valued system. The converse issue—viz. that every theorem is a tautology—is of course easily settled by checking that the axioms are tautologies and that the rules of inference are tautology-preserving. By such a procedure, the provability completeness of an axiom system for a many-valued logic originally defined by means of truth tables can be established.

25 Consistency, Negation Consistency, and Completeness

A system **X** of many-valued logic is said to be *consistent* if not every formula (wff) is an **X**-tautology, i.e., if some formula is nontautologous. This terminology is adopted on analogy with the standard conception of an axiom system's being (absolutely) *consistent* as regards provability if not every formula is a theorem.[1]

[10]To see the method at work in its full generality, one should consider formulas which, unlike "$\alpha \rightarrow \alpha$," involve two or more variables. The reader interested in fuller details should consult Wajsberg's classic paper of 1931 as tr. in S. McCall (ed.), *Polish Logic: 1920–1939* (Oxford, 1967), pp. 264–284.

[1]The ideas at issue in various concepts of consistency and completeness with respect to provability are discussed with clarity and precision in Alonzo Church, *Introduction to Mathematical Logic* (Princeton, 1956), pp. 108–110. In axiom systems having a rule of substitution, this absolute consistency is equivalent with Post consistency, a system of propositional logic being Post-consistent when it is not possible to prove as a theorem the

When *all* of the truth-values of the system **X** are designated, then the system will obviously be inconsistent (i.e., not consistent). In general, it is not difficult to see that a necessary and sufficient condition for the consistency of a many-valued logic is that some truth-value be nondesignated (since then the wff consisting of a propositional variable standing alone will be nontautologous). It is thus readily shown that *all* of the systems of many-valued logic that we have considered are consistent.

The conception of a tautologousness is a powerful tool for demonstrating the (absolute) consistency of axiom systems of propositional logic. For whenever one can show with regard to some such system that:

(1) Its axioms are all tautologies
(2) Its rules of inference are all tautology-preserving
(3) There is some formula (wff) that is not a tautology

then one has succeeded in showing that this formula cannot be a theorem, so that the axiom must be (absolutely) consistent as regards provability. (Cf. the discussion of Sec. 17.) By just this method Emil Post was able to show in his classic paper of 1921[2] that the orthodox two-valued truth tables serve to establish the consistency of the Russell-Whitehead axiomatization of C_2.

A system **X** of many-valued logic is said to be *negation-consistent* (or consistent with respect to its negation operator $\neg$) if it is such that the principle

If $p \in T(\mathbf{X})$, then $\neg p \notin T(\mathbf{X})$

obtains, that is, if it can never happen that both p and $\neg p$ are **X**-tautologies. (This concept is analogous with the standard conception of an axiom system's being *negation-consistent* as regards provability if it can never happen that both p and $\neg p$ are theorems.) It is readily seen that any **X** of many-valued propositional logic that includes the *modus ponens* principle for implication—in the specific form: Whenever $p \in T(\mathbf{X})$ and $p \to q \in T(\mathbf{X})$, then $q \in T(\mathbf{X})$—and that has the formula "$\alpha \to (\neg \alpha \to \beta)$" among its tautologies will be consistent iff it is negation-consistent. However, as we shall shortly see, in systems not asserting "$\alpha \to (\neg \alpha \to \beta)$" or

---

formula consisting of a propositional variable standing alone. I prefer to speak of what Church (and others) call *absolute consistency* (and *absolute completeness*) as *consistency* (or *completeness*) simple and unqualified. This leaves the label "absolute" open for general application to those modes of consistency (and completeness) which—like (absolute) consistency, Post consistency, and negation consistency—stand in generic contrast to the *relative* consistency (and completeness) that figures prominently in these discussions in ways we have already considered in the preceding sections.
[2]"Introduction to a General Theory of Elementary Propositions," *American Journal of Mathematics*, vol. 43 (1921), pp. 163–185.

something similar (and certainly in systems that lack negation altogether), consistency and negation consistency represent separate issues.

A system that is inconsistent is necessarily devoid of substantial logical interest: since *all* of its formulas are tautologies, it will be impossible to provide any workable sort of semantical interpretation for its asserted propositions. Since tautologousness and well-formedness then come to the same thing, the concept of tautologousness loses its logical bite.

Negation inconsistency, however, represents a far less serious flaw. Consider, for example, the 3-valued system S_3^*:

p	$\neg p$		$\backslash q$ $p\backslash$	$p \wedge q$ T I F	$p \rightarrow q$ T I F
$+T$	F		$+T$	T I F	T I F
$+I$	I		$+I$	I I F	T T F
$-F$	T		$-F$	F F F	T T T

This system has the standard 3-valued modes of negation and conjunction, and its implication operator has all the usual features of satisfying *modus ponens*, being transitive, reflexive, and asymmetric, etc.[3] Now let us add to the system the Słupecki T-operator (thus rendering the system truth-functionally complete[4]):

p	$\mathsf{T}(p)$
$+T$	I
$+I$	I
$-F$	I

It is readily seen that both "$\mathsf{T}(\alpha)$" and "$\neg\mathsf{T}(\alpha)$" are tautologies, so that the system is negation-inconsistent. (Note also that "$\mathsf{T}\alpha \wedge \neg\mathsf{T}\alpha$" is tautologous.) However, this inconsistency is in significant measure harmless. Specifically, it does not mean that any arbitrary formula is a tautology in the system, nor does it mean that the negation of every tautology is a tautology (as would be the case if I alone were designated).

An axiomatic system[5] is said to be *negation-complete* if no nontheorem can be added to its axioms without rendering the system negation-

---

[3]This system is identical with that of Łukasiewicz' $Ł_3$, except for having its $\rightarrow$ operator be such that F (rather than I) occurs at the $I \rightarrow F$ position.
[4]Note that we will have the constant truth functions "$\alpha \rightarrow \alpha$," "$\mathsf{T}(\alpha)$," and "$\neg(\alpha \rightarrow \alpha)$," which identically assume the truth-values T, I, and F.
[5]Which need not necessarily be a many-valued logic.

inconsistent, i.e., without making it possible to prove both p and $\neg p$ *for some (suitable) proposition p.*[6] Moreover, an axiom system is said to be *complete* (absolutely complete) if no nontheorem can be added to its axioms without rendering the system (absolutely) inconsistent, i.e., without making it possible to prove any arbitrary formula as a theorem. Note that both completeness and negation completeness are nonrelative or absolute matters, unlike the relative completeness considered in the last section (which requires reference to something outside the axiomatization itself, namely a certain separately given set of truth tables).

It is a significant fact that:

> Any axiomatization[7] of a system of finitely many-valued logic that is truth-functionally complete[8] and whose negation is "well behaved" (in a sense to be specified below) must be negation-complete.[9]

Thus let **X** be a truth-functionally complete system of many-valued logic based on the truth-values $1, 2, \ldots, n$. Let $D^+ = D^+(\mathbf{X})$ be the set of the designated truth-values of **X**, with respect to which the set $T(\mathbf{X})$ of all **X**-tautologies is then defined.[10] It is supposed that an axiom system is given that is characteristic of **X**, i.e., is such that:

$$\vdash p \text{ iff } p \in T(\mathbf{X})$$

We may suppose that this axiom system has the rule of substitution among its rules of inference.

Now the system **X** will be said to have a well-behaved mode of negation $(\neg)$ if this is such that the negation of a nondesignated truth-value is always designated, that is:

> (1) If $/p/ \notin D^+$, then $/\neg p/ \in D^+$

Moreover, it will (by the hypothesis of truth-functional completeness) be

---

[6]This concept of negation completeness differs from—and is weaker than—the standard one, according to which the axiom system is complete if no nontheorem can be added to its axioms without making it possible to prove both p and $\neg p$ *for every proposition p.* This *strong negation-completeness* is in general a more far-reaching feature of an axiom system, although the two modes of completeness will obviously coincide in axiom systems having *modus ponens* as a rule of inference and "$\alpha \rightarrow (\neg\alpha \rightarrow \beta)$" (or something similar) as an axiom or theorem.

[7]Which need not necessarily be finite.

[8]It will become apparent from the proof that full truth-functional completeness is not required but just sufficient completeness to obtain the constant-value truth functions.

[9]The argument we shall give for this thesis is adapted from that presented in N. D. Belnap, Jr., and S. McCall, "Every Functionally Complete *m*-Valued Logic Has a Post-Complete Axiomatization" (unpublished dittograph circulated in 1968).

[10]We can assume without loss of generality that there is some nondesignated truth-value (so that the system is Post-consistent). Otherwise *every* formula (wff) is a tautology and hence a theorem by the assumption of provability completeness.

possible to define in the system **X** a series of one-place connectives $\odot$ (where i ranges from 1 to n), having the following property:

(2) $/\odot p/ = i$ uniformly, regardless of $/p/$[11]

Consider now the given axiomatic system that is characteristic for **X**. We shall show that the addition of any nontheorem as axiom will render the axiom system inconsistent. Let q be some arbitrary nontheorem. Then $q \notin T(\mathbf{X})$. Thus, there is some assignment of truth-values to the variables of q such that $/q/ \notin D$ for this assignment. Let q' be the result of substituting for the variables of q the constant functions $\odot q$[12] corresponding to this specific assignment of truth-values to the variables of q. Then q' is itself a constant function and $/q'/ \notin D^+$. Now since q is to be added to the axioms for **X**, we shall have $\vdash q$ in the augmented axiom system, and hence we can obtain $\vdash q'$ by the rule of substitution. But since $/q'/ \notin D^+$, it follows from the well-behavedness of negation that $/\neg q'/ \in D^+$, and uniformly so (q' being a constant function), so that $\neg q' \in T(\mathbf{X})$. Hence $\vdash \neg q'$. Therefore the system is negation-inconsistent (since both q' and $\neg q'$ are provable in it). Since the result of adding any nontheorem q to the axiomatization for **X** creates a negation inconsistency, **X** must be negation-complete.

Moreover, if we add to the requirements of the hypothesis of the preceding result that the mode of implication at issue be such that (1) *modus ponens* obtains and (2) "$\alpha \rightarrow (\neg\alpha \rightarrow \beta)$" is a tautology, then we can obviously strengthen this finding to say that the system at issue must be complete.

An example of a many-valued system satisfying all the conditions of this last-indicated result ("well-behaved" negation, implication that satisfies *modus ponens*, and the tautologousness of "$\alpha \rightarrow (\neg\alpha \rightarrow \beta)$") is the system:

p	$\neg p$	Sp	$\diagdown \!\!\!{}^q_p$	$p \wedge q$			$p \vee q$			$p \rightarrow q$			$p \leftrightarrow q$		
				T	I	F	T	I	F	T	I	F	T	I	F
$+T$	F	I	$+T$	T	I	F	T	T	T	T	I	F	T	I	F
I	T	I	I	I	I	F	T	I	I	T	T	T	I	T	T
F	T	I	F	F	F	F	T	I	F	T	T	T	F	T	T

Like its close cognate $\mathbf{Ł}_3^S$, this system is thus such that its axiomatization must be complete.[13] (The details of this axiomatization must be left as an open question here.)

---

[11]That is, the $\odot$ operators are n distinct *constant* truth functions, taking the value i such that $/\odot p/ = i$ uniformly, for arbitrary p.

[12]We have q itself here for simplicity. But since the $\odot$'s are constant truth functions, it does not matter what stands in q's place.

[13]The completeness of Słupecki's axiomatization of $\mathbf{Ł}_3^S$ was first claimed by him in his 1931 paper, although he did not publish a demonstration until some years later.

In general, however, the preceding result will be inapplicable to many-valued logics whose negation is not "well behaved" in the sense at issue (e.g., Łukasiewicz' system $Ł_3$). Most of the systems of many-valued logic we have considered are *fragments* of C_2. Thus the axiomatization of any such system will not be complete or negation-complete, since any non-theorem that is C_2-tautologous could consistently be added as an axiom. However, Alan Rose has shown[14] that—while the Łukasiewicz systems $Ł_n$ are not complete (being fragments of C_2)—only a C_2-tautology can be added as a new axiom to an $Ł_n$ system without resulting in an inconsistency.[15] This result can without much difficulty be extended to other system families that are subsystems of C_2 (e.g., the systems S_n, G_n, etc.).

The situation with regard to $Ł_3^S$ is particularly interesting. As just remarked, Słupecki's axiomatization of this system is in fact complete. Thus if we add to the axioms of $Ł_s^S$ any C_2-tautology that is not an $Ł_3^S$-tautology, then the result is not a merely stronger system but an (absolutely) inconsistent one. We cannot (on pain of incurring inconsistency) add the $Ł_3^S$-tautology "$T(\alpha) \leftrightarrow \neg T(\alpha)$" to C_2; nor can we add the C_2-tautology "$(\neg\alpha \to \alpha) \to \alpha$" to $Ł_s^J$. This shows that $Ł_s^S$ is not to be regarded as somehow "weaker" than C_2, but that these are radically disjoint and fundamentally different systems.

26 Quasi-truth-functional Systems

Beginners in symbolic logic frequently, and quite rightly, experience difficulties in the transition from the informal "if . . . , then—" construction of common discourse to its replacement by material implication, the familiar '$\supset$' of C_2. There is relatively little trouble with motivating the idea that "if p, then q" must be so understood that if $/p/ = T$ and $/q/ = F$, then we must have it that $/p \supset q/ = F$. It is thus relatively unproblematic to lead the explanation to the point:

$\diagdown \, q$ p	$p \supset q$	
	T	F
T	?	F
F	?	?

---

[14]"Completeness in Łukasiewicz-Tarski Propositional Calculi," *Mathematische Annalen*, vol. 122 (1950), pp. 296–298.

[15]Of course one must consider here only the unmodified $Ł_n$ systems, not those which, like $Ł_3^S$, are supplemented by special connectives, so that "$T(\alpha) \leftrightarrow \neg T(\alpha)$" (for example) will be a theorem that has no counterpart in C_2.

But difficulty could arise in deciding how the question marks are to be filled in. For at this point someone could object: "Why must the truth table be so rigidly truth-functional as to permit only a single truth-value to occupy each place in the table, instead of permitting possible occurrence of either T or F in a given place, dependent upon the circumstances of the particular case at hand?" This question, surely a good one, leads us to envisage systems of two-valued (or many-valued) propositional logic *with truth tables that are not single-valued*, but permit multiple values to occur at least in some places.

For an example of such a system of propositional logic, consider the following two-valued system, to be designated as **Q**, obtained by retaining the usual two-valued truth tables for negation ($\sim$), conjunction (&), and disjunction ($\vee$), but replacing the usual truth table for material implication by:[1]

$_p\diagdown^q$	$p \supset q$	
	T	F
T	T	F
F	(T,F)	(T,F)

In this table, a bracketed entry (T,F) is to be considered disjunctively and means that either one of these two truth-values may occur in the various particular cases, depending upon (otherwise unspecified) circumstances regarding the specific cases. **Q** is thus a system of propositional logic based on the foregoing four connectives, of such a kind that: (i) the formulas of **Q** are identical with those of C_2; (ii) given an assignment of truth-values to its variables, the truth status of any formula can be worked out in the obvious way—so that, for example, if $/p/ = (T,F)$, $/q/ = T$, and $/r/ = F$, then $/\sim p/ = (T,F)$, $/p \& q/ = (T,F)$, $/p \& r/ = F$, $/p \vee q/ = T$, $/p \vee r/ = (T,F)$, etc.; (iii) consequently, the truth-functional interpretation of all formulas in which '$\supset$' does not occur is wholly identical with that of C_2. The foregoing truth table thus represents at least one alternative to material implication for giving something like a two-valued truth-functional repre-

[1]This truth table is closely related to that given by H. Reichenbach for what he calls quasi implication:

$_p\diagdown^q$	$p \rightarrow q$	
	T	F
T	T	F
F	I	I

See his *Philosophic Foundations for Quantum Mechanics* (Berkeley and Los Angeles, 1948), p. 168.

sentation of the common language notion of "implies." Note that the *modus ponens* principle will hold for this revised implication in the form:

If $/p/ = T$ and $/p \supset q/ = T$, then $/q/ = T$

In the subsequent discussion, we shall for the sake of concreteness use the system **Q** as a paradigm example of a quasi-truth-functional system. The usual notions of (two-valued) *tautology* and *contradiction* (i.e., as formulas uniformly taking the truth-value *T* or *F*, respectively, regardless of the particular truth-values assigned to their variables) apply without alternation to a quasi-truth-functional system such as **Q**. Note that the so-called "paradoxes of material implication"—the formulas "$\alpha \supset (\beta \supset \alpha)$" and "$\alpha \supset (\sim\alpha \supset \beta)$"—will not be tautologies of **Q**, i.e., will not inevitably take on the truth-value *T*. However, we do pay a price for this advantage, because many plausible tautologies of C_2 will also lose this status of tautologousness in **Q**. Indeed, all the following are nontautologous: "$\alpha \supset \alpha$," "$(\alpha \& \beta) \supset \alpha$," "$\alpha \supset (\alpha \lor \beta)$," "$(\alpha \supset \beta) \supset (\sim\beta \supset \sim\alpha)$," etc.[2]

We shall characterize as *quasi-truth-functional* systems of propositional logic defined by truth tables of this general type, in which some connectives are governed by (finitely) *many-valued* functions of the truth-values of their variables. (Such systems need not, of course, be two-valued, as our example happens to be.) Logical systems of this kind have not been intensively investigated.[3]

[2]This seemingly "unnatural" character of **Q** should not be considered an obstacle, since we are not concerned here to *advocate* **Q**, but to examine a whole family of systems of which **Q** serves merely as an example. All of these systems are fragments of propositional calculus, and of course in any *fragment* (proper), some "plausible" (two-valued) tautologies will inevitably be missing.

[3]They were first explored in detail by N. Rescher, "Quasi-Truth-Functional Systems of Propositional Logic," *The Journal of Symbolic Logic*, vol. 27 (1964), pp. 1–10. (The present section draws heavily on this article.) An early approach to quasi-truth-functionality is due to Hans Reichenbach. See Reichenbach (1932), (1935), (1935–36a), and (1935–36b). His starting point was the (by then well-known) observation that probability logic is not truth-functional. (See Sec. 27 below.) Specifically, since disjunction is not here truth-functional, Reichenbach had the idea of letting the truth-value of a disjunction depend on those of the two disjuncts, together with a third parameter ("Kopplungsgrad") whose value depends on the relation between them. This idea was developed by Zygmunt Zawirski. See "Les rapports de la logique polyvalente avec le calcul des probabilités," *Actes du Congrès International de Philosophie Scientifique*, IV (Paris, 1936), pp. 40–45. He suggested an *n*-valued logic in whose truth tables for disjunction (for example) there are in general $n - 1$ possible entries once the truth-values of both components have been determined, perhaps somewhat as follows:

$p \lor q$		
$\diagdown q$	1	2	3
p			
1	1	(1,2)	(1,2)
2	(1,2)	2	(2,3)
3	(1,2)	(2,3)	3

Zawirski did not develop any semantical basis for this proposal, and his suggestions bore no fruit. (This author's 1964 paper was written without awareness of Zawirski's work.)

A two-valued quasi-truth-functional truth table could be regarded as an *incomplete* version of some strictly truth-functional truth table, certain entries of which are simply not given. Thus if all that we are told regarding some two-place connective $\varnothing$ is that $T \varnothing F = F \varnothing T = F$, and no information is given us regarding the remaining, mixed cases, then we could substitute for the *incomplete* truth table

$_p\backslash^q$	$p \varnothing q$	
	T	F
T	?	F
F	F	?

the quasi-truth-functional one:

$_p\backslash^q$	$p \varnothing q$	
	T	F
T	(T,F)	F
F	F	(T,F)

Either way, we would know, for example, that "$\sim(\alpha \varnothing \sim\alpha)$" must be a tautology, and could proceed along these lines to develop the logic of the *incomplete* system by means of the quasi-truth-functional one.

In the consideration of such systems it is important to recognize that the bracketed pairing (T,F) that occurs in the truth tables is not a specific truth-value whose applicability represents *a distinct truth status* for a proposition. For if this were so, then a proposition's assuming this particular truth-value would preclude its simultaneous assumption of the other truth-values (T or F), and this is not the case. Rather its role is alternative-indicating: "the truth-value at issue may be T or it may be F."

The absence of certain plausible tautologies in such systems as **Q** can be mitigated if we adopt the conception of *quasi-tautologies*, i.e., formulas that invariably *do or can* take a designated truth-value for any and every given assignment of truth-values to its propositional variables. For example, "$\alpha \supset (\beta \supset \alpha)$" will then be a quasi-tautology of **Q**, as the following truth table shows:

p	q	$q \supset p$	$p \supset (q \supset p)$
T	T	T	T
F	T	F	(T,F)
T	F	(T,F)	(T,F)
F	F	(T,F)	(T,F)

In fact, it is possible to show that all tautologies of C_2 will be quasi-tautologies of **Q**. This can be done by verifying that all C_2-axioms are **Q**-quasi-tautologies, and establishing the applicability of the *modus ponens* principle that

If $p \supset q \in T'(\mathbf{Q})$ and $p \in T'(\mathbf{Q})$, then $q \in T'(\mathbf{Q})$

where $T'(\mathbf{X})$ is the set of quasi-tautologies of **X**. This last point can be shown as follows. If p is a quasi-tautology, then for any given assignment of truth-values to its variables either (1) $/p/ = T$ or (2) $/p/ = (T,F)$. But if $p \supset q$ is also a quasi-tautology, then $/q/$ cannot be F in case (1), and $/q/$ must be (T,F) in case (2), so that q must also be a quasi-tautology.

The conception of quasi-tautologousness is significant in militating against the idea that—since any formula either is or is not a tautology—many-valued logics are themselves inherently two-valued.

Let us now consider again the 3-valued connectives of Łukasiewicz' system $\mathbf{L}_3$:

p	$\neg p$	$\begin{smallmatrix}\backslash q\\ p\backslash\end{smallmatrix}$	$p \wedge q$			$p \vee q$			$p \rightarrow q$			$p \leftrightarrow q$		
			T	I	F	T	I	F	T	I	F	T	I	F
$+T$	F	$+T$	T	I	F	T	T	T	T	I	F	T	I	F
I	I	I	I	I	F	T	I	I	T	T	I	I	T	I
$-F$	T	$-F$	F	F	F	T	I	F	T	T	T	F	I	T

The entries for these truth tables can be arrived at by reasoning somewhat as follows in the $I \wedge I$ case: "If the truth-value of p is indeterminate (as between true and false), and the truth-value of q is indeterminate, then the truth-value of $p \wedge q$ must also be indeterminate." But this overlooks the fact that p and q may be interdependent, so that q may, for example, be $\neg p$.[4] Łukasiewicz' truth tables are thus unsatisfactory because they are inadequate to the purposes of his intended interpretation. While the idea of a logic based on three rather than two truth-values along the Łukasiewicz line of approach is not inherently unworkable, the resulting system must not be truth-functional, but quasi-truth-functional, along something like the following lines:

p	$\neg p$	$\begin{smallmatrix}\backslash q\\ p\backslash\end{smallmatrix}$	$p \wedge q$			$p \vee q$			$p \supset q$			$p \equiv q$		
			T	I	F	T	I	F	T	I	F	T	I	F
$+T$	F	$+T$	T	I	F	T	T	T	T	I	F	T	I	F
I	I	I	I	(I,F)	F	T	(I,T)	I	T	(I,T)	I	I	(I,T)	I
$-F$	T	$-F$	F	F	F	T	I	F	T	T	T	F	I	T

[4]This objection to $\mathbf{L}_3$ appears to have originated in the discussion of Łukasiewicz' 1938 paper in Zürich. See F. Gonseth (ed.), *Les entretiens de Zürich . . . décembre 1938* (Zürich, 1941), p. 105, n.

Łukasiewicz' own explanation of the rationale of this 3-valued logic would certainly call for a system that is not strictly truth-functional.

Note that this system, $\mathbf{L}_q$, as we shall call it, will *have no tautologies*. (A wff never yields an unqualified T output for uniformly I inputs.) It can, however, be shown that various two-valued tautologies are quasi-tautologies of $\mathbf{L}_q$ (for example, "$\alpha \supset \alpha$")—indeed if we were to designate I also, then the tautologies of this system would coincide with those of $\mathbf{C}_2$. Interestingly, if we add also the Słupecki operator

p	$\mathsf{T}p$
$+T$	I
I	I
F	I

then "$\mathsf{T}\alpha \vee \neg\mathsf{T}\alpha$" will be a quasi-tautology of $\mathbf{L}_q^{\mathrm{S}}$, but not of $\mathbf{L}_3^{\mathrm{S}}$, so that there is a substantial difference between those systems.

The preceding example shows how the concept of quasi-truth-functionality can be used to evade what might be called the "designation two-valuedness" of many-valued systems. What is at issue here is the feature of many-valued truth tables that for given input values a formula assumes either a designated truth-value or else a nondesignated one. For in accordance with this feature, the designated/nondesignated distinction comes to play a dichotomous role in many-valued logics analogous with the true-false dichotomy of two-valued logic. Quasi-truth-functionality affords a way of bypassing this vestigial two-valuedness. The concept of quasi-truth-functionality thus implements the idea of semantic indeterminacy. For example, if $/\alpha/ = I$, then in $\mathbf{L}_q$ we *simply cannot tell* whether "$\alpha \supset \alpha$" does or does not take a designated truth-value.

It may be noted further that various quasi-truth-functional connectives are of interest because they provide one way in which a counterpart can be had in the logic of two-valued truth functions to logical ideas of a fundamentally non-truth-functional character. Thus for "p conveys the same information as q" (symbolically: $p \ominus q$) and "p is (logically) incompatible with q" (symbolically: $p \parallel q$), we would obtain the following quasi-truth-functional approximations:

$p \backslash q$	$p \ominus q$		$p \parallel q$	
	T	F	T	F
T	(T,F)	F	F	(T,F)
F	F	(T,F)	(T,F)	F

It thus appears that various important logical relations between propositions can at least partially be approximated in two-valued logic by quasi-truth-functional representation.

Returning to the system **Q**, it is germane to examine the question of whether its lack of strict truth functionality can be overcome by reformulating **Q** as a many-valued strictly truth-functional system (using more than two truth-values), instead of a quasi-truth-functional two-valued one. At first sight, it would appear plausible and promising to remove the truth-value ambiguity of the bracketed pair (T,F) by replacing this through the introduction of a suitable "indeterminate" truth-value I. We would then obtain a 3-valued system, to be designated as **R**, characterized by the following truth tables, designed so as to be as closely compatible as possible with the defining truth tables of our system **Q**:

p	$\neg p$		$q \atop p$	$p \wedge q$			$p \vee q$			$p \to q$		
				T	I	F	T	I	F	T	I	F
$+T$	F		$+T$	T	I	F	T	T	T	T	I	F
I	I		I	I	I	F	T	I	I	I	I	I
$-F$	T		$-F$	F	F	F	T	I	F	I	I	I

This system **R** represents a 3-valued amplification of **Q** in that if we replace the truth-value I of **R** by the bracketed truth-value pairing (T,F), we will again obtain the system **Q**.[5]

It is readily seen, however, that the system **R** is thoroughly unsatisfactory as a many-valued reformulation of **Q**, because there is no way in which we can obtain the same concepts of "tautology" and "contradiction" in **R** that we have in **Q**. The following four alternatives exhaust the plausible possibilities:

(A)	(B)	(C)	(D)
$+T$	$+T$	$+T$	$+T$
I	$-I$	$+I$	$+I$
$-F$	$-F$	$-F$	$-F$

But here alternatives (A) and (C) are unsatisfactory because "α & $\sim\alpha$" is not a contradiction in **R** (as it is in **Q**), and alternative (B) because "$\alpha \vee \sim\alpha$" is not a tautology in **R** (as it is in **Q**). Alternative (D) is unac-

---

[5]Note that this system (and the others to be considered below) is of the following general type: between T and F are inserted a series of "intermediate" truth-values such that the ranking $T, I_1, I_2, \ldots, I_n, F$ may be viewed as a ranking in increasing order of "falsity" in the sense that (i) the truth-table column for negation is obtained by inverting this truth-value series, (ii) the truth-table entry for alternation is always the truth-values of the "truer" member, and (iii) the truth-table entry for conjunction is always the truth-value of the "falser" member.

ceptable because "$(\alpha \,\&\, \sim\alpha) \supset (\alpha \lor \sim\alpha)$" is *both* a tautology and a contradiction. Each of these four results seems undesirable in itself and is incompatible with the concepts of "tautology" and "contradiction" in the system **Q**, which **R** was intended to reproduce in many-valued form. Thus **R** does not represent a satisfactory many-valued truth-functional reformulation of the quasi-truth-functional system **Q**.

It should be remarked, however, that all of these unsatisfactory characteristics of **R** are traceable to the fact that **R** gives one and the same truth-value both to p and to $\neg p$ in certain cases (namely when $/p/ = I$).[6] This suggests the possibility of overcoming the shortcomings of **R** as a many-valued reformulation of **Q** by going over to a 4-valued system, in which the single *self-negating* truth-value I of **R** is split into *two mutually negating* truth-values, I_1 and I.

The idea of such a splitting and its reverse reidentifications suggests how many-valued systems can be related to one another by way of "expansion" and "compression." Consider, for example, the system $\mathbf{C_2} \times \mathbf{C_2}$ (cf. Sec. 16). The compression

  11 into T
  10 into I
  01 into I
  00 into F

will reduce this system to the quasi-truth-functional system

p	$\neg p$		q	$p \land q$			$p \lor q$			$p \to q$			$p \leftrightarrow q$		
		q / p		T	I	F	T	I	F	T	I	F	T	I	F
T	F	T		T	I	F	T	T	T	T	I	F	T	I	F
I	I	I		I	(I,F)	F	T	(I,T)	I	T	(I,T)	I	I	(T,F)	I
F	T	F		F	F	F	T	I	F	T	T	T	F	I	T

a system closely akin to $\mathbf{L}_q$. (Note that the indeterminacy here need not always involve I, but can—in the case of an equivalence—take the form of a vacillation between solely the classical truth-values.) On the other hand, the compression—and here cf. page 72—

  11 into T
  10 into T
  01 into F
  00 into F

---

[6]Difficulties of this nature have led Andrzej Mostowski to observe that he does not have "any hope that it will ever be possible to find a reasonable interpretation of the 3-valued logic of Łukasiewicz in terms of everyday language" (*The Journal of Symbolic Logic*, vol. 14 [1950], p. 223).

will take $\mathbf{C_2} \times \mathbf{C_2}$ into

p	$\sim p$	$p\backslash^{q}$	$p\,\&\,q$		$p \vee q$		$p \supset q$		$p \equiv q$	
			T	F	T	F	T	F	T	F
T	F	T	T	F	T	T	T	F	T	F
F	T	F	F	F	T	F	T	T	F	T

that is, back into $\mathbf{C_2}$ itself.

Consider one further example of the expansion-compression process. The 3-valued system

p	$\neg p$	$p\backslash^{q}$	$p \wedge q$			$p \vee q$			$p \to q$			$p \leftrightarrow q$		
			T	I	F	T	I	F	T	I	F	T	I	F
$+T$	F	$+T$	T	I	F	T	T	T	T	I	F	T	I	F
$+I$	F	$+I$	I	I	F	T	I	I	T	T	F	I	T	F
F	T	F	F	F	F	T	I	F	T	T	T	F	F	T

is related to $\mathbf{L_3}$—it would be identical with $\mathbf{L_3}$ if the four boxed F's were I's. This system is of interest in the present connection because the compression

T into T
I into T
F into F

will reduce it to the classical, two-valued propositional calculus $\mathbf{C_2}$. This 3-valued system is thus an expansion of $\mathbf{C_2}$ that results from it with an appropriate choice for splitting the T of $\mathbf{C_2}$ apart into two truth-values T and I.

The foregoing conception of how systems can be related by expansion and compression leads us to consider the following 4-valued system,[7] to be designated as $\mathbf{W}$, as a possibly suitable reformulation of $\mathbf{R}$:[8]

p	$\neg p$	$p\backslash^{q}$	$p \wedge q$				$p \vee q$				$p \to q$			
			T	I_1	I_2	F	T	I_1	I_2	F	T	I_1	I_2	F
$+T$	F	$+T$	T	I_1	I_2	F	T	T	T	T	T	I_1	I_2	F
I_1	I_2	I_1	I_1	I_1	I_2	F	T	I_1	I_1	I_1	I_1	I_1	I_2	I_2
I_2	I_1	I_2	I_2	I_2	I_2	F	T	I_1	I_2	I_2	I_1	I_1	I_1	I_1
$-F$	T	$-F$	F	F	F	F	T	I_1	I_2	F	I_1	I_1	I_1	I_1

[7]A many-valued *system*, in the sense of this discussion, is a set of truth tables (with specified designated and antidesignated truth-values) for the usual connectives of the propositional calculus.

[8]Note that $\mathbf{W}$, like $\mathbf{R}$, is built on the principles enunciated in note 5 with respect to the mode of many-valued generalization of the propositional connectives.

It is apparent that **W** is an "expansion" of **R**, in some sense. Indeed the precise sense in which this is so can be specified in general terms as follows.

We define (in general) the w-valued system $\mathbf{S}_w$ to be an "expansion" of the r-valued system $\mathbf{S}_r$ (with $r < w$) if there exists a (one-many) correspondence between the truth-values of $\mathbf{S}_r$ and those of $\mathbf{S}_w$ such that this correspondence satisfies four conditions: (i) it associates every $\mathbf{S}_r$ truth-value with some $\mathbf{S}_w$ truth-value, and, conversely, (ii) it never associates the same truth-value of $\mathbf{S}_w$ with distinct truth-values of $\mathbf{S}_r$, (iii) it always associates designated (or antidesignated) truth-values of $\mathbf{S}_w$ with designated (or antidesignated) truth-values of $\mathbf{S}_r$, and (iv) it is such that if we replace every $\mathbf{S}_w$ truth-value by the associated $\mathbf{S}_r$ truth-value throughout the truth tables of $\mathbf{S}_w$, these will be reduced to the truth tables of $\mathbf{S}_r$.

It should be observed that whenever $\mathbf{S}_w$ is an expansion of $\mathbf{S}_r$ in the sense of this definition, then every tautology (or contradiction) of $\mathbf{S}_w$ must also be a tautology (or contradiction) of $\mathbf{S}_r$ (though not necessarily conversely). We may thus speak of $\mathbf{S}_w$ as a *characteristic expansion* of $\mathbf{S}_r$, when it is not only an extension, but also when every tautology of $\mathbf{S}_r$ is a tautology of $\mathbf{S}_w$ (so that the tautologies of $\mathbf{S}_r$ and $\mathbf{S}_w$, according to the truth tables in question, will be precisely the same).[9] Further, we call $\mathbf{S}_w$ a *strongly characteristic* expansion when the same is true also with respect to contradictions.

It is readily shown that **W** is an expansion of **R**. If we associate I_1 and I_2 with I (in effect, make the identifications $I_1 = I_2 = I$)—letting both I_1 and I_2 have the same designation status in **W** that I has in **R**—then the system **W** reduces to the system **R**. Further, **W** is also a 4-valued expansion of the ordinary two-valued propositional calculus, for if we associate I_1 and T in **W** with T, and I_2 and F in **W** with F (i.e., set $I_1 = T, I_2 = F$), the truth tables of **W** are reduced to the familiar two-valued truth tables. Indeed this truth-value association leads to establishment of **W** as a *strongly characteristic expansion* of the propositional calculus. We thus obtain an adequate —indeed the usual—notion of "tautology" and "contradiction" for **W** by taking I_1 (and, of course, T) as designated, and I_2 (and, of course, F) as antidesignated. (We note also that **W** meets our initial requirement that $/p \rightarrow q/ = T$ can occur only when $/p/ = T$—and then $/q/ = T$—and so not when $/p/ = F$.)

However, it soon becomes clear that the system **W** has a major shortcoming from our standpoint. It cannot be viewed as an appropriate truth-

[9]In this usage, the term "characteristic" is analogous with the usual sense in which a system of truth tables is called *characteristic* of a system of propositional calculus if the tautologies according to these truth tables are the same as the original tautologies (i.e., theorems) of this system. Any characteristic extension of a *regular* system (i.e., one for which *modus ponens* applies) must be regular. Alonzo Church's paper "Non-Normal Truth-Tables for the Propositional Calculus," *Boletin de la Sociedad Matematica Mexicana*, vol. 10 (1953), pp. 41–52, contains an excellent survey of all the customary terminology relating to the logic of truth tables.

functional analogue of **Q**—which is what we have been seeking—for it fails to be an *expansion* of **Q** in the sense of our definition, but rather is an extension of the usual two-valued propositional calculus. However, to obtain this desideratum of a many-valued truth-functional extension of **Q**, it suffices to make one modification in **W**, namely to replace its truth table for implication by:

$p \backslash q$	$p \to q$: T	I_1	I_2	F
T	T	I_1	I_2	F
I_1	I_1	I_1	I_2	I_2
I_2	I_2	I_1	I_2	I_2
F	I_1	I_2	I_2	I_1

The resultant system, to be designated as **W***, is such that: (i) the identification $I_1 = I_2 = I$ yields **R**, so that **W*** is an expansion of **R** (with appropriate designations); (ii) the identification $I_1 = T, I_2 = F$ yields **Q**, so that **W*** is an expansion of **Q** (with T, I_1 designated; F, I_2 antidesignated) and indeed is a strongly characteristic expansion of **Q**. Thus the system **W*** constitutes a suitable many-valued, strictly truth-functional reformulation of the quasi-truth-functional two-valued system **Q**.

The question arises: Does *every* system of two-valued quasi-truth-functional propositional logic possess a strongly characteristic expansion which is a strictly truth-functional, many-valued system? This question can be answered affirmatively. As proof, consider the following construction procedure.

To transpose the two-valued (quasi-truth-functional) truth-table matrix for any two-place propositional connective[10] $\varnothing$

$p \backslash q$	$p \varnothing q$: T F
$+T$ $-F$	$\lVert v_{i,j} \rVert$

$j \in \{1,2\}$ $i \in \{1,2\}$ $v_{ij} \in \{T,F\}$

into a corresponding strictly truth-functional counterpart, we proceed to form a 4-valued matrix:

[10]To accommodate n-ary quasi-truth-functional connectives (with $n > 2$), we may reduce these to binary connectives. This calls for only minor and obvious modifications in the standard reduction procedure (see W. V. Quine, *Mathematical Logic*, §8).

$$
\begin{array}{c|cccc}
 & \multicolumn{4}{c}{p \oslash q} \\
\diagdown\!\!\!\!\!\!\!^{q}_{p} & T & F & I_1 & I_2 \\
\hline
+T & & & & \\
-F & & & & \\
+I_1 & \|u_{i,j}\| & & & \qquad i \in \{1,2,3,4\} \quad i \in \{1,2,3,4\} \ v_{ij} \in \{T,I_1,I_2,F\} \\
-I_2 & & & &
\end{array}
$$

This is to be done in accordance with the following rules:

(R1)   If $v_{i,j} = T$, then set $u_{i,j} = T$, and $u_{i+2,j+2} = u_{i,j+2} = u_{i+2,j} = I_1$

(R2)   If $v_{i,j} = F$, then set $u_{i,j} = F$, and set $u_{i+2,j+2} = u_{i,j+2} = u_{i+2,j} = I_2$

(R3)   If $v_{i,j} = (T,F)$, then set $u_{i,j} = I_1$, and set $u_{i+2,j+2} = u_{i+2,j} = u_{i,j+2} = I_2$

(R4)   At pleasure (i.e., where other considerations might indicate it desirable or appropriate) the truth table resulting from application of (R1) to (R3) may be altered by replacing (at any desired place within the matrix) I_1 by T, and I_2 by F.

The corresponding rules for a one-place connective are left as an exercise for the reader.

It is readily seen that the 4-valued truth table obtained in this manner will have the following two characteristics: (i) In collapsing the 4-valued truth table to a two-valued one by the identifications $I_1 = T$ and $I_2 = F$, we will always obtain the original two-valued truth table,[11] so that the 4-valued truth table is an expansion of the two-valued one, and therefore every 4-valued tautology (or contradiction) must also be a two-valued tautology (or contradiction). Further, (ii) every two-valued tautology (or contradiction) must also be a 4-valued tautology (or contradiction) so that the 4-valued truth table is also a *strongly characteristic* expansion.

The correctness of (ii) can be seen as follows. If a formula fails to be a 4-valued tautology, it must take on one of the truth-values F or I_2 for some assignment of truth-values to its variables, $p_1, p_2, \ldots, p_k$, let us say $/p_1/ = v_1$, $/p_2/ = v_2, \ldots, /p_k/ = v_k$, where the v_i are truth-values of the group $T, I_1, I_2,$ or F. But now, due to the very mode of construction of the 4-valued truth tables, the formula in question must take on the (two-valued) truth-value F when we assign to its variables the truth-values $/p_1/ = v'_1$, $/p_2/ = v'_2, \ldots, /p_k/ = v'_k$, where $v_i = T$ if v'_i is T or I_1, and $v'_i = F$ if v_i is F or I_2. Thus, every two-valued tautology must also be a 4-valued tautology. Further, if we substitute 'T' for 'F', 'F' for 'T', and "contradiction" for "tautology" throughout the foregoing argument, then it continues to be

---

[11]The upper left-hand 2×2 submatrix of the 4×4 matrix agrees completely with the two-valued matrix, except in those places where the latter has (T,F). Now in collapsing rows (and columns) 1 and 3, and 2 and 4, of the 4×4 matrix, by setting $I_1 = T$ and $I_2 = F$, the T's and F's must always agree pairwise, *except* where rule (R3) has led to opposites, which yield (T,F), as is appropriate.

applicable, and shows that every two-valued contradiction must also be a 4-valued contradiction. Thus the 4-valued extension must be strongly characteristic of the two-valued system on the basis of which it was constructed.

We have thus established the following principal result: *For every two-valued system of quasi-truth-functional propositional logic there exists a (strictly) truth-functional system of 4-valued logic which is a strongly characteristic expansion of the two-valued system.* And this result can readily be extended along analogous lines to show that many-valued quasi-truth-functional systems can always be represented by strictly truth-functional ones—systems which will in general, however, have a significantly greater number of truth-values. (If there are n truth-values in the initial system, the resultant expanded one will in general have $n \times n$ truth-values.)

An interesting variant of **Q** is the following quasi-truth-functional system **Q*** whose mode of implication is entirely non-truth-functional, except for the obviously truth-functional case of a true antecedent and a false consequent:

p	$\neg p$
T	F
F	T

${}^{q}\!\diagdown_{p}$	$p \wedge q$ T	F	$p \to q$ T	F
T	T	F	(T,F)	F
F	F	F	(T,F)	(T,F)

For this system—essentially the one with which we began in the first paragraph of this section—our specified expansion procedure yields the strictly truth-functional 4-valued (strongly characteristic) counterpart:

p	$\neg p$
$+T$	F
$+I_1$	I_2
I_2	I_1
F	T

${}^{q}\!\diagdown_{p}$	$p \wedge q$ T	I_1	I_2	F	$p \to q$ T	I_1	I_2	F
$+T$	T	I_1	I_2	F	I_1	I_1	I_2	F
$+I_1$	I_1	I_1	I_2	I_2	I_2	I_2	I_2	I_2
I_2	I_2	I_2	I_2	I_2	I_2	I_2	I_2	I_2
F	F	I_2	I_2	F	I_1	I_2	I_2	I_1

With permissible changes this can be altered to the normal and somewhat more standard-looking system:

p	$\neg p$
$+T$	F
$+I_1$	I_2
I_2	I_1
F	T

${}^{q}\!\diagdown_{p}$	$p \wedge q$ T	I_1	I_2	F	$p \to q$ T	I_1	I_2	F
$+T$	T	I_1	I_2	F	T	I_2	I_2	F
$+I_1$	I_1	I_1	I_2	F	I_2	I_2	I_2	I_2
I_2	I_2	I_2	I_2	F	I_2	I_2	I_2	I_2
F	F	F	F	F	T	I_2	I_2	T

This has the interesting feature that—though the rule of *modus ponens* applies, and though there are indeed tautologies [e.g., "$\neg(\alpha \wedge \neg\alpha)$]"—the most familiar implication tautologies of C_2 [e.g., "$\alpha \rightarrow \alpha$," "$(\alpha \wedge \beta) \rightarrow \alpha$," "$(\alpha \rightarrow \beta) \rightarrow (\neg\beta \rightarrow \neg\alpha)$"] will not be tautologous.

It is clear that the finding italicized above as a principal result can be generalized, *mutatis mutandis*, to cover many-valued systems of quasi-truth-functional propositional logic. In consequence, the logical theory of quasi-truth-functional systems introduces no fundamental novelty, but properly forms a part of the wider domain of many-valued (strictly) truth-functional logic. However, the truth-functional analogue of a quasi-truth-functional system will always be of a significantly higher order of many-valuedness than the quasi-truth-functional system it is intended to represent.[12] This added complexity is the price we pay in abandoning the simpler and conceptually perhaps more natural quasi-truth-functional systems for the greater mathematical convenience of strict truth functionality.

Finally, it should be noted that the idea of quasi-truth-functional systems of logic affords a new means for providing an interpretation for a large family of many-valued logic. By "compressing" the many-valued system through the identification of its designated truth-values with T, and its nondesignated truth-values with F, we will in many cases obtain quasi-truth-functional propositional connectives for which a "natural" interpretation exists. In such cases, the initial many-valued system can be construed as a means for accommodating these logical relationships in the manner of an approximation within the framework of truth-functional logic.

Consider, for the sake of illustration, the system of 3-valued logic obtained by replacing the truth table for implication in **R** by $\supset$-implication:

$\begin{smallmatrix}&&q\\p&&\end{smallmatrix}$	$p \supset q$		
	T	I	F
$+T$	T	I	F
$+I$	T	I	I
$-F$	T	T	T

Note also that I is now to be treated as designated. The truth tables of this system are of some interest because although characteristic for (ordinary, two-valued) propositional calculus, no Boolean algebra is homomorphic to them,[13] so that their interpretation as a system of propositional logic is problematic. (Note also that *modus ponens* does not hold in the form that if

---

[12]Thus in the case of a 3-valued (T,F,I) quasi-truth-functional system we would need seven truth-values to represent: (T,F,I), (T,F), (T,I), (F,I), and also T,F, and I.

[13]This was remarked by Alonzo Church and Nicholas Rescher in *The Journal of Symbolic Logic*, vol. 15 (1950), pp. 69–70.

an implication and its antecedent both assume a designated truth-value then the consequent must also do so.) However, if we set $I = T$, these truth tables reduce to the familiar two-valued system, except that the truth table for $\supset$-implication becomes:

$p \supset q$		
$\diagdown\!\!^q_p$	T	F
T	T	(T,F)
F	T	T

This is patently not identical with the truth table for material implication. It *is*, however, identical with the quasi-truth-functional truth table for $p \supset \Diamond q$, where '$\supset$' as usual represents material implication and '$\Diamond$' represents the modality of possibility, which, of course, is not truth-functional at all. Thus the 3-valued system in question could be construed as approximation to truth-functional representation of the logic of this (non-truth-functional) propositional relationship. This example illustrates the potential use of quasi-truth-functional systems as a vehicle for the interpretation of certain otherwise hard-to-interpret systems of many-valued logic.

An interesting perspective for viewing quasi-truth-functional systems can be developed in terms of a variation of the alternative worlds approach. (Compare Sec. 20.) Consider again a set W of possible worlds w_i:

$$W = \{w_1, w_2, \ldots\}$$

Let the truth-value of a proposition p now be a certain *pair of sets of possible worlds*, to be specified as follows:

$$/p/ = \langle T[p], F[p]\rangle$$

where

$$T[p] = \{w \mid w \in W \,\&\, p \text{ is } true \text{ in } w\}$$
$$F[p] = \{w \mid w \in W \,\&\, p \text{ is } false \text{ in } w\}$$

Let it be understood that:

1. Negation is such that $/\neg p/ = F$ iff $/p/ = T$, and $/\neg p/ = T$ iff $/p/ = F$
2. Conjunction is such that $/p \wedge q/ = T$ iff $/p/ = /q/ = T$, and $/p \wedge q/ = F$ iff either $/p/ = F$ or $/q/ = F$ or both
3. Disjunction is such that $/p \vee q/ = F$ iff $/p/ = /q/ = F$, and $/p \vee q/ = T$ iff either $/p/ = T$ or $/q/ = T$ or both

It is then clear that the following family of truth rules must obtain:

$$/\neg p/ \;= \langle F[p], T[p]\rangle$$
$$/p \wedge q/ = \langle T[p] \cap T[q], F[p] \cup F[q]\rangle$$
$$/p \vee q/ = \langle T[p] \cup T[q], F[p] \cap F[q]\rangle$$
$$/p \supset q/ = /\neg p \vee q/$$
$$/p \equiv q/ = /(p \supset q) \cap (q \supset p)/$$

Note that we shall have a two-valued or a many-valued system according as:

(A) For all p: $T[p] \cup F[p] = V (= W)$

is true or false. And we shall have a strictly truth-functional system only when it is true that:

(B) For all p: $T[p] \cap F[p] = \Lambda$

When condition (B) fails, the system will clearly be quasi-truth-functional, since it will then be possible for some proposition to assume *both the truth-values T and F.*

For the sake of an example, consider a system based on only two possible worlds w_1 and w_2. Four possible sets can then figure in the two places of the truth-value $/p/ = \langle T[p], F[p] \rangle$, namely:

$1 = \{w_1, w_2\} = W = V$
$2 = \{w_2\}$
$3 = \{w_1\}$
$4 = \Lambda$

There will then be 16 two-place truth-values:

$\langle 1,1 \rangle$ $\langle 2,1 \rangle$ $\langle 3,1 \rangle$ $\langle 4,1 \rangle$
$\langle 1,2 \rangle$ $\langle 2,2 \rangle$ $\langle 3,2 \rangle$ $\langle 4,2 \rangle$
$\langle 1,3 \rangle$ $\langle 2,3 \rangle$ $\langle 3,3 \rangle$ $\langle 4,3 \rangle$
$\langle 1,4 \rangle$ $\langle 2,4 \rangle$ $\langle 3,4 \rangle$ $\langle 4,4 \rangle$

Condition (A) will eliminate all the boxed truth-values, and condition (B) will eliminate all the shaded ones. Thus if one imposes both of these conditions, we have the following system (with $\langle 1,4 \rangle = T$, $\langle 4,1 \rangle = F$ and $\langle 2,3 \rangle$ and $\langle 3,2 \rangle$ as two distinct "intermediate" truth-values). [NOTE: In presenting this system we shall simply omit the brackets, thus writing $\langle 1,4 \rangle$ as 14.]

p	$\neg p$		$p \wedge q$ 14 23 32 41	$p \vee q$ 14 23 32 41	$p \supset q$ 14 23 32 41	$p \equiv q$ 14 23 32 41
		$\begin{array}{c} q \\ p \end{array}$				
14	41	14	14 23 32 41	14 14 14 14	14 23 32 41	14 23 32 41
23	32	23	23 23 41 41	14 23 14 23	14 14 32 32	23 14 41 32
32	23	32	32 41 32 41	14 14 32 32	14 23 14 23	32 41 14 23
41	14	41	41 41 41 41	14 23 32 41	14 14 14 14	41 32 23 14

The resulting system is therefore simply the product system $\mathbf{C}_2 \times \mathbf{C}_2$.

But if we now impose only condition (A), then a (somewhat complicated) 9-valued system results.[14] Although this system will on the surface of

---

[14]This 9-valued logic has the structure of the system $S_3^{\supset} \times S_2^{\supset}$. The correspondence between the truth-values goes as follows: $TT = 14$, $TI = 13$, $TF = 23$, $IT = 12$, $II = 11$, $IF = 21$, $FT = 32$, $FI = 31$, $FF = 41$, or else $TT = 14$, $TI = 12$, $TF = 32$, $IT = 13$, $II = 11$, $IF = 31$, $FT = 23$, $FI = 21$, $FF = 41$ (which is the preceding list with 2 and 3 interchanged).

it be strictly truth-functional, its violation of condition (B) makes it clear that the *underlying* semantic situation that it articulates is fundamentally non-truth-functional. For it admits such truth-values as $11 = \langle V,V \rangle$, so that its semantics contemplates propositions that are *both true and false* in the possible worlds at issue. On the other hand, if we now impose only condition (B), then a 9-valued system will also result.[15] Since this system admits such truth-values as $44 = \langle \Lambda,\Lambda \rangle$, its semantics contemplates the prospect of certain propositions as *neither true nor false* in either of the possible worlds, i.e., as indeterminate in both. In such a system, the underlying semantical situation is essentially 3-valued.

Appendix 1

There is yet another way in which a strictly truth-functional counterpart to a quasi-truth-functional system can be given. Let a truth-value in the "new," truth-functional system amount to a *set of truth-values* of the "old" quasi-truth-functional one, for example:

$$1 = \{T\}$$
$$2 = \{T,F\}$$
$$3 = \{F\}$$

And then use the basic quasi-truth-functional system, say

p	$\neg p$		$p \wedge q$		$p \vee q$		$p \rightarrow q$		$p \leftrightarrow q$	
		$^q_p\backslash$	T	F	T	F	T	F	T	F
$+T$	F	$+T$	T	F	T	T	T	F	T	F
$-F$	T	$-F$	F	F	T	F	(T,F)	T	F	T

as starting point for deriving a related strictly truth-functional one from the just-indicated identities:

p	$\neg p$		$p \wedge q$			$p \vee q$			$p \Rightarrow q$			$p \Leftrightarrow q$		
		$^q_p\backslash$	1	2	3	1	2	3	1	2	3	1	2	3
$+1$	3	$+1$	1	2	3	1	1	1	1	2	3	1	2	3
±2	2	±2	2	2	3	1	2	2	2	2	2	2	2	2
-3	1	-3	3	3	3	1	2	3	2	2	1	3	2	1

[15]This again has the structure $S_3^{\supset} \times S_3^{\supset}$. The correspondence between the truth-values can go either $TT = 14, TI = 24, TF = 23, IT = 34, II = 44, IF = 43, FT = 32, FI = 42, FF = 41$, or else $TT = 14, TI = 34, TF = 32, IT = 24, II = 44, IF = 42, FT = 23, FI = 43, FF = 41$ (which is again the preceding list with 2 and 3 interchanged).

Here the boxed entry means that from $2 \Rightarrow 2$, that is the combination $\{T,F\} \rightarrow \{T,F\}$, we will get—via the combinatorial possibilities $T \rightarrow T$, $T \rightarrow F$, $F \rightarrow T$, and $F \rightarrow F$—the truth-values of the set $2 = \{T,F\}$.

This procedure will also work if the initial system is strictly truth-functional. Thus for $\mathbf{C}_2$ we will obtain:

p	$\dashv p$		$\begin{array}{c}q\\p\end{array}$	$p \wedge\!\!\!\wedge q$ 1 2 3			$p \vee\!\!\!\vee q$ 1 2 3			$p \Rightarrow q$ 1 2 3			$p \Leftrightarrow q$ 1 2 3		
$+1$	3		$+1$	1	2	3	1	1	1	1	2	3	1	2	3
±2	2		±2	2	2	3	1	2	2	1	2	2	2	2	2
-3	1		-3	3	3	3	1	2	3	1	1	1	3	2	1

That is, we would obtain $\mathbf{K}_3 = \mathbf{S}_3^{\mathrm{p}}$ (with the indicated designations). As this shows, it is clear from the construction procedure that the tautologies of the derived system and those of the original system must be the same.

Appendix 2

Still another way of generating quasi-truth-functional systems will now be considered. The basis for this approach is the idea of multi-valued truth-value assignment operators considered in Sec. 14.

Suppose that we begin with logical operators that are two-valued and truth-functional—i.e., with the classical system $\mathbf{C}_2$—but superimpose a 3-valued truth-value assignment operator (in the manner of Sec. 14):

$\begin{array}{c}p\\v\end{array}$	$\mathbf{V}vp$ T I F		
T	T	I	F
I	I	T	I
F	F	I	T

It is possible on this basis to create "truth tables" by a somewhat novel procedure. Let us not proceed as with the orthodox truth table

$\begin{array}{c}q\\p\end{array}$	$p \supset q$ T F	
T	T	F
F	*T*	T

where the shaded entry means "If $/p/ = F$ and $/q/ = T$, then $/p \supset q/ = T$." Rather, let us use this two-valued truth table—along with the stipulated 3-valued matrix for $\mathbf{V}vp$—to create a 3-valued one:

$$\text{V}T(p \supset q)$$

$_p\backslash{}^q$	T	I	F
T	T	(T,F)	**F**
I	T	(T,F)	(T,F)
F	**T**	T	T

where the shaded entry means "If $/\text{V}Fp/ = T$ and $/\text{V}Tq/ = T$, then $/\text{V}T(p \supset q)/ = T$" and correspondingly the boxed entry means "If $/\text{V}Tp/ = T$ and $/\text{V}Fq/ = T$, then $/\text{V}T(p \supset q)/ = F$." In calculating entries regarding I, we interpret this as representing (T,F), i.e., as "undetermined as between the alternatives T and F." Using this procedure, we thus arrive at what is, in effect, a 3-valued logic of the type:

p	$\neg p$	$_p\backslash^q$	$p \wedge q$ T	I	F	$p \vee q$ T	I	F	$p \rightarrow q$ T	I	F	$p \leftrightarrow q$ T	I	F
T	F	T	T	(T,F)	F	T	T	T	T	(T,F)	F	T	(T,F)	F
I	(T,F)	I	(T,F)	(T,F)	F	T	(T,F)	(T,F)	T	(T,F)	(T,F)	(T,F)	(T,F)	(T,F)
F	T	F	F	F	F	T	(T,F)	F	T	T	T	F	(T,F)	T

That is, we obtain a 3-valued system which is decisive: the truth-table entries of its connectives are the classical T and F, but these will not occur in a strictly truth-functional way. Note, incidentally, that if we imposed strict truth functionality here by *identifying* the equivocal pair (T,F) with the specific truth-value I, then the resulting system is again $\mathbf{K}_3 = \mathbf{S}_3^{\supset}$, the 3-valued logic of Kleene.

27 Probability Logic: A Non-truth-functional System

The conception of probability as it is familiar from mathematical probability theory and its applications affords yet another way of obtaining a many-valued logic, indeed an infinite-valued one. In the present case of probability logic the usual historical preliminaries can be dispensed with since the matter has been treated in considerable detail in Chap. 1. Suffice it here to repeat that the first steps toward developing the probabilistic approach to many-valued logic were made in the 1932–1936 period by Hans Reichenbach and Zygmunt Zawirski.

The leading idea of this probabilistic approach to many-valued logic is that of assigning likelihood values or probabilities to *statements*. A measure function Pr is presupposed as given, which assigns some real-number value $Pr(p)$ to each and every member p of the domain of statements at issue. This numerical assignment is supposed to be of such a sort that the standard conditions imposed on a mathematical probability measure are all satisfied.

Specifically, the following basic conditions are postulated:

(P1) $0 \leq Pr(p)$, for any statement p
(P2) $Pr(p \lor \neg p) = 1$
(P3) $Pr(p \lor q) = Pr(p) + Pr(q)$, provided that p and q are mutually exclusive, i.e., that $p \land q$ is impossible (which could be taken to amount to $Pr(p \land q) = 0$)
(P4) $Pr(p) = Pr(q)$ when p and q are logically equivalent, i.e., both $p \land \neg q$ and $\neg p \land q$ are impossible

Given these postulates, the various usual relationships familiar from probability theory can readily be derived, specifically including the following:

1. $Pr(p \land \neg p) = 0$
2. $Pr(\neg p) = 1 - Pr(p)$
3. $0 \leq Pr(p) \leq 1$, for any statement p
4. $Pr(p) \leq Pr(q)$ when $p \land \neg q$ is impossible
5. $Pr(p \lor q) = Pr(p) + Pr(q) - Pr(p \land q)$

Several methods for securing a measure of the probability of statements in this fashion are in existence. For fuller details the reader may consult Rudolf Carnap's important treatise on the *Logical Foundations of Probability*,[1] where further references to the literature are also given. For present purposes, however, no particular, specific method for the assignment of probabilities need be assumed.

This machinery of statement probabilities can in effect be looked upon as a many-valued logic, with $Pr(p)$ in the role of $/p/$, that is, with probability construed as a "truth-value." As with the sequences $\mathbf{L}_n$ or $\mathbf{S}_n$, 1 will here play a part analogous to that of the classical truth-value T, and 0 a part analogous to that of the classical truth-value F. The truth-status of a compound proposition will conform to the following family of truth rules:

$$/p/ = Pr(p)$$
$$/\neg p/ = 1 - Pr(p)$$
$/p \lor q/ = Pr(p) + Pr(q)$ if p and q are mutually exclusive, and otherwise $/p \lor q/$ is a certain quantity λ such that $\lambda \leq Pr(p) + Pr(q)$, but $\lambda \geq Pr(p)$ and $\lambda \geq Pr(q)$[2]
$$/p \land q/ = Pr(p) + Pr(q) - Pr(p \lor q)$$
$$/p \supset q/ = /\neg p \lor q/$$
$$/p \equiv q/ = /(p \to q) \land (q \to p)/$$

---

[1]Chicago, 1950; 2d ed., 1960.
[2]It must be remembered that this vagueness is harmless because we are not claiming to *characterize Pr* at this juncture, but simply to note some of its features that derive from its previously fixed character as a *given* measure with certain properties.

By this line of procedure we obtain a method for assigning probabilistic "truth"-values to statements that results in a perfectly viable system of many-valued logic. We shall designate this system as the system **PL** ("probability logic").

However, the many-valued logic we obtain in this manner has the striking feature that *it is not truth-functional* at all. The essential feature of the truth-functional systems with which we have in the main been concerned—and which continues at least partially operative with respect to the quasi-truth-functional systems considered in the last section—is this:

> The truth-value-determining mechanism governing the *modus operandi* of $/p/$ is such that, for every connective $\varnothing$ there is a finitely pluri-valued function $\mathsf{F}_\varnothing$ (single-valued for the strictly truth-functional systems and at most n-valued for the finite quasi-truth-functional systems with n truth-values) such that:
>
> $$/\varnothing(p,q)/ = \mathsf{F}_\varnothing(/p/,/q/)$$

But this principle breaks down altogether for **PL**. This can readily be seen by considering the question of the value to be accorded to $\frac{1}{2} \wedge \frac{1}{2}$. Let $/p/ = Pr(p) = \frac{1}{2}$. Then if we use the previously specified conditions to reason as follows:

$$\frac{1}{2} \wedge \frac{1}{2} = /p \wedge p/ = Pr(p \wedge p) = Pr(p) + Pr(p) - Pr(p \vee p)$$
$$= 2Pr(p) - Pr(p) = Pr(p) = \frac{1}{2}$$

But on the other hand, when $Pr(p) = \frac{1}{2}$, then $/\neg p/ = Pr(\neg p) = 1 - \frac{1}{2} = \frac{1}{2}$. And then:

$$\frac{1}{2} \wedge \frac{1}{2} = /p \wedge \neg p/ = Pr(p \wedge \neg p) = Pr(p) + Pr(\neg p) - Pr(p \vee \neg p)$$
$$= \frac{1}{2} + \frac{1}{2} - 1 = 0$$

Thus $\frac{1}{2} \wedge \frac{1}{2}$ is not a fixed value at all, but is actually a quantity that *can vary over the entire range between* 0 *and* $\frac{1}{2}$. The many-valued logic at issue thus fails to be truth-functional.

The failure of truth functionality in **PL** might lead one to surmise that this system would differ wildly from other, seemingly more orthodox systems of propositional logics. That this seemingly plausible supposition is altogether wrong is shown by the following fact:

> The tautologies of **PL** (1 alone being designated) are exactly the same as the tautologies of C_2.

This can be shown in two stages:

The fact that every **PL**-tautology is a C_2-tautology is shown by the fact that the truth rules for C_2 will agree entirely with those for **PL** when the truth-values 0 and 1 alone enter upon the scene.

The fact that every C_2-tautology is a **PL**-tautology can be shown by going to an established axiomatization of C_2 using the connectives $\neg$ and $\vee$

(with *modus ponens* and substitution as the rules of inference), and then showing that all the C_2-axioms are **PL**-tautologies. (Since the rules of inference of **PL** are tautologousness-preserving, it will then follow that all C_2-tautologies will be **PL**-tautologies.) Such an axiomatization is that of Hilbert and Ackermann, based on the familiar definition of implication

$$p \supset q \quad \text{FOR} \quad \neg p \lor q$$

and the following four axioms:[3]

    (A1) $(\alpha \lor \alpha) \supset \alpha$
    (A2) $\alpha \supset (\alpha \lor \beta)$
    (A3) $(\alpha \lor \beta) \supset (\beta \lor \alpha)$
    (A4) $(\alpha \supset \beta) \supset [(\gamma \lor \alpha) \supset (\gamma \lor \beta)]$

These axioms are readily seen to be **PL**-tautologies. We shall verify this in detail only for (A1). We must show that:

    (1) $Pr(\neg[p \lor p] \lor p) = 1$, regardless of the value of $Pr(p)$

Now since $\neg(p \lor p)$ is mutually exclusive with p, we have by (P3) above that:

    (2) $Pr(\neg[p \lor p] \lor p) = Pr(\neg[p \lor p]) + Pr(p)$

But since $\neg(p \lor p)$ is logically equivalent with $\neg p$, we have by (P4) that:

    (3) $Pr(\neg[p \lor p]) = Pr(\neg p)$

Hence (2) yields:

    (4) $Pr(\neg[p \lor p] \lor p) = Pr(\neg p) + Pr(p)$

But since $\neg p$ and p are mutually exclusive, we have by (P3) that

    (5) $Pr(\neg p \lor p) = Pr(\neg p) + Pr(p)$

and from (4) and (5) we have:

    (6) $Pr(\neg[p \lor p] \lor p) = Pr(\neg p \lor p)$

But the right-hand side of (6) is uniformly 1 by (P2), so that (1) follows.

We can complete along such lines as these the demonstration that all the C_2-tautologies must also be **PL**-tautologies. And so the systems C_2 and **PL**, altogether different from one another in various fundamental respects, will wholly agree in their tautologies.

In the late 1920s and 1930s most writers of the Polish school questioned the conception of a probability logic: the influence of the *Principia Mathematica* systematization of classical logic was in its heyday, and some deemed it anomalous that a "logic" should fail to be truth-functional.[4] The reluc-

---

[3]For this axiom system see A. N. Prior, *Formal Logic* (Oxford, 1955), p. 301.
[4]See Ajdukiewicz (1928), Mazurkiewicz (1932) and (1934), and Tarski (1935–36).

tance of the Polish logicians to regard probability logic as a species of many-valued logic was also bound up with their regarding probabilities as not somehow representing values of a proposition, but measures of a *relationship* between propositions.[5] The later work of Rudolf Carnap was to undermine this view beyond restoration. But for a time, the idea of probability logic as a mode of many-valued logic was under a cloud from which it was to be redeemed only in part by the influence of the writings of H. Reichenbach.[6] From the historical point of view, the probabilistic approach was actually (in H. MacColl) one of the founding inspirations of many-valued logic, and it represents a recurrent background theme in the writings of other pioneers, including J. Łukasiewicz. Once truth-functionality is dropped as an essential feature of a "logic" (as it certainly ought to be), there is no longer any basis for failing to recognize the probabilistic logic as a system of many-valued logic.

Apart from probabilities, various other kinds of numerical-statement measures exist and can be used as a basis for a corresponding family of logical rules. For example, one can provide measures of the *desirability* or of the *cost* of the state of affairs represented by p's coming about.[7] However, these sorts of many-valued systems are hardly many-valued *logics* in the appropriate manner, because these measures lack the essential feature—demonstrably possessed by a *probability* measure—of maintaining an intimate linkage with the semantical concepts of truth and falsity. For a statement's assuring probability of 0 will (in finite alternative sets, at any rate) guarantee its falsity, and probability of 1 will guarantee its truth. It is the sort of relationship that entitles the probability values to be regarded as *truth*-values.

28 Modal Structures within Many-valued Logic

Given a system of many-valued logic, modal operators can be introduced within it as one-place propositional operators defined by a one-column

---

[5]See Z. Jordan, "The Development of Mathematical Logic in Poland between the Two Wars" in S. McCall (ed.), *Polish Logic: 1920–1939* (Oxford, 1967), pp. 338–345 (see pp. 392–393).

[6]See especially his *Wahrscheinlichkeitslehre* (Leipzig, 1935) and his brief but suggestive paper "Wahrscheinlichkeitslogik und Alternativlogik," *Erkenntnis*, vol. 5 (1935), pp. 177–178. A pioneering writer on probabilistic approaches to many-valued logic whose work is far less known than it deserves is Zygmunt Zawirski, who published a series of papers on this topic in the years 1934–1936. (For details see the Bibliography.)

[7]For the former conception see my "Semantic Foundations for the Logic of Preference" in N. Rescher (ed.), *The Logic of Decision and Action* (Pittsburgh, 1967). For the second see N. Rescher, "Notes on Preference, Utility, and Cost," *Synthèse*, vol. 16 (1966), pp. 332–343.

truth table in the manner of negation. Consider the three traditional alethic modal operators:

$\Box p$ FOR p is *necessary* (necessarily true)
$\Diamond p$ FOR p is *possible* (possibly true)
$\bigcirc p$ FOR p is *actual* (actually true)

In 3-valued logic, for example, one would expect these three modal operators to have the following truth table:

p	$\Box p$	$\Diamond p$	$\bigcirc p$
$+T$	T	T	T
I	F	T	I
$-F$	F	F	F

In general we would expect such modal operators to behave in accordance with the following rules:

($\Box$1) That whenever $/p/ \neq T$, then $/\Box p/ = F$
($\Box$2) That whenever $/p/ \notin D^+(\mathbf{X})$, then $/\Box p/ \notin D^+(\mathbf{X})$
($\Diamond$1) That whenever $/p/ \neq F$, then $/\Diamond p/ = T$
($\Diamond$2) That whenever $/p/ \notin D^-(\mathbf{X})$, then $/\Diamond p/ \in D^+(\mathbf{X})$
($\bigcirc$1) $/\bigcirc p/ = T$ iff $/p/ = T$
($\bigcirc$2) $/\bigcirc p/ = F$ iff $/p/ = F$
($\bigcirc$3) $/\bigcirc p/ \in D^+(\mathbf{X})$ iff $/p/ \in D^+(\mathbf{X})$
($\bigcirc$4) $/\bigcirc p/ \in D^-(\mathbf{X})$ iff $/p/ \in D^-(\mathbf{X})$

Rules ($\bigcirc$1) to ($\bigcirc$4) could always be assured by adopting the rule:

$$/\bigcirc p/ = /p/$$

But this stipulation is not an inevitable or necessary one, although it is obviously satisfied by the 3-valued truth table for $\bigcirc$ given above.

Again, if negation ($\neg$) has the reversal or mirroring property of taking D^+-values into D^--values, and conversely, then the $\bigcirc$-rules assure that:

$$/\bigcirc p/ = /\neg\bigcirc\neg p/$$

Moreover, in this case, the $\Box$-rules and the $\Diamond$-rules can be interrelated by stipulating:

$$/\Diamond p/ = /\neg\Box\neg p/$$
$$/\Box p/ = /\neg\Diamond\neg p/$$

But this condition is also not inevitable or necessary, although it too is obviously satisfied by the particular truth tables given above (if $\neg$ is standard 3-valued negation).

Examples of 4-valued truth tables for the modal operators satisfying all of the basic rules, but (subject to mirror-image negation) not those further relationships described as nonnecessary in the last two paragraphs, are:

p	$\Box p$	$\Diamond p$	$\bigcirc p$
$+T$	I_2	T	T
I_1	F	T	I_1
I_2	F	T	I_1
$-F$	F	F	F

It should be noted that in the two-valued case the only way of satisfying the basic rules is:

p	$\Box p$	$\Diamond p$	$\bigcirc p$
$+T$	T	T	T
$-F$	F	F	F

Considered as truth functions, the three modalities here become indistinguishable from one another (and from the unqualified assertion of a formula). Exactly this consideration was one of the factors that originally motivated Jan Łukasiewicz to introduce the 3-valued versions of $\Box$ and $\Diamond$ presented at the outset of the section.

Given the modalities defined by the truth tables of a many-valued logic, along with the usual connectives of propositional logic, the question arises:

> How can the tautologies of this many-valued modal system be axiomatized? That is, can we specify a finite list of axiomatic theses from which all—but only—the tautologies of the system can be derived as theorems by the usual rules of substitution and *modus ponens* for implication?

This question does not raise any issues of principle distinct from those noted in Sec. 24, and we shall not pursue it further here.

However, the converse of the question poses an interesting new issue. For if a system of modal logic has been presented in axiomatic development, we can raise the question:

> How can a characteristic set of truth tables (i.e., one whose tautologies will be exactly the set of theorems) be devised for this axiom system?

Now the best known and most thoroughly studied axiomatizations of modal logic are a group of five systems devised by C. I. Lewis between 1918 and 1932. These systems, designated S1 to S5, vary in their strength, which increases from that of the weakest S1 to that of the strongest S5. The axiomatic structure of these five systems is as follows:

Primitives: $\neg, \wedge, \square$
Definitions: $\lozenge p$ FOR $\neg \square \neg p$
$\qquad\qquad p \vee q$ FOR $\neg(\neg p \wedge \neg q)$
$\qquad\qquad p \supset q$ FOR $\neg(p \wedge \neg q)$
$\qquad\qquad p \equiv q$ FOR $(p \supset q) \wedge (q \supset p)$
$\qquad\qquad p \rightarrow q$ FOR $\square(p \supset q)$
$\qquad\qquad p \leftrightarrow q$ FOR $\square(p \equiv q)$
Rules of inference: (1) *Substitution*
$\qquad\qquad$ (2) *Modus ponens:* Given p and $p \rightarrow q$ to infer q
$\qquad\qquad$ (3) *Conjunction:* Given p and q to infer $p \wedge q$
$\qquad\qquad$ (4) *Replacement of equivalents:* Given $p \leftrightarrow q$ and
$\qquad\qquad\qquad\qquad (\ldots p \ldots)$ to infer $(\ldots q \ldots)$
Axioms for S1:   (1) $(\alpha \wedge \beta) \rightarrow (\beta \wedge \alpha)$
$\qquad\qquad$ (2) $(\alpha \wedge \beta) \rightarrow \alpha$
$\qquad\qquad$ (3) $\alpha \rightarrow (\alpha \wedge \alpha)$
$\qquad\qquad$ (4) $(\alpha \wedge [\beta \wedge \gamma]) \rightarrow (\beta \wedge [\alpha \wedge \gamma])$
$\qquad\qquad$ (5) $([\alpha \rightarrow \beta] \wedge [\beta \rightarrow \gamma]) \rightarrow (\alpha \rightarrow \gamma)$
$\qquad\qquad$ (6) $\alpha \rightarrow \lozenge \alpha$
Axioms for S2:   (1)–(6) plus (7.2) $\lozenge(\alpha \wedge \beta) \rightarrow \lozenge \alpha$
Axioms for S3:   (1)–(6) plus (7.3) $(\alpha \rightarrow \beta) \rightarrow (\lozenge \alpha \rightarrow \lozenge \beta)$
Axioms for S4:   (1)–(6) plus (7.4) $\lozenge \lozenge \alpha \rightarrow \lozenge \alpha$
Axioms for S5:   (1)–(6) plus (7.5) $\lozenge \alpha \rightarrow \square \lozenge \alpha$

It is easy to show that there are many-valued logics that *capture* the theorems of these systems in the sense that every theorem of the system will be a tautology subject to the many-valued truth tables. The strategy of demonstration here is simple and familiar: We simply verify that all the axioms are tautologies and that the rules of inference (substitution, *modus ponens*, etc.) are tautology-preserving. By way of example, it is readily checked that the following truth tables will capture the theorems of S5 and thus *a fortiori* those of the other four Lewis systems as well:

p	$\neg p$	$\square p$	$\lozenge p$	$\diagdown \!\! q \atop p$	$p \wedge q$				$p \rightarrow q$				$p \leftrightarrow q$			
					1	2	3	4	1	2	3	4	1	2	3	4
+1	4	1	1	+1	1	2	3	4	1	4	4	4	1	4	4	4
2	3	4	1	2	2	2	4	4	1	1	4	4	4	1	4	4
3	2	4	1	3	3	4	3	4	1	4	1	4	4	4	1	4
4	1	4	4	4	4	4	4	4	1	1	1	1	4	4	4	1

Although these truth tables yield all S5-theorems as tautologies, they will not so yield all C_2-tautologies. That these truth tables will yield all S5-theorems as tautologies can be seen by verifying the tautologousness of the axioms, and checking that the rules of inference—substitution and *modus ponens*—are tautologousness-preserving. But not all C_2-tautologies will be tautologous by the 4-valued truth tables, for specifically the modalized analogue of "$\alpha \supset (\beta \supset \alpha)$," namely

$$\alpha \rightarrow (\beta \rightarrow \alpha)$$

will not be a tautology according to these truth tables. (To see this, let $/\alpha/ = 2$ and $/\beta/ = 3$; then $2 \rightarrow (3 \rightarrow 2) = 2 \rightarrow 4 = 4$.) Thus not all C_2-theorems will be 4-valued tautologies, although all S5-theorems will be. However, the following important result can be established:

> There exists no finitely many-valued logic that is *characteristic* of any of the Lewis systems S1 to S5, because any finitely many-valued logic will contain tautologies that are not theorems of S5 (and *a fortiori* not of S1 to S4 either).

This fact was established in a 1940 paper by James Dugundji[1] applying a method developed some years before by Kurt Gödel in a very similar context.[2] It can be argued for as follows.

First, we observe that any many-valued logic **X** that is to capture all theorems of the modal logic at issue must have the features:

(F1) If $/p/ = /q/$, then $/p \leftrightarrow q/ \in D^+(\mathbf{X})$
(F2) If $/p/ \in D^+(\mathbf{X})$ or $/q/ \in D^+(\mathbf{X})$, then $/p \vee q/ \in D^+(\mathbf{X})$

If the first of these failed, then "$\alpha \leftrightarrow \alpha$" (which is a theorem) would not be a tautology. If the second failed, then "$\alpha \vee \tau$" would not invariably be a tautology when τ is a tautology (although it is automatically a theorem when τ is a theorem).

Now consider the following sequence of propositions (Δi) which we shall call the Gödel sequence:

($\Delta 2$) $(p_1 \leftrightarrow p_2) \vee (p_1 \leftrightarrow p_3) \vee (p_2 \leftrightarrow p_3)$
($\Delta 3$) $(p_1 \leftrightarrow p_2) \vee (p_1 \leftrightarrow p_3) \vee (p_1 \leftrightarrow p_4) \vee (p_2 \leftrightarrow p_3) \vee (p_2 \leftrightarrow p_4) \vee (p_3 \leftrightarrow p_4)$
(Δn) the disjunction of all terms $(p_i \leftrightarrow p_j)$ for $i \neq j$, $1 \leq i \leq n$, $1 \leq j \leq n$

It is readily seen that if there are just two distinct truth-values, then no assignment of truth-values to p_1, p_2, p_3 can possibly prevent one of the conjuncts of ($\Delta 2$) from taking the form $v \leftrightarrow v$. By (F1) and (F2), ($\Delta 2$) must therefore be a tautology. Similarly, if there are three truth-values, then ($\Delta 3$) must be a tautology. And in general, (Δn) must be tautologous whenever there are n or fewer truth-values—although it may (but need not) fail

[1]"Note on a Property of Matrices for Lewis and Langford's Calculi of Propositions," *The Journal of Symbolic Logic*, vol. 5 (1940), pp. 150–151.
[2]Kurt Gödel, "Zum intuitionistischen Aussagenkalkül," *Ergebnisse eines mathematischen Kolloquiums*, no. 4 (1933), p. 40. See the discussion of Gödel's ideas in Alonzo Church, *Introduction to Mathematical Logic* (Princeton, 1956), pp. 146–147.

to be a tautology when there are more than *n* truth-values. (This bears out the fact to which we have adverted in various contexts that a loss of tautologies generally accompanies an increase in truth-values—though this will not be so inevitably.[3])

Now it is not difficult to show that none of the (Δi) will be a theorem of S5. The strategy of argument will be as follows. To show that a given (Δi) is not an S5-theorem, we can produce a (sufficiently large) many-valued system in which:

1. the rules of inference for S5 will obtain
2. all the S5-axioms are tautologies
3. (Δi) is not a tautology

This can be done in a sufficiently large standard system (whose size will depend upon *i*), with the following truth rule for the modal operator or necessity:

$$/\Box p/ = \begin{cases} T \text{ if } /p/ = T \\ F \text{ if } /p/ \neq T \end{cases}$$

Thus any finitely many-valued logic satisfying (F1) and (F2) will contain tautologies—specifically members of the (Δi)-sequence—that are not theorems of any of Lewis's systems of modal logic. Thus no finitely many-valued logic can be *characteristic* of these modal logics.[4] (On the other hand, we did give earlier an example of a 4-valued truth table that *captures* all S5-theorems, as indeed we know C_2 to do also.)

The (Δi)-sequence is interesting quite apart from any issues of modal logic, because it exhibits the fact that in any finitely many-valued logic the relationships of equivalence and implication will have a certain unnaturalness in inevitably yielding (infinitely many) tautologies of this sort. It is a significant fact that these shortcomings can be avoided by going over to an infinite-valued logic.

This leads us to the question: Can an infinitely many-valued logic be characteristic of any of the Lewis systems of modal logic? This question can be answered in the affirmative. We shall consider two alternative many-valued—and necessarily infinite-valued—systems that are characteristic of S5:

---

[3]The many-valued truth tables could be characteristic of C_2, as is $S_4^{\supset}$ when *T* and I_1 are both designated. (Note that even Δ_2 is an $S_4^{\supset}$-tautology.)
[4]It must, of course, be granted that there will be some "modal logics" for which a many-valued logic is characteristic. We could, for example, simply *begin* with a truth-table representation of modal operators, and then axiomatize this.

1. The Modalized System $\Pi_{\aleph_0}(C_2)$ (Compare Sec. 16)

In this system, the truth-values are infinite strings of T's and F's of the type:[5]

$$T\ F\ T\ F\ T\ T\ T\ F\ F\ldots$$

The only designated value is $T\ T\ T\ldots$, the infinite string of T's. The truth rules for the usual propositional connectives $\neg$, $\wedge$, $\vee$, $\rightarrow$, $\leftrightarrow$ require the *place-by-place* calculation of the combined truth-values according to the classical, two-valued truth tables. The truth rules for $\square p$ and $\Diamond p$ are:

$$/\square p/ = \begin{Bmatrix} T\ T\ T\ T\ T\ T\ldots \\ F\ F\ F\ F\ F\ F\ldots \end{Bmatrix} \text{ according as } /p/ \begin{cases} = T\ T\ T\ T\ T\ T\ldots \\ \neq T\ T\ T\ T\ T\ T\ldots \end{cases}$$

$$/\Diamond p/ = \begin{Bmatrix} T\ T\ T\ T\ T\ T\ldots \\ F\ F\ F\ F\ F\ F\ldots \end{Bmatrix} \text{ according as } /p/ \begin{cases} \neq F\ F\ F\ F\ F\ F\ldots \\ = F\ F\ F\ F\ F\ F\ldots \end{cases}$$

Thus let it be that:

$$/p/ = T\ F\ T\ F\ T\ F\ T\ F\ldots$$
$$/q/ = F\ T\ F\ T\ F\ T\ F\ T\ldots$$

Then:

$$
\begin{aligned}
/\neg p/ &= F\ T\ F\ T\ F\ T\ F\ T\ldots \\
/p \wedge q/ &= F\ F\ F\ F\ F\ F\ F\ F\ldots \\
/p \vee q/ &= T\ T\ T\ T\ T\ T\ T\ T\ldots \\
/p \supset q/ &= F\ T\ F\ T\ F\ T\ F\ T\ldots \\
/p \equiv q/ &= F\ F\ F\ F\ F\ F\ F\ F\ldots \\
/p \rightarrow q/ &= F\ F\ F\ F\ F\ F\ldots \\
/(p \leftrightarrow q) \rightarrow p/ &= T\ T\ T\ T\ T\ T\ldots
\end{aligned}
$$

The system obtained in this way is the infinite-valued system $\Pi_{\aleph_0}(C_2)$, with modalities ($\square$ and $\Diamond$) added. It is possible to show that the tautologies of *this* system will be exactly the theorems of S5, although we shall not here present the rather complex demonstration of this fact.[6] (It should be noted that the situation is essentially the same in the system based on the modalities presented in note 13 of Sec. 18 [see page 115].)

---

[5] Bearing the time-interval interpretation in mind, it might be thought more natural to consider two-way infinite strings like

$$\overset{\downarrow}{\ldots F\ F\ F\ T\ T\ F\ T\ldots}$$

But these can always be transposed into a one-way string by picking an arbitrary starting point (marked by the arrow) and then alternating in the "next new entry forwards then next new entry backwards" principle to obtain:

$$T\ T\ F\ F\ F\ T\ F\ldots$$

We can thus proceed by means of one-way strings without any loss of generality.

[6] It can be shown by minor modifications of the argument given in Chap. 3 of A. N. Prior, *Time and Modality, op. cit.*

While the tautologies of $\Pi_{\aleph_0}$ ($\mathbf{C}_2$)—based on $\supset$ as implication—are simply the usual tautologies of $\mathbf{C}_2$, this set of tautologies will shrink to those of **S5** when we go over to the modalized implication:

$$p \to q \quad \text{FOR} \quad \square(p \supset q)$$

This finding raises the question:

> Consider the infinite-valued logic based on infinite strings formed from a 3-valued starting point: *T,I,F.* Again let
>
> $$/\square p/ = \begin{Bmatrix} T\ T\ T\ T\ldots \\ F\ F\ F\ F\ldots \end{Bmatrix} \text{ according as } /p/ \begin{cases} = T\ T\ T\ T\ldots \\ \neq T\ T\ T\ T\ldots \end{cases}$$
>
> with only $T\ T\ T\ldots$ as designated value, and let $\to$ be defined as above, as necessity-modalized implication. Let the truth rules be given in terms of place-by-place computation according to some 3-valued system such as $\mathbf{L}_3$, $\mathbf{B}_3$, or $\mathbf{K}_3$. Then what can be said about the modal structure of such a system?

It is not difficult to see that, if the initial 3-valued system is $\mathbf{X} = \mathbf{L}_3$ or $\mathbf{B}_3$ or $\mathbf{K}_3$, then the infinite-valued system constructed according to the rules just specified will be $\Pi_{\aleph_0}$ ($\mathbf{X}$). One thing is now clear: Since "$\alpha \to \alpha$" will not be a tautology of $\Pi_{\aleph_0}$ ($\mathbf{K}_3$), its modal logic will not be any of the Lewis systems. But beyond this meager—and negative—finding we shall not here offer any further discussion of this cluster of questions.

2. The Modalized System PL of Probabilistic Logic (Compare Sec. 27)

Let us introduce modalities into the system of probabilistic logic **PL** of Sec. 27 by the stipulation:

> $/\square p/ = 1$ or 0 according as $/p'/$ is (or is not) uniformly 1 for every substitution instance p' of p

That is to say that the truth-value of $\square p$ can only be 1 (true) or 0 (false), and moreover will be 1 only when there is no assignment of truth-values to the variables of p for which p will assume a truth-value different from 1.[7] The modality of possibility is then introduced by the definition:

$$\Diamond p \quad \text{FOR} \quad \neg\,\square\,\neg p$$

It will thus be subject to the truth rule:

> $/\Diamond p/ = 1$ or 0 according as $/p'/$ is (or is not) uniformly 0 for any substitution instance p' of p

---

[7] On this approach, modality is not at all treated as a truth-functional operator within the truth-functional structure of many-valued logic (as with Łukasiewicz' approach or even that of the previous section). Dealing with the truth-values of substitution instances, modality is here handled on close analogy with quantification. Cf. A. N. Prior, "On Propositions Neither Necessary nor Impossible," *The Journal of Symbolic Logic*, vol. 18 (1953), pp. 105–108, and *idem*, "Three-Valued Logic and Future Contingents," *The Philosophical Quarterly*, vol. 3 (1953), pp. 317–326 (see p. 324).

Correspondingly, the truth-value of $\Diamond p$ can only be 1 (true) and 0 (false), and moreover will be 1 only when there is some assignment of truth-values to the variable of p for which p will take on a truth-value different from 0. (This pair of truth rules is not, of course, strictly truth-functional—in keeping with the general non-truth-functionality of the system **PL**.)

Again, it is possible to show that the tautologies of this system will be exactly the theorems of S5, although we shall not here present the rather complex demonstration of this fact.[8]

We have thus seen that there are two systems of many-valued logic— neither of them finite, and indeed one of them not strictly truth-functional, which are both characteristic of Lewis' system S5 of modal logic. This establishes the fact that at least some of the classical systems of modal logic are such that their modal structure can be reproduced within appropriately designed systems of many-valued logic.

Appendix

Let us consider the modal structures of 4-valued logic in somewhat greater detail. We shall take as a basis the system $S_4^{\mathfrak{D}} = C_2 \times C_2$, whose interpretation was discussed in Sec. 18, and which is based on the following truth tables for the primitives $\neg$ and $\wedge$:

p	$\neg p$		$p \wedge q$			
		q \ p	0	1	2	3
$+0$	3	0	0	1	2	3
$(+?)1$	2	1	1	1	3	3
$(-?)2$	1	2	2	3	2	3
-3	0	3	3	3	3	3

Even after the alternative worlds interpretation of the four truth-values as proposed in Sec. 18 have been adopted, there still remain several distinct, more or less plausible and "natural" truth-table characterizations for the basic modality of necessity (we envisage the prospect of designating 0 and perhaps also 1 and antidesignating 3 and perhaps also 2).

Alternatives for $\Box p$

p	(A)	(B)	(C)	(D)	(E)
$+0$	0	0	0	1	1
1	3	2	2	3	2
2	3	2	2	3	2
-3	3	3	2	3	2

[8]See N. Rescher, "A Probabilistic Approach to Modal Logic," *Acta Philosophica Fennica*, fasc. 16 (1963), pp. 215–225.

The corresponding alternatives for $\Diamond p$ are as follows:

Alternatives for $\Diamond p$

p	(A)	(B)	(C)	(D)	(E)
+0	0	0	1	0	1
1	0	1	1	0	1
2	0	1	1	0	1
−3	3	3	3	2	2

Here the adoption of (A) leads to a system of many-valued truth tables coinciding with Lewis's "Group III."[9] Alternative (C) leads to his "Group IV" and (D) leads to "Group I." Cases (B) and (E) are not considered by Lewis. (Contrariwise, Lewis's "Group II" and "Group V" are incompatible with our proposed interpretation of the truth-values.[10]) The "Group III" system based on (A) has the feature that it renders tautologous all of the theorems of Lewis's modal system S5, if 0 is taken to be the only designated truth-value. (But, as we know, these truth tables must also render tautologous certain formulas that are not S5-theorems.)

It would appear that, in terms of the proposed semantical approach to the interpretation of the truth-values, alternative (A)—and thus "Group III"—is the most suitable choice of a 4-valued truth table for the possibility modality. It is based on a quite plausible construction of the modalities, namely the convention that: *A proposition asserting the possibility of some thesis is necessarily true if true, necessarily false if false, and true just in case the thesis at issue is not necessarily false.* None of the other alternatives (B) to (E) embodies a set of principles that can readily be defended—as alternative (A) can be—on the basis of traditional conceptions of the matter. (Still, the other alternatives are certainly not wholly devoid of claims to consideration.)

In general, the result of this discussion may be summarized by saying that the semantical approach to the intuitive interpretation of 4-valued logic (as described in Sec. 18) makes possible the interpretation of three of the classical "Groups" of many-valued logic originally proposed by C. I. Lewis, as well as several cognate systems.

29 Quantification in Many-valued Logic

In the context of orthodox two-valued logic, Andrzej Mostowski has introduced a very powerful generalization of the machinery of standard quanti-

---

[9]See the Appendix to C. I. Lewis and C. H. Langford, *Symbolic Logic* (New York, 1932). Actually, the truth tables of this group, and some others, are due to W. T. Parry.
[10]The system of alternative (B) is, as its characterization makes evident, intermediate between the systems of alternatives (A) and (C)—that is, between Lewis' "Group III" and "Group IV." This system may well repay further study. Suffice it here to remark that it resembles "Group IV" in that of Lewis' axioms, A7($\neg \Diamond \alpha \rightarrow \neg \alpha$) and B7(a *modus ponens* thesis) are not forthcoming as tautologies.

fication theory as typified by the familiar existential and universal quantifiers.[1] On Mostowski's conception, a quantifier is to be viewed as a *relation* (i.e., a two-parameter propositional function) of two *numbers* which are determined as follows: Given a one-place predicate (propositional function) P defined with respect to the individuals of a domain of discourse $\mathfrak{D}$, we are to conceive of a quantifier $\mathbf{Q}$ in such a way that

$(\mathbf{Q}x)Px$ amounts to $\mathbf{Q}(\xi,\eta)$

where $\mathbf{Q}$ is a (mathematical) propositional function of two quantities:

ξ = the cardinal number of the set of individuals x in $\mathfrak{D}$ for which Px is true:
$\xi = \#\{x \mid /Px/ = T\}$
η = the cardinal number of the set of individuals x in $\mathfrak{D}$ for which Px is false:
$\eta = \#\{x \mid /Px/ = F\}$

Thus, for example, to obtain the standard existential quantifier ($\exists$-quantifier) by this scheme, we simply take the condition $\mathbf{Q}(\xi,\eta)$ as:

$\xi \neq 0$

Again, to obtain the standard universal quantifier ($\forall$-quantifier), we take $\mathbf{Q}(\xi,\eta)$ as:

$\eta = 0$

One further example: to obtain the "plurality quantifier" ($\mathbf{M}$-quantifier) to represent "Most x's are P's"[2] we take $\mathbf{Q}(\xi,\eta)$ as:

$\xi > \eta$

This brief outline should suffice to exhibit the fundamental idea of Mostowski's approach.

We shall now consider a *generalization of quantifiers* (*in the sense of Mostowski*) *for many-valued logics*. Suppose, then, that in place of the usual two truth-values T (for truth) and F (for falsity) we have a series of n truth-values: $v_1, v_2, \ldots, v_n$. It seems natural to extend Mostowski's generalization of quantifiers as follows: Given a predicate P defined with respect to the individuals of a domain of discourse $\mathfrak{D}$, we are to conceive of a quantifier $\mathbf{Q}$ as a propositional function of n cardinal numbers (numerical parameters) in such a way that

$(\mathbf{Q}x)Px$ amounts to $\mathbf{Q}(\xi_1, \xi_2, \ldots, \xi_n)$

[1]A. Mostowski, "On a Generalization of Quantifiers," *Fundamenta Mathematicae*, vol. 44 (1957), pp. 12–36.
[2]Cf. N. Rescher, "Plurality—Quantification," *The Journal of Symbolic Logic*, vol. 27 (1962), pp. 373–374. Cf. also N. Rescher and C. A. Gallagher, "Venn Diagrams for Plurative Propositions," *Philosophical Studies*, vol. 16 (1965), pp. 49–55, reprinted in N. Rescher, *Topics in Philosophical Logic* (Dordrecht, 1968), pp. 126–133.

where

> ξ_i = the cardinal number of the set of individuals x in $\mathfrak{D}$ for which Px assumes the truth-values v_i: $\xi_i = \#\{x|/Px/ = v_i\}$

For convenience and simplicity we shall confine our attention to the 3-valued case, for the situation there is readily generalized. Consider a 3-valued logic with the truth-values T (true), F (false), and I (intermediate or neutral). One correspondingly obtains, for any predicate P, the three cardinal numbers:

> $\xi_1(P)$ = the cardinal number of the set of all x in $\mathfrak{D}$ for which Px takes the truth-value T
> $\xi_2(P)$ = the cardinal number of the set of all x in $\mathfrak{D}$ for which Px takes the truth-value I
> $\xi_3(P)$ = the cardinal number of the set of all x in $\mathfrak{D}$ for which Px takes the truth-value F

Using these quantities, such quantifiers as the following can now be introduced (for brevity we write simply ξ_i in place of $\xi_i(P)$):

(1) $(\exists^T x)Px$, $(\exists^I x)Px$, and $(\exists^F x)Px$ to correspond to the conditions that $\xi_1 \neq 0$, $\xi_2 \neq 0$, and $\xi_3 \neq 0$, respectively. That is, $(\exists^v x)Px$ is to be true iff $\#\{x\,|/Px/ = v\} \neq 0$ (i.e., this set is nonempty).

(2) $(\forall^T x)Px$, $(\forall^I x)Px$, and $(\forall^F x)Px$ to correspond to the conditions that $\xi_2 + \xi_3 = 0$, $\xi_1 + \xi_3 = 0$, and $\xi_1 + \xi_2 = 0$, respectively. Consequently, $(\forall^v x)Px$ is to be true in a finite domain $\mathfrak{D}$ iff $\#\{x|/Px/ = v\} = \#(\mathfrak{D})$.

(3) $(M^T x)Px$, $(M^I x)Px$, and $(M^F x)Px$ to correspond to the conditions that $\xi_1 > \xi_2 + \xi_3$, $\xi_2 > \xi_1 + \xi_3$, and $\xi_3 > \xi_1 + \xi_2$, respectively. That is, $(M^v x)Px$ is to be true iff $\#\{x|/Px/ = v\} > \#\{x|/Px/ \neq v\}$.

Quantifiers of this sort illustrate how the Mostowski approach to two-valued quantifiers can be redeployed to yield a generalization of the concept of quantification in the many-valued case.

It is clear that this extension of quantifiers affords highly flexible machinery for treating quantificational concepts in many-valued logics. The application of these ideas in special cases warrants further investigation. Interesting questions can be raised by its means—for example, that of the minimum number of independent (noninterdefinable) quantifiers that can be specified by certain given means in various systems of many-valued logic.

For the sake of illustration, consider the standard negation of 3-valued logic—like that of the systems $\mathbf{L}_3$, $\mathbf{B}_3$, and $\mathbf{K}_3$ of Łukasiewicz, Bochvar, and Kleene, though not that of Post's $\mathbf{P}_3$—whose truth table is as follows:

p	$\neg p$
T	F
I	I
F	T

Here there will be exactly six distinct (definition-independent) "*sum-inequality quantifiers*," i.e., quantifiers specifiable in terms of inequalities ($<$ or $\leq$) among sums or partial sums of the three ξ_i. This is so because the defining relationship for such a quantifier, $(Qx)Px$, must have one of the six forms (where r,s,t stand for distinct ξ_i):

(1)	(2)
$r < s$	$r \leq s$
$r < s + t$	$r \leq s + t$
$r + s < t$	$r + s \leq t$

We can immediately cut the number of possibilities in half, since any type-(2) quantifier (say the quantifier $(Qx)Px$ corresponding to $\xi_1 \leq \xi_2$) can be defined in terms of the negation of a type-(1) quantifier (in this case $\neg(Qx)Px$, where $(Qx)Px$ corresponds to $\xi_2 < \xi_1$).

We are left with twelve possibilities, as follows: (i) for $r < s$, there are three choices for r and two for s, for a total of six possibilities; (ii) for $r < s + t$, there are three possibilities, fixed by the three choices of r; and (iii) the case of $r + s < t$ is exactly like the preceding.

But these twelve possibilities can again be cut in half because any quantifier in the group (say $(Qx)Px$ corresponding to $\xi_1 < \xi_2$) gives rise to another quantifier of the group when we shift to $(Qx)\neg Px$ (and thus $\xi_1 > \xi_2$). For this shift—in virtue of the negation matrix—effects the substitutions

ξ_1 to ξ_3
ξ_2 to ξ_2
ξ_3 to ξ_1

and thus gives rise to a second, different inequality within the same family. *In the 3-valued logic at issue, there are thus exactly six distinct "sum-inequality" quantifiers on the basis of which all of the others can be introduced by definition.* This finding illustrates one kind of result that can be arrived at by the machinery here proposed for introducing quantifiers (of the Mostowski type) into many-valued logic.[3]

[3]The leading ideas of this discussion were originally presented in the writer's paper "Quantifiers in Many-Valued Logic," *Logique et Analyse*, vol. 7 (1964), pp. 181–184.

It should be noted that whenever the truth-values of one system $\mathbf{X}_1$ are included among those of another, $\mathbf{X}_2$, then all $\mathbf{X}_1$-quantifiers will automatically correspond to $\mathbf{X}_2$-quantifiers (although there will be some $\mathbf{X}_2$-quantifiers that do not correspond to $\mathbf{X}_1$-quantifiers).

It is a moot question how one ought to generalize the orthodox quantifiers $\forall$ and $\exists$ of two-valued logic in the many-valued case. Consider a many-valued logic based on the truth-values: $T, = +I_0, +I_1, +I_2, \ldots, +I_k,$ $I_{k+1}, I_{k+2}, \ldots, I_{k+m} = F$. Let us now define the "truth-status statistic" of a predicate as follows:

Given a predicate P, we obtain a corresponding list of $k + m + 1$ cardinal numbers

$$\langle \xi_0, \xi_1, \ldots, \xi_{k+m} \rangle$$

where

$$\xi_i(P) = \#\{x \mid /Px/ = v_i\}$$

We see that there are two alternative rivals as many-valued counterparts of the classical universal quantifier $\forall$, namely $\forall^+$ and $\forall^T$ defined as follows

$$(\forall^T x)Px \text{ amounts to } \xi_1(\overline{P}) + \xi_2(\overline{P}) + \cdots + \xi_{k+m}(\overline{P}) = 0$$
$$(\forall^+ x)Px \text{ amounts to } \xi_{k+1}(\overline{P}) + \xi_{k+2}(\overline{P}) + \cdots + \xi_{k+m}(\overline{P}) = 0$$

where $\overline{P}$ is the predicate complement of P (i.e., the predicate that applies whenever P does not). And correspondingly the classical existential quantifier $\exists$ has two counterparts:

$$(\exists^T x)Px \text{ amounts to } \xi_0(P) \neq 0$$
$$(\exists^+ x)Px \text{ amounts to } \xi_0(P) + \xi_1(P) + \cdots + \xi_k(P) \neq 0$$

Since, generally speaking, a many-valued logic may even fail to have a T-counterpart as a value, the $+$-indicated quantifiers are perhaps more plausible generalizations of $\forall$ and $\exists$ than the T-superscripted ones are.

In any normal system of many-valued logic, all the interrelations of the standard quantifier will be preserved by the T-superscripted ones. For example, we will have the inference:

From $(\exists^T x)(Px \wedge Qx)$ to infer $(\exists^T x)Px \wedge (\exists^T x)Qx$

To see that this is so consider the truth-status distribution statistic:

$P^{\backslash Q}$	T	I_1	$\cdots$	I_n	F
$0 = T$	$d_{0,0}$	$d_{0,1}$	$\cdots$	$d_{0,n}$	$d_{0,n+1}$
$1 = I_1$	$d_{1,0}$	$d_{1,1}$	$\cdots$	$d_{1,n}$	$d_{1,n+1}$
.	.	.	$\cdots$	.	.
.	.	.	$\cdots$	.	.
.	.	.	$\cdots$	.	.
$n = I_n$	$d_{n,0}$	$d_{n,1}$	$\cdots$	$d_{n,n}$	$d_{n,n+1}$
$n + 1 = F$	$d_{n+1,0}$	$d_{n+1,1}$	$\cdots$	$d_{n+1,n}$	$d_{n+1,n+1}$

Here $d_{i,j}$ is $\#\{x|/Px/ = i$ and $/Qx/ = j\}$. Then:

(1) $(\exists^T x)(Px \wedge Qx)$ iff $d_{0,0} \neq 0$
(2) $(\exists^T x)Px$ iff $d_{0,0} + d_{0,1} + d_{0,2} + \cdots + d_{0,n+1} \neq 0$
(3) $(\exists^T x)Qx$ iff $d_{0,0} + d_{1,0} + d_{2,0} + \cdots + d_{n+1,0} \neq 0$

Hence (given the normalcy of the truth table for $\wedge$), the indicated inference is valid in the case of T-superscripted quantifiers.

For $+$-superscripted quantifiers, however, the orthodox relationships may fail even in a normal many-valued system. Thus consider the equivalence:

(0) $(\forall^+ x)Px$ iff $\neg(\exists^+ x)\neg Px$

Let us suppose the many-valued logic at issue to be a 3-valued system with the indicated designations and the following normal negation matrix:

p	$\neg p$
$+T$	F
$+I$	I
F	T

Note that:

(1) $(\forall^+ x)Px$ amounts to $\#\{x \,|/Px/ = F\} = 0$
(2) $(\exists^+ x)\neg Px$ amounts to $\#\{x \,| /\neg Px/ = T\} + \#\{x|/\neg Px/ = I\} \neq 0$

But since $\neg p$ is true iff p is false, we have:

(3) $\neg(\exists^+ x)\neg Px$ iff $\#\{x \,| /\neg Px/ = T\} + \#\{x \,| /\neg Px/ = I\} = 0$

But by the truth table for $\neg$, $/\neg Px/$ will be T iff $/Px/ = F$, and further $/\neg Px/ = I$ iff $/Px/ = I$. Consequently, we have it from (3) that:

(4) $\neg(\exists^+ x)\neg Px$ iff $\#\{x \,| /Px/ = F\} + \#\{x \,| /Px/ = I\} = 0$

Now note that if the right-hand side of (4) obtains, then so must the right-hand side of (1), *but not conversely*. Hence,

$(\forall^+ x)Px$ if $\neg(\exists^+ x)\neg Px$

but not conversely, so that we have only one-half of (0).

On the other hand, it is not hard to see that if the truth tables for negation were changed to

p	$\neg p$
$+T$	F
$+I$	F
F	T

then the equivalence (0) would obtain in general. The lesson is clear: The fundamental equivalences of orthodox quantificational logic will not in general hold in many-valued logic, but will hold only if the truth tables for the logical connectives (negation, conjunction, etc.) are suitably well behaved.

We have so far left open the question of the truth-values of quantificational statements in many-valued logic, having simply observed that $(Qx)Px$ is to "amount to":

$$Q(\xi_1(P), \xi_2(P), \ldots, \xi_n(P))$$

This would seem to suggest that $(Qx)Px$ will in general behave in a two-valued way:

$/(Qx)Px/$ is T or F according as $(Q(\xi_1, \xi_2 \ldots, \xi_n))$ does or does not obtain

And this resolution of the question of the truth status of quantificational statements is a perfectly viable one. But of course it would be only fitting and proper if the issue of the truth-value of quantificational statements could be resolved in the context of many-valued logic in a less two-valued way.

Whenever satisfaction of the numerical condition Q can be construed as coming about in relevantly different ways, then we have room for the assignment of nonclassical truth-values to $(Qx)Px$. For example, consider a 3-valued logic based on T, I, F. Let the quantifier $\forall$ be defined so that:

$$(\forall x)Px \text{ amounts to } \#\{x \mid /Px/ = F\} = 0$$

Given this starting point, one can adopt the following truth-value specification for $(\forall x)Px$:

$$/(\forall x)Px/ = \begin{Bmatrix} T \\ I \\ F \end{Bmatrix} \text{ according as } \begin{cases} \#\{x \mid /Px/ = F\} = 0 \text{ and } \#\{x \mid /Px/ = I\} = 0 \\ \#\{x \mid /Px/ = F\} = 0 \text{ and } \#\{x \mid /Px/ = I\} \neq 0 \\ \#\{x \mid /Px/ = F\} \neq 0 \end{cases}$$

Along such lines, quantifiers can be so treated in many-valued logic that quantificational statements will themselves be many-valued.

This many-valued interpretation of the quantifiers is readily reconciled with the conjunction interpretation of $\forall$ and the disjunction interpretation of $\exists$, especially applicable in finite universes—i.e., the *substitution interpretation* of the quantifiers due to Ludwig Wittgenstein. On this approach we have:

($\forall$) $(\forall x)Px = Px_1 \wedge Px_2 \wedge \cdots \wedge Px_n$
($\exists$) $(\exists x)Px = Px_1 \vee Px_2 \vee \cdots \vee Px_n$

Let us assume, as in the preceding example, a 3-valued logic based on T, I, F, and let us suppose the truth tables for conjunction and disjunction to be as follows:

	$p \wedge q$			$p \vee q$		
$\overset{\diagdown q}{p\diagdown}$	T	I	F	T	I	F
T	T	I	F	T	T	T
I	I	I	F	T	I	I
F	F	F	F	T	I	F

It is then easy to show that the truth-value of $\forall$ as given in specification ($\forall$) will agree exactly with the stipulation of the preceding paragraph. Moreover, the truth rule for $\exists$ will now be as follows:

$$/(\exists x)Px/ = \begin{Bmatrix} T \\ I \\ F \end{Bmatrix} \text{ according as } \begin{cases} \#\{x \mid /Px/ = T\} \neq 0 \\ \#\{x \mid /Px/ = T\} = 0 \text{ and } \#\{x \mid /Px/ = I\} \neq 0 \\ \#\{x \mid /Px/ = T\} = 0 \text{ and } \#\{x \mid /Px/ = I\} = 0 \end{cases}$$

Whenever numerical truth-values are used and the truth tables for $\wedge$ and $\vee$ have the familiar feature,

$$/p \wedge q/ = \min [/p/,/q/]$$
$$/p \vee q/ = \max [/p/,/q/]$$

then one can set up the truth rules for quantified statements—in a way consonant with the preceding discussion—quite simply as

$$/(\forall x)Px/ = \min_{x \in \mathfrak{D}} /Px/$$
$$/(\exists x)Px/ = \max_{x \in \mathfrak{D}} /Px/$$

This procedure will preserve all of the usual relations among the quantifiers, when the other connectives are also suitably well behaved and will agree with the specifications of $\forall$ and $\exists$ if $\wedge$ and $\vee$ are of the standard type.

However, when the truth tables for $\wedge$ and $\vee$ are not sufficiently well behaved, the distribution-statistic approach to quantifiers can yield results substantially different from those obtained in the conjunction-disjunction construction. For example, if in some case we have it that $p \vee q$ can take a truth-value different from that for $q \vee p$ (or similarly for conjunction), then the application of the specifications ($\exists$) and ($\forall$) cannot be reproduced in a statistical way, since the application of ($\exists$) and ($\forall$) can then fail to yield a single determinate truth-value.[4]

One interesting application of this machinery must be indicated at least briefly. Consider the product logic $\Pi_n(C_2)$. Here a proposition p will have an n-place truth-value of the type:

$$\langle v_1, v_2, v_3, \ldots, v_n \rangle \text{ where every } v_i \text{ will be either } T \text{ or } F,$$

---

[4]This opens up the prospect of a many-valued logic that is strictly truth-functional at the propositional level, but quasi-truth-functional at the quantificational level.

We can thus look on a proposition p as a predicate $[\![p]\!]$ of a position indicator x ($x = 1$ or 2 or ... or n) such that: $/[\![p]\!]x/ = v$ iff $v_x = v$. On such an approach the modalities of Sec. 28 can be treated as quantified statements where:

$$\Box p \text{ iff } (\forall x)[\![p]\!]x, \text{ with } /(\forall x)[\![p]\!]x/ = \begin{Bmatrix} T \\ F \end{Bmatrix} \text{ according as } \#\{x \mid /[\![p]\!]x/ = F\} \text{ is } \begin{cases} = 0 \\ \neq 0 \end{cases}$$

$$\Diamond p \text{ iff } (\exists x)[\![p]\!]x, \text{ with } /(\exists x)[\![p]\!]x/ = \begin{Bmatrix} T \\ F \end{Bmatrix} \text{ according as } \#\{x \mid /[\![p]\!]x/ = T\} \text{ is } \begin{cases} \neq 0 \\ = 0 \end{cases}$$

In this way, the product-logic modalities of the type considered in Sec. 28 can be treated as quantifiers rather than as modalities proper. By such a procedure we can obtain modalities even in many-valued systems lacking the classical feature that modalized statements are invariably two-valued, and never assume a truth-value and distinct from T and F. (Just this would be the case with the necessity counterpart of the 3-valued $\forall$-quantifier described in the last paragraph.)

It remains to consider briefly the case of *propositional*—rather than *individual*—quantifiers. No fundamental novelty arises here. Such a statement as

(1) $(\forall\alpha)(\exists\beta)[\alpha \to (\alpha \wedge \beta)]$

is simply a claim verifiable in terms of the structure of the many-valued truth tables, subject to the conjunction-disjunction interpretation of the quantifiers. Thus (1) is valid (tautologous) in, say, all the systems $\mathbf{L}_n$ and $\mathbf{S}_n$, but not in $\mathbf{B}_3$ (with 1 alone designated)—as is readily checked—nor in the system:

p	$p \wedge q$			$p \vee q$			$p \to q$		
$\backslash q$	1	2	3	1	2	3	1	2	3
+1	1	2	3	1	1	1	1	2	3
2	2	2	2	1	2	2	1	2	3
3	3	2	3	1	2	3	1	2	2

For in this system

$(\exists\beta)[2 \to (2 \wedge \beta)]$

that is,

(2) $[2 \to (2 \wedge 1)] \vee [2 \to (2 \wedge 2)] \vee [2 \to (2 \wedge 3)]$

takes the truth-value

$2 \vee 2 \vee 2 = 2$

But now any conjunct involving (2) will take the nondesignated value 2, so that (1) cannot be tautologous on the conjunctive interpretation of $\forall$.

In certain families of systems, particularly interesting moves can be made by means of propositional quantification—moves that illuminate fundamental features of the many-valued logic at issue. Thus suppose we have a many-valued system with truth-values taken from the range from 0 to 1 (inclusive) and such that we have—or can define—connectives $\curlywedge$ and $\Rightarrow$ meeting the conditions:

(1) $/p \curlywedge q/ \in D^+$ iff $/p/ \in D^+$ and $/q/ \in D^+$
(2) $/p \Rightarrow q/ \in D^+$ iff $/p/ < /q/$[5]

As regards designation, we suppose only that some truth-values are designated and some are not. Now consider the thesis:

(t) $(\forall\alpha)(\forall\beta)(\exists\gamma)[(\alpha \Rightarrow \beta) \Rightarrow [(\alpha \Rightarrow \gamma) \curlywedge (\gamma \Rightarrow \beta)]]$

If this is to be tautologous, then whenever the antecedent is designated, i.e., whenever $/\alpha/ < /\beta/$, then there must be a 'γ' such that the consequent is also designated. So for this 'γ', both $/\alpha \Rightarrow \gamma/$ and $/\gamma \Rightarrow \beta/$ must be designated, and then $/\alpha/ < /\gamma/$ and $/\gamma/ < /\beta/$, so that we have inserted a new truth-value between $/\alpha/$ and $/\beta/$, one that is different from both of these. But if this is always possible, then there cannot be a finite number of truth-values. Thus, in any many-valued system satisfying the basic conditions enumerated above, (t) amounts to a stipulation of infinity. It is a thesis that cannot obtain in any finitely many-valued case but is valid (tautologous) in the infinitely many-valued case.

30 Applications of Many-valued Logic

The machinery afforded by systems of many-valued logic has been put to work in many highly diversified applications.[1] Many of these relate to very abstract contexts in logic and mathematics. The essential features of three such applications have already been considered in some detail:

1. The "purely abstract" use of many-valued logic as a tool for giving demonstrations of nonprovability, axiom independence, and consistency in the metalogic of axiomatizations of propositional logic. (See Sec. 15.)
2. Kleene's application of his 3-valued logic in studying the decidability of numerical predicates in the mathematical theory of partial recursive functions. (See Sec. 4.)

---

[5]Note that in $Ł_n$ or S_n, $p \Rightarrow q$ amounts to $(p \rightarrow q) \wedge \neg(q \rightarrow p)$.
[1]For information regarding contributions and contributors, the historical discussion of Chap. 1 as well as the Bibliography of Chap. 4 should be consulted.

3. The application of many-valued logics—already envisaged in the early papers of Łukasiewicz (see Sec. 2)—to the study of modal logics. (See Sec. 26.)

Going beyond this, other possibilities come to light. One of the most promising logical applications of many-valued logic arises in connection with the so-called semantical paradoxes. Consider, for example, the well-known *Liar paradox* already discussed on pages 87–90. The paradox is generated in a two-valued logic by the proposition:

(L_2) This proposition—viz. the proposition(L_2)—is false.

If we class (L_2) as true, then, strange to say, (L_2) must be false. And if we class (L_2) as false, then it will be true. Thus in a two-valued logic—where all propositions must be classed as either T or F—we have no choice but to reject (L_2) as meaningless, insisting that this formula not represent a proposition at all, since it must wholly lack a truth-value. On the other hand, in 3-valued logic based on T, F, and I, we can acknowledge (L_2) as a meaningful proposition but simply accord it the third, indeterminate truth-value. Unhappily, however, paradoxes of this sort will again recur within many-valued logic. In 3-valued logic we are embroiled in difficulty by:

(L_3) This proposition—viz. the proposition (L_3)—is false and not indeterminate.

Now:

(1) If $/(L_3)/ = T$, then (L_3) must be false, and hence $/(L_3)/ \neq T$
(2) If $/(L_3)/ = I$, then (L_3) must be false, and hence $/(L_3)/ \neq I$
(3) If $/(L_3)/ = F$, then (L_3) must be true, and hence $/(L_3)/ \neq F$

So we would need to resolve this version of the Liar paradox in a 4-valued logic based on T, F, I_1, and I_2, but here, instead of being put to difficulty by (L_3) in the formulation

(L_3) $/(L_3)/ = F$ and $/(L_3)/ \neq I$

we are embroiled by its analogue

(L_4) $/(L_4)/ = F$ and $/(L_4)/ \neq I_1$ and $/(L_4)/ \neq I_2$

One efficient way to overcome this regress of difficulties would be to go straightaway to an infinite-valued logic, proceeding along the lines sketched in Sec. 14 of Chap. 2.

Various writers have also attempted to use many-valued logic as a way of evading the paradoxes of the mathematical theory of sets.[2] Consider, for

[2]Pioneer work in this direction was done by D. A. Bochvar, detailed reference to whose work can be found in the Bibliography. See also the important papers by Moh Shaw-kwei, "Logical Paradoxes for Many-Valued Systems," *The Journal of Symbolic Logic*, vol. 19 (1954), pp. 37–39; T. Skolem, "Bemerkungen zum Komprehensionsaxiom," *Zeitschrift für mathematische Logik und Grundlagen der Mathematik*, vol. 7 (1957), pp. 1–17; and C. C. Chang, "Infinite-Valued Logic as a Basis for Set Theory" in Y. Bar-Hillel (ed.), *Logic, Methodology, and Philosophy of Science* (Amsterdam, 1965).

example, Russell's paradox of the set of all sets that are not members of themselves. Is this set a member of itself or not?

The set at issue is:

$$\Xi = \{x \mid x \notin x\}$$

Now suppose that "$\Xi \in \Xi$" is true, so that: $\Xi \in \Xi$. Then $\Xi \in \{x \mid x \notin x\}$, and then as a member of this set $\Xi \notin \Xi$. On the other hand, suppose that "$\Xi \in \Xi$" is false so that: $\Xi \notin \Xi$. Then $\Xi \in \{x \mid x \notin x\}$, and so since $\Xi = \{x \mid x \notin x\}$, we have $\Xi \in \Xi$. But if we go over to a 3-valued logic, we may avoid paradox by classing "$\Xi \in \Xi$" as neither true nor false but as indeterminate (neuter). In this way, by assuming the posture of an underlying logic that is not two-valued, it proves possible to bypass altogether the paradoxes of this sort, for whose avoidance mathematically far more cumbersome restrictions on set formation have to be devised.

When developing set theory in a 3-valued logic, three basic (mutually exclusive) situations have to be envisaged as regards the relationship between an arbitrary element x and a set S:

$x \in S$ or $/x{\in}S/ = T$

$x \notin S$ or $/x \in S/ = F$ (i.e., $x \notin S = \neg [x \in S]$)

$x \propto S$ or $/x \in S/ = I$ (i.e., $X \propto S = I$ $]x{\in}S[$ with I as defined below)

We face the possibility that a set has a fuzzy penumbra, so that a given element lying in this penumbra can be regarded neither as inside the set nor as outside it. The truth status of the various propositions will then be as follows:

The actual situation	$/x \in S/$	$/x \propto S/$	$/x \notin S/$
$x \in S$	T	F	F
$x \propto S$	I	T	I
$x \notin S$	F	F	T

We postulate the following truth tables for 3-valued logic at issue:

p	$\neg p$		p	Ip		q \ p	$p \wedge q$ T	I	F
T	F		T	F		T	T	I	F
I	I		I	T		I	I	I	F
F	T		F	F		F	F	F	F

We further postulate that whatever set-formation mechanism may be at issue is to adhere to the fundamental rule:

$$/y \in \{x \mid \ldots x \ldots\}/ = v \text{ iff } /\ldots y \ldots/ = v$$

In such a framework one can circumvent the paradoxicality engendered by the set $\Xi = \{x | x \not\subset x\}$ by classing the statement $\Xi \not\subset \Xi$ as neither true nor false, but indeterminate in truth-value (i.e., as *I*-assuming). So far, so good; but paradox now descends upon us by considering the set:

$$\Gamma = \{x \mid x \not\subset x \land \neg(x \propto x)\}$$

The argument that exhibits the paradoxicality runs as follows:

1. Assume $/\Gamma \in \Gamma/ = T$
   Then by the fundamentalrule, $/\Gamma \not\subset \Gamma \land \neg(\Gamma \propto \Gamma)/ = T$
   Then $/\Gamma \not\subset \Gamma/ = T$
   Thus $/\Gamma \in \Gamma = F$
   Hence this case cannot arise

2. Assume $/\Gamma \in \Gamma/ = F$
   Then by the fundamental rule, $/\Gamma \not\subset \Gamma \land \neg(\Gamma \propto \Gamma)/ = F$
   Then either $/\Gamma \not\subset \Gamma/ = F$ or $/\neg(\Gamma \propto \Gamma)/ = F$
   But since $/\Gamma \in \Gamma/ = F$, we must have $/\Gamma \not\subset \Gamma/ \neq F$
   Thus $/\neg(\Gamma \propto \Gamma)/ = F$
   Then $/\Gamma \propto \Gamma/ = T$
   Then both $\Gamma \not\subset \Gamma$ (since $/\Gamma \in \Gamma/ = F$) and $\Gamma \propto \Gamma$
   But these were assumed mutually exclusive
   Hence this case cannot arise

3. Assume $/\Gamma \in \Gamma/ = I$
   Then by the fundamental rule, $/\Gamma \not\subset \Gamma \land \neg(\Gamma \propto \Gamma)/ = I$
   Then one of the following must obtain:
   (a) $/\Gamma \not\subset \Gamma/ = T$ and $/\neg(\Gamma \propto \Gamma)/ = I$
   (b) $/\Gamma \not\subset \Gamma/ = I$ and $/\neg(\Gamma \propto \Gamma)/ = T$
   (c) $/\Gamma \not\subset \Gamma/ = I$ and $/\neg(\Gamma \propto \Gamma)/ = I$
   Case (a) cannot arise since $/\Gamma \in \Gamma/ = I$
   Case (b) cannot arise since it requires that $/\Gamma \in \Gamma/$ be T or F
   Case (c) cannot arise since it requires $/\Gamma \propto \Gamma/ = I$ which is not possible

Thus an analogue to the Russell paradox will arise also in 3-valued logic, and indeed such Russell-paradox analogues can be re-created in any finitely many-valued logic of the Łukasiewiczian group and its cognates.[3] Again, as with the Liar paradox, one can go to an infinite-valued logic to avoid the difficulty; or, alternatively, adopt initially the stance of a 3-valued logic with the very "strong" type of indeterminacy at issue in the system $\mathbf{B_3}$ of Bochvar.

Yet another interesting application of many-valued logic within the purely logical sphere relates to "nondesignating singular terms" represented by names (e.g., "Pegasus") or definite descriptions (e.g., "the present

---

[3]On the development of set theory within the framework of the infinite-valued Łukasiewiczian logic see Moh Shaw-kwei, "Logical Paradoxes for Many-Valued Systems," *The Journal of Symbolic Logic*, vol. 19 (1954), pp. 37–40; and Thoralf Skolem, "Mengenlehre gegründet auf einer Logik mit unendlich vielen Wahrheitswerten," *Sitzungsberichte der Berliner Mathematischen Gesellschaft* (1957–58), pp. 41–56.

king of France") which are vacuous and fail to have application. Statements about such nonexistent individuals, for example,

The present king of France is wise

can be viewed as representing a truth-value gap, at any rate from the classical, two-valued viewpoint. Correspondingly, the logic of such statements can be accommodated within a 3-valued system that resolves the question of their truth status by classing them as indeterminate (neuter, intermediate, or the like).[4]

Outside the abstract realm of logic and mathematics lies a substantial domain of *physical* applications of many-valued logic. Various writers have suggested that the realm of indeterminacy created by the fact that—according to the quantum theory—certain pairs of statements about the position and velocity of elementary particles cannot be maintained together can best be accommodated with a 3-valued logic (or a higher-valued logical one) rather than adopting Niels Bohr's suggestion that the trouble-creating sentences he discussed be viewed as meaningless (i.e., as *lacking* a truth-value). This application has been worked out most extensively by Hans Reichenbach,[5] who has depicted possible physical (or rather microphysical) situations in which a 3-valued logic would apply, in that statements about certain features of a physical would not be observationally verifiable or falsifiable, so that it would be pointless to class statements about these features as true or false. The "causal anomalies" of quantum theory create a situation where we appear to be faced with three alternatives:

(1) Adopt a two-valued logic and dismiss the paradox-generating statements as meaningless through an invocation of Bohr's principle of complementarity.

(2) Adopt a two-valued logic, retain the paradox-generating statements as meaningful, and admit the existence of "causal anomalies," simply swallowing the idea of occurrences incompatible with what we accept as the laws of nature.

(3) Adopt a 3-valued logic (or perhaps a higher-valued logic), retaining all (well-formed) physical sentences as meaningful while avoiding their anomalous consequences.

[4]For the basic ideas at issue here see P. F. Strawson, "On Referring," *Mind*, vol. 59 (1950), pp. 320–344. For the full-dress development of a logically sophisticated systematization of this approach see Bas van Fraassen, "Singular Terms, Truth-Value Gaps, and Free Logic," *The Journal of Philosophy*, vol. 63 (1966), pp. 481–495.

[5]See his *Philosophic Foundations of Quantum Mechanics* (Berkeley and Los Angeles, 1944), especially pp. 142–148 and 160–166. Cf. Paul Feyerabend, "Reichenbach's Interpretation of Quantum Mechanics," *Philosophical Studies*, vol. 9 (1958), pp. 49–59.

It is clear that alternative (3) will afford certain substantial systematic advantages. Going beyond this, Reichenbach has shown how the adoption of a 3-valued logic makes it possible to maintain at once both the laws of quantum mechanics and the principle that no causal chain travels with infinite speed, i.e., the proscription of "action at a distance." If ordinary two-valued logic is used, then this principle will be logically incompatible with the laws of quantum mechanics. (Although according to quantum mechanics no signal traveling faster than light can be detected, Einstein and collaborators have shown that specific mathematical features of quantum mechanics require that in certain situations a causal chain must have traveled with a velocity faster than that of light.[6]) In this way, a cohesive systematization appears to become possible in quantum physics which removes, or at any rate renders harmless, anomalies that amount to outright inconsistencies from the standpoint of two-valued logic. Beginning with Reichenbach, various writers have thus adopted the view that modern physics demands a logical apparatus that is at least 3-valued.[7]

Even more radically, the machinery of many-valued logic has been invoked to provide a way of reconciling the conflict of alternative theories that yield contradictory results with respect to a given domain of physical phenomena, such as the rival wave and particle theories in the quantum theory of light. The proposal is that since in 3-valued logics one does not —or need not—have such theses as

$$\neg(\alpha \leftrightarrow \neg\alpha)$$
$$\neg(\alpha \wedge \neg\alpha)$$

seemingly contradictory theories may somehow be in agreement. Similarly, the failure of the thesis

$$[\alpha \rightarrow (\beta \wedge \neg\beta)] \rightarrow \neg\alpha$$

to obtain in 3-valued systems (e.g., in $Ł_3$, the 3-valued logic of Łukasiewicz), has been construed to suggest that the presence of logical contradictions in a corpus of theory does not establish its falsity.[8] However, the ideas that have to date been proposed along these lines have not been worked out in detail

---

[6]See A. Einstein, B. Podolsky, and N. Rosen, "Can the Quantum Mechanical Description of Reality Be Considered Complete?" *Physical Review*, vol. 47 (1935), pp. 777 ff.

[7]Others, however, are skeptical. See H. Margenau, "Probability, Many-Valued Logics, and Physics," *Philosophy of Science*, vol. 6 (1939), pp. 65–87; and J. B. Rosser and A. R. Turquette, *Many-Valued Logics* (Amsterdam, 1952), pp. 2–3. Moreover, G. Birkhoff and J. von Neumann ("The Logic of Quantum Mechanics," *Annals of Mathematics*, vol. 37 (1936), pp. 823–843) have rightly stressed that as concerns quantum theory the distributive identities are the weakest link in logic, so that many-valuedness is not specifically required.

[8]See Z. Zawirski, "Les logiques nouvelles et le champ de leur application," *Revue de métaphysique et de morale*, vol. 39 (1932), pp. 503–519 (see especially pp. 512 ff).

sufficient to underwrite a favorable evaluation of a point of view departing so radically from established practices of thought about the nature of scientific knowledge.

Another area of application to physics arises with respect to the theory of switching circuits. The theory of simple on-off switches can most conveniently be represented by the two-valued machinery of classical propositional logic. But the theory of more complex, multichannel switching circuits can very conveniently be handled by the machinery of many-valued logic.

We come, last but not least, to the domain of *philosophical* applications of many-valued logics. The historically most venerable item here is the study of the problem of future contingency which—deeply rooted in the Aristotelian tradition—provided Jan Łukasiewicz with a prime motivation for developing his epoch-making 3-valued logic. (See Sec. 2.) A further philosophical application of many-valued logic arises in connection with the classical "laws of thought"—above all the Law of Excluded Middle and the Law of Noncontradiction. Considerations relevant to these themes were taken up in some detail in Secs. 20 and 21.

Moreover, by invoking the leading ideas of many-valued logic, we can throw substantial light upon those philosophical issues that revolve around our conception of the nature of logic itself. Of special importance here is the issue of relativism and conventionalism in logic, problems upon which our attention will turn in the ensuing chapter.

Chapter 3

The Question
of Relativism
in Logic

1 Introduction

The philosophical problems posed by the existence of many-valued systems of logic have a fundamental interest that far transcends that of the technical issues of logical theory involved. Looking backward toward the first impact of Łukasiewicz' work, Z. Jordan writes:

> But it is difficult to fully realize now all the consequences of Łukasiewicz's discovery. Investigations in this direction have gone little beyond the first shocking conclusion that logical truth has got a multi-form character and that there is a variety of ways in which it may be considered. In some respects the discovery and the foundation of many-valued logic makes us think of the shattering blow dealt by the discovery of the Non-Euclidean geometries to the deeply-rooted conviction that there is one and only one way of constructing the spatial reference-frame of our experiences. Similarly it was supposed that a consistent deductive system must follow the Aristotelian pattern, in accordance with his most general "law of thought." In particular it was be-

lieved that a statement must be either true or false. In some circles there arose doubts concerning this principle when Brouwer constructed definite examples of mathematical theorems—dealing with "the infinite" as it occurs in analysis—which are neither true nor false. The construction by Łukasiewicz of a self-consistent deductive system in which the proposition "a statement is either true or false" no longer holds turned the balance definitely against the Aristotelian assumption.[1]

The prospect of basically different alternatives to the traditional logic built up over the centuries upon the groundwork of Aristotle excited the imagination of many thinkers. But to what extent is this prospect posed by many-valued logics a reality and not a delusion?

Are there or are there not alternative logics? Within these restricted confines, one would surely have to answer the question in the affirmative. There is no balking the fact of *pluralism* in logic. Even just in the sphere of propositional logic, a plethora of systems confront us—the various many-valued logics, the intuitionistic propositional calculus, the proliferation of modal systems, the systems of material and strict implication, and other modes of entailment. In a persuasively argued article entitled "Are There Alternative Logics?" Friederich Waismann has put the matter trenchantly in supporting an affirmative answer to this question:

> . . . we do already possess distinct logics—if this term is used to denote precisely elaborated formalized systems; e.g., logics including or excluding a Theory of Types, systems admitting or barring the law of excluded middle, etc. Perhaps one might add that the rise of a conventionalistic mode of thinking—emanating from mathematics—today favours attempts to construct novel logics.[2]

How—outside the secure context of specialized purposes—is one to choose between these various systems, to elevate one as intrinsically superior to the rest?

Faced with the fact of pluralism, the step to relativism or conventionalism might seem short and easy. The choice between the plurality of systems might be regarded as essentially indifferent, or so the doctrinaire relativist would argue. And perhaps the way is now even paved from relativism via indifferentism to a kind of antilogic or even illogic and irrationalism. If there is no such thing as "the correct" logic, and the matter

---

[1] "The Development of Mathematical Logic in Poland Between the Two Wars" in S. McCall (ed.), *Polish Logic: 1920–1939* (Oxford, 1967), pp. 346–397 (see pp. 394-395).
[2] F. Waismann, "Are There Alternative Logics?" *Proceedings of the Aristotelian Society*, vol. 46 (1946), pp. 77–104; see p. 77.

is one of an arbitrary choice between conflicting but essentially indifferent systems, then whence arises the preeminent status of logic as such? Where are the credentials that establish logic as superior to illogic?

But other writers take the very opposite line: there is no plurality of genuine alternatives as regards logic. Thus the eminent late Polish logician Stanisław Leśniewski held (according to oral statements by J. M. Bocheński) that all many-valued systems are merely games: there is but one single authentic system of logic: the orthodox, standard one. In the same spirit Paul F. Linke relegates all the nonclassical pluri-valued logics to the position of "logic-like formalisms" (*logoide Formalismen*).[3]

These considerations provide the backdrop against which the present discussion obtains its point. Its task is to provide a detailed analysis of this problematic matter of "alternative logics."[4] It is our aim to furnish a clear picture regarding the exact sense in which there are "different, competing systems of logic." Then, but only then, will we be able to consider intelligently the implications of the incontestable facts of pluralism and to gain fertile insight into the many issues that hinge on the choice between alternative systems of logic. For the real issue cannot at this time of day be posed in terms of a question as to the *existence* of alternative systems. Rather, given the uncontestable reality of alternative systems of logic, the real issue is posed by such questions as: What is the basis for the existence of a plurality of logical systems? What makes them all systems of *logic?* Is the choice between them at bottom entirely arbitrary and strictly indifferent, or is it to be resolved preferentially? If so, is the preferability of certain systems such as to be based upon empirical grounds or is it fundamentally pragmatic or is it founded upon some other basis?

2 Two Modes of System Diversity

For two distinct systems to be *genuinely* alternative, some sort of actual conflict must be involved. The systems must at some place differ to the point

---

[3]"Die mehrwertigen Logiken und das Wahrheitsproblem," *Zeitschrift für philosophische Forschung*, vol. 3 (1948–49), pp. 376–398 and 530–546.

[4]Our discussion will in fact be confined to nonmodal systems of *propositional* logic. And we construe this to mean both a logic *for* propositions (i.e., with propositions for its objects) and *of* propositions (i.e., with formulas that bear a propositional interpretation). A proposition here is not a physical concretum (mark or sound) nor an overtly linguistic or symbolic entity (say, a sentence), but an abstract object that is not manifestly and overtly linguistic—the *meaning* of a declarative sentence. Throughout we shall assume that interpreted formulas (wffs) of the logic amount to propositions. Otherwise the whole semantical issue of their "*truth*-value" would be otiose.

of incompatibility. This can come about in two significantly different ways, according as alternative *doctrines* or alternative *instrumentalities* are at issue.

As regards *doctrine*, codified systems of assertions may clash with one another in a milder and in a stronger way. If one system asserts *P* and a second system *does not assert P*, the clash is mild or weak, while if the first system asserts *P* and the second system *asserts not-P*, the clash is strong. When there is a strong doctrinal conflict between two systems they will involve a conflict in truth claims: some thesis true according to one system is false according to the other. Various systems of geometry represent a doctrinal conflict of just this sort—Euclidean and Riemannian geometry, for example. For there will be theses (e.g., the Euclidean parallel postulate) which are true according to the one but false according to the other system. Again, two discordant theories in physics—classical and relativistic dynamics, for example—will also disagree in such a way that it is clear that conflicting assertions are involved.

On the other hand, diverse systematizations involve alternative *instrumentalities* when they provide different instruments or specify different procedures for the accomplishment of a task. The sets of instructions "Take first a pound of *A*, stir it up well, and then add an ounce of *B*" and "Take first an ounce of *B*, then add to it a pound of *A* and stir well" do not represent a logical conflict among contradictory *theses*, but rather a practical conflict among *procedures*. The conflict here is of the sort encountered among different languages or different codes of etiquette. It is not a clash of conflicting things *asserted* but one of conflicting things *to be done*. This type of alternativeness of instrumentalities can obviously come into play with respect to different systems of logic. Thus given, say, the desideratum of avoiding the semantical paradoxes, we may well consider whether this is more efficiently accomplished by adopting a many-valued logic (and accepting the added complications so introduced), or by keeping to a two-valued logic as our inferential apparatus and adopting a more complex theory of meaningfulness to rule out the paradox-generating statements.

The sharp difference between the cases of alternative doctrines and alternative instrumentalities may be brought out in yet another way. In the case of a doctrinal conflict we can appropriately ask the *dogmatic* question: *Which is correct?* This we cannot do in the case of an instrumental conflict. The question that can appropriately be raised with respect to alternative instrumentalities is the *pragmatic* question: *Which is optimal in being the most effective for specified purposes?*

There are thus two crucially different types of systematic diversity: the one involving a doctrinal conflict between supposedly available alternative sets of truths, and the other involving an instrumental conflict between actually available alternative sets of procedures. A pivotal question in the context of our inquiry is: Which of these two modes of conflict is at issue with respect to alternative logics? As long as systems disagree in the weak mode alone, it is always possible to regard them as fragments of one single, more inclusive system, and thus as not basically in conflict at all. Consequently, only the strong sort of doctrinal clash is relevant for our purposes, and it is this alone that we shall henceforth have in view when speaking of doctrinally conflicting systems.[5] At this juncture, the analogy of alternative sysemts of geometry—where, as we have seen, a strong conflict of the "doctrinal" variety arises—must be considered in some detail, since it has standardly provided the point of departure in discussions of "alternative logics."

3 The Geometric Analogy

The founding fathers of many-valued logic—V. A. Vasil'ev, Jan Łukasiewicz, Emil Post, and C. I. Lewis—all assimilated the diversity of logical systems to the existence of non-Euclidean geometries.[6] All these logicians were motivated by the idea of non-Aristotelian logic along lines analogous with the situation in geometry where one finds a proliferation of systems: not merely that of Euclid alone, but the variant geometries of Bolyai, Lobachevski, and Riemann, among others. On neither the geometric nor the logical side can a choice between alternative systems be validated on the basis of purely formal considerations. This comparison, upon which virtually all discussants alike have placed, largely independently, an explicit stress, represents a striking, almost astonishing convergency of perspective.

The distinction between a *pure* (i.e., wholly abstract and purely formal) and a *physical* (i.e., physically interpreted) geometry must play an important role in this analogy. For it is reasonably clear that only the physical sector of the geometric side is relevant to the analogy with logic. There can be

---

[5]In formulations of propositional logic, weak doctrinal conflicts often mask strong ones. Since theses are given with a tacit universal quantifier, a *failure* to assert, say, "$\alpha \lor \neg\alpha$"— that is, "$(\forall \alpha)[\alpha \lor \neg\alpha]$"—stands surrogate for a willingness to assert "$(\exists\alpha) \neg [\alpha \lor \neg\alpha]$" (although not for an assertion of "$\neg [\alpha \lor \neg\alpha]$" which would be tantamount to "$(\forall\alpha)\neg [\alpha \lor \neg\alpha]$").

[6]E. L. Post placed emphasis on one interesting feature of the analogy: From the standpoint of intuitive naturalness a three-dimensional space wins out on the geometric side of the analogy even as a two-dimensional truth space wins out on the logical side. But neither fact is to preclude the development of other systems of higher dimensionability. "Introduction to a General Theory of Elementary Propositions," *American Journal of Mathematics*, vol. 43 (1921), pp. 163–185. (see p. 182).

no "pure" (i.e., uninterpreted) logic. This point merits decisive emphasis. A "logic" is, after all, a very general, but all the same delimitable, *sort* of thing. Certain qualifications must be met by the axioms (if any) and inference rules of a system *of logic*. (An uninterpreted axiomatization of mathematical field theory or of classical mechanics would not qualify.) The—admittedly imprecise—requirement is that a semantical interpretation *along something like the usual lines* must be possible. (The italicized phrase here is indicative of a critical problem, or group of problems, to which we shall have to return.)

Thus we must wrestle with the difficult questions: What is a "system of logic"? In what sense can one system of logic be "alternative" to another?

Certainly a system of logic must have a bearing upon the formal structure of inference and reasoning. It must systematize our informal intuitions in this sphere in a way akin to that in which arithmetical calculating systems formalize the informal calculations we can "do in our head." Given an austerely formal system, a purely abstract calculus, we are not even entitled—and would not in the slightest be tempted—to speak of it as a "logic" until after the development of a semantical interpretation (involving such concepts as those of the *meaning* and *truth* of propositions, and relationships of *consequence* and *inconsistency* among groups thereof).[7] Only a system that achieves this objective of systematizing the formal, generic features of inference and reasoning as we conduct it in the context of precise inquiries like those of mathematics and science can qualify for characterization as a "system of logic."

The geometric analogy, then, must be construed as being drawn between logic, on the one hand, and, on the other, *physical* (i.e., interpreted) geometry. So drawn, the analogy suggests that in a choice between alternative logics empirical considerations will ultimately predominate. Just as one physical geometry must ultimately turn out to be the right one, the only one that correctly applies (under the specified conditions) to the actual world, so only one logic is acceptable as the actual logic (once all the relevant facts are known).[8] This suggestion would seem to be very much mistaken, and it will be criticized in detail below. However, the consideration that the analogy has such misleading consequences indicates that something is amiss with it, and in fact, I want to argue that it is quite inappropriate.

[7] Some formal systems, such as the many-valued systems of quantification theory developed by Rosser and Turquette, do not come with any semantic interpretation but base whatever claims they have to being a "logic" upon purely syntactical analysis. On our view such systems can be called "logics" only provisionally in the hope that the syntactic analogy gives grounds for expecting the future discovery of a workable semantics.

[8] See the claim in A. P. Ushenko, "The Many-Valued Logics," *The Philosophical Review*, vol. 45 (1936), pp. 611–615 (see p. 612).

The contention that the proliferation of logical systems is to be traced to sources similar to the multiplicity of non-Euclidean geometries is misguided because there is a crucial disanalogy between the two cases. The key point which—though it is generally neglected—cannot be given sufficient stress is this: *We cannot formulate* (*give exact articulation to*) *a system of logic without ourselves using logical principles.* The semantical factors of meaningfulness, truth, consequence, inconsistency, and their cognates must inevitably play an overt and prominent role in the development of a system *of logic*. In the course of formulating as a system the materials of "a logic" one must inevitably make use of logical principles. To articulate a *systematic* logic we necessarily employ some *presystematic* logical machinery. (The principles of the presystematic logic need not themselves be *formulated*—otherwise one would be caught up in an infinite regress—but they will surely be *formulatable*. In some cases—perhaps this is even the norm—the systematic logic at issue seeks to capture the presystematic logic used in its development—the formal system being so articulated that we can see intuitively that it largely or wholly succeeds in systematizing the logical principles employed in its own articulation.)[9]

Now this feature that a systematic logic is bound up with a presystematic logic as its *sine qua non* is a point of crucial disanalogy with geometry. It just is not the case that one need employ a presystematic geometry to formulate (give exact articulation to) a "system of geometry."

This disanalogy is highly significant from the standpoint of the present considerations of alternativeness and relativism. For the situation it puts before us is this: that the development of a geometric system is unfettered and free of involvement with presystematic geometric principles, while that of a logical system requires the use of a presystematic logic. And this latter fact suggests that there may be a hard core of *presystematic* logical principles that play a role in the articulation of all logical systems—even those which "internally" (so to speak) exclude them. This suggestion is doubtless mistaken, for reasons to which we shall return below. But the considerations that revolve about this critical disanalogy between the situation in logic and that in geometry do show that a different sort of alternativeness is at issue in the two cases, so that the nature of the

[9]The historic controversy—which raged both in antiquity and medieval times—as to whether logic is a *special branch* of knowledge or *general instrument* for the realization of knowledge throughout all its branches is to be resolved along just these lines. Systematized logic is a special branch of knowledge; but the presystematic logic used generically in the formulation of all branches of knowledge (systematized logic included) is a general instrument. (And, of course, a systematized logic can *also* be applied—say in mathematics —as an instrument in developing other branches of knowledge.)

choice between alternative systems in the two cases will in fact have to be quite different.

4 Absolutism and Relativism in Logic

The enterprise of logic itself may be viewed in substantially different perspectives, prominent among which are the *psychologistic*, the *Platonistic*, and the *instrumentalistic* points of view.

From the point of view of *psychologism*, logic is regarded as a fundamentally *descriptive* enterprise. The task of logic is taken to be the devising of a "theory of reasoning"—a formalized and systematized account of the way in which men actually proceed when reasoning successfully (i.e., when managing to avoid confusion and error). Logic is now construed as an empirical discipline: the logician studies the actually observed process of reasoning (perhaps only on the part of a very selective group of highly intelligent people—say mathematicians) exactly as the social sciences make a descriptive study of political or economic behavior.[10] Construed in this way, the question of the content of the appropriate system of logic is now an empirical issue. Alternative systems of logic stand in an outright doctrinal conflict. Logical principles are (for a given target group of reasoners to be studied) either correct or not.[11]

This conception of logic as the descriptive empirical science of *actual* (but correct or at any rate successful) reasoning stands in contrast with the position of *instrumentalism*. According to such a view, the task of logic lies in the construction of systems codifying *possible* instrumentalities for deductive (i.e., truth-preserving) inference. These would be *available* (should someone want to avail himself of them) for adoption as an organon of reasoning, but no empirical claims are made that anyone has (or will) avail himself of this opportunity. The logician devises a tool or instrument for correct reasoning, but does not concern himself about the uses of this instrument. That is the essence of the instrumentalist position.

This position embraces two distinct poles. At the *formalist* pole the construction of logical systems is regarded as a free exercise in creative ingenuity. We have to do with the unfettered construction of abstract procedures systematizing possible inferential practices.

---

[10]I do not actually know of any serious writer who has explicitly espoused this position in this extreme form, although perhaps certain Oxford philosophers in the entourage of the late J. L. Austin tended in this direction.

[11]The issue may of course become a ramified one: the "logic" of one group may go one way; that of another, another.

At the *pragmatist* pole, however, there is a strong injection of normative considerations, and great emphasis is placed on the convenient and efficient usability of some of these instruments as opposed to others. The case for pragmatism was clearly argued by C. I. Lewis.[12] Lewis maintains:

> Sufficiency for the guidance and testing of our usual deductions, systematic simplicity and convenience, accord with our psychological limitations and mental habits, and so on, operate as criteria in our conscious or unconscious choice of "good logic." Any current or accepted canon of inference must be pragmatically deteᵢmined. That one such system should be thus accepted does not imply that the alternative systems are false: it does imply that they are—or would be thought to be—relatively poorer instruments for the conduct and testing of our ordinary inferences.[13]

On this instrumentalistic approach, there is no danger of irrationalism, because one postulates at the metalogical level a clear, nonrelative criterion of *validity* of inference principles in an acceptable logic—viz. truth preservation, i.e., leading from true premises to true conclusions apart from this consideration, the choice between alternative systems is purely arbitrary for the formalist, but is for the pragmatist heavily hedged about by considerations of a functionalistic sort. With either mode of instrumentalism, however, logic is not conceived of as a theory descriptive of actual reasoning practices, but as something in the direction of the manufacture of intellectual tools.

The *Platonist* conceives of logic as descriptive, but as describing not human practices of reasoning but the geography of an abstract realm of concepts. The leading idea of Platonism is that there is a real but abstract realm of logical entities (say abstract propositions) and the aim of logical theory is to study the real but abstract interrelationships among the entities comprising this realm. The principles of logic are thus universal truths about one fundamental—though admittedly abstract—sector of reality.[14]

Psychologism and Platonism are both absolutistic and inherently monistic doctrines: they support the view that there is—actually or most probably—one single "correct" logic. Formalistic instrumentalism is inherently pluralistic: it envisages a virtually endless procession of logics, the choice between which is purely arbitrary and conventional and is guided by considerations of stylistic preference (if by anything at all). Pragmatism takes a more restrictive view. Admitting a plurality of logics, it regards the choice between them not as arbitrary and wide open, but as narrowly restricted by a whole host of *functional* or purpose-relative considerations of effectiveness, economy, and efficiency given the inferential

---

[12]"Alternative Systems of Logic," *The Monist*, vol. 41 (1931), pp. 481–507.
[13]*Op. cit.*, p. 484.
[14]See, for example, Morris R. Cohen's *Reason and Nature* (New York, 1931).

tasks and purposes upon which the logical apparatus at issue is to be deployed.

We may classify the approaches canvassed in this spectrum as follows:

Genus	Species	Difference: The choice between various systems of logic is—
1. Absolutism	Platonism	*determined*, being dictated by the abstract conceptual objects of logic
2. Absolutism	Psychologism	*determined*, being dictated by the empirical realities of human reasoning processes
3. Relativism	Conventionalism (formalistic instrumentalism)	*wholly free*, being unconstrained by any objective considerations; purely a matter of arbitrary preference, subjective taste, and personal "style"
4. Relativism	Pragmatism (functionalistic instrumentalism)	*guided*, being circumscribed by purpose-relative considerations of effectiveness, efficiency, convenience, economy, and the like

In the controversy between the absolutistic and the relativistic approaches to logic the correct position seems to us to lie somewhere in the middle—with the functionalistic or pragmatic version of the instrumental approach. Thus in the final analysis the question of doctrinal correctness as regards logic is—as we see it—to be taken to hinge upon that of instrumental superiority. But before considering the justification, and the ramifications of this position, a good deal of preliminary ground must be covered.

In traditional discussions of the matter, deriving from Aristotle and maintained within the Aristotelian tradition of antiquity and the Middle Ages, logic was held to be analogous not with geometry, but with *grammar*. The analogy of grammar may thus be regarded as the historically standard approach to the question of the nature of logic as a branch of knowledge. This analogy goes as follows:

> Both with grammar and with logic we begin with a pretheoretical corpus of practice: *speech* in the one case and *reasoning* in the other. In either case, a *theoretical systematization* of the (best and most correct) practice in this area can be made, codifying the procedural principles governing this practice in actual operation. With *speech* the framework of rules that present the theoretical systematization of the pretheoretical practice is *grammar*, and with *reasoning* it is *logic*. Logic is thus the systematic articulation of the principles of (correct) reasoning even as grammar is that of the principles of (correct) speech.

This classical analogy I believe to be not only in large measure true, but also very illuminating. Its main, but I think only major, shortcoming arises in connection with the normative qualifiers that occur in the characterization just given. For the modern grammarian has given up the normative emphasis of right and wrong whereas the logician (modern or otherwise) is neither willing nor able to do so. Traditional or classical grammar, conceiving its role normatively in terms of a search for the *correct* rules of usage of a given language, comes nearer to satisfying the conditions of a correct analogy.

Let us consider logic along grammatical lines, looking at grammar in the way of the traditional normative grammarians. We have to do, then, with a presystematic practice of reasoning in mathematics, political disputation, legal contexts, etc. This practice is very diversified, variegated, and inconsistent over a wide area (perhaps even much less well defined than the speech practices of grammatical relevance). This being the case, significant scope is left for divergent systematizations. For when a corpus of practice is inherently incoherent, different (mutually inconsistent) rule systematizations can organize various sectors of it. Not only may such divergences arise as between different groups of reasons and different subject-matter fields of inquiry—they can arise in the practice of one group within one area.

The resulting systems will be linked by a network of family resemblances based on the sharing of various principles by any two systems—although no particular group of principles will hold "all across the board." The lack of such an essentialistic "hard core" of logical principles—principles that will inevitably be features of any logical system—has significant consequences for the study of alternative logics. It means that in the study of alternative logics we cannot proceed essentialistically through the increasingly sufficient specifications of necessary conditions for what it is to be "a logic." We cannot say: "A logical system *must* embody the specific principles $P_1, P_2, \ldots, P_n$, and can then differ from others in other respects." However, subject to our family-resemblance concept of logic as the inevitably divergent systematization of an inherently discordant practice, such an essentialistic approach cannot be made to work. To take this view and to abandon the conception of a *hard* core of principles that *must inevitably be* present in all logical systems is not to deny that there may be a *statistical* core of principles that *will generally be* present in logical systems. For example, the rules of inference by substitution and *modus ponens* are almost universally present as inferential principles in propositional logic. But to say this is not to make the essentialistic contention that a system that wholly lacked these two principles could not conceivably count as a "logic."[15]

[15]In various contexts one speaks of "the principles of logic," and this mode of thought is not incompatible with the present analysis. For it is clear that one then has in mind inference processes such as those of substitution and *modus ponens* and conjunct separation (etc.) which obtain with respect to virtually all of the commonly encountered systematizations of logic. But one need not then espouse the essentialistic hard-core view of principles that must inevitably characterize any "genuine" logic.

In giving a central place to the idea of logic as the systematization of a presystematic practice of reasoning, normatively regarded, we must note the rule of various *regulative principles* in the construction of such a "systematization." I have in mind here such conceptions as those of *precision* and *exactness*, of *economy* and *simplicity*, and of *coherence* and *consistency*. Above all, one must here stress the regulative ideal of by-and-large *conformity* to the key features of the presystematic practice, of "saving the phenomena" that are involved in the presystematic practice. (It is here that the feature of *autodescriptivity*—among others—enters upon the scene, adding a requirement of substantive adequacy to the preceding primarily formal demands upon a logic.) Such regulative concepts will play a key role throughout the range of diverse "logics," and their employment will effectively condition our view of such systematizations.

Just here the difference from the situation of the purely descriptive grammar of the contemporary grammarians becomes crucial. With latter-day nonnormative grammar, the nature of the observed presystematic practice is decisive: the systematization must, on pains of inadequacy, conform to it. With grammar, then, the empirical aspects of the presystematic practice are the decisive consideration. But in logic the situation is otherwise. Early in the game, one abstracts certain of the key regulative features of the logical enterprise from an informal examination of the presystematic practice of reasoning. Thereupon one injects the requirement of conformity to the regulative features into the consideration of systematizations, as well as "pragmatic" considerations relating to the specific area of application at issue. In taking this stance, the logician (unlike the modern grammarian) veers away from primary emphasis upon the empirical features of the presystematic practice with which he deals: his insistence upon the regulative principles limits the extent to which he is satisfied with an empirical survey of inferential practice. Regulative and functional (and so teleologically oriented and normative) considerations gain a relatively greater weight. In this respect the logical situation is disanalogous with that of modern grammar. Our guiding analogy of the nature of logic is thus not with the modern descriptive, but with the traditional normative approach to the grammatical enterprise.

The fact of alternative systems of logic poses a real choice, and this choice—on the view we have propounded—is laden with function-oriented considerations. The prospect arises that one certain systematization is the optimal within one field of application (say classical logic in relation to ordinary discourse about everyday objects) and an alternative systematization is optimal within another field of application (say 3-valued logic in relation to the phenomena of quantum theory).

5 The Case for Relativism: The System
Relativity of Logical Principles

The Platonist conception of logic is inherently absolutistic. *If* there is one correct system of logic, *then* logical principles are in the final analysis either correct or not—and so certain logical principles will stand on a secure, uncontested footing. On the other hand, the instrumental conception of logic is inherently relativistic. If there is a plurality of viable systems of logic, then—even if some of them have, for certain purposes, an advantage in serviceability over others—logical principles are at the mercy of competing systematizations and principles standardly operative in some systems will fail to hold in others.

In putting forward the case for relativism in logic, let us (for the sake of having a concrete example) consider a particular logical principle, say the Law of the Excluded Middle in the form of the Principle of Bivalence asserting that every proposition either takes on the truth-value T (truth) or the truth-value F (false), in short, that every proposition is either true or false. Now consider the two questions:

(1) Does the Principle of Bivalence hold for system X?
(2) Does the Principle of Bivalence hold (*simpliciter*)?

These questions are strikingly different. The question of type (1) is obviously warranted and proper, for there are a variety of many-valued systems of logic and in some (e.g., the classical propositional calculus) the Principle of Bivalence obtains, whereas in others (e.g., the 3-valued system of Łukasiewicz) it does not. Everyone can agree with respect to considerations of this sort, regardless of any doctrinal position on the issue of the nature of logic.

But the case is altogether different with regard to the type (2) question. Here it may plausibly be argued that this whole class of questions is inappropriate and improper—as any instrumentalist would quite properly insist. Logical principles like that of Bivalence hold for some systems and not others (a universally admitted fact). And there is little alternative but to grant that the choice between logical systems is not dictated by any inevitable necessity, but is in the final analysis largely a matter of decision. The decision is not necessarily an arbitrary one, but may be guided by contextual considerations of purpose and functionality; all the same, it is a decision. We thus arrive at a version of the conventionalist position. Logical principles have a standing that is not absolute, but system-relative; and within a fairly wide range, the selection of a system is a matter of free choice; there are no inevitably "correct" axioms and no inevitably "correct" rules of inference (and so inevitably "correct" logical theses). Clearly the correctness of a controversial logical principle cannot be *demonstrated* satisfactorily, for to give a demonstration of it is to give a proof of it by the use of logical principles which then themselves take on the coloration of controversiality. At best the principle can be "vindicated" by invoking contextual considerations of a pragmatic sort. No doubt if we are not careful in selecting these axioms and rules, the resulting system may have some metalogical disadvantages—e.g., the system may be incomplete. But even this is not a decisive shortcoming: the system is simply a different system from its "complete" cognate and will doubtless have variant interpretations and applications of its own. This line of thought sets out the argument in support of the transition from instrumentalism to relativism in logic.

6 The Case for Absolutism: The Limits upon System Building

Our recognition of the merits of relativism with its emphasis upon the range of choice between alternative and mutually discordant systematizations must, however, be qualified by certain considerations of absolutistic tendency. The fact is that the area of choice between alternative systems of logic is limited. The room for maneuver is circumscribed by considerations which restrict what may at first sight appear as the systematizer's limitless freedom of choice. The limits are of two kinds, those relating to regulative *feasibility* and those relating to pragmatic *suitability*.

We need here to touch only lightly on considerations of suitability. Considering the inferential purposes upon which a system of logic is deployed, factors such as effectiveness, efficiency, convenience, economy, and the like enter upon the scene. They have already been discussed above in connection with the idea of a normatively conditioned instrumentalism.

Considerations of regulative *feasibility* must also be weighted heavily in the present context. For the fact is that proposed logical systems are never to be regarded as qualified for serious considerations if they do not meet minimal standards of precision (e.g., in avoiding ambiguity and equivocation). The feasibility aspects of the matter are seen in clearest focus by looking not so much at the specific content of the logical system from its own internal perspective, as by taking an essentially external perspective upon the metalogical aspects of the matter. Certain important features come immediately to the fore from this angle of approach. The first and most important of these is the need for meeting at least minimal regulative standards of coherence in the articulation and development of a logical system. The system must be consistent. (Regardless of whether or not the system contains something deserving of the name of a "Principle of

Noncontradiction," it must itself avoid self-contradiction.) Moreover, all the characterizing features of the system must be explicitly and unambiguously specified. Thus the systems themselves must be objective, in that they must hold interpersonally, obtaining with respect to *that system* for any person, regardless of his philosophico-logical perspective. We would not have succeeded in putting a well-defined system forward for consideration and discussion if this requirement were not satisfied. Let us designate this second requirement which we have added to that of coherence the requisite of *precision*.

In line with this requisite, it should be noted that if we are fully exact and explicit both in specifying the basic theses of any logical system (i.e., in stating its premisses) and in specifying the machinery of reasoning we are prepared to accept in developing the system, then the position we arrive at is an absolutistic and not a relativistic one. Only one answer is possible: both the intuitionist and the classical formalist can agree with one another as to what is classically and what is intuitionistically demonstrable. When a question is raised about a logical system after the fully explicit and precise statement of the appropriate inferential ground rules, only one "correct" answer is generally possible and the position of affairs is an essentially absolutistic one. There can be relativity in the sense of a genuine option among conflicting alternatives only when the situation is in some sense enthymematic, i.e., only where there is an element of ambiguity introduced at some point by a lack of explicitness or precision.

7 The Purported Primacy of Two-valued Logic

In view of the proliferation of many-valued alternatives to the classical two-valued logic, a degree of relativism seems to be warranted. All these systems, it might be held, are pretty well on a par: the choice between them largely a matter of convenience with respect to the particular purposes we have in hand at the moment. Against this sort of relativism, various writers have urged considerations that militate on behalf of the primacy of two-valued logic. William Kneale, for example, has argued as follows:

> ...even from the purely formal point of view the ordinary two-valued system has a unique status among deductive systems which can plausibly be called logic, since it contains all the others as fragments of itself.[16] In short, they are not alternatives to classical logic in the sense in which Lobachevski's geometry is alternative to Euclid's.

[16]William and Martha Kneale, *The Development of Logic* (Oxford, 1962), p. 575.

But this contention of Kneale's would seem to fall aside when one considers the possibility of (perfectly viable) systems of many-valued logic that are nonnormal and thus fail to be subsystems of ordinary two-valued logic. (The many-valued systems of Post are an extreme example.) Thus a 3-valued system with the truth tables

p	$\neg p$		$q \atop p$	$p \to q$ 1　2　3		
+1	3		+1	1	3	3
2	1		2	2	1	3
3	1		3	2	1	1

will have many appropriate features, but is such that "$\neg(\alpha \to \neg\alpha)$" will be tautologous, although it is not a tautology of C_2.

Going beyond this, there are yet other considerations that have been advanced on behalf of two-valued logic. Most significantly here, it has been argued that the various systems of strictly truth-functional many-valued logic depend, in their very mode of articulation at the metalogical level, upon principles inherent in, and codified by, two-valued logic. It is thus argued that the essentially dichotomous nature of the conception of true-false built into the standard two-valued logic is not abolished, but only modified when we take the step from two-valued to many-valued logic. The two-valued point of view—so it is said—stays with us throughout as a guiding principle. This inheres in the essentially dichotomous *modus operandi* of the truth-values. Given the set of truth-values $T, I_1, I_2, \ldots, I_n, F$, we do not, of course, have the "Principle of Bivalence" to the effect

That a proposition P must take either the truth-value T or F

but we do have its close cognate:

That a proposition P must take either the truth-value T or one of the remainder: $I, I_2, \ldots, I_n, F$.

Again, we still have intact the Law of the Excluded Middle—not of course in the classical form

That a proposition p cannot take on in the system any truth-value apart from the two possibilities: T, F

but rather, in the closely cognate form:

That a proposition p cannot take on in the system any truth-value apart from the n-plus-two possibilities: $T, I_1, I_2, \ldots, I_n, F$.

The root issue comes to be seen in the final analysis as the question of exactness, of precision. Unquestionably the classification of propositions into the true and the false has a basis deep-rooted in the nature of our discourse about things. A statement claims a possible state of affairs to obtain—and if this state is characterized with the requisite exactness, then circumstances are such that it either does or does not obtain: there is no intermediate possibility. But this whole line of approach is circular. If we insist upon setting out from a two-valued point of view, we will, of course, be able to regard the variant logical systems from its perspective. But as we saw in Chap. 2, there is no fundamental reason why we could not have set out from a multivalued point of view and then developed other pluri-valued systems—two-valued logic specifically included—from this vantage point.

It has again and again been insisted upon as the key point of fundamentality of two-valued logic that many-valued logics must be developed from a two-valued standpoint by means of a two-valued metalanguage.[17] We saw in detail in Sec. 14 of Chap. 2 that this contention is entirely erroneous. Within restricted confines, the correct approach was already clearly set forth in E. L. Post's 1921 paper:

> $_1T_2$ [i.e., $\mathbf{P}_2^1$] still appears to be the fundamental system since its truth-values correspond entirely to the [classical] truth-values of [completely] true and completely false whereas in $_\mu T_m$ [i.e., $\mathbf{P}_m^\mu$] . . . this equivalence no longer holds. We must however take into account the fact that our development [of pluri-valued systems of logic] has been given in the language $_1T_2$ and for this very reason every other kind of system appears distorted. This suggests that *if* we translate our entire development into the language of any one $_\mu T_m$ by means of its interpretation, then it would be the formal system [that appears] most in harmony with regard to the two systems [viz. as regards its own development and that of $_1T_2$].[18]

Someone might argue: "But mathematics—the most rigorously developed corpus of human reasoning—is two-valued. For any axiomatically developed theory is inherently two-valued, because in such a theory any given statement either is a theorem, or else it is not one.[19] And a similar situation obtains throughout axiomatically developed logic, and even in many-valued logic, where a given formula either is or is not tautologous."

---

[17]See, for example, Paul F. Linke, "Die mehrwertigen Logiken und das Wahrheitsproblem," *Zeitschrift für philosophische Forschung*, vol. 3 (1948–49), pp. 376–398 and 530–546.

[18]"Introduction to a General Theory of Elementary Propositions," *op. cit.*, p. 185.

[19]"Es bleibt also die vorhin ausgesprochene Tatsache bestehen, dass die Mehrwertigkeit einer Logik nur vom funktionellen [d.h. Wahrheitsfunktionellen] Standpunkt aus sinnvoll ist, während eine Logik vom axiomatischen Standpunkt aus immer aristotelisch, d.h. zweiwertig ist." Gerhard Frey, "Bemerkungen zum Problem der mehrwertigen Logiken," *Actes du XIème congrès international de philosophie*, vol. 5 (1953), pp. 53–58.

This contention is not correct. Axiomatic theories can readily be regarded from a many-valued point of view. Consider how this may be done:

Let $\vdash p$ (as usual) stand for "p is a theorem." Then consider the following assignment of truth-values in the context of an axiomatized system **X** (or in a many-valued system):

Truth-value		Status
T	$\vdash p$	$(p \in T(\mathbf{X}))$
F	$\vdash \neg p$	$(\neg p \in T(\mathbf{X}))$
I	Neither $\vdash p$ nor $\vdash \neg p$	$(p \notin T(\mathbf{X})$ and $\neg p \notin T(\mathbf{X}))$

With respect to these truth-values we will have the quasi-truth-functional system:

p	$\neg p$	$_p\!\diagdown^q$	$p \wedge q$ T	I	F	$p \vee q$ T	I	F	$p \supset q$ T	I	F	$p \equiv q$ T	I	F
$+T$	F	$+T$	T	I	F	T	T	T	T	I	F	T	I	F
I	I	I	I	(I,F)	F	T	(I,T)	I	T	(I,T)	I	I	(T,I,F)	I
F	T	F	F	F	F	T	I	F	T	T	T	F	I	T

Here we only need to assume about the axiomatic system that:[20]

1. It is consistent
2. $\vdash p$ iff $\vdash \neg \neg p$
3. $\vdash p \wedge q$ iff both $\vdash p$ and $\vdash q$
4. If $\vdash p$, then $\vdash p \vee q$ and $\vdash q \vee p$
5. If $\vdash \neg p$ and either $\vdash p \vee q$ or $\vdash q \vee p$, then $\vdash q$
6. $\vdash \neg (p \wedge)$ iff $\vdash \neg p \vee \neg q$ and $\vdash \neg (p \vee q)$ iff $\vdash \neg p \wedge \neg q$

Thus the result of adopting the proposed 3-valued perspective upon axiomatic (or many-valued) systems is a 3-valued (and moreover quasi-truth-functional) system of logic and not a two-valued one. This finding is quite contrary to the tenor of the initial contention that the theory of axiomatic systems must be articulated in terms of a two-valued logic. For the system in view is neither two-valued nor even truth-functional.

As we have seen again and again in Chap. 2, in many different contexts, there simply is no firm basis upon which an absolute claim of the classical two-valued logic over various many systems could be founded in any absolute way. A supporter of many-valued logic can always reply to the adherent of two-valued logic, "My system is capable of embracing and accommodating yours. Your system C_2 is simply a special case of mine."

---

[20]In case the system is many-valued rather than axiomatic, comparable assumptions must be made about many-valuedness.

All the classical tautologies of C_2, after all, will demonstrably also be many-valued tautologies of such systems as:

p	$\neg p$		q	$p \wedge q$			$p \vee q$			$p \rightarrow q$			$p \leftrightarrow q$		
		p		T	I	F	T	I	F	T	I	F	T	I	F
$+T$	F	$+T$		T	I	F	T	T	T	T	I	F	T	I	F
$+I$	I	$+I$		I	I	F	T	I	I	T	T	F	I	T	F
F	T	F		F	F	F	T	I	F	T	T	T	F	F	T

Moreover, an infinite variety of many-valued systems—e.g., all of the systems $\Pi_m(C_2)$—will have exactly the same tautologies as C_2. And various many-valued expansions of C_2 will be isomorphic with C_2 in a very thoroughgoing way. Thus the advocates of many-valued logics can always choose to regard classical two-valued logic as a special case of many-valued logic and so arrogate to their own position most or all of the considerations adduced on its behalf.

8 The Prominence of Two-valued Logic

But have we not ourselves seemingly adhered (in various places in Chap. 2) to the view that a formal system cannot qualify as a system of "logic" if it does not bear a sufficiently close relationship to classical logic? It would seem that the requirement of a "sufficiently close" relationship to the orthodox logic endows classical logic with a place of special preeminence.

This impression is unjustified. After all, it is necessary that one must have *some* criterion—or at least some cluster of partial criteria—for deciding what entitles a body of formal apparatus to be considered a "logic." In the final analysis this can only be done in terms of similarity—at least in certain fundamental respects—to orthodox "classical" logic. To ask whether something constitutes a "logic" can be done sensibly only in the context of *some* preexisting idea of what *logic* is. And this preexisting idea must be based upon the existing condition of the subject in whatever state the historical vagaries of its development has produced: it must, in short, be derived from the ongoing traditions of the discipline. This does, to be sure, endow orthodox, classical two-valued logic with a place of special prominence. But its claims in this regard will be a matter of historical accident and the result of contingent developments. As we have shown repeatedly and from the most various perspectives, there is nothing in the theoretical architecture of the situation—in its purely conceptual structure—that entitled the orthodox classical logic to advance claims of priority or preeminence.

In this respect the situation of *logic* is analogous to that of *arithmetic*, the theory of "calculation" with "numbers." No doubt the arithmetic of natural numbers came first historically. And so the machinery for calculation with fractions, real numbers, integers modulo *n*, complex numbers, and the like, which came historically later, came also to be subsumed under the rubric of "arithmetic." What entitled them to be so-called other than the patterns of their agreements and analogies with the previously known cases, especially the classical arithmetic of natural numbers? But few mathematicians (Kronecker apart) would incline to take this to mean that the arithmetic of the natural numbers is the one and only proper or true or correct arithmetic.

Moreover, it must not be forgotten that the historical claims of orthodox, two-valued logic to be the sole paradigm system by which alone all others must be judged are by no means irreproachable. Syllogistic and modal logic both antedate the Stoics' invention of a propositional calculus akin to the system C_2. Variant theories of (non-truth-functional) implication have deep historical roots. And the idea of denying certain propositions a definite truth status as T and F leading to some sort of 3-valued logic has (as we have seen) deep roots in classical antiquity and a notable place in medieval logic. Thus the "classical" two-valued logic can hardly with propriety arrogate to itself the role of sole or prime arbiter by reference to which alone the question of what is and what is not to qualify as a system of "logic" is to be resolved. The classical, two-valued propositional calculus C_2 can with propriety claim a place of special *prominence*, but it is certainly not the sole or even necessarily the *predominant* standard for making judgments about what is a system of logic.

9 Relativism vs. Absolutism

The question of relativism in logic is thus a complex one that is not to be answered by a simple *yes* or *no*. There certainly are genuinely alternative systems of logic: systems that are genuine *alternatives* because they disagree with one another about the acceptability of theses, and are *genuine* alternatives because the claims they can make upon us for acceptance are pretty much on a par. Thus, at the *constitutive* level of the issue, much can be said for the doctrine of relativism. There certainly are no logical principles which must indispensably figure as overt theses within any and every systematization deserving the name of a "logical system." But this doctrine of the *Constitutive Relativism of Logical Theses* (as we might call it) does certainly not entail results of an irrationalist tendency. For such results are precluded by the equally correct doctrine of (what we shall term) the *Regulative Absolutism of Metalogical Principles*.

We have had to distinguish between the "Principle of Contradiction" or "Principle of Excluded Middle" in two distinct guises: (1) On the one hand, as explicit formulas of a system (e.g., the analogues of "$\sim[\alpha \ \& \ \sim\alpha]$" and "$\alpha \lor \sim\alpha$").[21] (2) But on the other hand, such logical principles can be viewed as metasystematic principles ("Do not affirm a proposition and its negative," "If you class a proposition as true, you must class its negative false, and conversely"). In this second role, these principles have a very different sort of status. And in this essentially regulative role they cannot be written off as easily as in the first. Here logical precepts can be regarded as somehow basic regulative principles outside any specifically formulated system rather than as explicit members of an overt systematization.

A case can certainly be made out that analogues of some of the orthodox principles of two-valued logic are operative at the meta-level as regulative requirements upon all systems of logic, specifically including the many-valued systems. Thus, consider the principles of Excluded Middle and of Contradiction. Let $\neg$ be the negation operative in a formalized system. Then we shall have it that:

(1) For any *definite propositional formula p* of the system—i.e., closed formula which, like "$(\forall\alpha)\alpha$" or "$(\forall\alpha)(\exists\beta)(\alpha \to \beta),$" contains no free variables—either *p* or not-*p*.

(2) For any formula (wff) *p* of the system, the presence of both *p* and $\neg p$ among the assertions of the system is to be avoided.

In this metasystematic form these principles are certainly acceptable. (Actually they would be regarded as qualifiers for the concept of negation ($\neg$) or of the conception of an "assertion," or both.) But this regulative acceptability at the metasystematic level of *analogues* of various of the orthodox, two-valued principles clearly does not constitute the basis for a general claim of the preeminence of classical two-valued propositional logic.

The important feature of these regulative metaprinciples—convenience, economy, efficiency, effectiveness, and the rest—is that they represent constraints conformity to which leaves the content of any specific systematization of a "logic" *underdetermined*. The metaprinciples impose limiting conditions, without fixing a single solution—analogously with a

[21]It may be said that strictly speaking there is no such principle as that of the Excluded Middle, since there are many different logical systems in each of which there is (or may be) something akin to the principle. (One might even argue for a family-resemblance approach along the lines made familiar in philosophical discussions by the later work of Ludwig Wittgenstein.) But the fact is that there is a certain core idea operative throughout. Cf. M. Farber, "Logical Systems and the Principles of Logic," *Philosophy of Science*, vol. 9 (1942), pp. 40–54; see especially p. 52.

problem like constructing an equilateral triangle with two of three given points as vertices or solving n (independent) linear equations in $m < n$ unknowns. This analogy illustrates our own pragmatist approach to the matter that views the choice between various "alternative" logics as a *genuinely open* (non absolutist) choice—so much we must concede to relativism—but all the same a choice that is made within an (absolutistically) restricted range of viable alternatives and even within this range is *guided* by instrumentalistic, purpose-oriented considerations.

A "logical law," as we are now considering the matter, will not be a proposition that holds as an assertion of each and every system of logic. Rather it will be a regulative metasystematic principle. It must be *general* with respect to the various systems and *abstract*. It holds not *in*, but *with respect to*, the various systems. It is *regulative* in saying that such-and-such should be done. And it is normatively restrictive, having for its basis the contention that if such-and-such is not done, then these-and-those un-toward consequences ensue.

At the regulative level, every construction that can be put forward as a logical system must conform to certain general canons of rationality. These regulative canons underwrite a degree of metatheoretical uniformity across the whole wide range of diverse logical systems. In this sense we might adopt the doctrine of *una logica in systemarum varietate*, the conception of one "logic" that manifests itself through the variety of competing and mutually alternative systematizations.

10 Retrospect

Let us pause, then, for a retrospect over the preceding considerations. We began with the question "Are there alternative logics?" and answered this question in the affirmative, by embracing the doctrine of pluralism in logic. We saw that, although it is seriously deficient, the analogy of geometry does apply in at least a gross way: there are *genuine alternatives*. But our path grew more tortuous as we turned to the issue of relativism. There is indeed a choice between systems, but this choice is not wholly free and uncircum-scribed. In the first place, it is constrained by basic pragmatic considerations relating to the serviceability of the various systems to the purposes for which the systematization of logic is undertaken. And in the second place, there is the derivative fact that any proposed logical system that can be regarded as usable for these purposes must conform to regulative principles at the metasystematic level. Certain minimal but universal regulative standards of (*inter alia*) coherence and precision and *conformity with our presystematic understanding of what logic is all about* must be met at the metasystematic level. And this has important consequences for the issue of relativism. For it places certain absolutistic limits around the sort of logical relativism that can reasonably be put forward for acceptance.[22]

But in the final analysis we must come back to the same circumstance with which our considerations began: the reality of a plurality of viable systems of "logic" that are alternative to one another with respect to their common capacity to serve the fundamental objectives of any system of "logic": the systematization of the procedure's exact reasoning in general and the formal principles of successful reasoning in particular. This plurality of systems presents us with alternative instrumentalities. For certain specific purposes some of these instrumentalities may be better (e.g., two-valued logic for much of mathematics), for others, others may be superior (as 3-valued logic may turn out to be a better instrument for systematizing quantum theory, or infinite-valued logic may be the best medium for developing set theory). There can be no more question of the universally and generically "correct" logic than there can be of the universally and generically "correct" woodworking tool. (To say this is not to deny that a pencil will not be a woodworking tool at all, nor will an axiomatized theory of classical mechanics be a logic.) There will be a range of legitimate choice, with borders delimited by functionally grounded regulative principles, but within which the alternatives are, from a purely conceptual standpoint, equally viable. Within this range, then, a choice between systems cannot be made in a once-and-for-all fashion on the basis of abstract *theoretical* considerations, but must be made on the basis of *practical* (pragmatic or instrumentalistic) considerations regarding the specific, lower-level purposes at issue.[23] In this sense, then, we return to our initial affirmative answer to the question of the existence of alternative logics. The long journey has led back to this starting point of system pluralism. But the discussion has, I hope, shown this pluralism to be hedged in by regulative principles in such a way that it does not lead to a relativism or conventionalism of any unfortunate sort—to say nothing of illogic or irrationalism.

---

[22]We cannot here spell out in any detail the implications of this position for the concept of *logical truth* (and of *analytic propositions*). This will now *to some extent* become context-relative, being dependent upon the logical framework operative in a given context of discussion. Generally speaking, the range of application of the concept will now be fuzzy-edged: there will be a definite core and a definite exterior separated from one another by a wide penumbral border.

[23]Thus it is only with respect to this limited range that we are able to endorse the position of J. B. Rosser and A. R. Turquette in their book *Many-Valued Logics* (Amsterdam, 1952); see p. 1.

Chapter 4
A Bibliography of Many-valued Logic (to 1965)

1 Introduction

Many-valued logic is a field in which there are few books but a great journal literature with literally hundreds of papers. At this writing (1967), there exist only three books devoted to many-valued logic:

> James Barkley Rosser and Atwell R. Turquette, *Many-valued Logics* (Dordrecht, North-Holland Publishing Co., 1952).
>
> Aleksander Aleksandrovich Zinov'ev, *Philosophical Problems of Many-valued Logic*, ed. and tr. (from the Russian) by G. Küng and D. D. Comey (Dordrecht, D. Reidel Publishing Co., 1963).
>
> Robert Ackermann, *Introduction to Many-valued Logics* (London, Routledge & Kegan Paul, 1967).

One paper is so substantial and many-faceted as to approach monographic proportions:

> Arto Salomaa, "On Many-valued Systems of Logic," *Ajatus*, vol. 22 (1959), pp. 115–159.

Each of these works, however, deals with a very narrow range of topics, and none gives anything like a synoptic view of the field[1] The reader who wants to attain deeper familiarity with the subject must therefore grapple with its ramified literature, which consists almost entirely of specialized studies of particular problems. Our purpose in providing a comprehensive bibliography is to facilitate this step. For the user's convenience the reviews of these publications are cited whenever possible, drawing upon the three major reviewing organs that cover the field of symbolic logic:

JSL = *The Journal of Symbolic Logic*
MR = *Mathematical Reviews*
ZMG = *Zentralblatt für Mathematik und ihre Grenzgebiete*

2 Chronological Inventory of Contributions

MacColl (1877–78). Hugh MacColl: "The Calculus of Equivalent Statements and Integration Limits," *Proceedings of the London Mathematical Society*, vol. 9 (1877–78), pp. 9–20.

MacColl (1877–98). Hugh MacColl: "The Calculus of Equivalent Statements," *Proceedings of the London Mathematical Society*, vol. 9 (1877–78), pp. 177–186; vol. 10 (1878–79), pp. 16–28; vol. 11 (1879–80), pp. 113–121; vol. 28 (1896–97), pp. 156–183, 555–579; vol. 29 (1897–98), pp. 98–109.

MacColl (1880–1906). Hugh MacColl: "Symbolical Reasoning," *Mind*, vol. 5 (1880), pp. 45–60; vol. 6 (1897), pp. 493–510; vol. 9 (1900), pp. 75–84; vol. 11 (1902), pp. 353–368; vol. 12 (1903), pp. 355–364; vol. 14 (1905), pp. 74–81, 390–397; vol. 15 (1906), pp. 504–518.

MacColl (1899). Hugh MacColl: Review of Whitehead's *Universal Algebra*, *Mind*, vol. 8 (1899), pp. 108–113.

MacColl (1900–01). Hugh MacColl: A report on MacColl's 3-valued logic (invariably true, invariably false, and variable) in E. O. Lovett, "Mathematics at the International Congress of Philosophy, Paris 1900," *Bulletin of the American Mathematical Society*, vol. 7 (1900–01), pp. 157–183. [See pp. 166–168.]

MacColl (1901). Hugh MacColl: "La logique symbolique et ses applications," *Bibliothèque du Congrès International de philosophie*, vol. 3 (Paris, 1901), pp. 135–183.

---

[1]Ackermann's book, for example, is concerned almost exclusively with the systems of the Łukasiewiczian sequence $Ł_n$.

Peirce (1902). Charles Sanders Peirce: "Minute Logic," in *Collected Papers of Charles Sanders Peirce*, ed. by C. Hartshorne and P. Weiss, vol. IV (Cambridge, Mass., Harvard University Press, 1934). [See 4.308. Cf. also 4.12–20 and 4.257–265.]

MacColl (1903). Hugh MacColl: "La Logique Symbolique," *L'Enseignement mathématique*, vol. 5 (1903), pp. 415–430.

MacColl (1904). Hugh MacColl: "La Logique Symbolique," *L'Enseignement mathématique*, vol. 6 (1904), pp. 372–375.

MacColl (1906). Hugh MacColl: *Symbolic Logic and Its Applications* (London, New York, and Bombay, Longmans, Green & Co., 1906).

MacColl (1907). Hugh MacColl: "Symbolic Logic (A Reply)," *Mind*, vol. 16 (1907), pp. 470–472.

MacColl (1908). Hugh MacColl: " 'If' and 'Imply', " *Mind*, vol. 17 (1908), pp. 151–152.

Łukasiewicz (1910). Jan Łukasiewicz: "Über den Satz des Widerspruchs bei Aristoteles," *Bulletin international de l'Académie des Sciences de Cracovie, Classe de Philosophie* (Cracow, 1910), pp. 15–38.

Vasil'év (1910). Nikolai A. Vasil'év: "O častnyh suždéniáh, o tréugol'niké protivopoložnostéj, o zakoné isklúcënnogo čétvërtogo" (On particular propositions, the triangle of opposition, and the law of excluded fourth), *Učënié zapiski Kanzan'skogo Universitéte* (1910), 47 pp.

Vasil'év (1911). Nikolai A. Vasil'év: *Voobražaémaá logika: Konspékt léktsii* (Imaginary Logic: Abstract of a Lecture), (Kazan', 1911), 6 pp.

Jourdain (1912). P. E. B. Jourdain: "The Development of the Theories of Mathematical Logic and the Principles of Mathematics," *The Quarterly Journal of Mathematics*, vol. 43 (1912), pp. 219–314.

Vasil'év (1912). Nikolai A. Vasil'év: "Voobražaémaá (néaristotéléva) logika" (Imaginary [non-Aristotelian] logic), *Zurnal Ministérstva Narodnogo Prosvéščeniá*, vol. 40 (1912), pp. 207–246.

Vasil'év (1912–13). Nikolai A. Vasil'év: "Logika i métalogika" (Logic and metalogic), *Logos*, vols. 2–3 (1912–13), pp. 53–81.

Peirce (d. 1914). Charles Sanders Peirce: *Collected Papers of Charles Sanders Peirce*, vols. III–IV, ed. by C. Hartshorne and P. Weiss (Cambridge, Mass., Harvard University Press, 1933).

Guthrie (1916). Edwin Guthrie: "The Field of Logic," *Journal of Philosophy, Psychology and Scientific Methods*, vol. 13 (1916), pp. 152–158 and 336.

Łukasiewicz (1920). Jan Łukasiewicz: "O logice trójwartościowej" (On 3-valued logic), *Ruch Filozoficzny*, vol. 5 (1920), pp. 169–171. [Tr. in S. McCall (ed.), *Polish Logic: 1920–1939* (Oxford, 1967), pp. 16–18.]

Łukasiewicz (1921). Jan Łukasiewicz: "Logika dwuwartościowa" (Two-valued logic), *Przeglad Filozoficzny*, vol. 23 (1921), pp. 189–205.

Post (1921). Emil Post: "Introduction to a General Theory of Elementary Propositions," *American Journal of Mathematics*, vol. 43 (1921), pp. 163–185. Reprinted in J. van Heijenoort (ed.), *From Frege to Gödel: A Source Book in Mathematical Logic, 1879–1931* (Cambridge, Mass., 1967), pp. 265–283.

Wittgenstein (1922). Ludwig Wittgenstein: *Tractatus logico-philosophicus* (London, Routledge & Kegan Paul, 1922).

Łukasiewicz (1923). Jan Łukasiewicz: "O Determiniźmie" (On determinism), in J. Słupecki (ed.), Jan Łukasiewicz, *Z Zagadnień Logiki i Filozofii* (Warsaw, 1961); tr. in S. McCall (ed.), *Polish Logic: 1920–1939* (Oxford, 1967), pp. 19–39. [Lecture given from notes at Warsaw University and written out in 1923.]

Kolmogorov (1924–25). A. N. Kolmogorov: "O principé *tertium non datur*" (The *tertium non datur* principle), *Matématičéskij sbornik*, vol. 32 (1924–25), pp. 646–667. English tr. in J. van Heijenoort (ed.), *From Frege to Gödel: A Source Book in Mathematical Logic, 1879–1931* (Cambridge, Mass., 1967), pp. 414–437.

Vasil'ev (1924). Nikolai A. Vasil'ev: "Imaginary (Non-Aristotelian) Logic," *Atti del V Congresso Internazionale di Filosofia* (Napoli, 5–9 maggio, 1924) (Naples, 1925), pp. 107–109.

Brouwer (1925a). L. E. J. Brouwer: "Intuitionistische Zerlegung mathematischer Grundbegriffe," *Jahresbericht der deutschen Mathematiker-Vereinigung*, vol. 33 (1925), pp. 251–256. English tr. in J. van Heijenoort (ed.), *From Frege to Gödel: A Source Book in Mathematical Logic, 1879–1931* (Cambridge, Mass., 1967), pp. 334–341.

Brouwer (1925b). L. E. J. Brouwer: "Über die Bedeutung des Satzes vom ausgeschlossenen Dritten in der Mathematik, insbesondere in der Funktionentheorie," *Journal für die reine und angewandte Mathematik*, vol. 154 (1925), pp. 1–7. [Original in Dutch, 1923.]

Kaila (1926). Eino Kaila: *Die prinzipien der Wahrscheinlichkeitslogik*, Turun Suomalaisen Yliopiston julkaisuja (Annales Universitatis Fennicae Aboensis), ser. B, vol. 4, no. 1 (Abo, 1926), 171 pp.

von Neumann (1927). John von Neumann: "Zur Hilbertschen Beweistheorie," *Mathematische Zeitschrift*, vol. 26 (1927), pp. 1–46.

Ajdukiewicz (1928). Kazimierz Ajdukiewicz: *Glówne zasady metodologii i logiki formalnej* (Fundamental Principles of Methodology of the Sciences and Formal Logic), (Warsaw, 1928) mimeographed.

Bernstein (1928). B. A. Bernstein: "Modular Representations of Finite Algebras," *Proceedings of the International Mathematical Congress Held in Toronto*, August 11–16, 1924, vol. 1 (1928), pp. 207–216.

Weiss (1928). Paul Weiss: "Relativity in Logic," *The Monist*, vol. 28 (1928), pp. 536–548.

Łukasiewicz (1929). Jan Łukasiewicz: *Elementy Logiki Matematycznej* (Elements of Mathematical Logic), (Warsaw, Panstowowe Wydawnictwo Naukowe, 1929; 2d ed., 1958).

Skolem (1929). Thoralf Skolem: "Über einige Grundlagenfragen der Mathematik," *Skrifter utgitt av Det Norske Videnskaps-Akademi i Oslo*, no. 4 (1929), pp. 1–49.

Zawirski (1929). Zygmunt Zawirski: "Stosunek logiki do matematyki" (Relation of logic to mathematics), *Ksiega pamiatkowa Pierwszego Polskiego Zjazdu Matematycznego, Lwow, 7–10. IX. 1927* (Kraków, 1929), pp. 35–36.

Heyting (1930). Arend Heyting: "Die Formalen Regeln der intuitionistischen Logik," *Sitzungsberichte der Preussischen Akademie der Wissenschaften zu Berlin* (Berlin, 1930), pp. 42–46.

Lindenbaum (1930). Adolf Lindenbaum: "Remarques sur une question de la méthode axiomatique," *Fundamenta Mathematicae*, vol. 15 (1930), pp. 313–321.

Łukasiewicz (1930). Jan Łukasiewicz: "Philosophische Bemerkungen zu mehrwertigen Systemen des Aussagenkalküls," *Comptes rendus des séances de la Société des Sciences et des Lettres de Varsovie*, Classe III, vol. 23 (1930), pp. 51–77. Tr. in S. McCall (ed.), *Polish Logic: 1920–1939* (Oxford, 1967), pp. 40–65. Polish tr. in Łukasiewicz (1961).

Łukasiewicz and Tarski (1930). Jan Łukasiewicz and Alfred Tarski: "Untersuchungen über den Aussagenkalkül," *Comptes rendus des séances de la Société des Sciences et des Lettres de Varsovie*, Classe III, vol. 23 (1930), pp. 1–21, 30–50. English tr. in J. H. Woodger (tr.), Alfred Tarski: *Logic, Semantics, Metamathematics* (Oxford, 1956), pp. 38–59. Polish tr. in Łukasiewicz (1961).

Tarski (1930). See Łukasiewicz and Tarski (1930).

Wajsberg (1931). Mordchaj Wajsberg: "Aksjomatyzacja trójwartściowego rachunku zdań" (Axiomatization of the 3-valued propositional calculus), *Comptes rendus des séances de la Société des Sciences et des Lettres de Varsovie*, Classe III, vol. 24 (1931), pp. 126–148. Tr. in S. McCall (ed.), *Polish Logic: 1920–1939* (Oxford, 1967), pp. 264–284.

Weiss (1931a). Paul Weiss: "Two-Valued Logic: Another Approach," *Erkenntnis*, vol. 2 (1931), pp. 242–261.

Weiss (1931b). Paul Weiss: "Entailment and the Future of Logic," *Proceedings of the Seventh International Congress of Philosophy held at Oxford, England, September 1–6, 1930* (London, 1931), pp. 143–150.

Zawirski (1931). Zygmunt Zawirski: "Logika trójwartosciowa Jans Łukasiewicza. O logice L. E. J. Brouwera. Próby stosowania logiki wielowartosciowej do wspólczesnego przyrodoznawstwa" (Jan Łukasiewicz' 3-valued logic. On the logic of L. E. J. Brouwer. Attempts at applications of many-valued logic to contemporary natural science), *Sprawozdania Poznanskiego Towarzystwa Przyjaciol Nauk*, vol. 2 (1931), nos. 2–4.

Gödel (1932). Kurt Gödel: "Zum intuitionistischen Aussagenkalkül," *Anzeiger der Akademie der Wissenschaften Wien, mathematisch, naturwissenschaftliche Klasse*, vol. 69 (1932), pp. 65–66.

Kolmogorov (1932). A. N. Kolmogorov: "Zur Deutung der intuitionistischen Logik," *Mathematische Zeitschrift*, vol. 35 (1932), pp. 58–65.

Langford (1932). See Lewis and Langford (1932).

Lewis (1932). C. I. Lewis: "Alternative Systems of Logic," *The Monist*, vol. 42 (1932), pp. 481–507.

Lewis and Langford (1932). C. I. Lewis and Cooper H. Langford: *Symbolic Logic* (New York, The Century Co., 1932; reprinted, Dover Publications, 1951). [Reviewed by Alonzo Church in JSL, vol. 16 (1951), p. 225.]

Mazurkiewicz (1932). Stefan Mazurkiewicz: "Zur Axiomatik der Wahrscheinlichkeitslehre," *Comptes rendus des séances de la Société des Sciences et des Lettres de Varsovie*, Classe III, vol. 25 (1932), pp. 1–4.

Reichenbach (1932). Hans Reichenbach: "Wahrscheinlichkeitslogik," *Sitzungsberichte der Preussischen Akademie der Wissenschaften*, Physikalisch-mathematische Klasse, 1932, pp. 476–488.

Tarski (1932). Alfred Tarski: "Untersuchungen über der Aussagenkalkül," *Ergebnisse eines mathematischen Kolloquiums* (Vienna, 1932), pp. 13–14.

Zawirski (1932). Zygmunt Zawirski: "Les logiques nouvelles et le champ de leur application," *Revue de Métaphysique et de Morale*, vol. 39 (1932), pp. 503–519.

Gödel (1933a). Kurt Gödel: "Eine Interpretation des intuitionistischen Aussagenkalküls," *Ergebnisse eines mathematischen Kolloquiums*, vol. 4 (1933), pp. 33–40.

Gödel (1933b). Kurt Gödel: "Zum intuitionistischen Aussagenkalküls," *Ergebnisse eines mathematischen Kolloquiums*, vol. 4 (1933), p. 40.

Lewis (1933). C. I. Lewis: "Note Concerning Many-valued Logical Systems," *The Journal of Philosophy*, vol. 30 (1933), p. 364.

Ushenko (1933). Andrew Paul Ushenko: "Note on Alternative Systems of Logic," *The Monist*, vol. 42 (1933), pp. 319–320.

Weiss (1933). Paul Weiss: "On Alternative Logics," *The Philosophical Review*, vol· 42 (1933), pp. 520–525.

Zwicky (1933). Fritz Zwicky: "On a New Type of Reasoning and Some of Its Possible Consequences," *Physical Review*, vol. 43 (1933), pp. 1031–1033. Margenau (1934) offers a critique of this application of many-valued logics to physical reasoning.

Kalmár (1934). László Kalmár: "Über die Axiomatisierbarkeit des Aussagenkalküls," *Acta Scientiorum Mathematicarum*, vol. 7 (1934), pp. 222–243.

Łukasiewicz (1934). Jan Łukasiewicz: "Z historji logiki zdań" (From the history of the logic of propositions), *Przeglad Filozoficzny*, vol. 37 (1934), pp. 417–437. Tr. in S. McCall (ed.), *Polish Logic: 1920–1939* (Oxford, 1967), pp. 66–87.

Margenau (1934). Henry Margenau: "On the Application of Many-valued Systems of Logic to Physics," *Philosophy of Science*, vol. 1 (1934), pp. 118–121.

Mazurkiewicz (1934). Stefan Mazurkiewicz: "Über die Grundlagen der Wahrscheinlichkeitsrechnung," *Monatshefte für Mathematik und Physik*, vol. 41 (1934), pp. 343–352.

Zawirski (1934a). Zygmunt Zawirski: "Znaczenie logiki wielowartościowej dla poznania i zwiqzek jej z rachunkiem prawdopodobieństwa" (Significance of many-valued logic for cognition and its connection with the calculus of probability), *Przeglad Filozoficzny*, vol. 37 (1934), pp. 393–398.

Zawirski (1934b). Zygmunt Zawirski: "Stosunek logiki wielowartościowej do rachunku prawdopodobieństwa" (Le rapport de la logique à plusieurs valeurs au calcul des probabilités), *Prace Komisji Filozoficznej Poznanskiego Towarzystwa Przyjaciol Nauk*, vol. 4 (1934), pp. 155–240.

Gödel (1935). Kurt Gödel: "Eine Eigenschaft der Realisierungen des Aussagenkalküls," *Ergebnisse eines mathematischen Kolloquiums*, vol. 5 (1935), pp. 20–21.

Itô (1935). Makoto Itô: "Yûgenko-ryôiki ni okeru kansû ni tuite" (On the generation of all functions in the finitely many-valued algebra of logic), *Osaka shijô danwakai*, no. 58 (1935), pp. 27–35; no. 59, pp. 15–23; no. 60, pp. 6–15.

Łukasiewicz (1935–36). Jan Łukasiewicz: "Zur vollen dreiwertigen Aussagenlogik," *Erkenntnis*, vol. 5 (1935–36), p. 176.

Reichenbach (1935). Hans Reichenbach: *Wahrscheinlichkeitslehre* (Leyden, A. W. Süthoff's uitgeversmaatschappif N.V., 1935).

Reichenbach (1935–36a). Hans Reichenbach: "Wahrscheinlichkeitslogik," *Erkenntnis*, vol. 5 (1935–36), pp. 37–43.

Reichenbach (1935–36b). Hans Reichenbach: "Wahrscheinlichkeitslogik und Alternativlogik," *Erkenntnis*, vol. 5 (1935–36), pp. 177–178.

Schiller (1935). F. C. S. Schiller: "Multi-valued Logics—and Others," *Mind*, vol. 44 (1935), pp. 467–483.

Tarski (1935–36). Alfred Tarski: "Wahrscheinlichkeitslehre und mehrwertige Logik," *Erkenntnis*, vol. 5 (1935–36), pp. 174–175.

Wajsberg (1935). Mordchaj Wajsberg: "Beiträge zum Metaaussagenkalkül I," *Monatshefte für Mathematik und Physik*, vol. 42 (1935), pp. 221–242.

Webb (1935). Donald L. Webb: "Generation of Any *n*-Valued Logic by One Binary Operation," *Proceedings of the National Academy of Sciences*, vol. 21 (1935), pp. 252–254.

Zawirski (1935). Zygmunt Zawirski: "Über das Verhältnis mehrwertiger Logik zur Wahrscheinlichkeitsrechnung," *Studia Philosophia*, vol. 1 (1935), pp. 407–442. [Abridged German translation of above (1934b), with added *Ergänzung*.]

Baylis (1936). Charles A. Baylis: "Are Some Propositions Neither True nor False?", *Philosophy of Science*, vol. 3 (1936), pp. 156–166. [Reviewed by J. B. Rosser in JSL, vol. 1 (1936), p. 66.]

Birkhoff and von Neumann (1936). Garrett Birkhoff and John von Neumann: "The Logic of Quantum Mechanics," *Annals of Mathematics*, vol. 37 (1936), pp. 823–843. [Reviewed by A. Church in JSL, vol. 2 (1937), pp. 44–45.]

Habermann (1936). Edward Habermann: "Pojecie biegunowości i logika wielo-wartościowa" (The concept of polarity and many-valued logic), *Przeglad Filozo-ficzny*, vol. 39 (1936), pp. 438–441.

Hempel (1936–37). Carl G. Hempel: "Eine rein topologische Form nichtaristote-lischer Logik," *Erkenntnis*, vol. 6 (1936–37), pp. 436–442.

Jaśkowski (1936). Stanisław Jaśkowski: "Recherches sur le système de la logique intuitioniste," *Actes du Congrès International de Philosophie Scientifique*, vol. VI, Philosophie des mathématiques (Paris, 1936), pp. 58–61; tr. in S. McCall (ed.), *Polish Logic: 1920–1939* (Oxford, 1967), pp. 259–263. [Reviewed by S. C. Kleene in JSL, vol. 2 (1937), p. 55.]

Łukasiewicz (1936). Jan Łukasiewicz: "Bedeutung der logischen Analyse für die Erkenntnis," *Actes du Huitième Congrès International de Philosophie* (Prague, 1936), pp. 75–84. [See discussions by E. Harms, S. A. Kobylecki, I. M. Bocheński, K. Dürr, and J. Łukasiewicz on pp. 117–118. Reviewed by Ernest Nagel in JSL, vol. 2 (1937), p. 138.]

McKinsey (1936). J. C. C. McKinsey: "On the Generation of the Functions *Cpq* and *Np* of Łukasiewicz and Tarski by Means of a Single Binary Operation," *Bulletin of the American Mathematical Society*, vol. 42 (1936), pp. 849–851. [Re-viewed by W. V. Quine in JSL, vol. 2 (1937), p. 59.]

Malisoff (1936). William M. Malisoff: "Meanings in Multi-valued Logic (Toward a general semantics)," *Erkenntnis*, vol. 6 (1936), pp. 133–136.

von Neumann (1936). See Birkhoff and von Neumann (1936).

Schmierer (1936). Zygmunt Schmierer: "O funkcjach charakterystycznych w logi-kach wielowartościowych" (On characteristic functions in many-valued systems of logic), *Przeglad Filozoficzny*, vol. 39 (1936), p. 437. [Reviewed by A. Tarski in JSL, vol. 2 (1937), p. 92.]

Słupecki (1936). Jerzy Słupecki: "Der volle dreiwertige Aussagenkalkül," *Comptes rendus des séances de la Société des Sciences et des Lettres de Varsovie*, Classe III, vol. 29 (1936), pp. 9–11. [Reviewed by C. A. Baylis in JSL, vol. 2 (1937), p. 46.]

Sobociński (1936). Boleslaw Sobociński: "Aksjomatyzacja pewnych wielowartoś-ciowych systemów teorji dedukcji" (Axiomatization of certain many-valued systems of the theory of deduction), *Roczniki prac naukowych zrzeszenia asys-tentów Uniwersytetu Józefa Pilsudskiego w Warszawie*, vol. 1 (Warsaw, 1936), pp. 399–419. [Reviewed by A. Tarski in JSL, vol. 2 (1937), p. 93.]

Ushenko (1936). Andrew Paul Ushenko: "The Many-valued Logics," *The Philo-sophical Review*, vol. 45 (1936), pp. 611–615. [Reviewed by Paul Henle in JSL, vol. 2 (1937), p. 58.]

Webb (1936a). Donald L. Webb: "The Algebra of *n*-Valued Logic," *Comptes rendus des séances de la Société des Sciences et des Lettres de Varsovie*, Classe III, vol. 29 (1936), pp. 153–168. [Reviewed by Charles A. Baylis in JSL, vol. 3 (1938), p. 52.]

Webb (1936b). Donald L. Webb: "Definition of Post's Generalized Negative and Maximum in Terms of One Binary Operation," *Bulletin of the American Mathematical Society*, vol. 58 (1936), pp. 193–194. [Reviewed by Alonzo Church in JSL, vol. 1 (1936), p. 42.]

Zawirski (1936a). Zygmunt Zawirski: "Bedeutung der mehrwertigen Logik für die Erkenntnis und ihr Zusammenhang mit des Wahrscheinlichkeitsrechnung," *Actes du Huitième Congrès International de Philosophie* (Prague, 1936), pp. 175–180. [Reviewed by E. Nagel in JSL, vol. 2 (1937), p. 139.]

Zawirski (1936b). Zygmunt Zawirski: "Les rapports de la logique polyvalente avec le calcul des probabilités," *Actes du Congrès International de Philosophie Scientifique*, vol. IV (Paris, 1936), pp. 40–45. [Reviewed by Ernest Nagel in JSL, vol. 2 (1937), p. 54.]

Zawirski (1936–37). Zygmunt Zawirski: "Über die Anwendung der mehrwertigen Logik in der empirischen Wissenschaft," *Erkenntnis*, vol. 6 (1936–37), pp. 430–435. [Reviewed by C. H. Langford in JSL, vol. 2 (1937), p. 94.]

Février (1937a). Paulette Février: "Les relations d'incertitude de Heisenberg et la logique," *Comptes rendus hebdomadaires des séances de l'Académie des Sciences*, vol. 204 (1937), pp. 481–483. [Reviewed by Ernest Nagel in JSL, vol. 2 (1937), p. 88.]

Février (1937b). Paulette Février: "Sur une forme générale de la définition d'une logique," *Comptes rendus hebdomadaires des séances de l'Académie des Sciences*, vol. 204 (1937), pp. 958–959. [Reviewed by Ernest Nagel in JSL, vol. 2 (1937), p. 88.]

Feys (1937–38). Robert Feys: "Les logiques nouvelles des modalités," *Revue néoscolastique de philosophie*, vol. 40 (1937–38), pp. 517–553, and vol. 41 (1938), pp. 217–252. [Reviewed by C. A. Baylis in JSL, vol. 3 (1938), p. 120.]

Hailperin (1937). Theodore Hailperin: "Foundations of Probability in Mathematical Logic," *Philosophy of Science*, vol. 4 (1937), supplement, pp. 125–150. [Reviewed by P. Henle in JSL, vol. 2 (1937), pp. 95–96.]

Hempel (1937a). Carl G. Hempel: "A Purely Topological Form of Non-Aristotelian Logic," *The Journal of Symbolic Logic*, vol. 2 (1937), pp. 97–112. [Reviewed by Paul Bernays in JSL, vol. 3 (1938), pp. 91–92.]

Hempel (1937b). Carl G. Hempel: "Ein System verallgemeinerter Negationen," *Travaux du IXe Congrès International de Philosophie*, vol. VI (Paris, Hermann et Cie, 1937), pp. 26–32. [Reviewed by Paul Henle in JSL, vol. 3 (1938), p. 164.]

Jørgensen (1937). Jørgen Jørgensen: *Traek af deduktionsteoriens udvikling i den nyere tid* (Outline of the Recent Development of the Theory of Deduction), (Copenhagen, Levin & Munksgaard, 1937). [Reviewed by Alonzo Church in JSL, vol. 3 (1938), p. 43.]

Kattsoff (1937). Louis O. Kattsoff: "Modality and Probability," *The Philosophical Review*, vol. 46 (1937), pp. 78–85. [Reviewed by A. Church in JSL, vol. 2 (1937), p. 45.]

Łukasiewicz (1937). Jan Łukasiewicz: "Wobronie logistyki" (In defense of logistic), *Studia Gniesneusia*, vol. 15 (1937), 22 pp. [Reviewed by M. Kokoszyńska in JSL, vol. 3 (1938), pp. 43–44.]

Michalski (1937). Konstanty Michalski: "Le problème de la volonté à Oxford et à Paris au XIVe siècle," *Studia Philosophica*, vol. 2 (1937), pp. 233–365. [Reviewed by Robert Feys in JSL, vol. 11 (1946), p. 91.]

Moisil (1937–38). Grigor C. Moisil: "Sur le mode problématique," *Comptes rendus des séances de l'Académie des Sciences de Roumanie*, vol. 2 (1937–38), pp. 101–103. [Reviewed by C. A. Baylis in JSL, vol. 3 (1938), p. 162.]

Reichenbach (1937). Hans Reichenbach: "Les fondements logiques du calcul des probabilités," *Annales de l'Institut Henri Poincaré*, vol. 7 (1937), pp. 267–348. [Reviewed by Carl G. Hempel in JSL, vol. 3 (1938), pp. 114–115.]

Shirai (1937). Tameharu Shirai: "On the Pseudo-Set," *Memoirs of the College of Science, Kyoto Imperial University*, Series A, vol. 20 (1937), pp. 153–156. [Reviewed by A. Church in JSL, vol. 19 (1954), p. 221.]

Wajsberg (1937). Mordchaj Wajsberg: "Metalogische Beiträge," *Wiadomości Matematyczne*, vol. 43 (1937), pp. 131–168. English tr. in S. McCall (ed.), *Polish Logic: 1920–1939* (Oxford, 1967), pp. 285–318. [Reviewed by C. H. Langford in JSL, vol. 2 (1937), pp. 93–94.]

Destouches (1938). Jean-Louis Destouches: *Essai sur la forme générale des théories physiques* (Roumania, Cluj., 1938). [Reviewed by Saunders MacLane in JSL, vol. 5 (1940), p. 23.]

Frink (1938). Orrin Frink, Jr.: "New Algebras of Logic," *The American Mathematical Monthly*, vol. 45 (1938), pp. 210–219. [Reviewed by Everett J. Nelson in JSL, vol. 3 (1938), pp. 117–118.]

Kleene (1938). Stephen C. Kleene: "On a Notation for Ordinal Numbers," *The Journal of Symbolic Logic*, vol. 3 (1938), pp. 150–155. [Reviewed by R. Peter in JSL, vol. 4 (1939), pp. 93–94.]

Łukasiewicz (1938). Jan Łukasiewicz: "Die Logik und das Grundlagenproblem," *Les Entretiens de Zurich sur les fondements et la méthode des sciences mathématiques, 6–9 décembre 1938*, ed. by F. Gonseth (Zurich, S. A. Leemann Frères & Cie, 1941), pp. 82–100; "Discussion," pp. 100–108. [Reviewed by Saunders MacLane in JSL, vol. 7 (1942), p. 36; by H. B. Curry in MR, vol. 2 (1941), pp. 338–339.]

Moisil (1938). Grigor C. Moisil: "Sur la théorie classique de la modalité des jugements," *Bulletin Mathématique de la Société Roumaine des Sciences*, vol. 40 (1938), pp. 235–240. [Reviewed by C. A. Baylis in JSL, vol. 4 (1939), pp. 167–168.]

Shannon (1938). Claude E. Shannon: "A Symbolic Analysis of Relay and Switching Circuits," *Transactions of the American Institute of Electrical Engineers*, vol. 57 (1938), pp. 713–723. [Reviewed by C. A. Baylis in JSL, vol. 4 (1939), p. 103.]

Tarski (1938). Alfred Tarski: "Der Aussagenkalkül und die Topologie," *Fundamenta Mathematicae*, vol. 31 (1938), pp. 103–134. [Reviewed by Saunders MacLane in JSL, vol. 4 (1939), pp. 26–27.]

Vaidyanathaswamy (1938). R. Vaidyanathaswamy: "Quasi-Boolean Algebras and Many-valued Logics," *Proceedings of the Indian Academy of Sciences*, vol. 8 (1938), pp. 165–170. [Reviewed by J. C. C. McKinsey in JSL, vol. 4 (1939), pp. 27–28.]

Zich (1938). Otakar V. Zich: "Výrokový početás komplexními hodnotami" (Sentential calculus with complex values), *Česka Mysl*, vol. 34 (1938), pp. 189–196. [Reviewed by K. Reach in JSL, vol. 4 (1939), pp. 165–166.]

Bochvar (1939). D. A. Bochvar: "Ob odnom tréhznačnom isčislénii i égo priménénii k analizu paradoksov klassičéskogo rasširénnogo funkcional'nogo isčisléniá" (On a 3-valued logical calculus and its application to the analysis of contradictions), *Matématičéskij sbornik*, vol. 4 (1939), pp. 287–308. [Reviewed by Alonzo Church in JSL, vol. 4 (1939), pp. 98–99, and vol. 5 (1940), p. 119.]

Margenau (1939). Henry Margenau: "Probability, Many-valued Logics, and Physics," *Philosophy of Science*, vol. 6 (1939), pp. 65–87.

Metallmann (1939). Joachim Metallmann: *Wprowadzenie do zagadnién filozoficznych, Cześć I* (Introduction to Philosophical Problems, Part I), (Kraków, D. E. Friedlein, 1939). [Reviewed by H. Brodie in JSL, vol. 6 (1941), pp. 168–169.]

Moisil (1939a). Grigor C. Moisil: "Les principes de la logique et l'idée de chaîne," *Revista de filosofie*, vol. 24 (1939), pp. 3–12.

Moisil (1939b). Grigor C. Moisil: "Recherches sur le syllogisme," *Annales scientifiques de l'Université de Jassy*, vol. 25 (1939), pp. 341–384. [Reviewed by Ernest Nagel in JSL, vol. 4 (1939), p. 167.]

Moisil (1939c). Grigor C. Moisil: "La logique formelle et son problème actuel," *Istoria filosofiei moderne* (Bucharest), vol. 4 (1939), 28 pp. [Reviewed by R. Feys in JSL, vol. 13 (1948), p. 160.]

Rosser (1939). James Barkley Rosser: "The Introduction of Quantification into a Three-valued Logic," reprinted for the members of the Fifth International Congress for the Unity of Science (Cambridge, 1939) from *The Journal of Unified Science* (Erkenntnis), vol. 9 (never published). Abstracted in *The Journal of Symbolic Logic*, vol. 4 (1939), pp. 170–171. [Reviewed by Alonzo Church in JSL, vol. 4 (1939), p. 170.]

Rougier (1939). Louis Rougier: "La relativite de la logique," *The Journal of Unified Science*, vol. 8 (1939), pp. 193–217. [Reviewed by M. W. Gross in JSL, vol. 5 (1940), p. 124.]

Słupecki (1939a). Jerzy Słupecki: "Dowód aksjomatyzowalności pelnych systemów wielowartościowych rachunku zdań" (Proof of the axiomatizability of full many-valued systems of propositional calculus), *Comptes rendus des séances de la Société des Sciences et des Lettres de Varsovie*, Classe III, vol. 32 (1939), pp. 110–128. [Reviewed by Henryk Stonert in JSL, vol. 11 (1946), pp. 92–93.]

Słupecki (1939b). Jerzy Słupecki: "Kryterium pelności wielowartościowych systemów logiki zdań" (A criterion of completeness of many-valued systems of propositional logic), *Comptes rendus des séances de la Société des Sciences et des Lettres de Varsovie*, Classe III, vol. 32 (1939), pp. 102–110. [Reviewed by Jan Kalicki in JSL, vol. 11 (1946), p. 128.]

Wernick (1939). William Wernick: "An Enumeration of Logical Functions," *Bulletin of the American Mathematical Society*, vol. 45 (1939), pp. 885–887. [Reviewed by Alonzo Church in JSL, vol. 5 (1940), p. 31; by O. Frink in MR, vol. 1 (1940), p. 131.]

Birkhoff (1940). Garrett Birkhoff: *Lattice Theory*, American Mathematical Society Colloquium Publications (New York, 1940). [Reviewed by H. E. Vaughan in JSL, vol. 5 (1940), pp. 155–157; by O. Frink in MR, vol. 1 (1940), pp. 325–327.]

Dugundji (1940). James Dugundji: "Note on a Property of Matrices for Lewis and Langford's Calculi of Propositions," *The Journal of Symbolic Logic*, vol. 5 (1940), pp. 150–151. [Discussed in Prior's *Formal Logic* (Oxford, 1962), p. 326; reviewed by W. T. Parry in JSL, vol. 6 (1941), p. 37; by O. Frink in MR, vol. 2 (1941), p. 209.]

McKinsey (1940). J. C. C. McKinsey: "A Correction to Lewis and Langford's *Symbolic Logic*," *The Journal of Symbolic Logic*, vol. 5 (1940), p. 149. [Reviewed by O. Frink in MR, vol. 2 (1941), p. 209.]

Moisil (1940). Grigor C. Moisil: "Recherches sur les logiques non-chrysippiennes," *Annales scientifiques de l'Université de Jassy*, vol. 26 (1940), pp. 431–466. [Reviewed by Albert A. Bennett in JSL, vol. 13 (1948), p. 50; by G. Birkhoff in MR, vol. 8 (1947), p. 307.]

Moisil (1940–41). Grigor C. Moisil: "Sur la structure algébrique de la logique de M. Bochvar," *Disquisitiones mathematicae et physicae*, vol. 1 (1940–41), pp. 307–314. [Reviewed by A. R. Turquette in JSL, vol. 13 (1948), p. 116; by A. Heyting in MR, vol. 8 (1947), p. 557.]

Müller (1940). Hans R. Müller: "Algebraischer Aussagenkalkül," *Akademie der Wissenschaften in Wien, Mathematisch-naturwissenschaftliche Klasse, Sitzungsberichte*, Abteilung IIa, vol. 149 (1940), pp. 77–115. [Reviewed by Alonzo Church in JSL, vol. 7 (1942), p. 126; by O. Frink in MR, vol. 3 (1942), p. 130.]

Vrendenduin (1940). P. G. J. Vrendenduin: "Logistiek" (Logistic), *Christiaan Huygens*, vol. 18 (1940), pp. 170–211. [Reviewed by E. Beth in JSL, vol. 6 (1941), pp. 162–163.]

Weyl (1940). Hermann Weyl: "The Ghost of Modality," in M. Farber (ed.), *Philosophical Essays in Memory of Edmund Husserl* (Cambridge, Mass., 1940). [Reviewed by C. A. Baylis in JSL, vol. 8 (1943), p. 31.]

Ducasse (1941). Curt J. Ducasse: "Truth, Verifiability, and Propositions about the Future," *Philosophy of Science*, vol. 8 (1941), pp. 329–337. [Reviewed by E. Nagel in JSL, vol. 6 (1941), p. 160.]

Łukasiewicz (1941). Jan Łukasiewicz: "Die Logik und das Grundlagenproblem," in F. Gonseth (ed.), *Les Entretiens de Zurich sur les fondements et la méthode des sciences mathématiques* (Zurich, 1941). [Reviewed by S. MacLane in JSL, vol. 7 (1942), pp. 35–37.]

Malisoff (1941). William M. Malisoff: "Meanings in Multi-valued Logics," *Philosophy of Science*, vol. 8 (1941), pp. 271–274.

Moisil (1941a). Grigor C. Moisil: "Notes sur les logiques non-chrysippiennes," *Annales scientifiques de l'Université de Jassy*, vol. 27 (1941), pp. 86–98. [Reviewed by Albert A. Bennett in JSL, vol. 13 (1948), p. 50; by G. Birkhoff in MR, vol. 8 (1947), p. 307.]

Moisil (1941b). Grigor C. Moisil: "Recherches sur la théorie des chaînes," *Annales scientifiques de l'Université de Jassy*, vol. 27 (1941), pp. 181–240. [Reviewed by Albert A. Bennett in JSL, vol. 13 (1948), p. 50; by G. Birkhoff in MR, vol. 8 (1947), p. 308.]

Moisil (1941c). Grigor C. Moisil: "Contributions à l'étude des logiques non-chrysippiennes. I. Un nouveau système d'axiomes pour les algèbres Łukasiewicz-iennes tetra-valentes," *Comptes rendus des séances de l'Académie des Sciences de Roumanie*, vol. 5 (1941), pp. 289–293. [Reviewed by Robert Feys in JSL, vol. 13 (1948), p. 160.]

Moisil (1941d). Grigor C. Moisil: "Remarques sur la logique modale du concept," *Annales de l'Académie Roumanie, Mémoires de la section scientifique*, ser. 3, vol. 16 (1941), pp. 975–1012. [Reviewed by A. R. Turquette in JSL, vol. 13 (1948), pp. 161–162.]

Moisil (1941e). Grigor C. Moisil: "Sur les anneaux de caractéristique 2 ou 3 et leurs applications," *Bulletin de l'École Polytechnique de Bucarest*, vol. 12 (1941), pp. 66–90. [Reviewed by Robert Feys in JSL, vol. 13 (1948), pp. 160–161.]

Moisil (1941f). Grigor C. Moisil: "Sur les théories déductives à logique non-chrysippienne," *Comptes rendus des séances de l'Académie des Sciences de Roumanie*, vol. 5 (Bucharest, 1941), pp. 21–24.

Rosser (1941a). James Barkley Rosser: "Many-valued Logic," *School Science and Mathematics*, vol. 41 (1941), pp. 99–100.

Rosser (1941b). James Barkley Rosser: "On the Many-valued Logics," *American Journal of Physics*, vol. 9 (1941), pp. 207–212; reprinted in *Papers from the Second American Congress on General Semantics*, University of Denver, *August, 1941* (Chicago, 1943), pp. 79–86. [Reviewed by Alonzo Church in JSL, vol. 6 (1941), p. 109; by O. Frink in MR, vol. 3 (1942), p. 130; by A. Rose in ZMG, vol. 61 (1961), p. 8.]

Destouches (1942). Jean-Louis Destouches: *Principes fondamentaux de physique théorique* (Paris, Hermann, 1942). [Reviewed by J. B. Rosser in JSL, vol. 13 (1948), p. 213.]

Farber (1942). Marvin Farber: "Logical Systems and the Principles of Logic," *Philosophy of Science*, vol. 9 (1942), pp. 40–54. [Reviewed by C. G. Hempel in JSL, vol. 7 (1942), p. 99.]

Moisil (1942a). Grigor C. Moisil: "Logique modale," *Disquisitiones mathematicae et physicae*, vol. 2 (1942), pp. 3–98. [Reviewed by A. R. Turquette in JSL, vol. 13 (1948), pp. 162–163; by A. Heyting in MR, vol. 8 (1947), p. 557.]

Moisil (1942b). Grigor C. Moisil: "Contributions à l'étude des logiques non-chrysippiennes. II. Anneaux engendrés par les algèbres Łukasiewicziennes tetravalentes centrées," *Comptes rendus des séances de l'Académie des Sciences de Roumanie*, vol. 6 (1942), p. 9.

Moisil (1942c). Grigor C. Moisil: "Contributions à l'étude des logiques non-chrysippiennes. III. Anneaux engendrés par les algèbres Łukasiewicziennes tetravalentes axées," *Comptes rendus des séances de l'Académie des Sciences de Roumanie*, vol. 6 (1942), p. 14.

Rosenbloom (1942). Paul C. Rosenbloom: "Post Algebras. I. Postulates and General Theory," *American Journal of Mathematics*, vol. 64 (1942), pp. 167–188. [Reviewed by Saunders MacLane in JSL, vol. 7 (1942), pp. 124–125; by O. Frink in MR, vol. 3 (1942), p. 262.]

Wellmuth (1942a). John J. Wellmuth: "Some Comments on the Nature of Mathematical Logic," *The New Scholasticism*, vol. 16 (1942), pp. 9–15. [Reviewed by Alonzo Church in JSL, vol. 7 (1942), pp. 39–40.]

Wellmuth (1942b). John J. Wellmuth: "Philosophy and Order in Logic," *Proceedings of the American Catholic Philosophical Association*, vol. 17 (1942), pp. 12–18.

Bell (1943). Eric T. Bell: "Polynomials on a Finite Discrete Range," *Duke Mathematical Journal*, vol. 10 (1943), pp. 33–47. [Reviewed by H. E. Vaughan in JSL, vol. 9 (1944), p. 31; by I. Kaplanski in MR, vol. 4 (1943), pp. 129–130.]

Bochvar (1943). D. A. Bochvar: "K voprosu o néprotivoréčivosti odnogo tréhznačnogo isčisléniá" (On the consistency of a 3-valued calculus), *Matématičéskij sbornik*, vol. 12 (1943), pp. 353–369. [Reviewed by Wanda Szmielew in JSL, vol. 11 (1946), p. 129; by author in MR, vol. 5 (1944), p. 197; in ZMG, vol. 61 (1961), p. 8.]

Carnap (1943). Rudolf Carnap: *The Formalization of Logic* (Harvard, University of Harvard Press, 1943). [Reviewed by C. G. Hempel in JSL, vol. 8 (1943), pp. 81–83; by A. Church in *The Philosophical Review*, vol. 53 (1944), pp. 493–498.]

Dumitriu (1943). Anton Dumitriu: *Logica Polivalenta* (Many-valued Logic), (Bucharest, Viata Literara, 1943).

Moisil (1943). Grigor C. Moisil: "Contributions à l'étude des logiques non-chrysippiennes. IV. Sur la logique de Mr. Becker," *Comptes rendus des séances de l'Académie des sciences de Roumanie*, vol. 7 (1943), p. 9. [Reviewed by A. Heyting in MR, vol. 9 (1948), p. 1.]

Rosser (1943). James Barkley Rosser: "On the Many-valued Logics," *Papers from the Second American Congress on General Semantics, University of Denver, August, 1941* (Chicago, Institute of General Semantics, 1943), pp. 79–86. [Reprint of Rosser (1941b).]

Bochvar (1944). D. A. Bochvar: "K voprosu o paradoksah matématičéskoj logiki i téorii množéstv" (To the question of paradoxes of the mathematical logic and theory of sets), *Matématičéskij sbornik*, vol. 15 (1944), pp. 369–384. [Reviewed by W. Szmielew in JSL, vol. 11 (1946), p. 129.]

Chandrasekharan (1944). Komaravola Chandrasekharan: "Partially Ordered Sets and Symbolic Logic," *The Mathematics Student*, vol. 12 (1944), pp. 14–24. [Reviewed by Alonzo Church in JSL, vol. 11 (1946), pp. 100–101; by G. Birkhoff in MR, vol. 6 (1945), p. 143.]

Reichenbach (1944). Hans Reichenbach: *Philosophical Foundations of Quantum Mechanics* (Berkeley, Los Angeles, University of California Press, 1944). [Reviewed by C. G. Hempel in JSL, vol. 10 (1945), pp. 97–100.]

Turquette (1944). Atwell R. Turquette: "A Study and Extension of *m*-Valued Symbolic Logics," *Cornell University, Abstracts of Theses Accepted in Partial Satisfaction of the Requirements for the Doctor's Degree, 1943* (Ithaca, New York, Cornell University Press, 1944), pp. 49–51.

de Beauregard (1945). Olivier Costa de Beauregard: "Extension d'une théorie de M. J. de Neumann au cas des projecteurs non commutables," *Comptes rendus hebdomadaires des séances de l'Académie des Sciences*, vol. 21 (1945), pp. 230–231. [Reviewed by A. Borel and S. Specker in JSL, vol. 13 (1949), pp. 192–193; by O. Frink in MR, vol. 7 (1946), p. 356.]

Boehner (1945). Philotheus Boehner: The *"Tractatus de praedestinatione et de praescientia Dei et de futuris contingentibus" of William Ockham*, edited with a study on the medieval problem of a 3-valued logic (St. Bonaventure, New York; Franciscan Institute Publication, 1945). [Reviewed by Robert Feys in JSL, vol. 11 (1946), pp. 90–91.]

Helmer and Oppenheim (1945). Olaf Helmer and Paul Oppenheim: "A Syntactical Definition of Probability and Degree of Confirmation," *The Journal of Symbolic Logic*, vol. 10 (1945), pp. 25–60. [Reviewed by Max Black in JSL, vol. 11 (1947), pp. 17–18.]

Jordan (1945). Zbigniew A. Jordan: "The Development of Mathematical Logic and of Logical Positivism in Poland between the Two Wars," No. 6 in Anonymous (ed.), *Polish Science and Learning* (London, 1945). Reprinted in S. McCall (ed.), *Polish Logic, 1920–1939* (Oxford, 1967), pp. 346–406. [Reviewed by A. Mostowski in JSL, vol. 11 (1946), pp. 94–95.]

Lupasco (1945). Stéphane Lupasco: "Valeurs logiques et contradiction," *Revue philosophique de la France et de l'Étranger*, vol. 135 (1945),pp. 1–31. [Reviewed by C. A. Baylis in JSL, vol. 11 (1946), p. 134.]

Moisil (1945). Grigor C. Moisil: "L'algebra e la logica," *Atti del Congresso Matematico, tenuto in Roma 8–12 Novèmbre 1942* (Rome, Reale Instituto Nazionale di Alta Matematica, 1945), pp. 143–152. [Reviewed by A. Bennett in JSL, vol. 13 (1948), p. 118.]

Oppenheim (1945). See Helmer and Oppenheim (1945).

Rosser and Turquette (1945). James Barkley Rosser and Atwell R. Turquette: "Axiom Schemes for *m*-Valued Propositional Calculi," *The Journal of Symbolic Logic*, vol. 10 (1945), pp. 61–82. [Reviewed by Robert Feys in JSL, vol. 11 (1946), pp. 86–89; by J. C. C. McKinsey in MR, vol. 7 (1946), p. 185.]

Serrus (1945). Charles Serrus: *Traité de logique* (Paris, Editions Montaigne, 1945). [Reviewed by C. A. Baylis in JSL, vol. 12 (1947), p. 57; by G. R. Granger in *Philosophy and Phenomenological Research*, vol. 7 (1947), pp. 664–666.]

Turquette (1945a). Atwell R. Turquette: Review of Reichenbach's *Philosophical Foundations of Quantum Mechanics*, *The Philosophical Review*, vol. 54 (1945), pp. 513–516.

Turquette (1945b). See Rosser and Turquette (1945).

Destouches (1946). Jean-Louis Destouches: *Cours de logique et philosophie générale. I. Méthodologie de la physique: théorique moderne. II. Notions de logistique* (Paris, Centre de Documentation Universitaire, 1946). [Reviewed by Paul Bernays in JSL, vol. 13 (1948), pp. 118–120.]

Nagel (1946). Ernest Nagel: "Professor Reichenbach on Quantum Mechanics: A Rejoinder," *The Journal of Philosophy*, vol. 43 (1946), pp. 247–250.

Reichenbach (1946). Hans Reichenbach: "Reply to Ernest Nagel's Criticism of My Views on Quantum Mechanics," *The Journal of Philosophy*, vol. 43 (1946), pp. 239–247.

Shestakov (1946). V. I. Shestakov: "Prédstavlénié haraktérističéskih funkcij prédloženij posrédstvom vyražénij, réalizuémyh réléjno-kontaktymi shémani" (Representation of characteristic functions of propositions by expressions realizable by relay-contact circuits), *Izvéstiá Akadémii Nauk SSSR* (Bulletin de l'Académie des Sciences de l'URSS), Sériá matématičéskaá, vol. 10 (1946), pp. 529–554. [Reviewed by Andrzej Mostowski in JSL, vol. 12 (1947), p. 135; by A. Heyting in MR, vol. 8 (1947), p. 429.]

Słupecki (1946). Jerzy Słupecki: "Pelny trójwartościowy rachunek zdań" (The complete three-valued propositional calculus), *Annales Universitatis Mariae Curie-Sklodowska*, vol. 1 (1946), pp. 193–209. [Reviewed by Jan Kalicki in JSL, vol. 13 (1948), pp. 165–166; by H. Hiz in MR, vol. 10 (1949), p. 1.]

Storer (1946). Thomas Storer: "The Logic of Value Imperatives," *Philosophy of Science*, vol. 13 (1946), pp. 25–40. [Reviewed by C. G. Hempel in JSL, vol. 11 (1946), pp. 97–98.]

Waismann (1946). Friederich Waismann: "Are There Alternative Logics?," *Proceedings of the Aristotelian Society*, vol. 46 (1946), pp. 77–104. [Reviewed by C. A. Baylis in JSL, vol. 12 (1947), pp. 100–101.]

Zawirski (1946). Zygmunt Zawirski: "Geneza i rozwój logiki intuicjonistycznej" (Genesis and development of intuitionistic logic), *Kwartalnik filozoficzny*, vol. 16 (1946), pp. 165–222. [Reviewed by Andrzej Mostowski in JSL, vol. 12 (1947), pp. 26–27.]

Kiss (1947). Stephen A. Kiss: *Transformations on Lattices and Structures of Logic* (New York, 1947). (On sale by the author.) [Reviewed by H. E. Vaughan in JSL, vol. 13 (1948), pp. 159–160; by K. Chandrasekharan in MR, vol. 9 (1948), p. 76.]

Zich (1947). Otakar V. Zich: *Úvod do filosofie matematiky* (Introduction to the Philosophy of Mathematics), (Praha, Jednoto československých matematiků a Fysiků, 1947), Cesta k vědéni, vol. 34. [Reviewed by František Wolf in JSL, vol. 13 (1948), pp. 216–217.]

Aubert (1948). Karl E. Aubert: "Om presisering og generalisering av relasjons-begrepet" (A clarification and a generalization of the concept of relation), *Norsk matematisk tidsskrift*, vol. 30 (1948), pp. 33–53. [Reviewed by Thoralf Skolem in JSL, vol. 20 (1955), pp. 278–279.]

Klósak (1948). Kazimierz Klósak: "Teoria indeterminizmu ontologicznego a trójwartościowa logika zdań prof. Jana Łukasiewcza" (The theory of ontological indeterminism and the three-valued logic of propositions of Prof. Jan Łukasiewicz), *Ateneum Kaplanskie*, vol. 49 (1948), pp. 209–320. [Reviewed by I. M. Bocheński in JSL, vol. 14 (1949), p. 263.]

Linke (1948). Paul F. Linke: "Die mehrwertigen Logiken und das Wahrheits-problem," *Zeitschrift für philosophische Forschung*, vol. 3 (1948), pp. 378–398, 530–546. [Reviewed by Paul Bernays in JSL, vol. 17 (1952), pp. 276–277.]

Łoś (1948). Jerzy Łoś: "Logiki wielowartościowe a formalizacja funkcji intens-jonalnych" (Many-valued logics and the formalization of intensional functions), *Kwartalnik filozoficzny*, vol. 17 (1948), pp. 59–78. [Reviewed by R. Suszko in JSL, vol. 14 (1949), pp. 64–65; by H. Hiz in MR, vol. 10 (1949), pp. 1–2.]

McKinsey and Tarski (1948). J. C. C. McKinsey and Alfred Tarski: "Some Theorems about the Semantical Calculi of Lewis and Heyting," *The Journal of Symbolic Logic*, vol. 13 (1948), pp. 1–15. [Reviewed by Leon Henkin in JSL, vol. 13 (1948), pp. 171–172; by A. Heyting in MR, vol. 9 (1948), p. 486.]

Mostowski (1948). Andrzej Mostowski: *Logika matematyczna* (Mathematical logic), *Kurs uniwersytecki*, Monografie matematyczne, vol. 18 (Varsovie et Wroclaw, 1948). [Reviewed by O. V. Zich in JSL, vol. 14 (1949), pp. 189–190; by H. Hiz in MR, vol. 10 (1949), p. 229.]

Naess (1948). Arne Naess: *Symbolsk logikk* (Symbolic logic), (Oslo, Universitetes Studentkontor, 1948). [Reviewed by G. H. von Wright in JSL, vol. 14 (1949), pp. 185–186.]

Ridder (1948). Jacob Ridder: "Über mehrwertige Aussagenkalküle und mehr-wertige engere Prädikatenkalküle I–III," *Koninklijke Nederlandsche Akademie van Wetenschappen, Proceedings of the section of sciences*, vol. 51 (1948), pp. 670–680, 836–845, 991–995; also *Indagationes mathematicae*, vol. 10 (1948), pp. 221–231, 264–273, 324–328. [Reviewed by Boleslaw Sobociński in JSL, vol. 14 (1949), pp. 139, 261–262; by O. Frink in MR, vol. 10 (1949), pp. 230, 499.]

Rosser and Turquette (1948). James Barkley Rosser and Atwell R. Turquette: "Axiom Schemes for *m*-Valued Functional Calculi of First Order. Part I. Definition of Axiom Schemes and Proof of Plausibility," *The Journal of Symbolic Logic*, vol. 13 (1948), pp. 177–192. [Reviewed by Burton S. Dreben in JSL, vol. 14 (1949), pp. 259–260; by P. Lorenzen in MR, vol. 10 (1949), p. 420.]

Tarski (1948). See McKinsey and Tarski (1948).

Turquette (1948). See Rosser and Turquette (1948).

Vaccarino (1948). Giusseppe Vaccarino: "La scuola polacca di logica," *Sigma*, vol. 2 (1948), pp. 527–546. [Reviewed by Alonzo Church in JSL, vol. 14 (1949), p. 127.]

Aubert (1949). Karl E. Aubert: "Relations généralisées et indépendance logique des notions de réflexivité, symétrie et transitivité," *Comptes rendus hebdomadaires des séances de l'Académie des Sciences*, vol. 229 (Paris, 1949), pp. 284–286, 538–540. [Reviewed by A. R. Turquette in JSL, vol. 15 (1950), p. 71; by O. Ore in MR, vol. 11 (1950), p. 304.]

Bergmann (1949). Gustav Bergmann: "The Finite Representations of S5," *Methodos*, vol. 1 (1949), pp. 217–219. [Reviewed by W. T. Parry in JSL, vol. 15 (1950), pp. 224–225.]

Czeżowski (1949). Tadeusz Czeżowski: *Logika. Podrecznik dla studiujacych nauki filozoficzne* (Logic. Textbook for Students of the Philosophical Sciences), (Warsaw, Państwowe Zaklady Wydawnictw Szkolynch, 1949). [Reviewed by Jerzy Słupecki in JSL, vol. 15 (1950), p. 206.]

Destouches-Février (1949). Paulette Destouches-Février: "Logique et théories physiques," *Synthèse*, vol. 7 (1949), pp. 400–410. [Reviewed by A. R. Turquette in JSL, vol. 15 (1950), pp. 232–233; by C. C. Torrance in MR, vol. 12 (1951), p. 73.]

Dienes (P.) (1949). Paul Dienes: "On Ternary Logic," *The Journal of Symbolic Logic*, vol. 14 (1949), pp. 85–94. [Reviewed by Wilhelm Ackermann in JSL, vol. 15 (1950), p. 225; by A. Heyting in MR, vol. 11 (1950), p. 1; by K. Schröter in ZMG, vol. 41 (1952), p. 353.]

Dienes (Z. P.) (1949). Z. P. Dienes: "On an Implication Function in Many-valued Systems of Logic," *The Journal of Symbolic Logic*, vol. 14 (1949), pp. 95–97. [Reviewed by A. Church and N. Rescher in JSL, vol. 15 (1950), pp. 69–70; by A. Heyting in MR, vol. 11 (1950), p. 1; by K. Schröter in ZMG, vol. 37 (1951), pp. 3–4.]

Feys (1949). Robert Feys: *De ontwikkeling van het logisch denken* (The Development of Logical Thought), (Antwerp, Standaard-Boekhandel, 1949; Nijmegen, Dekker and van de Vegt, 1949). [Reviewed by Paul Bernays in JSL, vol. 16 (1951), pp. 55–56.]

Foster (1949). Alfred L. Foster: "The *n*-ality Theory of Rings," *Proceedings of the National Academy of Sciences of the United States of America*, vol. 35 (1949), pp. 31–38. [Reviewed by J. Dieudonné in MR, vol. 10 (1949), p. 349.]

Geach (1949). Peter T. Geach: "If's and And's," *Analysis*, vol. 9 (1949), pp. 58–62.

Halldén (1949a). Sören Halldén: "On the Decision-Problem of Lewis' Calculus S5," *Norsk matematisk tidsskrift*, vol. 31 (1949), pp. 89–94. [Reviewed by J. C. C. McKinsey in JSL, vol. 15 (1950), p. 224; by H. B. Curry in MR, vol. 11 (1950), p. 411.]

Halldén (1949b). Sören Halldén: "The Logic of Nonsense," *Uppsala Universitets årsskrift*, vol. 9 (1949), p. 132. [Reviewed by W. Ackermann in JSL, vol. 15 (1950), pp. 225–226.]

Hoo (1949). Tzu-hua Hoo: "*m*-Valued Sub-System of (*m* + *n*)-Valued Propositional Calculus," *The Journal of Symbolic Logic*, vol. 14 (1949), pp. 177–181. [Reviewed by A. R. Turquette in JSL, vol. 14 (1949), p. 261; by J. C. C. McKinsey in MR, vol. 11 (1950), p. 487; by G. Hasenjaeger in ZMG, vol. 36 (1951), p. 6.]

Klósak (1949). Kazimierz Klósak: "Konieczność wyjścia poza logike dwuwartościowq" (The necessity of going beyond the two-valued logic), *Ateneum Kaplanskie*, vol. 50 (1949), pp. 105–116. [Reviewed by I. M. Bocheński in JSL, vol. 14 (1949), p. 263.]

Martin (G.) (1949). Gottfried Martin: "Über ein zweiwertiges Modell einer vierwertigen Logik," *Methodos*, vol. 1 (1949), pp. 385–389. [Reviewed by A. Church in JSL, vol. 16 (1951), p. 150; by R. M. Martin in MR, vol. 12 (1951), p. 663; by K. Schröter in ZMG, vol. 37 (1951), p. 294.]

Meyer (1949). Herman Meyer: *Kennis en realiteit* (Knowledge and Reality), (Utrecht Uitgeversmaatschappij W. D. Haan, 1949). [Reviewed by R. Feys in JSL, vol. 15 (1950), p. 73.]

Reichenbach (1949a). Hans Reichenbach: *The Theory of Probability. An Inquiry into the Logical and Mathematical Foundations of the Calculus of Probability* (Berkeley and Los Angeles, University of California Press, 1949). [Reviewed by John G. Kemeny in JSL, vol. 16 (1951), pp. 48–51; by B. O. Koopman in MR, vol. 11 (1950), pp. 152–153.]

Reichenbach (1949b). Hans Reichenbach: *Philosophische Grunglagen der Quantenmechanic* (Basel, Verlag Birkhäuser, 1949). [Reviewed by G. Hasenjaeger in JSL, vol. 16 (1950), pp. 289–290; by Max Bense in *Deutsche Literaturzeitung*, vol. 71 (1950), pp. 5–10.]

Ridder (1949). Jacob Ridder: "Sur quelques logiques multivalentes," *Actes du Xme Congrès International de Philosophie* (Amsterdam, 11–18 août, 1948)—*Proceedings of the Tenth International Congress of Philosophy* (Amsterdam, North-Holland Publishing Company, 1949), pp. 728–730. [Reviewed by A. R. Turquette in JSL, vol. 14 (1949), p. 130; by O. Frink in MR, vol. 10 (1949), p. 585.]

Rosser and Turquette (1949). James Barkley Rosser and Atwell R. Turquette: "A Note on the Deductive Completeness of *m*-Valued Propositional Logic," *The Journal of Symbolic Logic*, vol. 14 (1949), pp. 219–225. [Reviewed by A. F. Bausch in JSL, vol. 15 (1950), pp. 137–138; by J. C. C. McKinsey in MR, vol. 11 (1950), p. 709; by G. Hasenjaeger in ZMG, vol. 36 (1951), p. 7.]

Turquette (1949). See Rosser and Turquette (1949).

Baudry (1950). Léon Baudry: *La querelle des futurs contingents: Louvain 1465–1475* (Paris, J. Vrin, 1950). [Reviewed by A. N. Prior in his *Formal Logic* (Oxford, 1962), p. 324.]

Boll and Reinhardt (1950). Marcel Boll and Jacques Reinhardt: "A propos des logiques polyvalentes: Les modalités et la vraisemblance," *Revue Philosophique de la France et l'Étranger*, vol. 140 (1950), pp. 143–179.

Carnap (1950). Rudolf Carnap: *Logical Foundations of Probability* (Chicago, University of Chicago Press, 1950; 2d ed., 1960). [Reviewed by J. G. Kemeny in JSL, vol. 16 (1961), pp. 205–207.]

Foster (1950). Alfred L. Foster: "On *n*-ality Theories in Rings and Their Logical Algebras, Including Triality Principle in Three-valued Logics," *American Journal of Mathematics*, vol. 72 (1950), pp. 101–123. [Reviewed by A. R. Turquette in JSL, vol. 15 (1950), p. 230; by J. Dieudonné in MR, vol. 11 (1950), p. 414.]

Kalicki (1950a). Jan Kalicki: "Note on Truth-tables," *The Journal of Symbolic Logic*, vol. 15 (1950), pp. 174–181. [Reviewed by J. C. C. McKinsey in JSL, vol. 16 (1951), p. 65; by O. Frink in MR, vol. 12 (1951), p. 663; by G. Hasenjaeger in ZMG, vol. 39 (1951), p. 6.]

Kalicki (1950b). Jan Kalicki: "A Test for the Existence of Tautologies According to Many-valued Truth-tables," *The Journal of Symbolic Logic*, vol. 15 (1950), pp. 182–184. [Reviewed by J. C. C. McKinsey in JSL, vol. 16 (1951), p. 65; by O. Frink in MR, vol. 12 (1951), p. 663; by G. Hasenjaeger in ZMG, vol. 39 (1951), p. 6.]

Margenau (1950). Henry Margenau: *The Nature of Physical Reality* (New York, McGraw-Hill, 1950). [Reviewed by J. G. Kemeny in JSL, vol. 18 (1953), p. 271; by C. C. Torrance in MR, vol. 11 (1950), p. 709.]

Martin (N. M.) (1950). Norman M. Martin: "Some Analogues of the Sheffer Stroke Function in *n*-Valued Logic," *Koninklijke Nederlandse Akademie van Wetenschappen, Proceedings of the section of sciences*, vol. 53 (1950), pp. 1100–1107; also *Indagationes Mathematicae*, vol. 12 (1950), pp. 393–400. [Reviewed by Alan Rose in JSL, vol. 16 (1951), pp. 275–276; by O. Frink in MR, vol. 12 (1951), p. 385; by W. Markwald in ZMG, vol. 39 (1951), p. 245.]

Rasiowa (1950). Helena Rasiowa: "Zdziedziny logiki matematycznej. II. Logiki wielowartościowe Łukasiewicza" (From the domain of mathematical logic. II. The many-valued logics of Łukasiewicz), *Matematyka*, vol. 3 (1950), pp. 4–11. [Reviewed by Andrzej Mostowski in JSL, vol. 15 (1950), p. 223.]

Reinhardt (1950). See Boll and Reinhardt (1950).

Rose (1950a). Alan Rose: "A Lattice-theoretic Characterization of Three-valued Logic," *Journal of the London Mathematical Society*, vol. 25 (1950), pp. 255–259. [Reviewed by Frederick B. Thompson in JSL, vol. 16 (1951), p. 151; by O. Frink in MR, vol. 12 (1951), p. 663; by G. Hasenjaeger in ZMG, vol. 39 (1951), p. 6.]

Rose (1950b). Alan Rose: "Completeness of Łukasiewicz-Tarski Propositional Calculi," *Mathematische Annalen*, vol. 122 (1950), pp. 296–298. [Reviewed by

A. R. Turquette in JSL, vol. 16 (1951), pp. 228–229; by R. M. Martin in MR, vol. 12 (1951), p. 662.]

Rosenbaum (1950). Ira Rosenbaum: *Introduction to Mathematical Logic and Its Applications* (Coral Gables, University of Miami Press, 1950). [Reviewed by A. R. Turquette in JSL, vol. 16 (1951), pp. 156–158.]

Rosenbloom (1950). Paul C. Rosenbloom: *The Elements of Mathematical Logic* (New York, Dover Publications, Inc., 1950). [Reviewed by Martin Davis in JSL, vol. 18 (1953), pp. 277–280; by P. Lorenzen in MR, vol. 12 (1951), p. 789.]

Sugihara (1950). Takeo Sugihara: "Tachi ronrigaku" (Many-valued logic), *Tetsugaku kenkyû*, vol. 33 (1950), pp. 684–703. [Reviewed by Z. Suetuna in JSL, vol. 16 (1951), p. 151.]

Wagner (1950). Klaus Wagner: "Zum Repräsentantenproblem der Logik für Aussagenfunktionen mit beliebig endlich oder unendlich vielen Wahrheitswerten," *Mathematische Zeitschrift*, vol. 53 (1950), pp. 364–374. [Reviewed by H. E. Vaughan in JSL, vol. 16 (1951), p. 227; by I. L. Novak in MR, vol. 12 (1951), p. 469; by W. Ackermann in ZMG, vol. 38 (1951), pp. 149–150.]

Wang (1950). Hao Wang: "A Proof of Independence," *American Mathematical Monthly*, vol. 57 (1950), pp. 99–100. [Reviewed by A. Church in JSL, vol. 15 (1950), p. 138; by O. Frink in MR, vol. 11 (1950), p. 411.]

Chen (1951). See Hu and Chen (1951).

Cohen (1951). Jonathan Cohen: "Three-valued Ethics," *Philosophy*, vol. 26 (1951), pp. 208–227.

Destouches-Février (1951). Paulette Destouches-Février: *La structure des théories physiques* (Paris, Presses Universitaires de France, 1951). [Reviewed by J. C. C. McKinsey and P. Suppes in JSL, vol. 19 (1954), pp. 52–55; by C. C. Torrance in MR, vol. 13 (1952), p. 424; by A. Kratzen in ZMG, vol. 45, Heft 7/10 (1954), pp. 293–294.]

Götlind (1951). Erik Götlind: "A Leśniewski-Mihailescu-theorem for *m*-Valued Propositional Calculi," *Portugaliae mathematica*, vol. 10 (1951), pp. 97–102. [Reviewed by Gene F. Rose in JSL, vol. 22 (1957), p. 329; by A. Robinson in MR, vol. 13 (1952), p. 615; by Alan Rose in ZMG, vol. 43 (1952), p. 249.]

Henle (1951). Paul Henle: "*n*-Valued Boolean Algebra," *Structure, Method, and Meaning, Essays in Honor of Henry M. Sheffer* (New York, Liberal Arts Press, 1951), pp. 68–73. [Reviewed by Alfred L. Foster in JSL, vol. 16 (1951), pp. 288–289.]

Hu and Chen (1951). Shih-hua Hu and Chiang-yeh Chen: "A Note on the 4-Valued Propositional Calculus and the Four Colour Problem," *Journal of the Chinese Mathematical Society*, vol. 1 (1951), pp. 243–246. [Reviewed by O. Frink in MR, vol. 17 (1956), p. 570.]

Kokoszyńska (1951). Maria Kokoszyńska: "A Refutation of the Relativism of Truth," *Studia Philosophica*, vol. 4 (1951), pp. 93–149. [Reviewed by C. G. Hempel in JSL, vol. 18 (1953), pp. 170–171.]

Leonard (1951). H. S. Leonard: "Two-valued Truth Tables for Modal Functions," in Paul Henle (ed.), *Structure, Method, and Meaning* (New York, 1951). [Reviewed by Jan Kalicki in JSL, vol. 16 (1951), p. 288.]

McNaughton (1951). Robert McNaughton: "A Theorem about Infinite-valued Sentential Logic," *The Journal of Symbolic Logic*, vol. 16 (1951), pp. 1–13. [Reviewed by H. E. Vaughan in JSL, vol. 16 (1951), pp. 227–228; by Alan Rose in MR, vol. 13 (1952), p. 3; by G. Hasenjaeger in ZMG, vol. 43 (1952), p. 9.]

Martin (N. M.) (1951). Norman M. Martin: "A Note on Sheffer Functions in *n*-Valued Logic," *Methodos*, vol. 3 (1951), pp. 240–242. [Reviewed by Alan Rose in JSL, vol. 17 (1952), pp. 204–205; by Alan Rose in MR, vol. 13 (1952), p. 3.]

Mora (1951). José Ferrater Mora: *Diccionario de filosofía* (Buenos Aires, Editorial Sudamericana, 1951), pp. 743–744, 762–765, 970–978. (Also several later editions, the 6th in 1966.) [Reviewed by W. V. Quine in JSL, vol. 17 (1952), pp. 129–130.]

Reichenbach (1951). Hans Reichenbach: "Über die erkenntnistheoretische Problemlage und den Gebrauch einer dreiwertigen Logik in der Quantenmechanik," *Zeitschrift für Naturforschung*, vol. 6a (1951), pp. 569–575. [Reviewed by O. Frink in MR, vol. 13 (1952), p. 716.]

Rose (1951a). Alan Rose: "Conditional Disjunction as a Primitive Connective for the *m*-Valued Propositional Calculus," *Mathematische Annalen*, vol. 123 (1951), pp. 76–78. [Reviewed by A. R. Turquette in JSL, vol. 16 (1951), p. 275; by O. Frink in MR, vol. 12 (1951), p. 790; by G. Hasenjaeger in ZMG, vol. 42 (1952), p. 7.]

Rose (1951b). Alan Rose: "A New Proof of a Theorem of Dienes," *Norsk Matematisk Tidsskrift*, vol. 33 (1951), pp. 27–29. [Reviewed by N. Rescher in JSL, vol. 16 (1951), p. 276; by O. Frink in MR, vol. 12 (1951), p. 790; by G. Hasenjaeger in ZMG, vol. 42 (1952), p. 245.]

Rose (1951c). Alan Rose: "Axiom Systems for Three-valued Logic," *The Journal of the London Mathematical Society*, vol. 26 (1951), pp. 50–58. [Reviewed by N. Rescher in JSL, vol. 16 (1951), p. 277; by O. Frink in MR, vol. 12 (1951), p. 663; by Heinrich Scholz in ZMG, vol. 43 (1952), p. 7.]

Rose (1951d). Alan Rose: "Systems of Logic Whose Truth-values Form Lattices," *Mathematische Annalen*, vol. 123 (1951), pp. 152–165. [Reviewed by A. R. Turquette in JSL, vol. 17 (1952), pp. 147–148; by P. Lorenzen in MR, vol. 13 (1952), p. 614; by Hans Hermes in ZMG, vol. 44 (1952), p. 2.]

Rose (1951e). Alan Rose: "A Lattice-Theoretic Characterization of the $\aleph_0$-Valued Propositional Calculus," *Mathematische Annalen*, vol. 123 (1951), pp. 285–287. [Reviewed by A. R. Turquette in JSL, vol. 17 (1952), pp. 147–148; by P. Lorenzen in MR, vol. 13 (1952), p. 614; by G. Hasenjaeger in ZMG, vol. 42 (1952), p. 245.]

Rose (1951f). Alan Rose: "The Degree of Completeness of Some Łukasiewicz-Tarski Propositional Calculi," *The Journal of the London Mathematical Society*, vol. 26 (1951), pp. 47–49. [Reviewed by A. R. Turquette in JSL, vol. 17 (1952), pp. 147–148; by O. Frink in MR, vol. 12 (1951), p. 662; by Heinrich Scholz in ZMG, vol. 41 (1952), p. 149.]

Rose (1951g). Alan Rose: "An Axiom System for Three-valued Logic," *Methodos*, vol. 3 (1951), pp. 233–239. [Reviewed by N. Rescher in JSL, vol. 18 (1953), p. 344.]

Rosser and Turquette (1951). James Barkley Rosser and Atwell R. Turquette: "Axiom Schemes for *m*-Valued Functional Calculi of First Order. Part II. Deductive Completeness," *The Journal of Symbolic Logic*, vol. 16 (1951), pp. 22–34. [Reviewed by Burton S. Dreben in JSL, vol. 16 (1951), p. 269; by P. Lorenzen in MR, vol. 12 (1951), p. 790; by Wilhelm Ackermann in ZMG, vol. 42 (1952), p. 244.]

Sugihara (1951). Takeo Sugihara: "Brouwer ronrigaku no tachi-ronrigaku-teki tokusei" (Many-valued logical characteristics of Brouwerian logic), *Kagaku*, vol. 21 (1951), pp. 294–295. [Reviewed by S. Kuroda in JSL, vol. 20 (1955), pp. 172–173.]

Turquette (1951). See Rosser and Turquette (1951).

Williams (1951). Donald Williams: "The Sea Fight Tomorrow," in P. Henle, H. M. Kallen, and S. K. Langer (eds.), *Structure, Method, and Meaning* (New York, 1951), pp. 280–306.

Wright (1951). Georg Henrick von Wright: *An Essay in Modal Logic* (Amsterdam, North-Holland, 1951). [Reviewed by A. R. Anderson in JSL, vol. 18, pp. 174–176; by R. M. Martin in MR, vol. 13 (1952), p. 614.]

Anonymous (1952). "Problemas de 'Theoria'. Problema no. I," *Theoria*, vol. 1 (1952), p. 7. [Reviewed by A. Church in JSL, vol. 20 (1955), p. 304.]

Aubert (1952). Karl E. Aubert: "On the Foundation of the Theory of Relations and the Logical Independence of Generalized Concepts of Reflexivity, Symmetry, and Transitivity," *Archiv for mathematik og naturvidenskab*, vol. 52 (1952), 48 pp. [Reviewed by Frank Harary in JSL, vol. 19 (1954), pp. 284–285; by G. Kreisel in MR, vol. 16 (1955), p. 324.]

Destouches-Février (1952). Paulette Destouches-Février: "Applications des logiques modales en physique quantique," *Theoria*, vol. 1 (1952), pp. 167–169. [Reviewed by Robert Feys in JSL, vol. 21 (1956), p. 106.]

Goodell (1952). John D. Goodell: "The Foundations of Computing Machinery," *The Journal of Computing Systems*, vol. 1 (1952), pp. 1–13.

Götlind (1952). Erik Götlind: "Some Sheffer Functions in *n*-Valued Logic," *Portugaliae Mathematica*, vol. 11 (1952), pp. 141–149. [Reviewed by Gene F. Rose in JSL, vol. 22 (1957), pp. 329–330; by O. Frink in MR, vol. 14 (1953), p. 834; by Alan Rose in ZMG, vol. 47 (1953), p. 16.]

Kleene (1952). Stephen C. Kleene: *Introduction to Metamathematics* (Amsterdam, Groningen, New York, 1952). [Reviewed by H. Rasiowa in JSL, vol. 19 (1954), pp. 215–216; by P. Lorenzen in MR, vol. 14 (1953), pp. 525–526; by W. Ackermann in ZMG, vol. 47 (1953), p. 7.]

Linke (1952). Paul F. Linke: "Eigentliche und uneigentliche Logik," *Methodos*, vol. 4 (1952), pp. 165–168. [Reviewed by R. M. Chisholm in JSL, vol. 22 (1957), pp. 383–384; by E. Löffler in ZMG, vol. 47 (1953), pp. 246–247.]

Łukasiewicz (1952). Jan Łukasiewicz: "On the Intuitionistic Theory of Deduction," *Indagationes Mathematicae*, vol. 14 (1952), pp. 202–212. [Reviewed by Gene F. Rose in JSL, vol. 19 (1954), p. 216; by A. Heyting in MR, vol. 14 (1953), p. 4; by H. Scholz in ZMG, vol. 48 (1953), p. 4.] Polish tr. in Łukasiewicz (1961).

Martin (N. M.) (1952). Norman M. Martin: "Sheffer Functions and Axiom Sets in *m*-Valued Propositional Logic," Ph.D. thesis (Los Angeles, University of California, 1952).

Prior (1952). Arthur Norman Prior: "In What Sense Is Modal Logic Many-valued?", *Analysis*, vol. 12 (1952), pp. 138–143. [Reviewed by A. R. Turquette in JSL, vol. 20 (1955), pp. 167–168.]

Reichenbach (1952–54). Hans Reichenbach: "Les fondements logiques de la théorie des quanta: Utilisation d'une logique à trois valeurs," *Applications scientifiques de la logique mathématique* (Actes du 2ème Colloque International de Logique Mathématique, Paris, 1952), pp. 103–114. (Paris, Gauthier-Villars and Louvain, E. Nauwelaerts, 1954). [Reviewed by O. Frink in MR, vol. 16 (1955), p. 782; by H. Hermes in ZMG, vol. 58 (1958), p. 3.]

Reiser (1952). Oliver Leslie Reiser: "Physics, Probability, and Multi-valued Logic," *The Philosophical Review,* vol. 61 (1952), pp. 147–159.

Rose (1952a). Alan Rose: "Some Generalized Sheffer Functions," *Proceedings of the Cambridge Philosophical Society*, vol. 48 (1952), pp. 369–373. [Reviewed by Norman M. Martin in JSL, vol. 18 (1953), pp. 344–345; by P. Lorenzen in MR, vol. 14 (1953), p. 3; by G. Hasenjaeger in ZMG, vol. 19 (1955), pp. 147–148.]

Rose (1952b). Alan Rose: "The Degree of Completeness of the *m*-Valued Łukasiewicz Propositional Calculus," *The Journal of the London Mathematical Society*, vol. 27 (1952), pp. 92–102. [Reviewed by Gene F. Rose in JSL, vol. 21 (1956), pp. 327–328; by O. Frink in MR, vol. 13 (1952), p. 811; by H. Scholz in ZMG, vol. 48 (1953), pp. 244–245.]

Rose (1952c). Alan Rose: "A Formalisation of Post's *m*-Valued Propositional Calculus," *Mathematische Zeitschrift*, vol. 56 (1952), pp. 94–104. [Reviewed by W. T. Parry in JSL, vol. 21 (1956), pp. 400–401; by P. Lorenzen in MR, vol. 14 (1953), p. 233; by H. Hermes in ZMG, vol. 48 (1953), p. 244.]

Rose (1952d). Alan Rose: "Le degré de saturation du calcul propositionnel implicatif à trois valeurs de Sobociński," *Comptes rendus hebdomadaires des séances de l'Académie des Sciences*, vol. 235 (1953), pp. 1000–1002. [Reviewed by G. F. Rose in JSL, vol. 19 (1954), p. 56; by O. Frink in MR, vol. 14 (1953), p. 834; by G. Hasenjaeger in ZMG, vol. 49 (1959), p. 147.]

Rose (1952e). Alan Rose: "Eight-valued Geometry," *Proceedings of the London Mathematical Society*, vol. 3 (1952), pp. 30–44. [Reviewed by P. Lorenzen in MR, vol. 13 (1952), p. 898; by H. Hermes in ZMG, vol. 48 (1953), p. 5.]

Rose (1952f). Alan Rose: "An Extension of Computational Logic," *The Journal of Symbolic Logic*, vol. 17 (1952), pp. 32–34. [Reviewed by F. B. Fitch in JSL, vol. 17 (1952), p. 204; by A. Robinson in MR, vol. 13 (1952), p. 811.]

Rose (1952g). Alan Rose: "Sur un ensemble de fonctions primitives pour le calcul des prédicats du premier ordre, lequel constitue son propre dual," *Comptes rendus hebdomadaires des séances de l'Académie des Sciences*, vol. 234 (1952), pp. 1830–1831). [Reviewed by A. Church in JSL, vol. 18 (1953), pp. 343–344; by P. Lorenzen in MR, vol. 14 (1953), p. 3; by H. Hermes in ZMG, vol. 48 (1953), p. 245.]

Rose (1952h). Alan Rose: "An Extension of the Calculus of Non-Contradiction," *Proceedings of the London Mathematical Society*, vol. 54 (1952), pp. 184–200. [Reviewed by F. B. Fitch in JSL, vol. 18 (1953), pp. 66–67; by H. Hermes in ZMG, vol. 49 (1955), p. 147.]

Rose (1952i). Alan Rose: "Extensions of Some Theorems of Schmidt and McKinsey," *Norsk Matematisk Tidsskrift*, vol. 34 (1952), pp. 1–9. [Reviewed by G. Hasenjaeger in ZMG, vol. 49 (1955), p. 148.]

Rosser and Turquette (1952). James Barkley Rosser and Atwell R. Turquette: *Many-valued Logics* (Amsterdam, North-Holland Publishing Co., 1952). [Reviewed by Boleslaw Sobociński in JSL, vol. 20 (1955), pp. 45–50; by R. Barcan Marcus in MR, vol. 14 (1954), p. 526; by Alan Rose in ZMG, vol. 47 (1953), pp. 15–16.]

Sobociński (1952). Boleslaw Sobociński: "Axiomatization of a Partial System of Three-valued Calculus of Propositions," *The Journal of Computing Systems*, vol. 1 (1952), pp. 23–55. [Reviewed by G. F. Rose in JSL, vol. 18 (1953), p. 283; by O. Frink in MR, vol. 14 (1953), p. 834; by H. Scholz in ZMG, vol. 49 (1959), p. 292.]

Sueki (1952–54). Takehiro Sueki: "The Formulization of Two-valued and n-Valued Systems, I, II, III," *Reports of the University of Electro-Communications* (Tokyo), vol. 4 (1952), pp. 1–24; vol. 5 (1953), pp. 1–18; vol. 6 (1954), pp. 1–19.

Sugihara (1952). Takeo Sugihara: "Negation in Many-valued Logic," *Memoirs of Liberal Arts College, Fukui University*, vol. 1 (1952), pp. 1–5. [Reviewed by Alan Rose in JSL, vol. 17 (1952), pp. 278–279; by O. Frink in MR, vol. 15 (1954), p. 91.]

Swift (1952). J. D. Swift: "Algebraic Properties of n-Valued Propositional Calculi," *American Mathematical Monthly*, vol. 59 (1952), pp. 612–621. [Reviewed by N. Rescher in JSL, vol. 18 (1953), p. 282; by Alan Rose in MR, vol. 14 (1953), p. 440; by Alan Rose in ZMG, vol. 49 (1959), p. 6.]

Tamari (1952–54). Dov Tamari: "Some Mutual Applications of Logic and Mathematics," *Applications scientifiques de la logique mathématique* (Actes du 2e Colloque International de Logique Mathématique, Paris, 1952), pp. 89–90. (Paris, Gauthier-Villars and Louvain, Nauwelaerts, 1954.) [Reviewed by Alan Rose in MR, vol. 16 (1955), p. 555.]

Turquette (1952). See Rosser and Turquette (1952).

Asser (1953). Günther Asser: "Die endlichwertigen Łukasiewiczschen Aussagenkalküle," *Bericht über die Mathematiker—Tagung in Berlin vom 14. bis 18. Januar 1953* (Berlin, 1953), pp. 15–18. [Reviewed by A. R. Turquette in JSL, vol. 21 (1956), p. 87.]

Behmann (1953). Heinrich Behmann: "Die typenfreie Logik und die Modalität," *Actes du XIème Congrès International de Philosophie, Bruxelles, 20–26 août 1953,* vol. 14, pp. 88–96 (Amsterdam, North-Holland Publishing Co., and Louvain, Editions E. Nauwelaerts, 1953). [Reviewed by R. Harrop in JSL, vol. 22 (1957), p. 326; by Alan Rose in MR, vol. 15 (1954), p. 386.]

Church (1953). Alonzo Church: "Non-normal Truth-tables for the Propositional Calculus," *Bolètin de la Sociedad Matematica Mexicana,* vol. 10 (1953), pp. 41–52. [Reviewed by Gene F. Rose in JSL, vol. 19 (1954), pp. 233–234; by Alan Rose in MR, vol. 15 (1954), p. 385.]

Frey (1953). Gerhard Frey: "Bemerkungen zum Problem der mehrwertigen Logiken," *Actes du XIème Congrès International de Philosophie,* vol. 5, *Logique, analyse philosophique, philosophie des mathématiques* (Amsterdam, North-Holland Publishing Co., and Louvain, Editions E. Nauwelaerts, 1953). [Reviewed by A. R. Turquette in JSL, vol. 19 (1954), pp. 131–132; by Alan Rose in MR, vol. 15 (1954), p. 278; by Alan Rose in ZMG, vol. 51 (1954), p. 245.]

Günther (1953a). Gotthard Günther: "Die philosophische Idee einer nicht-aristotelischen Logik," *Actes du XIème Congrès International de Philosophie,* vol. 5, *Logique, analyse philosophique, philosophie des mathématiques* (Amsterdam, North-Holland Publishing Co., and Louvain, Editions E. Nauwelaerts, 1953). [Reviewed by A. R. Turquette in JSL, vol. 19 (1954), p. 131.]

Günther (1953b). Gotthard Günther: "The Logical Parallax," *Astounding Science Fiction,* vol. 52 (1953), pp. 123–133. [Reviewed by A. R. Turquette in JSL, vol. 19 (1954), p. 131.]

Landsberg (1953). P. T. Landsberg: "On Heterological Paradoxes," *Mind,* vol. 62 (1953), pp. 379–381. [Reviewed by S. Orey in JSL, vol. 20 (1955), p. 293.]

Łukasiewicz (1953a). Jan Łukasiewicz: "A System of Modal Logic," *Actes du XIème Congrès International de Philosophie,* vol. 14, *Volume Complémentaire et communications du Colloque de Logique* (Amsterdam, North-Holland Publishing Co., 1953), pp. 82–87. [Reviewed by R. Harrop in JSL, vol. 25 (1960), pp. 293–296; by Alan Rose in MR, vol. 15 (1954), p. 189.]

Łukasiewicz (1953b). Jan Łukasiewicz: "A System of Modal Logic," *The Journal of Computing Systems,* vol. 1 (1953), pp. 111–149. Polish tr. in Łukasiewicz (1961). [Reviewed by R. Harrop in JSL, vol. 25 (1960), pp. 293–296; by Alan Rose in MR, vol. 15 (1954), p. 2.]

Prior (1953a). Arthur Norman Prior: "On Propositions Neither Necessary nor Impossible," *The Journal of Symbolic Logic,* vol. 18 (1953), pp. 105–108. [Reviewed by A. R. Turquette in JSL, vol. 20 (1955), pp. 167–168.]

Prior (1953b). Arthur Norman Prior: "Three-valued Logic and Future Contingents," *The Philosophical Quarterly,* vol. 3 (1953), pp. 317–326. [Reviewed by T. Sugihara in JSL, vol. 19 (1954), p. 294.]

Rose (1953a). Alan Rose: "The Degree of Completeness of the $\aleph_0$-Valued Łukasiewicz Propositional Calculus," *The Journal of the London Mathematical Society,* vol. 28 (1953), pp. 176–184. [Reviewed by Gene F. Rose in JSL, vol. 21 (1956), p. 328; by O. Frink in MR, vol. 14 (1953), p. 834; by G. Hasenjaeger in ZMG, vol. 53 (1961), p. 200.]

Rose (1953b). Alan Rose: "Conditional Disjunction as a Primitive Connective for the Erweiterter Aussagenkalkül," *The Journal of Symbolic Logic*, vol. 18 (1953), pp. 63–65. [Reviewed by N. Rescher in JSL, vol. 18 (1953), p. 344; by A. Robinson in MR, vol. 14 (1953), p. 936; by G. Hasenjaeger in ZMG, vol. 53 (1961), p. 199.]

Rose (1953c). Alan Rose: "The *m*-Valued Calculus of Non-contradiction," *The Journal of Symbolic Logic*, vol. 18 (1953), pp. 237–241. [Reviewed by B. Fitch in JSL, vol. 20 (1955), pp. 180–181; by G. Kreisel in MR, vol. 15 (1954), pp. 189–190; by H. Hermes in ZMG, vol. 53 (1961), p. 199.]

Rose (1953d). Alan Rose: "Fragments of the *m*-Valued Propositional Calculus," *Mathematische Zeitschrift*, vol. 59 (1953), pp. 206–210. [Reviewed by A. R. Turquette in JSL, vol. 23 (1958), pp. 64–65; by O. Frink in MR, vol. 15 (1954), p. 668; by H. Scholz in ZMG, vol. 52 (1955), p. 12.]

Rose (1953e). Alan Rose: "A Formalization of Sobociński's Three-valued Implicational Propositional Calculus," *The Journal of Computing Systems*, vol. 1 (1953), pp. 165–168. [Reviewed by G. F. Rose in JSL, vol. 19 (1954), p. 144; by O. Frink in MR, vol. 15 (1954), p. 91; by H. Scholz in ZMG, vol. 53 (1961), pp. 199–200.]

Rose (1953f). Alan Rose: "A Formalization of an $\aleph_0$-Valued Propositional Calculus," *Proceedings of the Cambridge Philosophical Society*, vol. 49 (1953), pp. 367–376. [Reviewed by P. Lorenzen in MR, vol. 14 (1953), p. 1052; by G. Hasenjaeger in ZMG, vol. 53 (1961), p. 200.]

Rose (1953g). Alan Rose: "Some Self-dual Primitive Functions for Propositional Calculi," *Mathematische Annalen*, vol. 126 (1953), pp. 144–148. [Reviewed by R. McNaughton in JSL, vol. 19 (1954), pp. 294–295; by O. Frink in MR, vol. 15 (1954,) p. 277; by G. Hasenjaeger in ZMG, vol. 53 (1961), p. 199.]

Rose (G. F.) (1953). Gene F. Rose: "Propositional Calculus and Realizability," *Transactions of the American Mathematical Society*, vol. 75 (1953), pp. 1–19. [Reviewed by David Nelson in JSL, vol. 19 (1954), p. 126; by A. Heyting in MR, vol. 15 (1954), p. 1.]

Rosser (1953). James Barkley Rosser: *Logic for Mathematicians* (New York, McGraw-Hill, 1953). [Reviewed by A. Robinson in JSL, vol. 18 (1953), pp. 326–327; by A. Heyting in MR, vol. 14 (1953), p. 935.]

Scholz (1953). Heinrich Scholz: Review of L. Baudry's *La querelle des futurs contingents: Louvain 1465–1475* (Paris, 1950), *Deutsche Literaturzeitung*, vol. 74 (1953), pp. 67–70.

Shestakov (1953). V. I. Shestakov: "Modélirovanié opéracij iscisléniá prédložénij posrédstvom prostéjših čétyréhpolúsynh shém" (Modeling the operations of the propositional calculus by means of the simplest four-pole networks), *Vyčislitel' naja matematika i vyčislitel' naja texnika*, vol. 1 (1953), pp. 56–89. [Reviewed by Z. Pawlak in JSL, vol. 22 (1957), pp. 332–333; by H. B. Curry in MR, vol. 18 (1957), pp. 272–273.]

Storer (1953). Thomas Storer: "A Note on Empiricism," *Philosophical Studies*, vol. 4 (1953), p. 78. [Reviewed by J. van Heijenoort in JSL, vol. 23 (1958), pp. 213–214.]

Vaccarino (1953). Giusseppe Vaccarino: "Le logiche polivalenti e non aristoteliche," *Archimede*, vol. 5 (1953), pp. 226–231. [Reviewed by E. J. Lemmon in JSL, vol. 21 (1956), p. 400; by H. Scholz in ZMG, vol. 51 (1954) p. 245.]

Hochberg (1954). Herbert Hochberg: "Professor Storer on Empiricism," *Philosophical Studies*, vol. 5 (1954), pp. 29–31. [Reviewed by J. van Heijenoort in JSL, vol. 23 (1958), pp. 213–214.]

Kalicki (1954a). Jan Kalicki: "On Equivalent Truth-tables of Many-valued Logics," *Proceedings of the Edinburgh Mathematical Society*, vol. 10 (1954), pp. 56–61. [Reviewed by Alan Rose in ZMG, vol. 57 (1956), p. 9.]

Kalicki (1954b). Jan Kalicki: "An Undecidable Problem in the Algebra of Truth-tables," *The Journal of Symbolic Logic*, vol. 19 (1954), pp. 172–176. [Reviewed by G. F. Rose in JSL, vol. 20 (1955), pp. 284–285; by Alan Rose in MR, vol. 16 (1955), p. 324.]

Kauf (1954). David Karl Kauf: "A Comment on Hochberg's Reply to Storer," *Philosophical Studies*, vol. 5 (1954), pp. 57–58. [Reviewed by J. van Heijenoort in JSL, vol. 23 (1958), pp. 213–214.]

Linsky (1954). Leonard Linsky: "Professor Donald Williams on Aristotle," *The Philosophical Review*, vol. 63 (1954), pp. 250–252. [Reviewed by E. J. Lemmon in JSL, vol. 22 (1957), pp. 384–385.]

McKinsey and Suppes (1954). J. C. C. McKinsey and Patrick Suppes: Review of Paulette Destouches-Février, *La Structure des Théories Physiques* (Paris, 1951), *The Journal of Symbolic Logic*, vol. 19 (1954), pp. 52–55.

Martin (N. M.) (1954). Norman M. Martin: "The Sheffer Functions of Three-valued Logic," *The Journal of Symbolic Logic*, vol. 19 (1954), pp. 45–51. [Reviewed by W. Wernick in JSL, vol. 21 (1956), p. 199; by Alan Rose in MR, vol. 15 (1954), p. 669; by Alan Rose in ZMG, vol. 55 (1955), p. 5.]

Moh Shaw-kwei (1954). Moh Shaw-kwei: "Logical Paradoxes for Many-valued Systems," *The Journal of Symbolic Logic*, vol. 19 (1954), pp. 37–40. [Reviewed by G. H. Müller in JSL, vol. 22 (1957), p. 90; by Alan Rose in MR, vol. 15 (1954), p. 669; by Alan Rose in ZMG, vol. 55 (1955), p. 5.]

Rose (1954). Alan Rose: "Sur les fonctions définissables dans une logique à un nombre infini de valeurs," *Comptes rendus hebdomadaires des séances de l' Académie des Sciences*, vol. 238 (1954), pp. 1462–1463. [Reviewed by G. Kreisel in MR, vol. 15 (1954), p. 925; by G. Hasenjaeger in ZMG, vol. 58 (1958), p. 245.]

Storer (1954). Thomas Storer: "The Notion of Tautology," *Philosophical Studies*, vol. 5 (1954), pp. 75–78. [Reviewed by J. F. Thomson in JSL, vol. 21 (1956), p. 380.]

Suppes (1954). See McKinsey and Suppes (1954).

Takekuma (1954). Ryōichi Takekuma: "On a Nine-valued Propositional Calculus," *The Journal of Computing Systems*, vol. 1 (1954), pp. 225–228. [Reviewed by Alan Ross Anderson in JSL, vol. 22 (1957), p. 330; by Alan Rose in MR, vol. 16 (1955), p. 555; by Alan Rose in ZMG, vol. 57 (1956), p. 9.]

Turquette (1954). Atwell R. Turquette: "Many-valued Logics and Systems of Strict Implication," *The Philosophical Review*, vol. 63 (1954), pp. 365–379. [Reviewed by Alan Ross Anderson in JSL, vol. 22 (1957), p. 328.]

Williams (1954). Donald Williams: "Professor Linsky on Aristotle," *The Philosophical Review*, vol. 63 (1954), pp. 253–255. [Reviewed by E. J. Lemmon in JSL, vol. 22 (1957), pp. 384–385.]

Yablonskii (1954). S. V. Yablonskii: "O funkcional'noj plonote v trehznacnom isčislenii" (On functional completeness in a three-valued calculus), *Doklady Akademii Nauk SSSR*, vol. 95 (1954), pp. 1153–1155. [Reviewed by A. Ehrenfeucht in JSL, vol. 20 (1955), p. 175; by H. B. Curry in MR, vol. 15 (1954), p. 925; by D. Tamari in ZMG, vol. 59 (1965), p. 15.]

Yonemitsu (1954). Naoto Yonemitsu: "Note on Completeness of *m*-Valued Propositional Calculi," *Mathematica Japonicae*, vol. 3 (1954), pp. 57–61. [Reviewed by Gene F. Rose in JSL, vol. 21 (1956), p. 328; by Alan Rose in MR, vol. 17 (1956), p. 224; by Alan Rose in ZMG, vol. 57 (1956), p. 247.]

Ballarat (Badillo) (1955a). Maria C. Badillo Ballarat: "Fundamentos en relación con lógica simbólica polivalente," *Gaceta matemática*, vol. 7 (1955), pp. 7–13. [Reviewed by John van Heijenoort in JSL, vol. 27 (1962), p. 112.]

Ballarat (Badillo) (1955b). Maria C. Badillo Ballarat: "Esquemas representativos de sistemas regidos por una lógica polivalente," *Revista de cálculo automático y cibernética*, vol. 4 (1955), pp. 54–62. [Reviewed by John van Heijenoort in JSL, vol. 25 (1960), pp. 184–185; by J. Riquet in MR, vol. 17 (1956), pp. 10–13.]

Butler (1955). Ronald J. Butler: "Aristotle's Sea Fight and Three-valued Logic," *The Philosophical Review*, vol. 64 (1955), pp. 264–274. [Reviewed by E. J. Lemmon in JSL, vol. 22 (1957), pp. 384–385.]

Greniewski (1955). Henryk Greniewski: *Elementy logiki formalnej* (Elements of Formal Logic) (Warsaw, Państwowe Wydawnictwo Naukowe, 1955). [Reviewed by J. Bendiek in JSL, vol. 21 (1956), p. 188; by A. Mostowski in *Studia Logica*, vol. 4 (1956), pp. 272–277.]

Günther (1955). Gotthard Günther: "Dreiwertige Logik und die Heisenbergsche Unbestimmtheitsrelation," *Actes du Deuxième Congrès International de l' Union Internationale de Philosophie des Sciences Zurich 1954, II Physique, mathématiques* (Neuchatel, Editions du Griffon, 1955), pp. 53–59.

Hu (1955). Shih-hua Hu: "Die endlichwertigen und funktionell vollständigen Sub-systeme $\aleph_0$-wertigen Aussagenkalküls," *Acta Mathematica Sinica*, vol. 5 (1955), pp. 173–191. [Reviewed by Hao Wang in MR, vol. 17 (1956), pp. 224–225.]

Itô (1955). Makoto Itô: "*n*-ti kansû soku (*n*-ti ronri) ni tuite" (On the "lattice of *n*-valued functions" [*n*-valued logic]), *Kyûsyû Daigaku kôgaku syûhô* (*Technology Reports of the Kyushu University*), vol. 28 (1955), pp. 96–101. [Reviewed by Katuzi Ono in JSL, vol. 22 (1957), pp. 100–101.]

Kurihara (1955). Toshihiko Kurihara: "Yûgen tatironri no denki kairo ni yoru hyôgen ni tuite" (On the representation of finitely many-valued logics by electric circuits), *Kyûsyû Daigaku kôgaku syûhô* (*Technology Reports of the Kyushu University*), vol. 28 (1955), pp. 102–106. [Reviewed by Katuzi Ono in JSL, vol. 22 (1957), p. 102.]

Mostowski (1955). Andrzej Mostowski and collaborators: *The Present State of Investigations on the Foundations of Mathematics* (Warsaw, Państwowe Wydawnictwo Naukowe, 1955). [Reviewed by L. Henkin in JSL, vol. 21 (1956), pp. 372–373.]

Prior (1955a). Arthur Norman Prior: "Many-valued and Modal Systems: An Intuitive Approach," *The Philosophical Review*, vol. 64 (1955), pp. 626–630. [Reviewed by Alan Ross Anderson in JSL, vol. 22 (1957), pp. 328–329.]

Prior (1955b). Arthur Norman Prior: "Curry's Paradox and 3-Valued Logic," *Australasian Journal of Philosophy*, vol. 33 (1955), pp. 177–182. [Reviewed by G. H. Müller in JSL, vol. 22 (1957), pp. 90–91.]

Prior (1955c). Arthur Norman Prior: *Formal Logic* (Oxford, Clarendon Press, 1955; 2d ed., 1962). See especially chap. ii of pt. III ("Three-Valued and Intuitionistic Logic"). [Reviewed by H. Leblanc in JSL, vol. 27 (1962), pp. 218–220.]

Rasiowa (1955). Helena Rasiowa: "O pewnym fragmencie implikacyjnego rachunku zdań" (On a fragment of the implicative propositional calculus), *Studia Logica*, vol. 3 (1955), pp. 208–226. [Reviewed by J. Bendiek in JSL, vol. 22 (1957), p. 330; by H. Hiż in MR, vol. 17 (1956), p. 226.]

Rescher (1955). Nicholas Rescher: "Some Comments on Two-valued Logic," *Philosophical Studies*, vol. 6 (1955), pp. 54–58. [Reviewed by E. J. Lemmon in JSL, vol. 24 (1959), p. 180.]

Rose (1955a). Alan Rose: "Le degré de saturation du calcul propositionnel implicatif à *m* valeurs de Łukasiewicz," *Comptes rendus hebdomadaires des séances de l'Académie des Sciences*, vol. 240 (1955), pp. 2280–2281. [Reviewed by Gene F. Rose in JSL, vol. 22 (1957), pp. 379–380; by O. Frink in MR, vol. 16 (1955), p. 892.]

Rose (1955b). Alan Rose: "A Gödel Theorem for an Infinite-valued Erweiterter Aussagenkalkül," *Zeitschrift für mathematische Logik und Grundlagen der Mathematik*, vol. 1 (1955), pp. 89–90. [Reviewed by L. N. Gál in MR, vol. 18 (1957), p. 866; by J. C. Shepherdson in ZMG, vol. 67 (1958), p. 250.]

Schaefer (1955). David H. Schaefer: "A Rectifier Algebra," *Transactions of the American Institute of Electrical Engineers*, vol. 74 (1955), pp. 679–682. [Reviewed by Raymond J. Nelson in JSL, vol. 21 (1956), p. 400.]

Schröter (1955). Karl Schröter: "Methoden zur Axiomatisierung beliebiger Aussagen- und Prädikatenkalküle," *Zeitschrift für mathematische Logik und Grundlagen der Mathematik*, vol. 1 (1955), pp. 241–251. [Reviewed by A. Robinson in MR, vol. 17 (1956), p. 1038.]

von Weizsäcker (1955). Carl F. von Weizsäcker: "Komplementarität und Logik," *Die Naturwissenschaften*, vol. 42 (1955), pp. 521–529, 545–555. [Reviewed by C. G. Hempel in JSL, vol. 23 (1958), pp. 65–66; by O. Frink in MR, vol. 17 (1956), p. 932.]

Yasuura (1955). Kamenosuke Yasuura: "Keidenkikairo ni yoru tatimeidaironri no hyôgen ni tuite" (On the representation of many-valued propositional logics by relay circuits), *Kyûsyû Daigaku kôgaku syûhô* (*Technology Reports of the Kyushu University*), vol. 28 (1955), pp. 94–96. [Reviewed by Katuzi Ono in JSL, vol. 22 (1957), p. 102.]

Áblonskij (1956). S. V. Áblonskij: "Funkcional' nyé postroéniá v mnogoznačnyh logikah" (Functional constructions in many-valued logics), *Trudy Trét'égo Vsésoúznogo Matématičéskogo Sézda, Moskva, iún-iúl' 1956*, vol. 2 (Moscow, 1956), pp. 71–73. [Reviewed by Andrzej Ehrenfeucht in JSL, vol. 23 (1958), p. 65.]

Ballarat (Badillo) (1956). Maria C. Badillo Ballarat: "Automatización de los silogismos en una lógica polivalente," *Revista de cálculo automático y cibernética*, vol. 5 (1956), pp. 1–10. [Reviewed by John van Heijenoort in JSL, vol. 27 (1962), p. 112.]

Bochénski (1956). Inocenty M. Bochénski: *Formale Logik* (Freiburg/München, K. Alber, 1956). English tr. Thomas Ivo, *A History of Formal Logic* (Notre Dame, 1961). [Reviewed by B. Mates in JSL, vol. 25 (1960), pp. 57–62; by A. N. Prior in MR, vol. 18 (1957), p. 1854.]

Church (1956a). Alonzo Church: *Introduction to Mathematical Logic* (Princeton, Princeton University Press, 1956). [Reviewed by Max Black in JSL, vol. 22 (1957), pp. 286–289; by I. N. Gál in MR, vol. 18 (1957), pp. 631–632; by G. H. Müller in ZMG, vol. 73 (1960), pp. 243–244.]

Church (1956b). Alonzo Church: "Laws of Thought," *Encyclopaedia Britannica*, vol. 22 (1956), p. 157. [Reviewed by A. R. Turquette in JSL, vol. 23 (1958), pp. 23–28.]

Greniewski (1956). Marek Greniewski: "Utilisation des logiques trivalentes dans la théorie des mécanismes automatiques. I. Réalisation des fonctions fondamentales par des circuits," *Comunicările Academiei Republicii Populare Romîne* (Bucharest), vol. 6 (1956), pp. 225–229. [Reviewed by E. Grosswald in JSL, vol. 24 (1959), p. 257.]

Heyting (1956). Arend Heyting: *Intuitionism: An Introduction* (Amsterdam, North-Holland, 1956). [Reviewed by Sigekatu Kuroda in JSL, vol. 21 (1956), pp. 367–371; by P. C. Gilmore in MR, vol. 17 (1956), pp. 698–699.]

Itô (1956a). Makoto Itô: "Itigen n-ti kansûsoku (ronri) hôteisiki no ippankai ni tuite" (On the general solution of the n-valued function-lattice [logical] equation in one variable), *Kyûsyû Daigaku kôgaku syûhô* (*Technology Reports of the Kyushu University*), vol. 28 (1956), pp. 239–243. [Reviewed by Katuzi Ono in JSL, vol. 22 (1957), p. 101.]

Itô (1956b). Makoto Itô: "Tagen *n*-ti kansûsoku (ronri) hôteisiki no ippankai ni tuite" (On the general solution of the *n*-valued function-lattice [logical] equation in several variables), *Kyûsyû Daigaku kôgaku syûhô* (*Technology Reports of the Kyushu University*), vol. 28 (1956), pp. 243-246. [Reviewed by Katuzi Ono in JSL, vol. 22 (1957), p. 101.]

Moch (1956a). François Moch: "La logique des attitudes," *Comptes rendus hebdomadaires des séances de l'Académie des Sciences*, vol. 242 (1956), pp. 1943–1945. [Reviewed by Alan Rose in MR, vol. 17 (1956), p. 1038; by J. C. Shepherdson in ZMG, vol. 71 (1958), p. 6.]

Moch (1956b). François Moch: "Des antinomies classiques à la Logique de Mme. Destouches-Février," *Comptes rendus hebdomadaires des séances de l'Académie des Sciences*, vol. 242 (1956), pp. 1562–1563. [Reviewed by P. C. Gilmore in MR, vol. 17 (1956), p. 818; by J. C. Shepherdson in ZMG, vol. 71 (1958), p. 6.]

Moisil (1956a). Grigor C. Moisil: "Utilisation des logiques trivalentes dans la théorie des mécanismes automatiques. II. Equation caractéristique d'un relai-paolarise," *Comunicările Academia Republicii Populare Romîne* (Bucharest), vol. 6 (1956), pp. 231–234.

Moisil (1956b). Grigor C. Moisil: "Sur l'application des logiques à trois valeurs à l'étude des schémas à contacts et relais," *Actes-Proceedings du Congrès International de l'Automatique* (Paris, June 18–24, 1956), p. 48.

Moisil (1956–1959). Grigor C. Moisil: "Intrebuintarea logicilor trivalente în teoriă algebrică a mecanismelor automate" (Use of 3-valued logic in the algebraic theory of automata), *Comunicările Academia Republicii Populare Romîne*, vol. 6 (1956), pp. 231, 285, 971; vol. 8 (1958), p. 1127; vol. 9 (1959), pp. 411–413, 531–532, 533–536, 665, 667. (A series of notes on the stated topic.)

Rose (1956a). Alan Rose: "An Alternative Formalisation of Sobociński's Three-valued Implicational Propositional Calculus," *Zeitschrift für mathematische Logik und Grundlagen der Mathematik*, vol. 2 (1956), pp. 166–172. [Reviewed by G. F. Rose in JSL, vol. 22 (1957), p. 380; by L. N. Gál in MR, vol. 20 (1959), p. 625; by Robert Feys in ZMG, vol. 74 (1962), p. 10.]

Rose (1956b). Alan Rose: "Formalisation du calcul propositionnel implicatif à $\aleph_0$ valeurs de Łukasiewicz," *Comptes rendus hebdomadaires des séances de l'Académie des Sciences*, vol. 243 (1956), pp. 1183–1185, 1263–1264 (à *m* valeurs). [Reviewed by E. Mendelson in MR, vol. 18 (1957), pp. 271–272, 633; by E. Specker in ZMG, vol. 73 (1960), p. 249.]

Rose (1956c). Alan Rose: "Some Formalisations of $\aleph_0$-Valued Propositional Calculi," *Zeitschrift für mathematische Logik und Grundlagen der Mathematik*, vol. 2 (1956), pp. 204–209. [Reviewed by P. Lorenzen in MR, vol. 19 (1958), p. 626; by Robert Feys in ZMG, vol. 74 (1962), p. 10.]

Sobociński (1956). Boleslaw Sobociński: "In memoriam Jan Łukasiewicz," *Philosophical Studies* (Maynooth), vol. 6 (1956), pp. 3–49. [Reviewed by K. Dürr in JSL, vol. 22 (1957), pp. 385–387.]

Sugihara (1956). Takeo Sugihara: "Four-valued Propositional Calculus with One Designated Truth-value," *Memoirs of the Liberal Arts College, Fukui University*, vol. 5 (1956), pp. 41–48. [Reviewed by R. Feys in JSL, vol. 23 (1958), p. 64.]

Tarski (1956). Alfred Tarski: *Logic, Semantics, Metamathematics: Papers from 1923 to 1938*. Tr. by J. H. Woodger (Oxford, Clarendon Press, 1956). See especially Paper IV.

Ballarat (Badillo) (1957). Maria C. Badillo Ballarat: "Lógica trivalente en la automatización de los circuitos," *Revista de cálculo automático y cibernética*, vol. 6 (1957), pp. 1–7. [Reviewed by J. van Heijenoort in JSL, vol. 27 (1962), pp. 112–113.]

Barker (1957). C. C. H. Barker: "Some Calculations in Logic," *The Mathematical Gazette*, vol. 41 (1957), pp. 108–111. [Reviewed by Alonzo Church in JSL, vol. 22 (1957), p. 379; registered in MR, vol. 19 (1958), p. 3.]

Christensen (1957). Neils E. Christensen: "Further Comments on Two-valued Logic," *Philosophical Studies*, vol. 8 (1958), pp. 9–15. (Reviewed by J. F. Thomson in JSL, vol. 24 (1959), p. 266.]

Evans and Hardy (1957). Trevor Evans and Lane Hardy: "Sheffer Stroke Functions in Many-valued Logics," *Portugaliae Mathematica*, vol. 16 (1957), pp. 83–93. [Reviewed by N. M. Martin in JSL, vol. 24 (1959), pp. 67–68; by Alan Rose in MR, vol. 21 (1960), pp. 234–235.]

Gazalé (1957). M. J. Gazalé: "Multi-valued Switching Functions," *Summaries of Talks Presented at the Summer Institute for Symbolic Logic, Cornell University* (1957), p. 147.

Greniewski (1957). Henryk Greniewski: "2^{n+1} wartości logicznych" (2^{n+1} logical values), *Studia filozoficzne*, no. 2 (1957), pp. 82–116, and no. 3, pp. 3–28. [Reviewed by A. Mostowski in JSL, vol. 29 (1964), pp. 109–110.]

Hardy (1957). See Evans and Hardy (1957).

Kotarbiński (1957). Tadeusz Kotarbiński: *Wylady z dziejów logiki* (Outlines of the History of Logic), (Lódź, Zaklad Narodowy in Ossolinskich we Wrolawicu, 1957). [Reviewed by R. Rand in JSL, vol. 25 (1960), pp. 62–67.]

Moisil (1957). Grigor C. Moisil: "Aplicatrile logicii trivalente in studiul functionarii reale a schemelor cu contacte si relee" (Application of three-valued logic in the study of the real operation of networks with contacts and relays), *Bulletin mathématique de la Société des Sciences Mathématiques et Physiques de la République Populaire de Roumanie*, vol. 1 (49), (1957), pp. 145–194. [Reviewed by E. F. Moore in MR, vol. 23 (1962), p. 1065.]

Mostowski (1957). Andrzej Mostowski: "L'oeuvre scientifique de Jan Łukasiewicz dans le domaine de la logique mathématique," *Fundamenta Mathematicae*, vol.

44 (1957), pp. 1–11. [Reviewed by K. Dürr in JSL, vol. 22 (1957), pp. 387–388; registered in MR, vol. 19 (1958), p. 722.]

Prior (1957a). Arthur Norman Prior: *Time and Modality* (London, Oxford University Press, 1957). [Reviewed by S. Kanger in JSL, vol. 25 (1960), pp. 342–343.]

Prior (1957b). Arthur Norman Prior: "The Necessary and the Possible: The First of Three Talks on 'The Logic Game,'" *The Listener*, vol. 57 (1957), pp. 627–628. [Reviewed by Tadeusz Czezowski in JSL, vol. 23 (1958), pp. 347–348.]

Prior (1957c). Arthur Norman Prior: "Symbolism and Analogy: The Second of Three Talks on 'The Logic Game,'" *The Listener*, vol. 57 (1957), pp. 675–678. [Reviewed by Tadeusz Czezowski in JSL, vol. 23 (1958), pp. 347–348.]

Prior (1957d). Arthur Norman Prior: "Many-valued Logics: The Last of Three Talks on 'The Logic Game,'" *The Listener*, vol. 57 (1957), pp. 717–719. [Reviewed by Tadeusz Czezowski in JSL, vol. 23 (1958), pp. 347–348.]

Putnam (1957). Hilary Putnam: "Three-valued Logic," *Philosophical Studies*, vol. 8 (1957), pp. 73–80. [Reviewed by L. Henkin in JSL, vol. 25 (1960), pp. 289–291.]

Scholz (1957). Heinrich Scholz: "In memoriam Jan Łukasiewicz," *Archiv für mathematische Logik und Grundlagenforschung*, vol. 3 (1957), pp. 1–18. [Reviewed by K. Dürr in JSL, vol. 22 (1957), pp. 385–387; registered in MR, vol. 19 (1958), p. 722.]

Skolem (1957a). Thoralf Skolem: "Mengenlehre gegründet auf einer Logik mit unendlich vielen Wahrheitswerten," *Sitzungsberichte der Berliner Mathematischen Gesellschaft* (1957–58), pp. 41–56. [Reviewed by J. R. Shoenfield in MR, vol. 27 (1964), p. 681.]

Skolem (1957b). Thoralf Skolem: "Bemerkungen zum Komprehensionsaxiom," *Zeitschrift für mathematische Logik und Grundlagen der Mathematik*, vol. 3 (1957), pp. 1–17. [Reviewed by H. B. Curry in MR, vol. 20 (1959), p. 508.]

Sobociński (1957a). Boleslaw Sobociński: "La génesis de la Escuela Polaca de Lógica," *Oriente europeo*, vol. 7 (1957), pp. 83–95. [Reviewed by J. Ferrater Mora in JSL, vol. 25 (1960), pp. 63–64.]

Sobociński (1957b). Boleslaw Sobociński: "Jan Łukasiewicz (1878–1956)," *Rocznik Polskiego Towarzstwa Naukowego Naukowego na Obczyźnie* (London, 1957), pp. 3–21.

Suszko (1957). Roman Suszko: "A Formal Theory of the Logical Values, I," *Studia Logica*, vol. 6 (1957), pp. 145–237. [Reviewed by L. Rieger in MR, vol. 21 (1960), p. 234.]

Taylor (1957). Richard Taylor: "The Problem of Future Contingencies," *The Philosophical Review*, vol. 66 (1957), pp. 1–28.

Törnebohm (1957). Hakan Törnebohm: "On Two Logical Systems Proposed in the Philosophy of Quantum Mechanics," *Theoria*, vol. 23 (1957), pp. 84–101. [Reviewed by H. Putnam in JSL, vol. 27 (1962), p. 115; by W. Salmon in MR, vol. 20 (1959), p. 375.]

Ballarat (Badillo) (1958). Maria C. Badillo Ballarat: "Aplicación de la lógicá polivalente a la teoría de números," *Gaceta Matemática* (Madrid), vol. 10 (1958), pp. 76–81. [Reviewed by J. van Heijenoort in JSL, vol. 27 (1962), p. 112.]

Borkowski and Słupecki (1958). Ludwik Borkowski and Jerzy Słupecki: "The Logical Works of J. Łukasiewicz," *Studia Logica*, vol. 8 (1958), pp. 7–56. [Reviewed by J. A. Faris in JSL, vol. 25 (1960), pp. 64–65; by H. Freudenthal in MR, vol. 21 (1960), p. 1024.]

Chang (1958a). Chen Chung Chang: "Proof of an Axiom of Łukasiewicz," *Transactions of the American Mathematical Society*, vol. 87 (1958), pp. 55–56. [Reviewed by A. R. Turquette in JSL, vol. 24 (1959), pp. 248–249; by E. J. Cogan in MR, vol. 20 (1959), p. 132.]

Chang (1958b). Chen Chung Chang: "Algebraic Analysis of Many-valued Logics," *Transactions of the American Mathematical Society*, vol. 88 (1958), pp. 467–490. [Reviewed by B. A. Galler in MR, vol. 20 (1959), p. 132; by Alan Rose in ZMG, vol. 84 (1960), pp. 7–8.]

Evans and Schwartz (1958). Trevor Evans and P. B. Schwartz: "On Słupecki T-functions," *The Journal of Symbolic Logic*, vol. 23 (1958), pp. 267–270. [Reviewed by Alan Rose in JSL, vol. 24 (1959), pp. 249–250; by E. Mendelson in MR, vol. 21 (1960), pp. 1174–1175; by K. Schütte in ZMG, vol. 88 (1961), p. 10.]

Feyerabend (1958). Paul Feyerabend: "Reichenbach's Interpretation of Quantum-Mechanics," *Philosophical Studies*, vol. 9 (1958), pp. 49–59. [Reviewed by L. Henkin in JSL, vol. 25 (1960), pp. 289–291.]

Goodstein (1958). R. L. Goodstein: "Models of Propositional Calculi in Recursive Arithmetic," *Mathematica Scandinavica*, vol. 5 (1958), pp. 293–296. [Reviewed by A. Mostowski in JSL, vol. 28 (1963), p. 291; by J. C. E. Dakker in MR, vol. 21 (1960), p. 1030; by K. Schütte in ZMG, vol. 88 (1961), p. 10.]

Günther (1958). Gotthard Günther: "Die aristotelische Logik des Seins und die nicht-aristotelische Logik der Reflexion," *Zeitschrift für philosophische Forschung*, vol. 12 (1958), pp. 360–407.

Harrop (1958). Ronald Harrop: "On the Existence of Finite Models and Decision Procedures for Propositional Calculi," *Proceedings of the Cambridge Philosophical Society*, vol. 54 (1958), pp. 1–13. [Reviewed by H. Arnold Schmidt in JSL, vol. 25 (1960), pp. 180–181.]

Margaris (1958). Angelo Margaris: "A Problem of Rosser and Turquette," *The Journal of Symbolic Logic*, vol. 23 (1958), pp. 271–279. [Reviewed by Alan Rose in MR, vol. 21 (1960), p. 901.]

Mlëziva (1958). Miroslav Mlëziva: "Teorie výroku" (Theory of propositions), *Moderni logica*, no. 7 (1958), pp. 29–75.

Meredith (1958). Charles A. Meredith: "The Dependence of an Axiom of Łukasiewicz," *Transactions of the American Mathematical Society*, vol. 87 (1958), p. 54. [Reviewed by A. R. Turquette in JSL, vol. 24 (1959), pp. 248–249; by E. J. Cogan in MR, vol. 20 (1959), p. 132.]

Moh Shaw-kwei (1958). Moh Shaw-kwei: "Yow-hsian-zhe fang-zhen hsi-t'ung ti kung-li-hua" (Axiomatization of many-valued logical systems), *Nan-king Ta-hsüeh hsüeh-pao tse-jan k'o-hsüeh pun*, vol. 1 (1958), pp. 791–800 (pp. 67–76). [Reviewed by Hao Wang in JSL, vol. 25 (1960), pp. 181–182.]

Prior (1958–59). Arthur Norman Prior: "Notes on a Group of New Modal Systems," *Logique et Analyse*, new series, vols. 1 and 2 (1958–1959), pp. 122–127.

Rose (1958a). Alan Rose: "Many-valued Logical Machines," *Proceedings of the Cambridge Philosophical Society*, vol. 54 (1958), pp. 307–321. [Reviewed by Robert McNaughton in JSL, vol. 27 (1962), p. 250; by R. M. Baer in MR, vol. 20 (1959), p. 376; by K. Schütte in ZMG, vol. 83 (1961), p. 244.]

Rose (1958b). Alan Rose: "Sur les définitions de l'implication et de la négation dans certains systèmes de logique dont les valeurs forment des treillis," *Comptes rendus hebdomadaires des séances de l'Académie des Sciences*, vol. 246 (1958), pp. 2091–2094. [Reviewed by G. F. Rose in JSL, vol. 24 (1959), p. 250; by P. Lorenzen in MR, vol. 20 (1959), p. 268.]

Rose (1958c). Alan Rose: "Applications of Logical Computers to the Construction of Electrical Control Tables for Signalling Frames," *Zeitschrift für mathematische Logik und Grundlagen der Mathematik*, vol. 4 (1958), pp. 222–243. [Reviewed by V. E. Beneš in MR, vol. 21 (1960), p. 363.]

Rose and Rosser (1958d). Alan Rose and James Barkley Rosser: "Fragments of Many-valued Statement Calculi," *Transactions of the American Mathematical Society*, vol. 87 (1958), pp. 1–53. [Reviewed by A. R. Turquette in JSL, vol. 24 (1959), pp. 248–249; by E. J. Cogan in MR, vol. 20 (1959), p. 132; by K. Schütte in ZMG, vol. 85 (1961), pp. 243–244.]

Schwartz (1958). See Evans and Schwartz (1958).

Słupecki (1958). See Borkowski and Słupecki (1958).

Sugihara (1958). Takeo Sugihara: "A Three-valued Logic with Meaning-Operator," *The Memoirs of Fukui University, Liberal Arts Department*, no. 8 (1958), pp. 59–60. [Reviewed by G. F. Rose in JSL, vol. 25 (1960), p. 293.]

Thiele (1958). Helmut Thiele: "Theorie der endlich-wertigen Łukasiewiczschen Prädikatenkalküle der ersten Stufe," *Zeitschrift für mathematische Logik und Grundlagen der Mathematik*, vol. 4 (1958), pp. 108–142. [Reviewed by W. Ackermann in ZMG, vol. 88 (1961), p. 247.]

Turquette (1958). Atwell R. Turquette: "Simplified Axioms for Many-valued Quantification Theory," *The Journal of Symbolic Logic*, vol. 23 (1958), pp. 139–148. [Reviewed by A. Rose in MR, vol. 21 (1960), p. 901; by A. Rose in ZMG, vol. 85 (1961), p. 245.]

Yablonskii (1958a). S. V. Yablonskii: "Funkcional' nye postroenija v k-znečnoj logike" (Functional constructions in a k-valued logic), *Trudy matematičeskogo instituta imeni V. A. Steklova*, vol. 51 (1958), pp. 5–142. [Reviewed by E. J. Cogan in MR, vol. 21 (1960), p. 620; by D. Tamari in ZMG, vol. 92 (1962), pp. 251–252.]

Yablonskii (1958b). S. V. Yablonskii: "Funktionale Konstruktionen in mehrdeutigen Logiken," *Trudy trét' égo vsésoúznogo matématičéskogo Sezda, Moskva*, vol. 3 (1958), pp. 425–431. [Reviewed by J. C. Shepherdson in ZMG, vol. 86 (1961), p. 245.]

Zinov'ev (1958). Aleksander Aleksandrovich Zinov'ev: "K problému abstraktního a konkrétniho poznatku" (On the problem of abstract and concrete knowledge), *Filosofický Časopis*, no. 2 (1958), pp. 201–212.

Bocheński (1959). Inocenty M. Bocheński: *A Precis of Mathematical Logic* (Dordrecht, D. Reidel, 1959). [Reviewed by N. M. Martin in JSL, vol. 25 (1960), pp. 78–79.]

Chang (1959). Chen Chung Chang: "A New Proof of the Completeness of the Łukasiewicz Axioms," *Transactions of the American Mathematical Society*, vol. 93 (1959), pp. 74–80. [Reviewed by A. Rose in MR, vol. 23 (1962), p. 7.]

Dummett (1959). Michael Dummett: "A Propositional Calculus with Denumerable Matrix," *The Journal of Symbolic Logic*, vol. 24 (1959), pp. 97–106. [Reviewed by G. Kreisel in MR, vol. 23 (1962), p. 139.]

Février (1959). Paulette Février: "Logical Structure of Physical Theories," in *The Axiomatic Method*, L. Henkin (ed.), (Amsterdam, 1959), pp. 376–389.

Gavrilov (1959). G. P. Gavrilov: "Certain Conditions for Completeness in Countable-valued Logic," *Doklady Akademii Nauk SSSR*, vol. 128 (1959), pp. 21–24. [Reviewed by E. Mendelson in MR, vol. 21 (1960), p. 1175; by D. Tamari in ZMG, vol. 124 (1964), pp. 5–6.]

Jordan (1959). Pascual Jordan: "Quantenlogik und das Kommutative Gesetz," in *The Axiomatic Method*, L. Henkin (ed.), (Amsterdam, 1959), pp. 365–375.

Kuznetzov (1959). B. G. Kuznetzov: "Ob osnovax kvantovo-reljativistakoj logiki" (On quantum and relativistic logic), *Logičeskie Issledovanija* (Moscow, Institut Filosofii, Izdatel'stvo Akademii Nauk SSSR, 1959), pp. 99–112.

Levi (1959). Isaac Levi: "Putnam's Three Truth-values," *Philosophical Studies*, vol. 10 (1959), pp. 65–69. [Reviewed by L. Henkin in JSL, vol. 25 (1960), pp. 289–291.]

Moisil (1959a). Grigor C. Moisil: "Rapport sur le développement dans la R.P.R. de la théorie algébrique des mécanismes automatiques," *Acta Logica* (Bucharest), vol. 2 (1959), pp. 145–199. [Reviewed by E. F. Moore in JSL, vol. 28 (1963), p. 174; by idem in MR, vol. 22 (1961), p. 1846.]

Moisil (1959b). Grigor C. Moisil: "Sur l'application de la logique à trois valeurs à l'étude des circuits électriques à contacts, redresseurs et résistances," *Revue de mathématiques pures et appliquées*, vol. 4 (1959), p. 173.

Moisil (1959c). Grigor C. Moisil: *Teoria algebrică a mecanismelor automate* (The Algebraic Theory of Automatic Machines), (Bucharest, Editura Technică, 1959). (See the bibliographic note No. VI on pp. 684–691 on many-valued logics.) [Reviewed by E. F. Moore in MR, vol. 22 (1961), p. 1846.]

Moisil (1959d). Grigor C. Moisil: "La logique à cinq valeurs et ses applications à l'étude des circuits électriques," *Praci o Automatisaci: Proceedings of the Automatic Control Conference, Prague, 1959* (Nakladatelsti Ceskozlovenske Akademie Ved, Prague, 1961).

Moisil (1959e). Grigor C. Moisil: "La logique à plusieurs valeurs et l'automatique," *Infinitistic Methods in Mathematics* (Warsaw, 1959; Proceedings of the Warsaw Conference on the Foundations of Mathematics, September, 1959).

Salomaa (1959). Arto Salomaa: "On Many-valued Systems of Logic," *Ajatus*, vol. 22 (1959), pp. 115–159. [Reviewed by A. R. Turquette in JSL, vol. 25 (1960), pp. 291–293.]

Umezawa (1959). Toshio Umezawa: "On Intermediate Many-valued Logics," *Journal of the Mathematical Society of Japan*, Rd. 11, Heft 2 (1959), pp. 116–128. [Reviewed by W. Ackermann in JSL, vol. 24 (1959), p. 250; by Alan Rose in MR, vol. 22 (1961), p. 1133; by Alan Rose in ZMG, vol. 86 (1961), p. 245.]

Zinov'ev (1959a). Aleksander Aleksandrovich Zinov'ev: "K otázce hodnocení soudů jako abstraktních a konkretních" (On the question of evaluating judgments as abstract and concrete), *Filosofický Časopis*, no. 6 (1959), pp. 848–850.

Zinov'ev (1959b). Aleksander Aleksandrovich Zinov'ev: "Problema značenij istinnosti v mnogoznačnoj logike" (The problem of truth-values in many-valued logic), *Voprosy Filosofii*, vol. 3 (1959), pp. 131–136.

Dreben (1960). Burton Dreben: "Relation of *m*-Valued Quantificational Logic to 2-Valued Quantificational Logic," *Summaries of talks presented at the Summer Institute for Symbolic Logic, Cornell University, 1957* (Princeton, N.J., 1960), pp. 303–304. [Reviewed by A. R. Turquette in JSL, vol. 30 (1965), pp. 375–376.]

Goddard (1960). Leonard Goddard: "The Exclusive 'Or', " *Analysis*, vol. 20 (1960), pp. 97–106.

Joja (1960). Athanase Joja: "About *tertium non datur*," *Acta Logica* (Bucharest), vol. 1 (1958), p. 11.

Martynjuk (1960). V. V. Martynjuk: "Investigation of Certain Classes of Functions in Many-valued Logics," *Problemy Kibernetiki*, vol. 3 (1960), pp. 49–60. [Reviewed by A. Salomaa in JSL, vol. 31 (1966), p. 502; by S. I. Adjan in MR, vol. 23 (1962), p. 699.]

Moisil (1960a). Grigor C. Moisil: "Sur les idéaux des algèbres Łukasiewicziennes trivalentes," *Analele Universitătii Bucuresti, Seria Acta Logica* (Bucharest), vol. 3 (1960), pp. 83–95. [Reviewed by G. F. Rose in JSL, vol. 27 (1962), pp. 367–368; by Alan Rose in MR, vol. 26 (1963), p. 691; by A. A. Mullin in ZMG, vol. 103 (1964), pp. 248–249.]

Moisil (1960b). Grigor C. Moisil: "Asupra logicii lue Bochvar" (On the logic of Bochvar), *Academia Republicii Populare Romîne; Analele Romîno-Sovietice Seria Matematica-Fizica* (Bucharest), vol. 14 (1960), pp. 19–25. [Reviewed by B. Germansky in MR, vol. 23 (1962), p. 138.]

Moisil (1960c). Grigor C. Moisil: *Logica matematica si teknica modernă: Logicile cu mai multe valori si circuitele cu contacte si relee* (Mathematical Logic and Modern Technology: Many-valued Logic and Relay-contact Circuits), *Probleme filosofice ale steintelor naturii* (Bucharest, Académie de la République populaire roumaine, 1960).

Rose (1960a). Alan Rose: "An Extension of a Theorem of Margaris," *The Journal of Symbolic Logic*, vol. 25 (1960), pp. 209–211. [Reviewed by B. A. Galler in MR, vol. 25 (1963), p. 390.]

Rose (1960b). Alan Rose: "Sur les schémas d'axiomes pour les calculs propositionnels à *m* valeurs ayant des valeurs sur désignées," *Comptes rendus hebdomadaires des séances de l'Académie des Sciences*, vol. 250 (1960), pp. 790–792. [Reviewed by E. Mendelson in MR, vol. 22 (1961), p. 109.]

Rosser (1960). James Barkley Rosser: "Axiomatization of Infinite-valued Logics," *Logique et Analyse*, vol. 3 (1960), pp. 137–153. [Reviewed by Robert McNaughton in JSL, vol. 27 (1962), p. 111–112.]

Rutledge (1960). Joseph D. Rutledge: "On the Definition of an Infinitely-Many-valued Predicate Calculus," *The Journal of Symbolic Logic*, vol. 25 (1960), pp. 212–216. [Reviewed by C. C. Chang in MR, vol. 25 (1963), pp. 391–392; by A. Salomaa in ZMG, vol. 105 (1964), p. 5.]

Shestakov (1960a). V. I. Shestakov: "O dvojnaj arixmetičeskoj interpretacii trexznačnogo isčislenija vyskazyvanij" in *Primenenie logiki v nauke i texnike*, ed. by P. V. Tavanec (Moscow, Institut Filosofii, Izdatél'stvo Akademii Nauk SSSR, 1960), pp. 341–376.

Shestakov (1960b). V. I. Shestakov: "A Dual Arithmetic Interpretation of the 3-valued Propositional Calculus Utilized in the Simulation of This Calculus by Relay-Contact Networks," *Applications of Logic in Science and Technology* (in Russian) (Moscow, Izdatél'stvo Akademii Nauk SSSR, 1960), pp. 341–376. *American Mathematical Society Translations*, vol. 48 (1965), pp. 45–72. [Reviewed by B. A. Galler in MR, vol. 33 (1967), p. 664.]

Sierpiński (1960–61). Warclaw Sierpiński: "Sur un problème de la logique à *n* valeurs," *Fundamenta Mathematicae*, vol. 49 (1960–61), pp. 167–170. [Reviewed by Alan Rose in MR, vol. 23 (1962), p. 700; by Alan Rose in ZMG, vol. 100 (1963), pp. 9–10.]

Skolem (1960). Thoralf Skolem: "A Set Theory Based on a Certain 3-Valued Logic," *Mathematica Scandinavica*, vol. 8 (1960), pp. 127–136. [Reviewed by W. Ackermann in ZMG, vol. 96 (1962), p. 243.]

Tavanec et al. (1960). P. V. Tavanec, È. Ja. Kol'man, G. N. Povarov, S. A. Janovskaja (eds.): *The Application of Logic to Science and Technology* (Moscow, Izdatél'stvo Akademii Nauk SSSR, 1960). [Reviewed in MR, vol. 26 (1963), p. 1147.]

Turowicz (1960). A. B. Turowicz: "Sur une méthode algébrique de vérification des théorèmes de la logique des énoncés," *Studia Logica*, vol. 9 (1960), pp. 27–36. [Reviewed by Gene F. Rose in MR, vol. 24 (1962), p. 335.]

Zinov'ev (1960). Aleksander Aleksandrovich Zinov'ev: *Filosofskié problémy mno-goznačnoj logiki* (Philosophical Problems of Many-valued Logic), (Moscow, Institut Filosofii, Izdatél'stvo Akademii Nauk SSSR, 1960); tr. by G. Küng and D. D. Comey (Dordrecht-Holland, 1963). [Reviewed by David D. Comey in JSL, vol. 28 (1963), pp. 255–256; by A. R. Turquette in JSL, vol. 29 (1964), pp. 213–214.]

Chang (1961). Chen Chung Chang: "Theory of Models of Infinite-valued Logics," I–IV, Abstracts in the *Notices of American Mathematical Society*, vol. 8 (1961), pp. 68 and 141.

Chang and Horn (1961). Chen Chung Chang and Alfred Horn: "Prime Ideal Characterization of Generalized Post Algebras," *Proceedings of the Symposium of Pure Mathematics*, vol. 2 (1961), pp. 43–48. [Reviewed by S. C. van Westrhenen in ZMG, vol. 108 (1964), pp. 5–6.]

Foxley (1961). Eric Foxley: "Testing the Independence of a System of Axioms, Using a Logical Computer," *Proceedings of the Cambridge Philosophical Society*, vol. 27 (1961), pp. 443–448. [Reviewed by P. C. Gilmore in MR, vol. 23 (1962), p. 5.]

Horn (1961). See Chang and Horn (1961).

Łukasiewicz (1961). Jan Łukásiewicz: *Z Zagadnień Logiki i Filozofii* (Logical and Philosophical Papers), edited by Jerzy Słupecki (Warsaw, Państwowe Wydawnictwo Naukowe, 1961).

Mittelstaedt (1961). Peter Mittelstaedt: "Quantenlogik," *Fortschritte der Physik*, vol. 9 (1961), pp. 106–147. [Reviewed by I. E. Segal in MR, vol. 23 (1962), p. 247.]

Mlëziva (1961). Miroslav Mlëziva: "On the Axiomatization of Three-valued Propositional Logic," *Casopis pro Pěstovani Matematiky* (Prague), vol. 86 (1961), pp. 392–403. [Reviewed by author in MR, vol. 24 (1962), p. 335; by J. Hořejš in ZMG, vol. 100 (1963), p. 9.]

Moisil (1961a). Grigor C. Moisil: "Les Logiques à plusieurs valeurs et l'automatique," *Proceedings of the Symposium on the Foundations of Mathematics, Warsaw, 1959* (Warsaw and Oxford, 1961), pp. 337–345.

Moisil (1961b). Grigor C. Moisil: "The Predicate Calculus in Three-valued Logic," *Analele Universitătii Bucuresti Seria Acta Logica* (Bucharest), vol. 4 (1961), pp. 103–112. [Reviewed by A. A. Mullin in ZMG, vol. 103 (1964), p. 247.]

Mostowski (1961a). Andrzej Mostowski: "Axiomatizability of Some Many-valued Predicate Calculi," *Fundamenta Mathematicae*, vol. 50 (1961), pp. 165–190. [Reviewed by G. Kreisel in MR, vol. 24 (1962), pp. 572–573; by A. Oberschelp in ZMG, vol. 99 (1963), pp. 7–8.]

Mostowski (1961b). Andrzej Mostowski: "An Example of a Non-axiomatizable Many-valued Logic," *Zeitschrift für mathematische Logik und Grundlagen der Mathematik*, vol. 7 (1961), pp. 72–76. [Reviewed by Alan Rose in MR, vol. 30 (1965), pp. 203–204; by J. J. F. Nieland in ZMG, vol. 124 (1966), p. 248.]

Rose (1961a). Alan Rose: "Self-dual Binary and Ternary Connectives for *m*-Valued Propositional Calculi," *Mathematische Annalen*, vol. 143 (1961), pp. 448–462.

[Reviewed by A. Salomaa in JSL, vol. 29 (1964), pp. 144–145; by E. Mendelson in MR, vol. 23 (1962), p. 138; by A. Salomaa in ZMG, vol. 107 (1964), p. 7.]

Rose (1961b). Alan Rose: "Sur certains calculs propositionnels à *m* valeurs ayant un seul foncteur primitif lequel constitue son propre dual," *Comptes rendus hebdomadaires des séances de l'Académie des Sciences*, vol. 252 (1961), pp. 3176–3178, 3375–3376. [Reviewed by A. Salomaa in JSL, vol. 29 (1964), pp. 144–145; by V. Devidé in MR, vol. 30 (1965), p. 374.]

Smetaníc (1961). Ja. S. Smetaníc: "Propositional Calculi with Additional Operations," *Doklady Akademii Nauk SSSR*, vol. 139 (1961), pp. 309–312. [Reviewed by Gene F. Rose in MR, vol. 26 (1963), p. 6.]

Smiley (1961). Timothy Smiley: "On Łukasiewicz's Ł-modal System," *Notre Dame Journal of Formal Logic*, vol. 2 (1961), pp. 149–153. [Reviewed by A. Church in JSL, vol. 27 (1962), p. 113; by Alan Rose in MR, vol. 26 (1963), p. 690.]

Sobociński (1961). Boleslaw Sobociński: "A Note Concerning the Many-valued Propositional Calculi," *Notre Dame Journal of Formal Logic*, vol. 2 (1961), pp. 127–128. [Reviewed by A. R. Turquette in JSL, vol. 31 (1966), p. 117; by Alan Rose in MR, vol. 28 (1964), p. 404; by Alan Rose in ZMG, vol. 121 (1966), p. 11.]

Turquette (1961). Atwell R. Turquette: "Solution to a Problem of Rose and Rosser," *Proceedings of the American Mathematical Society*, vol. 12 (1961), pp. 253–255. [Reviewed by L. Hay in JSL, vol. 31 (1966), p. 665; by Alan Rose in MR, vol. 23 (1962), p. 700; by K. Schütte in ZMG, vol. 106 (1964), p. 4.]

Wang (1961). Hao Wang: "The Calculus of Partial Predicates and Its Extension to Set Theory. I," *Zeitschrift für mathematische Logik und Grundlagen der Mathematik*, vol. 7 (1961), pp. 283–288. [Reviewed by Alan Rose in MR, vol. 26 (1963), p. 2.]

Zinov'ev (1961a). Aleksander Aleksandrovich Zinov'ev: *Logika vyskazyvanij i teorija vyvoda* (Moscow, Institut Filosofii, Izdatel'stvo Akademii Nauk SSSR, 1961).

Zinov'ev (1961b). Aleksander Aleksandrovich Zinov'ev: "Ob adnom sposobe obzora funkcij istinnosti *n*-značnogo isčislenija vyskazyvanij" (A method of describing the truth-functions of the *n*-valued propositional calculus), *Studia Logica*, vol. 11 (1961), pp. 217–222. [Reviewed by E. J. Cogan in MR, vol. 24 (1962), p. 6.]

Anderson and Belnap (1962). Alan Ross Anderson and Nuel D. Belnap, Jr.: "The Pure Calculus of Entailment," *The Journal of Symbolic Logic*, vol. 28 (1962), pp. 19–52. [Reviewed by J. Bennett in JSL, vol. 30 (1965), p. 240.]

Anderson and Johnstone (1962). John M. Anderson and Henry W. Johnstone, Jr.: *Natural Deduction. The Logical Basis of Axiom Systems* (Belmont, Calif., Wadsworth Publishing Co., 1962). [Reviewed by D. Kalish in JSL, vol. 29 (1964), pp. 93–94.]

Belnap (1962). See Anderson and Belnap (1962).

Bochénski and Menne (1962). Inocenty M. Bochénski and Albert Menne: *Grundriss der Logistik* (Paderborn, F. Schöningh, 1962).

Chang and Keisler (1962). Chen Chung Chang and H. Jerome Keisler: "Model Theories with Truth Values in a Uniform Space," *Bulletin of the American Mathematical Society*, vol. 68 (1962), pp. 107–109. [Reviewed by Alan Rose in MR, vol. 25 (1963), p. 2; by Alan Rose in ZMG, vol. 104 (1964), pp. 241–242.]

Clay (1962a). Robert E. Clay: "Note on Słupecki *T*-functions," *The Journal of Symbolic Logic*, vol. 27 (1962), pp. 53–54. [Reviewed by A. Salomaa in JSL, vol. 30 (1965), p. 105; by A. R. Turquette in MR, vol. 27 (1964), pp. 6–7; by A. Salomaa in ZMG, vol. 107 (1964), p. 8.]

Clay (1962b). Robert E. Clay: "A Simple Proof of Functional Completeness in Many-valued Logics Based on Łukasiewicz's *C* and *N*," *Notre Dame Journal of Formal Logic*, vol. 3 (1963), pp. 114–117. [Reviewed by A. Salomaa in JSL, vol. 30 (1965), pp. 105–106; by A. R. Turquette in MR, vol. 26 (1963), p. 934; by A. Salomaa in ZMG, vol. 118 (1965), p. 13.]

Fadini (1962). Angelo Fadini: "Il calcolo delle classi in una logica a tre valoridi verità," *Giornale di Matematiche di Battaglini* (Naples), vol. 10 (1962), pp. 72–92. [Reviewed by H. Riheiro in MR, vol. 30 (1965), p. 203.]

Foxley (1962). Eric Foxley: "The Determination of All Sheffer Functions in 3-Valued Logic, Using a Logical Computer," *Notre Dame Journal of Formal Logic*, vol. 3 (1962), pp. 41–50. [Reviewed by A. R. Turquette in JSL, vol. 28 (1963), p. 174; by Alan Rose in MR, vol. 27 (1964), p. 681; by A. Adam in ZMG, vol. 112 (1965), p. 5.]

Gnidenko (1962). V. M. Gnidenko: "Determination of Orders of Pre-complete Classes in Three-valued Logic," *Problemy Kibernetiki*, vol. 8 (1962), pp. 341–346. [Reviewed by V. Vuckovic in MR, vol. 29 (1965), p. 881.]

Jobe (1962). William H. Jobe: "Functional Completeness and Canonical Forms in Many-valued Logics," *The Journal of Symbolic Logic*, vol. 27 (1962), pp. 409–422. [Reviewed by A. Salomaa in JSL, vol. 29 (1964), pp. 143–144; by C. C. Chang in MR, vol. 31 (1966), p. 592; by G. Kreisel in ZMG, vol. 117 (1965), p. 253.]

Johnstone (1962). See Anderson and Johnstone (1962).

Keisler (1962). See Chang and Keisler (1962).

Kneale (1962). William and Martha Kneale: *The Development of Logic* (Oxford, Clarendon Press, 1962). See especially sec. 5, "Suggestions for Alternative Logics," of chap. IX. [Reviewed by B. Mates in JSL, vol. 27 (1962), pp. 213–217.]

Kreisel (1962). Georg Kreisel: "On Weak Completeness of Intuitionistic Predicate Logic," *The Journal of Symbolic Logic*, vol. 27 (1962), pp. 139–158. [Reviewed by A. Heyting in MR, vol. 28 (1965), p. 965.]

Menne (1962). See Bochenski and Menne (1962).

Moisil (1962a). Grigor C. Moisil: "Sur le principe du déterminisme," *Etudes de philosophie et d'histoire* (Bucharest, 1962), p. 33.

Moisil (1962b). Grigor C. Moisil: "Sur la logique à trois valeurs de Łukasiewicz," *Analele Universitătii Bucuresti Seria Acta Logica*, vol. 5 (1962), pp. 103–117. [Reviewed by G. F. Rose in JSL, vol. 27 (1962), p. 368; by A. R. Turquette in MR, vol. 26 (1963), pp. 1144–1145; by Alan Rose in ZMG, vol. 121 (1966), p. 11.]

Moisil (1962c). Grigor C. Moisil: "Les Logiques non-chrysippiennes et leurs applications," *Proceedings of a Colloquium on Modal and Many-Valued Logics* (Helsinki, 1962), pp. 137–149.

Nakamura (1962a). Akira Nakamura: "On the Infinitely Many-valued Threshold Logics and von Wright's System *M*," *Zeitschrift für mathematische Logik und Grundlagen der Mathematik*, vol. 8 (1962), pp. 147–164. [Reviewed by A. Salomaa in JSL, vol. 30 (1965), pp. 374–375; by Alan Rose in MR, vol. 26 (1963), p. 690; by A. Salomaa in ZMG, vol. 105 (1964), p. 5.]

Nakamura (1962b). Akira Nakamura: "On an Axiomatic System of the Infinitely Many-valued Threshold Logics," *Zeitschrift für mathematische Logik und Grundlagen der Mathematik*, vol. 8 (1962), pp. 71–76. [Reviewed by A. Salomaa in JSL, vol. 30 (1965), pp. 374–375; by A. R. Turquette in MR, vol. 26 (1963), p. 690; by Alan Rose in ZMG, vol. 103 (1964), p. 245.]

von Neumann (1962). John von Neumann: "Quantum Logics," unpublished, reviewed by A. H. Taub in *John von Neumann, Collected Works*, vol. 4 (New York, 1962), pp. 195–197.

Prior (1962). Arthur Norman Prior: "The Formalities of Omniscience," *Philosophy*, vol. 37 (1962), pp. 114–129.

Reichbach (1962). Juliusz Reichbach: "On the Connection of the First-order Functional Calculus with Many-valued Propositional Calculi," *Notre Dame Journal of Formal Logic*, vol. 3 (1962), pp. 102–107. [Reviewed by L. N. Gál in MR, vol. 26 (1963), p. 934.]

Rescher (1962). Nicholas Rescher: "Quasi-truth-functional Systems of Propositional Logic," *The Journal of Symbolic Logic*, vol. 27 (1962), pp. 1–10. [Reviewed by G. F. Rose in JSL, vol. 29 (1964), pp. 50–51; by A. R. Turquette in MR, vol. 27 (1964), p. 7; by A. Salomaa in ZMG, vol. 107 (1964), pp. 7–8.]

Rose (1962a). Alan Rose: "An Alternative Generalisation of the Concept of Duality," *Mathematische Annalen*, vol. 147 (1962), pp. 318–327. [Reviewed by S. Jaskowski in MR, vol. 27 (1964), p. 681.]

Rose (1962b). Alan Rose: "Extensions of Some Theorems of Anderson and Belnap," *The Journal of Symbolic Logic*, vol. 27 (1962), pp. 423–425. [Reviewed by A. R. Turquette in MR, vol. 30 (1965), p. 374; by A. Oberschelp in ZMG, vol. 118 (1966), p. 248.]

Rose (1962c). Alan Rose: "A Simplified Self *m*-al Set of Primitive Functors for the *m*-Valued Propositional Calculus," *Zeitschrift für mathematische Logik und Grundlagen der Mathematik*, vol. 8 (1962), pp. 257–266. [Reviewed by A. Salomaa in JSL, vol. 29 (1964), pp. 144–145; by E. Mendelson in MR, vol. 26 (1963), p. 452; by A. Salomaa in ZMG, vol. 108 (1964), p. 2.]

Rose (1962d). Alan Rose: "Sur un ensemble complet de foncteurs primitifs indé-pendants pour le calcul propositionnel trivalent lequel constitue son propre trial," *Comptes rendus hebdomadaires des séances de l'Académie des Sciences,* vol. 254 (1962), p. 2111. [Reviewed by A. Salomaa in JSL, vol. 29 (1964), pp. 144–145; by E. Mendelson in MR, vol. 24 (1962), p. 572; by A. Oberschelp in ZMG, vol. 116 (1965), p. 5.]

Rose (1962e). Alan Rose: "Sur les applications de la logique polyvalente à la construction des machines Turing," *Comptes rendus hebdomadaires des séances de l'Académie des Sciences,* vol. 255 (1962), pp. 1836–1838. [Reviewed by S. Huzino in MR, vol. 25 (1963), p. 969.]

Rose (1962f). Alan Rose: "Sur un ensemble de foncteurs primitifs pour le calcul propositionnel à *m* valeurs lequel constitue son propre *m*-al," *Comptes rendus hebdomadaires des séances de l'Académie des Sciences,* vol. 254 (1962), pp. 1897–1899. [Reviewed by A. Salomaa in JSL, vol. 29 (1964), pp. 144–145; by A. Salomaa in ZMG, vol. 114 (1965), p. 244.]

Scarpellini (1962). Bruno Scarpellini: "Die. Nichtaxiomatisierbarkeit des unend-lichwertigen Prädikatenkalküls von Łukasiewicz," *The Journal of Symbolic Logic,* vol. 27 (1962), pp. 159–170. [Reviewed by A. Rose in JSL, vol. 29 (1964), p. 145; by A. Salomaa in ZMG, vol. 112 (1965), pp. 245–246.]

Smiley (1962). Timothy J. Smiley: "Analytic Implication and 3-Valued Logic," *The Journal of Symbolic Logic,* vol. 27 (1962), p. 378.

Thomas (1962). Ivo Thomas: "On the Infinity of Positive Logic," *Notre Dame Journal of Formal Logic,* vol. 3 (1962), p. 108. [Reviewed by Gene F. Rose in MR, vol. 28 (1965), p. 403.]

Tîrnoveanu (1962). Mircea Tîrnoveanu: "Sur les extensions des types P et Q de la logique L_Ω^S," *Comunicările Academiei Republici Populare Romîne* (Bucharest), vol. 12 (1962), pp. 269–273. [Reviewed by H. W. Guggenheimer in MR, vol. 26 (1963), p. 239.]

Traczyk (1962). Tadeusz Traczyk: "On Axioms and Some Properties of Post Alge-bras," *Bulletin de l'Académie Polonaise des Sciences: Série des Sciences Mathé-matiques, Astronomiques et Physiques* (Warsaw), vol. 10 (1962), pp. 509–512. [Reviewed by G. Grätzen in MR, vol. 27 (1964), p. 147; by A. A. Mullin in ZMG, vol. 119 (1966), p. 11.]

Wilhelmy (1962). Alexander Wilhelmy. "Bemerkungen zur Semantik quantifizierter mehrwertiger logistischer Systeme," in Max Käsbauer (ed.), *Logik und Logik-kalkül* (Freiburg, München, K. Alber, 1962), pp. 179–188. [Reviewed by A. Salomaa in ZMG, vol. 119 (1966), p. 11.]

Zinov'ev (1962). Aleksander Aleksandrovich Zinov'ev. "Dvuznačnaja i mnogoz-načnaja logika" (Two-valued and many-valued logic), *Filosofskie Voprosy Sovremennoj Formal'noj Logiki* (Moscow, Institut Filosofii, Izdatel'stvo Akademii Nauk SSSR, 1962), pp. 111–139.

Anonymous (ed.) (1963). "Proceedings of a Colloquium on Modal and Many-valued Logics: Helsinki 23–26 August 1962," *Acta Philosophica Fennica*, fasc. 16 (1963), pp. 1–290.

Belluce and Chang (1963). L. P. Belluce and Chen Chung Chang: "A Weak Completeness Theorem for Infinite-valued First-order Logic," *The Journal of Symbolic Logic*, vol. 28 (1963), pp. 43–50. [Reviewed by Alan Rose in MR, vol. 34 (1967), p. 8; by Alan Rose in ZMG, vol. 121 (1966), p. 12.]

Caton (1963). Charles E. Caton: "A Stipulation of a Modal Propositional Calculus in Terms of Modalized Truth-values," *Notre Dame Journal of Formal Logic*, vol. 4 (1963), pp. 224–226. [Reviewed by A. R. Turquette in MR, vol. 29 (1965), p. 420; by K. Matsumoto in ZMG, vol. 119 (1966), pp. 11–12.]

Chang (1963a). Chen Chung Chang: "Logic with Positive and Negative Truth Values," *Acta Philosophica Fennica*, fasc. 16 (1963), pp. 19–39. [Reviewed by Alan Rose in MR, vol. 28 (1964), p. 578; by idem, in ZMG, vol. 129 (1967), pp. 256–257.]

Chang (1963b). Chen Chung Chang: "The Axiom of Comprehension in Infinite-valued Logic," *Mathematica Scandinavica*, vol. 13 (1963), pp. 9–30. [Reviewed by H. J. Keisler in MR, vol. 29 (1965), pp. 419–420.]

Chang (1963c). Chen Chung Chang and H. Jerome Keisler: "Continuous Model Theory," to appear in the *Proceedings of the Model Theory Symposium* held at Berkeley, June–July 1963 (Berkeley, 1966).

Chang (1963d). See Belluce and Chang (1963).

Clay (1963). Robert E. Clay: "A Standard Form for Łukasiewicz Many-valued Logics," *Notre Dame Journal of Formal Logic*, vol. 4 (1963), pp. 59–66. [Reviewed by A. R. Turquette in JSL, vol. 30 (1965), pp. 105–106; by *idem*, In MR, vol. 26 (1963), p. 1144; by Alan Rose in ZMG, vol. 118 (1965), p. 248.]

Fletcher (1963). T. J. Fletcher: "Models of Many-valued Logics," *American Mathematical Monthly*, vol. 70 (1963), pp. 381–391. [Reviewed by Alan Rose in MR, vol. 27 (1964), p. 681; by C. C. Chang in ZMG, vol. 118 (1965), p. 13.]

Hanson (1963). W. H. Hanson: "Ternary Threshold Logic," *IEEE Transactions on Electronic Computers*, EC–12 (1963), pp. 191–197. [Reviewed by A. Rose in JSL, vol. 29 (1964), pp. 110–111; by author in MR, vol. 27 (1964), p. 473.]

Hay (1963). Louise S. Hay: "Axiomatization of the Infinite-valued Predicate Calculus," *The Journal of Symbolic Logic*, vol. 28 (1963), pp. 77–86. [Reviewed by S. Jaśkowski in MR, vol. 31 (1966), p. 7; by C. C. Chang in ZMG, vol. 127 (1967), pp. 7–8.]

Jordan (1963). Zbigniew Jordan: "Logical Determinism," *Notre Dame Journal of Formal Logic*, vol. 4 (1963), pp. 1–38.

Keisler (1963). See Chang and Keisler (1963c).

Kirin (1963). Vladimr G. Kirin: "On the Polynomial Representation of Operators in the *n*-Valued Propositional Calculus," *Glasnik Matematičko-Fizički i Astronomski. Društvo Matematičara i Fizičara Hrvatske: Serija II*, vol. 18 (1963), pp. 3–12. [Reviewed by E. J. Cogan in MR, vol. 29 (1965), p. 420.]

Kneebone (1963). G. T. Kneebone: *Mathematical Logic and the Foundations of Mathematics: An Introductory Survey* London, Toronto, New York, Princeton, N.J., (D. Van Nostrand Co., Ltd., 1963). [Reviewed by J. Tucker in MR, vol. 27 (1964), pp. 4–6.]

Kripke (1963). Saul A. Kripke: "Semantical Analysis of Modal Logic. I. Normal Modal Propositional Calculi," *Zeitschrift für mathematische Logik und Grundlagen der Mathematik*, vol. 9 (1963), pp. 67–96. [Reviewed by D. Kaplan in JSL, vol. 31 (1966), pp. 120–122; by Alan Rose in MR, vol. 26 (1963), p. 688.]

Meredith and Prior (1963). Charles A. Meredith and Arthur Norman Prior: "Notes on the Axiomatics of Propositional Calculus," *Notre Dame Journal of Formal Logic*, vol. 4 (1963), pp. 171–187. [Reviewed by Alan Rose in MR, vol. 30 (1966), p. 203.]

Moisil (1963). Grigor C. Moisil: "Les Logiques non-chrysippiennes et leurs applications," *Acta Philosophica Fennica*, fasc. 16 (1963), pp. 137–152. [Reviewed by H. J. Keisler in MR, vol. 28 (1964), p. 579.]

Monteiro (1963). Antonio Monteiro: "Sur la définition des algèbres de Łukasiewicz trivalentes," *Bulletin mathématique de la Société des Science Mathématiques et Physiques de la Republique Populaire de Roumanie*, vol. 7 (55) (1963), pp. 3–12. [Reviewed by E. Mihăilescu in JSL, vol. 32 (1967), pp. 398–399; by C. C. Chang in MR, vol. 33 (1967), p. 6.]

Mostowski (1963). Andrzej Mostowski: "The Hilbert Epsilon Function in Many-valued Logics," *Acta Philosophica Fennica*, fasc. 16 (1963), pp. 169–188. [Reviewed by H. J. Keisler in MR, vol. 28 (1964), pp. 577–578; by Alan Rose in ZMG, vol. 121 (1966), p. 12.]

Nakamura (1963a). Akira Nakamura: "A Note on Truth-value Functions in the Infinitely Many-valued Logics," *Zeitschrift für mathematische Logik und Grundlagen der Mathematik*, vol. 9 (1963), pp. 141–144. [Reviewed by A. Salomaa in JSL, vol. 30 (1965), pp. 374–375; by Alan Rose in MR, vol. 28 (1964), p. 224; by Alan Rose in ZMG, vol. 113 (1965), p. 4.]

Nakamura (1963b). Akira Nakamura: "On an Axiomatic System of the Infinitely Many-valued Threshold Predicate Calculi," *Zeitschrift für mathematische Logik und Grundlagen der Mathematik*, vol. 9 (1963), pp. 321–329. [Reviewed by A. Salomaa in JSL, vol. 30 (1965), pp. 374–375; by A. R. Turquette in MR, vol. 28 (1964), p. 901.]

Nakamura (1963c). Akira Nakamura: "On a Simple Axiomatic System of the Infinitely Many-valued Logic Based on ∧, →," *Zeitschrift für mathematische Logik und Grundlagen der Mathematik*, vol. 9 (1963), pp. 251–263. [Reviewed by A. Salomaa in JSL, vol. 30 (1965), pp. 374–375; by C. C. Chang in MR, vol. 28 (1964), p. 681.]

Prior (1963a). Arthur Norman Prior: "The Theory of Implication," *Zeitschrift für mathematische Logik und Grundlagen der Mathematik*, vol. 9 (1963), pp. 1–6. [Reviewed by A. R. Anderson in JSL, vol. 31 (1966), pp. 665–666; by Alan Rose in MR, vol. 26 (1963), p. 691.]

Prior (1963b). See Meredith and Prior (1963).

Reichbach (1963). Juliusz Reichbach: "About Connection of the First-order Functional Calculus with Many-valued Propositional Calculi," *Zeitschrift für mathematische Logik und Grundlagen der Mathematik*, vol. 9 (1963), pp. 117–124. [Reviewed by Alan Rose in MR, vol. 28 (1964), p. 224.]

Rescher (1963). Nicholas Rescher: "A Probabilistic Approach to Modal Logic," *Acta Philosophica Fennica*, fasc. 16 (1963), pp. 215–226. [Reviewed by A. R. Turquette in MR, vol. 28 (1964), pp. 403–404.]

Salomaa (1963). Arto Salomaa: "Some Analogues of Sheffer Functions in Infinite-valued Logics," *Acta Philosophica Fennica*, fasc. 16 (1963), pp. 227–235. [Reviewed by N. M. Martin in JSL, vol. 31 (1966), pp. 118–119; by Alan Rose in ZMG, vol. 121 (1966), p. 11.]

Scarpellini (1963). Bruno Scarpellini: "Eine Anwendung der unendlichwertigen Logik auf topologische Räume," *Fundamentia Mathematicae*, vol. 52 (1963), pp. 129–150.

Summersbee and Walters (1963). Stuart Summersbee and A. Walters: "Programming the Functions of Formal Logic. II. Multi-valued Logics," *Notre Dame Journal of Formal Logic*, vol. 4 (1963), pp. 293–305. [Reviewed by B. A. Galler in MR, vol. 29 (1965), p. 881.]

Teh (1963). H. H. Teh: "On 3-Valued Sentential Calculus. An Axiomatic Approach," *Bulletin of Mathematical Society* (Singapore, Nanyang University, 1963), pp. 1–37. [Reviewed by S. Jaśkowski in MR, vol. 29 (1965), p. 2.]

Turquette (1963a). Atwell R. Turquette: "Modality, Minimality, and Many-valuedness," *Acta Philosophica Fennica*, fasc. 16 (1963), pp. 261–276. [Reviewed by Alan Rose in MR, vol. 28 (1964), p. 578; by Alan Rose in ZMG, vol. 121 (1966), p. 12.]

Turquette (1963b). Atwell R. Turquette: "Independent Axioms for Infinite-valued Logic," *The Journal of Symbolic Logic*, vol. 28 (1963), pp. 217–221. [Reviewed by L. Hay in JSL, vol. 31 (1966), p. 665; by C. C. Chang in MR, vol. 31 (1966), p. 593; by I. Rosenberg in ZMG, vol. 128 (1967), p. 12.]

Walters (1963). See Summersbee and Walters (1963).

Zinov'ev (1963). Aleksander Aleksandrovich Zinov'ev: *Philosophical Problems of Many-valued Logic*, ed. and tr. by Guido Küng and D. D. Comey (Dordrecht, D. Reidel Publishing Co., 1963). [Reviewed by J. Tucker in MR, vol. 28 (1964), pp. 2–3; by Alan Rose in ZMG, vol. 119 (1966), pp. 249–250.]

Zinov'ev (1963–64). Aleksander Aleksandrovich Zinov'ev: "Two-valued and Many-valued Logic," *Soviet Studies in Philosophy*, vol. 2 (1963–64), pp. 69–84.

Belluce (1964). L. P. Belluce: "Further Results on Infinite-valued Predicate Logic," *The Journal of Symbolic Logic*, vol. 29 (1964), pp. 69–78. [Reviewed by Alan Rose in MR, vol. 31 (1966), p. 209; by C. C. Chang in ZMG, vol. 127 (1967), p. 8.]

Bull (1964). R. A. Bull: "An Axiomatization of Prior's modal calculus *Q*," *Notre Dame Journal of Formal Logic*, vol. 5 (1964), pp. 211–214. [Reviewed by K. Ono in MR, vol. 34 (1967), p. 202.]

Fenstad (1964). Jens Erik Fenstad: "On the Consistency of the Axiom of Comprehension in the Łukasiewicz Infinite-valued Logic," *Mathematica Scandinavica*, vol. 14 (1964), pp. 64–74. [Reviewed by C. C. Chang in MR, vol. 30 (1965), p. 3.]

Fuchs (1964). W. R. Fuchs: "Ansätze zu einer Quantenlogik," *Theoria*, vol. 30 (1964), pp. 137–140.

Gonzalez Coppola (1964). See Monteiro and Gonzalez Coppola (1964).

Hartshorne (1964). Charles Hartshorne: "Deliberation and Excluded Middle," *The Journal of Philosophy*, vol. 61 (1964), pp. 476–477.

Menne (1964). Albert Menne: "Ueber monadische Valenzfunktionen," *Memorias del XIII Congresso Internacional de Filosofia*, vol. V (Mexico City, 1964).

Moisil (1964). Grigor C. Moisil: "Sur les logiques de Łukasiewicz à un nombre fini de valeurs," *Revue Roumanienne des mathématiques pures*, vol. 9 (1964), pp. 905–920. [Reviewed by A. R. Turquette in MR, vol. 32 (1966), p. 6.]

Moisil (1964–1965). Grigor C. Moisil: "The Interest of the Actual Operation of Switching Circuits for the Logician," *Acta Logica* (Bucharest), vols. 7–8 (1964–1965), pp. 131 ff.

Monteiro and Gonzalez Coppola (1964). Luiz F. T. Monteiro and Lorenzo Gonzalez Coppola: "Sur une construction des algèbres de Łukasiewicz trivalentes," *Portugaliae Mathematica*, vol. 23 (1964), pp. 157–167. [Reviewed by E. Mihăilescu in JSL, vol. 32 (1967), pp. 397–398; by J. E. Fenstad in MR, vol. 33 (1967), p. 448.]

Nakamura (1964). Akira Nakamura: "Truth-value Stipulations for the von Wright System *M'* and the Heyting System," *Zeitschrift für mathematische Logik und Grundlagen der Mathematik*, vol. 10 (1964), pp. 173–183. [Reviewed by A. Salomaa in JSL, vol. 30 (1965), pp. 374–375; by A. R. Turquette in MR, vol. 28 (1964), p. 757.]

Pogorzelski (1964). Nitold A. Pogorzelski: "The Deduction Theorem for Łukasiewicz' Many-valued Propositional Calculi," *Studia Logica*, vol. 15 (1964), pp. 7–23. [Reviewed by G. Rousseau in MR, vol. 33 (1967), p. 926.]

Reichbach (1964). Juliusz Reichbach: "A Note about Connection of the First-order Functional Calculus with Many-valued Propositional Calculi," *Notre Dame Journal of Formal Logic*, vol. 5 (1964), pp. 158–160. [Reviewed by Alan Rose in MR, vol. 31 (1966), p. 384.]

Rescher (1964). Nicholas Rescher: "Quantifiers in Many-valued Logic," *Logique et Analyse*, vol. 7 (1964), pp. 181–184. [Reviewed by A. R. Turquette in MR, vol. 30 (1965), p. 874.]

Rose (1964a). Alan Rose: "Formalisations de calculs propositionnels polyvalents à foncteurs variables," *Comptes rendus hebdomadaires des séances de l'Académie des Sciences*, vol. 258 (1964), pp. 1951–1953. [Reviewed by A. R. Turquette in MR, vol. 28 (1964), p. 579.]

Rose (1964b). Alan Rose: "Note sur la formalisation de calculs propositionnels polyvalents à foncteurs variables," *Comptes rendus hebdomadaires des séances de l'Académie des Sciences*, vol. 259 (1964), pp. 967–968. [Reviewed by M. J. Wicks in MR, vol. 29 (1965), p. 640.]

Scheibe (1964). Erhard Scheibe: *Die kontingenten Aussagen in der Physik* (Frankfurt a.M., etc., 1964).

Schock (1964a). Rolf Schock. "On Finitely Many-valued Logics," *Logique et Analyse*, vol. 7 (1964), pp. 43–58. [Reviewed by Alan Rose in MR, vol. 31 (1966), p. 209; by I. Rosenberg in ZMG, vol. 127 (1967), p. 8.]

Schock (1964b). Rolf Schock. "On Denumerably Many-valued Logics," *Logique et Analyse*, vol. 7 (1964), pp. 190–195. [Reviewed by Alan Rose in MR, vol. 31 (1966), p. 209.]

Schofield (1964). Peter Schofield: "On a Correspondence between Many-valued and Two-valued Logics," *Zeitschrift für mathematische Logik und Grundlagen der Mathematik*, vol. 10 (1964), pp. 265–274.

Shestakov (1964). V. I. Shestakov: "On the Relationship between Certain Three-valued Logical Calculi," *Uspehi Matematiceskih Nauk* (Moscow), vol. 19 (1964), pp. 177–181. [Reviewed by V. Devide in MR, vol. 31 (1966), p. 384.]

Siosen (1964). Federico M. Siosen: "Further Axiomatizations of the Łukasiewicz Three-valued Calculus," *Notre Dame Journal of Formal Logic*, vol. 5 (1964), pp. 62–70. [Reviewed by A. R. Turquette in JSL, vol. 31 (1966), pp. 500–501; by Alan Rose in MR, vol. 31 (1966), pp. 384–385; by Alan Rose in ZMG, vol. 137 (1967), p. 249.]

Turquette (1964). Atwell R. Turquette: "Independent Axioms for Infinite-valued Logic," *The Journal of Symbolic Logic*, vol. 28 (1964), pp. 217–221. [Reviewed by L. Hay in JSL, vol. 31 (1966), p. 665; by C. C. Chang in MR, vol. 31 (1966), p. 593; by I. Rosenberg in ZMG, vol. 128 (1967), p. 12.]

Aîzenberg (1965). N. N. Aîzenberg: "Representation of a Sum *mod m* in a Class of Normal Forms of Functions of *m*-Valued Logic," *Kibernetika* (Kiev), vol. 4 (1965), pp. 101–102. [Registered in MR, vol. 34 (1967), p. 8.]

Chang (1965). Chen Chung Chang: "Infinite-valued Logic as a Basis for Set Theory," in Y. Bar-Hillel (ed.), *Logic, Methodology, and Philosophy of Science: Proceedings of the 1964 International Congress* (Amsterdam, 1965), pp. 93–100. [Reviewed by A. Lévy in JSL, vol. 32 (1967), pp. 128–129; by G. Takeuti in MR, vol. 34 (1967), p. 429.]

Emch and Jauch (1965). Gérard Emch and J. M. Jauch: "Structures logiques et mathématiques en physique quantique," *Dialectica*, vol. 19 (1965), pp. 259–279.

Feys (1965). Robert Feys: *Modal Logics* (Louvain and Paris, 1965). [Reviewed by A. R. Turquette in MR, vol. 30 (1965), pp. 570–571.]

Jauch (1965). See Emch and Jauch (1965).

Klaus (1965). Georg Klaus: "Über einen Ansatz zur mehrwertigen Mengenlehre," *Monatsberichte der deutschen Akademie der Wissenschaften zu Berlin*, vol. 7 (1965), pp. 859–867. [Reviewed by A. Lévy in MR, vol. 33 (1967), pp. 218–219.]

Kline (1965). George L. Kline: "N. A. Vasil'év and the Development of Many-valued Logics," *Contributions to Logic and Methodology in Honor of J. M. Bocheński*, ed. by Anna-Teresa Tymieniecka in collaboration with Charles D. Parsons (Amsterdam, North-Holland Publishing Co., 1965), pp. 315–326.

Kochen and Specker (1965). Simon Kochen and E. P. Specker: "Logical Structures in Quantum Theory" in *The Theory of Models*, ed. by J. W. Addison (Amsterdam, 1965), pp. 177–189.

Moisil (1965). Grigor C. Moisil: *Încercari vechi si noi de logică neclasica* (Essays Old and New on Nonclassical Logic), (Bucharest, Editura Stüntifică, 1965). A collection of seventeen papers by Moisil, mostly published previously. [Reviewed by V. Poenaru in MR, vol. 35 (1968), pp. 5–6.]

Nakamura (1965). Akira Nakamura: "On the Infinitely Many-valued Double-threshold Logic," *Zeitschrift für mathematische Logik und Grundlagen der Mathematik*, vol. 11 (1965), pp. 93–101. [Reviewed by A. Salomaa in JSL, vol. 31 (1966), p. 665; by A. R. Turquette in MR, vol. 31 (1966), p. 209.]

Rescher (1965). Nicholas Rescher: "An Intuitive Interpretation of Systems of Four-valued Logic," *Notre Dame Journal of Formal Logic*, vol. 6 (1965), pp. 154–156.

Rose (1965). Alan Rose: "A Formalization of Post's m-Valued Propositional Calculus with Variable Functors," *Zeitschrift für mathematische Logik und Grundlagen der Mathematik*, vol. 11 (1965), pp. 221–226. [Reviewed by A. R. Turquette in MR, vol. 33 (1967), p. 6.]

Salomaa (1965). Arto Salomaa: "On Some Algebraic Notions in the Theory of Truth-functions," *Acta Philosophica Fennica*, fasc. 18 (1965), pp. 193–202. [Reviewed by V. Devidé in MR, vol. 32 (1966), p. 1258.]

Schock (1965). Rolf Schock: "Some Theorems on the Relative Strengths of Many-valued Logics," *Logique et Analyse*, vol. 8 (1965), pp. 101–104. [Reviewed by B. Lercher in MR, vol. 34 (1967), p. 1023.]

Specker (1965). See Kochen and Specker (1965).

3 Author Listing (*Alphabetical*)

Áblonskij, S. V.
(1956) "Funkcional' nyé postroénia v mnogoznačnyh logikah" (Functional constructions in many-valued logics).

Aîzenberg, N. N.
(1965) "Representation of a Sum **mod m** in a Class of Normal Forms of Functions of m-Valued Logic."

Ajdukiewicz, Kazimierz
(1928) *Główne zasady metodologii i logiki formalnej* (Fundamental Principles of Methodology of the Sciences and Formal Logic).

Anderson, Alan Ross
(1962) "The Pure Calculus of Entailment." (With Nuel D. Belnap, Jr.)

Anderson, John M.
Natural Deduction. The Logical Basis of Axiom Systems. (With Henry W. Johnstone, Jr.)

Anonymous
(1952) "Problemas de 'Theoria'. Problema no. I."

Anonymous (ed.)
(1963) "Proceedings of a Colloquium on Modal and Many-valued Logics: Helsinki 23–26 August 1962."

Asser, Günther
(1953) "Die endlichwertigen Łukasiewiczschen Aussagenkalküle."

Aubert, Karl E.
(1948) "Om presisering og generalisering av relasjonsbegrepet" (A clarification and a generalization of the concept of relation).
(1949) "Relations généralisées et indépendence logique des notions de réflexivité, symétrie et transitivité."
(1952) "On the Foundation of the Theory of Relations and the Logical Independence of Generalized Concepts of Reflexivity, Symmetry, and Transitivity."

Ballarat, Maria C. Badillo
(1955a) "Fundamentos en relación con lógica simbólica polivalente."
(1955b) "Esquemas representativos de sistemas regidos por una lógica polivalente."
(1956) "Automatización de los silogismos en una lógica polivalente."
(1957) "Lógica trivalente en la automatización de los circuitos."
(1958) "Aplicación de la lógica polivalente a la teoría de números."

Barker, C. C. H.
(1957) "Some Calculations in Logic."

Baudry, Léon
(1950) *La querelle des futurs contingents: Louvain 1465–1475.*

Baylis, Charles A.
(1936) "Are Some Propositions Neither True nor False?"

de Beauregard, Olivier Costa
(1945) "Extension d'une théorie de M. J. de Neumann au cas des projecteurs non commutables."

Behmann, Heinrich
(1953) "Die typenfreie Logik und die Modalität."

Bell, Eric T.
(1943) "Polynomials on a Finite Discrete Range."

Belluce, L. P.
(1963) "A Weak Completeness Theorem for Infinite-valued First-order Logic." (With C. C. Chang.)
(1964) "Further Results on Infinite-valued Predicate Logic."

Belnap, Nuel D., Jr.
(1962) "The Pure Calculus of Entailment." (With Alan Ross Anderson.)

Bermgann, Gustav
(1949) "The Finite Representations of S5."

Bernstein, B. A.
(1928) "Modular Representations of Finite Algebras."
Birkhoff, Garrett
(1936) "The Logic of Quantum Mechanics." (With John von Neumann.)
(1940) *Lattice Theory.*
Bochénski, Inocenty M.
(1956) *Formale Logik.*
(1960) *A Precis of Mathematical Logic*
(1962) *Grundriss der Logistik.* (With Albert Menne.)
Bochvar, D. A.
(1939) "Ob odnom tréhznačnom isčislénii i égo priménénii k analizu paradoksov klassičéskogo rasširénnogo funkcional'nogo isčislénia" (On a three-valued logical calculus and its application to the analysis of contradictions).
(1943) "K voprosu o néprotivoréčivosti odnogo tréhznačnogo isčislenia" (On the consistency of a 3-valued calculus).
Boehner, Philotheus
(1944) "K voprosu o paradoksah matématičéskoj logiki i téorii množéstv (To the question of paradoxes of the mathematical-logic and theory of sets).
(1945) *The "Tractatus de praedestinatione et de praescientia Dei et de futuris contingentibus" of William Ockham.*
Boll, Marcel
(1950) "A propos des logiques polyvalentes: Les modalités et la vraisemblance." (With J. Reinhardt.)
Borkowski, Ludwik
(1958) "The Logical Works of J. Łukasiewicz." (With J. Słupecki.)
Brouwer, L. E. J.
(1925a) "Intuitionistische Zerlegung mathematischer Grundbegriffe."
(1925b) "Über die Bedeutung des Satzes vom ausgeschlossenen Dritten in der Mathematik, insbesondere in der Funktionentheorie."
Bull, R. A.
(1964) "An Axiomatization of Prior's modal calculus *Q*."
Butler, Ronald J.
(1955) "Aristotle's Sea Fight and Three-valued Logic."
Carnap, Rudolf
(1943) *The Formalization of Logic.*
(1950) *Logical Foundations of Probability.*
Caton, Charles E.
(1963) "A Stipulation of Modal Propositional Calculus in Terms of Modalized Truth-values."
Chandrasekharan, Komaravola
(1944) "Partially Ordered Sets and Symbolic Logic."
Chang, Chen Chung
(1958a) "Proof of an Axiom of Łukasiewicz."
(1958b) "Algebraic Analysis of Many-valued Logics."
(1959) "A New Proof of the Completeness of the Łukasiewicz Axioms."
(1961a) "Theory of Models of Infinite-valued Logics."
(1961b) "Prime Ideal Characterization of Generalized Post Algebras." (With Alfred Horn.)
(1962) "Model Theories with Truth Values in a Uniform Space." (With H. Jerome Keisler.)
(1963a) "Logic with Positive and Negative Truth Values."

(1963b) "The Axiom of Comprehension in Infinite-valued Logic."
(1963c) "Continuous Model Theory." (With H. Jerome Keisler.)
(1963d) "A Weak Completeness Theorem for Infinite-valued First-order Logic." (With L. P. Belluce.)
(1965) "Infinite-valued Logic as a Basis for Set Theory."

Chen, Chiang-yeh
(1951) "A Note on the 4-Valued Propositional Calculus and the Four Colour Problem." (With Shih-hua Hu.)

Christensen, Neils E.
(1957) "Further Comments on Two-valued Logic."

Church, Alonzo
(1953) "Non-normal Truth-tables for the Propositional Calculus."
(1956a) *Introduction to Mathematical Logic.*
(1956b) "Laws of Thought."

Clay, Robert E.
(1962a) "Note on Słupecki *T*-functions."
(1962b) "A Simple Proof of Functional Completeness in Many-valued Logics Based on Łukasiewicz's *C* and *N*."
(1963) "A Standard Form for Łukasiewicz Many-valued Logics."

Cohen, Jonathan
(1951) "Three-valued Ethics."

Czeżowski, Tadeusz
(1949) *Logika. Podrecznik dla studiujacych nauki filozoficzne* (Logic. Textbook for Students of the Philosophical Sciences).

Destouches, Jean-Louis
(1938) *Essai sur la forme générale des théories physiques.*
(1942) *Principes fondamentaux de physique théorique.*
(1946) *Cours de logique et philosophie générale. I. Méthodologie de la physique: théorique moderne. II. Notions de logistique.*

Dienes, Paul
(1949) "On Ternary Logic."

Dienes, Z. P.
(1949) "On an Implication Function in Many-valued Systems of Logic."

Dreben, Burton
(1960) "Relation of *m*-Valued Quantificational Logic to 2-Valued Quantificational Logic."

Ducasse, Curt J.
(1941) "Truth, Verifiability, and Propositions about the Future."

Dugundji, James
(1940) "Note on a Property of Matrices for Lewis and Langford's Calculi of Propositions."

Dumitriu, Anton
(1943) *Logica Polivalenta* (Many-valued Logic).

Dummett, Michael
(1959) "A Propositional Calculus with Denumerable Matrix."

Emch, Gérard
(1965) "Structures logiques et mathématiques en physique quantique." (With J. M. Jauch.)

Evans, Trevor
(1957) "Sheffer Stroke Functions in Many-valued Logics." (With Lane Hardy.)
(1958) "On Słupecki *T*-functions." (With P. B. Schwartz.)

Fadini, Angelo
(1962) "Il calcolo delle classi in una logica a tre valori di verità."
Farber, Marvin
(1942) "Logical Systems and the Principles of Logic."
Fenstad, Jens Erik
(1964) "On the Consistency of the Axiom of Comprehension in the Łukasiewicz Infinite-valued Logic."
Février, Paulette (or Destouches-Février)
(1937a) "Les relations d'incertitude de Heisenberg et la logique."
(1937b) "Sur une forme générale de la définition d'une logique."
(1949) "Logique et théories physiques."
(1951) *La structure des théories physiques.*
(1952) "Applications des logiques modales en physique quantique."
(1959) "Logical Structure of Physical Theories."
Feyerabend, Paul
(1958) "Reichenbach's Interpretation of Quantum-Mechanics."
Feys, Robert
(1937–38) "Les logiques nouvelles des modalités."
(1949) *De ontwikkeling van het logisch denken* (The Development of Logical Thought).
(1965) *Modal Logics.*
Fletcher, T. J.
(1963) "Models of Many-valued Logics."
Foster, Alfred L.
(1949) "The *n*-ality Theory of Rings."
(1950) "On *n*-ality Theories in Rings and Their Logical Algebras, Including Triality Principle in Three-valued Logics."
Foxley, Eric
(1961) "Testing the Independence of a System of Axioms, Using a Logical Computer."
(1962) "The Determination of All Sheffer Functions in 3-Valued Logic, Using a Logical Computer."
Frey, Gerhard
(1953) "Bemerkungen zum Problem der mehrwertigen Logiken."
Frink, Orrin, Jr.
(1938) "New Algebras of Logic."
Fuchs, W. R.
(1964) "Ansätze zu einer Quantenlogik."
Gavrilov, G. P.
(1959) "Certain Conditions for Completeness in Countable-valued Logic."
Gazalé, M. J.
(1957) "Multi-valued Switching Functions."
Geach, Peter T.
(1949) "If's and And's."
Gnidenko, V. M.
(1962) "Determination of Orders of Pre-complete Classes in Three-valued Logic."
Goddard, Leonard
(1960) "The Exclusive 'Or'."
Gödel, Kurt
(1932) "Zum intuitionistischen Aussagenkalkül."
(1933a) "Eine Interpretation des intuitionistischen Aussagenkalküls."
(1933b) "Zum Intuitionistischen Aussagenkalkül."
(1935) "Eine Eigenschaft der Realisierungen des Aussagenkalküls."

Gonzalez, Coppola Lorenzo
  (1964) "Sur une construction des algèbres de Łukasiewicz trivalentes." (With Luiz F. T. Monteiro.)
Goodell, John D.
  (1952) "The Foundations of Computing Machinery."
Goodstein, R. L.
  (1958) "Models of Propositional Calculi in Recursive Arithmetic."
Götlind, Erik
  (1951) "A Lésniewski-Mihailescu-theorem for *m*-Valued Propositional Calculi."
  (1952) "Some Sheffer Functions in *n*-Valued Logic."
Greniewski, Henryk
  (1955) *Elementy logiki formalnej* (Elements of Formal Logic).
  (1957) "2^{n+1}wartości logicznych" (2^{n+1} logical values).
Greniewski, Marek
  (1956) "Utilisation des logiques trivalentes dans la théorie des mécanismes automatiques. I. Réalisation des fonctions fondamentales par des circuits."
Günther, Gotthard
  (1953a) "Die philosophische Idee einer nicht-aristotelischen Logik."
  (1953b) "The Logical Parallax."
  (1955) "Dreiwertige Logik und die Heisenbergsche Unbestimmtheitsrelation."
  (1958) "Die aristotelische Logik des Seins und die nicht-aristotelische Logik der Reflexion."
Guthrie, Edwin
  (1916) "The Field of Logic."
Habermann, Edward
  (1936) "Pojecie biegunowości i logika wielawartościowa" (The concept of polarity and many-valued logic).
Hailperin, Theodore
  (1937) "Foundations of Probability in Mathematical Logic."
Halldén, Sören
  (1949a) "On the Decision-Problem of Lewis' Calculus S5."
  (1949b) "The Logic of Nonsense."
Hanson, W. H.
  (1963) "Ternary Threshold Logic."
Hardy, Lane
  (1957) "Sheffer Stroke Functions in Many-valued Logics." (With Trevor Evans.)
Harrop, Ronald
  (1958) "On the Existence of Finite Models and Decision Procedures for Propositional Calculi."
Hartshorne, Charles
  (1964) "Deliberation and Excluded Middle."
Hay, Louise S.
  (1963) "Axiomatization of the Infinite-valued Predicate Calculus."
Helmer, Olaf
  (1945) "A Syntactical Definition of Probability and Degree of Confirmation." (With Paul Oppenheim.)
Hempel, Carl G.
  (1936–37) "Eine rein topologische Form nichtaristotelischer Logik."
  (1937a) "A Purely Topological Form of Non-Aristotelian Logic."
  (1937b) "Ein System verallgemeinerter Negationen."

Henle, Paul
(1951) "*n*-Valued Boolean Algebra."
Heyting, Arend
(1930) "Die Formalen Regeln der intuitionistischen Logik."
(1956) *Intuitionism: An Introduction.*
Hochberg, Herbert
(1954) "Professor Storer on Empiricism."
Horn, Alfred
(1961) "Prime Ideal Characterization of Generalized Post Algebras." (With Chen Chung Chang.)
Hu, Shih-hua (or Tzu-hua Hoo)
(1949) "*m*-Valued Sub-Systems of (*m* + *n*)-Valued Propositional Calculus."
(1951) "A Note on the 4-Valued Propositional Calculus and the Four Colour Problem." (With Chiang-yeh Chen.)
(1955) "Die endlichwertigen und funktionell vollständigen Sub-systeme $\aleph_0$-wertigen Aussagenkalküls."
Itô, Makoto
(1935) "Yûgenko-ryôiki mi okeru kansû ni tuite" (On the generation of all functions in the finitely many-valued algebra of logic).
(1955) "*n*-ti kansû soku (*n*-ti ronri) ni tuite" (On the "lattice of *n*-valued functions" [*n*-valued logic]).
(1956a) "Itigen *n*-ti kansûsoku (ronri) hôteisiki no ippankai ni tuite" (On the general solution of the *n*-valued function-lattice [logical] equation in one variable).
(1956b) "Tagen *n*-ti kansûsoku (ronri) hôteisiki no ippankai ni tuite" (On the general solution of the *n*-valued lattice [logical] equation in several variables).
Jaśkowski, Stanisław
(1936) "Recherches sur le système de la logique intuitioniste."
Jauch, Joseph M.
(1965) "Structures logiques et mathématiques en physique quantique." (With G. Emch.)
Jobe, William H.
(1962) "Functional Completeness and Canonical Forms in Many-valued Logics."
Johnstone, Henry W., Jr.
(1962) *Natural Deduction. The Logical Basis of Axiom Systems.* (With John M. Anderson.)
Joja, Athanase
(1960) "About *tertium non datur.*"
Jordan, Pascual
(1959) "Quantenlogik und das Kommutative Gesetz."
Jordan, Zbigniew A.
(1945) "The Development of Mathematical Logic and of Logical Positivism in Poland between the Two Wars."
(1963) "Logical Determinism."
Jørgensen, Jørgen
(1937) *Traek af deduktionsteoriens udvikling i den nyere tid* (Outline of the Recent Development of the Theory of Deduction).
Jourdain, P. E. B.
(1912) "The Development of the Theories of Mathematical Logic and the Principles of Mathematics."
Kaila, Eino
(1926) *Die Prinzipien der Wahrscheinlichkeitslogik.*

Kalicki, Jan

(1950a) "Note on Truth-tables."

(1950b) "A Test for the Existence of Tautologies According to Many-valued Truth-tables."

(1954a) "On Equivalent Truth-tables of Many-valued Logics."

(1954b) "An Undecidable Problem in the Algebra of Truth-tables."

Kalmár, László

(1934) "Über die Axiomatisierbarkeit des Aussagenkalküls."

Katsoff, Louis O.

(1937) "Modality and Probability."

Kauf, David Karl

(1954) "A Comment on Hochberg's Reply to Storer."

Keisler, H. Jerome

(1962) "Model Theories with Truth Values in a Uniform Space." (With Chen Chung Chang.)

(1963) "Continuous Model Theory." (With Chen Chung Chang.)

Kirin, Vladimir G.

(1963) "On the Polynomial Representation of Operators in the *n*-Valued Propositional Calculus."

Kiss, Stephen A.

(1947) *Transformations on Lattices and Structures of Logic.*

Klaus, Georg

(1965) "Über einen Ansatz zur mehrwertigen Mengenlehre."

Kleene, Stephen C.

(1938) "On a Notation for Ordinal Numbers."

(1952) *Introduction to Metamathematics.*

Kline, George L.

(1965) "N. A. Vasil'év and the Development of Many-valued Logics."

Klósak, Kazimierz

(1948) "Teoria indeterminizmu ontologicznego a trójwartościowa logika zdań prof. Jana Łukasiewcza" (The theory of ontological indeterminism and the three-valued logic of propositions of Prof. Jan Łukasiewicz).

(1949) "Konieczność wyjścia poza logike dwuwartościowa" (The necessity of going beyond the two-valued logic).

Kneale, William and Martha

(1962) *The Development of Logic.*

Kneebone, G. T.

(1963) *Mathematical Logic and the Foundations of Mathematics: An Introductory Survey.*

Kochen, Simon

(1965) "Logical Structures in Quantum Theory." (With E. P. Specker.)

Kokoszyńska, Maria

(1951) "A Refutation of the Relativism of Truth."

Kolmogorov, A. N.

(1924–25) "O principé *tertium non datur*" (The *tertium non datur* principle).

(1932) "Zur Deutung der intuitionistischen Logik."

Kotarbiński, Tadeusz

(1957) *Wylady z dziejów logiki* (Outlines of the History of Logic).

Kreisel, Georg

(1962) "On Weak Completeness of Intuitionistic Predicate Logic."

Kripke, Saul A.
(1963) "Semantical Analysis of Modal Logic. I. Normal Modal Propositional Calculi."
Kurihara, Toshihiko
(1955) "Yûgen tatironri no denki kairo ni yoru hyôgen ni tuite" (On the representation of finitely many-valued logics by electric circuits).
Kuznetzov, B. G.
(1959) "Ob osnovax kvantovo-reljativistakoj logiki" (On quantum and relativistic logic).
Landsberg, P. T.
(1953) "On Heterological Paradoxes."
Langford, Cooper H.
(1932) Symbolic Logic. (With C. I. Lewis.)
Leonard, Henry S.
(1951) "Two-valued Truth Tables for Modal Functions."
Levi, Isaac
(1959) "Putnam's Three Truth-values."
Lewis, C. I.
(1932) "Alternative Systems of Logic."
(1932) Symbolic Logic. (With Cooper H. Langford.)
(1933) "Note Concerning Many-valued Logical Systems."
Lindenbaum, Adolf
(1930) "Remarques sur une question de la méthode axiomatique."
Linke, Paul F.
(1948) "Die mehrwertigen Logiken und das Wahrheitsproblem."
(1952) "Eigentliche und uneigentliche Logik."
Linsky, Leonard
(1954) "Professor Donald Williams on Aristotle."
Łoś, Jerzy
(1948) "Logiki wielowartosćiowe a formalicacja funkcji intensjonalnych" (Many-valued logics and the formalization of intensional functions).
Łukasiewicz, Jan
(1910) "Über den Satz des Widerspruchs bei Aristoteles."
(1920) "O logice trojwartosciowej" (On three-valued logic).
(1921) "Logika dwuwartościowa" (Two-valued logic).
(1923) "O Determiniźmie" (On determinism).
(1929) Elementy Logiki Matematycznej (Elements of Mathematical Logic).
(1930a) "Philosophische Bemerkungen zu mehrwertigen Systemen des Aussagen-kalküls."
(1930b) "Untersuchungen über den Aussagenkalkül." (With Alfred Tarski.)
(1934) "Z historji logiki zdań" (From the history of the logic of propositions).
(1935-36) "Zur vollen dreiwertigen Aussagenlogik."
(1936) "Bedeutung der logischen Analyse für die Erkenntnis."
(1937) "Wobronie logistyki" (In defense of logistic).
(1938) "Die Logik und das Grundlagenproblem."
(1952) "On the Intuitionistic Theory of Deduction."
(1953a) "A System of Modal Logic."
(1953b) "A System of Modal Logic."
(1961) Z Zagadnién Logiki i Filozofii (Logical and Philosophical Papers).
Lupasco, Stéphane
(1945) "Valeurs logiques et contradiction."

MacColl, Hugh
(1877–78) "The Calculus of Equivalent Statements and Integration Limits."
(1877–98) "The Calculus of Equivalent Statements."
(1880–1906) "Symbolic Reasoning."
(1899) Review of Whitehead's *Universal Algebra.*
(1900–01) "Mathematics at the International Congress of Philosophy, Paris 1900."
(1901) "La logique symbolique et ses applications."
(1903) "La Logique Symbolique."
(1904) "La Logique Symbolique."
(1906) *Symbolic Logic and Its Applications.*
(1907) "Symbolic Logic (A Reply)."
(1908) " 'If' and 'Imply.' "

McKinsey, J. C. C.
(1936) "On the Generation of the Functions Cpq and Np of Łukasiewicz and Tarski by Means of a Single Binary Operation."
(1940) "A Correction to Lewis and Langford's *Symbolic Logic.*"
(1948) "Some Theorems about the Sentential Calculi of Lewis and Heyting." (With Alfred Tarski.)
(1954) Review of Paulette Destouches-Février, *La Structure des Théories Physiques.* (With Patrick Suppes.)

McNaughton, Robert
(1951) "A Theorem about Infinite-valued Sentential Logic."

Malisoff, William M.
(1936) "Meanings in Multi-valued logic (Toward a general semantics)."
(1941) "Meanings in Multi-valued Logics."

Margaris, Angelo
(1958) "A Problem of Rosser and Turquette."

Margenau, Henry
(1934) "On the Application of Many-valued Systems of Logic to Physics."
(1939) "Probability, Many-valued Logics, and Physics."
(1950) *The Nature of Physical Reality.*

Martin, Gottfried
(1949) "Über ein zweiwertiges Modell einer vierwertigen Logik."

Martin, Norman M.
(1950) "Some Analogues of the Sheffer Stroke Function in n-Valued Logic."
(1951) "A Note on Sheffer Functions in n-Valued Logic."
(1952) "Sheffer Functions and Axiom Sets in m-Valued Propositional Logic."
(1954) "The Sheffer Functions of Three-valued Logic."

Martynjuk, V. V.
(1960) "Investigation of Certain Classes of Functions in Many-valued Logics."

Mazurkiewicz, Stefan
(1932) "Zur Axiomatik der Wahrscheinlichkeitslehre."
(1934) "Über die Grundlagen der Wahrscheinlichkeitsrechnung."

Menne, Albert
(1962) *Grundriss der Logistik.* (With Inocenty M. Bocheński.)
(1964) "Ueber monadische Valenzfunktionen."

Meredith, Charles A.
(1958) "The Dependence of an Axiom of Łukasiewicz."
(1963) "Notes on the Axiomatics of Propositional Calculus." (With A. N. Prior.)

Metallmann, Joachim
(1939) *Wprowadzenie do zagadnień filozoficznych, Cześć I* (Introduction to Philosophical Problems, Part I).

Meyer, Herman
  (1949) *Kennis en realiteit* (Knowledge and reality).
Michalski, Konstanty
  (1937) "Le problème de la volonté à Oxford et à Paris au XIVe siècle."
Mittelstaedt, Peter
  (1961) "Quantenlogik."
Mlĕziva, Miroslav
  (1958) "Teorie výroku" (Theory of propositions).
  (1961) "On the Axiomatization of Three-valued Propositional Logic."
Moch, François
  (1956a) "La logique des attitudes."
  (1956b) "Des antinomies classiques à la Logique de Mme. Février-Destouches."
Moh Shaw-kwei
  (1954) "Logical Paradoxes for Many-valued Systems."
  (1958) "Yow-hsian-zhe fang-zhen hsi-t'ung ti kung-li-hua" (Axiomatization of many-valued logical systems).
Moisil, Grigor C.
  (1937–38) "Sur le mode problématique."
  (1938) "Sur la théorie classique de la modalité des jugements."
  (1939a) "Les principes de la logique et l'idée de chaîne."
  (1939b) "Recherches sur le syllogisme."
  (1939c) "La logique formelle et son problème actuel."
  (1940) "Recherches sur les logiques non-chrysippiennes."
  (1940–41) "Sur la structure algébrique de la logique de M. Bochvar."
  (1941a) "Notes sur les logiques non-chrysippiennes."
  (1941b) "Recherches sur la théorie des chaînes."
  (1941c) "Contributions à l'étude des logiques non-chrysippiennes. I. Un nouveau système d'axiomes pour les algèbres Łukasiewicziennes tetra-valentes."
  (1941d) "Remarques sur la logique modale du concept."
  (1941e) "Sur les anneaux de caractéristique 2 ou 3 et leurs applications."
  (1941f) "Sur les théories déductives à logique non-chrysippienne."
  (1942a) "Logique modale."
  (1942b) "Contributions à l'étude des logiques non-chrysippiennes. II. Anneaux engendrés par les algèbres Łukasiewicziennes tetravalentes centrées."
  (1942c) "Contributions à l'étude des logiques non-chrysippiennes. III. Anneaux engendrés par les algèbres Łukasiewicziennes tetravalentes axées."
  (1943) "Contributions à l'étude des logiques non-chrysippiennes. IV. Sur la logique de Mr. Becker."
  (1945) "L'algebra e la logica."
  (1956a) "Utilisation des logiques trivalentes dans la théorie des mécanismes automatiques. II. Equation caractéristique d'un relaipaolarise."
  (1956b) "Sur l'application des logiques à trois valeurs à l'étude des schémas à contacts et relais."
  (1956–59) "Intrebuintarea logicilor trivalente în teoriă algebrică a mecanismelor automate" (Use of three-valued logic in the algebraic theory of automata).
  (1957) "Aplicatrile logicii trivalente in studiul functionarii reale a schemelor cu contacte si relee" (Application of three-valued logic in the study of the real operation of networks with contacts and relays).
  (1959a) "Rapport sur le développement dans la R.P.R. de la théorie algébrique des mécanismes automatiques."
  (1959b) "Sur l'application de la logique à trois valeurs à l'étude des circuits électriques à contacts, redresseurs et résistances."

(1959c) *Teoria algebrică a mecanismelor automate* (The Algebriac Theory of Automatic Machines).

(1959d) "La logique à cinq valeurs et ses applications à l'étude des circuits électriques."

(1959e) "La logique à plusieurs valeurs et l'automatique."

(1960a) "Sur les idéaux des algèbres Łukasiewicziennes trivalentes."

(1960b) "Asupra logicii lue Bochvar" (On the logic of Bochvar).

(1960c) *Logica matematica si teknica modernă: Logicile cu mai multe valori si circuitele cu contacte si relee* (Mathematical Logic and Modern Technology: Many-valued Logic and Relay-contact Circuits).

(1961a) "Les Logiques à plusieurs valeurs et l'automatique."

(1961b) "The Predicate Calculus in Three-valued Logic."

(1962a) "Sur le principe du déterminisme."

(1962b) "Sur la logique à trois valeurs de Łukasiewicz."

(1962c) "Les logiques non-chrysippiennes et leurs applications."

(1963) "Les logiques non-chrysippiennes et leurs applications."

(1964) "Sur les logiques de Łukasiewicz à un nombre fini de valeurs."

(1964–65) "The Interest of the Actual Operation of Switching Circuits for the Logician."

(1965) *Încercări vechi si noi de logică neclasica* (Essays Old and New on Nonclassical Logic).

Monteiro, Antonio

(1963) "Sur la définition des algèbres de Łukasiewicz trivalentes."

Monteiro, Luiz F. T.

(1964) "Sur une construction des algèbres de Łukasiewicz trivalentes." (With L. Gongalez Coppola.)

Mora, José Ferrater

(1951) *Diccionario de filosofía.*

Mostowski, Andrzej

(1948) *Logika matematyczna* (Mathematical Logic).

(1955) *The Present State of Investigations on the Foundations of Mathematics.* (With collaborators.)

(1957) "L'oeuvre scientifique de Jan Łukasiewicz dans le domaine de la logique mathématique."

(1961a) "Axiomatizability of Some Many-valued Predicate Calculi."

(1961b) "An Example of a Non-axiomatizable Many-valued Logic."

(1963) "The Hilbert Epsilon Function in Many-valued Logics."

Müller, Hans R.

(1940) "Algebraischer Aussagenkalkül."

Naess, Arne

(1948) *Symbolsk logikk* (Symbolic Logic).

Nagel, Ernest

(1946) "Professor Reichenbach on Quantum Mechanics: A Rejoinder."

Nakamura, Akira

(1962a) "On the Infinitely Many-valued Threshold Logics and von Wright's System *M*."

(1962b) "On an Axiomatic System of the Infinitely Many-valued Threshold Logics."

(1963a) "A Note on Truth-value Functions in the Infinitely Many-valued Logics."

(1963b) "On an Axiomatic System of the Infinitely Many-valued Threshold Predicate Calculi."

(1963c) "On a Simple Axiomatic System of the Infinitely Many-valued Logic Based on $\wedge$, $\rightarrow$."

(1964) "Truth-value Stipulations for the von Wright System M' and the Heyting System."
(1965) "On the Infinitely Many-valued Double-threshold Logic."
von Neumann, John
(1927) "Zur Hilbertschen Beweistheorie."
(1936) "The Logic of Quantum Mechanics." (With G. Birkhoff.)
(1962) "Quantum Logics."
Oppenheim, Paul
(1945) "A Syntactical Definition of Probability and Degree of Confirmation." (With Olaf Helmer.)
Peirce, Charles Sanders
(1902) "Minute Logic."
(1914) *Collected Papers of Charles Sanders Peirce.*
Pogorzelski, Nitold A.
(1964) "The Deduction Theorem for Łukasiewicz' Many-valued Propositional Calculi."
Post, Emil
(1921) "Introduction to a General Theory of Elementary Propositions."
Prior, Arthur Norman
(1952) "In What Sense Is Modal Logic Many-valued?"
(1953a) "On Propositions Neither Necessary nor Impossible."
(1953b) "Three-valued Logic and Future Contingents."
(1955a) "Many-valued and Modal Systems: An Intuitive Approach."
(1955b) "Curry's Paradox and 3-Valued Logic."
(1955c) *Formal Logic.*
(1957a) *Time and Modality.*
(1957b) "The Necessary and the Possible: The First of Three Talks on 'The Logic Game'. "
(1957c) "Symbolism and Analogy: The Second of Three Talks on 'The Logic Game'."
(1957d) "Many-valued Logics: The Last of Three Talks on 'The Logic Game'."
(1958–59) "Notes on a Group of New Modal Systems."
(1962) "The Formalities of Omniscience."
(1963a) "The Theory of Implication."
(1963b) "Notes on the Axiomatics of Propositional Calculus." (With C. A. Meredith.)
Putnam, Hilary
(1957) "Three-valued Logic."
Rasiowa, Helena
(1950) "Zdziedziny logiki matematycznej. II. Logiki wielowartościowe Łukasiewicza" (From the domain of mathematical logic. II. The many-valued logics of Łukasiewicz).
(1955) "O pewnym fragmencie implikacyjnego rachunku zdań" (On a fragment of the implicative propositional calculus).
Reichbach, Juliusz
(1962) "On the Connection of the First-order Functional Calculus with Many-valued Propositional Calculi."
(1963) "About Connection of the First-order Functional Calculus with Many-valued Propositional Calculi."
(1964) "A Note about Connection of the First-order Functional Calculus with Many-valued Propositional Calculi."
Reichenbach, Hans
(1932) "Wahrscheinlichkeitslogik."
(1935) *Wahrscheinlichkeitslehre.*
(1935–36a) "Wahrscheinlichkeitslogik."
(1935–36b) "Wahrscheinlichkeitslogik und Alternativlogik."

(1937) "Les fondements logiques du calcul des probabilités."
(1944) *Philosophical Foundations of Quantum Mechanics.*
(1946) "Reply to Ernest Nagel's Criticism of My Views on Quantum Mechanics."
(1949a) *The Theory of Probability: An Inquiry into the Logical and Mathematical Foundations of the Calculus of Probability.*
(1949b) *Philosophische Grundlagen der Quantenmechanik.*
(1951) "Über die erkenntnistheoretische Problemlage und den Gebrauch einer dreiwertigen Logik in der Quantenmechanik."
(1952–54) "Les fondements logiques de la théorie des quanta: Utilisation d'une logique à trois valeurs."
Reinhardt, Jacques
(1950) "A propos des logiques polyvalentes: Les modalités et la vraisemblance." (With Marcel Boll.)
Reiser, Oliver Leslie
(1952) "Physics, Probability, and Multi-valued Logic."
Rescher, Nicholas
(1955) "Some Comments on Two-valued Logic."
(1962) "Quasi-truth-functional Systems of Propositional Logic."
(1963) "A Probabilistic Approach to Modal Logic."
(1964) "Quantifiers in Many-valued Logic."
(1965) "An Intuitive Interpretation of Systems of Four-valued Logic."
Ridder, Jacob
(1948) "Über mehrwertige Aussagenkalküle und mehrwertige engere Prädikaten-kalküle I–III."
(1949) "Sur quelques logiques multivalentes."
Rose, Alan
(1950a) "A Lattice-Theoretic Characterization of Three-valued Logic."
(1950b) "Completeness of Łukasiewicz-Tarski Propositional Calculi."
(1951a) "Conditional Disjunction as a Primitive Connective for the m-Valued Propositional Calculus."
(1951b) "A New Proof of a Theorem of Dienes."
(1951c) "Axiom Systems for Three-valued Logic."
(1951d) "Systems of Logic Whose Truth-values Form Lattices."
(1951e) "A Lattice-Theoretic Characterization of the $\aleph_0$-Valued Propositional Calculus."
(1951f) "The Degree of Completeness of Some Łukasiewicz-Tarski Propositional Calculi."
(1951g) "An Axiom System for Three-valued Logic."
(1952a) "Some Generalized Sheffer Functions."
(1952b) "The Degree of Completeness of the m-Valued Łukasiewicz Propositional Calculus."
(1952c) "A Formalisation of Post's m-Valued Propositional Calculus."
(1952d) "Le degré de saturation du calcul propositionnel implicatif à trois valeurs de Sobociński."
(1952e) "Eight-valued Geometry."
(1952f) "An Extension of Computational Logic."
(1952g) "Sur un ensemble de fonctions primitives pour le calcul des prédicats du premier ordre lequel constitue son propre dual."
(1952h) "An Extension of the Calculus of Non-Contradiction."
(1952i) "Extensions of Some Theorems of Schmidt and McKinsey."
(1953a) "The Degree of Completeness of the $\aleph_0$-Valued Łukasiewicz Propositional Calculus."

(1953b) "Conditional Disjunction as a Primitive Connective for the Erweiterter Aussagenkalkül."

(1953c) "The *m*-Valued Calculus of Non-Contradiction."

(1953d) "Fragments of the *m*-Valued Propositional Calculus."

(1953e) "A Formalization of Sobociński's Three-valued Implicational Propositional Calculus."

(1953f) "A Formalization of an $\aleph_0$-Valued Propositional Calculus."

(1953g) "Some Self-dual Primitive Functions for Propositional Calculi."

(1954) "Sur les fonctions définissables dans une logique à un nombre infini de valeurs."

(1955a) "Le degré de saturation du calcul propositionnel implicatif à *m* valeurs de Łukasiewicz."

(1955b) "A Gödel Theorem for an Infinite-valued Erweiterter Aussagenkalkül."

(1956a) "An Alternative Formalisation of Sobociński's Three-valued Implicational Propositional Calculus."

(1956b) "Formalisation du calcul propositionnel implicatif a $\aleph_0$ valeurs de Łukasiewicz."

(1956c) "Some Formalisations of $\aleph_0$-Valued Propositional Calculi."

(1958a) "Many-valued Logical Machines."

(1958b) "Sur les définitions de l'implication et de la négation dans certains systèmes de logique dont les valeurs forment des treillis."

(1958c) "Applications of Logical Computers to the Construction of Electrical Control Tables for Signalling Frames."

(1958d) "Fragments of Many-valued Statement Calculi." (With J. B. Rosser.)

(1960a) "An Extension of a Theorem of Margaris."

(1960b) "Sur les schémas d'axiomes pour les calculs propositionnels à *m* valeurs ayant des valeurs sur désignées."

(1961a) "Self-dual Binary and Ternary Connectives for *m*-Valued Propositional Calculi."

(1961b) "Sur certains calculs propositionnels à *m* valeurs ayant un seul foncteur primitif lequel constitue son propre dual."

(1962a) "An Alternative Generalisation of the Concept of Duality."

(1962b) "Extensions of Some Theorems of Anderson and Belnap."

(1962c) "A Simplified Self *m*-al Set of Primitive Functors for the *m*-Valued Propositional Calculus."

(1962d) "Sur un ensemble complet de foncteurs primitifs indépendants pour le calcul propositionnel trivalent lequel constitue son propre trial."

(1962e) "Sur les applications de la logique polyvalente à la construction des machines Turing."

(1962f) "Sur un ensemble de foncteurs primitifs pour le calcul propositionnel à *m* valeurs lequel constitue son propre *m*-al."

(1964a) "Formalisations de calculs propositionnels polyvalents à foncteurs variables."

(1964b) "Note sur la formalisation de calculs propositionnels polyvalents à foncteurs variables."

(1965) "A Formalisation of Post's *m*-Valued Propositional Calculus with Variable Functors."

Rose, Gene F.

(1953) "Propositional Calculus and Realizability."

Rosenbaum, Ira

(1950) *Introduction to Mathematical Logic and Its Applications.*

Rosenbloom, Paul C.

(1942) "Post Algebras. I. Postulates and General Theory."

(1950) *The Elements of Mathematical Logic.*

Rosser, James Barkley

(1939) "The Introduction of Quantification into a Three-valued Logic."

(1941a) "Many-valued Logic."

(1941b) "On the Many-valued Logics."

(1945) "Axiom Schemes for *m*-Valued Propositional Calculi." (With A. R. Turquette

(1948) "Axiom Schemes for *m*-Valued Functional Calculi of First Order. Part I. Definition of Axiom Schemes and Proof of Plausibility." (With A. R. Turquette.)

(1949) "A Note on the Deductive Completeness of *m*-Valued Propositional Logic." (With A. R. Turquette.)

(1951) "Axiom Schemes for *m*-Valued Functional Calculi of First Order. Part II. Deductive Completeness." (With A. R. Turquette.)

(1952) *Many-valued Logics.* (With A. R. Turquette.)

(1953) *Logic for Mathematicians.*

(1958) "Fragments of Many-valued Statement Calculi." (With Alan Rose.)

(1960) "Axiomatization of Infinite-valued Logics."

Rougier, Louis

(1939) "La relativité de la logique."

Rutledge, Joseph D.

(1960) "On the Definition of an Infinitely-Many-valued Predicate Calculus."

Salomaa, Arto

(1959) "On Many-valued Systems of Logic."

(1963) "Some Analogues of Sheffer Functions in Infinite-valued Logics."

(1965) "On Some Algebraic Notions in the Theory of Truth-functions."

Scarpellini, Bruno

(1962) "Die Nichtaxiomatisierbarkeit des unendlichwertigen Prädikatenkalküls von Łukasiewicz."

(1963) "Eine Anwendung der unendlichwertigen Logik auf topologische Raüme."

Schaefer, David H.

(1955) "A Rectifier Algebra."

Scheibe, Erhard

(1964) *Die kontingenten Aussagen in der Physik.*

Schiller, F. C. S.

(1935) "Multi-valued Logics—and Others."

Schmierer, Zygmunt

(1936) "O funkcjach charakterystycznych w logikach wielowartościowych" (On characteristic functions in many-valued systems of logic).

Schock, Rolf

(1964a) "On Finitely Many-valued Logics."

(1964b) "On Denumerably Many-valued Logics."

(1965) "Some Theorems on the Relative Strengths of Many-valued Logics."

Schofield, Peter

(1964) "On a Correspondence between Many-valued and Two-valued Logics."

Scholz, Heinrich

(1953) Review of Baudry's *La querelle des futurs contingents: Louvain 1465–1475.*

(1957) "In memoriam Jan Łukasiewicz."

Schröter, Karl

(1955) "Methoden zur Axiomatisierung beliebiger Aussagen–und Prädikaten-kalküle."

Schwartz, P. B.
(1958) "Om Słupecki *T*-functions." (With Trevor Evans.)
Serrus, Charles
(1945) *Traité de logique.*
Shannon, Claude E.
(1938) "A Symbolic Analysis of Relay'and Switching Circuits."
Shestakov, V. I.
(1946) "Prédstavlénié haraktérističéskih funkcij prédloženij posrédstvom vyraženij, réalizuémyh réléjno-kontaktymi shémani" (Representation of characteristic functions of propositions by expressions realizable by relay-contact circuits).
(1953) "Modélirovanié opéracij isčisléniá prédloženij posrédstvom prostéjših četyréhpolúsynh shém" (Modeling the operations of the propositional calculus by means of the simplest four-pole networks).
(1960a) "O dvojnaj arixmetičeskoj interpretacii trexznačnogo isčislenija vyskazyvanij."
(1960b) "A Dual Arithmetic Interpretation of the Three-valued Propositional Calculus Utilized in the Simulation of This Calculus by Relay-Contact Networks."
(1964) "On the Relationship between Certain Three-valued Logical Calculi."
Shirai, Tameharu
(1937) "On the Pseudo-Set."
Sierpiński, Warclaw
(1960–61) "Sur un problème de la logique à *n* valeurs."
Siosen, Federico M.
(1964) "Further Axiomatizations of the Łukasiewicz Three-valued Calculus."
Skolem, Thoralf
(1929) "Über einige Grundlagenfragen der Mathematik."
(1957a) "Mengenlehre gegründet auf einer Logik mit unendlich vielen Wahrheitswerten."
(1957b) "Bemerkungen zum Komprehensionsaxiom."
(1960) "A Set Theory Based on a Certain 3-Valued Logic."
Słupecki, Jerzy
(1936) "Der volle dreiwertige Aussagenkalkül."
(1939a) "Dowód aksjomatyzowalności pelnych systemów wielowartościowych rachunku zdań" (Proof of the axiomatizability of full many-valued systems of propositional calculus).
(1939b) "Kryterium pelności wielowartościowych systemów logiki zdań" (A criterion of completeness of many-valued systems of propositional logic).
(1946) "Pelny trójwartościowy rachunek zdań" (The complete three-valued propositional calculus).
(1958) "The Logical Works of J. Łukasiewicz." (With L. Borkowski.)
Smetanîc, Ja. S.
(1961) "Propositional Calculi with Additional Operations."
Smiley, Timothy
(1961) "On Łukasiewicz's Ł-modal System."
(1962) "Analytic Implication and 3-Valued Logic."
Sobociński, Boleslaw
(1936) "Aksjomatyzacja pewnych wielowartoś-ciowych systemów teorji dedukcji" (Axiomatization of certain many-valued systems of the theory of deduction).
(1952) "Axiomatization of a Partial System of Three-valued Calculus of Propositions."
(1956) "In memoriam Jan Łukasiewicz."
(1957a) "La génesis de la Escuela Polaca de Lógica."

(1957b) "Jan Łukasiewicz (1878–1956)."

(1961) "A Note Concerning the Many-valued Propositional Calculi."

Specker, E. P.

(1965) "Logical Structures in Quantum Theory." (With S. Kochen.)

Storer, Thomas

(1946) "The Logic of Value Imperatives."

(1953) "A Note on Empiricism."

(1954) "The Notion of Tautology."

Sueki, Takehiro

(1952–54) "The Formulization of Two-valued and *n*-Valued Systems, I, II, III."

Sugihara, Takeo

(1950) "Tachi ronrigaku" (Many-valued logic).

(1951) "Brouwer ronrigaku no tachi-ronrigaku-teki tokusei" (Many-valued logical characteristics of Brouwerian logic).

(1952) "Negation in Many-valued Logic."

(1956) "Four-valued Propositional Calculus with One Designated Truth-value."

(1958) "A Three-valued Logic with Meaning-Operator."

Summersbee, Stuart

(1963) "Programming the Functions of Formal Logic. II. Multi-valued Logics." (With A. Walters.)

Suppes, Patrick

(1954) Review of Paulette Destouches-Février, *La Structure des Théories Physiques.* (With J. C. C. McKinsey.)

Suszko, Roman

(1957) "A Formal Theory of the Logical Values, I."

Swift, J. D.

(1952) "Algebraic Properties of *n*-Valued Propositional Calculi."

Takekuma, Ryōichi

(1954) "On a Nine-valued Propositional Calculus."

Tamari, Dov

(1952–54)" "Some Mutual Applications of Logic and Mathematics."

Tarski, Alfred

(1930) "Untersuchungen über den Aussagenkalkül." (With J. Łukasiewicz.)

(1932) "Untersuchungen über der Aussagenkalkül."

(1935–36) "Wahrscheinlichkeitslehre und mehrwertige Logik."

(1938) "Der Aussagenkalkül und die Topologie."

(1948) "Some Theorems about the Sentential Calculi of Lewis and Heyting." (With J. C. C. McKinsey.)

(1956) *Logic, Semantics, Metamathematics: Papers from 1923 to 1938.*

Tavanec, P. V.

(1960) *The Application of Logic to Science and Technology.* (With È. Ja. Kol'man, G. N. Povarov, S. A. Janovskaja, eds.)

Taylor, Richard

(1957) "The Problem of Future Contingencies."

Teh, H. H.

(1963) "On 3-Valued Sentential Calculus: An Axiomatic Approach."

Thiele, Helmut

(1958) "Theorie der endlich-wertigen Łukasiewiczschen Prädikatenkalküle der ersten Stufe."

Thomas, Ivo

(1962) "On the Infinity of Positive Logic."

Tîrnoveanu, Mircea
  (1962) "Sur les extensions des types P et Q de la logique L_Ω^s."
Törnebohm, Hakan
  (1957) "On Two Logical Systems Proposed in the Philosophy of Quantum Mechanics."
Traczyk, Tadeusz
  (1962) "On Axioms and Some Properties of Post Algebras."
Turowicz, A. B.
  (1960) "Sur une méthode algébrique de vérification des théorèmes de la logique des énoncés."
Turquette, Atwell R.
  (1944) "A Study and Extension of m-Valued Symbolic Logics."
  (1945a) Review of Reichenbach's *Philosophical Foundations of Quantum Mechanics.*
  (1945b) "Axiom Schemes for m-Valued Propositional Calculi." (With J. B. Rosser.)
  (1948) "Axiom Schemes for m-Valued Functional Calculi of First Order. Part I. Definition of Axiom Schemes and Proof of Plausibility." (With J. B. Rosser.)
  (1949) "A Note on the Deductive Completeness of m-Valued Propositional Logic." (With J. B. Rosser.)
  (1951a) "Many-valued Logics and Systems of Strict Implication."
  (1951b) "Axiom Schemes for m-Valued Functional Calculi of First Order. Part II. Deductive Completeness." (With J. B. Rosser.)
  (1952) *Many-valued Logics.* (With J. B. Rosser.)
  (1954) "Many-valued Logics and Systems of Strict Implication."
  (1958) "Simplified Axioms for Many-valued Quantification Theory."
  (1961) "Solution to a Problem of Rose and Rosser."
  (1963a) "Modality, Minimality, and Many-valuedness."
  (1963b) "Independent Axioms for Infinite-valued Logic."
Umezawa, Toshio
  (1959) "On Intermediate Many-valued Logics."
Ushenko, Andrew Paul
  (1933) "Note on Alternative Systems of Logic."
  (1936) "The Many-valued Logics."
Vaccarino, Giusseppe
  (1948) "La scuola polacca de logica."
  (1953) "Le logiche polivalenti e non aristoteliche."
Vaidyanathaswamy, R.
  (1938) "Quasi-Boolean Algebras and Many-valued Logics."
Vasil'ev, Nikolai A.
  (1910) "O častnyh suždéniáh, o tréugol'niké protivopoložnostéj, o zakoné isklúcĕnnogo čétvĕrtogo" (On particular propositions, the triangle of opposition, and the law of excluded fourth).
  (1911) *Voobražáémaá logika: Konspékt léktsii* (Imaginary Logic: Abstract of a Lecture).
  (1912) "Voobražaémaá (néaristotéléva) logika" (Imaginary [non-Aristotelian] logic).
  (1912–13) "Logika i métalogika" (Logic and metalogic).
  (1924) "Imaginary (Non-Aristotelian) Logic."
Vrendenduin, P. G. J.
  (1940) "Logistiek" (Logistic).
Wagner, Klaus
  (1950) "Zum Repräsentantenproblem der Logik für Aussagenfunktionen mit beliebig endlich oder unendlich vielen Wahrheitswerten."
Waismann, Friederich
  (1946) "Are There Alternative Logics?"

Wajsberg, Mordchaj
(1931) "Aksjomatyzacja trójwartściowego rachunku zdań" (Axiomatization of the 3-valued propositional calculus).
(1935) "Beiträge zum Metaaussagenkalkül I."
(1937) "Metalogische Beiträge."
Walters, A.
(1963) "Programming the Functions of Formal Logic. II. Multi-valued Logics." (With S. Summersbee.)
Wang, Hao
(1950) "A Proof of Independence."
(1961) "The Calculus of Partial Predicates and Its Extension to Set Theory. I."
Webb, Donald L.
(1935) "Generation of Any n-Valued Logic by One Binary Operation."
(1936a) "The Algebra of n-Valued Logic."
(1936b) "Definition of Post's Generalized Negative and Maximum in Terms of One Binary Operation."
Weiss, Paul
(1928) "Relativity in Logic."
(1931a) "Two-valued Logic: Another Approach."
(1931b) "Entailment and the Future of Logic."
(1933) "On Alternative Logics."
von Weizsäcker, Carl F.
(1955) "Komplementarität und Logik."
Wellmuth, John J.
(1942a) "Some Comments on the Nature of Mathematical Logic."
(1942b) "Philosophy and Order in Logic."
Wernick, William
(1939) "An Enumeration of Logical Functions."
Weyl, Hermann
(1940) "The Ghost of Modality."
Wilhelmy, Alexander
(1962) "Bemerkungen zur Semantik quantifizierter mehrwertiger logistischer Systeme."
Williams, Donald
(1951) "The Sea Fight Tomorrow."
(1954) "Professor Linsky on Aristotle."
Wittgenstein, Ludwig
(1922) *Tractatus logico-philosophicus.*
von Wright, Georg Henrick
(1951) *An Essay in Modal Logic.*
Yablonski, S. V.
(1954) "O funkcional'noj plonote v trehznacnom iscislenii" (On functional completeness in a three-valued calculus).
(1958a) "Funkcional' nye postroenija v k-znečnoj logike" (Functional constructions in a k-valued logic).
(1958b) "Funktionale Konstruktionen in mehrdeutigen Logiken."
Yasuura, Kamenosuke
(1955) "Keidenkikairo ni yoru tatimeidaironri no hyôgen ni tuite" (On the representation of many-valued propositional logics by relay circuits).
Yonemitsu, Naoto
(1954) "Note on Completeness of m-Valued Propositional Calculi."

Zawirski, Zygmunt
(1929) "Stosunek logiki do matematyki" (Relation of logic to mathematics).
(1931) "Logika trójwartosciowa Jans Łukasiewicza. O logice L. E. J. Brouwera.
Próby stosowania logiki wielowartosciowej do wspólczesnego przyrodoznawstwa"
(Jan Łukasiewicz' 3-valued logic. On the logic of L. E. J. Brouwer. Attempts at applications of many-valued logic to contemporary natural science).
(1932) "Les logiques nouvelles et le champ de leur application."
(1934a) "Znaczenie logiki wielowarotściowej dla poznania i zwiqzek jej z rachunkiem
prawdopodobieństwa" (Significance of many-valued logic for cognition and its connection with the calculus of probability).
(1934b) "Stosunek logiki wielowartościowej do rachunku prawdowodobieństwa" (Le
rapport de la logique à plusieurs valeurs au calcul des probabilités).
(1935) "Über das Verhältnis mehrwertigen Logik zur Wahrscheinlichkeitsrechnung."
(1936a) "Bedeutung der mehrwertigen Logik für die Erkenntnis und ihr Zusammenhang mit des Wahrscheinlichkeitsrechnung."
(1936b) "Les rapports de la logique polyvalente avec le calcul des probabilités."
(1936–37) "Über die Anwendung der mehrwertigen Logik in der empirischen Wissenschaft."
(1946) "Geneza i rozwój logiki intuicjonistycznej" (Genesis and development of
intuitionistic logic).
Zich, Otakar V.
(1938) "Výrokový počets komplexními hodnotami" (Sentential calculus with complex
values).
(1947) *Úvod do filosofie matematiky* (Introduction to the Philosophy of Mathematics).
Zinov'ev, Aleksander Aleksandrovich
(1958) "K problému abstraktniho a konkrétniho poznatku" (On the problem of
abstract and concrete knowledge).
(1959a) "K otázce hodnocení soudů jako abstraktních a konkretních" (On the question
of evaluating judgments as abstract and concrete).
(1959b) "Problema značenij istinnosti v mnogoznačnoj logike" (The problem of
truth-values in many-valued logic).
(1960) *Filosofskié problémy mnogoznačnoj logiki* (Philosophical Problems of Many-
valued Logic).
(1961a) *Logika vyskazyvanij i teorija vyvoda.*
(1961b) "Ob adnom sposobe obzora funkcij istinnosti n-značnogo isčislenija
vyskazyvanij" (A method of describing the truth-functions of the n-valued propositional calculus).
(1962) "Dvuznačnaja i mnogoznačnaja logika" (Two-valued and many-valued Logic).
(1963) *Philosophical Problems of Many-valued Logic.*
(1963–64) "Two-valued and Many-valued Logic."
Zwicky, Fritz
(1933) "On a New Type of Reasoning and Some of Its Possible Consequences."

4 Topically Classified Register

I Basic Theory

1 TEXTS, GENERAL SKETCHES, AND HISTORICAL SURVEYS

Kazimierz Ajdukiewicz (1928). *Główne zasady metodologii i logiki formalnej* (Fundamental principles of methodology of the sciences and of formal logic).

John M. Anderson and Johnstone [Henry W., Jr.] (1962). *Natural Deduction. The Logical Basis of Axiom Systems.*

Anonymous (ed.) (1963). "Proceedings of a Colloquium on Modal and Many-valued Logics: Helsinki 23–26 August 1962."

Maria C. Badillo Ballarat (1955a). "Fundamentos en relación con lógica simbólica polivalente."

Inocenty M. Bochénski (1956). *Formale Logik.*

—— (1959). *A Precis of Mathematical Logic.*

—— and Menne [Albert] (1962). *Grundriss der Logistik.*

Alonzo Church (1956). *Introduction to Mathematical Logic.*

Tadeusz Czeżowski (1949). *Logika. Podrecznik dla studiujacych nauki filozoficzne* (Logic. Textbook for Students of the Philosophical Sciences).

Anton Dumitriu (1943). *Logica Polivalenta* (Many-valued Logic).

Robert Feys (1949). *De ontwikkeling van het logisch denken* (The Development of Logical Thought).

Henryk Greniewski (1955). *Elementy logiki formalnej* (Elements of Formal Logic).

Zbigniew A. Jordan (1945). "The Development of Mathematical Logic and of Logical Positivism in Poland between the Two Wars."

P. E. B. Jourdain (1912). "The Development of the Theories of Mathematical Logic and the Principles of Mathematics."

Stephen C. Kleene (1952). *Introduction to Metamathematics.*

George L. Kline (1965). "N. A. Vasil'ev and the Development of Many-valued Logics."

William and Martha Kneale (1962). *The Development of Logic.*

G. T. Kneebone (1963). *Mathematical Logic and the Foundations of Mathematics: An Introductory Survey.*

Tadeusz Kotarbiński (1957). *Wylady z dziejów logiki* (Outlines of the History of Logic).

Jan Łukasiewicz (1929). *Elementy Logiki Matematycznej* (Elements of Mathematical Logic).

—— (1934). "Z historji logiki zdań" (From the history of the logic of propositions).

—— (1936). "Bedeutung der logischen Analyse für die Erkenntnis."

Joachim Metallmann (1939). *Wprowadzenie do zagadnién filozoficznych, Cześć I* (Introduction to Philosophical Problems, Part I).

Andrzej Mostowski (1948). *Logika matematyczna* (Mathematical Logic).

—— and collaborators (1955). *The Present State of Investigations on the Foundations of Mathematics.*

—— (1957). "L'oeuvre scientifique de Jan Łukasiewicz dans le domaine de la logique mathématique."

Arne Naess (1948). *Symbolsk logikk* (Symbolic Logic).

Ira Rosenbaum (1950). *Introduction to Mathematical Logic and Its Applications.*

Paul C. Rosenbloom (1950). *The Elements of Mathematical Logic.*

James Barkley Rosser (1941a). "Many-valued Logic."

—— (1941b). "On the Many-valued Logics."

—— and Turquette [Atwell] (1952). *Many-valued Logics.*

Arto Salomaa (1959). "On Many-valued Systems of Logic."

F. C. S. Schiller (1935). "Multi-valued Logics—and Others."

Heinrich Scholz (1957). "In memoriam Jan Łukasiewicz."

Charles Serrus (1945). *Traité de logique.*

Jerzy Słupecki and Borkowski [L.] (1958). "The Logical Works of J. Łukasiewicz."

Boleslaw Sobociński (1956). "In memoriam Jan Łukasiewicz."
—— (1957a). "La génesis de la Escuela Polaca de Logica."

Takeo Sugihara (1950). "Tachi ronrigaku" (Many-valued logic).

Giusseppe Vaccarino (1948). "La scuola polacca de logica."
—— (1953). "Le logiche polivalenti e non aristoteliche."

P. G. J. Vrendenduin (1940). "Logistiek" (Logistic).

Zygmunt Zawirski (1932). "Les logiques nouvelles et le champ de leur application."

O. V. Zich (1947). *Úvod do filosofie matematiky* (Introduction to the Philosophy of Mathematics).

Aleksander Aleksandrovich Zinov'ev (1960). *Filosofskié problémy mnogoznačnoj logiki* (Philosophical Problems of Many-valued Logic).
—— (1963). *Philosophical Problems of Many-valued Logic.*

2 THE 3-VALUED SYSTEM OF ŁUKASIEWICZ

Robert E. Clay (1962b). "A Simple Proof of Functional Completeness in Many-valued Logics Based on Łukasiewicz's *C* and *N*."

Robert Feys (1937–38). "Les logiques nouvelles des modalités."

Jan Łukasiewicz (1920). "O logice trojwartościowej" (On three-valued logic).
—— (1921). "Logika dwuwartościowa" (Two-valued logic).
—— (1930a). "Philosophische Bemerkungen zu mehrwertigen Systemen des Aussagenkalküls."
—— (1935–36). "Zur vollen dreiwertigen Aussagenlogik."
—— (1938). "Die Logik und das Grundlagenproblem."

J. C. C. McKinsey (1936). "On the Generation of the Functions of *Cpq* and *Np* of Łukasiewicz and Tarski by Means of a Single Binary Operation."

Grigor C. Moisil (1941c). "Contributions à l'étude des logiques non-chrysippiennes. I. Un nouveau système d'axiomes pour les algèbres Łukasiewicziennes tetra-valentes."
—— (1941d). "Remarques sur la logique modale du concept."
—— (1962b). "Sur la logique à trois valeurs de Łukasiewicz."
—— (1963). "Les logiques non-chrysippiennes et leurs applications."

Andrzej Mostowski (1957). "L'oeuvre scientifique de Jan Łukasiewicz dans le domaine de la logique mathématique."

Arthur Norman Prior (1957d). "Many-valued Logics: The Last of Three Talks on 'The Logic Game'."

Helena Rasiowa (1950). "Zdziedziny logiki matematycznej. II. Logiki wielowartościowe Łukasiewicza" (From the domain of mathematical logic. II. The many-valued logics of Łukasiewicz).

Alan Rose (1955a). "Le degré de saturation du calcul propositionnel implicatif à *m* valeurs de Łukasiewicz."

Bruno Scarpellini (1962). "Die Nichtaxiomatisierbarkeit des unendlichwertigen Prädikatenkalküls von Łukasiewicz."

Federico M. Siosen (1964). "Further Axiomatizations of the Łukasiewicz Three-valued Calculus."

Jerzy Słupecki and Borkowski [L.] (1958). "The Logical Works of J. Łukasiewicz."

Boleslaw Sobociński (1956). "In memoriam Jan Łukasiewicz."

———— (1957b). "Jan Łukasiewicz (1878–1956)."

Alfred Tarski (1956). *Logic, Semantics, Metamathematics: Papers from 1923 to 1938.*

Mordchaj Wajsberg (1931). "Aksjomatyzacja trójwartściowego rachunku zda í" (Axiomatization of the 3-valued propositional calculus).

Zygmunt Zawirski (1931). "Logika trójwartościowa Jans Łukasiewicza. O logice L. E. J. Brouwera. Próby stosowania logiki wielowartosciowej do wspólczesnego przyrodoznawstwa" (Jan Łukasiewicz' 3-valued logic. On the logic of L. E. J. Brouwer. Attempts at applications of many-valued logic to contemporary natural science).

3 FINITELY AND INFINITELY MANY-VALUED SYSTEMS OF PROPOSITIONAL LOGIC

Günther Asser (1953). "Die endlichwertigen Łukasiewiczschen Aussagenkalküle."

Maria C. Badillo Ballarat (1955b). "Esquemas representativos de sistemas regidos por una lógica polivalente."

D. A. Bochvar (1939). "Ob odnom tréhznaćnom isčislénii i égo priménénii k analizu paradoksov klassičéskogo rasširénnogo funkcional'nogo isčisléniá" (On a 3-valued logical calculus and its application to the analysis of contradictions).

———— (1943). "K voprosu o néprotivoréčivosti odnogo tréhznaćnogo isčisléniá" (On the consistency of a 3-valued calculus).

Chen Chung Chang (1963a). "Logic with Positive and Negative Truth Values."

Alonzo Church (1953). "Non-normal Truth-tables for the Propositional Calculus."

Robert E. Clay (1963). "A Standard Form for Łukasiewicz Many-valued Logics."

Paul Dienes (1949). "On Ternary Logic."

Michael Dummett (1959). "A Propositional Calculus with Denumerable Matrix."

Angelo Fadini (1962). "Il calcolo delle classi in una logica a tre valori di verità."

Robert Feys (1965). *Modal Logics.*

V. M. Gnidenko (1962). "Determination of Orders of Pre-complete Classes in Three-valued Logic."

Kurt Gödel (1932). "Zum intuitionistischen Aussagenkalkül."

—— (1935). "Eine Eigenschaft der Realisierungen des Aussagenkalküls."

R. L. Goodstein (1958). "Models of Propositional Calculi in Recursive Arithmetic."

Erik Götlind (1951). "A Lésniewski-Mihailescu-theorem for m-Valued Propositional Calculi."

Henryk Greniewski (1957). "2^{n+1} wartości logicznych" (2^{n+1} logical values).

Shih-hua Hu = Tzu-hua Hoo (1949). "m-Valued Sub-Systems of $(m + n)$-Valued Propositional Calculus."

—— and Chen [Chiang-yeh] (1951). "A Note on the 4-Valued Propositional Calculus and the Four Colour Problem."

—— (1955). "Die endlichwertigen und funktionell vollständigen Sub-systeme $\aleph_0$-wertigen Aussagenkalküls."

Stanisław Jaśkowski (1936). "Recherches sur le système de la logique intuitioniste."

Jørgen Jørgensen (1937). *Traek af deduktionsteoriens udvikling i den nyere tid* (Outline of the Recent Development of the Theory of Deduction).

Jan Kalicki (1954a). "On Equivalent Truth-tables of Many-valued Logics."

László Kalmár (1934). "Über die Axiomatisierbarkeit des Aussagenkalküls."

Stephen C. Kleene (1938). "On a Notation for Ordinal Numbers."

—— (1952). *Introduction to Metamathematics.*

Paul F. Linke (1952). "Eigentliche und uneigentliche Logik."

Jan Łukasiewicz (1930a). "Philosophische Bemerkungen zu mehrwertigen Systemen des Aussagenkalküls."

—— and Tarski [Alfred] (1930b). "Untersuchungen über den Aussagenkalkül."

—— (1935–36). "Zur vollen dreiwertigen Aussagenlogik."

Hugh MacColl (1906). *Symbolic Logic and Its Applications.*

J. C. C. McKinsey (1940). "A Correction to Lewis and Langford's *Symbolic Logic.*"

Robert McNaughton (1951). "A Theorem about Infinite-valued Sentential Logic."

Gottfried Martin (1949). "Über ein zweiwertiges Modell einer vierwertigen Logik."

Albert Menne (1964). "Ueber monadische Valenzfunktionen."

Charles A. Meredith (1958). "The Dependence of an Axiom of Łukasiewicz."

Miroslav Mlёziva (1958). "Teorie výroku" (Theory of propositions).

Grigor C. Moisil (1939b). "Recherches sur le syllogisme."

—— (1939c). "La logique formelle et son problème actuel."

—— (1940). "Recherches sur les logiques non-chrysippiennes."

—— (1941a). "Notes sur les logiques non-chrysippiennes."

—— (1941f). "Sur les théories déductives à logique non-chrysippienne."

—— (1943). "Contributions à l'étude des logiques non-chrysippiennes. IV. Sur la logique de Mr. Becker."

—— (1960b). "Asupra logicii lue Bochvar" (On the logic of Bochvar).

—— (1962c). "Les logiques non-chrysippiennes et leurs applications."

—— (1964). "Sur les logiques de Łukasiewicz à un nombre fini de valeurs."

—— (1965). *Încercări vechi si noi de logică neclasica* (Essays Old and New on Nonclassical Logic).

Andrzej Mostowski (1957). "L'oeuvre scientifique de Jan Łukasiewicz dans le domaine de la logique mathématique."

Akira Nakamura (1963a). "A Note on Truth-value Functions in the Infinitely Many-valued Logics."

—— (1963c). "On a Simple Axiomatic System of the Infinitely Many-valued Logic Based on $\wedge$, $\rightarrow$."

Nitold A. Pogorzelski (1964). "The Deduction Theorem for Łukasiewicz' Many-valued Propositional Calculi."

Arthur Norman Prior (1955c). *Formal Logic*.

—— (1957a). *Time and Modality*.

—— (1957c). "Symbolism and Analogy: The Second of Three Talks on 'The Logic Game'."

Nicholas Rescher (1962). "Quasi-truth-functional Systems of Propositional Logic."

Jacob Ridder (1948). "Über mehrwertige Aussagenkalküle und mehrwertige engere Prädikatenkalkule I–III."

—— (1949). "Sur quelques logiques multivalentes."

Alan Rose (1950b). "Completeness of Łukasiewicz-Tarski Propositional Calculi."

—— (1951b). "A New Proof of a Theorem of Dienes."

—— (1951c). "Axiom Systems for Three-valued Logic."

—— (1951f). "The Degree of Completeness of Some Łukasiewicz-Tarski Propositional Calculi."

—— (1952b). "The Degree of Completeness of the m-Valued Łukasiewicz Propositional Calculus."

—— (1952c). "A Formalisation of Post's m-Valued Propositional Calculus."

—— (1952d). "Le degré de saturation du calcul propositionnel implicatif à trois valeurs de Sobociński."

—— (1952f). "An Extension of Computational Logic."

—— (1952h). "An Extension of the Calculus of Non-Contradiction."

—— (1952i). "Extensions of Some Theorems of Schmidt and McKinsey."

—— (1953a). "The Degree of Completeness of the $\aleph_0$-Valued Łukasiewicz Propositional Calculus."

—— (1953d). "Fragments of the m-Valued Propositional Calculus."

—— (1953e). "A Formalization of Sobociński's Three-valued Implicational Propositional Calculus."

—— (1953f). "A Formalization of an $\aleph_0$-Valued Propositional Calculus."

—— (1953g). "Some Self-dual Primitive Functions for Propositional Calculi."

—— (1955a). "Le degré de saturation du calcul propositionnel implicatif à *m* valeurs de Łukasiewicz."

—— (1956a). "An Alternative Formalisation of Sobociński's Three-valued Implicational Propositional Calculus."

—— (1964a). "Formalisations de calculs propositionnels polyvalents à foncteurs variables."

—— (1965). "A Formalization of Post's *m*-Valued Propositional Calculus with Variable Functors."

Rolf Schock (1964a). "On Finitely Many-valued Logics."

—— (1964b). "On Denumerably Many-valued Logics."

—— (1965). "Some Theorems on the Relative Strengths of Many-valued Logics."

Peter Schofield (1964). "On a Correspondence between Many-valued and Two-valued Logics."

Karl Schröter (1955). "Methoden zur Axiomatisierung beliebiger Aussagen und Prädikatenkalküle."

V. I. Shestakov (1964). "On the Relationship between Certain Three-valued Logical Calculi."

Warclaw Sierpiński (1960–61). "Sur un problème de la logique à *n* valeurs."

Thoralf Skolem (1960). "A Set Theory Based on a Certain 3-Valued Logic."

Jerzy Słupecki (1936). "Der volle dreiwertige Aussagenkalkül."

—— (1939a). "Dowód aksjomatyzowalności pelnych systemów wielowartościowych rachunku zdań" (Proof of the axiomatizability of full many-valued systems of propositional calculus).

—— (1939b). "Kryterium pelności wielowartościowych systemów logiki zdań" (A criterion of completeness of many-valued systems of propositional logic).

—— (1946). "Pelny trójwartościowy rachunek zdań" (The complete three-valued propositional calculus).

—— and L. Borkowski (1958). "The Logical Works of J. Łukasiewicz."

Ja. S. Smetanič (1961). "Propositional Calculi with Additional Operations."

Boleslaw Sobociński (1956). "In memoriam Jan Łukasiewicz."

—— (1961). "A Note Concerning the Many-valued Propositional Calculi."

Takeo Sugihara (1956). "Four-valued Propositional Calculus with One Designated Truth-value."

—— (1958). "A Three-valued Logic with Meaning-Operator."

Roman Suszko (1957). "A Formal Theory of the Logical Values, I."

Ryōichi Takekuma (1954). "On a Nine-valued Propositional Calculus."

—— (1932). "Untersuchungen über der Aussagenkalkül."

Alfred Tarski (1956). *Logic, Semantics, Metamathematics: Papers from 1923 to 1938.*

H. H. Teh (1963). "On 3-Valued Sentential Calculus: An Axiomatic Approach."

Ivo Thomas (1962). "On the Infinity of Positive Logic."

Mircea Tîrnoveanu (1962). "Sur les extensions des types P et Q de la logique L_Ω^S."

Atwell R. Turquette (1944). "A Study and Extension of m-Valued Symbolic Logics."

Klaus Wagner (1950). "Zum Repräsentantenproblem der Logik für Aussagenfunktionen mit beliebig endlich oder unendlich vielen Wahrheitswerten."

Naoto Yonemitsu (1954). "Note on Completeness of m-Valued Propositional Calculi."

O. V. Zich (1938). "Výrokový počets komplexními hodnotami" (Sentential calculus with complex values).

Aleksander Aleksandrovich Zinov'ev (1961a). *Logika vyskazyvanij i teorija vyvoda.*

4 SPECIAL CONNECTIVES IN MANY-VALUED LOGIC (FUNCTIONAL COMPLETENESS, SPECIAL MODES OF NEGATION, SHEFFER STROKE FUNCTIONS)

S. V. Áblonskij (1956). "Funkcional' nyé postroénia v mnogoznačnyh logikah" (Functional constructions in many-valued logics).

D. A. Bochvar (1939). "Ob odnom tréhznačnom isčislénii i égo priménénii k analizu paradoksov klassičéskogo rasšírénnogo funkcional'nogo isčisléniá" (On a 3-valued logical calculus and its application to the analysis of contradictions).

────── (1943). "K vorposu o néprc.i oréčivosti odnogo tréhznačnogo isčislenia" (On the Consistency of a 3-valued Calculus).

Robert E. Clay (1962a). "Note on Słupecki T-functions."

Z. P. Dienes (1949). "On an Implication Function in Many-valued Systems of Logic."

Trevor Evans and Hardy [Lane] (1957). "Sheffer Stroke Functions in Many-valued Logics."

────── and Schwartz [P. B.] (1958). "On Słupecki T-functions."

Eric Foxley (1962). "The Determination of All Sheffer Functions in 3-valued Logic, Using a Logical Computer."

Peter T. Geach (1949). "If's and And's."

Erik Götlind (1952). "Some Sheffer Functions in n-Valued Logic."

Carl G. Hempel (1937a). "A Purely Topological Form of Non-Aristotelian Logic."

────── (1937b). "Eine System verallgemeinerter Negationen."

Makoto Itô (1935). "Yûgenko-ryôiki mi okeru kansû ni tuite" (On the generation of all functions in the finitely many-valued algebra of logic).

William H. Jobe (1962). "Functional Completeness and Canonical Forms in Many-valued Logics."

Jerzy Łoś (1948). "Logiki wielowartosćiowe a formalicacja funkcji intensjonalnych" (Many-valued logics and the formalization of intensional functions).

Norman M. Martin (1950). "Some Analogues of the Sheffer Stroke Function in *n*-Valued Logic."

—— (1951). "A Note on Sheffer Functions in *n*-Valued Logic."

—— (1952). "Sheffer Functions and Axiom Sets in *m*-Valued Propositional Logic."

—— (1954). "The Sheffer Functions of Three-valued Logic."

V. V. Martynjuk (1960). "Investigation of Certain Classes of Functions in Many-valued Logics."

Grigor C. Moisil (1960b). "Asupra logicii lue Bochvar" (On the logic of Bochvar).

Emil Post (1921). "Introduction to a General Theory of Elementary Propositions."

Alan Rose (1951a). "Conditional Disjunction as a Primitive Connective for the *m*-Valued Propositional Calculus."

—— (1952a). "Some Generalized Sheffer Functions."

—— (1953b). "Conditional Disjunction as a Primitive Connective for the Erweiterter Aussagenkalkül."

—— (1953g). "Some Self-dual Primitive Functions for Propositional Calculi."

—— (1954). "Sur les fonctions définissables dans une logique à un nombre infini de valeurs."

—— (1958b). "Sur les définitions de l'implication et de la négation dans certains systèmes de logique dont les valeurs forment des treillis."

—— (1961a). "Self-dual Binary and Ternary Connectives for *m*-Valued Propositional Calculi."

—— (1961b). "Sur certains calculs propositionnels à *m* valeurs ayant un seul foncteur primitif lequel constitue son propre dual."

—— (1962a). "An Alternative Generalisation of the Concept of Duality."

—— (1962c). "A Simplified Self *m*-al Set of Primitive Functors for the *m*-Valued Propositional Calculus."

—— (1962d). "Sur un ensemble complet de foncteurs primitifs indépendants pour le calcul propositionnel trivalent lequel constitue son propre trial."

—— (1962f). "Sur un ensemble de foncteurs primitifs pour le calcul propositionnel à *m* valeurs lequel constitue son propre *m*-al."

—— (1964b). "Note sur la formalisation de calculs propositionnels polyvalents à foncteurs variables."

Arto Salomaa (1963). "Some Analogues of Sheffer Functions in Infinite-valued Logics."

V. I. Shestakov (1964). "On the Relationship between Certain Three-valued Logical Calculi."

Warclaw Sierpiński (1960–61). "Sur un problème de la logique à *n* valeurs."

Takeo Sugihara (1952). "Negation in Many-valued Logic."

Donald L. Webb (1935). "Generation of Any *n*-Valued Logic by One Binary Operation."

—— (1936a). "The Algebra of *n*-Valued Logic."

———— (1936b). "Definition of Post's Generalized Negative and Maximum in Terms of One Binary Operation."

William Wernick (1939). "An Enumeration of Logical Functions."

S. V. Yablonskii (1954). "O funkcional'noj plonote v trehznacnom iscislenii" (On functional completeness in a three-valued calculus).

———— (1958a). "Funkcional' nye postroenija v k-znečnoj logike" (Functional constructions in a k-valued logic).

———— (1958b). "Funktionale Konstruktionen in mehrdeutigen Logiken."

Aleksander Aleksandrovich Zinov'ev (1961b). "Ob adnom sposobe obzora funkcij istinnosti n-značnogo isčislenija vyskazyvanij" (A method of describing the truth-functions of the n-valued propositional calculus).

5 QUANTIFICATION THEORY IN MANY-VALUED LOGIC

Karl E. Aubert (1948). "Om presisering og generalisering av relasjonsbegrepet" (A clarification and a generalization of the concept of relation).

Maria C. Badillo Ballarat (1956). "Automatización de los silogismos en una lógica polivalente."

L. P. Belluce and Chang [Chen Chung] (1963). "A Weak Completeness Theorem for Infinite-valued First-order Logic."

———— (1964). "Further Results on Infinite-valued Predicate Logic."

Burton Dreben (1960). "Relation of m-Valued Quantificational Logic to 2-Valued Quantificational Logic."

Louise S. Hay (1963). "Axiomatization of the Infinite-valued Predicate Calculus."

Georg Kreisel (1962). "On Weak Completeness of Intuitionistic Predicate Logic."

Grigor C. Moisil (1961b). "The Predicate Calculus in Three-valued Logic."

Andrzej Mostowski (1961a). "Axiomatizability of Some Many-valued Predicate Calculi."

———— (1963). "The Hilbert Epsilon Function in Many-valued Logics."

Akira Nakamura (1963b). "On an Axiomatic System of the Infinitely Many-valued Threshold Predicate Calculi."

Nicholas Rescher (1964). "Quantifiers in Many-valued Logic."

Jacob Ridder (1948). "Über mehrwertige Aussagenkalküle und mehrwertige engere Prädikatenkalkule I–III."

Alan Rose (1952g). "Sur un ensemble de fonctions primitives pour le calcul des prédicats du premier ordre lequel constitue son propre dual."

———— (1953b). "Conditional Disjunction as a Primitive Connective for the Erweiterter Aussagenkalkül."

———— (1955b). "A Gödel Theorem for an Infinite-valued Erweiterter Aussagenkalkül."

James Barkley Rosser (1939). "The Introduction of Quantification into a Three-valued Logic."

—— and Turquette [A. R.] (1951). "Axiom Schemes for *m*-Valued Functional Calculi of First Order. Part II. Deductive Completeness."

Joseph D. Rutledge (1960). "On the Definition of an Infinitely-Many-valued Predicate Calculus."

Bruno Scarpellini (1962). "Die Nichtaxiomatisierbarkeit des unendlichwertigen Prädikatenkalküls von Łukasiewicz."

Helmut Thiele (1958). "Theorie der endlich-wertigen Łukasiewiczschen Prädikatenkalküle der ersten Stufe."

Atwell R. Turquette (1958). "Simplified Axioms for Many-valued Quantificational Theory."

Hao Wang (1961). "The Calculus of Partial Predicates and Its Extension to Set Theory I."

Alexander Wilhelmy (1962). "Bemerkungen zur Semantik quantifizierter mehrwertiger logistischer Systeme."

6 AXIOMATIZATION OF MANY-VALUED LOGIC (FORMAL RESULTS; METALOGICAL THEORY)

L. P. Belluce and Chang [Chen Chung] (1963). "A Weak Completeness Theorem for Infinite-valued First-order Logic."

—— (1964). "Further Results on Infinite-valued Predicate Logic."

Rudolf Carnap (1943). *The Formalization of Logic*.

Chen Chung Chang (1958a). "Proof of an Axiom of Łukasiewicz."

—— (1959). "A New Proof of the Completeness of the Łukasiewicz Axioms."

—— (1963a). "Logic with Positive and Negative Truth Values."

Alonzo Church (1953). "Non-normal Truth-tables for the Propositional Calculus."

Michael Dummett (1959). "A Propositional Calculus with Denumerable Matrix."

Eric Foxley (1961). "Testing the Independence of a System of Axioms, Using a Logical Computer."

G. P. Gavrilov (1959). "Certain Conditions for Completeness in Countable-valued Logic."

Gotthard Günther (1953a). "Die philosophische Idee einer nicht-aristotelischen Logik."

—— (1953b). "The Logical Parallax."

—— (1958). "Die aristotelische Logik des Seins und die nicht-aristotelische Logik der Reflexion."

Louise S. Hay (1963). "Axiomatization of the Infinite-valued Predicate Calculus."

Jan Kalicki (1950a). "Note on Truth-tables."

—— (1950b). "A Test for the Existence of Tautologies According to Many-valued Truth-tables."

—— (1954b). "An Undecidable Problem in the Algebra of Truth-tables."

László Kalmár (1934). "Über die Axiomatisierbarkeit des Aussagenkalküls."

Georg Kreisel (1962). "On Weak Completeness of Intuitionistic Predicate Logic."

Adolf Lindenbaum (1930). "Remarques sur une question de la méthode axiomatique."

Jan Łukasiewicz (1936). "Bedeutung der logischen Analyse für die Erkenntnis."

Robert McNaughton (1951). "A Theorem about Infinite-valued Sentential Logic."

Angelo Margaris (1948). "A Problem of Rosser and Turquette."

Charles A. Meredith (1958). "The Dependence of an Axiom of Łukasiewicz."

—— and Prior [Arthur Norman] (1963). "Notes on the Axiomatics of Propositional Calculus."

Miroslav Mlěziva (1961). "On the Axiomatization of Three-valued Propositional Logic."

Moh Shaw-kwei (1958). "Yow-hsian-zhe fang-zhen hsi-t'ung ti kung-li-hua" (Axiomatization of many-valued logical systems).

Andrzej Mostowski (1961b). "An Example of a Non-axiomatizable Many-valued Logic."

Akira Nakamura (1962b). "On an Axiomatic System of the Infinitely Many-valued Threshold Logics."

—— (1963c). "On a Simple Axiomatic System of the Infinitely Many-valued Logic Based on ∧, →."

Nitold A. Pogorzelski (1964). "The Deduction Theorem for Łukasiewicz' Many-valued Propositional Calculi."

Emil Post (1921). "Introduction to a General Theory of Elementary Propositions."

Helena Rasiowa (1955). "O pewnym fragmencie implikacyjnego rachunku zdań" (On a fragment of the implicative propositional calculus).

Jacob Ridder (1948). "Über mehrwertige Aussagenkalküle und mehrwertige engere Prädikatenkalküle I–III."

Alan Rose (1950b). "Completeness of Łukasiewicz-Tarski Propositional Calculi."

—— (1951c). "Axiom Systems for Three-valued Logic."

—— (1951f). "The Degree of Completeness of Some Łukasiewicz-Tarski Propositional Calculi."

—— (1951g). "An Axiom System for Three-valued Logic."

—— (1952b). "The Degree of Completeness of the m-Valued Łukasiewicz Propositional Calculus."

—— (1952c). "A Formalisation of Post's m-Valued Propositional Calculus."

—— (1953a). "The Degree of Completeness of the $\aleph_0$-Valued Łukasiewicz Propositional Calculus."

────── (1953c). "The *m*-Valued Calculus of Non-Contradiction."

────── (1953d). "Fragments of the *m*-Valued Propositional Calculus."

────── (1953e). "A Formalization of Sobociński's Three-valued Implicational Propositional Calculus."

────── (1953f). "A Formalization of an $\aleph_0$-Valued Propositional Calculus."

────── (1953g). "Some Self-dual Primitive Functions for Propositional Calculi."

────── (1955b). "A Gödel Theorem for an Infinite-valued Erweiterter Aussagenkalkül."

────── (1956a). "An Alternative Formalisation of Sobociński's Three-valued Implicational Propositional Calculus."

────── (1956b). "Formalisation du calcul propositionnel implicatif a $\aleph_0$ valeurs de Łukasiewicz."

────── (1956c). "Some Formalisations of $\aleph_0$-Valued Propositional Calculi."

────── and Rosser [James Barkley] (1958d). "Fragments of Many-valued Statement Calculi."

────── (1960a). "An Extension of a Theorem of Margaris."

────── (1960b). "Sur les schémas d'axiomes pour les calculs propositionnels à *m* valeurs ayant des valeurs sur désignées."

────── (1964b). "Note sur la formalisation de calculs propositionnels polyvalents à foncteurs variables."

James Barkley Rosser (1960). "Axiomatization of Infinite-valued Logics."

────── and Turquette [Atwell R.] (1945). "Axiom Schemes for *m*-Valued Propositional Calculi."

────── and ────── (1948). "Axiom Schemes for *m*-Valued Functional Calculi of First Order. Part I. Definition of Axiom Schemes and Proof of Plausibility."

────── and ────── (1949). "A Note on the Deductive Completeness of *m*-Valued Propositional Logic."

────── and ────── (1952). *Many-valued Logics.*

Zygmunt Schmierer (1936). "O funkcjach charakterystycznych w logikach wielowartościowych" (On characteristic functions in many-valued systems of logic).

Karl Schröter (1955). "Methoden zur Axiomatisierung beliebiger Aussagen -und Prädikatenkalküle."

Federico M. Siosen (1964). "Further Axiomatizations of the Łukasiewicz Three-valued Calculus."

Jerzy Słupecki (1939a). "Dowód aksjomatyzowalności pelnych systemów wielowartościowych rachunku zdań" (Proof of the axiomatizability of full many-valued systems of propositional calculus).

────── (1946). "Pelny trójwartościowy rachunek zdań (The complete three-valued propositional calculus).

Boleslaw Sobociński (1936). "Aksjomatyzacja pewnych wielowartościowych systemów teorji dedukcji" (Axiomatization of certain many-valued systems of the theory of deduction).

—— (1952). "Axiomatization of a Partial System of Three-valued Calculus of Propositions."

H. H. Teh (1963). "On 3-valued Sentential Calculus: An Axiomatic Approach."

Atwell R. Turquette (1944). "A Study and Extension of *m*-Valued Symbolic Logics."
—— (1958). "Simplified Axioms for Many-valued Quantification Theory."
—— (1961). "Solution to a Problem of Rose and Rosser."
—— (1963b). "Independent Axioms for Infinite-valued Logic."

Mordchaj Wajsberg (1931). "Aksjomatyzacja trójwartściowego rachunku zdań" (Axiomatization of the 3-valued propositional calculus).
—— (1935). "Beiträge zum Metaaussagenkalkül I."
—— (1937). "Metalogische Beiträge."

Hao Wang (1950). "A Proof of Independence."

Naoto Yonemitsu (1954). "Note on Completeness of *m*-Valued Propositional Calculi."

7 SEMANTIC INTERPRETATIONS OF MANY-VALUED LOGIC

Anonymous (1952). "Problemas d 'Theoria'. Problema no. I."

D. A. Bochvar (1939). "Ob odnom tréhznačnom isčislénii i égo priménénii k analizu paradoksov klassičéskogo rasširénnogo funkcional'nogo isčisléniá" (On a 3-valued logical calculus and its application to the analysis of contradictions).
—— (1943). "K voprosu o néprotivoréčivosti odnogo tréhznačnogo isčislenia" (On the consistency of a 3-valued calculus).

Jonathan Cohen (1951). "Three-valued Ethics."

Gerhard Frey (1953). "Bemerkungen zum Problem der mehrwertigen Logiken."

Edward Habermann (1936). "Pojecie biegunowości i logika wielawartościowa" (The concept of polarity and many-valued logic).

Sören Halldén (1949b). "The Logic of Nonsense."

Paul F. Linke (1948). "Die mehrwertigen Logiken und das Wahrheitsproblem."

Jan Łukasiewicz (1936). "Bedeutung der logischen Analyse für die Erkenntnis."

Stéphane Lupasco (1945). "Valeurs logiques et contradiction."

William M. Malisoff (1936). "Meanings in Multi-valued Logics (Toward a general semantics)."
—— (1941). "Meanings in Multi-valued Logics."

François Moch (1956a). "La logique des attitudes."

Emil Post (1921). "Introduction to a General Theory of Elementary Propositions."

Arthur Norman Prior (1953a). "On Propositions Neither Necessary nor Impossible."

Jacques Reinhardt and Boll [Marcel] (1950). "A propos des logiques polyvalentes: Les modalités et la vraisemblance."

Nicholas Rescher (1962). "Quasi-truth-functional Systems of Propositional Logic."
—— (1963). "A Probabilistic Approach to Modal Logic."
—— (1965). "An Intuitive Interpretation of Systems of Four-valued Logic."

Alan Rose (1952e). "Eight-valued Geometry."

James Barkley Rosser (1953). *Logic for Mathematicians.*

Thomas Storer (1946). "The Logic of Value Imperatives."

Atwell R. Turquette (1954). "Many-valued Logics and Systems of Strict Implication."

N. A. Vasil'ev (1912). "Voobražaémaá (néaristotéléva) logika" (Imaginary [non-Aristotelian] logic).
—— (1912–13). "Logika i métalogika" (Logic and metalogic).

Alexander Wilhelmy (1962). "Bemerkungen zur Semantik quantifizierter mehrwertiger logistischer Systeme."

Aleksander Aleksandrovich Zinov'ev (1959b). "Problema značenij istinnosti v mnogoznačnoj logike" (The problem of truth-values in many-valued logic).

II Logical Ramifications

8 USES OF MANY-VALUED LOGICS IN THE STUDY OF MODAL LOGICS

Alan Ross Anderson and Belnap [Nuel D., Jr.] (1962). "The Pure Calculus of Entailment."

Heinrich Behmann (1953). "Die typenfreie Logik und die Modalität."

Gustav Bergmann (1949). "The Finite Representations of S5."

R. A. Bull (1964). "An Axiomatization of Prior's modal calculus *Q*."

Charles E. Caton (1963). "A Stipulation of Modal Propositional Calculus in Terms of Modalized Truth-values."

James Dugundji (1940). "Note on a Property of Matrices for Lewis and Langford's Calculi of Propositions."

Robert Feys (1937–38). "Les logiques nouvelles des modalités."

Sören Halldén (1949). "On the Decision-Problem of Lewis' Calculus S5."

Louis O. Katsoff (1937). "Modality and Probability."

Saul A. Kripke (1963). "Semantical Analysis of Modal Logic. I. Normal Modal Propositional Calculi."

Henry S. Leonard (1951). "Two-valued Truth Tables for Modal Functions."

C. I. Lewis and Langford [Cooper H.] (1932b). *Symbolic Logic.*

Jan Łukasiewicz (1953a). "A System of Modal Logic."
—— (1953b). "A System of Modal Logic."

Grigor C. Moisil (1937–38). "Sur le mode problématique."
——— (1938). "Sur la théorie classique de la modalité des jugements."
——— (1941d). "Remarques sur la logique modale du concept."
——— (1942a). "Logique modale.",
——— (1963). "Les logiques non-chrysippiennes et leurs applications."

Akira Nakamura (1962a). "On the Infinitely Many-valued Threshold Logics and von Wright's System *M*."
——— (1964). "Truth-value Stipulations for the von Wright System *M'* and the Heyting System."

Arthur Norman Prior (1952). "In What Sense Is Modal Logic Many-valued?"
——— (1955a). "Many-valued and Modal Systems: An Intuitive Approach."
——— (1957a). *Time and Modality.*
——— (1957b). "The Necessary and the Possible: The First of Three Talks on 'The Logic Game'."
——— (1958–59). "Notes on a Group of New Modal Systems."
——— (1963a). "The Theory of Implication."

Jacques Reinhardt and Boll [Marcel] (1950). "A propos des logiques polyvalentes: Les modalités et la vraisemblance."

Nicholas Rescher (1963). "A Probabilistic Approach to Modal Logic."

Alan Rose (1962b). "Extensions of Some Theorems of Anderson and Belnap."

Timothy Smiley (1961). "On Łukasiewicz's Ł-modal System."
——— (1962). "Analytic Implication and 3-Valued Logic."

Atwell R. Turquette (1954). "Many-valued Logics and Systems of Strict Implication."
——— (1963a). "Modality, Minimality, and Many-valuedness."

Hermann Weyl (1940). "The Ghost of Modality."

Georg Henrick von Wright (1951). *An Essay in Modal Logic.*

9 USES OF MANY-VALUED LOGIC IN THE STUDY OF INTUITIONISTIC LOGIC AND PROOF THEORY

Kurt Gödel (1932). "Zum intuitionistischen Aussagenkalkül."
——— (1933a). "Eine Interpretation des intuitionistischen Aussagenkalküls."
——— (1933b). "Zum Intuitionistischen Aussagenkalkül."
——— (1935). "Eine Eigenschaft der Realisierungen des Aussagenkalküls."

Ronald Harrop (1958). "On the Existence of Finite Models and Decision Procedures for Propositional Calculi."

Arend Heyting (1930). "Die Formalen Regeln der intuitionistischen Logik."
——— (1956). *Intuitionism: An Introduction.*

Stanisław Jaśkowski (1936). "Recherches sur le système de la logique intuitioniste."

Jørgen Jørgensen (1937). *Traek af deduktionsteoriens udvikling i den nyere tid* (Outline of the Recent Development of the Theory of Deduction).

A. N. Kolmogorov (1924–25). "O principé *tertium non datur*" (On the *tertium non datur* principle).

—— (1932). "Zur Deutung der intuitionistischen Logik."

Georg Kreisel (1962). "On Weak Completeness of Intuitionistic Predicate Logic."

Jan Łukasiewicz (1937). "Wobronie logistyki" (In defense of logistic).

—— (1938). "Die Logik und das Grundlagenproblem."

—— (1952). "On the Intuitionistic Theory of Deduction."

J. C. C. McKinsey and Tarski [Alfred] (1948). "Some Theorems about the Sentential Calculi of Lewis and Heyting."

Akira Nakamura (1964). "Truth-value Stipulations for the von Wright System *M'* and the Heyting System."

John von Neumann (1927). "Zur Hilbertschen Beweistheorie."

Gene F. Rose (1953). "Propositional Calculus and Realizability."

James Barkley Rosser (1953). *Logic for Mathematicians.*

Thoralf Skolem (1929). "Über einige Grundlagenfragen der Mathematik."

Takeo Sugihara (1951). "Brouwer ronrigaku no tachi-ronrigaku-teki tokusei" (Many-valued logical characteristics of Brouwerian logic).

Toshio Umezawa (1959). "On Intermediate Many-valued Logics."

Zygmunt Zawirski (1931). "Logika trójwartosciowa Jans Łukasiewicza. O logice L. E. J. Brouwera. Próby stosowania logiki wielowartosciowej do wspólczesnego przyrodoznawstwa" (Jan Łukasiewicz' 3-valued logic. On the logic of L. E. J. Brouwer. Attempts at applications of many-valued logic to contemporary natural science).

—— (1946). "Geneza i rozwój logiki intuicjonistycznej" (Genesis and development of intuitionistic logic).

10 MANY-VALUED LOGIC AND THE LOGICAL PARADOXES

Charles A. Baylis (1936). "Are Some Propositions Neither True nor False?"

D. A. Bochvar (1944). "K voprosu o paradoksah matématičéskoj logiki i téorii množéstv" (To the question of paradoxes of the mathematical logic and theory of sets).

Ronald J. Butler (1955). "Aristotle's Sea Fight and Three-valued Logic."

Curt J. Ducasse (1941). "Truth, Verifiability, and Propositions about the Future."

Charles Hartshorne (1964). "Deliberation and Excluded Middle."

Athanase Joja (1960). "About *tertium non datur*."

Zbigniew A. Jordan (1963). "Logical Determinism."

P. T. Landsberg (1953). "On Heterological Paradoxes."

Leonard Linsky (1954). "Professor Donald Williams on Aristotle."

Jan Łukasiewicz (1910). "Über den Satz des Widerspruchs bei Aristoteles."
—— (1923). "O Determiniźmie" (On determinism).

Grigor C. Moisil (1937–38). "Sur le mode problématique."
—— (1962a). "Sur le principe du déterminisme."

Arthur Norman Prior (1953b). "Three-valued Logic and Future Contingents."
—— (1957a). *Time and Modality.*
—— (1957b). "The Necessary and the Possible: The First of Three Talks on 'The Logic Game'."
—— (1962). "The Formalities of Omniscience."

Richard Taylor (1957). "The Problem of Future Contingencies."

Donald Williams (1951). "The Sea Fight Tomorrow."
—— (1954). "Professor Linsky on Aristotle."

III Philosophical Ramifications

11 FUTURE CONTINGENCY AND A NEUTRAL TRUTH-VALUE

Charles A. Baylis (1936). "Are Some Propositions Neither True nor False?"

L. E. J. Brouwer (1925a). "Intuitionistische Zerlegung mathematischer Grundbegriffe."
—— (1925b). "Über die Bedeutung des Satzes vom ausgeschlossenen Dritten in der Mathematik, insbesondere in der Funktionentheorie."

Neils E. Christensen (1957). "Further Comments on Two-valued Logic."

Marvin Farber (1942). "Logical Systems and the Principles of Logic."

William and Martha Kneale (1962). *The Development of Logic.*

Isaac Levi (1959). "Putnam's Three Truth-values."

C. I. Lewis (1932a). "Alternative Systems of Logic."
—— (1933). "Note Concerning Many-valued Logical Systems."

Hilary Putnam (1957). "Three-valued Logic."

Nicholas Rescher (1955). "Some Comments on Two-valued Logic."

Thomas Storer (1954). "The Notion of Tautology."

Andrew Paul Ushenko (1933). "Note on Alternative Systems of Logic."
—— (1936). "The Many-valued Logics."

Friederich Waismann (1946). "Are There Alternative Logics?"

Paul Weiss (1928). "Relativity in Logic."
—— (1931). "Two-valued Logic: Another Approach."
—— (1933). "On Alternative Logics."

John J. Wellmuth (1942b). "Philosophy and Order in Logic."

Aleksander Aleksandrovich Zinov'ev (1958). "K problému abstraktniho a konkrétniho poznatku" (On the problem of abstract and concrete knowledge).

———— (1959a). "K otázce hodnocení soudů jako abstraktních a konkretních" (On the question of evaluating judgments as abstract and concrete).

———— (1960). *Filosofskié problémy mnogoznačnoj logiki* (Philosophical Problems of Many-valued Logic).

———— (1962). "Dvuznačnaja i mnogoznačnaja logika" (Two-valued and many-valued logic).

———— (1963). *Philosophical Problems of Many-valued Logic.*

———— (1963–64). "Two-valued and Many-valued Logic."

12 PHILOSOPHICAL CONTROVERSIES OVER "ALTERNATIVE" LOGICS

D. A. Bochvar (1939). "Ob odnom tréhznačnom isčislénii i égo priménénii k analizu paradoksov klassičéskogo rasširénnogo funkcional'nogo isčislénia" (On a 3-valued logical calculus and its application to the analysis of contradictions).

Alonzo Church (1956b). "Laws of Thought."

Herbert Hochberg (1954). "Professor Storer on Empiricism."

David Karl Kauf (1954). "A Comment on Hochberg's Reply to Storer."

Kazimierz Klósak (1948). "Teoria indeterminizmu ontologicznego a trójwartościowa logika zdań prof. Jana Łukasiewcza" (The theory of ontological indeterminism and the three-valued logic of propositions of Prof. Jan Łukasiewicz).

———— (1949). "Konieczność wyjścia poza logike dwuwartościowa" (The necessity of going beyond the two-valued logic).

Maria Kokoszyńska (1951). "A Refutation of the Relativism of Truth."

Herman Meyer (1949). *Kennis en realiteit* (Knowledge and Reality).

Francois Moch (1956b). "Des antinomies classiques à la Logique de Mme. Février-Destouches."

Moh Shaw-kwei (1954). "Logical Paradoxes for Many-valued Systems."

Arthur Norman Prior (1955b). "Curry's Paradox and 3-valued Logic."

Louis Rougier (1939). "La relativité de la logique."

Thomas Storer (1953). "A Note on Empiricism."

J. D. Swift (1952). "Algebraic Properties of *n*-Valued Propositional Calculi."

Paul Weiss (1931b). "Entailment and the Future of Logic."

IV Ramifications in Mathematics and Physics

13 APPLICATIONS OF MANY-VALUED LOGIC IN SET THEORY

Chen Chung Chang (1963b). "The Axiom of Comprehension in Infinite-valued Logic."

———— (1965). "Infinite-valued Logic as a Basis for Set Theory."

Georg Klaus (1965). "Uber einen Ansatz zur mehrwertigen Mengenlehre."

Tameharu Shirai (1937). "On the Pseudo-Set."

Thoralf Skolem (1957a). "Mengenlehre gegründet auf einer Logik mit unendlich vielen Wahrheitswerten."

——— (1957b). "Bemerkungen zum Komprehensionsaxiom."

——— (1960). "A Set Theory Based on a Certain 3-Valued Logic."

14 ALGEBRAIC, ALGORITHMIC, AND TOPOLOGICAL MODELS OF AND APPLICATIONS IN MANY-VALUED LOGICS

N. N. Aîzenberg (1965). "Representation of a Sum *mod m* in a Class of Normal Forms of Functions of *m*-Valued Logic."

Karl E. Aubert (1949). "Relations généralisées et indépendence logique des notions de réflexivité, symétrie et transitivité."

——— (1952). "On the Foundation of the Theory of Relations and the Logical Independence of Generalized Concepts of Reflexivity, Symmetry, and Transitivity."

Maria C. Badillo Ballarat (1958). "Aplicación de la lógica polivalente a la teoría de números."

C. C. H. Barker (1957). "Some Calculations in Logic."

Eric T. Bell (1943). "Polynomials on a Finite Discrete Range."

B. A. Bernstein (1928). "Modular Representations of Finite Algebras."

Garrett Birkhoff (1940). *Lattice Theory*.

Komaravola Chandrasekharan (1944). "Partially Ordered Sets and Symbolic Logic."

Chen Chung Chang (1958b). "Algebraic Analysis of Many-valued Logics."

——— (1961a). "Theory of Models of Infinite-valued Logics."

——— and Horn [Alfred] (1961b). "Prime Ideal Characterization of Generalized Post Algebras."

——— and Keisler [H. Jerome] (1962). "Model Theories with Truth Values in a Uniform Space."

——— and ——— (1963c). "Continuous Model Theory."

Chiang-yeh Chen and Hu [Shih-hua] (1951). "A Note on the 4-Valued Propositional Calculus and the Four Colour Problem."

Jens Erik Fenstad (1964). "On the Consistency of the Axiom of Comprehension in the Łukasiewicz Infinite-valued Logic."

Alfred L. Foster (1949). "The *n*-ality Theory of Rings."

——— (1950). "On *n*-ality Theories in Rings and Their Logical Algebras, Including Triality Principle in Three-valued Logics."

Orrin Frink, Jr. (1938). "New Algebras of Logic."

John D. Goodell (1952). "The Foundations of Computing Machinery."

W. H. Hanson (1963). "Ternary Threshold Logic."

Carl G. Hempel (1936–37). "Eine rein topologische Form nichtaristotelischer Logik."
—— (1937a). "A Purely Topological Form of Non-Aristotelian Logic."

Paul Henle (1955). "*n*-Valued Boolean Algebra."

Makoto Itô (1955). "*n*-ti kansû soku (*n*-ti ronri) ni tuite" (On the "lattice of *n*-valued functions" [*n*-valued logic]).
—— (1956a). "Itigen *n*-ti kansûsoku (ronri) hôteisiki no ippankai ni tuite" (On the general solution of the *n*-valued function-lattice [logical] equation in one variable).
—— (1956b). "Tagen *n*-ti kansûsoku (ronri) hôteisiki no ippankai ni tuite" (On the general solution of the *n*-valued lattice [logical] equation in several variables).

Jan Kalicki (1954b). "An Undecidable Problem in the Algebra of Truth-tables."

Vladmir G. Kirin (1963). "On the Polynomial Representation of Operators in the *n*-Valued Propositional Calculus."

Stephen A. Kiss (1947). *Transformations on Lattices and Structures of Logic.*

Stephen C. Kleene (1938). "On a Notation for Ordinal Numbers."
—— (1952). *Introduction to Metamathematics.*

Moh Shaw-kwei (1954). "Logical Paradoxes for Many-valued Systems."

Grigor C. Moisil (1939a). "Les principes de la logique et l'idée de chaîne."
—— (1940–41). "Sur la structure algébrique de la logique de M. Bochvar."
—— (1941b). "Recherches sur la théorie des chaînes."
—— (1941e). "Sur les anneaux de caractéristique 2 ou 3 et leurs applications."
—— (1942b). "Contributions à l'étude des logiques non-chrysippiennes. II. Anneaux engendrés par les algèbres Łukasiewicziennes tetravalentes centrées."
—— (1942c). "Contributions à l'étude des logiques non-chrysippiennes. III. Anneaux engendrés par les algèbres Łukasiewicziennes tetravalentes axées."
—— (1945). "L'algebra e la logica."
—— (1956–59). "Intrebuintarea logicilor trivalente în teoriă algebrică a mecanismelor automate" (Use of 3-valued logic in the algebraic theory of automata).
—— (1959a). "Rapport sur le développement dans la R.P.R. de la théorie algébrique des mécanismes automatiques."
—— (1959c). *Teoria algebrică a mecanismelor automate* (The Algebraic Theory of Automatic Machines).
—— (1959e). "La logique à plusieurs valeurs et l'automatique."
—— (1960a). "Sur les idéaux des algèbres Łukasiewicziennes trivalentes."
—— (1965). *Încercări vechi si noi de logică neclasica* (Essays Old and New on Nonclassical Logic).

Antonio Monteiro (1963). "Sur la définition des algèbres de Łukasiewicz trivalentes."

Luiz F. T. Monteiro and Lorenzo Gonzalez Coppola (1964). "Sur une construction des algèbres de Łukasiewicz trivalentes."

Hans R. Müller (1940). "Algebraischer Aussagenkalkül."

Akira Nakamura (1962a). "On the Infinitely Many-valued Threshold Logics and von Wright's System *M*."

——— (1962b). "On an Axiomatic System of the Infinitely Many-valued Threshold Logics."

——— (1963b). "On an Axiomatic System of the Infinitely Many-valued Threshold Predicate Calculi."

——— (1965). "On the Infinitely Many-valued Double-threshold Logic."

Juliusz Reichbach (1962). "On the Connection of the First-order Functional Calculus with Many-valued Propositional Calculi."

——— (1963). "About Connection of the First-order Functional Calculus with Many-valued Propositional Calculi."

——— (1964). "A Note about Connection of the First-order Functional Calculus with Many-valued Propositional Calculi."

Alan Rose (1950a). "A Lattice-Theoretic Characterization of Three-valued Logic."

——— (1951d). "Systems of Logic Whose Truth-values Form Lattices."

——— (1951e). "A Lattice-Theoretic Characterization of the $\aleph_0$-Valued Propositional Calculus."

——— (1958a). "Many-valued Logical Machines."

——— (1958b). "Sur les définitions de l'implication et de la négation dans certains systèmes de logique dont les valeurs forment des treillis."

——— (1962e). "Sur les applications de la logique polyvalente à la construction des machines Turing."

——— (1962f). "Sur un ensemble de foncteurs primitifs pour le calcul propositionnel à *m* valeurs lequel constitue son propre *m*-al."

Paul C. Rosenbloom (1942). "Post Algebras. I. Postulates and General Theory."

James Barkley Rosser (1953). *Logic for Mathematicians.*

Arto Salomaa (1965). "On Some Algebraic Notions in the Theory of Truth-functions."

Bruno Scarpellini (1963). "Eine Anwendung der unendlichwertigen Logik auf topologische Raüme."

Stuart Summersbee and Walters [A.] (1963). "Programming the Functions of Formal Logic. II. Multi-valued Logics."

J. D. Swift (1952). "Algebraic Properties of *n*-Valued Propositional Calculi."

Dov Tamari (1952–54). "Some Mutual Applications of Logic and Mathematics."

Alfred Tarski (1938). "Der Aussagenkalkül und die Topologie."

Tadeusz Traczyk (1962). "On Axioms and Some Properties of Post Algebras."

A. B. Turowicz (1960). "Sur une méthode algébrique de vérification des théorèmes de la logique des énoncés."

R. Vaidyanathaswamy (1938). "Quasi-Boolean Algebras and Many-valued Logics."

Donald L. Webb (1936a). "The Algebra of *n*-Valued Logic."

John J. Wellmuth (1942a). "Some Comments on the Nature of Mathematical Logic."
—— (1942b). "Philosophy and Order in Logic."

Zygmunt Zawirski (1929). "Stosunek logiki do matematyki" (Relation of logic to mathematics).

15 PROBABILISTIC VARIANTS OF MANY-VALUED LOGIC

Rudolf Carnap (1950). *Logical Foundations of Probability*.

Paulette Février (or Destouches-Février) (1937a). "Les relations d'incertitude de Heisenberg et la logique."
—— (1937b). "Sur une forme générale de la définition d'une logique."
—— (1959). "Logical Structure of Physical Theories."

Theodore Hailperin (1937). "Foundations of Probability in Mathematical Logic."

Olaf Helmer and Oppenheim [Paul] (1945). "A Syntactical Definition of Probability and Degree of Confirmation."

Eino Kaila (1926). *Die Prinzipien der Wahrscheinlichkeitslogik*.

Louis O. Katsoff (1937). "Modality and Probability."

Henry Margenau (1939). "Probability, Many-valued Logics, and Physics."

Stefan Mazurkiewicz (1932). "Zur Axiomatik der Wahrscheinlichkeitslehre."
—— (1934). "Über die Grundlagen der Wahrscheinlichkeitsrechnung."

Hans Reichenbach (1932). "Wahrscheinlichkeitslogik."
—— (1935). *Wahrscheinlichkeitslehre*.
—— (1935–36a). "Wahrscheinlichkeitslogik."
—— (1935–36b). "Wahrscheinlichkeitslogik und Alternativlogik."
—— (1937). "Les fondements logiques du calcul des probabilités."
—— (1949). *The Theory of Probability: An Inquiry into the Logical and Mathematical Foundations of the Calculus of Probability*.

Jacques Reinhardt and Boll [Marcel] (1950). "A propos des logiques polyvalentes: Les modalités et la vraisemblance."

Nicholas Rescher (1963). "A Probabilistic Approach to Modal Logic."

Zygmunt Zawirski (1934a). "Znaczenie logiki wielowartościowej dla poznania i związek jej z rachunkiem prawdopodobieństwa" (Significance of many-valued logic for cognition and its connections with the calculus of probability).
—— (1934b). "Stosunek logiki wielowartościowej do rachunku prawdowodobieństwa" (Le rapport de la logique à plusieurs valeurs au calcul des probabilités).
—— (1935). "Über das Verhältnis mehrwertigen Logik zub Wahrscheinlichkeitsrechnung."

———— (1936a). "Bedeutung der mehrwertigen Logik für die Erkenntnis und ihr Zusammenhang mit des Wahrscheinlichkeitsrechnung."

———— (1936b). "Les rapports de la logique polyvalente avec le calcul des probabilités."

16 APPLICATIONS OF MANY-VALUED LOGIC IN PHYSICS

Olivier Costa de Beauregard (1945). "Extension d'une théorie de M. J. de Neumann au cas des projecteurs non commutables."

Garrett Birkhoff and von Neumann [John] (1936). "The Logic of Quantum Mechanics."

Jean-Louis Destouches (1938). *Essai sur la forme générale des théories physiques.*

———— (1942). *Principes fondamentaux de physique théorique.*

———— (1946). *Cours de logique et philosophie générale. I. Méthodologie de la physique: théorique moderne. II. Notions de logistique.*

Gérard Emch and Jauch [J. M.] (1965). "Structures logiques et mathématiques en physique quantique."

Paulette Février [or Destouches-Février] (1949). "Logique et théories physiques."

———— (1951). *La structure des théories physiques.*

———— (1952). "Applications des logiques modales en physique quantique."

Paul Feyerabend (1958). "Reichenbach's Interpretation of Quantum Mechanics."

W. R. Fuchs (1964). "Ansätze zu einer Quantenlogik."

Gotthard Günther (1955). "Dreiwertige Logik und die Heisenbergsche Unbestimmtheitsrelation."

Pascual Jordan (1959). "Quantenlogik und das Kommutative Gesetz."

Simon Kochen and Specker [E. P.] (1965). "Logical Structures in Quantum Theory."

Toshihiko Kurihara (1955). "Yûgen tatironri no denki kairo ni yoru hyôgen ni tuite" (On the representation of finitely many-valued logics by electric circuits).

B. G. Kuznetzov (1959). "Ob osnovax kvantovo-reljativistakoj logiki" (On quantum and relativistic logic).

Isaac Levi (1959). "Putnam's Three Truth-values."

J. C. C. McKinsey and Suppes [Patrick] (1954). Review of Paulette Destouches-Février, *La Structure des Théories Physiques.*

Henry Margenau (1934). "On the Application of Many-valued Systems of Logic to Physics."

———— (1939). "Probability, Many-valued Logics, and Physics."

———— (1950). *The Nature of Physical Reality.*

Peter Mittelstaedt (1961). "Quantenlogik."

Ernest Nagel (1946). "Professor Reichenbach on Quantum Mechanics: A Rejoinder."

John von Neumann (1962). "Quantum Logics."

Hilary Putnam (1957). "Three-valued Logic."

Hans Reichenbach (1944). *Philosophical Foundations of Quantum Mechanics.*

—— (1946). "Reply to Ernest Nagel's Criticism of My Views on Quantum Mechanics."

—— (1949). *Philosophische Grundlagen der Quantenmechanik.*

—— (1951). "Über die erkenntnistheoretische Problemlage und den Gebrauch einer dreiwertigen Logik in der Quantenmechanik."

—— (1952–54). "Les fondements logiques de la théorie des quanta: Utilisation d'une logique à trois valeurs."

Oliver Leslie Reiser (1952). "Physics, Probability, and Multi-valued Logic."

James Barkley Rosser (1941a). "Many-valued Logic."

—— (1941b). "On the Many-valued Logics."

Erhard Scheibe (1964). *Die kontingenten Aussagen in der Physik.*

P. V. Tavanec (1960). *The Application of Logic to Science and Technology.* (With È. Ja. Kol'man, G. N. Povarov, S. A. Janovskaja, eds.)

Hakan Törnebohm (1957). "On Two Logical Systems in the Philosophy of Quantum Mechanics."

Atwell R. Turquette (1945a). Review of Reichenbach's *Philosophical Foundations of Quantum Mechanics.*

Carl F. von Weizsäcker (1955). "Komplementarität und Logik."

Zygmunt Zawirski (1936–37). "Über die Anwendung der mehrwertigen Logik in der empirischen Wissenschaft."

Fritz Zwicky (1933). "On a New Type of Reasoning and Some of Its Possible Consequences."

17 CIRCUITRY AND SWITCHING-THEORY APPLICATIONS OF MANY-VALUED LOGIC

Maria C. Badillo Ballarat (1957). "Lógica trivalente en la automatización de los circuitos."

T. J. Fletcher (1963). "Models of Many-valued Logics."

M. J. Gazalé (1957). "Multi-valued Switching Functions."

Marek Greniewski (1956). "Utilisation des logiques trivalentes dans la théorie des mécanismes automatiques. I. Réalisation des fonctions fondamentales par des circuits."

Grigor C. Moisil (1956a). "Utilisation des logiques trivalentes dans la théorie des mécanismes automatiques. II. Equation caractéristique d'un relaipaolarise."

—— (1956b). "Sur l'application des logiques à trois valeurs à l'étude des schémas à contacts et relais."

—— (1957). "Aplicatrile logicii trivalente in studiul functionarii reale a schemelor cu contacte si relee" (Application of three-valued logic in the study of the real operation of networks with contacts and relays).

—— (1959b). "Sur l'application de la logique à trois valeurs à l'étude des circuits électriques à contacts, redresseurs et résistances."

—— (1959c). *Teoria algebrică a mecanismelor automate* (The Algebraic Theory of Automatic Machines).

—— (1959d). "La logique à cinq valeurs et ses applications à l'étude des circuits électriques."

—— (1960c). *Logica matematica si teknica modernă: Logicile cu mai multe valori si circuitele cu contacte si relee* (Mathematical Logic and Modern Technology: Many-valued Logic and Relay-contact Circuits).

—— (1961a). "Les Logiques à plusieurs valeurs et l'automatique."

—— (1964–65). "The Interest of the Actual Operation of Switching Circuits for the Logician."

—— (1965). *Încercări vechi si noi de logică neclasica* (Essays Old and New on Nonclassical Logic).

Alan Rose (1958c). "Applications of Logical Computers to the Construction of Electrical Control Tables for Signalling Frames."

David H. Schaefer (1955). "A Rectifier Algebra."

Claude E. Shannon (1938). "A Symbolic Analysis of Relay and Switching Circuits."

V. I. Shestakov (1946). "Prédstavlénié haraktéristićéskih funkcij prédložénij posrédstvom vyražénij, réalizuémyh réléjno-kontaktymi shémani" (Representation of characteristic functions of propositions by expressions realizable by relay-contact circuits).

—— (1953). "Modélirovanié opéracij isčisléniá prédložénij posrédstvom prostéjših čétyréhpolùsynh shém" (Modeling the operations of the propositional calculus by means of the simplest four-pole networks).

—— (1960a). "O dvojnaj arixmetičeskoj interpretacii trexznačnogo isčislenija vyskazyvanij."

—— (1960b). "A Dual Arithmetic Interpretation of the Three-valued Propositional Calculus Utilized in the Simulation of This Calculus by Relay-Contact Networks."

Takehiro Sueki (1952–54). "The Formulization of Two-valued and *n*-Valued Systems, I, II, III."

Kamenonsuke Yasuura (1955). "Keidenkikairo ni yoru tatimeidaironri no hyôgen ni tuite" (On the representation of many-valued propositional logics by relay circuits).

Appendix: A Survey of Pluri-valued Systems

The aim of this Appendix is to bring together the most important of the many-valued systems or types of many-valued systems discussed in Chap. 2. This not only serves a reference function, but facilitates comparison of the various systems in an instructive way. For completeness a few non-pluri-valued systems to which frequent reference was made are also included.

1 The Classical Propositional Calculus C_2 and Its Implication Fragment $C_2^{\supset}$

Truth-values:

T (true), F (false)

Truth tables:

p	$\sim p$
$+T$	F
$-F$	T

$p \backslash^q$	$p \,\&\, q$ T	F	$p \lor q$ T	F	$p \supset q$ T	F	$p \equiv q$ T	F
$+T$	T	F	T	T	T	F	T	F
$-F$	F	F	T	F	T	T	F	T

Axiomatizations:[1]

Group 1. C_2 with $\sim$ and $\vee$ primitive. (Hilbert and Ackermann, 1928)

Definitions:

$p \supset q$ FOR $\sim p \vee q$
$p \mathbin{\&} q$ FOR $\sim(\sim p \vee \sim q)$
$p \equiv q$ FOR $(p \supset q) \mathbin{\&} (q \supset p)$

Axioms:

1. $(\alpha \vee \alpha) \supset \alpha$
2. $\alpha \supset (\alpha \vee \beta)$
3. $(\alpha \vee \beta) \supset (\beta \vee \alpha)$
4. $(\alpha \supset \beta) \supset [(\gamma \vee \alpha) \supset (\gamma \vee \beta)]$

Group 2. C_2 with $\sim$ and $\supset$ primitive. (Łukasiewicz, 1929)

Definitions:

$p \vee q$ FOR $\sim p \supset q$
$p \mathbin{\&} q$ FOR $\sim(p \supset \sim q)$
$p \equiv q$ FOR $(p \supset q) \mathbin{\&} (q \supset p)$

Axioms:

1. $(\sim\alpha \supset \alpha) \supset \alpha$
2. $\alpha \supset (\sim\alpha \supset \beta)$
3. $(\alpha \supset \beta) \supset [(\beta \supset \gamma) \supset (\alpha \supset \gamma)]$

Group 3.   The $\supset$-fragment of C_2 ($\supset$ the only primitive). (Tarski and Bernays, 1930)

Axioms:

1. $\alpha \supset (\beta \supset \alpha)$
2. $[(\alpha \supset \beta) \supset \alpha] \supset \alpha$
3. $(\alpha \supset \beta) \supset [(\beta \supset \gamma) \supset (\alpha \supset \gamma)]$

2 C. I. Lewis's Systems of Strict Implication S1 to S5

The Lewis systems S1 to S5 (C. I. Lewis, 1918 for S3, 1932 for the other S*i*) are developed axiomatically (not as many-valued logics). They are based on the following primitives: $\neg$ (negation), $\wedge$ (conjunction), $\square$ (the modality of necessity).

---

[1]Substitution (i.e., uniform substitution of wffs for variables) and *modus ponens* (in the form: given *p* and *p*-implies-*q*, to infer *q*) will be assumed as rules of inference for all the axiomatizations discussed throughout this appendix, unless a different stipulation is explicitly made.

Definitions:

$$
\begin{array}{lll}
\Diamond p & \text{FOR} & \neg\;\Box\;\neg p \\
p \lor q & \text{FOR} & \neg(\neg p \land \neg q) \\
p \supset q & \text{FOR} & \neg(p \land \neg q) \\
p \equiv q & \text{FOR} & (p \supset q) \land (q \supset p) \\
p \to q & \text{FOR} & \Box(p \supset q) \\
p \leftrightarrow q & \text{FOR} & \Box(p \equiv q)
\end{array}
$$

Rules of inference:

    (1) *Substitution*
    (2) *Modus ponens:* Given p and $p \to q$ to infer q
    (3) *Conjunction:* Given p and q to infer $p \land q$
    (4) *Replacement of equivalents:* Given $p \leftrightarrow q$ and some propositional context $(\ldots p \ldots)$ involving 'p' to infer $(\ldots q \ldots)$, where 'q' has replaced 'p' in one of its occurrences in the initial context.

Axioms for S1:

    (1) $(\alpha \land \beta) \to (\beta \land \alpha)$
    (2) $(\alpha \land \beta) \to \alpha$
    (3) $\alpha \to (\alpha \land \alpha)$
    (4) $(\alpha \land [\beta \land \gamma]) \to (\beta \land [\alpha \land \gamma])$
    (5) $([\alpha \to \beta] \land [\beta \to \gamma]) \to (\alpha \to \gamma)$
    (6) $\alpha \to \Diamond \alpha$

Axioms for S2:
    (1)–(6) plus (7.2) $\Diamond(\alpha \land \beta) \to \Diamond \alpha$
Axioms for S3:
    (1)–(6) plus (7.3) $(\alpha \to \beta) \to (\Diamond \alpha \to \Diamond \beta)$
Axioms for S4:
    (1)–(6) plus (7.4) $\Diamond \Diamond \alpha \to \Diamond \alpha$
Axioms for S5:
    (1)–(6) plus (7.5) $\Diamond \alpha \to \Box \Diamond \alpha$

3 The Intuitionistic Propositional Calculus IPC

IPC, Intuitionistic Propositional Calculus (Heyting, 1930, and reaxiomatized by Łukasiewicz in 1953). The system **IPC** is developed axiomatically (not as a many-valued logic). Negation ($\neg$), conjunction, ($\land$), disjunction ($\lor$), and implication ($\to$) are all primitives.

Axioms:

    1. $(\alpha \land \beta) \to \alpha$
    2. $(\alpha \land \beta) \to \beta$
    3. $\alpha \to (\alpha \lor \beta)$
    4. $\beta \to (\alpha \lor \beta)$
    5. $\alpha \to (\beta \to \alpha)$
    6. $\alpha \to (\neg \alpha \to \beta)$

7. $\alpha \to (\beta \to [\alpha \wedge \beta])$
8. $(\alpha \to \neg\beta) \to (\beta \to \neg\alpha)$
9. $[\alpha \to (\beta \to \gamma)] \to [(\alpha \to \beta) \to (\alpha \to \gamma)]$
10. $(\alpha \to \gamma) \to [(\beta \to \gamma) \to [(\alpha \vee \beta) \to \gamma]]$

4 The Family of Lukasiewiczian Systems

(A) Ł$_3$. *The 3-valued System of Lukasiewicz (1920)* (Pp. 22–28.)
  Truth-values:
    T (true), I (indeterminate or neuter), F (false). (Only T is designated.)

p	$\neg p$		q	$p \wedge q$			$p \vee q$			$p \to q$			$p \leftrightarrow q$		
		p		T	I	F	T	I	F	T	I	F	T	I	F
$+T$	F	$+T$		T	I	F	T	T	T	T	I	F	T	I	F
I	I	I		I	I	F	T	I	I	T	T	I	I	T	I
$-F$	T	$-F$		F	F	F	T	I	F	T	T	T	F	I	T

Negation ($\neg$) and implication ($\to$) may be taken as primitives.

Definitions:

  $p \vee q$ FOR $(p \to q) \to q$
  $p \wedge q$ FOR $\neg(\neg p \vee \neg q)$
  $p \leftrightarrow q$ FOR $(p \to q) \wedge (q \to p)$

Axioms (Wajsberg, 1931):

  (W1) $\alpha \to (\beta \to \alpha)$
  (W2) $(\alpha \to \beta) \to [(\beta \to \gamma) \to (\alpha \to \gamma)]$
  (W3) $(\neg\beta \to \neg\alpha) \to (\alpha \to \beta)$
  (W4) $[(\alpha \to \neg\alpha) \to \alpha] \to \alpha$

(B) Ł$_q^S$. *Słupecki's Variant of* Ł$_3$ *(1936)* (P. 64.)
  To Ł$_3$ above add:

p	Tp
T	I
I	I
F	I

Axioms: To those for Ł$_3$ add:

  (S1) T$\alpha \to \neg$Tα
  (S2) $\neg$T$\alpha \to$ Tα

(C) Ł$_3^W$. *The "Weak" Variant of Lukasiewicz' 3-Valued System* Ł$_3$ (Pp. 32–33.)

Introducing the one-place connective **W** by the truth table:

p	$\mathbf{W}p$
T	T
I	T
F	F

new connectives are defined in terms of $\mathbf{L}_3$-connectives as follows:

$\neg p$	FOR	$\neg \mathbf{W}p$
$p \barwedge q$	FOR	$\mathbf{W}p \wedge \mathbf{W}q$
$p \veebar q$	FOR	$\mathbf{W}p \vee \mathbf{W}q$
$p \Rightarrow q$	FOR	$\mathbf{W}p \rightarrow \mathbf{W}q$
$p \Leftrightarrow q$	FOR	$\mathbf{W}p \leftrightarrow \mathbf{W}q$

Truth tables:

p	$\neg p$	${}^q_p\diagdown$	$p \barwedge q$ T	I	F	$p \veebar q$ T	I	F	$p \Rightarrow q$ T	I	F	$p \Leftrightarrow q$ T	I	F
$+T$	F	$+T$	T	T	F	T	T	T	T	T	F	T	T	F
$+I$	F	$+I$	T	T	F	T	T	T	T	T	F	T	T	F
$-F$	T	$-F$	F	F	F	T	T	F	T	T	T	F	F	T

Axioms:
Exactly the same as for $\mathbf{C}_2$.
Note:
The systems $\mathbf{K}_3^{\mathbf{W}}$ and $\mathbf{B}_3^{\mathbf{W}}$—obtained by introducing the **W**-operator (and consequent redefinitions of connectives) into $\mathbf{K}_3$ and $\mathbf{B}_3$, respectively—will be identical with $\mathbf{L}_3^{\mathbf{W}}$.

(D) $\mathbf{L}_n$. *The Finitely Many-Valued Systems of Lukasiewicz (1930)* (Pp. 36–40.)
Truth-values:

$$0 = \frac{0}{n-1}, \frac{1}{n-1}, \frac{2}{n-1}, \frac{3}{n-1}, \cdots, \frac{n-2}{n-1}, \frac{n-1}{n-1} = 1 \qquad \text{(Only 1 is designated.)}$$

Truth rules:

$$/\neg p/ = 1 - /p/$$
$$/p \wedge q/ = \min [/p/, /q/]$$
$$/p \vee q/ = \max [/p/, /q/]$$
$$/p \rightarrow q/ = \begin{cases} 1 \\ 1 - /p/ + /q/ \end{cases} \text{according as} \begin{cases} /p/ \leq /q/ \\ /p/ > /q/ \end{cases}$$
$$/p \leftrightarrow q/ = /(p \rightarrow q) \wedge (q \rightarrow p)/$$

Axioms:
As for $\mathbf{L}_{\aleph_0}$ below *plus certain added characteristic axioms depending upon the specific value of n.*

(E) $\mathbf{Ł}_{\aleph_0}$. *The Denumerably Infinite System of Lukasiewicz* (*1930*) (Pp. 36–40.)
  Truth-values:
    The rational numbers (i.e., fractions) of the interval from 0 to 1 (inclusive).
    (Only 1 is designated.)
  Truth rules:
    Exactly as for $\mathbf{Ł}_n$.
  Axioms:

  (L1) $\alpha \to (\beta \to \alpha)$ [=(W1)]
  (L2) $(\alpha \to \beta) \to [(\beta \to \gamma) \to (\alpha \to \gamma)]$ [=(W2)]
  (L3) $(\neg\beta \to \neg\alpha) \to (\alpha \to \beta)$ [=(W3)]
  (L4) $[(\alpha \to \beta) \to \alpha] \to [(\beta \to \alpha) \to \alpha]$

(F) $\mathbf{Ł}_{\aleph_1}$ ($= \mathbf{Ł}_{\aleph_0} = \mathbf{Ł}_{\aleph}$). *The Nondenumerably Infinite System of Lukasiewicz* (*1930*)
    (Pp. 37–40.)
  Truth-values:
    The real numbers of the interval from 0 to 1 (inclusive). (Only 1 is designated.)
  Truth rules:
    Exactly as for $\mathbf{Ł}_n$.
  Axioms:
    Exactly as for $\mathbf{Ł}_{\aleph_0}$.

(G) $\mathbf{V}_{\aleph_1}$. *A variant of* $\mathbf{Ł}_{\aleph_1}$ (Not discussed in text.)
  Truth-values:
    The real numbers of the interval from -1 to $+1$ (inclusive). (See below re
    designation.)
  Truth rules:

$$/\neg p/ = -/p/$$
$$/p \wedge q/ = \min [/p/, /q/]$$
$$/p \vee q/ = \max [/p/, /q/]$$
$$/p \to q/ = \begin{cases} 1 \\ 1 - /p/ + /q/ \end{cases} \text{ according as } /p/ \text{ is } \begin{cases} \le /q/ \\ > /q/ \end{cases}$$
$$/p \leftrightarrow q/ = /(p \to q) \wedge (q \to p)/$$

  Axioms:
    1. If $+1$ alone is designated, the tautologies of this system are the same as
       those for $\mathbf{Ł}_{\aleph_0} = \mathbf{Ł}_{\aleph_1}$.
    2. If 0 is deleted from the range of truth-values to obtain the system $\mathbf{V}_{[\aleph]}$, and
       all values >0 are designated, then the tautologies of this system are the
       same as those of $\mathbf{C}_2$.

(H) *The Finitely Valued* $\mathbf{V}_n$ (Not discussed in text.)
  Truth-values:
    (i) When n is odd, the truth-values will be:

$$-1 = -\frac{n-1}{2} \times \frac{2}{n-1}, \cdots, -3 \times \frac{2}{n-1}, -2 \times \frac{2}{n-1}, -1 \times \frac{2}{n-1}, 0,$$

$$1 \times \frac{2}{n-1}, 2 \times \frac{2}{n-1}, 3 \times \frac{2}{n-1}, \cdots, \frac{n-1}{2} \times \frac{2}{n-1} = +1$$

(ii) When n is even, then the truth-values will be as determined by (i) for $n + 1$, but with 0 deleted. (Designation is left open apart from the stipulation that $+1$ is designated.)

Truth rules:

Exactly as for $\mathbf{V}_{\aleph_1}$.

Axioms:

1. Exactly as for $\mathbf{L}_n$ if 1 alone is designated.
2. If 0 is deleted from the range of truth-values (and thus in all the even-valued $\mathbf{V}_n$), and if all the values >0 are designated, then the tautologies of these systems are the same as those of $\mathbf{C}_2$.

5 *A Variant System Family That Is a Generalization of* $\mathbf{L}_3$

(A) *The Sequence* $\mathbf{U}_n$ ($\mathbf{U}_2 = \mathbf{C}_2$, $\mathbf{U}_3 = \mathbf{L}_3$) (Pp. 40–41.)

Truth-values:

(i) When n is odd, the truth-values will be all the integers between $-\dfrac{n-1}{2}$ and $+\dfrac{n-1}{2}$ (inclusive). (All numbers > 0 are designated.)

(ii) When n is even, then the truth-values will be as determined by (i) above for $(n + 1)$, but with 0 deleted.

Truth rules:

$$/\neg p/ = -/p/$$
$$/p \wedge q/ = \min \left[/p/, /q/ \right]$$
$$/p \vee q/ = \max \left[/p/, /q/ \right]$$

$$/p \to q/ = \begin{cases} +\dfrac{n-1}{2} \\[2mm] 0 \\[2mm] -\dfrac{n-1}{2} \end{cases} \text{according as } /p/ - /q/ \text{ is } \begin{cases} \leq 0 \\ > 0 \text{ but } \leq 1 \\ > 1 \end{cases}$$

Axioms:

The same as for $\mathbf{C}_2$.

(B) *The System* $\mathbf{U}_{\aleph_0}$ (Pp. 40–41.)

Truth-values:

All positive and negative integers with $+\infty$ and $-\infty$ added.

Truth rules:

Exactly as for $\mathbf{U}_n$.

Axioms:

The same as for $\mathbf{C}_2$.

(C) *The System* $\mathbf{U}_{\aleph_1}$ (Pp. 40–41.)

Truth-values:

All real numbers of the interval -1 to $+1$ (inclusive).

Truth rules:

Exactly as for $\mathbf{U}_3$.

Axioms:

The same as for $\mathbf{C}_2$.

(D) *The Systems* $\mathbf{U}_n^{\supseteq}$ (P. 40.)

These systems $\mathbf{U}_n^{\supseteq}$ result from the corresponding systems $\mathbf{U}_n$ by replacing the mode of implication ($\rightarrow$) at issue by:

$p \supseteq q$ FOR $\neg p \vee q$

The truth-values are thus exactly as above and so are the truth rules, apart from the revised mode of implication ($\supseteq$).

Axioms:

The same as for $\mathbf{C}_2$.

6 The 3-valued Systems of Bochvar

(A) $\mathbf{B}_3$. *The 3-valued "Internal" System of Bochvar* (*1939*) (Pp. 29–34.)

Truth-values:

T, *I*, *F*. (Only *T* is designated.)

Truth tables:

p	$\neg p$
$+T$	F
I	I
F	T

$p \backslash q$	$p \wedge q$: T	I	F	$p \vee q$: T	I	F	$p \rightarrow q$: T	I	F	$p \leftrightarrow q$: T	I	F
$+T$	T	I	F	T	I	T	T	I	F	T	I	F
I	I	I	I	I	I	I	I	I	I	I	I	I
F	F	I	F	T	I	F	T	I	T	F	I	T

Axioms:

None (there are no tautologies). But note: if *I* were also designated, then the axioms would be exactly as for $\mathbf{C}_2$.

(B) $\mathbf{B}_3^{\mathrm{E}}$. *The 3-valued "External" System of Bochvar* (*1939*) (Pp. 30–33)

Truth-values:

T, *I*, *F*. (Only *T* is designated.)

Truth tables:

p	$\neg p$
$+T$	F
I	T
F	T

$p \backslash q$	$p \wedge q$: T	I	F	$p \vee q$: T	I	F	$p \rightarrow q$: T	I	F	$p \leftrightarrow q$: T	I	F
$+T$	T	F	F	T	T	T	T	F	F	T	F	F
I	F	F	F	T	F	F	T	T	T	F	T	T
F	F	F	F	T	F	F	T	T	T	F	T	T

Axioms:

The same as for $\mathbf{C}_2$

7 The Bochvarian Sequence $\mathbf{B}_n$ and Its Variants

(A) *The Sequence* $\mathbf{B}_n$ (Pp. 43–44.)
   Truth-values:

$$0 = \frac{0}{n-1}, \frac{1}{n-1}, \frac{2}{n-1}, \cdots, \frac{n-2}{n-1}, \frac{n-1}{n-1} = 1 \qquad \text{(Only 1 is designated.)}$$

Truth rules:

$/{\neg}p/ = 1 - /p/$

$/p \wedge q/ = \begin{cases} /p/ \times /q/ \\ Z(n) \end{cases}$ according as $\begin{cases} \text{both } /p/ \text{ and } /q/ \text{ belong to } [0,1] \\ \text{otherwise} \end{cases}$

$/p \vee q/ = \begin{cases} \min\,[1, /p/ + /q/] \\ Z(n) \end{cases}$ according as $\begin{cases} \text{both } /p/ \text{ and } /q/ \text{ belong to} \\ \;[0,1] \\ \text{otherwise} \end{cases}$

$/p \rightarrow q/ = \begin{cases} \min\,[1, 1 - /p/ + /q/] \\ Z(n) \end{cases}$ according as $\begin{cases} \text{both } /p/ \text{ and } /q/ \text{ belong} \\ \;\text{to } [0,1] \\ \text{otherwise} \end{cases}$

$/p \leftrightarrow q/ = \begin{cases} 1 - /p/ - /q/ + 2/p/ \times /q/ \\ Z(n) \end{cases}$ according as $\begin{cases} \text{both } /p/ \text{ and} \\ \; /q/ \text{ belong to} \\ \;[0,1] \\ \text{otherwise} \end{cases}$

Note:

$$Z(n) = \tfrac{1}{2} \text{ or } \frac{n-2}{2(n-1)} \text{ according as } n \text{ is odd or even}$$

(B) *The System* $\mathbf{B}_{\aleph}$ (Pp. 43–44.)
   Truth-values:
   All real numbers from 0 to 1 (inclusive). (Only 1 is designated.)
   Truth rules:
   The same as for $\mathbf{B}_n$ with $\tfrac{1}{2}$ in place of $Z(n)$ throughout.
   Axioms:
   None (there are no tautologies).

8 The 3-valued Systems of Kleene

(A) $\mathbf{K}_3$. *The 3-valued System of Kleene* (Kleene, 1938) (Pp. 34–36.)
   Truth-values:
   T, I, F (See below re designation.)

p	$\neg p$		$q \atop p$	$p \wedge q$			$p \vee q$			$p \rightarrow q$			$p \leftrightarrow q$		
				T	*I*	*F*	*T*	*I*	*F*	*T*	*I*	*F*	*T*	*I*	*F*
+*T*	*F*		+*T*	*T*	*I*	*F*	*T*	*T*	*T*	*T*	*I*	*F*	*T*	*I*	*F*
I	*I*		*I*	*I*	*I*	*F*	*T*	*I*	*I*	*T*	*I*	*I*	*I*	*I*	*I*
F	*T*		*F*	*F*	*F*	*F*	*T*	*I*	*F*	*T*	*T*	*T*	*F*	*I*	*T*

Axioms:
  1. None if T alone is designated. (There are no tautologies.)
  2. The same as for $\mathbf{C}_2$ if both T and I are designated.

(B) $\mathbf{K}_3{}^*$. *The "Weak" 3-valued System of Kleene* (Kleene, 1952)
   This system is identical with Bochvar's $\mathbf{B}_3$.

9 Further 3-valued Systems

(A) *The 3-valued T-split System*

p	$\neg p$	$p\backslash{}^q$	$p \wedge q$			$p \vee q$			$p \to q$			$p \leftrightarrow q$		
			T	I	F	T	I	F	T	I	F	T	I	F
$+T$	F	$+T$	T	I	F	T	T	T	T	I	F	T	I	F
$+I$	F	$+I$	I	I	F	T	I	I	T	I	F	I	I	F
$-F$	T	$-F$	F	F	F	T	I	F	T	T	T	F	F	T

Axioms:
  The same as for $\mathbf{C}_2$.

(B) *The 3-valued F-split System* (Not discussed in text.)

p	$\neg p$	$p\backslash{}^q$	$p \wedge q$			$p \vee q$			$p \to q$			$p \leftrightarrow q$		
			T	I	F	T	I	F	T	I	F	T	I	F
$+T$	F	$+T$	T	I	F	T	T	T	T	I	F	T	I	F
$-I$	T	$-I$	I	I	F	T	I	I	T	I	I	I	I	I
$-F$	T	$-F$	F	F	F	T	I	F	T	T	T	F	I	T

Axioms:
  The same as for $\mathbf{C}_2$.

(C) *Reichenbach's 3-valued Quantum Logic* (Reichenbach, 1946)

p	$\neg p$	$\daleth p$	$\overline{}p$	$p\backslash{}^q$	$p \vee q$			$p \wedge q$			$p \to q$			$p \Rightarrow q$			$p \mapsto q$		
					T	I	F	T	I	F	T	I	F	T	I	F	T	I	F
$+T$	F	I	I	$+T$	T	T	T	T	I	F	T	I	F	T	F	F	T	I	F
I	I	F	T	I	T	I	I	I	I	F	T	T	I	T	T	T	I	I	I
F	T	T	T	F	T	I	F	F	F	F	T	T	T	T	T	T	I	I	I

(D) *Słupecki's 3-valued System of 1946* (Słupecki, 1946)
   In his 1946 paper, Słupecki established the truth-functional completeness of the following system and provided a complete axiomatization for it:

				$p \to q$		
p	$\neg p$	$\dashv p$	$p \backslash ^q$	T	I	F
$+T$	F	I	$+T$	T	I	F
I	I	T	I	T	T	T
F	T	T	F	T	T	T

(E) *Sobociński's 3-valued System of 1952* (Sobociński, 1952)

In his 1952 paper, Sobociński axiomatized the following 3-valued system:

			$p \wedge q$			$p \vee q$			$p \supset q$			$p \equiv q$		
p	$\neg p$	$p \backslash ^q$	T	I	F	T	I	F	T	I	F	T	I	F
$+T$	F	$+T$	T	T	F	T	T	T	T	F	F	T	F	F
$+I$	I	$+I$	T	I	F	T	I	F	T	I	F	F	I	F
F	T	F	F	F	F	T	F	F	T	T	T	F	F	T

10 The Gödelian Sequence G_n with Its Variants

(A) *The Sequence* G_n (Gödel, 1932) (Pp. 44–45.)

Truth-values:

$$0 = \frac{0}{n-1}, \frac{1}{n-1}, \frac{2}{n-1}, \cdots, \frac{n-2}{n-1}, \frac{n-1}{n-1} = 1 \qquad \text{(Only 1 is designated.)}$$

Truth rules:

$$/\neg p/ \;=\; \begin{Bmatrix} 1 \\ 0 \end{Bmatrix} \text{according as} \begin{cases} /p/ = 0 \\ /p/ \neq 0 \end{cases}$$

$$/p \wedge q/ = \min\,[/p/,/q/]$$
$$/p \vee q/ = \max\,[/p/,/q/]$$

$$/p \to q/ \;=\; \begin{Bmatrix} 1 \\ /q/ \end{Bmatrix} \text{according as} \begin{cases} /p/ \leq /q/ \\ /p/ > /q/ \end{cases}$$

$$/p \leftrightarrow q/ \;=\; \begin{Bmatrix} 1 \\ \min\,[/p/,/q/] \end{Bmatrix} \text{according as} \begin{cases} /p/ = /q/ \\ /p/ \neq /q/ \end{cases}$$

Axioms:

G_3 is axiomatized by supplementing the axioms of **IPC** (the Intuitionistic Propositional Calculus) by the axiom:

$$(\neg\alpha \to \beta) \to [([\beta \to \alpha] \to \beta) \to \beta]$$

(B) *The System* $G_\aleph$ (Gödel, 1932) (Pp. 44–45.)

Truth-values:

All real numbers from 0 to 1 (inclusive). (Only 1 is designated.)

Truth rules:

Exactly as for G_n.

Axioms:

$\mathbf{G}_{\aleph}$ is axiomatized—as shown in Dummett (1959)—by supplementing the axioms of **IPC** by the axiom:

$$(\alpha \to \beta) \lor (\beta \to \alpha)$$

11 The Standard Sequence $\mathbf{S}_n$ and Its Variants

(A) *The Sequence* $\mathbf{S}_n$ (Pp. 46–52.)

Truth-values:

$$0 = \frac{0}{n-1}, \frac{1}{n-1}, \frac{2}{n-1}, \cdots, \frac{n-2}{n-1}, \frac{n-1}{n-1} = 1 \qquad \text{(Designation left open.)}$$

Truth rules:

$$/\neg p/ \;\; = 1 - /p/$$
$$/p \land q/ = \min [/p/,/q/]$$
$$/p \lor q/ = \max [/p/,/q/]$$
$$/p \to q/ = \begin{Bmatrix} 1 \\ 0 \end{Bmatrix} \text{according as} \begin{cases} /p/ \leq /q/ \\ /p/ > /q/ \end{cases}$$
$$/p \leftrightarrow q/ = /(p \to q) \land (q \to p)/ = \begin{Bmatrix} 1 \\ 0 \end{Bmatrix} \text{according as} \begin{cases} /p/ = /q/ \\ /p/ \neq /q/ \end{cases}$$

Axioms:

The same as for $\mathbf{C}_2$ if n is even and all values $> \frac{1}{2}$ are designated.

(B) *The Sequence* $\mathbf{S}_n^{\supset}$ (Dienes, 1949) (Pp.49–51.)

Truth-values:

Exactly as for $\mathbf{S}_n$.

Truth rules:

$\neg$, $\land$, $\lor$ exactly as for $\mathbf{S}_n$.

$$/p \supset q/ = /\neg p \lor q/$$
$$/p \equiv q/ = /(p \supset q) \land (q \supset p)/$$

Axioms:

1. None if 1 alone is designated. (There are no tautologies.)
2. The same as for $\mathbf{C}_2$ if all values $\geq \frac{1}{2}$ are designated.

Note: $\mathbf{S}_n^{\supset} = \mathbf{U}_n^{\supset}$.

(C) *The Sequence* $\mathbf{S}_n^*$ (P. 52.)

Truth-values:

Exactly as for $\mathbf{S}_n$.

Truth rules:

$\neg$, $\land$, $\lor$ exactly as for $\mathbf{S}_n$.

$$/p \to q/ = \begin{Bmatrix} 1 \\ /q/ \end{Bmatrix} \text{according as} \begin{cases} /p/ \leq /q/ \\ /p/ > /q/ \end{cases}$$
$$/p \leftrightarrow q/ = /(p \to q) \land (q \to p)/ = \begin{Bmatrix} 1 \\ \min [/p/,/q/] \end{Bmatrix} \text{according as} \begin{cases} /p/ = /q/ \\ /p/ \neq /q/ \end{cases}$$

Axioms:
   The same as for C_2 if n is even and all values $> \frac{1}{2}$ are designated.

(D) *The Systems* $S_{\aleph}$ *and* $S_{[\aleph]}$ (Pp. 47–48.)
   Truth-values:
      All the real numbers from 0 to 1 (inclusive), with $\frac{1}{2}$ deleted for $S_{[\aleph]}$.
   Truth rules:
      Exactly as for S_n.
   Axioms:
      The axioms of $S_{[\aleph]}$ are the same as those for C_2 if all truth-values $> \frac{1}{2}$ are designated.

(E) *The Systems* $S_{\aleph}^{\supset}$ *and* $S_{[\aleph]}^{\supset}$ (Pp. 49–50.)
   Truth-values:
      All the real numbers from 0 to 1 (inclusive), with $\frac{1}{2}$ deleted for $S_{[\aleph]}^{\supset}$.
   Truth rules:
      Exactly as for $S_n^{\supset}$.
   Axioms:
      1. None if 1 alone is designated. (There are no tautologies.)
      2. For $S_{[\aleph]}^{\supset}$ exactly the same as for C_2, provided all values $> \frac{1}{2}$ are designated.

(F) *The Systems* $S_{\aleph}^{*}$ *and* $S_{1[\aleph]}^{*}$ (P. 52.)
   Truth-values:
      All the real numbers from 0 to 1 (inclusive), with $\frac{1}{2}$ deleted for $S_{[\aleph]}^{*}$.
   Truth rules:
      Exactly as for S_n^{*}.
   Axioms:
      The axioms of $S_{[\aleph]}^{*}$ are the same as those for C_2 if all truth-values $> \frac{1}{2}$ are designated.

(G) *The System* $S_{\measuredangle}^{t}$ (Not discussed in text.)
   Truth-values:
      All real numbers from 0 to 1 (inclusive). (Only 1 is designated.)
   Truth rules:
      $\neg$, $\wedge$, $\vee$ exactly as for S_n.

$$/p \to q/ = \begin{Bmatrix} 1 \\ 0 \end{Bmatrix} \text{according as} \begin{cases} \text{either } /p/ \neq 1 \text{ or } /q/ = 1 \\ \text{otherwise} \end{cases}$$
$$/p \leftrightarrow q/ = /(p \to q) \wedge (q \to p)/$$

   Axioms:
      Exactly as for C_2.

12 The Postian Family of Many-valued Systems

(A) *The Sequence* P_n (Post, 1920) (Pp. 52–55.)
   Truth-values:
      $1, 2, 3, \ldots, n$ (P_n^{μ} with $1, 2, \ldots, \mu < n$ designated.)

Truth rules:

$$/\neg p/ \;\; = /p/ + 1 \;(\text{mod } n)$$
$$/p \lor q/ = \min \;[/p/,/q/]$$
$$/p \land q/ = /\neg(\neg p \lor \neg q)/$$
$$/p \supset q/ = /\neg p \lor q/$$
$$/p \equiv q/ = /(p \supset q) \land (q \supset p)/$$

Axioms:

The axiomatization of these systems is discussed in Post's 1920 paper.

(B) *The System* $\mathbf{P}_{\aleph_0}$ (Pp. 54–55.)

Truth-values:

$$1,\tfrac{1}{2},\tfrac{1}{4},\tfrac{1}{8},\tfrac{1}{16}, \ldots, \tfrac{1}{2^n}, \ldots, 0$$

Truth rules:

$$/\neg p/ = \tfrac{1}{2} \times /p/$$
$$/p \lor q/ = \max \;[/p/,/q/]$$
$$\land, \supset, \text{ and } \equiv \text{ as for } \mathbf{P}_n.$$

Axioms: See (A).

(C) *The System* $\mathbf{P}_{\aleph_1}$ (Pp. 54–55.)

Truth-values:

All real numbers from 0 to 1 (inclusive).

Truth rules:

Exactly as for $\mathbf{P}_{\aleph_0}$.

Axioms: See (A).

13 Systems Generated as Extension Series

(A) *Jaśkowski's E-series* (Jaśkowski, 1936) (Pp. 91–94.)

Truth-values:

$$1,2,3, \ldots, n, n+1$$

Truth rules:

Let $\neg$, $\land$, $\lor$, $\to$, and $\leftrightarrow$ be the connectives of the given n-valued logic (whose truth-values are, we shall assume, $1,2,\ldots,n$). Correspondingly, $\eqcolon$, $\tilde{\land}$, $\tilde{\lor}$, $\Rightarrow$, and $\Leftrightarrow$ are to be the connectives of the $(n+1)$-valued system being constructed. Moreover, if i and j are two n-valued truth-values then:

(1) $\langle \neg i \rangle$ is to be the truth-value assigned by the n-valued truth table for negation ($\neg$) to the negation of the truth-value i.

(2) $\langle i \oslash j \rangle$ is to be the truth-value assigned by the n-valued truth table for the binary connective $\oslash$ (any arbitrary binary connective) to the truth-value combination i,j.

We now construct our $(n+1)$-valued truth tables as follows:

p	$\eqcolon p$	$\begin{smallmatrix}\\ \diagdown q \\ p \diagdown \end{smallmatrix}$	$p \tilde{\land} q$ $j(\neq n+1)$	$n+1$	$p \tilde{\lor} q$ $j(\neq n+1)$	$n+1$	$p \Rightarrow q$ $j(\neq n+1)$	$n+1$
1	$n+1$	$i(\neq n+1)$	$\langle i \land j \rangle$	$n+1$	$\langle i \lor j \rangle$	i	$\langle i \to j \rangle$	$\langle i \to n \rangle + 1$
$i(\neq 1)$	$\langle \neg(i-1) \rangle$	$n+1$	$n+1$	$n+1$	j	$n+1$	1	1

Note: $E^n(\mathbf{C_2}) = \mathbf{L}_n$

(B) *The F-series* (Pp. 94–95.)

This series is exactly like the E-series except for changing the extension rule for implication to:

$_p\!\diagdown^{\,q}$	1	$p \Rightarrow q$ $j \neq 1$
$i(\neq n + 1)$	1	$\langle i \to (j - i)\rangle + 1$
$n + 1$	1	1

Note: $F^n(\mathbf{C_2}) = \mathbf{S}_n^{\supset}$

(C) *The G-series* (Pp. 95–96)

If $\perp$ is an arbitrary one-place connective, an ϕ an arbitrary binary connective, for which n-valued truth tables are already given, then the extended $(n + 1)$-valued truth tables are:

p	Ψp
$i \leq n$	$z_i = \langle \perp i \rangle$
$n + 1$	z_n

$_p\!\diagdown^{\,q}$	$j \leq n$	Φp	$n + 1$
$i \leq n$	$x_{i,j} = \langle i\,\phi\,j\rangle$		$x_{i,n}$
$n + 1$	$x_{n,j}$		$x_{n,n}$

where $1 \leq i, j \leq n$, and Ψ and Φ are the $(n + 1)$-valued counterparts to $\perp$ and ϕ.

14 Product Systems

(A) *The General Principle* (Jaśkowski, 1936) (Pp. 97–101.)

Truth-values:

Let $/p/_1$ be the truth-value of p in the system $\mathbf{X}_1$ and $/p/_2$ be p's truth-value in the system $\mathbf{X}_2$; then the truth-value of p in the product system $\mathbf{X}_1 \times \mathbf{X}_2$ is to be the ordered pair $\langle /p/_1, /p/_2 \rangle$.

Truth rules:

$$/\neg p/\ = \langle /\neg p/_1, /\neg p/_2 \rangle$$
$$/p \wedge q/ = \langle /p \wedge q/_1, /p \wedge q/_2 \rangle$$
$$/p \vee q/ = \langle /p \vee q/_1, /p \vee q/_2 \rangle$$
$$/p \to q/ = \langle /p \to q/_1, /p \to q/_2 \rangle$$
$$/p \leftrightarrow q/ = \langle /p \leftrightarrow q/_1, /p \leftrightarrow q/_2 \rangle$$

(B) *The System* $\mathbf{C_2} \times \mathbf{C_2}$ (Pp. 97–98.)

p	$\neg p$	$_p\!\diagdown^{\,q}$	$p \wedge q$ 11 10 01 00	$p \vee q$ 11 10 01 00	$p \supset q$ 11 10 01 00	$p \equiv q$ 11 10 01 00
11	00	11	11 10 01 00	11 11 11 11	11 10 01 00	11 10 01 00
10	01	10	10 10 00 00	11 10 11 10	11 11 01 01	10 11 00 01
01	10	01	01 00 01 00	11 11 01 01	11 10 11 10	01 00 11 10
00	11	00	00 00 00 00	11 10 01 00	11 11 11 11	00 01 10 11

15 The Boolean Systems

The leading idea of the Boolean systems is due to Church (1953).

(A) *The Simple Boolean Systems* (Pp. 116–119.)

Given a set W of possible worlds $w_1, w_2, \ldots$, a proposition p is assumed to have a "basic" truth-value $/p/_w$ with respect to each possible world w. These truth-values are to include T and F (among others). On the basis of the "basic" truth-values, "derived" ones may be obtained according to the following:

Truth rules:

$$/p/ \quad = \{w| \ /p/_w = T\}$$
$$/\neg p/ \quad = /p/ \qquad \text{where } S' \text{ is the set complement of } S \text{ (in } V = W)$$
$$/p \wedge q/ = /p/ \cap /q/$$
$$/p \vee q/ = /p/ \cup /q/$$
$$/p \supset q/ = /\neg p \vee q/$$
$$/p \equiv q/ = /(p \supset q) \wedge (q \supset p)/$$

When there are n elements in W, these truth rules will lead to the system $\Pi_n(\mathbf{C}_2)$.

(B) *The Two-place Boolean Systems* (Pp. 180–182.)

On the same basis as before, we now specify:

$$/p/ = \langle \{w| \ /p/_w = T\}, \ \{w| \ /p/_w = F\} \rangle$$

Now if $/p/ = \langle P_1, P_2 \rangle$ and $/q/ = \langle Q_1, Q_2 \rangle$, we have:

Truth rules:

$$/\neg p/ = \langle P_2, P_1 \rangle$$
$$/p \wedge q/ = \langle P_1 \cap Q_1, P_2 \cup Q_2 \rangle$$
$$/p \vee q/ = \langle P_1 \cup Q_1, P_2 \cap Q_2 \rangle$$
$$/p \supset q/ = /\neg p \vee q/$$
$$/p \equiv q/ = /(p \supset q) \wedge (q \supset p)/$$

When there are n elements in W, these truth rules will also lead to the system $\Pi_n(\mathbf{C}_2)$.

(C) *Complex Boolean Systems* (Pp. 119–120.)

On the same basis as before, now assuming the basic truth-values to be *numerical* truth-values $1, 2, \ldots, n$, we define:

$$i(p) = \{w| \ /p/_w = i\}$$

We now specify for propositions an n-place derived truth-value:

$$/p/ = \langle 1(p), 2(p), \ldots, n(p) \rangle$$

The truth rules for these complex truth-values must be adapted to the truth rules for the initial truth-values $/p/$. If these latter are governed by the many-valued system $\mathbf{X}$ and the adaptation is suitably adjusted, then when there are n elements in the set W of possible worlds, we shall in general be led to the system $\Pi_n(\mathbf{X})$ by this mode of construction.

16 Quasi-truth-functional Systems

(A) *The System* **Q** (Pp. 167–168.)

p	$\sim p$		q	$p \& q$		$p \lor q$		$p \supset q$		$p \equiv q$	
		p		T	F	T	F	T	F	T	F
$+T$	F		$+T$	T	F	T	T	T	F	T	F
$-F$	T		$-F$	F	F	T	F	(T,F)	(T,F)	F	(T,F)

Axioms:
The tautologies of this system—which will include all those of the ($\sim$, &, $\lor$)-fragment of C_2—have not yet been axiomatized. Its "quasi-tautologies" (i.e., formulas that invariably do *or may* take on the truth-value *T* for any and every assignment of truth-values to its variables) are the same as the C_2-tautologies.

(B) *The System* **Q*** (Pp. 178–179.)

p	$\sim p$		q	$p \& q$		$p \lor q$		$p \supset q$		$p \equiv q$	
		p		T	F	T	F	T	F	T	F
$+T$	F		$+T$	T	F	T	T	(T,F)	F	(T,F)	F
$-F$	T		$-F$	F	F	T	F	(T,F)	(T,F)	F	(T,F)

Axioms:
The tautologies of this system will include those of the ($\sim$, &, $\lor$)-fragment of C_2. Its quasi-tautologies will again be the same as those of C_2.

(C) *The 3-valued "Lukasiewiczian" System* L_q (Pp. 170–171.)

p	$\neg p$		q	$p \land q$			$p \lor q$			$p \to q$			$p \leftrightarrow q$		
		p		T	I	F	T	I	F	T	I	F	T	I	F
$+T$	F		$+T$	T	I	F	T	T	T	T	I	F	T	I	F
I	I		I	I	(I,F)	F	T	(I,T)	I	T	(T,F)	(I,F)	I	(T,I)	(I,F)
$-F$	T		$-F$	F	F	F	T	I	F	T	T	T	F	(I,F)	T

Axioms:
The quasi-tautologies of this system will be the same as those of L_3.

17 The System PL

For historical and other details, see Pp. 184–188.
Truth-values:
The real numbers from 0 to 1 (inclusive). (Designation is left open apart from the stipulation that 1 is designated.)

Truth rules:

$/p/$ is to be the probability of p. In consequence:

$$/\neg p/\quad = 1 - Pr(p)$$

$/p \lor q/ = Pr(p) + Pr(q)$ if p and q are mutually exclusive, and otherwise a certain quantity λ such that $\lambda \le Pr(p) + Pr(q)$, but $\lambda \ge Pr(p)$ and $\lambda \ge Pr(q)$

$$/p \land q/ = Pr(p) + Pr(q) - Pr(p \lor q)$$

$$/p \supset q/ = /\neg p \lor q/$$

$$/p \equiv q/ = /(p \supset q) \land (q \supset p)/$$

Axioms:

The tautologies of this system are exactly the same as those of $\mathbf{C}_2$.

Index of
Many-valued
Logic

$\mathcal{N}$ame Index

Subject Index

This book was set in Times Roman, printed on permanent paper and bound by The Maple Press Company. The editors were James Mirrielees and Judy Reed. Robert R. Laffler supervised the production.